"My first thought on seeing these pages was that perhaps not since Richard Baxter penned his massive *Christian Directory* has a book like *Ask Pastor John* been offered to Christians. From the vast number of questions to which John Piper has responded over a decade of podcasting, these pages contain 750 of the most listened-to answers. And while Piper's ministry is separated from Baxter's by more than three centuries, a common thread binds them together—the deep-seated conviction that the God-breathed Scriptures make us '*wise* for salvation' in the fullest sense because, in providing teaching, reproof, correction, and training in righteousness, they are sufficient to equip us 'for every good work' (2 Tim. 3:15–17). The value of these pages is as evident as it is manifold. At one level, theological, pastoral, and ethical questions are assessed, analyzed, and consistently answered by bringing them to the touchstone of Scripture. But in addition, this is done with a rigorous and determined attention to both the wording and the interior logic of God's word with a desire to help us to think God's thoughts after him. And this in turn serves all of us as a pattern to learn and apply in our own Bible reading, and as a model that encourages us to live according to Scripture. In addition, the step-by-step care with which John Piper seeks to handle Scripture helps us—as he would wish—to discern how what he says applies in our own lives, and, indeed, where it might not. And so as a theologian he guides our understanding, and as a pastor he encourages us to grow in discernment so that we are not simply becoming automatons but are learning to think through and apply God's word by ourselves, for ourselves, and to ourselves. We owe a debt of grateful thanks to John Piper for the labor of love and devotion of time and pastoral care this book reflects, and to his long-time colleague Tony Reinke, who—from an archive of over two million words!—has expertly selected and edited these pages. Here is one of those rare contemporary books that can be described as 'should be in every Christian home,' and to which we can turn again and again for guidance from God's word, encouragement in Christ, and challenge to walk according to the Spirit."

Sinclair B. Ferguson, Chancellor's Professor of Systematic Theology, Reformed Theological Seminary; author, *The Whole Christ* and *Worthy*

"I don't know what is more remarkable, that the *Ask Pastor John* podcast has nearly two thousand episodes and over 230 million listens or that Tony Reinke has distilled all that content in order to give us a guided tour of 220 hours of audio recordings. Have you ever wished you could sit down with John Piper (or any wise, seasoned pastor) and ask him all your practical, nitty-gritty questions about life, ministry, parenting, sex, Bible reading, divorce, abuse, dating, gambling, eating, drinking, movies, demons, depression, poetry, and selfie sticks? Then this is the book for you. Even if you don't agree with Piper on every jot and tittle of application, you will find that he is always thoughtful, always careful, always pastoral, and always tied to the Bible. Read the book straight through, a little each day, or use these five hundred pages as an encyclopedia on situational ethics and practical theology. Either way, I can't imagine any Christian who wouldn't be helped (and fascinated) by the hundreds of topics covered in this amazing resource."

Kevin DeYoung, Senior Pastor, Christ Covenant Church, Matthews, North Carolina; Associate Professor of Systematic Theology, Reformed Theological Seminary, Charlotte

"Throw a hard question at John Piper and he will isolate the main challenge and address it with a sage answer, drawn from the Bible, delivered in a kind tone that lacks even a hint of hubris. He willingly answers all sorts of dilemmas, from hard Bible verses to the daily struggles of the Christian life to culturally charged questions that border on the embarrassing to the bizarre. For years I have been an avid listener because each episode draws me deeper into God's word. Pastor John has spoken so wisely on such a wide array of topics that I am always ferreting through past episodes to learn more. But that vast archive can be daunting. With many years of experience as the host, Tony Reinke has pulled together the 750 most popular episodes from their first decade together into a single guide touching on dozens of themes. This book is an index to the podcast archive, drawing together multiple episodes on single topics, making it easy for me to find the audio I need, when I need it. As a podcast listener, I couldn't be more pleased. I'm thankful to Reinke for compiling this encyclopedia and—now for over a decade—drawing out, documenting, and helping us all more richly benefit from America's most beloved theologian!"

    Joni Eareckson Tada, Founder and CEO, Joni and Friends International Disability Center

"This book is a remarkable achievement, cataloging John Piper's answers to hundreds of challenges and dilemmas in the Christian life. A modern-day *Table Talk*, reminiscent of Martin Luther, this book is like sitting across a table from a Bible-saturated pastor addressing issues that are timely and issues that are timeless. You likely won't agree with every answer. I didn't. But what I appreciate about this book is how, even when I disagreed, Pastor John pointed me back to the Scriptures and pressed my nose deeper into those pages where, through studying and savoring, I find the unerring words of life. I am thankful for this encyclopedia of wisdom and insight. It increases my love for God and his word."

    Trevin Wax, Vice President of Research and Resources, The North American Mission Board; Visiting Professor, Cedarville University; author, *The Thrill of Orthodoxy*; *Rethink Your Self*; and *This Is Our Time*

"For years, the *Ask Pastor John* podcast has served me as a go-to reservoir for pastoral encouragement and practical help. There is nothing else like it. If you're serious about your joy in Jesus, turn these pages and find accessible, God-centered answers to life's biggest questions. The book is brilliantly organized; few will sufficiently appreciate what Reinke has pulled off here."

    Matt Smethurst, Lead Pastor, River City Baptist Church, Richmond, Virginia; author, *Before You Open Your Bible* and *Before You Share Your Faith*

Ask Pastor John

Other Books by Tony Reinke

Competing Spectacles: Treasuring Christ in the Media Age (2019)

God, Technology, and the Christian Life (2022)

Lit! A Christian Guide to Reading Books (2011)

Newton on the Christian Life: To Live Is Christ (2015)

12 Ways Your Phone Is Changing You (2017)

Ask Pastor John

750 Bible Answers to Life's Most Important Questions

TONY REINKE

Foreword by John Piper

∷ CROSSWAY®

WHEATON, ILLINOIS

Ask Pastor John: 750 Bible Answers to Life's Most Important Questions

© 2024 by Tony Reinke

Published by Crossway
    1300 Crescent Street
    Wheaton, Illinois 60187

Cover design: Desiring God, Jordan Singer

First printing 2024

Printed in the United States of America

Hardcover ISBN: 978-1-4335-8126-7
epub ISBN: 978-1-4335-8129-8
PDF ISBN: 978-1-4335-8127-4

Library of Congress Cataloging-in-Publication Data

Names: Reinke, Tony, 1977– author. | Piper, John, 1946– Ask Pastor John.
Title: Ask Pastor John : 750 Bible answers to life's most important questions / Tony Reinke ; foreword by John Piper.
Description: Wheaton, Illinois: Crossway, 2024. | Includes bibliographical references and index.
Identifiers: LCCN 2023013611 (print) | LCCN 2023013612 (ebook) | ISBN 9781433581267 (hardcover) | ISBN
    9781433581274 (pdf) | ISBN 9781433581298 (epub)
Subjects: LCSH: Christian life—Biblical teaching.
Classification: LCC BS680.C47 .R45 2024 (print) | LCC BS680.C47 (ebook) | DDC 248.4—dc23/eng/20230722
LC record available at https://lccn.loc.gov/2023013611
LC ebook record available at https://lccn.loc.gov/2023013612

Crossway is a publishing ministry of Good News Publishers.

SH		34	33	32	31	30	29	28	27	26	25	24
15	14	13	12	11	10	9	8	7	6	5	4	3

To each of Desiring God's precious ministry partners who carried this podcast through its first decade. This book testifies to your faithful response to the call of our Savior through your faithful prayers, personal encouragements, and monetary investments over these ten years. Together we are extending God's grace around the world and adding new voices to the global chorus of souls thankful to God, all to the praise of his majesty (2 Cor. 4:15).

"All learning is the fruit of question-asking and answer-seeking."

JOHN PIPER (1975)

Contents

Foreword by John Piper

AFTER SPENDING EIGHT HOURS PREPARING to record answers to five *Ask Pastor John* questions, I come downstairs at six o'clock and say to my wife, "What would we do if we did not have the Bible?"

The answer is, we would presume that our own wisdom could penetrate the mysteries of life and point people to their eternal good. That is not what we presume. Our assumption is that God alone has the wisdom we need to honor him, love people, and be eternally happy in his presence. That wisdom is recorded infallibly in one place, the Bible. God's word is the foundation and motivation of *Ask Pastor John* (APJ).

Christ has given to his church "shepherds and teachers" (Eph. 4:11). I believe he called me to be one in 1966. Tony tells the story in his introduction. It is a dangerous calling. The very Bible that warrants the call, warns the called: "Not many of you should become teachers, my brothers, for you know that we who teach will be judged with greater strictness" (James 3:1).

A podcast that presumes to answer some of the hardest questions of life would be utter folly without the word of God. And even with the word, and the help of the Holy Spirit, it is a trembling work: "This is the one to whom I will look," declares the Lord, "he who is humble and contrite in spirit and trembles at my word" (Isa. 66:2).

For all the danger and all the trembling, it is a joyful work. The teacher always learns more than the student. This is God's way: it is always more blessed to give than to receive (Acts 20:35). But the joy is not just in learning; it is even more in tasting its fruit in the lives of those who listen. For example, one young woman said to me, "My parents are not believers. I am a new Christian. I do not know how to do life. But when I hear your voice on APJ, it sounds like a soothing grandfather helping me know how to live."

There are advantages to being old. Sounding like a trusty grandfather is one. Another is recognizing rare gifts when you see them. The gift of synthesis manifested in this book is astonishing. For ten years I have watched Tony Reinke evaluate questions, record answers, edit recordings, host the podcast, and schedule the episodes. It is a precious partnership. But the skill you see in this book is of another order. Weaving hundreds of thousand-word answers into topical, coherent, readable chapters inspires my seasoned admiration.

One of our hopes for this book is that you will be drawn into the audio podcast. Not because spoken words are truer than written words. But because the living voice carries the affections of the heart more effectively. Why does that matter?

It matters because love is the goal of knowledge, not the other way around (1 Tim. 1:5). Christ-exalting behavior flows from Christ-cherishing hearts, not just Christ-knowing minds. Tony and I are Christian Hedonists.[1] Therefore, this podcast flows from the conviction that God is most glorified in our listeners when they are most satisfied in him. So, we can't settle for imparting new ideas. We aim to impart new affections. A miracle. Such affections can be heard more readily than read. We hope you can hear our hearts. There is a melody there. We call it the glory of God in the gladness of God-centered souls.

---

1 See APJ 1913: "Christian Hedonism in Two Minutes" (March 15, 2023).

A Little History of APJ
(And Why I Wrote This Book)

THIS BOOK TELLS THE STORY OF ONE PODCAST—*Ask Pastor John* (APJ).
Every day our audience sends us hard questions about life. I read the questions,
select a few, and ask them to longtime author and pastor John Piper. We call
him Pastor John. And we ask him about everything—smartphones, shopping,
sex, self-pity, swearing, Satan, and salvation. Nothing is off-limits. He takes his
answers from the Bible.

I submitted this book to the publisher in the first week of 2023, just a few
days after we broadcasted our final episode of 2022—the bookend to our first
decade. We have released 1,881 episodes, which have now been played over
230 million times, or about 125,000 times each. In the story of the universe
these numbers are trivial, but in the story of this podcast they are remarkable
reminders of God's kindness to us.

The stats give a sense of the number of lives impacted over the years. Five
years into the podcast, Pastor John began to notice that "of a constellation of
influences people receive from Desiring God, APJ is one that people mention
to me as much as any other—from moms shuttling their kids to school and
playing the podcast on the way, to lawyers building it into their early morning
exercise routines, to high school students taking a break from homework, to
eighty-somethings whose eyes won't read anymore."[1] The podcast's rise has
drawn other notice. As I was wrapping up this book, I heard Kevin DeYoung
publicly celebrate Desiring God's many valuable labors. Then he singled out

---

1 John Piper, email to author, July 11, 2018.

the podcast as "chief among their media content."[2] So it's no surprise that when he now travels, Pastor John is thanked for the podcast more than anything else he does. In conference venues, the most common badge of affiliation and appreciation he hears is from people who approach him simply to say, "I listen to APJ every week!"[3]

The podcast serves a steady diet of content to a growing audience that's becoming increasingly diverse and international. It gathers older listeners, church leaders, and young adults, many of whom were raised in nominal or non-Christian homes and are now trying to navigate life as new believers. Across the generations, Pastor John's voice is that of a (nearly eighty-year-old) mentor. One regular listener, a wife and mother, called APJ an "audible daily moment of gospel-centered encouragement, like a quick coffee with a dear friend who stirs my affections for Christ."[4] It is the unique power of persistent, steady, audio podcasting over the years to forge deep connections with listeners.[5] So it's also not a surprise when listeners tell us that Pastor John's voice is like heeding the voice of a father, grandfather, mentor, or friend.

An Origin Story

To understand APJ's success you need to understand one part of John Piper's life. The part about why he thinks *asking good questions* is essential to succeeding in life. And that story begins with an awkward teenager—insecure, pimple-faced, and nervous—by the name of Johnny Piper, as he was first known to the world.[6] The son of a respected preacher and traveling evangelist, Johnny was unable to talk in front of groups and deathly afraid of public speaking from grade five to his sophomore year in college.[7] In front of others, he froze. An "intense nervousness" haunted him as his chief boyhood burden. But despite the debilitating limitation, his local church became for him "an oasis" where he gained respect for a growing knowledge of Scripture. While he couldn't

---

Kevin DeYoung, "Positive World, Negative World, and Christian Nationalism with Justin Taylor and Collin Hansen," *Life and Books and Everything*, podcast, November 8, 2022, episode 87.

Point made in his debrief after T4G's final conference in the spring of 2022, where he intentionally invested extra time meeting attendees (John Piper, private meeting [April 28, 2022]).

APJ 1558: "How Do I Battle Imposter Syndrome?" (December 7, 2020).

True for me as the host too. When I first meet listeners face-to-face, I'm often met with a contorted look, the outward expression of an internal calculation processing how a total stranger could speak with the voice of an old friend.

APJ 1: "Reflections from John Piper on His Birthday" (January 11, 2013).

APJ 228: "How Did You Learn to Preach?" (December 3, 2013) and APJ 1730: "Should I Become a Preacher?" (January 12, 2022).

stand up and speak in front of a group—any group—he *could* answer Bible questions in his youth group.[8]

Johnny became John around the time he entered Wheaton College (1964–1968; BA), the scene of a tumultuous 1966 that would change his course forever. As the year began, John was completing his second year of a lit major. But by May he took a sharp turn toward medicine and jumped into a premed track. On June 6, 1966, the aspiring doctor met his future wife, Noël, on campus.[9] Just weeks later John was asked to pray in chapel, a request he surprisingly agreed to do with a vow to God: "If you will just get me through it so that I don't freeze and my voice doesn't stop, I will never turn down a speaking opportunity for you again out of fear." It worked. He prayed in chapel (and has kept his vow ever since).[10] That fall he was hospitalized for three weeks with mononucleosis. Lying in bed with "big yellow tonsils and palpitating spleen," he heard compelling preaching on the radio that ignited a new fire within him.[11] A passion to preach "that has never died."[12] In that hospital bed his calling moved from medicine to ministry,[13] an inadvertent "bait and switch" on his new girlfriend, who "thought she was falling in love with a medical doctor." She was understanding. John's new calling was undeniable and clear: "You're not going to be a medical doctor; you're going to be a Bible guy. And your job for the rest of your life is going to be to *look at it*, see what's there, try to *savor it* according to its value, and then *say it* for other people to enjoy."[14] Tongue loosed, he aspired to Bible scholarship, a decision driven by many factors including "an unceasing desire to have some questions answered" for himself and an urge to "help others answer them" too.[15] In these formative years, Wheaton's English department had awakened his heart's affection for God and sharpened his mind to read texts more carefully.[16]

John graduated with a literature degree and enrolled at Fuller Seminary (1968–1971; BD). There he was first exposed to a quote attributed to John Dewey: "We never think until we have been confronted with a problem."[17] And there he first read Mortimer J. Adler's book *How to Read a Book* in its original

---

8   John Piper, personal journal, November 27, 1990.

9   APJ 1382: "When to Stop Listening to This Podcast" (October 16, 2019).

10 APJ 1730: "Should I Become a Preacher?" (January 12, 2022).

11 APJ 1373: "Who Is John Piper?" (September 25, 2019).

12 APJ 1382: "When to Stop Listening to This Podcast" (October 16, 2019).

13 APJ 1405: "I'm Not Good at My Job—Is the Lord Telling Me to Quit?" (December 9, 2019).

14 APJ 1382: "When to Stop Listening to This Podcast" (October 16, 2019).

15 John Piper, personal journal, August 16, 1970.

16 APJ 1713: "John Piper's Ministry in One Bible Text" (December 3, 2021).

17 As cited in Daniel P. Fuller, *Thinking God's Thoughts: The Hermeneutics of Humility* (np; 2020), 66.

1940 edition. "Wonder is the beginning of wisdom in learning from books as well as from nature," Adler wrote. "If you never ask yourself any questions about the meaning of a passage, you cannot expect the book to give you any insight you do not already possess."[18]

Dewey and Adler entered John's life through a seminary professor who would permanently alter Piper's entire approach to Bible study—Daniel Fuller, who quickly became the most influential character in Piper's formation, second only to his parents (Bill and Ruth).[19] Fuller modeled a "rigorous attention to the text."[20] He called it arcing, the act of writing out every proposition of a Bible text on a different line to figure out how those propositions relate to each other.[21] The approach demands attention to detail as it "takes every word, every phrase, every sentence in the Bible with blood-earnest seriousness, and wrings it until every drop of life-giving blood falls out of it on the page," Piper said. "And I've never been the same since." His own transformation was rapid. By Dr. Fuller's influence, between the age of twenty-two and twenty-three, Piper became, in his own words, "a different human being."[22] The rapid metamorphosis was driven by laborious practice. Proposition by proposition, Piper plodded through courses on Romans 9, Romans 1–8, Galatians, the Sermon on the Mount, and 1 Corinthians—the whole time "Dan Fuller pushing my nose down in the nitty-gritty of the conjunctions and the connectors."[23]

Arcing is a surgical skill that asks and answers questions within the ligaments of the Bible's connective tissue. But it's more than a sophisticated academic tool. It sustains faith. Over time, John came to discover that Christian learning is the process of heart convictions gained by asking great questions and finding convincing answers in the Bible. Whether a scholar investing in Christian minds, a preacher seeking to mature a congregation, or a parent seeking to raise his child in the Lord, all three must labor to avoid the deadly trap of authoritarianism. Answers must be rooted in the Bible's authority, not the expertise of the scholar

18 Mortimer J. Adler, *How to Read a Book: The Art of Getting a Liberal Education* (New York: Simon & Schuster, 1940), 219–20. Read for the first time in his early twenties (APJ 1244: "How Do I Choose Good Books and Grow My Library?" [August 31, 2018]).

19 APJ 107: "Who Has Been Most Influential in Your Life?" (June 7, 2013).

20 APJ 1713: "John Piper's Ministry in One Bible Text" (December 3, 2021).

21 APJ 107: "Who Has Been Most Influential in Your Life?" (June 7, 2013) and APJ 127: "Advice for Better Bible Reading" (July 8, 2013). On arcing, see APJ 395: "What Tools Do I Need to Study the Bible?" (July 29, 2014), APJ 1056: "How Can I Better Study a Bible Passage?" (June 19, 2017), APJ 1141: "Deep Bible Reading Strategies for the Tired and Busy" (January 3, 2018), and John Piper, *Reading the Bible Supernaturally* (Wheaton, IL: Crossway, 2017), 395–411.

22 APJ 1373: "Who Is John Piper?" (September 25, 2019).

23 APJ 311: "How Piper Learned Reformed Theology" (April 2, 2014).

or preacher or parent. Failure here will "sow the seeds of apostasy," because the student, the congregant, and the child must find their own way to their own convictions. To this end, question-asking is essential for an enduring faith.[24]

John found himself developing into "two kinds of person in one: a highly analytical question asker and a romantic pursuer of deep and authentic, satisfying emotional responses to what I see and experience." Rightly stewarded, curiosity must lead to worship. At Wheaton College, Piper found "the deepening and intensifying of my affections—my emotions, my heart response—to the good, the true, and the beautiful, and ultimately, of course, of the highest good and the highest affections for God himself and his word." Likewise, he found an intensifying "analytical bent toward probing, questioning, scrutinizing, and dissecting" texts. By Dr. Fuller's influence, "I had formed habits of observation and analysis and text querying that were very fixed in my methodology." From here on, "everything I have done, written, or spoken has been shaped by the double grasp of God's word in these two ways"—in the "double response" of Psalm 119:97. Rigorous *meditation* in search of truths to *love*.[25]

John took his question-centric probing of Scripture and his love for the resulting answers into three years of graduate school at the University of Munich (1971–1974; DTheol). But following his deeply transformative years at Fuller Seminary, the move to Germany was an exegetical disappointment. German academia was stuck on "textual gamesmanship" that never "pushed through the words to *the reality* that was driving and animating everything in the Bible." Arcing had given Piper a method of discovery that kept him from being intimidated by his learned professors (Ps. 119:99). In Germany, he couldn't outread his liberal professors by volume of reading, but he could outmeditate them with an open Bible. With this conviction from the psalmist, Piper knew that "one true citation from God's word may silence a whole semester of human speculation."[26]

Academic games were powerless to forge convictions. Instead, as a twenty-six-year-old Sunday school teacher, John was convinced that the deepest questions of the human soul were often the simplest in form. The *why* questions. So he prodded his class to ask them, the *why* questions, until one man finally mustered the courage to raise his hand and ask, "*Why* do we go to church anyway?" It was a great question, a dangerous question, the kind of question that makes the asker vulnerable. But the honest question set Piper's mind to work. Such basic inquiries must be asked (and never assumed) because "the person who does

24 John Piper, personal journal, April 7, 1972.
25 APJ 1713: "John Piper's Ministry in One Bible Text" (December 3, 2021).
26 APJ 1713: "John Piper's Ministry in One Bible Text" (December 3, 2021).

not know *why* he believes something or does something is like a robot: he does not know from whence his thought or action springs nor where it is headed."[27]

In response, Piper turned the attention of his class to the brimming affection of the psalmist (in Ps. 116:12–14). Like this psalmist, Christians gather with God's people because our hearts are filled with a gratitude bursting to expression. To this question (why do we go to church?), and to every other question, mere intellectual answers are insufficient. "The psalmist was not solving a riddle or a mind teaser. He was giving expression to a heart delighted with real bounty, not mere thoughts about bounty: he *felt* the goodness and beauty of God in his own life."[28] So he had to express it. Hence, he had to be with the people of God. That's why we go to church. This Sunday-school-class moment illustrates an essential conviction in Piper. Whether standing behind a music stand in a Sunday school class, teaching behind an academic lectern, laboring over the exegetical point of a biblical text at a desk, or standing in the pulpit preaching—true Christian communication aims to persuade by satisfying the *regenerate heart* with divine glory, not simply by addressing the *curious mind* with articulate reasoning. The *why* question may simply be the product of a curious brain, but its *answer* should appeal to the capacities of the thirsting heart. True in the early 1970s. True today.

John Piper graduated from the University of Munich and became Dr. Piper, a Bible and Greek professor in Minnesota. And to prep for his inaugural semester as a professor he returned to Adler's book on reading, newly minted in a revised version. Added to the new edition of the book (likely by its new coauthor, Charles Van Doren) was one sharp prescription for active reading: "*Ask questions while you read—questions that you yourself must try to answer in the course of reading.*"[29] To this newly added line, printed on the page in italics, Piper eagerly underlined it with a pencil and added five emphatic symbols in the outside margin, two stars and three vertical lines (★ ★ |||). The hand-drawn ciphers codify a multilayered ah-ha moment—a "revelation."[30] The line struck him (and still does), because "no one *thinks* (which is the key to understanding) until they have a problem; and the best way to have problems for the mind is to ask questions. Questions are the best steady-state way of creating problems for the mind" because "a question-free mind is a thinking-free mind and a discovery-free mind." Without this engagement, "reading becomes passive

---

27 APJ 1713: "John Piper's Ministry in One Bible Text" (December 3, 2021).
28 John Piper, personal journal, July 29, 1972.
29 Mortimer J. Adler and Charles Van Doren, *How to Read a Book: The Classic Guide to Intelligent Reading*, rev. ed. (New York: Touchstone, 1972), 46; emphasis original.
30 John Piper, personal journal, January 27, 1975.

entertainment, rather than growth in understanding reality." It's great advice from Adler to every reader, but "when the book is *the Bible*—O my, the implications for soaring in conversation with the inspired writers and God!"[31]

Adler simply confirmed what had already been operating in Dr. Piper's mind for many years: "all learning is the fruit of question-asking and answer-seeking." But like his Sunday school class, he would soon find that his college students asked too few of them. "It is astonishing how many only make assertions of what they presently think rather than posing questions in order to make their thinking better." Why didn't they? Two reasons. One, asking questions creates problems and adds to the workload. It's academically easier to make assertions based on present knowledge. And, two, questions expose ignorance and require humility. The greater temptation is to make quick assertions on the fly, to avoid the embarrassment of "not knowing," and to appear sharp and intelligent before others. The "questioning mind" must cut against these twin-sin tendencies: laziness and pride. Asking honest questions, in other words, requires childlikeness. "That a child asks so many questions shows his boundless energy and his unawareness of the adult shame of ignorance. Hence *childlikeness* in this sense is a prerequisite of a lifetime of learning." To *not* ask questions is to stagnate, to never have the mind and heart refreshed as if by a mountain stream, a refreshment reserved only for those willing to ask "eager questions." Such an unquestioning mind can only grow "more and more bigoted" as it becomes more sold out to the "correctness" of its past assumptions. To such a mind comes a damning end: "Hearing they do not hear and seeing they do not see" (Matt. 13:13).[32]

Dr. Piper came to understand that one of his main tasks as professor was to impart a "dramatic reorientation" to the lives of even his most pious students, "who have imbibed from childhood an 'unquestioning' approach to the New Testament." His challenge: convince students that question-asking was not to cast doubt on God and his revelation but to honor him and his word. By his own example, Piper would prove that "posing questions is not inimical to an open, docile, childlike spirit toward the Scripture." So while many Christians associate these interrogations "with unbelief and doubt," in reality "without questions, *earnestly asked*, there is rarely any true conviction of truth. There may be much espousing of ideas inherited or picked up along life's way; but that does not make for deep hearty union with the God of truth and whole-souled *amen* to his counsels."[33] The sturdiest faith-convictions, the ones that cut deep

31 John Piper, email to author, May 5, 2022.
32 John Piper, personal journal, January 27, 1975.
33 John Piper, personal journal, November 27, 1976.

and hold fast in the hungry heart like a fishhook, are convictions that start as childlike questions, earnestly asked in faith and resolved by Scripture. These answers convince the mind and feed the heart. For short, I'll call this four-step approach "question-resolution-conviction-worship" (or QRCW).

It's not irreverent to question the Bible's claims, if we are eager to receive the Bible's answers. In fact, "reverence for God's word *demands* that we ask questions and pose problems *and* that we believe there are answers and solutions which will reward our labor with treasures new and old (Matt. 13:52)."[34] Reverent questions can only come from minds and hearts seeking answers. Irreverent "questions" come from a skeptical and antagonistic heart that has already closed itself to answers. God is most attentive to questions that are personal, honest, earnest, and urgent.[35]

When done humbly and expectantly, this reverent and childlike approach (QRCW) proved superior to and more fruitful than all other forms of teaching— a result confirmed to Dr. Piper one evening in 1976, in a formal debate with another professor before students. This strict and proper debate structure was never his style, as he later reflected. He preferred more open and free-flowing dialogue. "What I really enjoy is question-and-answer sessions. There is where I am at my best, I think, and there is where *understanding* really happens."[36] To teach and persuade is to answer questions with the aim of worship. And Dr. Piper's aptitude for answering such difficulties—questions on texts, theology, and ethics—was confirmed over time. Three years after his formal debate, God called him out of academia and into the pulpit.[37] The teaching assistants in his department sent him off with a custom T-shirt that read: "Asking questions is the key to understanding."[38] It wasn't a reminder. It was his brand.

Dr. Piper became Pastor John in 1980. His eight-mile move to become the senior pastor of Bethlehem Baptist Church caught the attention of one local reporter who predicted that his methodology wouldn't change much. "Piper's preaching style will be similar to his classroom teaching style. In the classroom, Piper asks questions and makes his students do part of the answering. Behind the pulpit, he will ask questions and do the answering himself. 'The way I study the Bible,' said Piper, 'is to ask questions of the text to try to get out its meaning.

---

34 John Piper, *Brothers, We Are Not Professionals: A Plea to Pastors for Radical Ministry* (Nashville, TN: B&H, 2002), 91; emphasis added.

35 APJ 1707: "Is Violent Crime under God's Providence?" (November 19, 2021).

36 John Piper, personal journal, August 30, 1976; emphasis added.

37 Justin Taylor, "'This Word Must Be Preached': John Piper's Call to the Pastorate," Desiring God, October 14, 2019, https://www.desiringgod.org/.

38 John Piper, *Brothers, We Are Not Professionals*, 74–75.

It is natural that my sermons will be a systematic exposition of the meaning of biblical texts. That is what I think good preaching is."[39]

But good preaching must be more than resolving mental curiosities. Good preaching isn't Socratic dialogue reduced to monologue, nor is good preaching like a classroom lecture. The preacher may raise and answer questions to help explain the text, but all with an eye to "the first aim of preaching"—not education, but a "supernatural encounter with the living God." Asking the right questions is essential for arcing, exegesis, and sermon prep, and those questions may sometimes emerge in the sermon itself. But the *final task* of the preacher is to herald the glorious news that the living God of the universe is "calling his people to the fullest enjoyment of his kingdom." That's the sermon's main goal. "I call it *expository exultation*."[40] In the sermon, questions are answered, the congregation is shown truth from Scripture, and then they are invited to be "caught up with the preacher in his love affair with God and his salvation."[41] Affectionate worship is the final aim of QRCW, whether in preaching a sermon or answering pastoral questions. The regenerate heart's search for satisfying divine answers was—and remains—the pedagogical foundation from which Piper's entire ministry is built.

As predicted, in the transition from academic lectern to church pulpit, Pastor John never stopped asking and answering questions. The discipline shaped how he prepared his sermons and pastored his flock. Live and in-person Q&A sessions became a staple for Piper, both at home and on the road, as his preaching ministry rose to national and international notoriety in the early 2000s.

In 1998, a new website launched to host Piper's popular sermons (desiringGod.org). And as the volume of online listeners increased, so too rose the volume of theological inquiries. Email questions arrived about everything—Calvinism, eschatology, infant salvation, marriage and divorce, "just war" (in light of 9/11), and Bible reading tips. In the early days, these inquiries were answered by his assistants. With the website in place, it made sense to publish written responses to the most common questions as a digital FAQ. The site became an online hub of answers.

Beginning in 2007, these questions were posed to Pastor John by radio host Bob Allen, who edited Piper sermons into radio broadcasts. In a ten-month span between June 2007 and April 2008, he produced 132 episodes.[42] Several of these broadcasts included bonus in-studio audio, with Allen posing questions to Piper. Those responses were later excerpted from the radio programs

---

39 Ken Wanovich, "Piper Accepts Senior Pastorate," *Clarion* 55 (March 21, 1980): 4.
40 APJ 118: "Is the 40-Minute Sermon Passé?" (June 24, 2013).
41 APJ 1877: "What Makes for a Good Musical Worship Experience?" (December 21, 2022).
42 Bob Allen, email to author, July 19, 2018.

and indexed as audio files at desiringGod.org under a new banner: "Ask Pastor John"—a heading first coined and added to the website in August 2007.

After the radio program ended, Desiring God launched a livestream video format called *Ask Pastor John Live*.[43] On a makeshift set, Piper answered real-time questions from viewers through a novel social-media platform called Twitter. Sometimes the live video format used a host to read questions,[44] and other times the questions were printed on cards or flashed on a screen to Pastor John, who read the questions and answered them all on the fly, consecutively, one after another, without advance preparation. The videos ended abruptly a few years later, canceled in the spring of 2010 to make room for Pastor John's eight-month ministry leave to focus on his heart, his marriage, and his family.[45]

Podcasting
The leave ended at the conclusion of 2010, and Pastor John returned to ministry rejuvenated and renewed. But no radio or video manifestation of APJ resumed.

In January of 2012, I joined the team at Desiring God and launched my first longform podcast, *Authors on the Line* (AOTL). I interviewed authors over the telephone and handled the planning, hosting, writing, producing, recording, postproduction, sound engineering, and marketing. By the end of that first year, I completed eleven longform episodes and had settled on a process for efficiently getting conversations recorded, transcribed, edited, and published through a syndicated audio channel. I called John Piper's home landline phone for the very first time at the end of November 2012 to record a special holiday episode of AOTL.[46] Technologically, everything worked.

Entering 2013, Desiring God faced a new challenge. In the spring, Piper's pastorate at Bethlehem Baptist Church would end. And to allow the new church leadership to gel, he planned a year away in Knoxville, Tennessee, with wife, Noël, and daughter, Talitha, from June 2013 to August 2014.[47] He would use the time to work on various book projects and to dream about the next decade of ministry ahead, a rural "retooling" for his next season of urban ministry.[48] But the temporary move left Desiring God in a bind because we had never experienced ministry

43 First envisioned by Lukas Naugle.
44 Often moderated by David Mathis.
45 May to December 2010. For details, see his bookended updates: John Piper, "John Piper's Upcoming Leave," Desiring God, March 28, 2010, https://www.desiringgod.org/; John Piper, "John Piper's Report on His Leave of Absence," Desiring God, January 1, 2011, https://www.desiringgod.org/.
46 John Piper and Paul Maier, "Christmas and the Sting of Personal Loss," podcast interview, *Authors on the Line*, December 4, 2012.
47 APJ 111: "Our Move to Tennessee and New Projects" (June 13, 2013).
48 APJ 112: "Adjusting to Life in the Country" (June 14, 2013).

with Pastor John so long absent from Minneapolis. How could we keep his voice close to our audience while he lived and worked eight hundred miles away?

With my little podcast experience, at a ministry team lunch on January 7, 2013, I proposed a new podcast with an old title: *Ask Pastor John*. Podcast delivery would follow the popular Q&A format, reminiscent of the old radio program and the livestream video, but could now geographically detach Pastor John from the host. It would replace eye contact and attentiveness to a video camera with the freedom to work remotely and to work from detailed notes. It eliminated the uncertainties of live and impromptu sessions. Now every episode could be preplanned and every question more carefully selected and studied. Pastor John would now have between forty-five and sixty minutes of prep time for each reply. No cold questions; no cold answers. A time investment made possible when Pastor John became a full-time employee at Desiring God a few months later.[49] Providentially, at the same time, audio-only podcasting was becoming popular among Christian listeners.

In the podcast proposal, I suggested that topics "could include leadership coaching, pastoral and exegetical and theological questions, responses to con-temporary events, autobiographical details of public value, updates on current reading and thinking, responses to listener questions, as well as travel plans and personal and writing updates." Pastor John *could* cover all those topics. That was clear. And I had a goal in mind: to "connect Pastor John to the Desiring God audience each week from now until the conclusion of his leave." The podcast would then terminate after eighteen months, giving us about 390 episodes. Surely by then, I thought, every question would be answered.

That evening I sent a formal proposal to Pastor John, and two hours later he eagerly replied: "This sounds excellent. Let's pray that it will not just be interesting or informative, but spiritually awakening and Christ-exalting, and soul-sanctifying, and mission advancing, and that it would spread a passion for the supremacy of God in all things through Jesus Christ, and abundantly more." Because the goal of human curiosity is not just right answers in the brain, but joy in the satisfied heart (QRCW). Then he asked: "Any suggested regular hour of the week. Like this week, starting Friday????"[50] John Piper doesn't use emojis and rarely repeats punctuation. Four repeated question marks translated into an eagerness to launch this podcast. Just four days after I sent my proposal, we launched episode 1 on January 11, 2013: "Reflections from John Piper on His [Sixty-Seventh] Birthday."

---

49 Which began April 1, 2013.
50 John Piper, email to author, January 7, 2013.

Our initial pace was brisk. Episode 100 released *before* the Pipers left for Knoxville. In our eager jump, we released 245 episodes in 2013 alone, one new episode from Pastor John every weekday. In due time we slowed the pace, but Pastor John's voice remained very close to Desiring God's audience. As the Pipers packed up to leave Knoxville and return to Minneapolis, we published episode 400 (on, of all things, a very sensitive marital intimacy question). No topic was taboo, and this episode proved it. The more willingly we embraced awkward situational topics, the quicker our audience grew.

But episode 400 did not become our finish line; it became our tipping point (now the most played episode in the history of the podcast, with around 2.5 million plays and growing). By the time the Pipers returned home to Minneapolis, the podcast had registered nine million episode plays, and—thanks to episode 400—that number quickly rocketed past ten million.[51] New daily emails from listeners increased from ten to twenty to thirty.[52] We decided to ride out the growth momentum, and we never stopped. Here we are, ten years later.

In the inaugural episode I called APJ a "relaunch" of the previous radio and video formats, but in fact the podcast version developed into a unique product within John Piper's ministry legacy. The prep time allotted to Pastor John was a big reason why. After a decade, and nearing two thousand episodes, our basic premise remains unchanged, though we've modified various aspects of the podcast over the years. Early on we moved our landline phone calls to Skype and then to Zoom. Since Knoxville, Piper has always recorded in his upstairs office in Minneapolis in an urban home on a busy street, and not far from a hospital. Plenty of road noises and sirens have interrupted recordings. To combat the commotion, we experimented with various studio mics that helped but never totally silenced the clamor (most obvious the morning when city workers arrived unannounced to chainsaw down his beloved front-yard tree[53]).

I also record in my home office, first in Minneapolis and then in Phoenix, always remotely. The exception being August 21, 2019, when Pastor John and I appeared on stage to record our first-ever APJ live in Nashville in front of

---

51 A few milestones to note, based on the total times our episodes were played. Even before the Pipers moved out of Minneapolis, APJ crested one million total episode plays all-time (July 2013). Shortly after they returned from Knoxville, we hit ten million (October 2014). We hit fifty million in July 2016, one hundred million in July 2018, and two hundred million in July 2021.

52 An email load that soon exceeded our capacity to answer. In total, in our first decade, we averaged thirty emails per day, 216 per week, 936 per month, 11,237 per year—or sixty-three questions *in* per Piper episode *out*.

53 APJ 1615: "Did Abraham Laugh at God's Promise?" (April 19, 2021).

about two thousand podcast listeners at the Getty Sing! conference. It resulted in five episodes.[54] And it worked so well, we repeated it three years later.[55]

To make our publishing pace sustainable over the years, we introduced seasons of guests and sermon extracts, and later scaled to a format of three episodes per week—two new studio episodes from Piper (on Mondays and Fridays), and one curated sermon-clip episode (on Wednesdays). When we launched a new sermon-clip podcast in 2023, we dropped the clips and settled on two episodes per week (on Mondays and Thursdays).

Over time, the podcast proved useful for field recordings of Piper audio that wouldn't fit other content channels. This included his prayer at a local pro-life rally outside a Planned Parenthood facility, simply recorded on an iPhone.[56] Also on an iPhone, at a Desiring God staff meeting, we captured his prayer for the president, minutes after the staff watched Donald Trump's inauguration together.[57] And a local church captured an unforgettable prayer at the funeral for a family of five who had been in training to become missionaries to Japan when they were all killed in a single car accident.[58] Each of these historic audio moments in Pastor John's ministry found a ready home in APJ.

APJ's Goal

The growth of the podcast was great, but it also led to occasional friendly emails from church leaders who feared that APJ's widespread use was subverting the wisdom of local churches, pastors, and Christian friends in our lives who are better suited to help us in our struggles. So at the end of our first year, I asked Pastor John how he wanted listeners to engage with APJ. How should listeners balance the podcast with the voices immediately around us? "In the spirit of 1 Thessalonians 5," he said. "Test everything; hold fast what is good"

---

54 Sing 2019 episodes were released as APJ 1379: "How Do We Respond When a Pastor Leaves the Faith?" (October 9, 2019), APJ 1382: "When to Stop Listening to This Podcast" (October 16, 2019), APJ 1386: "Should Anyone Say, 'I Am of Calvin'?" (October 25, 2019), APJ 1418: "What Every Marriage Needs Most" (January 8, 2020), and APJ 1421: "How Should I Parent My Non-Christian Teen?" (January 15, 2020).

55 Sing 2022 episodes were released as APJ 1861: "Let the Nations Be Glad!—Thirty Years Later" (November 14, 2022), APJ 1877: "What Makes for a Good Musical Worship Experience?" (December 21, 2022), APJ 1882: "John Piper's Favorite Things" (January 2, 2023), APJ 1885: "Getting the Tone Right on Sunday Morning" (January 9, 2023), and APJ 1887: "When Does Despondency Become Sin?" (January 13, 2023).

56 APJ SE06: "John Piper's Prayer at Planned Parenthood" (August 22, 2015).

57 APJ SE11: "John Piper's Prayer for President Trump" (January 20, 2017).

58 APJ SE10: "John Piper's Funeral Prayer for a Family of Five" (August 6, 2016), a risky episode we debriefed a few weeks later (APJ 931: "How Do You Pray in Public, without Performing?" [August 31, 2016]).

(1 Thess. 5:21). Test everything by the Bible. "That's where I try to find all my responses to people's questions." Second, "I hope they esteem the spiritual leaders of their own churches highly and talk to them about the issues they face—which is also in 1 Thessalonians 5 (1 Thess. 5:13)! There is one final authority and it's God's word, not mine. I want to exalt God's word over and over as true and wise and sweet."[59]

A few years later, Pastor John mentioned his hope that the podcast was equipping listeners to think for themselves. "My prayer is that, besides the immediate guidance and encouragement it may give, over time, people will absorb a way of thinking and a way of using the Bible so that in the decades to come they will become the sages in their churches where younger people come for wise, Bible-saturated, gospel-rich counsel."[60] The purpose of APJ is to disciple Christians into mentors who can better serve the people around them. The podcast doesn't subvert local churches; it fortifies them. We pray the Christians who listen will be equipped to better serve the many nonlisteners in their lives. Based on our emails, this is happening. (And equipping pastors to be better pastors too.)

The podcast doesn't replace pastors or friends, because our episodes are not infallible. APJ is one source of wisdom, not a single decoder ring to solve all of life's riddles. We don't make decisions for listeners. Our aim is to equip and empower Christians to answer their own questions with an open Bible.

To avoid religious authoritarianism (mentioned above), listeners must be equipped to find answers from Scripture on their own. Pastor John has explained how. Begin with a question and find the corresponding Bible terms. Run a digital concordance word study of those terms. Isolate five (or so) key texts, print them, study their context, and then circle and underline words that seem especially relevant for answering the question. With these texts in place, build your biblical convictions. Knowing most listeners could do this on their own, Piper seeks to "empower" listeners to engage the word for themselves. "You could make your own podcast," he said with a smile.[61]

Why This Book?
John Piper is a pastor-theologian. Decades of pastoral ministry trained him for this podcast. I'm a journalist-teacher. Several years in the print-news industry trained me how to report events and conduct interviews, skills I now use to capture and curate pastoral wisdom to serve APJ's audience. Reading audience emails, choosing the best questions, scheduling the episodes—my podcast

59 John Piper, email to author, March 10, 2014.
60 John Piper, email to author, July 11, 2018.
61 APJ 1084: "If Someone Doesn't Like Me, Have I Ruined My Christian Witness?" (August 23, 2017).

labors are just an excuse to pull off a 220-hour interview with a pastor-theologian (and friend) who endlessly fascinates me. After a full decade, we have accumulated a huge archive of over 2.3 million published words.

My book is a guided tour, a narrated synthesis of our 750 most popular episodes, mostly on situational ethics, published in the *Ask Pastor John* audio podcast over the course of its first decade (from January 11, 2013 to December 30, 2022). This book is a core sample of John Piper's mind and theology. I pray it serves four purposes.

1. I want to map the ground we have covered so I don't repeat questions. With such a vast archive, about a third of new listener emails have been sufficiently covered in the past, either directly or indirectly. This suggests to me that even though we maintain a huge digital archive—fully transcribed and searchable—many people cannot easily find those episodes when they need them. Even I sometimes forget which questions have already been covered. So I pray this book matches our archive to new and future questions you will face. And helps me avoid repetition.

2. I want to topically curate our episodes. As the podcast archive grew, I also noticed a sharp uptick in requests from friends and ministry partners asking me to point them to past APJ answers to specific questions they are facing. I did. And as I did, I discovered how each question is best answered from various angles in multiple episodes. The overlapping value of multiple episodes proved daunting at first. But to each request I responded with an abstract, a summary and synthesis of multiple episodes that I thought could help. In return, I was told these summaries did help. So I kept a running document to collect them over the years. That document became the genesis of this book. And when our international partners heard about these abstracts, they requested them for another reason. Translators interested in bringing the podcast archive to a new language (and APJ now exists in ten languages!) told me that they would benefit from a topical guide to help them triage episodes on given topics and subtopics to guide their work and cluster their focus.

3. I want to celebrate Pastor John's investment in this podcast. APJ is a one-of-a-kind pastoral resource. As inspiring as he is in explaining his do-it-yourself method, he does so by leaving out his own resume. His answers are not simply the product of a concordance. John Piper is a renowned New Testament scholar, world-class preacher, and veteran pastor with over three decades of church leadership practice added to his personal experience in marriage, parenting, and grandparenting. He watches his life and doctrine more closely than anyone else I've known (1 Tim. 4:16). And he was born to answer Bible questions.[62]

---

62 In keeping, you'll find references to Scripture and Scripture quotations throughout. Many of these cited scriptures are not direct quotes but paraphrases or original translations. The

He has a keen eye for the crux, skilled in rapidly pinpointing the core problem in a given dilemma—a gift I've seen operate in tense meetings, complex email chains, and now in hundreds of APJ responses. While there's always much more to say on a topic, he can isolate the main thing that needs to be said in a ten-minute episode. His willingness to invest hundreds of hours of preparation into his responses, personal piety, earnestness, devotion to Scripture, skill in pinpointing core issues, and deep experience are the ingredients to the secret sauce of the podcast's popularity now, and of its potential to endure for decades ahead.

4. I want to acquaint you with the scope and depth of the podcast archive. My fifteen years in curating pastoral wisdom is now employed in the goal of adding value to APJ. This book doesn't replace the podcast; it complements it as an easily browsable companion guide, a summary of our most popular episodes, particularly focused on the situational dilemmas we will face. It's a CliffsNotes version of our most popular episodes to aid meditation, retainment, and recall. Books can be easily stacked on shelves. Even magazines can be kept in a box or basket. But podcasts are strictly digital things—ephemeral audio files meant to stream, play, and then disappear like a soundwave in the air. But APJ was designed, from the start, to endure as a permanent audio archive. What you hold in your hands is a guided tour— a topically arranged encyclopedia to a podcast archive. I don't intend for that to make immediate sense, because I think this book inaugurates a new genre. Basically, my prayer is that by making dozens of the major podcast themes browsable in print, this book will make the archive more useful to you at the very moment you need it. This book doesn't *have* an index; it *is* the index, an index to serve you as you serve others. So for example, if you're counseling someone (or a couple), don't simply copy and assign pages from this book. Instead, assign specific podcast episodes. Use this book to find your assignments.

As we build this podcast into a single content library, our first decade lays the groundwork for everything else to come. For current listeners, the book rehearses key highlights from the past. For future listeners, the book is an on-ramp to summarize the ground we've already covered. This book will immediately serve thousands of current listeners who found their way *from* the podcast *to* this book. But perhaps, if the Lord is gracious, the current will reverse in due time, and thousands of readers will find their way *from* this book *to* the podcast.

___

quotation marks surrounding Scripture verses frequently indicate Pastor John's speaking from the Scripture rather than the actual Scripture text.

That's my prayer. As you gift this book to not-yet-listeners, you're helping me fulfill this dream. Think of this book as a podcast promo made of paper and ink that you can physically hand to others.

Getting to the Audio

I want to show you around these 220 hours of audio recordings. I'll again be your host, not from behind a mic but from behind a keyboard.

The audio recording and transcript for each episode is housed at the Desiring God website (desiringgod.org). To move from the book to the episode, follow my footnotes. A footnote for "APJ 1173" means everything paraphrased or quoted *before that footnote* is from episode 1173. To find the full episode, go to the APJ homepage—AskPastorJohn.com—and simply type "1173" in the search bar. To find episodes in Google or YouTube, use the full episode titles in your search.

Find the episode number in the footnote, flip to the episode index in the back of this book, and find the episode's full title to use in your search.

Speaking of that index in the back, over the years several APJ listeners have emailed to let us know they have listened to *every episode* of the podcast. You can, too, with that full title index as a guide to every episode featuring Pastor John over the course of our first decade, 2013–2022. It can be used to tick off episodes as you listen through the entire archive. And just browsing the title list is a great way to discover episodes too.

The archive is overwhelming. I want it to feel more manageable through my book, first inspired by Richard Baxter's classic *A Christian Directory* (1673), which weighs in at 1.3 million words (six times longer than this book). Forced in his introduction to address the elephant in the room—its enormous size!—Baxter lamented that it was to his "own great trouble" that "the world cannot be sufficiently instructed and edified in fewer words."[63] Ha! Yes. Now zooming past 2.3 million published words, the APJ archive dwarfs Baxter's book. As it does, I'll echo his sentiment. Instructing and edifying the world is wordy work.

Thank-Yous

But the labor involved in publishing APJ is no trouble or burden. It's a joyful labor, largely because our listeners eagerly listen and enthusiastically participate. But it *is* work. *Hard* work. Firsthand, I've watched John Piper pour himself into every APJ recording session. In the summer of 2018, he bought a Fitbit heart

---

63 Richard Baxter, *The Practical Works of the Rev. Richard Baxter* (London: James Duncan, 1830), 1:546.

monitor. A couple of weeks later, as we ended our recording of one particularly grueling series of questions, I said: "Wow, that was a lot!" He agreed. "Whew— I feel like I just ran a marathon!" he replied, with a joy-filled laugh as he looked down at the Fitbit on his wrist. "I have been stunned—stunned—when I look at the graph of my day. I have a lot of 60 bpm. And then spikes go up to 100 or 125 bpm. Of course, the spikes are there when I jog and when I lift. But they're also there when I preach and record APJs. But I don't feel out of breath like when I jog. It's adrenaline—an adrenaline high, I guess."[64]

That summer we reached 100 million episodes played, and at this benchmark I discovered another side to his exertion. I asked Pastor John to reflect on what it had been like for him working on the podcast. "There are times I put my face in my hands and shake my head when I read the questions you send me from our listeners," he said of his prep days. "So much suffering. So much sorrow. So many imponderable relational tangles with seemingly no human solution. So the effect of *Ask Pastor John* on my life is first to soften me for people's suffering, and then anger me at sin and Satan. It drives me not only to the word of God, my only hope of helping anybody, but also to prayer and to the Holy Spirit. In other words, the podcast makes me feel helpless."[65]

Pouring our lives into the work, in a spirit of desperation, we depend wholly on God for this podcast to continue. Ten years old, nearing two thousand episodes, passing 230 million episode plays—all of it is grace. We charge no fees. We use no sidebar ads or paid sponsors. We depend wholly on God, putting it on listeners' hearts to pray for us and to financially support us, so that we can—together—make the podcast free and accessible to millions of listeners around the world. APJ has the potential to serve the church for decades ahead, and it has been the honor of a lifetime to play my part in it. For all of it, I'd like to personally say thank you! To *you*—Desiring God's precious ministry partners—I dedicate this book.

64 John Piper, raw recording session outro, June 6, 2018.
65 John Piper, email to author, July 11, 2018.

A Word before We Begin

DON'T STOP LISTENING TO THE PODCAST! What you hold is a companion guide, a thematic synthesis, an easy-to-browse encyclopedia, to make the audio archive more valuable and useful. My book is intentionally brief, blunt, and to the point. The audio recordings are fuller, warmer, and more pastoral. Use them in tandem.

You probably won't agree with everything in this book or on the podcast. That's okay. Read and listen as a good Berean with an open Bible and active discernment.

You won't need everything in this book. Not immediately. It covers a broad swath of situational ethics on our most popular themes.

If you are a Christian leader and pastor, however, you should consider every word of this book. These topics will introduce you to the mind of John Piper as he addresses situational, ethical dilemmas from the Bible. By them I hope you will more clearly see how he processes challenging questions. It's formative. While I am forever grateful to God that Piper writes books and preaches sermons, I have learned the most from Pastor John in his answers to great questions. Those answers help me contextualize his complete works.

Study Pastor John's text-first approach to ethics. With a question on the table, Pastor John begins with the clearest biblical texts on the topic first, then reasons out to proper application. The church can sometimes rush too quickly to discuss and debate very specific ethical *applications*, too often running past the first step of getting clear on the *baseline relevant texts*, which are the ground of all else. For the sake of the church, this text-first approach will remain an essential discipline for Christian authors, professors, journalists, counselors, pastors, preachers, parents, and anyone who describes or prescribes Christian ethics. The goal of the podcast is the aim of this book—to help you form your own ethical synapses, new junctions where Scripture connects to daily life in the twenty-first-century world.

Most importantly, desire God. God *is*—"absolute, self-existent, and independent of all other reality" (Exod. 3:14). He has no beginning and no end. He experiences no need, no change, no improvements.[1] Behind, under, over, and around the entire APJ podcast looms this self-sufficient Creator of the universe, infinitely happy in himself. Every other topic—from salvation to smartphones to sulking to sex—can only be handled Christianly in the presence of our triune Creator's bliss. "From all eternity, before all time, God was alive with volcanic joy. Joy is essential to the very nature of God in the fellowship of the infinitely happy and holy Trinity. The Father loves the Son and finds him supremely well pleasing. The Son loves the Father and delights in all that he is. The Holy Spirit streams omnipotently with his joy between the Father and the Son. So God needs nothing. He has no deficiencies. He is free from all evil and full of all good."[2]

All of God's subsequent sovereign actions display his all-powerful independence. God is "completely happy" within himself, "happy at the core of his being in his all-sufficiency." From his self-sufficiency he creates the world, in love, a place "to share with creatures in his own image the very joy that he has in himself." God doesn't need creation. Or you. Or me. And yet he is so "perfectly happy" in himself that he chooses to create us and to redeem us from our sin through Christ's blood so that we can experience the eternal bliss of delighting in him. And so arises "this great circle of *enjoying* God and *glorifying* God."[3] The two aims become one. Thus, second only to the happiness he enjoys in himself, "there is no higher or greater happiness that God is looking forward to" than "the delight that he takes in the echoes of his excellence in the supremely happy praises of the saints."[4] Only to this ultimate and eternal end—God glorified by our satisfaction in him—should each of our life decisions be considered and each of the following episodes be consumed.[5]

1 APJ 1600: "Who Is God?" (March 15, 2021).
2 APJ SE09: "The Joy Project" (September 21, 2015).
3 APJ 116: "God's Joy and the Joy of the Calvinist" (June 20, 2013).
4 APJ 958: "The Heart of Christian Hedonism—and the Bible and Creation and Everything" (November 2, 2016).
5 To flesh out John Piper's "favorite slogan" ("God is most glorified in us when we are most satisfied in him"), see APJ 30: "Three Levels of God-Glorifying Emotion" (February 19, 2013), APJ 194: "Is God an Egomaniac?" (October 15, 2013), APJ 482: "Are We Satisfied 'in God' or 'by God'?" (December 1, 2014), APJ 497: "Is God Less Glorified in the Judgment of Sinners?" (December 22, 2014), APJ 702: "Is God Only Glorified by People Who Love Him?" (October 8, 2015), APJ 1096: "What's the Origin of Desiring God's Slogan?" (September 20, 2017), APJ 1201: "Is My Joy Essential in Glorifying God?" (May 23, 2018), and APJ 1215: "Is God Glorified in Those Who Reject Him?" (June 25, 2018).

On Bible Reading, Bible Neglect, and Bible Memory

Why do we read the Bible?

We prioritize daily Bible reading because without it we fail to achieve life's great purpose: "to make God in Christ look magnificent—to make him look precious and valuable, to look like the supreme treasure that he is" (Phil. 1:20). And yet, "there's so much in us that is inclined to think or feel or act in ways that *don't* make Christ look great." To accomplish our great purpose, we must see glory. "If we don't desire and cherish and enjoy and savor and treasure Christ, we will not commend him as magnificent in what we feel and say and do. Christ is most magnified in us when we are most satisfied in him, and we cannot be daily satisfied in the depths of our soul in Christ if we don't *see* him and *savor* him." And that will "only happen" by a "steady meditation on the word of God in the Bible." In Scripture we behold Christ's glory, and this glory transforms us from the inside out (2 Cor. 3:18; 4:4).

Proper Bible reading is motivated by a desperation to see God. "The reason I read the Bible is because I am stone-cold dead without Christ and his word. But I want all my life—every part of it—to be glorious. I want life to be beautiful. I want life to be vastly more than it is if I'm left to myself. I want to see how astonishing reality is at every turn—every person, every rock, every tree, every animal, every work of salvation. I know that, left to myself, I am an absolute dud. I am blank, nothing deep, nothing moving, nothing intense, nothing beautiful, nothing precious, nothing sweet or wonderful— just empty, blank, unmoved, coasting along from one worldly preoccupation to another." There's "one hope for John Piper: that I would have eyes to see the God-entranced magnificence of everything—namely, that God would be pleased in my Bible reading to cause me to see the glory that is really there." We must see and savor the glory that shapes us into redeemed sinners who magnify God by being satisfied in him. Set in this context, Bible reading is truly an "awesome quest."[1]

Why read the Bible daily?

To a new believer who asked why daily Bible reading is so essential to a fruitful life: "I have never met a mature, fruitful, strong, spiritually discerning Christian who is not full of Scripture, devoted to regular meditation on Scripture, and given to storing it in the heart through Bible memorization—and that's not a coincidence." Indeed, "it is absolutely essential, after coming to faith in Christ, to be radically, deeply, experientially devoted—unshakably, unwaveringly per-suaded—that reading and meditating on and understanding and memorizing and enjoying the Scriptures is absolutely essential for the Christian life." It calls for daily practice.

Here are ten reasons we need the word daily. (1) Scripture is a means of preserving our salvation. Salvation is a dynamic reality that functions in three tenses: past, present, and future. And in the present reality, "God saves us daily by Scripture" (1 Tim. 4:16). (2) Scripture meets Satan's temptations (John 8:32, 44; 1 John 2:14). "Every time Jesus was tempted by the devil, he struck back with 'the sword of the Spirit, which is the word of God'" (Eph. 6:17). And he had it memorized "so he didn't have to carry a book in the wilderness." (3) Scripture is a means of grace and peace to us (2 Pet. 1:2). (4) Scripture is meant to sanctify our lives, to make us more and more holy (John 17:17). "We don't become perfect in this life, but we do become holy" through the Spirit's work in our lives via the word. (5) Scripture gives us joy (Ps. 1:2; 1 Thess. 1:6). "Life without joy is unbearable. The Christian life is filled with afflictions. But in them all, God sustains joy, and he does it by the Scriptures." (6) Scripture protects from error (Eph. 4:13–14). How do Christians avoid becoming leaves blown around by all the cultural winds of opinions? The answer: "The unity of the faith and of the knowledge of the Son of God—knowledge that they experience not as the opinion of man, but as the word of God. That's found in one place: the scriptures." (7) Scripture gives us hope for eternity. Scripture promises us that the frustrations that limit our joy in this life will be removed in the age to come. (8) Scripture keeps us from being startled by false teachers and apostates (2 Tim. 4:3). (9) The Bible calls for careful handling, which we can only learn through day-by-day familiarity with the word (2 Tim. 2:15). (10) The Bible sustains our lives (Matt. 4:4). "Spiritual life—eternal life—just like physical life, must be fed, not by bread, but by the word of God. If you think

---

1   APJ 1140: "A New Year, A New Bible Reading Plan" (January 1, 2018).

that you have eternal life as a kind of vaccination against hell, which needs no nourishment, you don't know what spiritual life is." Spiritual life is sustained by the daily bread of God's word.[2]

How do I get the most from my Bible reading?

With all these convictions in place, how do we maximize the impact of our daily Bible reading?

People are very different, and Bible reading will be a different experience for everyone, including the man who initially asked the question. "How disciplined is he? How much time does he have available? What skill does he have in reading—what speed and comprehension? How familiar is he with all the parts of the Bible, even those maybe he hasn't read at all? What level of curiosity does he have that might drive him to slow down and figure things out that are puzzling to him?" Our Bible reading experiences differ because "our capacities for reading and comprehending, our speed, and our life situations are different."

Despite the variables, here are common helps.

1. Belong to a great church that models careful Bible reading by preaching verse by verse. "Few things are more helpful in grasping the totality of Scripture than a steady, week in and week out, month in and month out, year in and year out, decade in and decade out feeding on the preached word of God. Oh, this is so important. If your pastor doesn't preach Bible texts and explain to you what they mean, please try to find another church. Because the decades of your life will be gloriously transformed if you sit under the preaching of the word like that for a long, long time." What you hear preached on Sunday morning should illuminate what you read on Monday morning.

2. Find friends who offer accountability and ask you how your reading is going.

3. Set your routine. "Set aside a place and a time where you're going to read your Bible every day. If you don't have a set place and a set time, Satan—along with your own flesh—will almost certainly push your Bible reading right out of your schedule and out of your space."

4. Pray. "Pray earnestly over your Bible reading before you read, while you're reading, and after you read. Pray that God would show you what's really there and make it real for you."

5. Appreciate the deep change that comes from persistence. The Bible is huge. In a given day you'll read four chapters, most of which you will forget in

2   APJ 1512: "Ten Reasons to Read the Bible Every Day" (August 14, 2020).

an hour. In this sense, daily reading will soon feel "absolutely overwhelming and pointless." But in the discipline, Scripture is "lodging itself in your mind and in your heart in ways you cannot comprehend. The so-called forgotten *language*, the forgotten *paragraphs*, the forgotten *words*, the forgotten *stories*, the forgotten *points* are becoming a repository from which the Holy Spirit can draw out things you do not even know are there."

6. Take something specific from your reading. More practically, aim to "take one crisp, clear sentence with you—something encouraging, something motivating, something strengthening, something guiding. Write it down on a little piece of paper, stick it in your pocket, stick it in your purse, whatever. Say it to yourself over and over again during the day. Those sentences accumulated—365 of them—are an amazing power and stockpile of truth over time."

7. Very practically, use the Discipleship Journal Bible Reading Plan to read from four places in the Bible, with the benefit of catch-up days built into the monthly rhythms. But read it. Read all of it. Because "if we leave out big parts of the Bible, we probably won't know God the way we should."[3]

What should we expect on our first read through the Bible?
The Bible daunts any first-time reader, so it's natural to feel intimidated from the start. Here are three negatives to "scare you off," and then nine positives to "suck you back in."

Expect three challenges that will dampen your desire to read the Bible cover to cover.

1. You will be opposed. "Satan hates the word of God and will disincline you, blind you, distract you, bore you." He will do anything to keep you from the word. Pray for his subversive aims to backfire. "Ask God to keep your heart inclined, remove your blindness, grant you focus instead of distraction, and give you excitement instead of boredom."

2. You will be shocked. The Bible is raw and honest about life and eternal matters. It's "stunningly graphic in its description, both of our outrageous sin and God's breathtaking judgment on sin. If you have any kind of sympathetic engagement with the Bible, you will want to throw up at times when you see what God ordains against sin in this world." Brace yourself.

3. You will be confused. Expect to come away from Bible reading with unanswered questions, because God does not reveal to us everything we want to know (Deut. 29:29). And what he does reveal is sometimes hard to understand (2 Pet. 3:16). You will need preachers and teachers in your life to make

3   APJ 1296: "How Do I Make the Most of Daily Bible Reading?" (December 31, 2018).

progress in the challenging parts of Scripture. Press through the confusion. "Put things together that you can put together. And what you can't figure out, put on the shelf for later attention, and keep on moving." Don't let any question stop your progress.

If you press on, expect nine experiences to bless your efforts. (1) Your faith will be deepened. Faith comes from hearing the word, because the Bible was written to give us hope (Rom. 10:17; 15:4). (2) You will experience new liberation from lies and sins that have plagued you (John 8:32). (3) You will be outfitted with new weapons to withstand Satan (Matt. 4:1–11). (4) You will be made more holy (John 17:17). (5) You will become more loving (Phil. 1:9). (6) You will be sustained. "The Bible is the means of God by which he goes on saving us" (1 Tim. 4:16). (7) You will be given an indestructible joy (John 15:11). (8) You will meet God directly, because he meets us in his word (1 Sam. 3:21). (9) And you will behold more and more of Christ's radiant glory (2 Cor. 3:18). These nine blessed experiences make the challenges of daily Bible reading worthwhile.[4]

How do we stay passionate about Bible reading for a full year?

We don't follow Bible reading plans to tick off a daily checklist or to meet an external law. We do it to meet an internal necessity, because "feeding upon the word of God day-by-day is built into God's way of saving you." We are born again by the word that awakens our spiritual appetite (1 Pet. 1:23–2:3). In this new condition, Peter tells us to *keep on desiring* this word. This is no auto-appetite. We "stoke this desire for spiritual food in the word of God by which you were born again." The pure word saved us (1 Pet. 1:23–25). And because of it, we can long for the pure milk of the word, "that by it you may grow up into salvation" (1 Pet. 2:1–3). James makes the same point. The word made you alive (James 1:18). Therefore, go on receiving the word with meekness (James 1:21). "The evidence of your new birth will be shown by your ongoing feeding on the word of God, which works in you all the kinds of things that keep you on the narrow road that leads to life and final salvation." If you neglect the word, "what's your alternative strategy for making it home?"

Peter and James remind us that the Christian life starts with a new birth brought about by the word, and it is sustained by receiving the word humbly and regularly. Our spiritual lives are not preserved automatically; they are preserved by the means of God's word. "I love to get up early in the morning,

4   APJ 1416: "What Should I Expect My First Time through the Bible?" (January 3, 2020).

grab my cup of hot tea in the wintertime, sit in my chair for an hour, and enjoy fellowship with Jesus, the living King of the universe, in four different places of the Bible. It is my life. May I say it again? It is my life. Oh, may God cause you to experience his word as life!"[5]

Where should I help a new believer begin his journey into the Bible?

The Gospel of John is celebrated as a good place to start, given that its purpose is clearly to introduce the life and work of Christ (John 20:30–31). But you can go broader and begin with some sense of familiarity with the New Testament. The Bible is meant for a lifetime of exploration and daily discipline. John Piper's sixty years as a believer have been sustained by this discipline of daily Bible reading. "Wherever you start, you are going *forever* in the Bible. This is not about merely starting."

Another place to start is with an overview of the New Testament's structure. It begins with four Gospels, "the books about the historical foundations of the life, death, and resurrection of Jesus." And then comes the book of Acts, "the story of how the early church got started and launched by the power of the Holy Spirit after Jesus went back to heaven, and how the church took root because of what Jesus had done." Next comes a bunch of letters written by "the authoritative apostles—the spokesmen for the risen Christ—teaching the church how to live in the church and in society." Finally, the "strange book" of Revelation finishes the New Testament with "the victory of God at the end of the age."

Or you can start with Luke and Acts, one book in two volumes. See the opening of the book and their united purposes as "one man writing a double volume about the foundations and then about the expansion of the church" (Luke 1:1–4; Acts 1:1–3). Then move to Paul's letters.

Every reader brings different intellectual capacities and reading abilities. Some will struggle to read, and that's okay. Essential to Bible reading is also finding a church "with solid preaching, vital corporate worship, and a small group of relationships where you can ask lots of questions" and "get all the help in the world" as you make your way through the canon "little by little."[6]

Another consideration. If you've never read the Bible, start with Jesus. Begin with two books about his life and work. Start with the Gospel of Mark and then read the Gospel of John. Then read an epistle that puts all the implications of

5 APJ 1569: "How Do I Become Passionate about Bible Reading?" (January 1, 2021).
6 APJ 284: "Where Should a New Believer Start in the Bible?" (February 24, 2014).

Christ's life and work together, particularly Romans. Then consider a historical book about the early church, called Acts. And then read from the middle of the Bible, the Psalms, ancient songs that "capture all the moods and the ups and downs and the struggles of God's people."[7]

Three essential components to daily Bible reading

We need three essential components "to ongoing fruitful encounters with God and his intended truth through the Bible." (1) *Motivation*, (2) *skill*, and (3) *illumination*. Or (1) the "want to," (2) the "able to," and (3) the "see through." Or the (1) *desire*, (2) *act*, and (3) *reward* of Bible reading.

Essential Bible reading component 1 is the motivation—the "want to," the desire for Bible reading. "If we lose motivation, we will not read the Bible. And if we don't read the Bible, we miss everything God has for us through the word." We *must* be motivated for the task, with motivation like Jesus offers in John 17. "There is a fullness of joy that we will miss if we don't continually listen to what Jesus speaks—that is, listen to the Bible" (John 17:13). And there's a life transformation we will miss if we don't read the Bible (John 17:17). And there's a strengthening of our faith that comes through the testimony of Christ and his apostles via Scripture (John 17:20). "If you want faith, if you want holiness, if you want joy—they all come through encountering God in his word, Jesus says. That's how we get motivated."

Essential Bible reading component 2 is the skill—the "able to," the act of Bible reading. "Something mysterious happens when we pick up a pen or a pencil—not a keyboard, but a pen or a pencil—and we either write out the text, or if it's too long, write down questions you have or observations you make about the things that you're reading in the text." The act of writing out the text will cause you to have new thoughts about the text you would not have had otherwise. Write out your thoughts and questions. Note-taking cultivates careful Bible reading.

Essential Bible reading component 3 is illumination—the "see through," the reward of Bible reading. The payoff. The *realities* of God—his character, will, and ways—"shine through the Scriptures." We see these divine glories by the Holy Spirit (Eph. 1:18).[8]

Component 3 is subtle, profound, and expounded elsewhere more fully. It means we don't grow content with checking off daily readings, or marking up our Bible for Instagram, or even arcing or diagraming texts. Press "through

---

7   APJ 464: "I've Never Read the Bible. Where Should I Start?" (November 3, 2014).
8   APJ 1297: "Three Reasons to Read the Bible Every Day in 2019" (January 2, 2019).

the words" to get into "the *reality*" that was "driving and animating" the Bible's words.[9] "Massive realities are *behind* these words." So push yourself "*through* words into reality."[10] "Push through" the Bible's words and grammar and logic until you see "the *reality* behind all the words and grammar and logic." And then dwell on that illuminated divine *reality* until it becomes "an *emotionally experienced reality*."[11]

How many Bible versions should I read?

Settle on one main translation. The English Standard Version is Piper's choice. The ESV is not perfect (no translation is), but it "strikes such a good balance between formal equivalence to the original language as far as possible and readability and appropriate dignity, while being accessible, for the most part, to ordinary folks," a rare translation broadly useful for personal study, the church's gathered life, and for memorization by both children and adults. That's "asking a lot of a translation, to cover all of those bases."

Good Bible translations don't overinterpret or oversimplify challenging texts. And yet, with all the varying philosophies behind each work, no contemporary English translation will "lead people into serious doctrinal error." So it's a great question: Read one or multiple? "The rule of thumb that I would suggest is this: use multiple translations for the purpose of *increased understanding*—for instance, use them as commentaries—and use one main translation for the purpose of *memorization* and *the saturation of your mind*."[12]

Ink or pixels?

Is a Bible on-screen or a Bible on paper best for personal devotions?

"I have done all my reading—Bible reading, devotional reading—on an iPad for several years now" and it's a "wonderful" reading experience, having original-language resources and commentaries available with a screen tap. "So the digital word has made the Bible more accessible, and it has made helps easier to use. Those are some of the upsides." Apps provide immediate access to tools to enhance our Bible reading experience.

But the digital convenience has two drawbacks.

1. The downside of transience. "I want to see the highlighting and underlining and note-taking with a digital Bible as more secure and more permanent. When I have a paper Bible in front of me, I can be underlining it, taking notes

---

9 APJ 1713: "John Piper's Ministry in One Bible Text" (December 3, 2021).
10 APJ 1268: "How to Read the Bible for Teenagers" (October 26, 2018).
11 APJ 1197: "How to Read the Bible—and Preach It" (May 14, 2018).
12 APJ 1003: "How Many Bible Versions Should I Read?" (February 15, 2017).

in the margin, and that Bible can go on a shelf, and forty years later—which is what I do with my King James Bible from when I was fifteen years old—fifty years later I can take that down and look at what God was doing, at what he was showing me." Instead, there's a lingering suspicion that digital notes are doomed to be deleted over time. A "lack of permanence." We need software that "takes this seriously" by allowing users to export all personal notes and highlights into a file you can save, archive, and return to years later.

2. The downside of immediate distractions. Digital Bible reading requires special focus because we're just a click away from social media or texts or emails, or a pop-up notification away from having our screen intruded upon. Bible reading easily gets co-opted as we jump back and forth from app to app, a communion-killing compulsion. "Real change happens in the human soul when God shows up in his almighty, authoritative word and works on you. And that is just diminished when we are jumping around looking at other things." It's a serious downside. If you cannot overcome this app-jumping impulse, "I would say that it might be better not to even put yourself at risk."[13]

Yet again, digital Bible programs on a tablet add expediency at several levels. Daily readings are made convenient by an app like Logos where the Bible plan readings are hyperlinked to make it easy to flip to and read. You can copy, paste, highlight, and save verses for meditation later in the day. You can share Bible verses and brief meditations to Twitter and social media. You can click on English words to see their Greek or Hebrew origin. You can earmark texts for future writing projects. And you can reference Bible commentaries with a tap.[14]

How do I find the meaning of a Bible text?

Seven stages of discovery will unlock a text. (1) Define key words. Every word has a meaning, often derived from the context—from the immediate context, the paragraph, and the book overall. Find these keywords with Bible software or a concordance, "my most commonly used tool in Bible study." Rather than turning to commentaries or Bible dictionaries, gather up texts to get you into the author's head. "What issues all the insight, almost 90 percent of the time, is looking up words that put me onto the trains of thought in an author's mind." (2) Find the propositions. Propositions, "the basic building blocks of meaning," tie those words together, usually with a subject, a verb, and some modifiers. (3) Relate the propositions. Look for these connections in words like *because, therefore, in order that, although,* or *when.* "This is the way an author

---

13 APJ 275: "Digital or Paper Bible for Devotions?" (February 11, 2014).
14 APJ 828: "How Do You Use Your iPhone and iPad in Christian Growth?" (April 1, 2016).

communicates his meaning. He puts words together in propositions, then he puts propositions together in certain logical relationships." (4) Determine the main point of the text flow. The propositions will link together into a logical flow, revealing the author's point. (5) Compare different texts with similar themes. Find other texts that carry similar terms or similar logical flows, and compare and contrast how they convey the same meaning. (6) Stop to appreciate the reality behind the text. This is a serious step, too often neglected by even the most serious students. "Lots of young people, and older people, when they're getting excited about seeing the meaning of words, seeing how propositions work, seeing how logical flows of thought develop, get all excited about words and logic. Suddenly they're playing a game, and they're forgetting about heaven and hell, life and death, God and Satan—the massive realities behind these words. So I want to push myself through words into reality." (7) Make life application. Apply your discoveries to your own life. So run a Bible app search for keywords or get a good concordance—the "most helpful" and "most commonly used tool in my Bible study. Commentaries don't even come close."[15]

Often the meaning of a complicated verse will come only by studying the larger context. When you're stumped by a text, "step back and look at the larger flow" of the author's thinking. This will often help resolve the meaning and purpose of a verse or phrase.[16]

Too many Christians assume that others must tell them what a text means before they can start thinking about it. That's false. God gave us "a huge, untapped resource for Bible study: our minds." So think over texts as you write verses out by hand into a personal notebook. In seminary, Pastor John began writing the text out, and in "writing every proposition of every paragraph on a different line and figuring out how those propositions relate to each other—the very writing caused me to see things." Writing slows us down, enhances learning, and improves retention. It allows you to write and retain your response. On the same page as the Bible text you copied out, write out implications you see or questions the text raises in your mind. The goal is communion. "We want to meet God in the Bible. And in my experience, slow, meditative, commenting, question-asking reading is where I meet God. I don't meet God when I am rushing through a text. So get a pen and paper. Open your Bible and copy out a paragraph."[17]

---

15 APJ 1268: "How to Read the Bible for Teenagers" (October 26, 2018). On studying isolated texts, see APJ 1056: "How Can I Better Study a Bible Passage?" (June 19, 2017).

16 APJ 1863: "Do Unbelievers Get a Second Chance after Death?" (November 18, 2022).

17 APJ 127: "Advice for Better Bible Reading" (July 8, 2013). Piper alludes here to the discipline of arcing. On arcing see APJ 395: "What Tools Do I Need to Study the Bible?" (July 29, 2014),

Should we read the Bible for breadth or depth?

The Bible is a huge book. So how do we enjoy it: *verse by verse* to uncover important details or *chapter by chapter* to understand the sweeping storyline? We need skills to do both. Some days you will not finish your entire reading, and that's okay. Imagine you wake up one morning, get to your Bible reading, and read Romans 12:9–13, a text with thirteen exhortations in it! What do you do? Breeze past them to finish your daily reading? Or stop and focus on one command to take into your day? "And the answer is *both*. And I don't know how. I just know I've got to read the Bible fast and I've got to read the Bible slow, because if you don't read the Bible fast to get through it in a year or two, you can't get the big picture." Imagine a jumbo jet flying 560 miles per hour at 38,000 feet over Florida. "You look down and say, 'Wow, that's an amazing orange grove. Very nourishing. Really tastes good. Really gives me energy.' Wrong! It doesn't. You're just flying tens of thousands of feet overhead. And that's the way we read the Bible: flying overhead." Eventually you must land, go to the orange grove, and pick one orange. So "let love be genuine" (Rom. 12:9). Pick one command from the cluster of thirteen and take it into your day. Be willing to stop and ask, What does this mean? Then pray. "I want to be like that. Holy Spirit, please kill the disease of hypocrisy in my life." In Bible reading, know when to stop and meditate.[18]

A decade later, Piper worked out a clearer process for doing both.

To read for *depth* means stopping to reflect deeply on the words and phrases and propositions in a particular text. You can read through a few verses per day, but at that pace "it will take you eighty years or more to read your Bible. I am a great believer in slowing down and thinking, thinking, thinking."

But given the length of the Bible we must also read for *breadth*. "By *breadth* I mean reading broadly enough so that you take in the entire five-hundred-year period, say, of the divided kingdom in Israel, from Rehoboam right down to the end of the exile. In 1 and 2 Kings and 1 and 2 Chronicles we have king after king after king rising, falling, succeeding, and failing. Good and evil. Evil then good. A rotten father followed by a good son. A good father followed by a rotten son and on and on." In this case, "I don't know of any other way but reading through those books broadly to get the profound sense of both the repeated failure and rebellion of God's people over centuries and the extraordinary mercy and patience of God." There's no replacement for taking a month to consume

APJ 1056: "How Can I Better Study a Bible Passage?" (June 19, 2017), APJ 1141: "Deep Bible Reading Strategies for the Tired and Busy" (January 3, 2018); and John Piper, *Reading the Bible Supernaturally* (Wheaton, IL: Crossway, 2017), 395–411.
18 APJ 1670: "How Can I Make Daily Bible Reading Authentic?" (August 25, 2021).

the breadth of these four historic books to fully appreciate God's patience with them—and by implication his patience with us.

Practically, three considerations. (1) Alternate mornings and evenings. Go for *depth* in the mornings and for *breadth* in the evenings. (2) Alternate by month. One month read for *depth*, the next read for *breadth*. (3) Alternate by year. One year read the whole Bible and the next year study only Romans. But whatever path you choose, "never stop reading. This is God's very word. Broad or deep, it is his transforming voice."[19]

Reading broadly *and* deeply is part of the natural rhythm of reading the whole Bible in a year in the Discipleship Journal Bible Reading Plan, a favorite of Pastor John's. Every day you read in four areas: two long Old Testament readings for broader study and two shorter readings in the New Testament for deeper reflection. "This has the great advantage of combining both a broad scope of reading and a narrow, intensified reading." As an added help, catch-up days are scheduled into the monthly plan.[20]

Balance deep reading with devotional reading

How do we accomplish *deep reading* with pens and paper and marked-up texts, but also simply read the Bible *devotionally*?

Bible reading is about life stability. "My goal in everything I've ever done with regard to the Bible is not to produce a lot of Bible nerds, but the kind of Christians who are so deep and unshakable in their convictions about eternal reality that they are not blown over by the winds of trouble and don't simply float mindlessly along, conforming to the currents of contemporary culture." The aim is to be an oak tree, "withstanding the winds of adversity" (Ps. 1:3). Or a dolphin, "cutting through the currents of culture." To these ends, the Bible calls us to first become gold diggers, seeking after buried treasure (Pss. 19:10; 119:72, 127; Prov. 2:1–5). Imagine a treasure was hidden long ago in your backyard. Would you dig out this wealth? Yes, of course. That's what Scripture is: a treasure of spiritual wealth beyond imagination, worthy of the grime, sweat, and excavation. So it's "a matter of how desperate we are to get rich with true riches—the riches of Christ and the wealth of his glory, and his wisdom and his power for living the kind of radical Christian life this world so desperately needs."

Practically speaking, do both kinds of study: deep *and* devotional. Set aside one day to excavate deep into the word. And then read more devotionally throughout the week. "Find a slot in your week, early, before you have to do

19 APJ 606: "How Do I Study Bible Verses and the Bible Storyline Together?" (May 28, 2015).
20 APJ 1140: "A New Year, A New Bible Reading Plan" (January 1, 2018).

lots of stuff with the kids or work in the yard. Find a slot—maybe Saturday morning early or Sunday afternoon or Sunday evening—where you do some serious digging in God's backyard once a week. But on most mornings, give yourself to a more devotional kind of meditation on the word. It's never one or the other. It's always both-and."[21]

How do we piece together chapters of Scripture?

Reading whole chapters is hard work, especially when connecting propositions and finding the logical flow of arguments. Think of a whole chapter, or a whole psalm, like a jigsaw puzzle. "There are five hundred pieces laid in front of you, and as you look at them, they do not look at all like the painting on the front of the box. They are just one big jumble. That's how the words and phrases and clauses might look to you in a chapter in the Bible when you try to think of the chapter as a whole." So how do we start, when the Bible offers no overall picture on the cover to make sense of the pile of pieces?

You examine one piece. "You notice that half of this piece is solid red and the other half is solid gold. You notice that the little protrusion at the top is split in half, and half of it is gold and half of it is red. From this, you infer with careful thinking that there is another piece somewhere that will be half red and half gold." Of the five hundred pieces, maybe six meet this design. You isolate them, fit them together, and make one "mid-size unit." Then you look for another unit. And build another. And another. Later you begin to fit the units together.

Such work is tactile, too demanding for most of us to do in our heads. So print the text on paper, draw circles and lines on it, and make summaries of the mid-sized pieces. And then fit those larger units together to see their logical coherence. So "look at the pieces very carefully. Fit them together in mid-size units. Jot down the main points of the mid-size units until you have them all on a half-sheet of paper, and then think and think, and pray and pray, and think and pray and think and pray, and organize and draw lines, and try to fit them all together until they fall into place and you see how these five, six, seven, eight, nine points of the mid-size units are in a flow that make one big overarching point. You will be surprised, if you take a pencil and paper and do this, what you will see."[22]

---

21 APJ 1141: "Deep Bible Reading Strategies for the Tired and Busy" (January 3, 2018). For more on the dolphin/jellyfish contrast between those who "cut a path against the current" versus those who "float in the current of culture," see APJ 683: "How to Engage Culture and Swim against It" (September 11, 2015) and APJ 1141: "Deep Bible Reading Strategies for the Tired and Busy" (January 3, 2018).

22 APJ 1049: "How Do I Follow Big Sections of Scripture?" (June 2, 2017).

How do I read the Bible topically?

"I love this question because I think many people sell themselves short when it comes to what they can glean from the Scriptures—for their own spiritual enrichment in depth and for their life in a morally complex world. I think most of us doubt our capacities to find answers for ourselves. Others of us are lazy—let's be honest—and we want somebody else to do the work for us. So we try to get a quick answer from somebody else rather than do it ourselves with rigorous study." But the Bible will not give its riches to people who refuse to dig (Prov. 2:3–6). Over all of our Bible study waves the flag of Jeremiah 29:13: "You will seek me and find me, when you seek me with all your heart."

From this motivation, get to work and isolate your topic by a keyword, like *money* or *marriage*. Use a concordance or a Bible program. You could limit your study to one book, one author, or just the New Testament. But keep it manageable and don't get overwhelmed. Once you have a list of verses, jot them all down and read each one. Write out the connections you see in the word as it appears in the same author or across Scripture. "Many people have the notion that simply reading and observing the Bible causes insight and wisdom. It doesn't. It doesn't. You've got to think." You must *think over* (νόει) what you read (2 Tim. 2:7). To do this, you must keep your eye on the context and logic of each text. And follow the footnoted related texts to the one you're studying.

Keep paper and pens handy. "Be writing, writing, writing, either in a file on your computer or, like I do often, with a folded half-sheet of paper. I'm doodling and I'm constantly writing because when I write, I'm able to hold more things in my head. Without writing, everything tends to be a muddle. It's just so complex. People that aren't writing aren't going to go very far in bringing a coherent picture of some reality." Then, later in the process, consult commentaries, books, or web resources on your theme. But in everything, preserve what you have seen so that you can easily return to your discoveries later.[23]

What happens when you pray over Scripture?

Prayer is an essential component of Bible reading, but often ignored. "It is amazing, after all these years, how many times I simply start reading without praying. And I can tell the difference, profoundly."[24] Maybe this is one reason why our delight in God from our Bible reading is so short-lived.

We read with the foundational conviction that we are called to focus our lives—our attention and our delight—on heavenly things (Col. 3:1–2). And we

---

23 APJ 1058: "How Do I Study a Specific Topic in the Bible?" (June 23, 2017).
24 APJ 903: "Why Is My Delight in God So Short-Lived?" (July 22, 2016).

are to avoid setting our attention and delight on the things of man (Matt. 16:23). So what's the solution to an enduring encounter with the word? "I think maybe the most helpful thing I could do is to bring you into a lesson God is teaching me afresh at age seventy that I should not have to be taught again after sixty years as a Christian. I have one tip for you that is just so front-burner for me right now." The tip: pray, before you read your Bible, that God "would come and meet you in the reading of Scripture and open the eyes of your heart and show you what is really there, and make himself real, and bring about amazing changes in your life" (Eph. 1:18). It makes a real difference.

If we pause and pray before we read, God will answer us in six ways. (1) We will hear. By our pre–Bible reading prayer, "God creates a supernatural atmosphere" to remind us "this moment is not just about you and a book. It is about you and the living God." (2) We will see. God will answer and show us new things in Scripture. "Most of us are blind to the glories embedded by God in the very words that he has given us. We read them so casually. Reading the word *Spirit*, the word *glory*, the word *cross*, the word *sin* without praying is one experience. Reading those words after praying may be cataclysmically different, a different kind of *seeing* in those same words." Divine weightiness attends to God's word as it is prayed over. (3) We will feel. We want the right affections to attend our reading. "If you pray, God will open your heart to feel the preciousness of glorious things and the horror of evil things that you would not otherwise feel," because "most of us do not feel emotions that accord with the realities we are thinking about. This is a work of the Spirit, and he does it in answer to prayer." (4) We will be changed. By praying before reading, "God will work changes in you that you would not otherwise experience," changes in your war against sin, desires for holiness, conquering of bad habits, recharging new resources for your relationships, and increased experience of the fruits of the Spirit. (5) We will be guided. "If you pray this prayer at the beginning of your Bible reading, God will from time to time provide the very guidance and leading that you have been longing for in regard to big decisions in your life. God delights to bring fresh vision and guidance into the life of his children while they are spending time with him in his word." (6) We will recalibrate to true reality. Reading the Bible will give us new eyes to see spiritual realities, the lostness of the world, and the eternal future we each have.

So each day, "pause before you read, and earnestly—with as much heartfelt longing as you can muster—pray to God that he would come and meet you in the reading of Scripture and open the eyes of your heart and show you what is really there and make himself real and bring about amazing changes in your life."[25]

---

25 APJ 903: "Why Is My Delight in God So Short-Lived?" (July 22, 2016).

A one-minute prayer before you read your Bible

So what does this prayer look like? Before opening your Bible, pray a one-minute prayer of desperation, organized by the acronym IOUS: *Incline* my heart (Ps. 119:36). *Open* my eyes (Ps. 119:18). *Unite* my heart (Ps. 86:11). *Satisfy* my soul (Ps. 90:14).

Find comfort that such an acrostic of desperation was pulled directly from the Bible. "I take unbelievably strong encouragement from the fact that the psalmists had to pray this way." *Incline my heart.* "It is amazing that the psalmist would ask God to incline his heart to the word. What? You are not inclined to the Bible sometimes, Mr. Psalmist?!" *Open my eyes.* The psalmist opens the word but looks at basically a blank page and feels horrible about his spiritual insensitivity. We do too. *Unite my heart.* "My heart is all fragmented; it is going every direction. I am looking at a fly on the wall or hearing something on my driveway, and I get distracted in a hundred ways. And the psalmist does too." *Satisfy my soul.* This final plea is "maybe the most important one of all," as we join the psalmist in praying: "O God, don't leave me in this season of boredom or blankness or deadness."[26]

Step 3 (*U*) applies especially to those with a divided heart, a normal experience of the Christian life. We want God to draw near to us, but we also have a heart that pulls back from him when he does.[27]

In sum, I.O.U.S. ("my favorite acrostic") is "my prayer virtually every day over the word of God," says Pastor John.[28] Without this little prayer, "I might blunder into God's word in a spiritually self-sufficient frame of mind, in which I am not at all listening to God or hearing God." And it's a short prayer. "I'm talking about one minute. You say to God, 'I am about to read your word, and I need your help.'" Bible reading is not for satisfying curious minds but for feeding hungry souls. "I am here to eat. I am not here to stockpile arguments. I am not here to get a lesson. I am hungry for *you*, God. I need to eat truth here!" This is the desperation behind the little one-minute prayer.[29]

The acrostic is not only built from the psalmist's spiritual vulnerability, but also from his darkest struggles. Together they make a prayer of desperation for the believer. "I have gone through very dark and cold seasons, and I want to make sure that when I say that, people realize that we are not talking about a simple, two-phased Christianity, as if there is really red-hot, devoted, vital Christianity, and then there is cold, dead, dark Christianity. The fact is, there

---

26 APJ 166: "When I'm Bored of the Bible—What Can I Do?" (September 5, 2013).
27 APJ 1719: "Is It Normal to Have a Divided Heart?" (December 17, 2021).
28 APJ 27: "Fighting for Joy in Pastoral Ministry" (February 14, 2013).
29 APJ 496: "How Does Scripture Serve Our Prayers?" (December 19, 2014).

are infinite gradations in between those two extremes." And those gradations change all day long. "I wake up needing to become alive. And my strategy has been the same pretty much all the way along in trying to fight this fight for joy, and that is to pray earnestly while I look at the Bible." This struggle is the heart of the acrostic prayer. "I want to see Jesus. I need Jesus. I don't need mere propositions. I need an encounter with the living Christ, and I believe it comes through the word."[30]

A similar strategy works well when the Bible feels boring. When it does, simply recount its own testimony about itself. "I look at things that the Bible says about the Bible to rekindle my love for the Bible" (especially Ps. 119:25, 98; John 5:24; 6:68; 8:32; 17:17; Rom. 10:17; and 2 Tim. 3:16–17). But the bottom line is that for those who find the Bible boring, "you are not alone. We all are up and down in the degree to which we love to read the Bible." But "even when you don't feel like it, keep tending the garden like a farmer who has to get out there every day and pull the weeds and till the soil—not because that day the fruit is going to grow up, but because sooner or later, in God's sovereign timing, if you tend your garden, it will grow."[31]

I read the Bible but I don't feel anything—what do I do?

Given the high calling of our emotional engagement with the word, what if I read my Bible, but I don't feel anything in my affections that resonates with the worth, the value, the preciousness, the beauty, the pleasures of what those words are supposed to communicate? Is there anything I can do next?

Yes, there is, because Scripture calls us to *incline* our ears and apply our hearts to knowledge so that it will be pleasant to the taste and fixed in the memory (Prov. 22:17–18). From this text we see that Scripture is meant to move from the head to the heart in three stages. (1) We *incline* our ear. When we struggle to hear someone, we lean in and listen more attentively. Same with the Bible. (2) We *incline* so that we can *hear* wisdom. (3) After *inclining* and *hearing* we then *apply* our heart to what's been heard. This means, literally, "you take your heart and you *push it*—you *push* the nose of your heart into the beauty of the knowledge. If the heart is not feeling anything, you say to your heart, 'Heart, wake up!' And you take hold of the heart and you apply. You push it. You place it in the knowledge. You *push* on it."

The word of God is a precious diamond. It's a gift. And if your heart doesn't feel the preciousness of this, *push* it into the diamond to look at it from every

30 APJ 27: "Fighting for Joy in Pastoral Ministry" (February 14, 2013).
31 APJ 166: "When I'm Bored of the Bible—What Can I Do?" (September 5, 2013).

direction, "and say to your heart: 'Heart, move around this diamond. Look at the diamond from that side and look at the diamond from that side.'" Preach to your heart: "Come on, heart, wake up. Come on, heart, *look* at this. Come on heart, *feel* this. This is beautiful. Wake up, heart!" Make this the instinctive cry of your heart when spiritual affections wane over God's word.[32]

Prep your soul to encounter Christ

Bible reading is for encountering Christ. So how do we know that we are not just connecting prepositions but beholding glory? Some thoughts on *seeking* out this encounter with God.

1. Sync your soul. It can take a long time to sync our souls with divine glory. "One of the reasons we don't meet God profoundly in his word as often as we would like is because our hearts are so unprepared and out of sync with the spiritual reality when we come." It may take reading fifty chapters of the Bible before the sync happens! "I say it to point out the fact that we may be that out of sync spiritually and emotionally and psychologically with the Bible so that when we read, our frame of mind and the disposition of our heart and the spiritual receptivity of our heart are so out of step with the Spirit of the passage that nothing happens." To sync, consider personal retreats, rare times set aside to read fifty chapters of the Bible and go hard after God.

2. Draw from writers who have beheld Christ's glory. Give them the first fifteen or twenty minutes of your time before you open the Bible. This will help sync your soul (1).

3. Taste joy in the longing. We have no greater desire than to see our Savior. But this "perfect fullness of the enjoyment of Christ" is reserved for when we see him face-to-face (1 John 3:2). And yet this joy of Christ's presence is something we taste now—"really, substantively, authentically, spiritually in the very longings for it." Meaning it's "artificial" to separate "our deepest yearnings and achings and longings and cryings for Christ from his presence, his sweetness, the tastes of his visits, and his love. That's an artificial distinction. The *longings* are themselves a sweet taste of the bread of heaven. The *yearnings* are themselves a sweet detection of the aroma of paradise. The *inconsolable desires* of your soul for Christ are themselves a divine work of the Holy Spirit communicating to you in advance some measure of the sweetness of Christ himself in heaven."

4. Open your Bible and read. Use a plan to read the whole Bible in a year, something like the Discipleship Journal Bible Reading Plan. And anticipate that God will meet you—maybe in just one of the four readings in any given day. And

---

32 APJ 748: "I Read the Bible and Feel Nothing—What Should I Do?" (December 11, 2015).

that's okay. Don't expect God to make every Bible reading time unforgettable. But expect a few of them to be especially sweet. Read with this anticipation. And "even if God only shows up once a year, it's worth a year's reading. I mean, if he showed up once a year, it would be worth reading every day, wouldn't it?"[33]

Isn't the Bible old and irrelevant?

The Bible is old, but motivation for Bible reading is built on the conviction that its ancient pages are ongoingly relevant to our lives today. So how do we respond when it doesn't *feel* relevant? Listeners ask this question about (1) the Old Testament, (2) the New Testament, and (3) the whole Bible.

1. Is the Old Testament relevant to our lives? What do we gain by reading difficult Old Testament books like Leviticus, where the glory of Christ is not obvious and personal application for our postmodern lives seems unclear? The Bible is always relevant, but we should never imagine that the Bible was entirely written only for us today. The Bible, "with all of its many wonderful and strange parts, is designed by God, inspired by God, put together by God, not just for twenty-first-century, Western, middle-class culture but for thousands of cultures around the world, spread over thousands of years, with all of those centuries and all of those cultures being dramatically different." Only God could pull off a task this huge. So the Bible is relevant for every culture, but it will not apply the same to each generation. For us, "there are going to be parts of the Bible that I as a twenty-first-century, middle-class, White guy find difficult to find relevance in or any kind of echo of my own present concerns. When that happens, I don't think I should neglect any part of the Bible. I think I should be patient and pursue it all."[34]

2. Are Paul's epistles from the first century applicable to twenty-first-century life? Yes, they remain relevant for several reasons. Some of Paul's letters were intentionally circular, so their contents were not limited to a single church. This is also true of letters from James and Peter. Paul knew that his letters were from God, "words valid and relevant for his people of all time" (1 Cor. 2:12–13). As an apostle, Paul often spoke about the church universal because he knew that his teaching was "foundational and useful for the church's whole existence" (see Eph. 2:19–20). And several New Testament texts deal with transcendent themes that will never change: the nature of God, the nature of man, and the truths of the gospel. Nothing about the gospel that we read is "time-bound or situation-bound," but is equally true and valid and important for us today (see 1 Cor. 15:3). And many points of application for our lives are built on eternal truths that remain "valid

---

33 APJ 1216: "What Does It Feel Like to See the Beauty of Christ?" (June 27, 2018).
34 APJ 864: "How Do I Feed My Soul in the Hard Books of the Old Testament?" (May 23, 2016).

across time." So Christians still shouldn't lie to one another, because we belong to one another (Eph. 4:25). We don't avenge ourselves, because God is still our avenger (Rom. 12:19). Women don't preach, because the creation order holds firm today (1 Tim. 2:12–14). And we still love through appeals rather than by commands (Philem. 8–9). Our situational ethics today are held firm by ancient truths.[35]

3. How do we overcome the perpetual, low-grade feeling that the whole Bible is too long and old and irrelevant for us today? "What I would like to do is help this person get over the hump of feeling like the Bible is over their head or from another planet or just totally irrelevant. The real answer to the question of 'Why press on?' is this. It is worth it. The Bible has so much to give, and what it has to give can be found *only* in the Bible. If you turn away from it, it can't be found anywhere else. Nothing can compare to it." The Bible is "better than gold, better than silver, better than honey" (Pss. 19:10; 119:72). Only in the Bible do we find the truth that will save us eternally (1 Tim. 4:16). Only in the Bible do we find the truth that "liberates us from sin and Satan," gives peace with God, empowers holiness, motivates love, and sustains our souls in life's hardest trials. "It really is the greatest book in the world because it is the only book inspired by God Almighty, the Creator of the universe, and the only one that can make us wise unto everlasting life" (2 Tim. 3:15–16).

With those convictions in place, here are six simple steps for overwhelmed Bible readers. (1) Find a modern translation like the ESV. (2) Get a good study Bible, like the ESV Study Bible with notes that will help answer the perplexing questions you meet along the way. (3) Write out the most challenging passages you stumble over and work through them with a pen in hand. (4) Watch *Look at the Book* episodes, video tutorials "for me to help guide you through texts that I hope will instill habits of reading in you that will make the Bible live and will make it understandable for you." (5) Find your way to an expositional church that preaches through the Bible text slowly. (6) "Pray for God to give you light. God loves to make his Son known. He sent him into the world at the cost of his life so that he could be known and loved. He is not interested in holding back from you the light that he gave with his Son and gave with his word."[36]

Battling doubt and cynicism in Bible reading

A woman wrote in to admit that her Bible reading is often "hijacked" by a sense of doubt and cynicism about Scripture, a spiritual battle more than an intellectual one.

---

35 APJ 904: "How Do I Know Paul's Epistles Are Relevant for My Life?" (July 25, 2016).
36 APJ 438: "6 Tips If You Find the Bible Hard to Read" (September 26, 2014).

It's never automatic that we believe the Bible to be true. All our Bible reading is spiritual warfare. "The devil really hates the Bible. He hates truth. He is a deceiver from the beginning, and he can make things look merely intellectual when, in fact, some pretty heavy spiritual stuff is going on." But we can respond with prayer, asking that God "would fight your doubts and cynicism" as you also fight. In battling our inner cynic, we pray for God to "help my unbelief" (Mark 9:24). "Help your unbelief do what? Die. That's what." Unbelief must die for us to see divine beauty, the beauty that validates itself. "Seek in all your reading and praying in the Bible not just to know truth but to see the glory of Christ. There is a spiritual light shining from Christ that is self-authenticating if you see it."

In the believer's battle with doubt and cynicism with the Bible, we must remember that Christ is kind and patient with us. Think and pray on this as you look to authors, teachers, local church leaders, and Christians around you who have a robust spiritual life.

But never stop reading the Bible in the fight of faith, because the fight of faith is fought *in the reading*. "This is one of Satan's main aims in your doubt and your cynicism. He wants to get you to stop reading when, in fact, the Bible says faith comes by hearing and hearing by the word of Christ" (Rom. 10:17). Read on despite the inevitable dry seasons. "The dry desert winds blow. And those whose roots are not planted by the streams wither by cynicism and doubt. But those whose roots have gone down meditating day and night on the word of God are like trees that have roots way down by the water so that they are not killed by the droughts of doubt" (Ps. 1:1–3).[37]

Why is the Bible so violent?

The Bible features some shockingly violent texts, like Judges 19:22–30. Few Christians would approve of watching such violence on a movie screen. So why is it in our Bibles?

We know that "all Scripture is breathed out by God and profitable" (2 Tim. 3:16). "All of it is profitable and God-inspired—and that includes the most violent parts." Yet the violence on a page is different from the violence on a screen. Gratuitous onscreen violence is "not profitable and should be avoided." But on the page, "God's presentation of these things in writing in the inspired Scripture is no mistake. He presents the world in divine, context-laden, interpretive words—not lurid videos of blood and gore that preempt and replace the God-intended movement from reading written words to having word-built images in the mind. Verbal descriptions with divine explanations are not the

---

37 APJ 651: "Battling Doubt and Cynicism in Our Bible Reading" (July 30, 2015).

same as worldly depictions for entertainment or education with no ultimate divine meaning."

The shocking violence of Scripture awakens us from dreamlike fiction. "We live in a very soft, easily offended, emotionally fragile culture that unfits us to grasp what most of history has been like, and what most of the world is still like. I think God gave us the Bible the way it is, with all the horrors, partly because he knew the day would come when we would be so spoiled, so cocooned, so overprotected, so coddled that we would not have the emotional and mental capacities to grasp utterly crucial realities in the Bible and in the world."

So what's the meaning of biblical violence?

1. Violence exposes the ugliness of unrestrained rebellion. Particularly in the book of Judges, we witness broken civil authority (Judg. 17:6; 18:1; 19:1; 21:25). "Violence signifies what happens to a society when the river of evil flowing from the human heart runs wild without a dam of civil authority to keep it from spilling out over the whole earth and corrupting with violent effects. That's the point: There was no king. 'Everyone did what was right in his own eyes'" (Judg. 17:6; 21:25). Thus, "the book of Judges is written to demonstrate what happens when human beings, in all our sinful rebellion against God, have no restraints." The human heart is so evil that civil authority is essential.

2. Violence exposes sin's wickedness. The world is violent because of human rebellion and the fall (Gen. 3:1–24). After the fall, "when God-opposing, God-rejecting, God-disparaging, God-demeaning treason against God entered the world—God responded not simply by judging man's *emotions* and *thinking* and *willing* and *relationships*, but he also responded by subjecting the human body and the entire material and physical creation to his judgment" (Gen. 3:14–19; Rom. 8:20).

So why did God curse the whole creation? "Why did he ordain that the effect of moral evil would be displayed in the horrors of physical evil—earthquakes, floods, famines, pandemics, wars, and every manner of horrible mistreatment of man on man? Oh, my. He did it because he knew that people who are dead in their trespasses and sins would never comprehend the moral outrage of treason against God unless they saw it reflected in the physical outrage of violence against men." No sinner "loses sleep" over his cosmic treason against God. "But let their physical body be touched with cancer or their house be touched with rioting, and then their emotions rise up with moral indignation. Violence and suffering exist in this world as a divine witness to the meaning and the seriousness and the outrage of sin against God."

3. The Bible's violence showcases the bloodiness of our faith. Our gospel is the message of "the Lamb who was slain" (Rev. 13:8). We're saved through

violence. This text reminds us that "God's plan before the foundation of the world" was that the center of our salvation would be "one of the grossest, most violent and gory events in the history of the world—namely, the crucifixion of the Son of God." For us there's "no salvation without this violence." And in a gloriously subversive way, we will celebrate this violence forever (Rev. 5:9–10) because in this "gruesome death of his infinitely precious Son," we come to appreciate the greatness of God's love to us (Rom. 5:8).[38]

So pastors should read the Bible cover to cover to be reminded of the violent sinfulness of the world and of God's global sovereignty over it all. "How easy it is to put the sovereignty of God to the side while lamenting the miseries and wickedness of this world. God is in charge of the world. This is one of the great benefits of reading the whole Bible cover to cover every year," something Piper has done for decades. "You watch the terrible sweep of evil in the world, and the Bible portrays it better than anybody—the sweep of evil from century to century in the world. And you have this rugged, unwavering, biblical perspective that God is on his throne and is in charge over the world, and evil does not, will not, triumph. So that note must be struck. The sovereignty of God must be struck by a pastor over and over again because his people are going to start losing it as things get bad."[39]

Indeed, "the murder of the Son of God" was "the worst act in human history." And God planned it (Acts 4:27–28).[40] He remains "sovereign over all sin," and in that governance "he never sins."[41] That's because there are two wills in God. The sin of murder can, at the same time, (1) contradict God's moral will (Exod. 20:13; Deut. 5:17) and (2) fulfill God's sovereign purposes (Acts 4:27–28). In God, there are two wills: (1) A will of command—a moral, revealed will. And (2) a will of decree—a sovereign, ultimate will (Eph. 1:11).[42]

Let the Bible demolish your theology

Reckoning honestly with the Bible forces us to purge old errors we cherished. In his twenties, Pastor John's theology was tormented by new biblical realities in Scripture that contradicted his understanding of God's goodness, especially over questions like whether God predestines some for eternal wrath. "I know what it is like to see these things at first and not see how they fit with his justice and goodness. And I have wept. My early twenties was a season of great torment

---

38 APJ 1530: "Why Is the Bible So Violent?" (September 24, 2020).
39 APJ 817: "Gospel Hope for Cultural Pessimists" (March 17, 2016).
40 APJ 85: "How Do You Process Public Tragedy?" (May 7, 2013).
41 APJ 749: "Where Did Satan's First Desire for Evil Come From?" (December 14, 2015).
42 APJ 1122: "Does God Decree Events He Doesn't Want to Happen?" (November 20, 2017).

mentally and emotionally over theological issues like this. I have tasted what it means to put my hands on my desk, face in my hands, and cry out to God, 'I don't get this!'"[43]

This testimony prompted an email from a listener whose theology was likewise being deconstructed.

Getting theology right is something like a dynamic puzzle, where one key piece that seems to hold together a whole theology in our mind can be dislodged and everything else moves. Perhaps you learned something as a child and believed it. "And now you are reading your Bible and you say, 'That is not a Bible piece.' And it comes out. Then what happens?" The other pieces shift, "because you might have to jostle fifteen pieces to put the new Bible piece back in. And here is what I think makes us frightened to the point of weeping: it feels as though all of those fifteen pieces might be wrong. They moved. They shifted out of the position that they had. The thing that was giving them coherence just suddenly was gone." But in the shift, the Holy Spirit brings a new coherence built on biblical truth that brings freedom and peace.

To this aim of theological coherence, the Bible calls for us to add theological knowledge (Phil. 1:9; Col. 1:10; 2 Pet. 3:18). But it also demands that our theological knowledge be refined and any false notions we have about God be *destroyed* (καθαιροῦντες; 2 Cor. 10:5). And that's why the growing pains hurt. "I assume that not every opinion in my brain is a perfect opinion, and there may be some lofty opinions that get in there from time to time or left over from when I was a kid that need to be torn down." As these errors are purged from us, it stings, "especially if they are old or cherished or from mom and dad." As you construct a better and more cohesive biblical vision of God," pray that he would give understanding and lead you to an eternally beautiful and biblically accurate picture of God—beautiful in its biblical accuracy (Ps. 118:5–6; 2 Tim. 2:7).[44]

Is Bible reading only profitable if we come away with application?
No. "And here is why I feel strongly about it. I would say that probably 99 percent of our lives is lived without immediate reflection upon a life principle. Rather, we just act. If you think about your day, there are maybe a hundred big decisions you make in a day. And by *big*, I just mean *conscious*." We don't have time to weigh every decision. And in this light, Jesus made it clear that *what we do* is an expression of *who we are*. "The good person out of the good

---

43 APJ 450: "Does God Predestine People to Hell?" (October 14, 2014).
44 APJ 609: "When Scripture Demolishes Your Theology" (June 2, 2015).

treasure of his heart produces good, and the evil person out of his evil treasure produces evil, for out of the abundance of the heart his mouth speaks" (Luke 6:45). Out of the heart's abundance we speak, either from an abundance of evil or of good (Matt. 12:33–37; 15:18–20).

"Well, that is scary, right?" Yes, a scary heart-abundance paradigm with two big implications for our lives. It means that "most of our lives are lived spontaneously. Most of our lives are *not* lived after ten seconds of reflection on a biblical principle. So where do they come from? They come from being a *kind* of person." So "how do you become a *kind* of person so that you are a good tree that bears spontaneous good fruit instead of a bad tree that bears spontaneously bad fruit? You soak in the Scriptures, and you let your sight of Jesus and your taste of Jesus and his ways in the Bible affect and shape your soul. Your soul marinates in the sauces of grace until the soul is made soft and tender and supple and sensitive to the leadings of the Holy Spirit so that in a kind of spontaneous way, it responds." Basically, we aim to live out the Christian life, in most of life, from the heart, through an informed, Spirit-filled subconscious.[45]

"I'm a Christian Hedonist for theological reasons. I'm after people's affections—their hearts, their emotions, their feelings." Maybe a few things we say or do "by dint of willpower against our passions," but "very few." Ninety-nine percent of what we do and say comes from the abundance of what's inside our hearts (Matt. 12:34). Therefore, "the number-one issue in life is having new passions." Or to say it another way, God coaxes our daily holiness by feeding our passions with the lavish, eternal promises we discover in his word. A dynamic on full display in 1 Peter 1:1–25.[46]

How do we avoid intellectualism with the Bible?

The Bible calls for hard thinking *and* deep feeling. But each of us tends to fall on one side or the other, either toward an anti-intellectual feeling, or an antifeeling intellectualism. So how do we avoid a cold, academic study of our Bible? Five strategies.

1. Read as a life-and-death battle. There are many people in the church who, for "personality reasons" or "theological reasons," think emotions are unimportant—just "the caboose at the end of the train." Not so. Love is essential. Loving God with all your heart is essential (Matt. 22:36–37; 1 Cor. 16:22). Love for Christ above all others is essential (Matt. 10:37). Love for God is a matter of life and death. The "deepest, heartfelt, affectionate, relative kind of love" that

45 APJ 26: "Must Bible Reading Always End with Application?" (February 13, 2013).
46 APJ SE07: "The Passions That Prevent Adultery" (September 4, 2015).

we can imagine for a mother or father or son or daughter is the love we are to have for Christ—but intensified. If Christ is not our supreme love, "we are not worthy of Jesus." So we must become "totally persuaded" that knowledge of God without love for God is "eternally deadly. Deadly! So, I am trembling at the thought that I could go about my academic work or my scholarly work or writing work or preaching work or study work in some kind of cold frame with no awakened love for God, affection for God." Making the quest to overcome intellectualism is "a life-and-death battle."

2. Read for more than truth. We are looking for *value* to adore and love. The devil "probably knows more true things about God than we do," but he will never worship God as "supremely valuable and supremely satisfying." If Satan refuses to treasure what he knows about God, then "our aim in reading the Bible should not be demonic." Instead, we read "with a view to *feeling* what is valuable about God, *treasuring* the treasure that God is. The aim is to see the millions of reasons why God is a treasure, not just the millions of evidences that God exists or has certain attributes. All of our theological refinement should be for the sake of doxological embrace and enjoyment." We don't just drink in the word; we drink to *taste* God's goodness for ourselves because "*the tasting is the nutritional encounter* with the living God that grows us up into salvation" (1 Pet. 2:2–3).

3. Read in desperation. Pray before reading. "You can make yourself read. You can make a list of God's attributes. You can make lists of ways that God behaves. But you can't make yourself *feel* how wonderful they are." So we must pray that God would satisfy us (Ps. 90:14). Why? Because "the human heart doesn't naturally feel it when it hears and sees the beauties of God." Prayer "is absolutely essential, not only that my eyes would be open, but that my affections would be awakened." To that end we pray. "We ask God to make us satisfied in God."

4. Read others. Read authors who express beautifully the spiritual realities they see and feel deeply, voices like John Owen, Jonathan Edwards, John Newton, and C. S. Lewis.

5. Share your joy. "Open your mouth and bear witness to family and friends and neighbors and colleagues to the beauty of God and your joy in him. It is precisely in giving expression to our joy that intensifies the joy itself. A shared joy is a doubled joy. God loves mission. God loves witness. God loves sharing. God loves loving people. And he does not love hoarding." We glorify God and intensify our own joy as we share the joy he gives us in our Bible reading.[47]

---

[47] APJ 939: "Five Strategies for Avoiding Intellectualism" (September 19, 2016).

Does John Piper overthink the Christian life?

No, and the nature of Bible reading explains one reason why not. Much life application flows from the careful reading of the Bible, in tracing lengthy arguments and logical connections. If God didn't want our serious thinking, he would not have given us such a long book. Based purely on the nature of Scripture, serious thinking is essential. "It was a huge moment in my life when I woke up to the fact that the Bible is not just a string of pearls to be admired one at a time, or a package of Life Savers to be dissolved on the tongue of my soul one at a time. Rather, the Bible, in most of its writings, forges a chain of arguments connected by words like *because* and *therefore* and *although* and *in order that.*" By this design, God expects us to work hard to follow the "argument chains" in the text.

As one example, Paul chains together five arguments against sexual sin in 1 Corinthians 6:18–20. (1) Such sin violates your own body; (2) your body is a temple of the Spirit; (3) you were redeemed at a cost; and (4) you are not your own. Therefore (5) glorify God with your body. Our sex ethics require us to trace these progressive connections in the text.[48]

Paul chains together another argument in Romans 1:15–17. He makes four statements that build through three "because" statements, or "for" statements ("*For* I am . . . *for* it is . . . *For* in it . . ."). "I read my Bible for two decades before I discovered that's the way Paul wrote. You can't understand Paul's intention, what he's trying to communicate, unless you understand the logical relationships between those four statements." And he "signals those relationships, loud and clear, by using the word *because* [γὰρ] three times" as he builds "from foundations to conclusions."[49]

Do I love Bible insights more than I love God?

A young woman who highlights and writes notes and draws multicolored diagrams on her Bible has been warned by older Christian women that her study of Scripture is too academic. It lacks devotional warmth. Too much *head* and not enough *heart*, they say.

The core question for all serious Bible students is whether we have committed "a slight misplacement of affections onto what is discovered more than the one who revealed it." Or, do we have "an excitement more with intellectual insights than with God himself?" This danger is not often obvious to us at first.

Or to ask the question another way: Can we honor God through a detailed study of Scripture? Absolutely. For example, watch how Paul employs typology,

---

48 APJ 900: "Can We Overthink the Christian Life?" (July 19, 2016).
49 APJ 1696: "How Do You Find Meaning in the Bible's Narratives?" (October 25, 2021).

drawing from the Old Testament to shape Christian desires and affections (evidenced in 1 Cor. 10:1–5). In Paul's words, Old Testament events are recorded as "examples" (τυπος) for us so that "we might not desire evil as they did" (1 Cor. 10:6). In other words, "typology is about emotions." To cultivate healthy loves within us, we study Old Testament and New Testament connections.

The rigorous study of Scripture honors Christ when done authentically. "I want to glorify God by serious, rigorous, detailed study of the Bible that owns up to all that God put there. But here is something we need to remember: some people are wired by God in their genetic makeup that if they themselves make that effort at detailed study, their heads shut down their hearts. It does. As soon as they try their best to think hard, they start feeling cold." To such a person, the detailed study of Scripture by others would trigger a false alarm.

So for those who love deep Bible study, what can be done? The one who studies most rigorously should *love* most rigorously too. "In other words, if others think that our study will damage us, we must prove to them that it does the opposite." Among the older Christian women concerned for a too-academic approach to the Bible, this young woman's call is to "out-love them, out-rejoice them, out-repent them, and out-serve them. And how will they then be able to say that study is hurting her if all the evidence is in the other direction?"[50]

Later in the year came a more specific question. In Bible reading, how do I fight the temptation to glory in the novelty of personal discovery? How do I kill the impulse to study only to impress others on social media?

It's a two-part danger—one part *cerebral* and one part *vainglory*.

1. The cerebral trap. As we're reading our Bible, "we see something new and fresh and amazing" and taste "a flash of genuine enjoyment of what it shows us about God. And then there is an almost immediate impulse to begin shaping it for a conversation or an email or a devotional thought or a sermon or a lecture or a blog post or a poem or a tweet. This is real dangerous stuff. And it can feel in that moment as though we have lost the authenticity of our enjoyment of communion with God in the truth we have seen." The danger here is that "the impulse to plan to teach or restate in some way what I have seen may reveal that my enjoyment is not really in the Lord himself at that moment, but rather in the intellectual process of making the discovery and in the impulse." In this case, pray: "Lord, deliver me from the bondage to that kind of intellectualism that finds more pleasure in the processes of intellectual discovery in the Bible than the glorious one we have discovered!"

50 APJ 634: "Is My Bible Reading Too Academic?" (July 7, 2015).

2. The vainglory trap. The second danger is that "the impulse to turn my insights into, say, a teaching plan or a blog or something may signal that I crave recognition from an audience for what I have seen. So my pleasure is not so much in what I have seen as in the approval others are going to give me for seeing it. Oh, how horribly insidious and dangerous this is! If my impulse to teach reveals that to me, I am on my face pleading, 'O God, deliver me from that kind of vainglory!'"

Despite the dangers, these impulses to see, discover, and share truth, bring four benefits too. (1) Healthy discovery should lead to an impulse to put words to it, to "turn *seeing* into *saying*." (2) Healthy discovery should lead to *sharing*. This is how divine beauty works. "As our minds circle and orbit around some glorious sight, some discovery about God and his word, viewing it with joy from all the angles as we orbit the thing we have seen, the very circling of the mind to see the beauty of the truth tends to fling the mind outward where people are, so that they can be drawn into this orbit of seeing." To *see* beauty is to be compelled to *share* beauty. To *share* beauty is to *see more* beauty. "I think that belongs to the very nature of the truth of God, the very nature of God. He is not a privatistic God. He is a very public God. He is a displaying God, a communicating God, an expansive God. So it is not surprising to me that not only would our seeing become centrifugal almost immediately, but that he would design for that centrifugal impulse to become a way of seeing more." (3) Taught truth is enjoyed truth because "teaching is not strictly a mere second step after enjoyment but is an extension of the enjoyment itself. Otherwise, I think teaching becomes inauthentic." Failing to enjoy a truth *in the act of teaching* is nearly as bad as the original inauthenticity of merely enjoying the discovery. "So it cuts both ways. For teaching to be authentic, it must be an extension of that joy, I think. Otherwise, it is just not Christian teaching of glorious truth." (4) For all Christian communicators, our calling is to see and enjoy divine glory as we seek to shape others by what we have seen.

So self-test to ensure you're not "enjoying the process of discovering things about God" more than you are "enjoying God authentically and supremely." If you sense this to be a problem, "the most practical thing" you can do is stop. "Pause repeatedly" to tell God how much you enjoy what you see. "Tell him. Talk to him about how *good* he is, and *beautiful* he is, and *wise* he is, and *just* he is." Halt the impulsive desire to share or write a new point into a sermon. This worship-pause is "a great test of my soul." Build into your Bible discipline time to sing to him. And when it comes to sharing with others, see it (1) "not merely as a way of *saying*, but as a way of *seeing* more of God by saying." And

(2) see the joy-filled act of teaching as the "authentic overflow" of enjoyment in God that began in private.[51]

Bible reading in dark seasons

Don't neglect the Bible during spells of discouragement and depression. Bible reading is *for* seasons of testing, and particularly *for* seasons when we feel dejected. As Paul says, "For whatever was written in former days was written for our instruction, that through *endurance* and through the encouragement of the Scriptures we might have hope" (Rom. 15:4). "This is amazing; this is sweeping!" The keyword is *endurance* for getting through tough seasons. For the suffering, Bible reading is not irrelevant and optional but appropriate and essential. "If you can, insomuch as you can just make it a few verses, be in the word every day. Even though you don't feel like fighting, give yourself that medicine every day."[52]

Bible reading, meditating in the mind, and stirring your affections by biblical truth—as a daily discipline—is "the central biblical strategy" for escaping discouragements, disappointments, and the dark seasons of life—a point made and embodied by Asaph in Psalm 77.[53] It is also a point embodied by a friend of Pastor John's, a "seriously depressed" man who endured an eight-year darkness—"almost to the point of immobilization"—who never stopped reading and memorizing Scripture until one day God "broke in" and delivered him. The friend "always chalked up" his escape "to the fact that he continued in the word, even when he didn't feel much and could barely function."[54]

I'm too busy and exhausted—when should I read the Bible?

This question came from three listeners: a pastor, a single woman, and a mom.

First, a tired pastor wrote in asking how he could recharge his body and soul after being depleted by the demands of ministry.

Pastor John applied thirty years of pastoral experience and told him to plan his devotional Bible reading when he has the most energy and focused attention. Likely, first thing in the morning. "Take your best times of the day with your best energy and feed your soul. Worship the Lord over his word with

---

51 APJ 727: "Do I Delight in God or in Others Being Impressed by My Discovery about God?" (November 12, 2015).

52 APJ 1046: "God's Work in Your Depression" (May 26, 2017).

53 APJ 1883: "The Bible's Main Road Out of Discouragement" (January 4, 2023). On Psalm 77, see also APJ 1880: "Beat a Path to the Word in 2023" (December 28, 2022), APJ 1886: "How Do I Push Truth from My Head to My Heart?" (January 11, 2023), APJ 1887: "When Does Despondency Become Sin?" (January 13, 2023), and APJ 1889: "Fight for Delight by Planning Your Devotions" (January 18, 2023).

54 APJ 542: "What to Do When God Feels Distant" (February 27, 2015).

your best energy, not the dregs at the end of the day. Any pastor who says, 'I work so hard at the demands of the church ministry that I don't have energy for feeding my own soul through Scripture and Scripture-saturated books,' has got his day backward. If there are parts of the day with *much energy* and parts with *little energy*, then let one of the parts with *much energy* be given to what is absolutely indispensable: communion with God in his word for the sake of seeing and savoring the King of heaven. If this personal joy, personal fellowship, and personal hope languish, everything languishes—and worse than languishes usually. It's *deadly*. What our people need from us more than anything is the aroma of Christ."

The tired pastor must steward his affections carefully, ensuring that he does not allow his affections for Christ to be deadened by a steady diet of popular media. "I believe we live in a day where immersion in popular culture—with all of its God-ignoring, sin-enjoying, pride-exalting assumptions—is not only assumed to be harmless but assumed to be necessary. Both of those assumptions are wrong—deadly wrong." Pop media is an affection killer.[55]

Second, a female listener wrote in to say that she feels spiritually stuck and too tired for edifying Bible reading. God's word has been pushed to the margins of a life filled with cooking, cleaning, exercising, running errands, getting food, and shopping—all "classic, good, valuable things."

Jesus understood these realities when he entered the house of Martha and Mary. Martha welcomed Jesus into her home. And while she was "anxious and troubled," frantically trying to pull off the impromptu hospitality and "distracted with much serving," her sister Mary "sat at the Lord's feet and listened to his teaching." Martha complained that she was left "to serve alone." To which Jesus replied: "Martha, Martha, you are anxious and troubled about many things, but *one thing is necessary*. Mary has chosen the good portion, which will not be taken away from her" (Luke 10:38–42). There are many things, but only one thing is necessary. "*More needful* than your pattern of cooking, *more needful* than your pattern of cleaning, *more needful* than your pattern of exercising, *more needful* than your pattern of errand-running and shopping—it's just plain *more needful*." You need to hear the voice of God. And yet, since the time of Christ, the word is often choked out by the busyness and cares of life (Luke 8:14).

So, very practically, go to bed earlier, wake up forty-five minutes earlier, shower earlier, and then hit the coffee to "let caffeine do its magic." But if this doesn't solve the drowsiness problem, "get up out of your comfortable chair and walk around

---

55 APJ 988: "I'm Exhausted—How Do I Recharge My Body without Neglecting My Soul?" (January 11, 2017).

the room in circles, reading your Bible. There's nothing sacred about sitting, and it's much harder to fall asleep while you're walking. I did it just the other day."

But "more important than these nitty-gritty, practical suggestions is the foundational experience that the word of God is more precious than anything" (Ps. 19:9–10). "Don't let gold and don't let food feel more valuable or sweeter than the word of God. They're not."[56]

Third, the question from a mom who struggles to get time in the word. Her husband must step in. Single moms will face particular challenges here, but "God's idea for marriage and parenting is two parents. That is his ideal. And one of the reasons for this is so that one can cover for the other and make sure that both are connecting with God through Jesus in the word every day."

For the sake of mom's soul, dad should work especially hard to establish parental order. "My impression is that way too many parents today think their children should be allowed to control the atmosphere of the house. That is a big mistake on a lot of levels. So, dad, step up. Partner with your wife in establishing routines, and expect obedience—expect submission to her and to your authority." Bring "the whole atmosphere of the house" under "parental order." Next, set a playtime. In the Piper home, Pastor John took the kids for an hour after dinner. "Noël had done it all day. I can do it for an hour, and she can do whatever she wants. And if it is time to read the Bible, there she has it." Also, build in short retreats for mom (and for dad). Lead your wife in the word. Give her adult conversation in the word. Pray for her regularly.

In the end, consider the discipline of Susanna Wesley, the busy mother of Charles and John Wesley and seventeen other children. "Nine of them died in infancy. That left ten. She promised the Lord that she would spend time in prayer and the word every day, and at one point, her strategy was this: she taught the older children and the younger children that the younger ones were responsible to the older. And when you see mom with an apron over her head at the table, don't bother her. Keep the kids quiet. 'That is my time with God,' she said. So train your children with that kind of rigor. Expect obedience. Find your apron or your closet. But, dad, I am looking to you for the major support."[57]

When reading disabilities intrude on Bible reading

Dyslexia and other mental and physical challenges make reading painfully hard. So how can a reader who is plagued by limits of concentration work through the Bible in short spurts?

56 APJ 1299: "I'm Tired and Busy—How Do I Make Time for the Bible?" (January 7, 2019).
57 APJ 437: "Bible Time for Busy Moms" (September 25, 2014).

The first step is convictional. "We live by faith or we don't live at all. And faith comes by hearing and hearing by the word of God" (see Rom. 10:17). As Jesus said, we don't live only by physical food, but from every word spoken to us by God in his word (Matt. 4:4). "Faith cannot be sustained without the word of God." If faith dies, holiness dies, and holiness is essential to our final salvation (Heb. 12:14). So Bible reading "goes right to the heart of what it means to be a Christian and how to sustain faith."

Whatever physical challenges some readers face, every Bible reader can expect massive spiritual resistance. "The big ones are sin, indifference, love for the world, and spiritual blindness to the glory of Christ."

But then come challenges that are physiological (like dyslexia) or due to age (like senility). For those challenges, Pastor John offered five pieces of advice.

1. Read to savor. "The goal is not just to put in a certain amount of time or to cover a certain amount of material. The goal is to see and savor God, his ways, and his promises. The goal is to fight for faith and to walk in obedience by faith. Be sure to keep that mindset. Go to the Bible to get food for your faith."

2. Plead for healing. Ask God for supernatural help. "I'm dismayed how many Christians are fatalistic, materialistic, and humanistic when it comes to their disability." Don't just think of your disability in terms of medicines or therapies (which are important). Pray for full healing.

3. Work harder. "There are some strengths we'll never have and some things we'll never accomplish. But, oh, what amazing things people with disabilities have accomplished by refusing to be dominated by the negative implications of their weaknesses." Instead of reading for an unbroken ideal of thirty minutes, you may need alarms throughout the day to read the Bible ten times for three minutes. Think about strategies to read small portions more frequently.

4. Lean on audio Bibles. You may comprehend better by following the text with your eyes as you listen to an audio Bible with your ears. "I do that. When I'm especially tired, I let the audio read for me while I read with my eyes."

5. Lean on others. "Cultivate deep friendships in the body of Christ and in your family. Do this so that when you're old and can't do hardly anything for yourself, others will be there for you to read to you, and to perhaps, in that last comatose hour, say glorious words really loud into your seemingly deaf ear: 'Even to your old age I am he, and to gray hairs I will carry you. I have made, and I will bear; I will carry and will save' (Isa. 46:4)."[58]

58 APJ 1099: "Reading Is Agonizing for Me—How Can I Study the Bible in Small Bits?" (September 27, 2017).

Should we use audio Bibles for daily devotions?

Speaking of audio Bibles, a long-haul trucker asked if simply listening to the Bible is sufficient for his daily Bible intake. Obviously, it suits his lifestyle well.

Such a desire shows a wonderful hunger for the word in his life. But the practice comes with many pros and cons, raising six questions. (1) Can you recall what you hear? We process audio inputs differently. "Some people can remember almost everything that they hear." Is this you? Or do you forget everything you hear? Know how well audio mediums stick. (2) Is the audio Bible reader accurate? How the text is read is a form of interpretation. Pace, cadence, emphasis, pauses, emotional tone, soft voice, loud voice, pronunciation—all of it is an interpretation of the text. "If the interpretation is perceptive and penetrating and true and powerful, that's a benefit to the hearing listener. If the interpretation is contrary to the author's intention in meaning or tone, it can be a great hindrance from profiting the way God intended us to profit when we read or hear the word." (3) Can you stop? God will meet you and move you in his word. In that moment, what will you do? Will you let the audio run and the moment pass? Or will you be in a position to pull over, stop, and embrace the moment? (4) How much focus can you give the Bible? As you work, can you give the text your full attention? The Bible will compete for the attention you need to safely drive. This is not evil; "it's just a limitation of all that the word might accomplish if it had our full and complete attention." (5) Can you look up cross-references to other related texts in the Bible as you go? No. (6) Can you take notes as you go? No, not easily.

"Because of everything I've said, I would suggest that listening to the Bible not be the *only* way we fellowship with God in the word. Listening is a great way to meet God. It has its own advantages and benefits, but it also has limitations. So why not both?" Listen to the Bible and find time to read the text itself. Benefit from the strengths of both mediums. And in whatever way you do it, keep pressing into the word to be filled with glorious truths from its pages (Ps. 119:18; Eph. 1:17).[59]

I have one hour to read. How much Bible? How much other books?

It's dangerous to get too specific to any one person's life and needs in answering this question. But there are broad applications.

First, the Bible calls us to learn outside the Bible. "I can imagine a person saying, 'Well, if the Bible is the very word of the Creator of the universe, why would you not just stay with your Bible all day and listen to God? For goodness' sake—he's God!' The answer to that question is that the Bible tells you not to:

---

59 APJ 1575: "Is an Audio Bible Sufficient for Devotions?" (January 15, 2021).

'Go to the ant, O sluggard; consider her ways, and be wise' (Prov. 6:6). In other words, close your Bible and go out and look at anything and learn something from the world." Close your Bible and look at the lilies (Matt. 6:28). Close your Bible and study the birds (Matt. 6:26). "Don't just read the Bible. Read God's *world* as well as God's *word*."

This holds true in our vocations. The Bible calls us to work diligently (1 Thess. 4:10–12). "But you learn how to be a tentmaker like Paul, or a doctor like Luke, or a carpenter like Jesus's father, or a professional fisherman like Peter *not* by reading your Bible. The Bible doesn't tell you which stitches hold tents together when the leather gets wet. It doesn't do that. It's not designed for that." Listen to the wise, study nature, "and figure things out." So the very Bible itself tells us to pay attention to other sources of knowledge as it "instructs us to learn about the world, learn about people, learn about vocations, and learn about society and social processes that God made."

With this principle in place, learn from edifying books. If you have a copy of John Calvin's *Institutes* or J. I. Packer's *Knowing God*, and you also want to read your Bible, how do you divvy up the hour? It's practical math. A slow reader reading at two hundred words a minute for fifteen minutes a day can cover over one million words per year. A serious book with 360 words per page translates into 3,041 pages read per year at this pace. Averaging books to 250 pages each, "that's twelve very substantial books, all in fifteen minutes a day for the average slow reader." This leaves forty-five minutes per day to read Scripture slowly, thoughtfully, meditatively, prayerfully—and at a pace to get through the entire Bible in one year.

So make both readings work in tandem. "My experience, and the Bible itself, tells me that other people's vision of what they have seen in the Bible can be a great means of seeing more in the Bible. I know this is true. If I take ten minutes in the morning to read John Owen or Jonathan Edwards, I see more in my Bible."[60]

If I listen carefully to sermons, why do I need to read my Bible?

Eager listeners on Sunday encourage pastors. But pastors are not encouraged if their sermons fail to breed eager Bible readers the other six days of the week. Faithful preaching "doesn't just *satisfy* hunger—it *creates* hunger. I would have felt like a total failure if my people said, 'Because of your preaching, we don't read our Bibles!'" Faithful preaching creates new longings for the word.

Evaluate your Bible appetite with two questions.

---

60 APJ 1298: "I Have an Hour a Day to Read—How Much Should Be Bible?" (January 4, 2019).

1. How much of the Bible do you *want*? Imagine being in love. "'My girl-friend writes me every day. But I would rather just read her letters once a week. And I think I would like somebody else to read them for me and give me a digest of what she said.' Are you kidding me? I was in love in the summer of 1967 while working as a water safety instructor. I was eager to go off every day with these lavender envelopes to smell them for five minutes before I opened them. I am not going to give those letters to anybody else." In the same way, Scripture is "an unparalleled love letter to the people of God." Its words are sweet every day, not just on Sundays (Ps. 119:103). Scripture is our daily delight and daily meditation (Ps. 1:2), more desirable than the gold that greedy treasure hunters seek daily (Ps. 19:10; Prov. 2:4). "So why would you only want one glimpse a week of this beauty, one taste a week of this honey, one deposit a week of this silver in your bank, one letter from your lover?"

2. How much Bible do you *need*? Scripture is our *daily* sustenance, more necessary than bread (Matt. 4:4). "Temptations are too relentless. Doubt is too frequent. Satan is too active. Tribulations are too heavy. Conflicts are too many. Emotions are too volatile. Perplexities are too difficult. Faith, hope, and love are too threatened to think I can deal with these all week long, simply from one word I got on Sunday. I can't do it. And I don't think anybody can."[61]

If I read my Bible, why do I need preachers?

On the flip side, if we're faithful Bible readers, why do we need preachers?

God designed it like this. The church is given the "infallible word of God in the Bible" and then later, and underneath its authority, God gives the church "fallible elders" who are gifted to lead and teach the flock. Even Paul, the "'in-fallible' apostle," entrusted the ministry of the word to fallible pastors (1 Thess. 5:12–14). In this text, Paul is "telling the teachers how to *minister* the word, and he's telling the members how to *receive* the word and how to *respect* the teachers." In another place, Paul commands one pastor, Timothy, to herald that infallible word (2 Tim. 4:1–5). Whether or not the believers in Ephesus each had a copy of the epistle written to the church (which we now call Ephesians), they're called to attend to Timothy in Ephesus as he heralds that epistle and equips his church for the work of ministry (Eph. 4:11–12). This was God's design.

So why did God design for his infallible word to be handed off to fallible teachers? Five answers.

---

61 APJ 435: "If I Listen to Sermons, Why Do I Need to Read My Bible?" (September 23, 2014).

1. Preachers make new discoveries. God gifts preachers and teachers and makes them "apt to teach" (διδακτικόν) the Bible, "which means that they should have the time, the inclination, the skill, and the spiritual discernment to see things in God's infallible word that many ordinary folks just don't see" (1 Tim. 3:2).

2. Preachers train new discoverers. Preachers who are disciplined to discover truth for their congregation train that congregation to see more truth on their own, in their private reading.

3. Preachers stoke new affections. Good preaching (that is, expository exultation) means that "the preacher himself *feels* and *communicates* the *worth* of what he's seeing." It's a preaching that both *sees* and *savors* the realities of the text. "This means that those who listen to such preaching, over time, will not only have their *heads* stocked with new thoughts, but will have their *hearts* awakened to new affections for God and his word and his ways and his people." For example, the preached word is meant to encourage the fainthearted (1 Thess. 5:14). "Affections are changed—not just minds—through God-ordained preaching."

4. Preaching saves (1 Cor. 1:21). "We might imagine that all the world needs are Bibles dropped from airplanes into people's lives," but God's plan is to save people through the word preached.

5. Preachers are indispensable. God designed that we be mutually encouraged by the expressions of others' gifts (1 Cor. 12:21), including preachers. "God has determined that Jesus Christ, through the ministry of the Holy Spirit, will get *more glory* through the Christ-exalting, Spirit-dependent, word-saturated, mutual ministry in the church than he would if people only read their Bibles, rather than hearing other believers speak the word into their lives. That's the bottom line: Christ is *more glorified* through doing it God's way than by forsaking God's way while presuming to love the Bible."[62]

John Piper's whole ministry methodology in one text

In exploring the role of Bible teachers in our personal reading of the text, we meet one of the most influential paradigms for understanding John Piper's Bible-centered ministry methodology—Psalm 119:97–100.

"When I was in graduate school in Germany, forty-five years ago or so, I was in my twenties. I was surrounded by world-class, high-powered scholarship in people who did not believe the Scriptures as God's word or share my love for the gospel." He knew that his limited reading capacity could be overcome by careful attention to the word, and he drew tremendous comfort from Psalm 119:99.

---

62 APJ 1659: "If We Read Our Bibles, Why Do We Need Sermons?" (July 30, 2021).

There David makes the claim: "I have more understanding than all my teachers, for your testimonies are my meditation" (Ps. 119:99). His teachers had God's word. But David believed that "direct, sustained, personal, love-filled meditation on the word of God itself would produce, in his mind and in his heart, a kind of discernment and a kind of insight that would protect him from errors in his teachers, and would give him an authentic, personal, true understanding of God and his ways that would go beyond what he got from his teachers, or what they got from their way of study." Freed from being "at the mercy of scholarship," he experienced "personal, prayerful, sustained, thoughtful, rigorous, love-soaked meditation." By it, he could outsee his teachers. "And, frankly, looking back fifty years now, I believe it's true. I believe God granted me to see beautiful things that many of my more sophisticated, even more intelligent, teachers did not see."

We listen to teachers, but we test everything according to the word (1 Cor. 14:37–38; 1 Thess. 5:21; 1 John 4:1). But we must also find delight in reading the word itself, without aid. "Something's wrong with the taste-palate of the tongue of your soul if you need to have the food of God's word always spiced with the words of a fallible human being." True Bible scholarship is driven by an affectional dynamic. "If every time a lover gets a letter from his beloved, instead of reading it—reading it slowly as if to savor every word, revealing the heart and the mind of the beloved—he goes searching for somebody else to read the letter to him and then talk to him about the letter, that's a defective relationship. I mean, this is serious." Careful Scripture reading is about feeding delight, not simply accumulating knowledge.[63]

To further understand John Piper's entire ministry approach, consider these two provocative tweets. "In my twenties, I knew I could not outread my liberal professors. But I took heart from this verse that I could outmeditate them. So can you."[64] Two years earlier he tweeted: "One true citation from God's word may silence [a] whole semester of human speculation."[65]

I asked Piper to expand on these tweets and the key texts that inspired them both (Ps. 119:97–100). These verses "are very, very precious to me," he said. Psalm 119:97 defines the *practices*. It sets the stage as David celebrates God's *law*—or more literally God's *torah* (תּוֹרָה), all of his *teachings* (Ps. 119:18). David is celebrating all of God's revelation, not simply his rules. He's saying: "Oh, how I love everything you say!" So David *loves* God's teaching as he *meditates* on it

63 APJ 1533: "Why Do I Need to Read the Bible When We Have Bible Teachers Online?" (October 2, 2020).
64 John Piper (@JohnPiper), Twitter, June 15, 2020.
65 John Piper (@JohnPiper), Twitter, June 16, 2018.

all day long. During his college years, Piper experienced this double focus. He meditated deeply on texts. And what he saw, he loved. A "double response" that "set the course of my life." It set it to the point that "everything I have done, written, or spoken has been shaped by the double grasp of God's word in these two ways." This dual discipline paid off in his next six years of higher education. He became more confident in dealing with the biblical text directly, finding that "spending long hours staring at the texts—wrestling, digging, querying, praying—paid more dividends for me than if I had spent all of that time reading secondary sources."

So when future professors put more emphasis on secondary resources, he wasn't impressed. He knew that direct engagement with Scripture (with head and heart) makes one wiser than (1) enemies, (2) teachers, and (3) the aged. Those *practices* of Psalm 119:97 bear their *fruit* in Psalm 119:98–99. Hence, "the more seriously and diligently and lovingly you dig into God's word, and let it dig into you, the more likely it is that you will be wiser and more insightful than those who get their learning another way—no matter how much older than you they are." So read the Bible for yourself. And to any aspiring pastor: "If they will *love* God and *love* his word, and if they will give themselves untiringly to careful handling, *meditation*, on God's text, they will never have to be cowed by their enemies, their teachers, or the aged—even the aged John Piper. They will be able, on their own, to get what they need and preach the word."[66]

When does my Bible neglect become sin?

Here are five symptoms, determined by key internal spiritual shifts, we should be aware of.

1. When you lose your desperation. Only the Bible can give us a glimpse of God himself, feed our faith, give us joy, and sanctify us (1 Sam. 3:21; John 17:13, 17, 20; Rom. 10:17). "Wherever diminishing Bible reading is owing to a loss of desperation for seeing God, trusting God, rejoicing in God, and holiness—as if those things don't matter or can be found without the word—sin is taking hold."

2. When you read without faith. "Diminishing Bible reading and meditation is becoming sinful when it is owing to disillusionment with the Bible, because it has not been pursued by faith but rather as a performance to win God's favor." Self-righteous Bible reading is destined to fail. In contrast, consistent discipline of Bible reading can only flourish in our Bible reading if we know "the great reality that in Christ God is 100 percent for us." When faith wanes,

---

66 APJ 1713: "John Piper's Ministry in One Bible Text" (December 3, 2021). A related point from Ps. 119:100—age doesn't equate to wisdom (APJ 1867: "Give Young Christians a Chance to Lead" [November 28, 2022]).

and we stop reading the Bible from our full justification by the blood of Christ, our reading will diminish.

3. When you stop living from the fruit of your reading. When our morning reading is done, we close our Bibles and go off to work or school to live out the fruit of what we have seen and savored. "God did not design the Bible to be read eighteen hours a day so that we do nothing else. He designed the Bible as a tree that produces delicious fruit of living for the glory of God and the good of others." Failing to live fruitfully from our reading will undermine our reading over time.

4. When you lose a taste for the preciousness of God's revealed words. Bible reading will not endure if we cease to experience the preciousness of divine things in the Bible. We will drift away from Scripture when it's no longer "something more precious than gold and sweeter than honey" (Ps. 19:10). "This preciousness and this sweetness are meant to entice us back, freely and joyfully, to the word." But when we "no longer embrace this preciousness, or taste this sweetness, the diminishing is sin."

5. When you tie daily reading to failed examples. You might know a man who prided himself on daily Bible reading but was a jerk. His sin shouldn't cause you to neglect the Bible. "That's idiotic. That's immature. Don't be like that. This includes refusing to read your Bible daily because your dad did, and he beat your mom. He was abusive, and he read his Bible. That kind of immaturity is a tactical triumph of Satan. You don't want to be Satan's lackey, an immature, adolescent follower of the evil one."[67]

The final goal of Bible reading

When the story of the world is complete, what's the point of all the hours invested in our Bible reading? That end is being unveiled now as God acts in and through his word. It's not a dead book. "God doesn't set out his word in the world and then walk away and watch from a distance to see what is going to come of it." No. "He watches over his word to perform it" (Jer. 1:12). He's performing his word right now, in us. As we read our Bibles we are being permanently changed. And this transformation culminates into an ultimate purpose—which is that God be "worshiped with white-hot affection as the supreme excellence and value of the universe, by a people gathered from all the nations and tribes of the world. The Bible is the place where people see God clearly enough, that the Holy Spirit might be moving them to savor him supremely enough, that they will be changed enough

---

67 APJ 1300: "When Does Bible Neglect Become Sinful?" (January 9, 2019).

into his likeness so that he will get the white-hot worship that he deserves." Thus, in bringing about this ultimate end, "Bible reading is a necessary, indispensable instrument in the hand of God."[68] So God doesn't merely *predict* the future, he *knows* the future. And he *knows* the future "because he *plans* it and *performs* it." And he *plans* and *performs* it through his word" (Jer. 1:12; Ezek. 12:25).[69] In Bible reading, we participate in God's unfolding of his final design for the cosmos.

Moving from Bible reading to Bible memory

After completing your daily Bible reading in the morning, go back, isolate one verse or phrase, memorize it, and take it into your day. Make this phrase "the main message you will preach to yourself during the day. Set yourself a reminder on your phone to go ding every hour or buzz on your wrist to tell you to pull out that sword from your morning reading, say it to yourself, preach it to yourself, and tell Jesus 'thank you' for it and that you really believe it."[70]

The power of Bible memory

"I have never met a mature, fruitful, strong, spiritually discerning Christian who is not full of Scripture, devoted to regular meditation on Scripture, and given to storing it in the heart through Bible memorization. And that's not a coincidence."[71] Bible memorization is a "signature of sanctified people." On the flip side, "low-level interest in the Bible and Bible memory almost always goes hand in hand with high-level interest in superficial things."[72] Bible memory is a pivotal priority in the authentic Christian life. It serves the soul. But the discipline is uniquely positioned to serve the souls of others.

Knowing Scripture by heart leads to "immeasurable moments" when you draw a key text "from your heart, eyeball to eyeball, without having to open a book and read it, coming from your soul," an impromptu moment that "explodes with significance." Key texts include Psalms 16, 46, 121, and 130. "How many times have I knelt down, put my arm on somebody who has just been broken for some sin that they have committed, and I have been able to just pray, 'Lord, if you would mark iniquities, who could stand?'" (Ps. 130:3).[73]

---

68 APJ 837: "Sneak Peek of Pastor John's Next Book" (April 14, 2016).
69 APJ 1010: "Is God Ever Surprised?" (March 3, 2017).
70 APJ 1245: "How Do I Feed My Joy in Jesus Every Morning?" (September 3, 2018).
71 APJ 1512: "Ten Reasons to Read the Bible Every Day" (August 14, 2020).
72 APJ 257: "Bible Memory: Essential or Optional?" (January 16, 2014).
73 APJ 131: "Bible Memory as Ministry to Others" (July 15, 2013).

We minister grace to our friends through the memorized word. In 2013, in a small prayer gathering, Pastor John prayed over his friend Dave, an older man, nervous about his upcoming flight to India to serve pastors. "We got around Dave, people prayed, and I closed it by saying, 'Dave, fear not for I am with you. Be not dismayed. I am your God. I will help you. I will strengthen you. I will hold you up with my righteous right hand. Amen.' I spoke God's promise from Isaiah 41:10. I spoke it to him. And I hope ringing in his mind at that moment was: 'God is going to help me. God is strong for me. God doesn't want me to be dismayed.'"[74]

Piper discovered the power of recited texts firsthand as a twenty-eight-year-old, when he first heard someone recite a large section of Scripture from memory. A Bible professor recited Jesus's words against anxiety (Matt. 6:25–34). "Oh, the effect it had on me!" It was "paradigm-changing."[75] It became a commitment he deployed as a pastor years later when he recited Isaiah 53 during a Communion service. A woman in the congregation broke down in tears over the power of the moment.[76] She later said it was the power of pastor-to-congregation eye contact in hearing Scripture, made possible by memorization. The practice is potent in public and in private. If you're standing beside the bed of a dying man and a passage comes to mind, "you could look a dying man right in the face and recite to him the last five verses of Romans 8. It is so much more powerful than if you say, 'Well, let me reach in here and get my phone—*click, click, click, click, click.* At that moment, that just feels so distant and so artificial."[77]

Bible apps don't replace memorization, because memorization is more than simple recall. Memorization restructures our brains through "immersion in the mind of God." By it, our minds are renewed (Rom. 12:2).[78] Indeed, "nothing can replace Bible memory in doing what it was designed to do—forge a connection between the Bible, our minds, and our hearts."[79] These connections are essential because daily we're forced to make decisions under pressure. Too much of our life is spontaneous. Most of what we decide is not premeditated. Our lives are 95 percent "spillover." If what's in our hearts is good, goodness spills out of our life. If what's in our hearts is evil, evil will spill out. The same is true of the connection between what's in our hearts and what comes out of our mouths (Luke 6:45). Deep change must happen within us if holiness is to

74 APJ 39: "How Can I Help My Friends Stay Satisfied in God?" (March 4, 2013).

75 APJ 690: "Seven Tips for College Students" (September 22, 2015).

76 APJ 257: "Bible Memory: Essential or Optional?" (January 16, 2014).

77 APJ 276: "Do Digital Bible Searches Relativize Memorization?" (February 12, 2014).

78 APJ 276: "Do Digital Bible Searches Relativize Memorization?" (February 12, 2014).

79 APJ 1727: "Let God's Word Dwell in You Richly This Year" (January 5, 2022).

spill out of us in our decisions, actions, and speech. To state the urgency bra-zenly: we don't have "the chance of a snowball in hell to be holy" if we're not memorizing and meditating deeply on God's word.[80]

Bible memory accomplishes many things. It makes Scripture accessible when we are away from our Bible, sweetens our communion with God, and conforms our minds to God's mind. It gives us truth to heal the hurting, ammunition to conquer temptations, a shield to deflect lies, and power to resist the devil. "Memorizing Scripture enables me to hit the devil in the face with a force he cannot resist, to protect myself and my family from his assaults. What are you hitting him with? He is a million times stronger than you. And he hates you and your family and your marriage and your church and your God. How anybody walks through this devil-ruled world without a sword in hand is beyond me."[81]

College students should be memorizing Scripture, because ten minutes of morning devotions is woefully inadequate to confront the temptations they face daily. Spiritual warfare calls for serious Bible memory. "Memorize chapters. Memorize whole books. Memorize the Sermon on the Mount. Memorize particular psalms. I doubt that anyone will be an effective Chris-tian in our day standing *against* the culture—and *for* the culture—without much Bible memory."[82]

Memorization suggestions

Bible memory is "a signature of sanctified people." So where do we begin? Start with a whole chapter, and make it Romans 8, "probably the greatest chapter in the Bible" and one that's "always relevant." Romans 8 covers everything from our justification, the peace it brings, the end of fearing condemnation, the weakness of the flesh, and our hope of the resurrection and glorification—all within the present reality of our suffering and groaning as we await Christ's return.[83] At the outset of the coronavirus lockdown (2020), Pastor John suggested that we all use the extra time at home to memorize Romans 8, a bedrock passage for fighting off the fears and unknowns of the looming pandemic.[84]

Love is also relevant, an ingredient so essential to the successful Christian life that "most of us should memorize all of 1 Corinthians 13," the Bible's "most important chapter on love." The text is especially important for anyone strug-gling with a critical spirit. Memorize the chapter and watch it change your

---

80 APJ 411: "The Key to Christian Obedience" (August 20, 2014).
81 APJ 476: "Good Motives for Bible Memory" (November 19, 2014).
82 APJ 690: "Seven Tips for College Students" (September 22, 2015).
83 APJ 257: "Bible Memory: Essential or Optional?" (January 16, 2014).
84 APJ SE18: "How to Talk to Children about the Coronavirus" (March 31, 2020).

entire life. "Good night! Say it and say it, pray it and pray it, until it's *you*. And God will heal you of much of your hypercritical spirit."[85]

Beyond key psalms, Isaiah 53, Romans 8, and 1 Corinthians 13, memorize smaller and more specific promises. Isaiah 41:10 has proven to be Pastor John's "most commonly used" promise "over the last fifty years."[86] Facing the pains and struggles of life, he's wielded the text "a thousand times."[87] A text with historical significance traced back to a critical transition in his life at the age of twenty-five.[88] Ever since the weapon of choice against anxiety. Whenever he feels nervous before preaching, he turns his mind to Isaiah 41:10 to hear God's voice. "I did that many times as I stood up to preach. It was as though the Lord just looked me right in the face and said, 'I will help you.' I didn't make that up. He said that to me. That's what I mean by *meeting* the Lord in his word."[89] This text's relevance for life is proven by its three verbs corresponding to "every challenge" we will face. You can use it in weakness ("I will strengthen you"), in need ("I will help you"), or when life beats you up ("I will uphold you"). Three "awesome verbs" God uses to speak his comforting presence directly to your soul.[90] Speak the text verbally, as an act of faith, and you will hear God audibly speaking to you.[91]

Be sure to memorize Romans 8:32—"the most prominent promise in my heart,"[92] and "perhaps my favorite verse in all the Bible."[93] Additionally, consider memorizing Matthew 28:20, Romans 8:28, 2 Corinthians 1:20, 9:8, Galatians 2:20, Philippians 4:19, and Hebrews 13:5–6. "I think it is good to memorize a handful of promises so that you can always call them to mind, no matter what your situation, for encouragement and protection and strength."[94]

Essential Bible texts for life's hardest battles

Speaking of key texts to memorize, these sixteen have proven most useful to Pastor John over the decades, each "tailor-made for living the Christian life through all of its ups and downs."

85   APJ 1714: "How Can I Resist a Critical Spirit?" (December 6, 2021).
86   APJ 1858: "What Makes My Life Christian?" (November 7, 2022).
87   APJ 799: "How Do I Live the Authentic Christian Life?" (February 22, 2016).
88   APJ 1232: "John Piper's Most-Used Promises" (August 3, 2018).
89   APJ 589: "Have I Cast My Anxieties or Hoarded Them?" (May 5, 2015).
90   APJ 1232: "John Piper's Most-Used Promises" (August 3, 2018).
91   APJ 1232: "John Piper's Most-Used Promises" (August 3, 2018) and APJ 1798: "Crucial Texts for Our Hardest Battles" (June 20, 2022).
92   APJ 1232: "John Piper's Most-Used Promises" (August 3, 2018).
93   APJ 536: "The Dangers of Nostalgia" (February 19, 2015).
94   APJ 1232: "John Piper's Most-Used Promises" (August 3, 2018).

1. Texts for battling lust. First, a warning text, a "very powerful disincentive" to seeking online porn (Matt. 5:29). Then a promise text, that not lingering over sexual stimulation will preserve my vision of God (Matt. 5:8). Then a provision text (1 Pet. 2:24). The power of sin over me has been broken. Why would I grieve Christ with this sin?

2. A text for affliction (Ps. 34:19). We don't necessarily suffer because we've sinned. The righteous suffer too. And their suffering will end in God's timing.

3. A text for when you're mistreated (Rom. 12:19–20). When false things are said about us, how do we find peace? We leave the retribution with God. "Oh, how many times I have been set free from bitterness" by this text.

4. Texts for when you feel weak. God works for us (Isa. 64:4). This is "the glorious uniqueness of our God" compared to the ancient gods. Our God does not recruit slave labor to work *for him*, he's eager to work *for us*! Indeed, God's eyes scan the globe for his righteous children, "looking for people for whom— with omnipotence—he can work for today" (2 Chron. 16:9).

5. Texts for when you feel inadequate. When you feel short on money, time, or help, there are "two go-to verses I have used hundreds of times." God promises that *every need* we have *will be met* (Phil. 4:19). Bank on it. So don't love money. Don't fear man. Be content. Why? Because God is with you (Heb. 13:5–6). And to *have* God "is as sweet as it gets."

6. A text for when you feel alone (1 Pet. 5:6–7). God has a mighty, omnipotent hand. And he cares for *you—little you*. "So don't shrink back from humility, thinking that you're going to be too vulnerable if you're humble." No. Your "every single anxiety goes onto his broad shoulders." Because he cares for *you!*

7. Texts for when you think God is begrudging toward you. In truth, God is *eager* to bless you from his "good pleasure" (Luke 12:32). "He *loves* to care for you." He *rejoices* in doing us good (Jer. 32:41). "What more can God say than that *he rejoices to do good to us*, with *all his heart* and *all his soul*? There isn't anything conceivably bigger than *all* of God's heart and *all* of God's soul. And that's what he says is behind his doing good for us!"

8. A text for fear (Isa. 41:10). This is the verse "I've gone to more than any other in all my seventy-six years of life." It's verse "number one for the struggle with fear." It is the voice of God directed right at you with "I will . . . I will . . . I will . . ." Recite the text verbally to hear God speak directly to you.

9. A text for depression (Ps. 42:11). Yet another text that speaks directly. An interrogation. Why, soul, are you cast down? Hope in God! "Oh, my goodness. I have preached that to myself in low times, hundreds and hundreds of times."

10. A text for facing death (1 Thess. 5:9–10). At the age of seventy-six, "I recite this to myself before I go to sleep every night," akin to a "Now I Lay

Me Down to Sleep" bedtime prayer. The text tells us we are free from wrath and safe forever in Christ, whether alive or dead. So powerful is this text, he says, unless he changes his mind in the meantime, "it's going onto my gravestone."

11. The promise of all promises (Rom. 8:32). This is the "all-encompassing" promise, the fountain, "the Vesuvius" of all the other promises on this list. Because Christ shed his blood for us, "God will give his children everything—absolutely everything—we need to be supremely holy and happy forever."[95]

Scripture memory how-to

So how does one memorize the whole chapter of Romans 8? Start by breaking it down into thirty-nine verses over thirty-nine days. On day one, read verse 1 ten times. Study each different word. Each time, read the verse with an emphasis on a different word in the sentence. Squeeze as much possible meaning from each text. Then close your eyes and recite the verse ten times. The next day, recite verse 1 from memory ten times. Make sure you got it. Then work on verse 2. The next day recite verses 1 and 2 ten times from memory. And so on.[96]

What translation should we use for Bible memory? Pastor John vividly remembers his two translation moves—first from KJV to RSV; then from RSV to ESV. Contrary to using multiple translations in Bible reading, in memorization you should settle on one translation: "If you are going to do significant long-term memory, it will be very difficult to jump around in translations because the mind gets locked in—and it *needs* to get locked in—to certain wording, so that it doesn't have to be self-conscious as it is reciting the Bible and can focus on the meaning." Consistency is important. Ask your church leaders which translation is going to be used over the long haul. Avoid using "idiosyncratic translations" and keep to those proven over the years: NIV, NKJV, NASB, and ESV. "My own vote is for the ESV, but, boy, it is far better to be memorizing *any* version than to be memorizing *none*."[97] Best of all, memorize for a long time from *one* proven translation because "I just don't know any who have done serious, long-term, extensive Bible memory by using several translations."[98]

95 APJ 1798: "Crucial Texts for Our Hardest Battles" (June 20, 2022).
96 APJ 258: "Practical Tips for Bible Memory" (January 17, 2014).
97 APJ 259: "What Translation for Bible Memory?" (January 20, 2014).
98 APJ 1003: "How Many Bible Versions Should I Read?" (February 15, 2017).

On Politics, Patriotism, and Culture Wars

On church, state, and politics

Christ entered into this world as a figurative sword to divide. "He comes into the world as the supreme beauty and supreme joy and supreme value of the universe (Matt. 10:34–39). And he comes with absolute supreme authority. Therefore, he claims in every family, and in every business, and in every school, and in every church, and in every political party, and in every nation a superior allegiance, a superior love. And so, with the sword of his supremacy, he cuts every affection and every allegiance to family or business or school or church or political party or nation which would compete with him for supreme place in our hearts."[1]

Decisions of eternal consequence play out every moment. Pastor John witnessed the weight of this truth early in life. "My father's prayers when I was a little boy were laden with the glory of God." Bill Piper's life and ministry witnessed to "the fallen creation of God in desperate need of rescue by the gospel. In other words, I grew up in a home with big things going on. The home was not about the latest TV show. It wasn't about the latest political shenanigans. It was about the latest rescue from hell for heaven for a glorious God who made the universe, who exists for his own glory."[2]

On theocracy

No single nation carries out God's work on earth. "God no longer works through a people who are a political state or an ethnic entity to perform his kingdom-spreading, saving work." More particularly, he no longer deals with Israel "as the embodiment—ethnically and politically—of his kingdom on the earth (Matt.

---

1 APJ 1447: "Jesus Came to Bring Violence—but What Does That Mean for Us?" (March 16, 2020).
2 APJ 192: "How Did Your Vision for Missions Develop?" (October 11, 2013).

21:43). He is giving the kingdom to a people who produce its fruits—namely, the church of Jesus Christ. And since God works through his Spirit by his word in a people called the church, they have no status as a political state, and they have no singular ethnic identity." In Christ, "God no longer works as a king exerting immediate authority over a people gathered as a political state or as a single ethnic identity."[3]

So the church marks "a dramatic change from the old theocratic, ethnic orientation on one people group—namely, Israel—to a new kind of people who are not a political entity," and "not an ethnic entity ruled by a political or governmental leader." Instead, "they are a people scattered like exiles away from heaven, their homeland, on the earth, mingling among all the ethnic groups of the world with a King in heaven and not on earth." The church doesn't function "like Israel did, as a national or political governmental agency," and therefore it doesn't "coerce its beliefs with the sword."[4]

This change affects the civic role of the Mosaic law—"the laws which dealt with Israel as a state are no longer applied that way, since the people of God are no longer a political entity." God now works in the world through his church. For example, the *excommunication* protocols of the New Testament church replace the *execution* protocols of Old Testament Israel. And Jesus declares all food clean, "meaning those laws which once defined Israel as a people of ethnic, religious, and political distinction from the world don't function that way anymore" (Mark 7:19).[5]

Should Christians ignite revolutions or live quietly?

Christ came to bring a sword of division into the world (Matt. 10:34). But Paul commands us to live quiet lives (1 Thess. 4:11). So do Christians trigger revolutions or work in silence?

This isn't simply a Jesus-versus-Paul tension. Jesus drove out money-changers (Matt. 21:12). *And* Jesus told us to turn the other cheek (Matt. 5:39). These two texts leave us with a puzzle. Paul called the church "to live quietly, and to mind your own affairs, and to work with your hands, as we instructed you" (1 Thess. 4:11). This same church struggled with lazy people meddling in others' affairs (2 Thess. 3:10–12). "Some in the church seem to be idlers, lazy, not working for a living, mooching off of others, and bringing the church and the name of Jesus into disrepute among outsiders. And the quietness that Paul has in mind seems to be the opposite of bothersome talk—when you hang around others who

---

3 APJ 468: "Did God Commission Terrorism in the Bible?" (November 7, 2014).
4 APJ 795: "Doesn't the Bible Tell Christians to Put Homosexuals to Death?" (February 16, 2016).
5 APJ 632: "Why Are Old Testament Commands No Longer Binding?" (July 3, 2015).

are trying to do their work and you aren't doing any work. All you are is talk." Instead, says Paul, get to work, support yourself, and "stop making Christianity look like the birthplace of laziness." Perhaps these meddling Christians had quit working, assuming that Christ's return was soon. In any case, the quietness Paul envisions "is the opposite of—or it flows from—focused, diligent, gainful employment. If you are laying bricks all day or digging a ditch or winnowing grain, then you are not a nuisance, gadding about and gossiping about other people while they are trying to work."

So did Paul contradict his quiet-life principle by preaching Christ and inciting a riot in Ephesus (Acts 19:21–41)? No. Paul's main concern in Thessalonica "was that the saints walk in love and that they truly exalt Christ in the community, so the outsiders see what he is really like." That's ministry. And if ministry causes a riot, so be it. Let's be sure any "public uproar" is ignited by our love to people and exultation of Christ.[6]

On patriotism in the sanctuary and pastors in politics

The Sunday church gathering "should be wonderfully and gloriously vertical in its focus." We gather to focus on God. But those gatherings can get horizontally hijacked by other good things: community life, art, drama, children, evangelism, concerts, or political activism. If the Godward focus gets lost, Sunday becomes "man-centered" and "the vertical focus is blunted." We need political activism, but not on Sunday morning.[7] The Pledge of Allegiance, even American flags, "do not belong in a worship service that is called to highlight the absolute allegiance that we have to Jesus."[8]

Pastors who lead overly patriotic churches can reframe the focus over the years and decades. (1) Preach the lordship of Christ. "Patiently, week in and week out, preach Bible-saturated, God-centered, Christ-exalting, man-humbling sermons that by implication so elevate the lordship of Christ over every detail of life with such majesty that, little by little, the church begins to absorb the mindset that our highest affections and our only absolute allegiance belongs to Jesus Christ—willingly, eagerly, joyfully, no regrets, no restraint." (2) Be open about your discomfort with fellow leaders, because "until you get some of them on board with you, any change is probably going to be futile and may be destructive." (3) Communicate gratitude to military veterans in the church. Let them know that you love them and appreciate their sacrifices. See if a few of them will affirm your vision and help redirect the church's Sunday focus. (4) In light of militaristic valor, celebrate

6 APJ 695: "Should Christians Start Revolutions or Just Live Quietly?" (September 29, 2015).
7 APJ 106: "How Evangelistic Should Sundays Be?" (June 6, 2013).
8 APJ 1060: "Should Patriotism Have a Place in Church?" (June 28, 2017).

the missional courage of those who lived and died, "not to advance the American way, but to advance an even greater good." (5) Remove flags from the sanctuary. Put flags in common areas, the places where people transition from the world into worship, and then transition from worship back into the world.[9]

Such buffers don't excuse pastors from cultural awareness. Pastors must address at least "the few" issues from the news that seem particularly "urgent and major." Use these few issues to disciple your people in how to think of social issues. Address the issues, not as a politician but as a pastor, "aiming to show how to think and pray and act from the roots of things"—the root of human nature and the root of biblical revelation. Pastor, "go deep with your Bible and with human nature," because those two topics are your "bread and butter" and "expertise" and what people most need from you.[10]

The government exists to punish evil and praise good. And when a nation's leaders get these duties backward, praising evil and punishing good, the church speaks up. "Yes, the disposition of a Christian should be to support and be submissive to governments—local governments and national governments. This is part of God's will. On the other hand, we should—in writing, in speaking, and in conversation (I would include preaching in all of this)—publicly confront governors and presidents who do not punish evil and do not praise good, especially when we reverse the pattern and notice that they start participating in the very evil they are supposed to punish."[11] For example, this conviction was on display four years earlier. "It galls me that, in front of his daughters, he [President Barack Obama] would say that equal rights for women means that they must have access to abortion, which really means equal rights to have sex outside of marriage without any more consequences than the man has. That is what he means, which is horrific to say." And worthy of public rebuke.[12]

But in a world driven by political correctness at every level—from gender studies,[13] public school instruction, media reporting,[14] and even Bible translations[15]—don't be surprised if our public rebuke of sin gets interpreted as a political move. Particularly when it comes to celebrating the biblical truth on sexuality and gender, the world will charge us with partisan motives. "There will always be people who twist what you say to have connotations and implications

9   APJ 1061: "How Would You Lead an Overly Patriotic Church?" (June 30, 2017).
10 APJ 662: "How Culturally Up-to-Date Must My Pastor Be?" (August 14, 2015).
11 APJ 1127: "When Do Christians Resist a Government That Kills Its Citizens?" (December 1, 2017).
12 APJ 31: "How Do Rape, Incest, and Threat to the Mother's Life Affect Your Pro-Life Stance?" (February 20, 2013).
13 APJ 989: "Are Men Superior to Women?" (January 13, 2017).
14 APJ 1739: "Embracing Unpopular Truth in an Age of Political Correctness" (February 2, 2022).
15 APJ 259: "What Translation for Bible Memory?" (January 20, 2014).

that you don't want them to have and you didn't intend. That's exactly the way people treated the preaching of Jesus." And it got him killed. "The day is long gone in America where it is possible to be publicly faithful as a Christian to the truth of God and not be excoriated."[16]

Here's the key difference. "Our political voice should be so permeated by the announcement of the horrors of divine wrath over the human race and the glories of the gospel of divine rescue and the unsearchable riches of Christ, the ruler of the nations, and the demand for repentance and faith from every citizen and every politician—so permeated with all that—that it is evident to all that political concerns for the true Christian fade into mists compared to these vastly greater realities."[17]

In general, the pastor can celebrate the work of Christians in politics, and can extract himself from ongoing political discussions online. So "I am one hundred times more passionate about creating Christians and churches that will be faithful, biblical, countercultural, and spiritually minded in a socialist America, in a Muslim America, in a communist America, than I am in preventing a Muslim America or a communist America. That puts me in a very different ballpark than many public voices. My main calling is not to help America be anything, but to help the church be the church. I want to help the church be the radical outpost of the kingdom of Christ, no matter what kind of America it happens to be in or any other people group or country in the world."[18]

On Inauguration Day 2017, Pastor John prayed for the salvation and protection of Donald Trump. He prayed for the church and the work of the gospel. "I pray for evangelical leaders not to celebrate Donald Trump's presidency with no apparent qualification, no tears, no brokenness, no sadness that he sets such an awful example for this land." But considering the rise and fall of American presidents, our mission is rooted in something greater. "Lord, don't let us exhaust our energies fretting about the little molehill of this presidency when we have a Himalayan mountain range of blessings in Christ Jesus." Then he prayed over the staff at Desiring God, that "together we might make the greatest possible impact to spread a passion for your supremacy, not American supremacy or Trump supremacy or Republican or Democratic supremacy. May it always feel like a heavenly orientation rather than an earthly orientation."[19]

16 APJ 1125: "Did Public Controversy over the Nashville Statement Hurt the Cause?" (November 27, 2017).
17 APJ 1419: "How Do We Respond to Claims That Christianity Is Dangerous?" (January 10, 2020).
18 APJ 1263: "Why Does Piper Avoid Politics and What's Trending?" (October 15, 2018).
19 APJ SE11: "John Piper's Prayer for President Trump" (January 20, 2017).

On global missions and narrowed nationalism

As hinted above (in APJ 1061), a church captive to political nationalism will prove weak on missional resolve. Repeatedly in history the church has become "ingrown" and "indifferent to the world." Missions dies when professing Christians take their status as divinely chosen and combine it with an ethnocentric nationalism. "Jesus saw it in his day," in Jewish biases against Gentiles. So from the church's inception, Christ taught his people to think globally by appreciating how he was drawing his church from other folds and foreign nations (John 10:16; Rev. 5:9). Such an inclusive vision would help guard his church from global indifference. "Oh, there is so much racism, so much ethnocentrism left over in America. We thought we finished it off forty years ago. We didn't. And you know we didn't. It's in your heart. It's in my heart." It's in the church. We need a worldwide worldview to see that—in Christ—the bloodline linking us with a brother or sister in Africa "is a thicker bloodline" than the bond between you and your unbelieving mother or father or brother or sister.[20]

The same lesson was illustrated in Billy Graham's friendship with Martin Luther King Jr. The men were "not on the same page culturally or experientially." And they "were not on the same theological page—not by a long shot." But they were friends. And Graham leveraged his influence to help ease race tensions in America. He "absolutely refused" to hold Christian crusades that were not racially integrated, even across the South, a decision "simply unheard of" at the time. From the pulpit, Graham made it clear that Jesus was not a White man. And he was not a Black man. "Christ belongs to all people," he preached. "He belongs to the whole world." In this way, Graham proclaimed "the global, pan-ethnic glory of Jesus. Jesus does not belong to America but to the world. Therefore, to belong to Jesus is also to belong to the world. The more Billy Graham walked with Jesus among the peoples of the world, the less distinctly American he felt, the less decisively defined he was by his nation and his ethnicity or his race." The takeaway: "a spirit of confined, narrow, limited parochialism that has no glad heart, no biblical heart for the thousands of peoples of the world, is going to be missing one of the great healing impulses for ethnic challenges in our day here in America, or wherever you live around the world."[21]

Particularly after 9/11, the world needs to be reminded that *American* is not a synonym for *Christian*.[22] We "are not first Americans, or Canadians, or British, or Russians, or Nigerians. In every nation, we are exiles (1 Pet. 2:11). Let that

---

20 APJ 1922: "Christ's Plan for the Globe—and You" (April 5, 2023).
21 APJ 1576: "Martin Luther King and His Partner in the Cause" (January 18, 2021).
22 APJ SE30: "John Piper's 9/11 Radio Interview" (September 11, 2021).

sink in. I want to scream that from the top of a building to every nationalistic tendency: 'In every nation, we are exiles!'"[23] Exiles, meaning "I'm a foreigner in America."[24] This alien identity broadens the scope of John Piper's ministry ambitions from Minneapolis. "God does not endorse or encourage any kind of nationalistic or ethnocentric focus in his people. We belong to his kingdom first and foremost. That shapes everything. He is pursuing all the nations, peoples, languages, and cultures of the world. I want my life to count for the world, not just for my national or ethnic or geographic or cultural tribe."[25]

Because the impulse to "confuse and combine" our Christian identity with political, ethnic, or national identities is "so strong" and "so destructive" to our gospel witness, the church needs "steadfast resistance" in every generation. We need a Christian identity that will "survive and thrive with faith and hope and joy and love and purity, whether America survives, or Brazil survives, or Britain survives, or China survives, or Russia survives, or India survives. Or not."

We find our identity in seven texts. (1) We are not of this world (John 18:36). Jesus warns his people to be "very, very careful" not to employ fighting (ἠγω-νίζοντο), force, or coercion to establish his kingdom. "In this age, King Jesus is creating a people in a very different way." (2) We are identified in Christ, who is hidden (Col. 1:13; 3:1–4). "Our most fundamental and defining identity and location is the kingdom of Christ," in heaven, at the right hand of God—"not the right hand of any earthly power." And that means, for now, our identity is mostly veiled to the watching world. Only when Christ "appears" will we "be openly known for who we really are." (3) We are citizens of heaven (Phil. 3:20–21). "No earthly citizenship, whether American or Russian or Chinese, has any ultimate allegiance over those who are in Christ Jesus. No party, no nation, no ethnicity, no ideology has any ultimate claim on us. Our decisive constitution is the word of God, and no human document." (4) We belong to a brand-new race and nation (1 Pet. 2:9). These are "ethnically and politically shattering words." Our past identities—ethnic and national—are superseded by a new identity in Christ. "Christians are a new thing, a new reality, a new people, a new nation, a new ethnicity and race." (5) We are resident aliens on earth (John 15:19; 1 Pet. 2:11). For now, we live as sojourners and exiles in this world. In every nation, Christians are aliens. (6) We are God's servants (1 Pet. 2:13–16). As Christians, we are free—"free from emperors, free from governors, free from presidents, free from worldly powers and parties. We belong to God. We are slaves of God, not any man. We are his servants. He owns us. We do his

---

23 APJ 1804: "Politics, Patriotism, and the Pulpit" (July 4, 2022).
24 APJ SE30: "John Piper's 9/11 Radio Interview" (September 11, 2021).
25 APJ 1552: "God's Providence in 2020" (November 16, 2020).

bidding." We pay taxes and abide by laws because God is our authority, and he tells us to abide by just laws. We submit ourselves to state authority "for his sake and in his limits." (7) We are globally ambitious (Matt. 28:19–20). Our aim is not to Christianize nations. We are called to baptize and disciple nations. Namely, we baptize and disciple *them* (αὐτοὺς), the *plural people* living in those nations. God's new "holy nation" is comprised of "every race, ethnicity, and nation."

Of course, Christians will disagree about how all this plays out on social media, in the voting booth, and at work. But pastors don't need to figure out the "thousands of ways" your diverse people will meet dilemmas in their "cultural and professional and political endeavors." Instead, "speak these biblical truths and others that you see as relevant from Scripture. Call your people to radical allegiance to King Jesus. Set them on a quest of lifelong learning, and trust the Spirit of God in their lives."[26]

On patriotic Christians

With national flags out of the sanctuary, should Christians ever voice patriotism?

"We are exiles, sojourners, refugees ourselves in a very refugee-heightened culture" (Phil. 3:20; 1 Pet. 2:11). We await someplace new. But we don't aspire to prematurely escape the world (John 17:15–19). In the waiting, we love the people of God, our nation, our city, and our neighbors. We experience the love of *storge* (στοργή)—"this kind of affection for a tree or a city or a fatherland or a language or a culture because it fits you. When you leave it, you get on a plane, you go to another country, yeah—there is an excitement and a challenge and a stimulation of going other places, but there is something inside, that when you come home, it just feels wonderful to eat the food and lie in your own bed and be in your own living room and walk your own streets and hear your own language. All that seems to be something that God puts his approval on."

Holy patriotism is only possible after God claims our ultimate allegiance. We are exiles here, and we reckon with the fact that our country is going to change in a lot of ways. But we commit not to wield patriotism as a weapon against others. "Whatever form your patriotism takes, let it be with a deep sense that we are more closely bound to brothers and sisters in Christ in other countries and other cultures than we are to our closest unbelieving compatriot or family member in the fatherland or in the neighborhood."[27]

---

26 APJ 1804: "Politics, Patriotism, and the Pulpit" (July 4, 2022).
27 APJ 893: "Should Christians Be Patriotic?" (July 1, 2016). On *storge* love, affection for a city or fatherland or language or culture, see APJ 125: "Patriotism and the Christian" (July 4, 2013), APJ 378: "Pilgrims and Patriots" (July 4, 2014), APJ 893: "Should Christians Be Patriotic?" (July 1, 2016), and APJ 1494: "How Much Patriotism Is Too Much Patriotism?" (July 3, 2020).

So "never feel more attached to your fatherland or your tribe or your family or your ethnicity than you do to the people of Christ. Everyone who is in Christ is more closely and permanently united to others in Christ, no matter the other associations, than we are to our nearest fellow citizen or party member or brother or sister or spouse. Oh, how many horrible indignities, injustices, contradictions of Christianity have been perpetrated because believers have failed to realize this. We are more bound together with other believers—no matter their ethnicity or their political alignments or their nationality—than we are to anybody in our own fatherland." Christ "has relativized all human allegiances, all human loves. Keeping Christ supreme in our affections makes all our lesser loves better, not worse. Under his flag, it is right to be thankful to God that we have a fatherland, a tribe, a family, an old pair of slippers that just fit right."[28]

On voting for degenerate politicians

Our political voice must be "permeated" with truth—the horrors of divine wrath, the glorious rescue of the gospel, the unsearchable riches of Christ, and his radical demands on every citizen and politician.[29] In light of these priorities, it's appalling that Christians would eagerly vote for politicians who would have been called, in previous generations, "lechers and perverts." We must show great care with voting because "those who put immoral people in office reveal that their strategy prioritizes political power over the fruits of godliness as a way to make the world a better place," showing that "trust has shifted from the power of God to work through the humility of holiness onto the power of our own cleverness, whether it be political shrewdness or cultural savvy. I regard this approach to life and transformation as hopelessly flawed. It will not bring the kingdom. It will not transform culture. It will not convict sinners. It will backfire and destroy the credibility of the Christian church."[30]

Political pragmatism can backfire on the Christian life. Feeding on urgent, politically driven media hype can misdirect our attention away from personal holiness. Biblical priorities certainly "have a bearing on public life and political issues," but Scripture places "overwhelming emphasis" on the believer's pursuit of God-patterned purity (Lev. 11:44–45; 19:2; 20:7; 1 Pet. 1:16). This holiness priority includes everything: how we speak to one another, love others, endure suffering, fight sexual temptation, tend our marriages, work with integrity, and honor Christ in all of life. And yet "I've seen, over my fifty years of adult life, how

28 APJ 1494: "How Much Patriotism Is Too Much Patriotism?" (July 3, 2020).
29 APJ 1419: "How Do We Respond to Claims That Christianity Is Dangerous?" (January 10, 2020).
30 APJ 1187: "Will Profanity Make Us More Relevant in Reaching Our Culture?" (April 20, 2018).

presumed public virtue and public position-stating can conceal much private corruption and unholiness. People like to think that they have seized the moral high ground in public, but, in fact, the foundations are crumbling." Beware of any media diet where you "find yourself endlessly pondering public issues while losing battle after battle at the level of personal holiness and integrity."[31]

On slavery

Jonathan Edwards's (1703–1758) deep influence on Piper's life and ministry reminds us that even our greatest theologians are plagued by besetting sins and blind spots. Edwards purchased and owned household and farming slaves, perhaps as many as six in total over his lifetime. Such participation in the slave trade revealed in him a "blind spot" of fallibility, a "blank spot" in his maturity, an ethical "flaw" in his heart, a moral "mess," and a "failure" where he simply "blew it." His failures teach us five lessons. (1) Don't idolize any man but Jesus. Measure your admiration of fallible teachers. (2) Read with discernment. Edwards had this blind spot in his life, so watch out for other blind spots in his writings. (3) Be amazed that God uses any of us. After an eight-month leave of absence to deal with his own heart, Pastor John's "sobering season" led him to marvel "that I survived thirty-three years in the pastorate as an imperfect man." And yet God worked through him. "So, I am not quick to point my finger at Edwards, but I am quick to marvel that *he was used*—and *I have been used*—and I am amazed." (4) Search out and address your own sins. Find the blind spots you don't see and work to root them out. Don't settle for holiness in five areas and ignore the sixth area. Go after every sin. (5) Be driven to prayer for discernment with your own heart. Pray with the psalmist: "Who can discern his errors? Declare me innocent from hidden faults" (Ps. 19:12). Even as you grow in sanctification, assume personal blind spots you don't yet see.[32]

The weight of our fathers' sins—our national forefathers' sins—weighed heavily on Piper as he walked around Andrew Jackson's Hermitage, a huge plantation outside Nashville that drew from the labor of at least five hundred documented slaves. Jackson (1767–1845) was a war hero, the seventh president of the US, a wealthy slave owner, and "the main force" behind the Indian Removal Act of 1830, booting Cherokee, Chickasaw, Choctaw, Creek, and Seminole Indians from southeastern states to clear the land for White settlers, land in South Carolina where Piper's childhood home would sit. "I watched this twenty-minute

31 APJ 1665: "Six Dangers of Podcasts" (August 13, 2021).
32 APJ 138: "Slavery and Jonathan Edwards" (July 26, 2013).

video of Jackson's life and presidency, then I read the plaques in the museum, and then I strolled through all the grounds and gardens of the mansion and the slave quarters. The heavy realization came again that our country is built in significant part *on the soil of stolen land and the backs of stolen men*—land taken from Native Americans and cultivated with African American slaves."

So how should the racial sins of our fathers—the sins of our forefathers—be visited today? (1) We are all sinners in Adam (Rom. 5:12–21). He's our head. (2) The son *is not guilty* for his father's sin (Deut. 24:16). "It seems like God has established in the beginning a kind of union with Adam and all humans, but not in such a way that all sons fall in all fathers. We fell *in Adam*, but I didn't fall *in Bill Piper* in the same way." (3) Only when the son is *guilty* of the same sins does Scripture say that the father's sins are visited on his son (Exod. 20:5).

Confronted with Andrew Jackson's sins, Pastor John processed his thoughts in two responses. (1) A *chastened gratitude* for America's present prosperity. "I enjoy hundreds of benefits for being an American just because I was born here—in the skin I have, at the time I was born, in the place I was born, to the parents I was born. I had nothing to do with any of that, and yet I benefit from it." And yet it's a "*chastened* gratitude" because "I am prospering from the sins of national forefathers. I may not be guilty of their guilt, but I do benefit from the country they built on their guilt." (2) A *shame* for the behavior of others. When our kids misbehave, we feel shame. When a minority is mistreated inside our high school, we feel shame. When Christians "act ugly toward Muslims," we feel shame. We express sorrow for the injustice, renounce the sin, and resolve to make it right.[33]

The killing of Michael Brown by a White police officer in Ferguson, Missouri (2014), fed longstanding outrage in the Black community. It evoked a long train of American history that includes slavery and Jim Crow laws, a story that's "ugly, horrible, and demeaning—I mean to a degree that one can hardly imagine the indignities of it." These abuses "are part of the matrix of that minority self-consciousness: 'We have been hated. We have been abused. We have been mistreated for a long time.'" Other voices say, "'Come on. If we don't get beyond that, we won't make any progress.' That is true. But it is not canceling out the reality of the consciousness, which we need to handle. Whites need to be aware that we never had to deal with that [history], and they [Blacks] still do."[34]

Another listener asked a more technical question. If Paul laid out ethics for the slave-master relationship in the New Testament, which he did, and if we

---

33 APJ 248: "Slavery, Oppression, and America's Prosperity" (January 3, 2014).
34 APJ 424: "What Whites Can Learn from Ferguson" (September 8, 2014).

denounce the institution of slavery as sin, won't this subjectify other institution-based ethics, like complementarity, in the future? No, it won't. (1) Paul rooted male-female relationships, both in the church and home, firmly within the created order (1 Tim. 2:12–13). In stark contrast, (2) Paul "did not treat the institution of slavery as *normative* or as *desirable* or as *right* in the way it functioned. Paul did not say that slavery—as it existed in his day or in most of history and especially in America—was the way Christians should relate to each other. In other words, you don't need a trajectory hermeneutic to see in Paul that slavery is not the way it should be" (1 Cor. 7:21–23; Eph. 6:9–10; Philem. 1:16).[35]

Slavery was a broken system. Enslaving is evil. And yet God remains sovereign over enslavement. He alone can *intend* evil for a future good. In the testimony of an enslaved man named Joseph, speaking to his enslavers: "As for you, *you meant* evil against me, but *God meant* it for good" (Gen. 50:20). "When Joseph's brothers in the Old Testament sold him into slavery, they sinned." And yet such abuse did not break God's good plan. Joseph doesn't say that God *used it* for good, but that he *intended it* for good. His brothers *intended* a meaning (evil). God *intended* a meaning (good). Through such evil, God "brought about salvation for the people of God and the redemption that would one day come through the seed. So, yes, God was in, on, controlling, governing, bringing about what happened there."[36] "God had an agenda. God had a plan."[37] And he revealed that plan to us so that we can say, more broadly and personally, "the very same thing that is evil in someone's intention—the same event God intends for good."[38]

Joseph's testimony dovetails with the story of God's sovereignty told in the rich theology of Black spiritual songs. "The preaching and the singing of Black slaves and post–Civil War Black churches virtually never questioned God in the miseries of their lives." Slavery was unthinkable; Whites were culpable. "But God? He was the deliverer, and he was never portrayed as helpless—like, 'Where was God while we were in chains?'" Instead, "the spirituals are shot through with the sovereign Lord of history."[39]

On racial progress, President Barack Obama's election (2008) was a stunning development. "If you had told plantation owners 150 years ago, or members of the Ku Klux Klan in the 1920s, or White Southerners I grew up with—including

---

35 APJ 492: "Are New Testament Ethics Final or Trajectory-Setting?" (December 15, 2014).

36 APJ 697: "Can God Be Sovereign over All Sin and Still Be Good?" (October 1, 2015).

37 APJ 1170: "God's Sovereign Plans behind Your Most Unproductive Days" (March 12, 2018).

38 APJ 1327: "What Is the Sovereignty of God?" (April 8, 2019).

39 APJ 512: "Why So Few African-American Calvinists?" (January 16, 2015).

me—that this would be true, none would have believed it. It is astonishing and wonderful in itself, quite apart from any moral or philosophical differences we may have with President Obama. The President of the United States is Black, and he couldn't even drink out of the same fountain with me in 1959 at the Kress Five-and-Ten Cent store."[40]

On abortion

Every day in America, the strong murder the weak. And it's legal. Legal because Americans have grabbed for a godlike power to determine who is human and who is subhuman. "In Minnesota, and lots of states, it's *illegal* to take the life of an unborn child if the mother *wants* the baby. And it's *legal* to take the life of an unborn child if she *doesn't*. In the first case, the law treats the fetus as a *human* with rights. In the second case, the law treats the fetus as *nonhuman* with no rights. Humanness, the existence of a human being, is decreed by the will of a mother." This "right" to confer (or withhold) personhood "is legally enshrined self-deification. The strong decide which of the weak are persons. We reject that in the case of Nazi anti-Semitism. We reject that in the case of Confederate, race-based slavery. We reject that in the case of the Soviet Gulag. But in the case of the unborn, millions of people—millions in the church, which is what I care about most—embrace the self-deifying principle that the human will of the strong confers personhood. If she wants the baby, it's a baby. If she doesn't, it's not. She's God." No. She's not God. According to Scripture, God grants personhood to every child—in the womb and outside it (Ps. 139:13–16).[41]

Abortion is a dehumanizing moral outrage. It angers us, and it should. But we must display the right kind of anger. The anger of man achieves nothing (Eph. 4:31; James 1:19–20). But the "appropriate anger" over abortion "may communicate *more* truth about God, about the Christian faith, about Scripture, and about Christ than *the absence of anger* communicates." There's a time and place to voice anger over abortion (and other injustices), a controlled anger, a righteous anger—an anger that can still love its enemy, voice sorrow and brokenheartedness, won't poison us to become angry people, and accord with the outrage of God being dishonored by this murder and dishonored by those indifferent to God being dishonored. "My guess is that most people have never seen anything like that. They don't have any categories for that kind of anger. In other words, our anger may bear witness to the character of God who

40 APJ 331: "Civil Rights 50 Years Later" (April 30, 2014). On the stark moral differences, see APJ 31: "How Do Rape, Incest, and Threat to the Mother's Life Affect Your Pro-Life Stance?" (February 20, 2013).
41 APJ 1655: "The Strong Murder the Weak Every Day in America" (July 21, 2021).

has created these little ones in his image and is knitting them together in the mother's womb (Ps. 139:13). When the lacerations and the chopping begins from the abortionist, it is not just the babies that are being shredded, but God is being assaulted as his knitting needles are pitched aside and his hands are being thrust back from what he has been doing there."[42]

Piper's biblical convictions, namely Proverbs 24:11–12, led him to participate in anti-abortion demonstrations in the late 1980s and early 1990s. "We would get up early, pile into buses, and sit in front of an abortion clinic so that nobody could get in or open the door without stepping on us. Eventually, we'd be accused of trespassing, and they would tell us to leave. But we wouldn't because we believed that we were there trying to rescue children from being aborted. So the police would come haul us down, tell us not to do it anymore, and let us go. That happened maybe half a dozen times, and one of those times we were sentenced to a night or two in jail." It was a civil disobedience in fear of God, not man (Est. 4:16; Acts 5:29; Rom. 13:1–4). But the demonstrations were unsustainable, mainly "because we, the Christians, could not maintain the kind of suffering, humble, quiet attitude that would win the day as in the civil rights movement. There were just too many loud-mouth, feisty pro-life people that couldn't keep their mouths shut when we were mistreated by the police or those who were pro-abortion. Since the spirit was lacking in so many, it backfired and ceased to be an effective tool in the rescue."[43]

Abortion's evil is reminiscent of the Holocaust. Both kill God's image bearers. Both slaughter people like animals—no, "worse than animals." This evil correlation sank in when Piper visited the Dachau concentration camp in Germany. "I have read and seen the pictures of people frozen to death to experiment with how quickly people would freeze to death, or hanging, or asphyxiation, or all kinds of horrible experiments that were done. It was a kind of slaughter that was worse than the killing of animals. And so it is with babies in the womb; most of them are dismembered limb from limb." Both slaughters measure in the millions. Both trample human personhood. "The non-Aryan race was deemed increasingly subhuman, or at least not the kind of human who was worthy of life. And that is exactly the same rationale for the killing of the unborn." Both slaughters will one day be looked on with horror. "The time will come when the generations will look back on ours with even more unbelief that we could

---

42 APJ 672: "When Should We Vent over Social Sins?" (August 27, 2015). On the dangers of "righteous anger" suffocating holy affections and subverting our delight in God, see APJ 1711: "Does Righteous Anger Kill Our Joy?" (November 29, 2021).

43 APJ 9: "Arrests and Imprisonments in Opposing Abortion" (January 22, 2013).

have let it happen than when we look back on Germany in the 1930s and 1940s and marvel that it happened." God will avenge it all.[44]

Related to these Holocaust experiments, we must resist any medical innovation that requires babies to be aborted. Abortion's evil is never justified by the good medical benefits that may result (Rom. 3:8). We must be willing to stand against these practices in principle, with a vision set on eternal life, lest we shrug off evil means by idolizing our temporal health.[45]

The womb is "God's workplace" (Job 31:15; Ps. 139:13). Conception inaugurates a human life in the womb—a son or daughter from the beginning (Luke 1:36, 41). As the incarnation proves, full personhood begins in the womb, making *Roe v. Wade* the "most wicked of all Supreme Court decrees ever," and "a direct assault on the Son of God. Not only because the Son of God is the Creator of all children—and therefore *Roe v. Wade* is assaulting person-creating rights when it kills children that he is creating—but also because this law that they passed, if enforced in the first century, would have endorsed the legal killing of Jesus in the womb. And Jesus in the womb is the Son of God." So, "I would say that every lover of the incarnation of Jesus should hate abortion and what it stands for, and I hope that the Lord keeps us prayerful and keeps us active until the day comes when abortion will be as unthinkable as slavery is today, because it is a far more destructive action."[46]

But doesn't conception due to rape or a pregnancy threatening a mother's life change your stance? No, rape and incest are not warrants for killing the baby. "The baby is not the criminal here." The perpetrator is the criminal to bear the punishment. Even in worst-case scenarios, the conceived child is indivisibly the product of the mother. "Yes, it was conceived by a man whom she didn't want to have anything to do with, but the baby is hers just like it would be hers if it was conceived by her husband." Whatever scenario brought about conception, mother and child are uniquely bound. There are ways forward with single motherhood or adoption because—"whether by caring for the baby herself or giving the baby to a loving family because she is in a situation where she can't raise it—that would be less damaging to her soul" than the rupture of abortion. And in the rare event when a pregnancy threatens the mother's life, in determining the line between "a certain death" for mom or baby, I will "lean heavy on the wisdom of Christian doctors to help me discern."[47]

---

44 APJ 160: "Is Abortion Like the Holocaust?" (August 28, 2013).
45 APJ 1570: "Can I Take a Vaccine Made from Aborted Babies?" (January 4, 2021).
46 APJ 261: "*Roe v. Wade* Assaults the Incarnation of Christ" (January 22, 2014).
47 APJ 31: "How Do Rape, Incest, and Threat to the Mother's Life Affect Your Pro-Life Stance?" (February 20, 2013).

But if babies go to heaven, why fundamentally oppose abortion? It's an argument against evangelical pro-lifers. "I have argued numerous times that infants who die do go to heaven," not based on cuteness, but on the fact that God "makes the rejection of observable evidences of truth the basis for his final condemnation," which is not possible for the unborn and infants (Rom. 1:20). There are six reasons why aborting the heaven-bound is a huge violation. (1) Murder is murder, and murder is always a big deal (Gen. 9:6). (2) The logic would hold for killing infants and toddlers. (3) The logic would hold for murdering any heaven-bound Christian. (4) Such abortion would violate the prohibition against grace abounding because sin abounds (Rom. 3:8; 6:1). (5) Abortion violates the goodness of life on earth, even for the heaven-bound (Phil. 1:21–25). (6) Abortion violates God, playacting a godlike role of judge.[48]

So if abortions are wicked, and my government subsidizes them, should I stop paying taxes? The Bible distinguishes between "intentional evil" and "unknowing participation in evil" (Deut. 19:4–5). In general, paying taxes is just (Rom. 13:1–7). "I think it is fair to say that when this letter was written, the Roman Caesar did not use all of that money for actions Christians would have approved of." In practice, all tax expenditures run together. We don't pay an abortion tax or social security tax or military tax or welfare tax that we can give to or not. It's all funneled together. "So my practice is, yes, I keep giving money to a government that is funding abortion." But two questions remain about when government fails to function to punish evil and reward the good (1 Pet. 2:14). When do we stop paying taxes? And when do we overthrow the government entirely? "I am not sure where that line is. In fact, I tremble at the possible necessity of making that decision someday."[49]

For those guilty of abortion, God's word offers hope for those willing to embrace "gutsy guilt" (Mic. 7:8–9). "Micah owns his sin. He owns his guilt. He's in darkness, sitting there under the Lord, and the Lord is disciplining him. He's under God's judgment." He makes no excuses. He doesn't shift blame. "He knows this is from the Lord, and it's awful. He owns his sin. He owns his guilt. Then he says, 'I will sit in this darkness under the Lord's displeasure until he pleads my cause and executes judgment for me.' Not *against* me—*for* me." The only way "to survive as a saved sinner" is with "real guilt, real sorrow, real pain, real darkness under God's discipline, and real gutsy faith. Gutsy faith that the very God who is disciplining me and displeased with me is on my side and will vindicate me." Gutsy guilt like this knows that

48   APJ 684: "If Babies Go to Heaven, Why Oppose Abortion?" (September 14, 2015).
49   APJ 685: "If My Government Funds Abortions, Why Pay Taxes?" (September 15, 2015).

we should be punished forever for our sin. But we won't, because of Christ's sacrifice for sinners (Isa. 53:5; Gal. 3:13). By faith, you belong to him. And you belong in the church with fellow sinners washed pure in Christ (1 Cor. 6:9–11). To seek forgiveness is not selfish. "It would be selfish if you just wanted to use God to get a relieved conscience. But if you want forgiveness because you want God, that's not selfish. That's what you were made for. It honors God, not you. It honors God. God is glorified when you want to be satisfied in God." Your future hope is warranted by the blood of Christ. Come to him. Your story is not over. Your life is not wasted. He has good plans for your future (Jer. 29:11).[50]

Rivers of desire and dams of legislation

Christians esteem God-given gifts in the military, the police, and "the common grace of retributive justice."[51] A just government rewards good behavior and punishes evil behavior.[52] By God's design, it "enforces laws with coercion, fines, imprisonment, bodily harm, and even death."[53] This role differs from the church. The church excommunicates; it doesn't execute.[54] Blasphemy was met in the Old Testament with execution (Lev. 24:16) and is met in the New Testament with excommunication (1 Tim. 1:20). The church focuses on the more important heart work that new legislation cannot accomplish. Laws exist because hearts are hard (Mark 10:5). But the church's main mission is not to hold hard hearts accountable but to see dead hearts come alive by the resurrecting power of the gospel.

This may mean that Christians partner with unbelievers in social causes, "wherever the *external behavior* we are advocating or restraining overlaps with *their convictions about that external behavior.*" But external change is not our final aim. "As a Christian, I will always desire and pray that people do the right thing out of faith in Jesus, not just because it is legal or illegal. Who cares about that in the long run? If they don't do it because they are a Christian, they go to hell. Then I have done a not very good thing for them." So we agree that murder is sin, and murderers should be prosecuted by the state (Rom. 13:1–7; 1 Pet. 2:14). But we also believe lust is spiritually damning. Legislation won't

---

50 APJ 1067: "'I Had an Abortion'" (July 14, 2017).
51 APJ 1635: "Should Christian Jurors Show Mercy to the Guilty?" (June 4, 2021).
52 APJ SE08: "Is Kim Davis Right to Refuse Marriage Licenses?" (September 11, 2015).
53 APJ 1621: "How Can I Protect My Child from State Indoctrination?" (May 3, 2021).
54 APJ 632: "Why Are Old Testament Commands No Longer Binding?" (July 3, 2015), APJ 1635: "Should Christian Jurors Show Mercy to the Guilty?" (June 4, 2021), and APJ 1782: "Would You Have Supported Prohibition in 1913?" (May 13, 2022).

prosecute lust. Laws can restrain some sins. But laws don't change hearts, and that's what we seek. Changed hearts.[55]

The attempt to use legal pressure to suppress alcoholism by making alcohol illegal, called Prohibition (1920–1933), was doomed to fail. And seeking to recriminalize recreational marijuana use today would likely meet the same fate. The social pressure is too strong. The church's focus (for pastors and for parents) is the miracle of creating a generation of believers who don't *want* the escape of recreational pot use.[56]

Indeed, Prohibition failed because "long-term societal support was simply not there." The masses didn't want it. Pent-up desire in society will collapse the dam of any law. So the church acknowledges the limits of legislation. "Christian faith, and all the heart obedience of faith that flows from it, cannot be coerced by the sword—that is, by the state. The entire history of Christendom by force, from Constantine to the Puritans, was misguided." It backfired. "Any arrangement of church-state relations that sanctions state penalties to promote true heart faith and the heart obedience of faith will eventually corrupt the church."[57]

On the flip side, the overturning of *Roe v. Wade* (2022) marked a major victory for the pro-life movement. But again, the Supreme Court will never change souls by adding or canceling laws. "We can build legal dams to keep the river of sin that pours out of the human heart from flooding the world with actual behaviors like abortion. And that's a good thing. That's what all good laws do. They make it harder for the sinful heart to overflow in outward crimes. But if the river of sin that flows from the human heart is simply dammed up, and nothing changes the heart, that river is going to build behind the dam until the reservoir is so deep and so heavy that no legal dam, no mere law, can hold it back." And then "a tidal wave of wickedness will overflow the land." No matter the wins or losses in culture, "our main job is not *new laws*—good as they may be—but *new hearts*" (John 3:3, 7; 2 Cor. 3:18). Because "if that doesn't happen, new laws will collapse under the pressure of unchanged hearts. It's only a matter of time." More importantly, "without a Christ-exalting heart change, people perish. We perish." So "it is *loving* to work for good laws. But it is *more loving* to help people enter the kingdom of God." Indeed, the "real post–*Roe v. Wade* challenge will not be how to make abortions *hard to get*, but how to make them *hard to approve of* in the human heart." Laws can make sin illegal for a sinner. But laws don't make a sin repulsive to a sinner. Making abortion

---

55 APJ 845: "Should Christians Partner with Non-Christians on Social Issues?" (April 26, 2016).
56 APJ 1698: "The Church's Calling in an Age of Recreational Pot" (October 29, 2021).
57 APJ 1782: "Would You Have Supported Prohibition in 1913?" (May 13, 2022).

unthinkable is the pro-life miracle we ultimately seek, possible only by the grace of God in Christ.[58]

Eventually, abortion will be as "unthinkable" as slavery is unthinkable today.[59]

On the dangers of socialism

After a disclaimer, misgivings, and admitting that he's "not an expert in political science or economics," Pastor John offered a few thoughts on socialism, "for what it's worth." The question arose after socialist Bernie Sanders launched a serious run at the presidency (2015), raising concerns of a system that "through legal or governmental or military coercion, establishes social ownership at the expense of private or personal ownership." The system controls the means of production in society. "And thus, through control, you effectively eliminate many of the implications and motivations of private ownership." At its best, "socialism borrows the compassionate aims of Christianity in meeting people's needs while rejecting the Christian expectation that this compassion not be coerced or forced. Socialism, therefore, gets its attractiveness at certain points in history where people are drawn to the entitlements that socialism brings, and where people are ignorant or forgetful of the coercion and the force required to implement it—and whether or not that coercion might, in fact, backfire and result in greater poverty or drab uniformity or, worse, the abuse of the coercion as we saw in murderous states like the USSR and Cambodia."[60]

Coercive, socialist cultures raise all sorts of challenges for Christians. Particularly in how to best educate children.[61] We need Christians to address these social pressures, though Piper himself remains "one hundred times more passionate about creating the *kind* of Christians and the *kind* of churches that stand with unshaken, faithful, biblical, countercultural spiritual-mindedness in a socialist America than I am in preventing a socialist America."[62]

On tolerance, religious liberty, human rights, and God's rights

Baptists tend to be more "disentangled" from civil government.[63] And they affirm that religious liberty is woven into the gospel's fabric. So when it comes to debates with adherents to other religions, we need thick skin and for tolerance to allow for "an ongoing relationship of open, honest, rough-and-tumble give-and-take."

58 APJ SE31: "*Roe v. Wade* Has Ended—Our Pro-Life Work Has Not" (June 30, 2022).
59 APJ 261: "*Roe v. Wade* Assaults the Incarnation of Christ" (January 22, 2014).
60 APJ 710: "How Should Christians Think about Socialism?" (October 20, 2015).
61 APJ 1621: "How Can I Protect My Child from State Indoctrination?" (May 3, 2021).
62 APJ 1263: "Why Does Piper Avoid Politics and What's Trending?" (October 15, 2018).
63 APJ 1629: "What Is a Baptist?" (May 21, 2021).

We seek to persuade and to woo others. "We hold out warnings of what we think God or circumstances may bring about, and we plead. But we do not persecute, and we do not force. And we do not manipulate or do anything underhanded or try to bribe or do political maneuvering or do violence to change a person's mind." Religious tolerance goes beyond preserving "civil order in a pluralistic society." It's necessary because "genuine faith in God, genuine allegiance to Jesus, genuine Christ-exalting obedience to God's word, is only possible if it is uncoerced and free." Thus, religious tolerance "is built into the very nature of Christianity."[64]

And yet, standards of political tolerance and intolerance will change with the winds. "Sixty years ago in America, adultery would have ruined a man in office and racism would not have. Today it is exactly flipped. Now adultery won't ruin you—witness Bill Clinton. Racism will. You drop the N-word one time, and your political career is over. That was not true sixty years ago. That is how democracy works. Cultural shifts dictate tolerance shifts and legal shifts."[65]

In the end, the universe is centered on *God's rights* not *human rights*. The world, the flesh, and our media tell us to make the universe all about our own rights, needs, and expectations. But "you see the universe totally differently when you begin with God at the center—*his* rights and *his* goals as the assumption of the universe. Is the basic riddle of the universe to preserve man's rights and solve man's problems? Or is the basic riddle of the universe how an infinitely worthy God, in complete freedom, can display the whole range of his perfections adequately for all to see and—if they will—to worship and enjoy? Is his holiness and power and wisdom and justice and wrath and goodness and truth and grace the agenda of the universe? Is the meaning and purpose of everything to manifest *God*, to display *God*, to exalt *God*? Or are *we* the center? Are *we* the measure? Are *our rights* the thing to be guarded? How you answer these questions will determine whether or not you can understand the biblical teaching about justification." Our riveted focus on God's rights, not our rights, will prove to be "an absolutely foreign concept in this nation." But such a radical concept will protect the church's gospel proclamation to this nation.[66]

64 APJ 794: "Should Christians Tolerate False Religious Beliefs?" (February 15, 2016).
65 APJ 511: "How Local Church Trumps Twitter and Facebook" (January 15, 2015).
66 APJ 1901: "The God-Centeredness of God Unlocks the Gospel" (February 15, 2023).

On Careers, Calling, and Overworking

Made to make; remade to better make

God made us to make. He created a garden. Then he created Adam and Eve "to make something good and beautiful and useful" out of that garden. The same is true for us. God made us to "make a rocky field into a garden, or a stick into a spear, or a rock into a hammer, or an empty apartment into a home, or a cow into a steak."

After the fall, God redeems his children. He remakes us. In Christ, we become God's poem (ποίημα), his "workmanship" (Eph. 2:10). As *creatures* we are made to be makers. But as *new creatures* we are remade to make with God in a new way, "called to take what God has made in all of its now-present falseness and remake it into something Godward and beautiful and Christ-honoring, with a deep sense of fulfillment of who we are, created in the image of our Maker." In Christ—as God's poem—we find our identity focused and our calling sharpened.[1]

How do I glorify God at work?

Paul tells us to "work heartily, as for the Lord and not for men" (Col. 3:22–24). So how does this apply to cleaning our home, writing a paper for school, or working our nine-to-five job? How do we fight against personal laziness?

Fundamentally, Christ's blood covers all our guilt. "None of us does our work as well as we could. We're always falling short of the ideal." We rest in his forgiveness as we resolve to work more faithfully. The gospel is not a "free pass" to excuse sinful laziness. Our conscience will not allow it. But if we seek to work hard without relying on Christ for our failures, "we will either fail in despair, or we will look like we succeed and become proud." Both operate together—peace-giving forgiveness and gospel-resolved diligence.

God owns us, and he lays claim on our lives, including our work (Prov. 3:5–6; 16:3; Rom. 14:6–9; 1 Cor. 10:31; Col. 3:17). "All those texts have one basic

---

1   APJ 17: "We Are Makers—Lessons on Vocation from Dorothy Sayers" (January 31, 2013).

message: we belong to God; we're not our own. Everything we do, from morning till night, is to be done in a Godward way, before his face, in reliance on his grace, guided by his will, and aiming to make him look magnificent and glorious as our all-satisfying treasure. That's what work is for. That's what all of life is for."

So what does it mean to "work heartily, as for the Lord and not for men," particularly in the broader context of Colossians 3:22–25? Note five modifiers. (1) Don't work for eye service and to please men. Work for God first and foremost, to honor him. (2) Work with sincerity, the opposite of man-pleasing and eye service—which amounts to insincere work. We don't work to impress others but to serve others. (3) We work in fear of the Lord. We are not fearful of displeasing man but of displeasing God. (4) We work "heartily," putting our whole soul into the work. (5) We work for God's reward. Any recompense in this life is a secondary motivator to our greater future reward from God. God needs nothing we produce (Acts 17:25). We exist to magnify him. "Paul gave us these instructions because this will bring the greatest joy to us when we work this way. And it will show that God is our greatest treasure."[2]

Work is one area where we show the world that Christ is our greatest treasure. Such an aim is not forced; it emerges from the Christian's "great vocation"—beholding the glory of Christ (2 Cor. 3:18). "This is the fountain of all the godliness in your life, seeing the Lamb as supremely beautiful and satisfying and compelling. The devil knows this. And that is why Paul said in 2 Corinthians 4:4, '[Satan] has blinded the minds of the unbelievers, to keep them from seeing the light of the gospel of the glory of Christ.' This is the most terrifying thing in the world to me, that people I love (or I myself) may be so blinded by the devil that they look at Jesus and he is *not* beautiful. He is *not* their treasure. Money is their treasure. Videos are their treasure. Making grades is their treasure. Their boyfriend is their treasure. . . . Death is not terrifying. To be so deceived that you can't see Jesus as the treasure of your life, that is the most terrifying thing." Treasuring Christ is our "great vocation" and ultimate calling that gives shape to our careers in this world.[3]

Should I follow my heart to find my dream career?

When seeking out a career path, is there a difference between pursuing a dream, following our heart, and walking in obedience to God with the gifts he gave us? Or should this be the same thing for the Christian?

2   APJ 1121: "How Do I Glorify God in My Job?" (November 17, 2017).
3   APJ 796: "The Christian's Great Vocation" (February 17, 2016).

Two points about our desires need to be in place first. (1) We *can* find enjoyment in our acts of obedience, leadership, and service to others (Ps. 40:8; Rom. 12:8; Heb. 13:17; 1 Pet. 5:2). However, Scripture never makes "our delight in doing something the sole criterion for deciding whether that something is right to do." That's because (2) we must also learn to deny certain desires in the path of obedience (Matt. 16:24). "The life of obedience to Jesus will never be a life of only doing what we love to do. There will always be some measure of denying ourselves. The world is too harsh, pain is too real, and we are too sinful to think otherwise." So the better question to ask is: "Are my dreams and my passions and my gifting—are they all being transformed by a radically God-centered, Christ-exalting, Bible-saturated vision of reality?"

To embody the answer to this question, and to find your way to the right career, here are three suggestions.

1. Leave complex calculations to God. It's impossible for us to compute our dreams, passions, giftings, and "what precise path will be *most fruitful* for people and *most faithful* to God." No finite mind can figure all this out. In the end, we must entrust our future to his wisdom. He will open the right doors.

2. Shape yourself. Instead of making calculations, "pour your energy into becoming a radically God-centered person, a radically Christ-exalting person, a radically Bible-saturated person, a radically loving person, a radically risk-taking, servantlike person." The "lion's share" of our work is becoming a *kind* of person. "Then, in ways that to me appear increasingly mysterious, God guides his radically crazy, God-entranced, Christ-treasuring, Bible-permeated people into some of the most surprising vocational pathways that we can imagine." Seek to become a type of person, and God will open the right doors for you.

3. Be driven by gospel-sized ambitions. Whatever vocational field is ahead for you, meditate deeply on Paul's stated ambitions for his own life, and let his aims shape your ambitions (Acts 20:24; Rom. 15:20; Phil. 1:20–21; 3:13–14). "If your dreams become as drenched with gospel zeal, and your gifts become as fervently bent toward magnifying Christ, and your passions become as thrilled with the glory of God as Paul's, then yes, you can follow your dream."[4]

Speaking of (3), our colossal ambitions, Paul is our model (Rom. 15:20, 23–24). Within these dreams he *abounded* (περισσεύοντες) in the work, meaning he did lots and lots of it (1 Cor. 15:58). Paul outworked everyone, and he attributed this entirely to God's grace (1 Cor. 15:10). We follow his model. "Go ahead. Dream your big dream. Do your work—lots and lots of it! But never, never presume that you are doing it on your own. Every dream is a gift. Every

---

4 APJ 1593: "Should I Ever Pursue My Dreams?" (February 26, 2021).

accomplishment of a dream is a gift" (1 Cor. 4:7). Dream huge, gospel-saturated dreams and let your humble dependence on God keep your ego in check.[5]

Speaking of (2), shaping the self, this is how we prepare to face two good career options in the future. Make it your aim now to become a *kind* of person, in six ways. (i) Aim for radical holiness in all of life. (ii) Aim to be regularly and deeply shaped by Scripture. (iii) Aim to know God's gifts in you. (iv) Become sensitive to the needs of the world. (v) Pray for God to lead you, as modeled by David (Ps. 25:1–22). (vi) Belong to a "worshiping community of love" where other believers regularly speak into your life. With these disciplines in place, when two good career options sit before you, rate the pros/cons, decide, and proceed.[6]

Overcoming indecision

On questions of indecision, Pastor John is quick to turn to Psalm 25—a "precious promise of guidance"[7] and "precious psalm of guidance" that speaks to the heart.[8] In a sermon he called it "just about the best passage on guidance in the Bible," and he encouraged his church to memorize it.[9] He's rememorized it over the years.[10] Now he says, "I don't know any other passage of Scripture that is better for putting into words our cry for guidance and wisdom from God."[11] When faced with two good choices, Psalm 25 proves "especially valuable."[12] It tells us that God loves to lead the humble.[13] Not the perfect. He leads *sinners.* Sinners like us. Sinners who are humble, "people who know they are sinners and admit it and cry out" (25:8–9).[14] So "if Satan discourages you from seeking God's guidance because you are a sinner, you know where to tell him to go."[15] Friendship with God is for those who fear him (25:14). God's friendship makes us stable as he holds us and guides us.[16] It is a friendship of fear so that when you meet a fork in the road, "reverence will reveal what's right."[17]

5   APJ 1064: "Should I 'Dream Big' for God When I Have a Huge Ego?" (July 7, 2017).

6   APJ 1381: "How Do I Follow God's Will in the Face of Two Good Options?" (October 14, 2019).

7   APJ 973: "I'm Paralyzed by Indecision—What Should I Do?" (December 7, 2016).

8   APJ 1255: "My Funding Dried Up—Is This My Sign to Leave the Ministry?" (September 26, 2018).

9   APJ 1888: "Eight Counsels for Those Thinking of Quitting" (January 16, 2023).

10 APJ 1140: "A New Year, A New Bible Reading Plan" (January 1, 2018) and APJ 1296: "How Do I Make the Most of Daily Bible Reading?" (December 31, 2018).

11 APJ 1761: "On Permanent Birth Control" (March 25, 2022).

12 APJ 1381: "How Do I Follow God's Will in the Face of Two Good Options?" (October 14, 2019).

13 APJ 1431: "How Do I Find a Good Church?" (February 7, 2020).

14 APJ 1120: "How Do I Process Personal Criticism?" (November 15, 2017).

15 John Piper (@JohnPiper), Twitter, June 28, 2018.

16 APJ 1120: "How Do I Process Personal Criticism?" (November 15, 2017).

17 John Piper (@JohnPiper), Twitter, May 28, 2020.

Related, a question came from a pair of empty nesters, paralyzed by indecision for how to invest the last season of life. Overcome this "perfectionist fear of making a mistake" by realizing that "deciding *nothing* is the biggest mistake. There is your deal breaker. That will get you going. In other words, you are not in a neutral zone. There are no neutral zones. Not to move toward a God-sized goal in this next season of your life is to disobey." God loves to guide ships in motion. So investigate and explore, but begin moving and expect God to direct you as you launch out into this new season. And dream big—"don't let the fatalism of aging limit your dreams of fruitfulness." Ask, "'What new vision for our next chapter of life would cause us to taste most fully the power of God, the wisdom of God, and the grace of God in our lives? How can we get more of God?' And I think if that is the passion, God will show you the answer."[18]

How Christ changes our careers

Do we go too far when we press Paul's gospel aspirations into secular career choices? No, not for the Christian. To the crowd who ate the feast of loaves and fish, Christ commanded them: "Do not work for the food that perishes, but for the food that endures to eternal life, which the Son of Man will give to you" (John 6:27). Christ himself is the all-satisfying bread. So does this mean that once we trust in Christ, we stop laboring for the bread we buy at the store? Obviously not. "The whole New Testament assumes and commends the dignity of work" (Eph. 4:28; 2 Thess. 3:10).

So what changes when we believe in Christ and find him to be "glorious, all-satisfying, eternal bread"? (1) A new chapter is added to our lives: eternity. The bread of Christ leads to eternal life. Retirement is not our final chapter. (2) A new treasure is added to our lives: the bread of life. "This bread, when you eat it and discover who he is and over a lifetime discover more and more of how deeply nutritional this is for souls that were made for God, all other values go down, down, down as he goes up, up, up!"

Christ doesn't withdraw us from the job market. We remain employed. And in those jobs, we "remain with God" (1 Cor. 7:24). "Staying where you are is ordinary, normal, steady-state Christianity, and *something about everything* in that job changes. That's carefully said. I'm tempted to say that *everything* changes. I will say that eventually. But what I mean when I say it is this: *something about everything* changes." Christ is our greatest treasure. So "if things look bleak in work or at home, you remember that you're going to live forever. So you go to work not dominated by the desire for the bread that perishes or

---

18 APJ 973: "I'm Paralyzed by Indecision—What Should I Do?" (December 7, 2016).

for the fear of losing it. You go to work knowing him, trusting him, treasuring him, being satisfied in him with your heart set on making much of him. That's how you go to work now." Such a discipline "will not make you a lazy worker; it will not make you a shoddy worker; it will not make you a gloomy worker. You will bring zeal and excellence and joy to your work because you know him, you trust him, you treasure him. You want to make much of him in all that you do. You know that everything—everything—done in the name of Jesus and for the glory of Jesus, from the washing of the bathroom to the running of the boardroom, will be rewarded forever with ten-thousandfold, undeserved joy."[19]

To remain in a career because God *remains* with us (μενέτω; 1 Cor. 7:24) means "whatever work we have, the greatest joy about the job is that we get to be there with God. He is with us every day." He is present to help us reach good ends in our careers.[20] He is present to help us endure and thrive in less-than-ideal careers if we must.[21]

Will God give me a job I don't like?

Would God call you to a job you *cannot* enjoy? Or will God call you to a job that he *will not enable you* to enjoy?

Three factors answer these questions.

1. Serve with cheerfulness (Ps. 100:2; Rom. 12:8). All our giving and serving should be marked by joy (Eccl. 3:22; 2 Cor. 9:7; 1 Thess. 5:18). By implication, we shouldn't refuse to work until we land a job that "we think we can enjoy." Instead, "we should take the work that we can for the good of the family, the good of the community, the glory of God, and then *pray our way into the enjoyment of it* and shape it in whatever way we can so that it becomes more fruitful and more enjoyable."

2. Be instructed by slaves. Many of the first Christians were enslaved in the Roman Empire, an unpleasant life of "often terrible" mistreatment (1 Pet. 2:18–25). Of course, if slaves could get free, they should, showing that "Paul did not consider it ideal that we labor in a miserable role" (1 Cor. 7:21). But in whatever role we find ourselves, we "have God," Paul says (1 Cor. 7:24). "In other words, whatever work we have, the greatest joy about the job is that we get to be there *with God*. He has come to us. He is with us every day. Whatever we are doing, he is there. He will help us. He will turn it for our good."

3. Be thankful for options. "In most places in the world, people do not have one hundred possibilities in front of them for how to make a living. They may

19 APJ 1511: "How Does Christ Change How I Work?" (August 12, 2020).
20 APJ 768: "Will God Call Me to a Career I Don't Enjoy?" (January 8, 2016).
21 APJ 1519: "Is My Career in Marketing Vain?" (August 31, 2020).

ON CAREERS, CALLING, AND OVERWORKING   73

have one or two or three options, given their village and the family they are in
and the society they are in." The question is "very Western." But whether in the
West or the East, in prosperity or in lack, "this is the essence of the Christian
life: finding contentment in Christ and turning every circumstance, and all of
our work, into living worship" (Phil. 4:11).[22]

How do I learn to enjoy God in my work?

God calls us to *learn to enjoy* our work. How do we do this?

Four keys. (1) Know that God is greater than all his gifts to us (Ps. 73:25–26;
Phil. 3:8). "I think the point of those passages is not to say that there can be no
legitimate pleasure in God's gifts. Too many other texts contradict that idea.
But the point is that *only in God*, or *supremely in God*, we find our pleasure."
(2) See everything as rubbish that does not magnify Christ, and see why this
conviction doesn't nullify our nine-to-five labors (Phil. 3:8; 4:1). (3) Give with
joy and cheerfulness (Acts 20:35; 2 Cor. 9:7). (4) Enjoy your labor and work
with your whole heart (Eccl. 2:24; 3:13; 5:19).

To put these four points in a "short," "tangled," and "exciting" conclusion: our
enjoyment of our work "should be an enjoyment of honoring what God has given
us and what he has done for us." We labor *from* our enjoyment in God. Our self-
giving is "overflow" (περισσεύω; 2 Cor. 8:2). In the context of meaningful labor,
we not only taste the goodness of God to us (labor is a divine gift), but then our
joy in him overflows in serving others. So "*conscious* of being created by God,
dependent on God, *gifted* by God for certain work, *motivated* by God, being
eager to do it as to God, then we can say that our very work is an embodiment
or an incarnation of the very glory of God that delights us." Everything we use
in our work—our mind, muscles, nerves, eyes, ears, and emotions—is "designed
by God to show the glory of God." In this way, our daily labors not only express
but also enlarge our enjoyment of God. So we aim to see "the fruit of our lives
to be such a display of the all-satisfying glory of God that other people see it"
and "come to share in it so that our joy in God is enlarged by their joy in God."[23]

Is the missionary greater than the algebra teacher?

Most Christians are not missionaries and cannot invest most of their hours in
ministry. But isn't the missionary's work superior to the algebra teacher's work?

All Christians are equal in Christ (Gal. 3:28). Yet we're prone to sinfully rank-
ing each other (James 1:9–11). Even so, is there a basis in which one vocation

---

22 APJ 768: "Will God Call Me to a Career I Don't Enjoy?" (January 8, 2016).
23 APJ 730: "Four Key Ways We Enjoy God in Our Work" (November 17, 2015).

could be considered "greater" than another? Paul seemed to do this very thing in ascribing honor to those who teach the word (1 Thess. 5:12–13; 1 Tim. 5:17). He sees "some roles or activities or vocations as having a certain kind of honor or esteem that other roles or activities don't have." Learn to distinguish by two comparisons.

1. Compare the inner dispositions. First, picture a preacher standing before "unbelievers in a hostile missionary setting." And compare that to an algebra teacher teaching "a class of compliant teenagers in a Christian school." There's an inner faith, trust, and Godward humility required in both, and the algebra teacher may have more of it. That's because "no activity in and of itself is a greater activity in the measure of its worship and devotion and faith than any other if you just consider that: the devotion, the worship, the faithfulness."

2. Compare the potential impact. "Algebra is good. Algebra is God's creation. Algebra is needed. But algebra is not the gospel, and algebra does not save sinners." So "the likelihood of miracles of eternal significance happening are greater in the preaching of the sermon—and the risking of life is also greater in that audience." So (1) the missionary isn't necessarily more holy. But (2) the missionary's ambitions are superior.

"So, at least for myself, as a pastor for thirty-three years who was basically surrounded by people who loved and approved me and who paid me well in a society that didn't put me in jail, in a city with ample medical care, central air-conditioning, functioning infrastructures—in view of all of that, I have always felt that missionaries who have taken more risks, gone into harder places, enduring greater trials with less affirmation, are worthy of a kind of esteem and honor of which I am not worthy. I think that is true. And when I say that, I am not belittling the value of my thirty-three years in ministry."[24]

Am I wasting my life in any vocation other than missions?

If we don't become martyrs for Christ, have we really done all that we could do for the kingdom? The question came from a successful man working in corporate America. Pastor John shared three cautions and two exhortations.

Caution 1: Don't make a missionary decision that indicts other Christians who remain in business. Choosing missions because a corporate job feels sub-Christian is an invalid argument. It's clear that the apostles "do not intend that all Christians should leave their ordinary employment." Paul calls Christians to "remain in the condition" of their calling, and to remain so "with God" (1 Cor. 7:20, 24). "Now, 'with God' changes everything. Oh, my goodness, it's not as though the apostles

---

24 APJ 942: "Is the Missionary Greater Than the Artist?" (September 26, 2016).

don't want there to be radical change in your life and in the way you relate to people in your job. But you don't have to leave your job in order to be a faithful Christian, according to those principles." Don't reason your way into missions by thinking that those who remain in corporate work are sinfully disobedient.

Caution 2: Being spent for the kingdom doesn't favor the missionary. You can move into a hostile environment and be martyred "even though you, in fact, were not using every ounce of your strength and not using every fiber of your being in devotion to Jesus—but were in fact wasting a lot of time, acting in a worldly way, with great timidity, and caring very little about the people around you. That's possible; that happens. Missionaries can become like that." On the other hand, in corporate America you can be "using more of your strength, more fibers of your being, more ounces of your strength for the sake of the kingdom than if you were a missionary." There's "no necessary correlation" between where you work and how wholeheartedly you work.

Caution 3: Martyrdom isn't mandated. Such an aspiration is presumptive, because "aiming to be a martyr is turning a God-decided result of faithfulness into a self-decided definition of faithfulness. You shouldn't do that. It may be that the path of obedience God assigns to you will end in martyrdom." Or not. "That's not your call." Our call is "obedience and faithfulness and love and zeal. How it ends is his business, not ours." And keep in mind that many martyrs were "weak and worldly Christians who happened to be in the wrong place at the wrong time." And many who died natural deaths "were vastly more fruitful and effective Christians than some martyrs." There's "no necessary correlation" between your fruitfulness and your cause of death.

Exhortation 1: Expect restlessness to drive you to missions. God has "mysteriously, wonderfully led thousands of people to leave ordinary jobs in their homeland in order to move them on to frontline missionary work" through "a sense of restlessness." But this restlessness isn't an indictment on Christians who don't feel it.

Exhortation 2: Be called to mission in community with other believers. Every missionary needs to be "embedded in a fellowship of believers, where other people can discern his gifts and his passions and his maturity, and in that way confirm for him God's call on his life."[25]

How do I climb the corporate ladder and reach the lost?

This question is essentially, how do we live our faith sincerely at work? We all want "a life that is so integrated—with Christ as the agent of the integration—

25 APJ 1503: "Am I Wasting My Life in a Secular Job?" (July 24, 2020).

that we don't feel pulled in separate directions." We seek a life that feels "cohesive," "whole," and brings "integrity to all the pieces of my life." Climbing the corporate ladder and caring for the eternal needs of others: how do these two aims become an integrated whole? Ponder eleven questions.

(1) Can you see your labor and the purpose of your company within an ultimate, Christ-exalting outcome? (2) Can you see the excellence of what you do in a way that honors Christ, not merely positions you for promotions? (3) Can you see your labors as a means of serving others? (4) Can you see your personal integrity at work as the expression of your love to Christ? (5) Can you thank God for the skills and abilities he's given you? (6) Can you imagine what your work would look like if it was done in a spirit of humility? (7) Can you see the joy of Christ permeating your workdays? (8) Can you appreciate the importance of working without murmuring and complaining? (9) Can you see the importance of patience with others? (10) Can you see the Creator and his glory shining in your skills and work? (11) Can you see your vocation as a place of love? This point summarizes the previous ten: "Ponder how everything you do is an expression of love: love to God, love to people."[26]

Am I overworking or underworking?

The Bible commands a six-day workweek. So how do we know if we're overworking or underworking?

After the resurrection, the Lord's Day moved from the Saturday Sabbath to Sunday. And it's now observed less rigorously. "I don't take the Old Testament command to keep the Sabbath as binding on the church today with the same strictness it had in the Old Testament." Jesus was already "loosening the strictness of Sabbath" in his ministry (Matt. 12:1–8), because *Christ is our Sabbath rest.* Paul, too, seems less strict about holy days (Rom. 14:5; Gal. 4:10–11; Col. 2:16). Yet the church retains the six-day workweek and one day of rest, rooted in the created order. "So my view is that, with a lot of flexibility, we should keep the Lord's Day for rest and for worship—for spiritual renewal."

Interestingly, it's not the *one day of rest* but the *six days of work* that gets the emphasis in the Old Testament commands (Exod. 20:9; 34:21; Deut. 5:13). "All my ministry I have assumed that I work six days. I rest on one." As for many pastors, Monday is his day of rest.

With this conviction for six days of work, here are seven qualifiers. (1) Our work includes more than formal vocations. We also maintain our lives, cut our lawns, and fix our cars, squeaky doors, and leaky faucets. That, too, is work.

---

26 APJ 1174: "How to Climb the Corporate Ladder—for Jesus's Sake" (March 21, 2018).

(2) Five days could be spent in the corporate office, and then a sixth day devoted to ministry or civic work. (3) You may put in fifty or sixty hours of work in five workdays, completing a full six-day workload in five days. (4) If you love your work, *work* and *leisure* may become hard to distinguish. (5) On the contrary, a man may work an extra-long week to escape his home life, stoke his ego, feed his love of money, or catch up from five days of lazy working. (6) You can love your job and enjoy doing it six days a week. (7) Most of all, Christ is our Sabbath rest, "which means pervading all our work—five, six, four days—we are restful in Christ."

In sum, each of us must answer this question: "Have we found the rhythm of work and refreshment that points to the greatness of the risen Christ and leads to strong faith and sustained energy for joyfully fulfilling all the various callings (plural!) that a person has to the glory of God?"[27]

When has my career become my idol?

In highly competitive career fields, employees are pressed to work seven days a week. For one young woman, the texts and emails never stop. If she stopped for a day, she would immediately begin losing ground to colleagues who would outpace her in the race toward career advancement. In such competition, when has career become an idol?

The Ten Commandments warn us, "You shall not covet" (Exod. 20:17). And that word for *covet* is the same word used for the *good desire* we should have for the Bible (Ps. 19:10). So if a desire can be virtuous or sinful, what turns desire into coveting? The first commandment sets the stage. "You shall have no other gods before me" (Exod. 20:3). Thus, "a desire becomes covetousness when it begins to displace God as your *chief* desire. So in our workplace, we always have a measuring rod for idolatry. Is my work starting to feel *more precious*, *more satisfying*, and *more valuable* than God?"

In a competitive workplace we'll be tempted toward idolatry in three ways. (1) Work pressure-tests our faith. Do the tests at work deepen my faith, or do they make me more self-dependent? Do you stay up late, overwork, and trust in your own competencies? Or does the pressure you feel at work cause your faith to arise to say, "God is enough, and he will help me"? (2) Work pressure-tests our jealousy. Be zealous, not jealous. Ask, is my life passion about God's fame or my own? An honest answer here can disclose jealousy, the "resentful desire that someone else got some glory or some reward that I wanted for myself." We know that jealousy has taken hold "when we don't rejoice at other people's

27 APJ 658: "Am I Overworking?" (August 10, 2015).

successes and rewards," but resent them. (3) Work pressure-tests our security. We were redeemed for the good works that cannot redeem us (Eph. 2:8–10). And yet our works can become sinful works. How? "Your work is becoming *works* when you begin to feel that your work is earning your acceptance with God." In other words, "your work has become idolatry when it's the *root* and not the *fruit* of your acceptance—your status, your riches, your identity, which are all free in Christ." Christ grounds our work. Only in Christ do we find "the greatest acceptance, the greatest status, the greatest wealth, the greatest identity. If we shift from seeing our work as the *overflow* of that and start seeing our work as the *basis* of that, we have turned our work into grace-belittling idolatry."[28]

If I'm not good at my job, is the Lord telling me to quit?

A teacher wrote in because her lack of effectiveness is hurting her students academically. None of the feedback from her superiors has helped. Should she quit? Two guidelines.

Guideline 1: Our abilities must match our aspirations. Elders are representative. A man who "aspires" and "desires" to become an elder has a subjective aspiration (1 Tim. 3:1). To this subjective aspiration, Paul puts "fifteen measurable qualifications" for eldership (1 Tim. 3:2–7). The personal aspirations are essential. So too are the objective qualifications, particularly that the man be a competent and helpful teacher (1 Tim. 3:2). You don't need to be a great preacher to be a competent pastor, but you need to be helpful. "People get help when you open the Bible." If he cannot help people understand their Bibles, then he is not called to eldership.

Guideline 2: Our ability must serve the goal of our team. We're not self-sufficient, and that's on purpose. Our strengths come with weakness. God "intends every human being to be *good* at some things and *not good* at other things, so that they fit together like a diverse body—like body parts, not like links in a chain. Links in a chain are all the same, and the chain works precisely because each link does the same thing: it holds." As in the workplace, so also the church, we hold together as a team—not in our similarity but in our diversity of gifting and need for one another (1 Cor. 12:14–20). The ear is a terrible eye. And the eye is a terrible ear. Our weaknesses don't condemn us; they help us perceive how we fit with others and their gifts. Such a recognition "does require some humility, because you can ruin your life with envy of others' competencies." Our vocational fitness is not based on self-sufficiency, but on whether or not our particular strengths work toward the final goal of the team.

---

28 APJ 1390: "When Has My Career Become My Idol?" (November 4, 2019).

We commonly misread our callings, so God sends us detours to move us away from careers that fit badly and into careers that will prove more fruitful. "To adjust our sense of calling and to find a new job is nothing to be ashamed of, if we are humble enough to admit that we're fallible and that we're not omnicompetent."[29]

Is my career in marketing vain?

The question came from a Nike marketer, a Christian who pushes luxury goods on people "who don't need them and often can't afford them." Can he glorify God in his marketing job?

Marketers should ask themselves five questions. (1) Do I tell the truth? God is a God of truth and we must speak the truth to one another. "Christians are radically truth-driven people. We really believe there is such a thing as truth. So we should ask regularly, Is my messaging always truthful?" (2) Do I help people? We must love others and meet their needs (Mark 9:35; Rom. 13:10; 1 Cor. 16:14). So "is my service or is my product doing good for people, or hurting them, or confirming them in some hurtful pattern of behavior or thinking?" (3) Do I influence my workplace? "Am I in a position to significantly change the way my company does business so that people will be helped rather than hurt by what we do and the way we do it?" (4) Do I magnify Christ in my work? Is the result of my labor "showing more clearly that Christ is supremely valuable, more valuable than anything?" This was Paul's goal, and it should inform our own goals (Phil. 1:20; 3:8). "I don't claim that any of that is easy or obvious. But I do claim that we should ask that question. And I do think that in asking it, God will help us get a read on whether we are doing his revealed will in our job." (5) Could my gifts be used more fruitfully somewhere else? An employee is not responsible for all the misdeeds of his company. "The more he knows, the more responsible he is. The more power he has, the more responsible he is. But I don't think it is automatic that one must leave a job because there is sin in the company." Paul says to stay in the job gratefully, or leave if you can gracefully (1 Cor. 7:21, 24).

Specifically, when it comes to personal uneasiness about reinforcing consumerism, listen to your conscience. "The Bible is very serious about not acting against our conscience" (Rom. 13:5). Our conscience can be "distorted" or need calibration to God's will if it becomes "too loose" or "too tight" (Acts 10:9–16). But even as the conscience is being informed and shaped, the general principle holds. To contradict your conscience, to say: "'God, I don't mind risking displeasing you,'" is "a very dangerous" place to be.

---

29 APJ 1405: "I'm Not Good at My Job—Is the Lord Telling Me to Quit?" (December 9, 2019).

Finally, when it comes to consumerism and pushing products to people who cannot afford them, let "the relentless stream of New Testament texts about money" wash over you (like Matt. 6:19–20; Luke 6:20, 24; 8:14; 9:58–59; 12:15, 20–21, 33; 14:33; 18:24; 2 Cor. 8:2; 1 Tim. 6:7–8; Heb. 13:5). "The New Testament is relentless in pushing us *toward* a wartime simplicity and economy for the sake of the kingdom, and *away from* luxury and *away from* affluence and *away from* finery and opulence." Combined, all these texts ask for a response: "Is what we do and say about money communicating that Christ is more precious than money, his security is better than the security of money, his power is better than the power of money, his preciousness is better than the preciousness of money? That's what our life is supposed to say to the world."[30]

I have no energy, direction, or purpose in life—what do I do?

A recent college grad is supposed to transition into the workforce, but he feels energy-less, directionless, and purposeless. It feels like a quarter-life crisis.

"The first thing to say is that this season *will pass*," while engaging "in the kind of spiritual warfare that God will use *to make it pass*." It's a crisis season that needs to be handled with four strategies.

Strategy 1: Name the crisis. This appears to be *acedia*, "a state of listlessness or torpor, of not caring or not being concerned with one's position or condition in the world." Not depression. The goal of step one is to "identify the crisis, look it full in the face, make no denials, identify its nature, and make plans for war."

Strategy 2: "Set one's face for a patient, God-centered waiting upon the Lord—not that the waiting will be inactive, but rather that it will be a recognition that the victory may take time and that in the meanwhile we will not give in to despair" (Ps. 40:1–3). "However long we may have to be in the pit or in the miry bog of *acedia*—listlessness, directionlessness—we will not despair, but will look expectantly to God to act in his time."

Strategy 3: Know that this crisis is common to genuine Christians. Paul calls the church to admonish the idle (ἄτακτος)—those whose lives are chaotic and disordered, full of malaise and out of whack (1 Thess. 5:14). In the church we will find the idle, the fainthearted, and the weak who "need to be cared for."

Strategy 4: Put Bible truth to each loss. The losses are threefold: (1) lost energy, (2) lost direction, and (3) lost purpose. And the Bible gives a command to fight each one.

1. Seek strength (Neh. 8:10; Ps. 28:7; 1 Cor. 15:10). The popular refrain: "God helps those who help themselves" is "a kind of secular effort to express

30 APJ 1519: "Is My Career in Marketing Vain?" (August 31, 2020).

a biblical truth," that "God helps the weak and paralyzed and dead to help themselves, so that in all our so-called self-help God will get the glory because all our self-help turned out to be God-help."

2. Seek direction (2 Thess. 3:5). God is "the great heart director." So we pray that "God would direct the heart, first to the love of God and then to the steadfastness of Christ" and from there to bring "the clarity you need for your life's work."

3. Seek purpose (1 Pet. 2:9; 4:10). "Whatever else God has for you in life, this is crystal clear: you exist to make the excellencies of God known, especially the excellencies by which he calls people from darkness to light. And it is a *marvelous* light." So it is "your God-appointed purpose to see it, to savor it, and to make it known" according to the particular gifts God gave you. We need energy, direction, and purpose. And we must battle against the helplessness we can sometimes feel by reminding ourselves who God is (Lam. 3:20–24). Hope in him, move in him, and find strength from him. In due time, he will restore in you a "joyful sense of energy and direction and purpose."[31]

How do I battle perfectionism and the "imposter syndrome" at work?

A woman in medicine is a perfectionist. She feels anxious about her incompetence and writes off her vocational successes as luck. She feels like a fraud, plagued by "imposter syndrome."

Pastor John encouraged her with three responses.

1. Die to perfectionism by living in the gospel. The "imposter syndrome" is likened to "professional anorexia." Anorexia is to the body what imposter syndrome is to professional competence. "With anorexia, a ninety-pound, twenty-five-year-old woman stands in front of a mirror and sees an overweight woman. With the imposter syndrome, a competent, successful, responsible, helpful woman stands in front of the mirror and sees an incompetent, irresponsible, unhelpful, fraudulent employee. The challenge in both cases is to overcome the illusions and live in reality with Jesus Christ at the center."

The plague of perfectionism is the root here, the desire "to always do better and to do more is the deep uncertainty of being loved and accepted and approved—most deeply by God, but also by other significant people in our lives, like parents or friends or supervisors." The basis for our lives is that *we are already* loved and accepted and approved in Christ. We seek vocation excellence because we're fully secure in him. "By grace alone, through faith alone, on the basis of the work of Christ alone, we stand on the glorious rock of the

---

31 APJ 767: "Strategies for When Life Seems Aimless" (January 7, 2016).

forgiveness of our sins, our acceptance with God, the removal of our guilt, the canceling of our debts—all of it rooted in the love of God, who chose us for himself before the foundation of the world. That's where every day starts." We're not working *for* God's acceptance, forgiveness, or love. We work *from* them.

2. Die to feeling like a fraud. A fraud intentionally deceives others. "If you come into work every day with a good will, not a deceptive will, and at the end of the day you are perceived as competent, responsible, and helpful because there's been no evidence to the contrary, you're not a fraud—no matter what your feelings are."

3. Witness God's providence over your life. Our vocational successes are not luck. "There is no such thing as *luck*—period." It's God's providence. "So what you're dealing with is not several thousand professional instances of luck, in which you lucked out and proved competent and responsible and helpful by accident." No. "God, not luck, brought about those thousands of moments of competency and responsibility and helpfulness. This is a pattern of divine sustaining, divine support, divine help, divine guidance, which bears all the marks of a calling, a vocation from God." So when you awaken, "and you feel anxiety that your luck might run out today," preach to yourself this truth. Luck is fiction. "It doesn't exist. God has sustained me in all these thousands of moments of competency that I've been calling 'luck.'" Added up, these three points kill "imposter syndrome."[32]

Should pastors have all the answers?

It is impossible for pastors to have all the answers. Yet some Christians imagine that "if a big ethical issue comes up in their vocation, the pastor should have the answer." On the contrary—lawyers, doctors, carpenters, computer programmers, and salesmen—"they bear the main responsibility to think through how Christianity bears on the nitty-gritty of their vocation." Pastors certainly help as they deliver "rich biblical insights week in and week out from the Scriptures." But it's "naive" and "disenchanting" to think that pastors will be the experts for all vocational challenges. Instead, "pastors empower, and we encourage our *people* to become the experts on how faith and work fit together. All the while, the pastor is pointing and encouraging and pointing them to the Scriptures and feeding their souls."

The same point applies to social issues. Strategically positioned congregants "should be studying health care and immigration issues and racial profiling and police reform and the roots of poverty in their neighborhood and so on.

---

32 APJ 1558: "How Do I Battle Imposter Syndrome?" (December 7, 2020).

There are just dozens of social, ethical, moral justice issues in the world that our people ought to be engaged with and that vastly outstrip the ability of the pastor to be up-to-date on all of them."[33] Pastors are not called to resolve every complexity that comes from trying to live out the Christian life inside politically hot and nationalistic environments.[34]

33 APJ 662: "How Culturally Up-to-Date Must My Pastor Be?" (August 14, 2015).
34 APJ 1804: "Politics, Patriotism, and the Pulpit" (July 4, 2022).

On Purpose, Productivity, and Laziness

Why do I exist?

Our personal productivity is always framed by God and his purposes. Most fundamentally, he *is*. God is from himself. He is self-sufficient and "exists without influence or input or resources or forces or anything from outside himself." Before creation, and independent of creation, "God was completely and flawlessly God." And his holy name—Yahweh—makes this same point, built on the verb "I am," and used thousands of times in the English Bible, whenever you see the small-caps Lord. The name "bears witness to the absolute existence of God in and of himself" (Exod. 3:14). It is God saying, "I am absolute reality. I had no beginning. I will have no ending. And in relation to creation, I am not becoming what I am." Our God is un-improvable. Creation is unessential to his happiness because his full triune love precedes all that he made.

So then by what purpose would God create me if he had nothing to gain? Am I an accident? Am I the product of a whim? Neither. He created you for his glory, from his love (Isa. 43:6–7). He creates out of the overflow of who he is. "He gave to all who would have it—all who would receive it as their treasure—he gave us a share in the God-displaying, God-glorifying delight that God has in God. And if you press even harder on me and say, 'But why did he do this if he was so full and happy without creation?' I would say it's the nature of the fullness of the divine love to share itself. That's just what love is like in God. And this sharing is not the completion of God or the improvement of God."

This high theology matters in everyday life. When the alarm goes off tomorrow morning, know that this is why we exist. "We exist to bring our lives into alignment with the purpose of God in creation—namely, his purpose to communicate his glory in the overflow of his God-exalting, soul-satisfying love. And what that alignment looks like is this: our magnifying God's glory by finding him to be the most satisfying reality in the universe" (1 Cor. 10:31).[1]

What is my purpose in life?

How do we write a personal mission statement, one that's concrete but not so complex that it proves improbable, impractical, and useless?

Like God, we should act with purpose (Isa. 14:24; 37:26; 46:9–10). He makes plans and he carries them out. It's why we have the gospel (Acts 4:27). But *how* we create a personal mission statement requires answers to three important questions. (1) What is God's ultimate plan? (2) How do I live in sync with his ultimate plan? (3) How do I adapt my statement to the changing seasons of life? Unlike God, we change all the time. "You change. Your job changes. You have kids. You get sick. You move." So "if you want your mission statement to last more than a few years, it will need to be high-level and general," at least from the outset.

The short answer to (1): "God's ultimate purpose is to be seen and savored and shown as infinitely glorious." God is no megalomanic. "God is the *one* being in all the universe—and he is the *only one*—for whom self-communication *and* self-exaltation are the highest virtues and the most loving acts" (Isa. 43:6–7).

The short answer to (2): "The essence of every biblical personal mission statement" is the first petition of the Lord's Prayer: "Hallowed be your name" (Matt. 6:9). God is to be hallowed—"that is, glorified, treasured, loved, honored, praised, admired, enjoyed." We pray to this end: "May others hallow your name because I exist." Texts abound on the actions we do to bring God glory (Rom. 10:9; 12:13; 15:7; 1 Thess. 5:18; 1 Pet. 2:12). "Everything we should be doing with our bodies and our minds and our hearts should be something that makes God look glorious, because he really is. We're helping people see him, savor him, show him for what he's really like." But texts also remind us that *how* we do those things honors God. He is glorified in *how* we live and depend on him (2 Thess. 1:11–12; 1 Pet. 4:11).

The short answer to (3): Work down from the big picture. "God is infinitely glorious. God means to communicate that glory to his people—to see it, savor it, show it. He means for us to join him in that purpose. That applies to absolutely everything we do. And we do it in humble reliance upon his grace and power, which come through Jesus Christ in the service of others. That will make him look great."

1   APJ 1579: "Why Did God Create Us?" (January 25, 2021).

Then focus on the short term. Make a mission statement for the year ahead, with concrete goals that "draw particularities up into that mission statement according to the season of your life."[2]

Speaking of 2 Thessalonians 1:11–12, there we find "the two most important verses in the Bible on New Year's resolutions."[3] A whole "theology of resolutions."[4] And the eight essentials we need for year-round success in the Christian life.[5]

On Isaiah 43:6–7

Since it appears in every episode on finding personal purpose, here's a handful of related points on this (gloriously versatile) text.

1. See how it shaped twenty-something Piper. Isaiah 43:6–7 sank in for him when he first read Jonathan Edwards's dissertation titled, *Concerning the End for Which God Created the World*[6] (later: *God's Passion for His Glory*[7]). His first reading of it, in Germany (1972), "simply blew me away with the God-centeredness of God's purpose in this universe." Notably in Isaiah 43:6–7 and Ephesians 1:11–12. Then "I began to see it everywhere."[8] God's ultimate plan *for* his creation—to glorify himself *in* creation—"runs like a golden thread from Genesis to Revelation." So there's no confusion about *why* we exist. "It's gloriously clear. We exist for the praise of his glory—the meaning of the universe."[9]

Between 1968 and 1972, Piper's world was "destroyed and rebuilt by an understanding of the overarching, sovereign purposes of God to be glorified in this world," a "Copernican revolution" thanks to Edwards's book, but first ignited by professor Daniel Fuller in his seminary course and essay on Isaiah 43:6–7. From childhood, Piper knew that he should live for God's glory (1 Cor. 10:31). "But what I had not seen was that this was God's design for himself, not just my duty toward him. God's purpose in creating the universe was that

---

2 APJ 1710: "How Do I Write a Personal Mission Statement?" (November 26, 2021). *How* do we serve? "First Peter 4:11 is my favorite expression of the answer" (APJ 1059: "How Is Jesus Both Joy and Master?" [June 26, 2017]).

3 APJ 246: "A Little Theology of Resolutions" (January 1, 2014).

4 APJ 1415: "Are Personal Resolutions Effective or Futile?" (January 1, 2020).

5 APJ 1793: "Eight Essentials for Christian Living" (June 8, 2022).

6 Jonathan Edwards, *Ethical Writings*, ed. Paul Ramsey and John E. Smith, vol. 8, *The Works of Jonathan Edwards* (New Haven, CT: Yale University Press, 1989), 403–536.

7 John Piper and Jonathan Edwards, *God's Passion for His Glory: Living the Vision of Jonathan Edwards* (Wheaton, IL: Crossway, 1998).

8 APJ 192: "How Did Your Vision for Missions Develop?" (October 11, 2013).

9 APJ 1748: "God's Providence in the Ministry of Crossway Books" (February 23, 2022).

he would glorify himself in all that he does in creation and providence and redemption."[10] God lives for God's glory. "The duty that I grew up with expanded into a full-blown view of the universe."[11]

2. See the potent simplicity of the text. Why do we exist? Isaiah 43:6–7 is "gloriously clear,"[12] and "probably the simplest, most straightforward sentence in the Bible in answer to the question."[13] "The deepest longing of the human heart is to know and enjoy the glory of God. We were made for this."[14] Use the text as a gospel ice breaker. Make it your starting point when you share the good news, to frame your entire presentation correctly.[15]

3. See the self-destructive sinfulness of sin. To rebel against God's good design in Isaiah 43:6–7 and to center your life on yourself—or anything other than God—destroys his beautiful design for your life. God-belittling sin infects and poisons everyone and everything. We feel the fallout. "There is dysfunction and chaos and misery all over the world because the whole world is in rebellion against valuing the glory of God above all things."[16]

4. See God's plan override our vain desires. The text illustrates "how wonderful and satisfying and significant is the identity that God offers us in Jesus," over the alluring power of scintillating immodesty, relationship idols, and infatuation with personal attraction and sex appeal. In light of vanity's allure, God can make Isaiah 43:1–7 "deeply, personally, even sexually sufficient."[17]

5. See the centrality of our worship in God's desire to glorify himself. Creation was made to worship God. Worship is essential to our design. God seeks our worship—"not because it meets his need, but because it meets our need." Worship fulfills his design in and for us.[18]

6. See God's total sovereignty. God's desire to glorify himself in all of his works reveals him to be "totally free and sovereign," a point "at the center of Reformed theology." God "is not decisively constrained or controlled by any force from outside himself. He can overcome every obstacle to his purposes and do everything he pleases."[19]

---

10 APJ 1233: "What's the Point of My Life?" (August 6, 2018).

11 APJ 1701: "Does God Command Our Praise for His Sake or Ours?" (November 5, 2021).

12 APJ 1748: "God's Providence in the Ministry of Crossway Books" (February 23, 2022).

13 APJ 1329: "How Does God Answer Today's Skeptics?" (April 12, 2019).

14 APJ 1406: "What's the Deepest Desire of My Heart?" (December 11, 2019).

15 APJ 1510: "How Do I Lead Someone to Christ?" (August 10, 2020).

16 APJ 1847: "Becoming Unshakable in a World of Pain" (October 12, 2022).

17 APJ 1144: "What's Wrong with Dressing Immodestly for Attention?" (January 10, 2018).

18 APJ 1111: "Is God a Megalomaniac?" (October 25, 2017).

19 APJ 341: "What Is Calvinism?" (May 14, 2014).

Productivity tips

John Piper is celebrated for his prolific, high-volume output of writing, speaking, and teaching. Few can match it. Just in its first decade, the *Ask Pastor John* podcast amounts to over 2.3 million words. (Roughly the length of this book *times ten*!) So how is he so productive with podcasting, book writing, articles, and social media? I asked. Here are ten productivity tips.

1. Don't compare. Admire Pastor John's productivity, but don't romanticize it. "You don't know how much I have neglected. You don't know what the costs have been. The real question is how to be the fullest, most God-centered, Christ-exalting, Bible-saturated, loving, humble, mission-advancing, justice-seeking, others-serving person you—*you*—can be. Don't measure yourself by others. Measure yourself by your potential in Christ."

2. Focus on your vision. "Very few people become productive by avoiding obstacles to productivity." Business gurus make millions writing books about avoiding obstacles. But in reality, "getting things done—things that count—come from great, glorious, wonderful future possibilities that take you captive and draw your pursuit with all your might." Read productivity books to eliminate the impediments to productivity as part of "the 10 percent of broom work that you have to do."

3. Factor in your seasons. Certain seasons will demand more of your focus. If you have little kids, it might be hard to write a long book. By nature, some seasons will seem unproductive. But in truth, "the Lord will be pleased if you focus on the chapter you are in and live according to the demands of that chapter with all your might."

4. Determine your aim. For Piper, "magnifying Christ in living and dying, and spreading a passion for Christ into the lives of others—that is my goal" (Phil. 1:20–21). "Find yours, and make it work in everything you do."

5. Prepare to give an account. Work hard, and work hard *out of* your justification, not *for* your justification. Work hard because you know that God is for you, and his grace is working in you (1 Cor. 15:10; Phil. 2:12–13). And work hard because you know that you will give an account for your life. Let Jesus "intensify this sense of accountability" through his parable of the talents (Matt. 25:14–30). Don't be found lazy; be found wise and diligent and faithful (Luke 12:42).

6. Work with urgency. The days are evil. Life is short. Feel this urgency in every resolve (John 9:4; Eph. 5:15–16; Col. 4:5).

7. Kill half-heartedness. The resolution of Jonathan Edwards that "probably had more impact on me in the last thirty years than any other" was this one: "Resolved, to live with all my might, while I do live." This resolution "took

hold of me a long time ago." By contrast, study the fourteen mentions of "the sluggard" in Proverbs (6:6, 9; 10:26; 13:4; 15:19; 19:24; 20:4; 21:25; 22:13; 24:30; 26:13–16). And kill half-heartedness.

8. Persevere. We're easily discouraged, especially after we set out to meet a large goal. Like chopping down a huge tree, it may require many chops of the axe. Small trees—small goals—will look more appealing. But don't go for easy. "Many chops fell a big tree. Do you want to do something great? Don't quit. Keep chopping."

9. Meet the hardest tasks with joy. "There is no worthwhile role in life that does not require you to do things you don't at first feel like doing or that only let you do what comes naturally." Meet your hardest tasks with the right attitude, with the joy of faith.

10. Specialize your focus. Over time, "find your niche—that is, find the thing you love to do. With all your weaknesses and all your strengths, put most of your energies and your love there, for Christ and his kingdom."[20]

Four years later, to commemorate episode 1500 (and clearly having forgotten that we covered this topic already), I looked back on God's grace over the podcast and asked Pastor John, then seventy-four, to dwell on principles of his personal productivity.

Productivity requires a team, he said. "I think the first lesson, the first piece of wisdom, perhaps, that any productive person needs to learn is that no man is an island." We are part of a body. Other parts are essential to the whole (1 Cor. 12:21). We have nothing that has not been given to us as a gift (1 Cor. 4:7). And we work hard because God is working in us (1 Cor. 15:10). "Paul is so eager *not* to take any credit for his productivity as an apostle." Productivity requires colleagues, friends, spouses, and of course God working in us.

With that, here are seven thoughts on productivity (not entirely overlapping his previous list).

1. Know why you exist. Go big picture and get "a clear vision for why everything exists, including yourself." Study the vision of Jonathan Edwards in his classic *Concerning the End for Which God Created the World*. And personalize your purpose. "I used to carry around in my wallet a piece of paper that basically said, 'You exist to spread a passion for the supremacy of God in all things for the joy of all peoples.' Never, never, never, never forget it. Carry it in your wallet, if not in your conscious head, all the time. Know why you are on this planet."

2. Embrace your role as a subcreator. "God is the great Creator-maker, and he created humans in his image as secondary creator-makers." It means

---

20 APJ 839: "Ten Principles for Personal Productivity" (April 18, 2016).

that "every time we act, every time we do anything, we make something into something else—some situation into something different than it was: a rocky field into a garden, a stick into a spear, a room into a home, a cow into a steak, flour and sugar and fruit into an apple pie, snow into a snowman, sounds into melody, fire into lamps and heaters and locomotion, eleven men into a football team." This role as subcreator "has settled into me in such a way as to make me find tremendous pleasure in creating things—in my case, mainly with words: sermons, articles, books, poems, and *Ask Pastor John* episodes." And it includes order. "Piper has a low tolerance level for chaos," he admitted. "I really do; I don't like it. Anywhere I find it, I'm on it." Messy thinking, messy rooms, messy yard—"I don't like to leave the world the way it is. It ought to be a better place: more beautiful, more orderly, more wonderfully fruitful."

3. Study the distinction between *sloth* and *rest*. Everyone knows that "there's a place—an absolutely crucial place—for rest and leisure. The Sabbath principle holds." But we must also learn to carefully distinguish between *sloth* and *rest*, *laziness* and *leisure*.

4. Make peace with imperfection. "If we're going to do our work faithfully and abundantly," as Paul calls us to in 1 Corinthians 15:58, we're going to do a lot of it. To be prolific in our work, we cannot get "paralyzed by perfection." Indeed, "I think one of the main reasons that I have been as productive as I have is that I made peace decades ago with imperfection and finitude. I have no illusions that I will say the last word about anything. My job, while I live, is to speak the truth—as I see it in God's word—as well as I can say it, and let God do what he wants to with that imperfection."

5. Act quickly and capture your thoughts. Write down what comes to mind because "seminal ideas, far-reaching fruitful thoughts, come to us at night, while we're reading, meditating, praying, walking, playing. If you don't capture those in some way, in writing, you'll almost certainly lose them."

6. Chop daily. "I told Noël last night, 'Did you know that we're at fifteen hundred *Ask Pastor John* episodes?' And she laughed and said, 'Just like reading fifteen minutes a day.'" Yes! You can read large books by reading them for just fifteen minutes a day.

7. Let the future capture you. Forget what's behind, press forward to what is ahead (Phil. 3:13–14). "Never get to the point in your life where you are more contented with what you *have already done* than you are excited with what is *yet to be done*. At every stage—twenty-four, forty-four, sixty-four, seventy-four, eighty-four—pray with all your heart, 'O God, make the next season of my life the most fruitful season ever for the supremacy of God in all things for the joy of all people.'"

"So, it's been a good run, Tony; fifteen hundred episodes is a good run. But now we start the beginning of the second fifteen hundred. 'If the Lord wills, we will live and do this or that'" (James 4:15). Amen.[21]

How do I respond to my most unproductive days?

As much as we love planning and productivity, we often find ourselves unproductive, facing days when all of our plans go wrong. So where's God in our disastrous days?

"God's priorities for efficiency in this life are not ours." To see the distinction, here's a story. Imagine you're a busy mom and you must rush to the bank one morning to get cash to pay the teenager who is now mowing your lawn. The neighbor next door watches your youngest children, and you head out for a quick errand. Things are going great until you find yourself locked in freeway traffic due to a major accident ahead. You're stuck and helpless. Finally, after an hour, you return home without the cash. The neighbor was forced to miss a house showing because of it, the teenager isn't paid, and you now feel awful. "Your efficiency proved utterly useless to accomplish your priorities. You failed, but God's priorities totally succeeded." How so? Because perhaps, in this scenario, God wanted to prevent the teen from getting money he would use to buy pot, prevent the neighbor from buying a new home with a failed foundation, and "grow your faith in his sovereign wisdom and sovereignty.

"That's what I mean by 'God's priorities for efficiency in this life are not ours.' In my view, this isn't happening just now and then; it's happening all the time." And it's proven in Scripture. God seems perfectly fine in frustrating human efficiency on purpose, and he does so regularly. "God almost never takes the shortest route between point A and point B. The reason is that such efficiency— the efficiency of speed and directness—is not what he's about. His purpose is to sanctify the traveler, not to speed him between A and B. Frustrating human efficiency is one of God's *primary*—I say *primary*, not *secondary*—means of sanctifying grace."

Joseph's story is a great example from the Old Testament (Gen. 37–50), with its moral lesson in Genesis 50:20. In all of Joseph's inefficiencies, detours, and testings, and in all the evils done to him, "God had an agenda." God *meant it*, and he meant it for a good end. Paul's story is a great example from the New Testament. Paul planned to go to Rome, gather support, and live out his days in Spain. Instead, he found himself imprisoned in Rome. Yet even this detour "served to advance the gospel" (Phil. 1:12).

---

21 APJ 1500: "Seven Lessons for Productivity" (July 17, 2020).

Here's the lesson. "By all means, make your list of to-dos for the day." Make a plan. Prioritize your day. Read books about efficiency. "Then walk in the peace and freedom that, when your plan shatters on the rocks of reality—which it will most days—you're not being measured by God by how much you get done. You're being measured by whether you trust the goodness and the wisdom and the sovereignty of God to work this new mess of inefficiency for his glory and the good of everyone involved, even when you can't see how."[22]

Fighting laziness

Laziness is the lack of ambition toward future fruit. Jesus pulls no punches here. For his followers, laziness is inexcusable (Matt. 25:26).[23] Yet it plagues us all. We naturally slide into becoming mentally lazy readers of the Bible.[24] Pastors get lazy with their Bible reading, exegesis, and affectional engagement with the text.[25] Oversleeping can be a sign of laziness.[26] Physical exertion, like going to the gym, is a direct way to confront personal laziness (Prov. 20:4; 21:25; 1 Cor. 9:26–27).[27]

To fight laziness, consider four factors. (1) Physical issues. Is your body right? Is your thyroid broken? Are you short on sleep? Eating poorly? (2) Build a theology of work from the Bible. The fall has made work harder, but work retains its dignity. God designed us to work (Gen. 2:15). His original design is still good. "God put us on the planet to be comakers, cocreators, coworkers with him." He created us to be creators. We are his workmanship to work (Eph. 2:10). Do your work with diligence before him (Eccl. 9:10; Col. 3:23). (3) Heed the biblical warnings against slacking (2 Thess. 3:10). (4) Draw on God's grace. God's grace was the engine that generated the horsepower for Paul's work (1 Cor. 15:10). "Discover how to apply your will to a task in hard work in such a way that, as you do it and after you do it, you know: 'God is at work in me!' This is what I think gives the work life its greatest meaning" (Phil. 2:12–13).[28]

Acquaint yourself with the distinctions between *rest* and *sloth*, *leisure* and *laziness*.[29] Do it through the terms of Proverbs: the *sluggard* and the *diligent* (Prov. 13:4). What distinguishes the restfulness of the *diligent* believer from the laziness of the *sluggard*? Both sit in chairs and sleep in beds. Both recline in the

---

22 APJ 1170: "God's Sovereign Plans behind Your Most Unproductive Days" (March 12, 2018).
23 APJ 839: "Ten Principles for Personal Productivity" (April 18, 2016).
24 APJ 277: "'Piper Is Too Intellectual'" (February 13, 2014).
25 APJ 1114: "Six Common Ways Preachers Dishonor God's Word" (November 1, 2017).
26 APJ 1063: "How Much Sleep Is Too Much Sleep?" (July 5, 2017).
27 APJ 1042: "Is Body Image My Idol?" (May 17, 2017).
28 APJ 79: "How to Fight Laziness" (April 29, 2013).
29 APJ 1500: "Seven Lessons for Productivity" (July 17, 2020).

same leisurely postures. But here's the essential difference. "The laziness of the *sluggard* is owing to his overpowering aversion to work. And the restfulness of the *diligent* is received as a gracious reward for the gift of God-glorifying work and a pleasant preparation for renewed productivity. Or let me say it another way: the laziness of the *sluggard* is a capitulation to his disinclination to exertion. And the restfulness of the *diligent* is a sweet compensation for God-honoring exertion and thankful renewal for more usefulness." The diligent see God behind their work. He makes their sleep sweet (Ps. 127:1–2; Eccl. 5:12). The posture of sleep is the same to both. But the diligent want to get back to work so they pose no financial burden on others (2 Thess. 3:8). They're motivated to support themselves and others (Eph. 4:28). Such diligence shines as an example to unbelievers (1 Thess. 4:12), for others to see "our good deeds, our exertions, for the glory of God" (Matt. 5:16).[30]

---

30 APJ 1672: "What's the Difference between Sloth and Rest?" (August 30, 2021).

On Money, Shopping, and the Prosperity Gospel

The love of money and its opposite

In a heart of grateful worship, Mary bent to the floor and poured perfume on Christ's feet. This small bottle was worth a year's wages, and Judas became incensed by the exorbitant waste (John 12:1–8). But here's the difference. Mary loved Christ, not money. Judas loved money, not Christ—and it was killing him. "If you want to be rich, you are on a suicidal track. The love of money is suicidal. Jesus said it. Paul said it. Judas proved it." You can't serve two masters. You can't serve God and money. In effect, Jesus said to him, "'You are devoted to *money*, Judas. You get up in the morning, you think *money*. You go to bed at night, you think *money*. You open the newspaper and go to the stock page, you think *money, money, money*. It's the hope and the god that you have. It's your security. It's your pathway to pleasure. If that is true, you are dead. You are going to die, Judas, and never see me again.'"[1]

Use the world, but don't treasure it

With eternity at stake, we handle our possessions with Paul's confession: "Indeed, I count everything as loss because of the surpassing worth of knowing Christ Jesus my Lord" (Phil. 3:8). All else is rubbish compared to Christ. It means that Christians should "buy as though they had no goods, and those who deal with the world as though they had no dealings with it. For the present form of this world is passing away" (1 Cor. 7:30–31). "That is pretty provocative. Be married as though you were not. Do business as though you were not doing

---

1 APJ 706: "Loving Money Is Suicide" (October 14, 2015). See also APJ 1499: "What Does Freedom from the Love of Money Look Like?" (July 15, 2020).

it. Buy things as if you had no possessions. This is crazy, wonderful Christianity. Use a car, use a coat, use a computer in such a way that people around you assume that it is not your treasure."[2]

Do I love the giver more than his material gifts to me?

So how do I know if, like Mary, God is truly my treasure, more than my wealth and possessions?

As creatures, we experience God in this world in many indirect ways. "He is not his gifts. He is different from his gifts. And yet we experience him *through* his gifts." Similarly, we know that "love *for a person* and the love *for their gifts* are not the same. Yet we experience love through gifts—through touch, through sight, through Christmas presents under the tree." If you love a person, you react to the gift and bless the giver, but no one would treasure the gift more than the giver. Except with God we do, because we are creatures who sin, creatures "spring-loaded to turn gifts into alternatives to God." So in this case, how does God respond? "Well, in this age between our fall and our perfection at the second coming, God uses *pleasure* and *pain* to provide us with revelations of his goodness and protect us from loving substitutes." He uses this mixture "in order to show us that he is more important than the things." God pours out good gifts on unbelievers to get them to repent (Rom. 2:4). He lavishes us with "sunrises and sunsets to get attention for his glory" (Ps. 19:1). He gives us marriage and food to enjoy in thankfulness to the giver (1 Tim. 6:17). But in all these gifts, he also calls for self-denial (2 Cor. 1:8–9). God uses trials and losses because they serve a greater good in our lives, namely, to deter us from idolizing his gifts (Rom. 5:3; Phil. 3:8).

In every gift, see the giver. Be willing to lose it all for the "gain" of Christ. And look forward to the new creation where all our losses are restored with an unimaginable wealth to be enjoyed by creatures who are "suited and fit to receive it without any idolatry."[3]

As Christmas 2017 approached, we talked about gift-giving and gift-receiving. Specifically, how can we know that we love God himself, not just his benefits?

It's like if you gave an engagement ring to a woman. If she took the ring and ran off, showing everyone the ring but neglecting you, that would be a loss. Obviously, you wanted her to love and enjoy the ring. "And then you wanted her to put it on her hand, take your hand across the table, and look you in the eye and say, 'I would love to spend the rest of my life with you. You are ten thousand times

---

2   APJ 696: "Does Netflix Make Christ More Precious to You?" (September 30, 2015).
3   APJ 55: "How Do I Know If I Love the Gifts More Than the Giver?" (March 26, 2013).

more precious to me than this beautiful ring."' It's like the story of the ten lepers healed by Jesus. Only one came back to worship the giver (Luke 17:11–19). Nine of the ten healed lepers missed the fact that physical healing was an invitation for something greater than healing—some*one* greater than healing: Jesus himself.

The beautiful logic of Romans 8:32 shows us that every good gift from God is the *fruit* of Christ's finished work on the cross. Every gift should remind us of Christ crucified for sinners. More than that, Christ is not only the *channel* of our gifts; he himself is our greatest gift! This is what the nine lepers missed. They wanted the healing but missed the healer—the greater gift, a self-given gift (Mark 10:45; Rom. 8:32; Gal. 1:4; 2:20; Eph. 5:2; 5:25; 1 Tim. 2:6; Titus 2:14). Think about it for a moment. "If God gives his Son, and the Son gives himself *for you*, and *to you*, then it doesn't even make sense to say that we love the gift more than the giver. The gift *is the giver*; the giver *is the gift*."[4]

Is enjoying our possessions a divine gift?

It is. The writer of Ecclesiastes suggests that God gives two things independently: (1) material wealth, and (2) the ability to enjoy that material wealth (Eccl. 5:19; 6:2). Both are divine gifts. At his discretion, (1) God dispenses the material possessions we enjoy. And (2) he determines whether we are given the power to enjoy (or not enjoy) that wealth. "What this means is that in God's providence, you can miss out on pleasure in more ways than one. You can be deprived of material things that you want, or you can get them and be deprived of the power to enjoy them because they are snatched away."

Like the story of a couple who designed and built a dream home and lived in a trailer on site to watch the progress, "and just when it was finished and they were about to move in, she died of a heart attack. That is Ecclesiastes. And his purpose in pointing out these miseries, the grievous evils—or these 'sore afflictions,' as the writer calls them—is not to make us godless or cynical or hopeless. His point is to make us despair that meaning and joy can finally be found in this world under the sun—that is, as naturalists, as godless. One man gets rich and *gets* the ability to enjoy his riches. Another man gets rich and *loses* his ability to enjoy it. And the lesson for both is: Don't set your heart on riches."

That's Paul's solution too. Charge the wealthy not to "set their hopes on the uncertainty of riches, but on God, who richly provides us with everything to enjoy," and to be rich in good works and to store up treasures in heaven, "so that they may take hold of that which is *truly life*" (1 Tim. 6:17–19).[5]

---

4   APJ 1135: "Do I Love God for His Gifts or for Who He Is?" (December 20, 2017).
5   APJ 453: "When Enjoying Money and Possessions Is a Work of Grace" (October 17, 2014).

Such a *true* (ὄντως) life is not found in accumulated wealth. And hope is never found in the uncertainties (μηδέ) of worldly wealth (1 Tim. 6:17). That's because eternity "is not a postscript to *this true life*. Rather, *this life* is a prelude to *real life*" (1 Tim. 6:19). Plan your finances accordingly (1 Tim. 6:17–19).[6]

Is wartime living cheap or expensive?

Take Christian conferences as an example. Tabulating the venue and music and lighting and production costs, the final bill gets expensive. Is it worth it? Or wasteful?

Most of us face this question daily because we are incredibly wealthy compared to the people of the New Testament. "Everything in modern life looks out of character with Jesus's way of life. Simply having a car looks wildly out of character." As does living in a house with heating, cooling, plumbing, electricity, lighting, refrigeration, phones, computers, access to police and firefighters and EMTs. Not to mention hundreds of books and Bible software programs and everything available on the internet. All of these gifts are "stunningly different" and "out of character with the lifestyle of a first-century Palestinian peasant." So it's right to ask this about conferences, and personal spending habits, too. "The main aim of Scripture is to magnify the supreme truth and beauty and worth of Jesus Christ." Our goal is to "spend money in a way that shows that Jesus is better than money" and "better than life." From this universal truth come two lifestyle guidelines.

Guideline 1: Enjoy your possessions in faith. "God gives us good gifts of creation to be enjoyed as expressions of his own all-satisfying nature" (1 Tim. 6:17). "In other words, enjoy God's gifts in creation without experiencing them as more satisfying than God or separated from God. Be thankful to God *for them* and taste God *in them*."

Guideline 2: Employ your possessions for war. This life is not for leisure but for winning the world to Christ. "We are at war with the god of this world, the stakes are eternal, and the weapons are spiritual—and how we live should reflect this wartime mindset." But this wartime living is not about simplicity and bare minimalism. In a war you may choose not to replace your car's tires because the war effort needs the rubber. And you may pay taxes to fund a huge and expensive B-52 bomber that may "deliver the knockout blow to the enemy that ends the war." In other words, wartime living "does not romanticize" simplicity as if "the world, in its lost condition, benefited from my growing vegetables in the backyard or my having only two pairs of jeans I wear every

---

6   APJ 1286: "I Will Die Young—How Do I Fight for Hope?" (December 7, 2018).

other day." Neither serve the world's eternal needs. Serving the eternal needs of the world may require a lot of money—like in national conferences, major book projects, global translations initiatives, complex ministry websites, and global missions endeavors.

So don't let your salary determine your lifestyle. "That's the American lie. God is calling us to be conduits of grace and resources, not cul-de-sacs. Our danger today is thinking that the conduit has to be gold-lined. It shouldn't be. Copper will do. Copper will do as we channel a $500,000 salary into good for others while we live at a $60,000, $50,000, or $40,000 lifestyle."[7]

Is wartime living the same as a "minimalist" lifestyle?

Minimalism is a cultural desire to own only a few things, to strip life to its bare necessities, and to embrace asceticism in the name of self-optimization. But the discipline is nothing new. "In the 1970s—I can remember so clearly because I was part of it—there was a great outburst of simple living."[8]

So if minimalism is not the essence of wartime living, how do these ideas differ? Wartime living holds to these six convictions.

1. The world is a gift. The wartime worldview sees the world as a *good gift* to be received in Godward gratitude (1 Tim. 4:4–5). "Any kind of austerity pursued in a wartime lifestyle is not based on any intrinsic evil in the created world."

2. The war is real. We find ourselves in the middle of a cosmic battle (Eph. 6:11–13). "One of the aims of wartime teaching, as I have tried to represent it, is to wake up the church, especially in the West, that has simply settled into a peacetime mentality with no sense of urgency for the warfare we are in." The "military-warfare temperature" of the average Western Christian is low.

3. The world entices the sin in us. "Since we are fallen now and sinful in our desires, the world that God created around us—with all of its cares and pleasures—is not only a created *good* to be subdued and enjoyed, but also a *danger* to be guarded against." The daily cares of this world are strong enough to choke out the gospel (Luke 8:14). "The ordinary riches that I have all around me—the ordinary pleasures of life—are not simply *good*; they are also *mortally dangerous* to the soul." Wartime puts us on "red alert to not be naive." God's creation is good. But because of sin and Satan, those good gifts can destroy us if we abuse them.

4. Self-denial is essential. In light of all our gifts and the internal temptation to misuse those good gifts, we are called to self-denial (Matt. 16:24). "Our aim

---

7   APJ 780: "How Do You Synthesize Your Simple Lifestyle and Speaking at Expensive Conferences?" (January 26, 2016).

8   APJ 1085: "Is Wartime Living the Same as Minimalism?" (August 25, 2017).

here is to glorify Christ by showing *him* to be supremely valuable—not our possessions." This end goal demands a certain abstinence.

5. Worldly wealth gets deployed on mission. In World War II, a luxury liner was converted into a troop transport ship, a vivid illustration of wartime living, of wealth deployed in service. "This is where the truth of wartime living really took root in my teaching thirty years ago. The aim of wartime living is not that we go without." Wartime living is convinced that "we are able to accomplish more things by a reallocation of resources from self-gratification to mission penetration." So we pool our resources because "we have the most powerful, liberating bomb in the world." The gospel.

6. We seek more joy by giving more. "It is more joyful to advance the cause of Christ than accumulate wealth and comforts" (Acts 20:35). We're on a quest to maximize our present joy.[9]

Am I wartime enough?

How do I know if my life decisions reflect *wartime simplicity* or *peacetime luxury*?

(1) The reason "I refer to 'wartime simplicity' as opposed to 'simplicity' by itself is that simplicity alone might lead you to renounce all modern appliances and devices and machines for the smallest possible carbon footprint." (2) The Bible doesn't offer us a percentage, prescription, or optimized figure. It doesn't resolve this question easily "in quantitative numbers." No, "it gives a relentless push" in the form of several warning texts (Matt. 6:19, 33; Luke 8:14; 9:58; 12:15, 20, 33; 18:24; Acts 2:45; 2 Cor. 6:10; 8:2; Eph. 4:28; 1 Tim. 6:7–8; Heb. 13:5; James 2:5; 1 John 3:17).

"I don't think it's possible to take all that biblical teaching about money and find a clear line between *wartime simplicity* and *peacetime luxury*." So the answer is best found in living out a "loving, fruitful, others-oriented, sacrificial simplicity for the sake of kingdom advance." We know that "riches are dangerous." Yes, "that message is everywhere." And we know that "simplicity for its own sake is worthless because love is what counts." In fact, "I know there are people who've given themselves to way more simplicity than others, and they're loveless, while people who have more are more loving, and good comes from their lives."

So live under the "relentless push" of Scripture's teaching on wealth. Love people, not money. Love simple beauty, not "luxurious status symbols." And learn the secret of such a profound contentment in Jesus that you can "know how to be brought low" and "how to abound" (Phil. 4:12).[10]

---

9   APJ 1085: "Is Wartime Living the Same as Minimalism?" (August 25, 2017).

10 APJ 1185: "Do the Biblical Warnings against Riches Apply to Most Americans?" (April 16, 2018).

What luxuries in my life are sinful?

So many of life's "needs" began as luxuries enjoyed only by the very wealthy. Refrigerators, for example, were first amenities reserved for the richest. As they got cheaper, more people bought them. Now they're a *necessity* in the modern kitchen. So in a world where *expensive luxuries* eventually become *affordable necessities*, how can we discern *needs* from *wants*?

The very category of "luxuries" is relative. But "here is my best shot to guide John Piper in what to avoid as a sinful luxury," a guide in five questions. (1) Does it serve souls—mine and others? "I am thinking here of beauty and various kinds of artwork that you would hang on your walls. You could live without it, but you hang a picture up or plant flowers in your garden. We are more than biological, physical people. We are created in God's image. We are made to see and know and love beauty." You can "surround yourself with beauty without being rich." (2) Is it efficient for ministry? Without a refrigerator, you'd be required to shop for groceries more frequently. So it saves time that we can employ for ministry. (3) What does it communicate? "Is it affordable without saying to the world that you love things?" Or does the purchase proclaim to the world that you have a "pride in possessions" (1 John 2:16)? What does your purchase disclose about what *you* want the world to say about *you*? (4) Does it keep you from loving others? "Is the money you just spent on this nonessential item hindering you from a lifestyle or act of love? You could always say, 'Well, I could have given that money to a missionary.' And that is true. The money you use to buy every ice cream cone you could have sent somewhere else. But would you have? Has buying things gotten in the way of your heartfelt calling to do a good thing?" (5) Is it a special gift? Large, medium, and small expenses mark special celebrations. Everything from weddings, wedding rings, birthday presents, and simple acts of kindness let others know that you love them.[11]

On tithing

Tithing was commanded of Jewish believers in the Old Testament. Is it commanded of Christians today?

Christians are no longer under the Mosaic law (Rom. 6:15; 7:4–6; Gal. 2:19; Eph. 2:15). Meaning, "in the new relationship to God through the Messiah who has fulfilled the law for us, we are not under the law. It is not the *primary* way by which we relate to God, or by which we discern and find strength to do what is pleasing to God." In its place has arrived "the law of Christ" (Rom. 13:8; 1 Cor. 9:21; Gal. 6:2).

---

11 APJ 419: "What Luxuries in My Life Are Sinful?" (September 1, 2014).

So within this change, where does tithing fit? The Old Testament Levite worship leaders received the people's 10 percent tithe, "a way of supporting the covenantal religious system of that era" (Exod. 35:4–36:38). And we know New Testament pastors who gave their lives to gospel labor were worthy of a wage (Luke 10:7; 1 Tim. 5:17–18). Instead of a tithe, Paul wants churches funded by a heartfelt bounty, by givers not under compulsion but who give cheerfully (2 Cor. 9:6–7). "I think I preached on tithing two or three times in thirty-three years at Bethlehem. I mean, I talked about giving and sacrifice all the time"—but rarely tithing. The "gist" of his sermons on financial giving: "Brothers and sisters, why would we *want* to do less? I mean, the person who is saying: 'Do I *have* to?' They are getting off on the wrong foot immediately. Everything is greater in the new covenant. We have better *promises*, a better *covenant*, Hebrews says. Why wouldn't there be better *sacrifice*, better *giving*?"[12]

So a 10 percent tithe is simply "a starting point for Christians."[13] Even a pastor who gives away 30 percent of a $1 million royalty check in order to spend 70 percent on luxuries, "I'm not impressed with."[14]

As we give to the church, we give to God. It's horizontal and vertical at the same time. Paul interpreted the money sent through Epaphroditus "as sacrifices and gifts and offerings to God himself" (Phil. 4:18). Of course, we never enrich God. "Everything we give is his already. Our giving never improves him or puts us in his debt (1 Chron. 29:14; Ps. 50:9–15; Acts 17:25; Rom. 11:35–36). "In fact, God is so completely self-sufficient that even *our act of giving*—not just the *gift*, but *the act of giving*—is *God's gift to us*, not vice versa." This glorious truth is revealed in 1 Chronicles 29:14–18. "Our offering *willingly* is a *gift* we don't deserve." So, yes, "you are giving to God, and, oh, that we might always know that *our gifts* are a gift from God, and *our giving to God* is a gift from God, so that only God gets the glory."[15]

So can we split the figure? Can we give 5 percent to our local church and 5 percent to another ministry? Again, we're not bound to Mosaic obligations. In financial contexts, Paul instructs us to give, but "he never instructs us to lay aside a tithe" (1 Cor. 16:2). We give according to our means (2 Cor. 8:3). We don't give under compulsion, but from a willing heart that is eager to give abundantly, not sparingly (2 Cor. 9:6–7). "The point is not that we be governed by percentages. They are not mandated. Rather, we should be governed by lavish, sacrificial generosity that overflows freely and joyfully." So, "a middle-class

12 APJ 182: "Is Tithing Commanded for Christians?" (September 27, 2013).
13 APJ 1185: "Do the Biblical Warnings against Riches Apply to Most Americans?" (April 16, 2018).
14 APJ 290: "Pastor of World's Largest Church Convicted of Embezzlement" (March 4, 2014).
15 APJ 543: "Do I Tithe to My Church or to God?" (March 2, 2015).

American who is only tithing 10 percent is probably robbing God." But such giving is not legislated by careful calculations; it's encouraged from eager hearts. In the end, give as if the local church is the epicenter of all missions on earth, because she is. And "if the church fails, all other ministries become unbiblical." So as a general guideline, "start your giving by tithing to the local church and then give over and above elsewhere. But that is not a rule or a mandate." Be lavishly generous, sacrificially giving, loyal to your church, and visionary with other ministries, and let God handle the percentages.[16]

Prosperity preachers like to tie future material prosperity to the present discipline of tithing to a church, and that's "really dangerous." God does "often regularly bless people who give sacrificially in ways they could never imagine, because he delights in cheerful givers and he loves Christlike, generous hearts. But instead of attaching a sure material blessing to an act of tithing, I think we need to cultivate a love for Christ—not his gifts, but for Christ—that would tithe and double and triple and quadruple the tithe that God prospers, even when the hoped-for physical blessing does not come." At the same time, Christ-centered joy can abound in the generosity of the poorest giver (2 Cor. 8:2).[17]

Our sacrificial giving doesn't manipulate God or buy his protection. Contrary to the false promises of prosperity preachers (and illustrated by a true story), you can set out to give above and beyond your normal giving, write a check, and set out to drive your check to the church office, and find all your plans complicated because your car got pinched. Check in hand, and "God ordains for your car to be stolen."[18]

So if true, worshipful giving flows from an abounding heart, should we tithe even when we don't feel like tithing? On the spectrum is a perfunctory giving from a dead heart (on one end), and a spontaneous giving from a grateful heart (on the other). But there's a third way to give—in the middle, a giving that gives while regretting the absence of proper affections—a giving in hope that the act of giving will help restore the heartfelt affections of future giving.[19]

Did Jesus command us to sell all our possessions?

The line between *wartime simplicity* and *peacetime luxury* is not entirely clear. But didn't Jesus call his disciples to give away 100 percent of their worth, to liquidate their assets and give it all to the needy (Luke 12:33; 18:22)? So how much should I give away on mission? Is 10 percent enough? Or 20 or 40 or 80 percent?

---

16 APJ 792: "May I Split My Giving between My Church and Another Ministry?" (February 11, 2016).
17 APJ 968: "Are We Overdoing the Anti-Prosperity Gospel Theme?" (November 25, 2016).
18 APJ 1880: "Beat a Path to the Word in 2023" (December 28, 2022).
19 APJ 1280: "Should I Ever Go through the Motions in Worship?" (November 23, 2018).

It is certainly true that Jesus celebrated the widow who didn't merely give from her *abundance* but from her *total assets* (Mark 12:41–44). And yet we cannot take from this a "biblical obligation or duty of Christians in general to give away all that they have." Why not? Seven reasons.

(1) The command to sell everything and give it all to the poor was never considered "a duty for all followers of Christ," but was given to a specific few during the ministry of Christ. (2) Zacchaeus was commended for giving away *half* of his riches to the poor (Luke 19:8–9). (3) Barnabas was celebrated for selling off *one* of his fields, giving the proceeds to the apostles (Acts 4:36–37). (4) Paul tied increased financial prospering to increased giving (1 Cor. 16:1–4). Put aside for the Lord "not everything—just *more* for those who *earn more*; *less* for those who *earn less*." (5) Christian financial independence is celebrated (1 Thess. 4:11–12). "That means you need to have enough to pay your bills. You don't give everything away. You invest and create a life that keeps you from being dependent on others." (6) Christian financial independence is what makes donating possible (Eph. 4:28). In other words, "enough of our income is supporting us so that we can give and give" and not become "moochers" off others. (7) Christian financial independence is key to ministry that does not require financial support (2 Thess. 3:8–12). It is honorable for missionaries to seek financial support, but Paul didn't need it. "The normal pattern in the early church—and in Christianity—for day-to-day life is to make a living, pay your own way, and turn your whole life into a ministry." Together these points show that "owning nothing and giving away everything was not, in the New Testament, the way Jesus and the apostles conceived of the ongoing, corporate Christian life."

Giving is not about the percentages but about the heart of love behind the sacrifice (Luke 10:30–35). "Do not merely think, 'What percentage can I get rid of?' But rather, 'The people that I deal with and that I'm aware of—do I love them as I ought with my resources?'" In sum, "remember that all of your money is God's, not just what you give to the Lord. This means that we should think of every expenditure in a kingdom-advancing way, not just what we give away. It is all Christ's. He owns you. He owns it." Every penny can magnify Christ.[20]

Can I pray for a doubled income?

Job was a wealthy man whose life was shattered overnight and then slowly restored over time. More than restored. In the end, God *doubled* Job's original wealth (Job 42:10–17). So can Christians pray for doubled incomes today?

20 APJ 1368: "Does Jesus Teach Us to Sell All Our Possessions?" (July 12, 2019).

The desire for a doubled income is relative. "I'm absolutely certain it would be a sin for me to pray that my resources be doubled now, because as an American living a comfortable middle-class lifestyle, I am by global standards vastly wealthier than billions of poor people around the world. The burden on me in prayer should not be that I amass and lay up more treasures on earth, but that by giving away more and more, and investing more and more in other people, I lay up treasures in heaven (Matt. 6:19–20), and that I use what I have for the greatest good of others, and that I beware, because it is hard for the rich to get into heaven, Jesus said (Luke 18:24)." On the other end of the economic spectrum, if an impoverished Christian makes one dollar a day, a doubled income is still poverty.

And there's a redemptive-history factor. The Old Testament was a come-and-see religion, "stressing prosperity as a witness to the world about God's faithfulness to Israel" (1 Kings 10:1–13). But the New Testament is a go-and-tell religion, "stressing simplicity and sacrifice and generosity to accomplish the mission to reach all the nations of the world and to show that our treasure is not in this world but in Christ in heaven." Not surprisingly, the New Testament is "relentless" in encouraging us to "simplicity and economy for the sake of kingdom advance" (Matt. 6:19; Luke 6:20, 24; 8:14; 12:33; 14:33; 18:24; 2 Cor. 6:10; Eph. 3:8). So, no, Job's example should not be used to justify a Christian asking for a doubled income.

So should we only embrace loss and suffering? No. We pray for healing, increased joy, greater fruitfulness, relational peace, and for victory over personal sin (Rom. 6:12–14; 15:13; Phil. 1:11; 4:6–7; Col. 1:10; James 5:16). Each prayer answers to personal loss.

So then, finally, if my salary isn't doubled, can I at least pray for a more comfortable income? Again, it's relative. Does comfort for you mean that you want a second T-shirt or a second house? We entered the world with nothing. We leave it with nothing. So be content with what you have (1 Tim. 6:7–8). "It's not wrong to want the basics of life." As for comfort, it's a matter of the heart. Is Christ so precious to you that you can be content with a comfortable life or an uncomfortable life—whether you feast or starve, or own more or less stuff than you need (Phil. 4:11–13)? Or is contentment *only* aspirational, in something you don't yet have? This is the "real battle." So "may God make it plain to all of us how much more of our resources we can put to use for his gospel-spreading purposes, and how much we may rightfully use for ourselves."[21]

---

21 APJ 1633: "Is It Sinful to Pray for a Larger Income?" (May 31, 2021).

The false gospel of the prosperity gospel

The prosperity gospel promises that God will give you wealth and health—if you have enough faith. But the prosperity gospel is an antigospel.

1. Prosperity preachers peddle the antigospel of self-destruction. Lust for wealth is self-destructive (1 Tim. 6:6–10). So any gospel according to wealth is the antigospel. "The very thing that leads people to suicidal piercings of pangs—namely, the desire to be rich—is nurtured and cultivated by the prosperity preachers." To encourage spiritual suicide from a pulpit is "abominable." Feeding the heart's desire for wealth is to push people *into* the snares and temptations and "many senseless and harmful desires that plunge people into ruin and destruction" (1 Tim. 6:9). It's anti-Christ, who said riches are "dangerous," destructive, and "usually a curse," not a blessing. Souls are eternally destroyed by the love of money (Matt. 19:24). "I don't mean it is sinful to *make* a lot of money. I just mean it is sinful to want to *keep* a lot of money." It's spiritual suicide to want "bigger barns and bigger cars and bigger houses and bigger portfolios and finer clothes. Everything is growing with your income so that your conscience is getting harder and harder," all to justify a growing lifestyle and to ignore Christ's commands for cross-carrying self-denial (Luke 12:13–21).

2. Prosperity preachers peddle propaganda to swindle the globally poor. They "don't just talk to Americans who are already fairly well off and try to help them become a little richer. They get on their jets—their personal jets—and they fly to Africa or the Philippines. And they land, and they gather a stadium full of one hundred thousand desperately poor people and tell them that if they believe in Jesus, they will get rich, and all of their needs will be met, and their wives won't have miscarriages anymore, and blah, blah, blah. And then they get on their jets, with their pockets full, and go home."

3. Prosperity preachers fail to prepare Christians for reality. "Normal Christianity is pain." God promises that his children will suffer in this world (Acts 14:22; 2 Cor. 4:17; 6:10). Such preachers "do not prepare new converts in third-world countries to endure the realities of what it will cost them to be a Christian."

4. Prosperity preachers fail to feed missions. It will never fuel years of selfless sacrifice to reach hard places. The only people who will carry the torch of global missions "are the people that have been taught that to follow Christ is to suffer," and who know that this life is short. "Only eighty years. And then comes heaven."

5. Prosperity preachers promise wealth too quickly. They peddle an "over-realized eschatology" that "promises wealth too soon." God does promise us

riches beyond our wildest imagination in possessing the world (1 Cor. 3:19–23). But this wealth (beyond imagination) is our eternal future. Not yet.

Summed up, "it is a tragic thing that one of our greatest exports from America is the prosperity gospel. People are being destroyed by it. Christians are being weakened by it. God is being dishonored by it. Souls are perishing because of it. And a lot of guys are getting rich on it."[22]

We will not win the world with wealth

Saving faith is about treasuring Christ for who he is, not for what he gives. Prosperity preachers fall into one fundamental missiological failure by assuming that "the world will see the material prosperity of Christians and be motivated to embrace Christ. Well, that's not the way it works." Christ cannot be turned into a means to get something other than Christ (John 6:22–27). So "if Christ can be a good stock investment to get that, they will use Christ for that—to get what they really want. That's not saving faith." Instead, "if we have food and clothing, with these we will be content" (1 Tim. 6:8). The world takes notice of contentment in our simplicity—simplicity made possible because (1) Christ has "made an incredible future for us" and because (2) he now provides for all our needs. "*That* might cause the world to wake up and ask a reason for the hope that is in us, because it seems to them like we're not hoping in the same stuff they're hoping in—namely, the accumulation of wealth."[23]

"Gratitude for luxury impresses no one with our Savior. No matter how grateful we are, lining our lives with gold will not make the world think that *our God is great*. It will make the world think that *our god is gold*. That is no honor to the supremacy of his worth. None! But his supremacy, his being infinitely more valuable than gold, is why we live."[24]

The universe exists to express God's glory, and to do it "supremely in the suffering of his Son. Will you join the Son in displaying the supreme satisfaction of the glory of grace, in joining him on the Calvary road of suffering? Because there's no other way the world is going to see the supreme glory of Christ today, except that we break free from the Disneyland of America and begin to live lifestyles of missionary sacrifice," lifestyles that show the world that "our treasure is in heaven and not on earth. It's the only way. The prosperity gospel will not make anybody praise Jesus. It will make people

22 APJ 231: "Why I Abominate the Prosperity Gospel" (December 6, 2013).
23 APJ 1211: "Does Scripture Forbid Entrepreneurs from Raising Big Money?" (June 15, 2018).
24 APJ 780: "How Do You Synthesize Your Simple Lifestyle and Speaking at Expensive Conferences?" (January 26, 2016).

praise prosperity. 'Of course, I'll have a Jesus who'll give me a car.' Who wouldn't want a Jesus who gives me health, a car, a fine marriage?! 'I'll take your Jesus if the payoff is right.'" But "that's not going to get any praise for the suffering Christ."[25]

Prosperity gospel warning signs

What symptoms would reveal a "soft prosperity gospel" emerging inside my local church?

Watch for six warning signs. (1) No doctrine of suffering. "Tribulations are necessary, and there are many, and you must walk through them." From the pulpit, are the inevitabilities of persecution and physical pain presented as *normal* and even *necessary* to the Christian life (John 15:20; Acts 14:21; Rom. 8:23)? (2) No calls for self-denial. "Normal progress in the Christian life comes by saying no to lesser values and yes to Christ. Many of those lesser values are the kinds of pleasures that prosperity preachers don't like to say *no* to" (Matt. 16:24; Rom. 8:13; Phil. 3:8). Is there a robust doctrine of self-denial in your church? (3) No exposition. "Does the preaching take the Bible seriously by explaining what is really there in texts? Does it work through passages of Scripture, explaining the flow of thought? Or does it feel like the pastor has his favorite topics—he circles around to them over and over, making a few texts serve his purpose?" This pattern is especially troubling if the topics begin to sound like self-help or prosperity seeking. (4) No wrestling with tensions. A faithful preacher will wrestle with biblical texts to make them harmonize with other texts that seem to contradict. It's a "serious problem" for any preacher who is content to say what he wants while ignoring the difficult texts. (5) Exorbitant lifestyles celebrated. Do the preachers "drive cars, live in houses, wear clothes, and travel to places to which only the very wealthy can go or that only the very wealthy can possess? Is the pastor living above the average person in his parish?" (6) Self-centeredness over God-centeredness. "Does the preacher seem to parade himself? Does he figure into the talk too much?" Or "is the greatness and majesty and glory of God the centerpiece of all he says and does? Is the preacher in love with the glory of God in the gospel? Is he brokenhearted for his sin? Is he contrite and humble? Is he publicly self-effacing? Does he repent of his sins and model how to appropriate daily the sweetness of what Jesus did for us on the cross? Or is the majesty of grace marginalized while he exalts himself?"[26]

---

25 APJ 1442: "Will Suffering Weaken My Ministry?" (March 4, 2020).
26 APJ 320: "Six Keys to Detecting the Prosperity Gospel" (April 15, 2014).

How do I deliver my family from the prosperity gospel?
An international listener asked how he can rescue loved ones from the entrapments of prosperity preaching. Such a work begins with three litmus tests.

1. The prosperity gospel downplays "the vast scriptural theology of suffering that is *expected of* Christians and *promised to* Christians" (1 Pet. 4:19). Not just suffering from persecution but also "body-wasting-away, disease-type suffering in Romans 8:23 and 2 Corinthians 4:16. So Christians in prosperity churches are often profoundly unprepared for what life under God's providence is going to deal them—and that is a tragedy."

2. "The prosperity gospel reduces the glorious gospel to earthly betterment. The dominant gift of the gospel in the New Testament is *not* earthly betterment. The dominant gift is the joy of reconciliation with God and eternal joys at his right hand forever through Jesus Christ (Ps. 16:11)." The new creation will be glorious, "but that is not the immediate payoff of the gospel" in this life. "The biggest problem in the world is that God is angry at his creatures for rebelling against him, and the central good of the good news is that, in Christ, God took the initiative to satisfy that anger and make himself our treasure and not our terror." Prosperity preachers major on the gospel's secondary effects and apply them prematurely.

3. "Prosperity teachers distort the ground of our salvation by putting the emphasis on whether we can produce the *kind of faith* that gets hailed and gets rich, rather than putting it on the glorious work of Christ in dying and rising to bear the guilt of our sin and propitiate the wrath of God."

With these three convictions in place, to help others break free from the lies of prosperity preaching consider these four approaches. (1) Celebrate God's intent that his children be healthy and wealthy—not here, but later. We enjoy the settled promise of a future reality (Rev. 21:4). "Prosperity preachers get the timing of this all wrong." (2) Celebrate God as our treasure. Joy in God is meant to abound *during* suffering and loss, not *despite* it (Ps. 73:25–26; Hab. 3:17–18). (3) Love the disabled, and don't shun them. Show that disability is not the result of failed faith but that "it is a sign of great faith that these people, while not healed, are rejoicing in the hope of the glory of God rather than being miserable and angry at God." (4) Show that the Bible promises suffering. Share stories of those who served God and suffered greatly in life. And rejoice in the sufferings of Christ. As Peter says, "Rejoice insofar as you share Christ's sufferings, that you may also rejoice and be glad when his glory is revealed" (1 Pet. 4:13).[27]

---

27 APJ 689: "How to Help Friends Escape the Prosperity Gospel" (September 20, 2015).

Isn't all this anti-prosperity talk overdoing it?

Psalm 35:27 says that the Lord has "pleasure in the *prosperity* of his servant" (KJV). So can we go too far and undermine God's will that his people prosper *in this life* by constantly attacking the prosperity gospel?

As a baseline, the Lord's Prayer sets our life's priorities. We are to seek God's kingdom first, hallow God's name, pursue his saving rule, do his holy will, pursue purity, seek to rescue the perishing, and love our neighbor as ourselves. "These are the great, all-consuming goals of life. Whether we are *rich* or *healthy* or *safe* is a secondary issue. Praying that God would give us our daily bread—just our daily bread, let alone *lots* of bread—is subordinate to praying that his name would be hallowed and his kingdom would come." In this light, prosperity preaching is off in three ways.

1. Prosperity preaching has the *wrong timing.* Yes, "the gospel does include health, wealth, and prosperity." But it saves it for "the age to come, when we are so spiritually mature and perfected that we are suited to enjoy these things to the full, with no hint of idolatry. Prosperity preachers tend to bring this promise into the present in a way that is out of proportion with the way the New Testament describes the embattled position of the Christian in this fallen world." And not only the prosperity preachers, but "most of the modern church, as far as my limited eyes can see. Most of us—*us*—love this world too much and live in a compromised situation that does not comport with the wartime situation in which we find ourselves, with millions of people perishing eternally and millions suffering in this life, and most of us using our resources to make ourselves more comfortable rather than relieving temporal and eternal suffering." Each of us must be delivered from the love of this world (1 John 2:15).

2. Prosperity preaching has the *wrong perspective.* It fails to see God's providence over the *necessity* of suffering in this life. The promise that "through many tribulations we must enter the kingdom" is "Discipleship 101" (Acts 14:22). That's why the New Testament is "replete" with promises that "nothing can separate us from the love of Christ, including tribulation, persecution, famine, nakedness, danger, sword, even—Paul says—when we are being killed all day long (Rom. 8:35–36). And right alongside those assurances—that faithfulness will be accompanied by suffering—are the promises of forgiveness and acceptance with God and peace and joy and hope that are worth ten thousand times more than physical prosperity and health and safety in this life."

3. Prosperity preaching offers the *wrong comfort.* The problem is that prosperity preachers "comfort people not with the presence of Christ in suffering and his rescue from suffering in the age to come, but rather with the assurance that they will *get out of suffering in this life* if they follow the right prescription."

They treat blessing like a formula. If you tithe right, they say, God will bless you and give you a "sure material blessing." No. That's not how it works. Paul praises the joyful giving of the poorest Christians (2 Cor. 8:2).

So what about Psalm 35:27? How is God delighting in our welfare, or prosperity, now? The answer is Romans 8. "There is no greater chapter to prove that God is for us—100 percent for us, not 99 percent—and not against us. There is no greater chapter to show that when he gave Christ for us, it was not to remove suffering in this life, but to assure us with unshakable joy and hope that, in all our pain and in all our sorrow and frustration and disappointment, nothing can separate us from the love of God in Christ." So let this chapter—"perhaps the greatest chapter in the Bible—put Christian *gladness* and Christian *groaning* in their painful and precious relationship in this age." Let God's word define true prosperity in this life.[28]

Speaking of (3), poor and suffering Christians model true love. To motivate generosity, Paul pointed to "the poorest church" to showcase how their happiness in God "*overflowed* in a wealth of generosity" (2 Cor. 8:1–5).[29] The text is "one of my favorite expressions of this dynamic."[30] Macedonian Christians were "hurting" and "poverty-stricken"—poignant pains that were unalleviated. Yet they modeled joy-driven love in their eager financial giving. It is the very definition of love: a "gladness in God that overflows in the act—the behaviors of love—in the hope of including others in it, that is, in our gladness in God."[31] The "blood-bought joy" of Christ flows in us to overflow in love to others.[32] "God-exalting love for people is the overflow of joy in God that meets the needs of others."[33] It's a love that meets temporal needs with the aim of drawing others into an eternal wealth, "into sharing our joy in God, which doesn't just last for eighty years but for eighty thousand years."[34] Joyful generosity, in light of eternity, protects the hurting from becoming infatuated with life's pains. Because "if our suffering turns us in on ourselves, we will not love others in the midst of our affliction." To have a joy in God that overflows in generous giving to others—as we ourselves suffer—"is the beauty of Christian love."[35] This Macedonian generosity is, for any generation of Christians facing economic setback, "the clearest recession text in the Bible."[36]

28 APJ 968: "Are We Overdoing the Anti-Prosperity Gospel Theme?" (November 25, 2016).

29 APJ 289: "Biblical Hope for Christians Facing Poverty" (March 3, 2014).

30 APJ 1289: "Why Do We Give Christmas Gifts?" (December 14, 2018).

31 APJ 953: "Is It Love If I Don't Feel It?" (October 21, 2016).

32 APJ 1819: "What Makes Christian Love Different?" (August 8, 2022).

33 APJ 1193: "Isn't God Most Glorified in Me When I Am Most Self-Giving?" (May 4, 2018).

34 APJ 1106: "Is Anyone Born a Racist? Or Is It Learned?" (October 13, 2017).

35 APJ 1589: "Sustained through the Hardest Suffering" (February 17, 2021).

36 APJ 1472: "Could a Recession Serve Our Joy?" (May 13, 2020).

Behold the one who never loved money

Jesus was poor. Of himself he said, "Foxes have holes, and birds of the air have nests, but the Son of Man has nowhere to lay his head" (Matt. 8:20; Luke 9:58). Or as Paul said of Christ: "Though he was rich, yet for your sake he became poor, so that you by his poverty might become rich" (2 Cor. 8:9). "My amazement at his poverty—poverty that made many rich—moves me. It moves me. It shapes me. It frees me from my love affair with money. I admire it." And "I love him. I love his simplicity. I love his freedom from the love of money. I love his readiness to risk all for the mission." Beholding the glory of Christ, "in his freedom from money, starts to give me freedom from money. And his vastly more admirable beauty so far surpasses the tycoons of Wall Street." He is "so free, so loving, so bold, so sacrificial. Everything about him is more attractive than all the rich people I have ever known. So that is the way it works for me. Beholding the glory of the Lord, I am changed into a person who doesn't love money (2 Cor. 3:18)."[37]

Coveting is idolatry

The first commandment forbids idolatry: "You shall have no other gods before me" (Exod. 20:3). The last commandment forbids coveting: "You shall not covet" (Exod. 20:17). And Paul merges the commandments when he calls Christians to "put to death therefore what is earthly in you," including "covetousness, which is idolatry" (Col. 3:5). Coveting *is* idolatry. It includes more than money. It covers any disordered desire in our lives that diminishes the worth of God. *Coveting*, in both Hebrew and Greek, is a word of *desire*. Coveting is a *wrong desiring*, and it certainly applies to money. "Don't desire anything in a way that would express lack of contentment in God." To covet is to desire anything else *more* because our desire for God is *less*. "That is covetousness. That is evil. It doesn't matter what you are desiring," even otherwise good things. It is "our exchange for the glory of God, the value of God, the beauty of God, the all-satisfying worth of God. Where that exchange is happening and our desire for him and our satisfaction in him is getting weaker, other desires are going to come in to fill the void, and they get stronger. All of that is called *covetousness*."[38]

Paul's text bridges Old Testament idols (of statues and trinkets) to contemporary greed. Idolatry has always been about our interior lust for the world (Col. 3:5).[39] The apostle John says the same thing. Idolatry is a love of the world (1 John 2:15–16; 5:21). So from ancient pagan superstitions to corporate

---

37 APJ 850: "Can Pleasure in God Really Compete with the Pleasures of Porn?" (May 3, 2016).
38 APJ 872: "Are the First and Last Commandments the Same?" (June 2, 2016).
39 APJ 410: "What Is Idolatry?" (August 19, 2014).

kleptocracy now, idols are the same thing—any substitute for "wholehearted reliance on the true and living God." It could be a religious statue, a trinket, praise, power, career, sex, productivity, or wealth. An idol remains what it has always been. The object of a disordered heart seeking God-replacements for its "greatest blessing, help, guidance, and satisfaction."[40]

When has my online shopping gone too far?

Buying new things and having them delivered to our doorstep can be an addictive thrill. Why? "It seems to me that the pleasure rises mainly from the elusive sense that buying and receiving things is life-giving. It feels life-giving. Or it feels like I get a sense of empowerment."

For example, book buying delivers an "amorphous euphoric sense that life is going to be better for me now. My knowledge is going to be larger. My influence is going to be greater. Some of my weaknesses and limitations of ignorance and looking foolish because I have never heard of this book are going to be overcome." Self-image drives our book buying, not to mention clothes, tools, electronics, and other gadgets. Some purchases may help us improve, but, honestly, the pleasures they bring "are not often totally noble."

Contrasted to the *buzz* we get from Amazon, Jesus warns us to "take care, and be on your guard against all covetousness, for one's life does not consist in the abundance of his possessions" (Luke 12:15). "It seems to me that Jesus strikes right at the heart of the matter. Life does not consist in the abundance of possessions. That feeling—that arrival of the package in the mail—is an illusion. The euphoria is short-lived. It is shallow. It keeps us from deeper pleasures that we were made for." This hunger for materialism reveals a "void in our hearts—some measure of emptiness that Jesus intends to satisfy by himself, his fellowship, his ministry" (Phil. 4:11–13). So when we "get more pleasure out of *receiving* than *giving*, it shows that something has gone wrong in our hearts. We were designed as followers of Christ to experience even greater euphoria in *giving* than in the doorbell ringing and a new package *coming*" (Acts 20:35).

We only win the battle against covetousness when our true wealth is settled. "If you are a Christian, you already possess all material things (1 Cor. 3:21–23). You really do. Your Father created and owns everything—everything in the universe! And as his child, you will inherit it, and it will be at your disposal in the age to come in the new earth, in the new heavens. And you will be able to do with it as you please." So we do not lay up for ourselves treasures on earth, but in heaven (Matt. 6:19–20). "In heaven we will have them forever. We won't lose

40 APJ 1726: "What Is an Idol?" (January 3, 2022).

them. No rust. No theft. And we will be able for the very first time to use them with joy without any greed, without any covetousness, without any idolatry. So in a sense, abundance of material things can wait. We have more important things to do right now. Love God, love people, and find the greatest pleasure in giving."[41]

Is greed as damning as homosexual sin?

Yes, they're equally damning. A life of greed kills the soul like a life of homosexual sin. Paul says, "Do not be deceived: neither the sexually immoral, nor idolaters, nor adulterers, nor *men who practice homosexuality*, nor thieves, nor *the greedy*, nor drunkards, nor revilers, nor swindlers will inherit the kingdom of God" (1 Cor. 6:9–10). In other words, "greed and homosexual practice have the same horrific outcome when they are embraced in a lifelong lifestyle."[42]

But while one sin is more perverse, the other is more pervasive. "I do not doubt that millions more people are ruined in this life and the next through greed, covetousness, pride, selfishness, and excessive anger than are ruined through same-sex orientation or through homosexual behavior." These sins are far more widespread because "the sins of greed and pride and selfishness and anger are more subtle and disguise themselves more easily as acceptable." And yet, *unlike* the sins of greed, stealing, arrogance, exploiting others, anger, malice, and abusiveness, "homosexual behavior has articulate and forceful advocates and defenders." Only one sin on this list gets a sin-pride rally. But greed is not so blatantly celebrated. It operates more subtly, yet its corruption is more pervasive. So it stands statistically that "the number of people who are ruined in this life and the next by the sins of greed, pride, selfishness, and anger is vastly greater than the number of people ruined by same-sex orientation or sinful homosexual behavior." Thus, the "social miseries" brought about through a sin like greed is "vastly greater in scope than any brought about through homosexual sin."[43]

Learning the secret to financial contentment

So the love of money is dangerous and disordered, revealing a spiritual emptiness within us. But the problem is not the money. Possessions are good gifts

41 APJ 743: "Counsel for Online Shopping Addicts?" (December 4, 2015). Other episodes on consumerism, materialism, and the love of possessions include APJ 345: "Do I Love God or Just Love Loving Him?" (May 20, 2014), APJ 419: "What Luxuries in My Life Are Sinful?" (September 1, 2014), APJ 1185: "Do the Biblical Warnings against Riches Apply to Most Americans?" (April 16, 2018), APJ 1460: "More Precious Than Praise and Possessions" (April 15, 2020), APJ 1493: "How Can I Be Free from Materialism?" (July 1, 2020), and APJ 1534: "Why Did Demons Ask Jesus for Pigs?" (October 5, 2020).
42 APJ 950: "Little Ears, 'Big Church,' and Sensitive Sermons" (October 14, 2016).
43 APJ 1038: "Is Homosexuality Really the Worst Sin?" (May 8, 2017).

when we don't love them inordinately. Our interests "start with legitimate love—proper and proportional and Christ-exalting and God-rooted—for something innocent that God has given for our enjoyment. But then they become improper, disproportionate. They cease to exalt Christ. They cease to have their root in God."

Paul tells us that "godliness with contentment is great gain" (1 Tim. 6:6). "This is precisely what acts as the governor, moderator, regulator, or guide in all of our other desires." Here's what happens. "The use of money governed by a sweet, deep, pervasive contentment in God has been replaced by the loss of that contentment and the emergence of a powerful love for money and craving for money, as Paul calls it. So the use of money has been disconnected or uncoupled from contentment in God." Our loves become disordered when our Godward love ebbs. "Supreme contentment or happiness or joy or satisfaction in God ceases to be the great guide or ballast or moderator or regulator of our souls. And when that goes, everything goes bad."

When it comes to our money and possessions, we must *learn* contentment (Phil. 4:11–13). Paul calls it the Christian's "secret" (μυέω; Phil. 4:12). The *secret* is in weighing all of our present possessions in comparison to "the surpassing worth of knowing Christ Jesus my Lord," until we can say that we are willing to suffer "the loss of all things and count them as rubbish, in order that I may gain Christ" (Phil. 3:8). The secret is Christ. Paul finds in him "a satisfaction that is so profound and so pervasive that even if everything else is lost, he doesn't lose this contentment or this satisfaction." When this secret of Christ-centered contentment is present, "it functions as a wonderful governor and moderator and regulator and guide and control on the use of all good things."[44]

Money love dies only by better love for a greater treasure. Or as the writer of Hebrews commands: "Keep your life free from love of money, and be content with what you have, for he has said, 'I will never leave you nor forsake you'" (Heb. 13:5). We are told to get rid of this "deep, dysfunctional craving love of money" by treasuring our omnipotent God. "It is amazing that the Bible talks this way." Get rid of your love for money. And be content with what you have. Why? Because God promised to never leave you. "In other words, God's *presence* and God's *promise* make a powerful emotional difference in resisting wrong desires and finding contentment in really painful and difficult situations." God's promises "sever the power of disordered desires."[45] So when the love of money "starts to raise its ugly head," how do we respond? We hear God say

44 APJ 752: "Four Signs Food Has Become an Idol" (December 17, 2015).
45 APJ 358: "Counsel for Those Considering Transgender" (June 6, 2014).

to us: "I will never leave you. I will never forsake you. I will be your sufficient helper. Man cannot destroy you. He cannot ruin you. I am for you." When we trust the promises of Scripture, that God is our great treasure, we kill our love of money—or our love for any sin—by the Spirit (Rom. 8:13).[46]

Should wealthy Christians intentionally live below their means?

Paul commissions wealthy Christians to be known for their good deeds (1 Tim. 6:17–19). He doesn't call them to downgrade their lifestyle. So could a wealthy Christian, living in a mansion and driving sports cars, fulfill Paul's vision for a life of good works?

Paul didn't simply tell wealthy Christians to get rid of their wealth. (Nor did he tell slave owners to free their slaves.) His words were subtler, but he—like Christ—still manages to "disturb the wealthy." Jesus's warnings to the wealthy were point-blank. It's hard for the rich to be saved (Luke 18:24), hard for four reasons. (1) Wealth gags our faith (Luke 8:14). Wealth isn't neutral. It "chokes the vitality of radical Christian living" and endangers authentic faith. (2) Wealth hinders our radical obedience (Luke 14:33). Jesus didn't forbid us from owning material things (see above). But he does call us to be "radically free from the control of possessions and always ready to do the most life-threatening acts of obedience." The wealthier we become, the fewer risks we embrace for him, the more in bondage to materialism our lives will appear to others. (3) Wealth confuses our treasure (Phil. 1:20; 3:8). In life and in death, Paul desired to magnify Christ. "He wanted to live and die in a way that would appear to the world that Christ was magnificent to him—more satisfying than possessions or life." (4) Wealth distorts our motives. "Why would a Christian—whose treasure is in heaven, and whose life is devoted to doing as much good as he can, and whose desire is to show the world that Christ is more precious than things—want to look like riches are his treasure? What would be the motive for buying a mansion and surrounding yourself with more and more and more than you need?"

In sum: "Without specifying what measure of wealth is destructive to the soul or to our witness, the New Testament relentlessly pushes us toward simplicity and economy for the sake of the gospel and away from luxury and affluence."[47]

Christians using wealth to make more wealth

If it is not sinful to *make* a lot of money, but it is sinful to *keep* a lot of money, are there any scenarios where *keeping* a lot of money is a wise investment strategy?

---

46 APJ 422: "What Does It Mean to 'Kill Sin by the Spirit'?" (September 4, 2014).
47 APJ 1680: "Should Rich Christians Downgrade Their Lifestyle?" (September 17, 2021).

Would this be wise for Christians who want to expand their businesses and build wealth in order to give more in the future?

First, the warning of 1 Timothy 6:6–10 stands as "about as strong a warning about the desire to be rich as I could imagine." With that said, no, "wartime lifestyle does not mean that, after providing yourself and your family with modest housing, food, and clothing, you are then obliged to give all the surplus away immediately. That is not what the wartime lifestyle says." Instead, the call for a wartime way of life says that the remaining resources beyond necessities—whether ten dollars or ten million dollars—is "managed and stewarded for the good of others, the glory of God, and the advancement of his saving and sanctifying and healing purposes in the world rather than for personal aggrandizement."

Stewardship may mean giving away a "huge and immediate sacrificial gift. You may give all your surplus away when profits rise or you get a windfall." Or it may mean you don't give it all away, but instead "build a large capital reserve for starting a foundation or for accomplishing some larger, longer-term goal for the good of the culture or the society."

On the spiritual side, no time is more expensive than wartime, requiring huge investments (like conferences, addressed above). But even on the business side of things, "many legitimate businesses depend on large concentrations of capital. You can't build a new manufacturing plant without millions of dollars in equity. And therefore, financial officers in these big businesses have the responsibility to build those reserves." So "when the Bible condemns the desire to get rich, it is not necessarily condemning a business that aims to expand and, therefore, seeks larger capital reserves." Now, it may be the case that the officers within that corporation are greedy for personal wealth or power. But amassing capital is not sinful if it seeks to create jobs that meet needs. "So what Paul is warning against is not the desire to earn money to meet our needs and the needs of others. He is warning against the desire to have more and more money for the security and the ego boost and the material luxuries it can provide, with no plan for loving other people with your increase. That is what my effort to teach a wartime lifestyle is aiming to avoid."[48]

Christian entrepreneurs seeking wealth for missions
Speaking of capital investments, a Christian entrepreneur wants to generate surplus profit to fund missions. Is aggressive capital accumulation sinful?

First, we need to be clear that Jesus warns us about accumulating money into larger and larger barns (Luke 12:19–20). "Now, the problem here is not that

---

48 APJ 420: "Wartime Wisdom for the Wealthy" (September 2, 2014).

this man's business prospered. It's almost inevitable that gifted, hard-working business people with integrity are going to run businesses that prosper." Jesus doesn't condemn the success; he condemns the excessive accumulation. "The problem was that the accumulation was accompanied by—I say 'accompanied by' because it could be both cause or effect—a sense of self-reliant, self-satisfied ease in this world" as if eternity doesn't matter, nor the needs of my neighbors. Endless accumulation of profits reveals a self-sufficiency and a heart that treasures the world, not Christ (Matt. 6:21; Luke 12:19).

Honest, hard-working Christians can make a lot of money. Business success is not evil. But the accumulation of wealth for the purposes of self-security, or boasting, or out of "indifference" to the world's needs and your future accountability to God, means that "something else should be done with the proceeds from all that God-given success."

Christians are to be content with daily food and clothing (1 Tim. 6:6–8). Such faithful simplicity catches the attention of the world (1 Pet. 3:15). The prosperity gospel offers Christ as a means of wealth and grabs the eyes of the wealth-seeking world. True Christianity seeks contentment in simple provisions—and that hope-filled contentment serves as a countercultural witness. "If we have food and clothing, with these we will be content, because Christ has made an incredible future for us and provided all our needs. That might cause the world to wake up and ask a reason for the hope that is in us because it seems to them like we're not hoping in the same stuff they're hoping in—namely, the accumulation of wealth." The prosperity gospel is powerless to produce this countercultural contentment.

Here's the personal temptation. As the business succeeds and wealth accumulates, we are led to believe that we need to also "continually increase" our lifestyle choices according to growing "symbols of wealth and power," in clothing and homes and cars and vacations. They all get more expensive over time. Seeking after these growing symbols of wealth is the root of "all kinds of evil" (1 Tim. 6:10).

There is a radical "alternative vision for the successful Christian entrepreneur," and it's this: Don't let your success make you arrogant or self-sufficient (1 Tim. 6:17). Life is fragile. "Mr. Rich Man," your body is fragile—and so is the world, the culture, the economy, and all economic theories. Embrace the fragility of all things so that "you cannot be so foolish as to bank on something so fragile as riches."

Instead, enjoy the simple pleasures of eating, drinking, reading, gardening, and giving away your resources to others (Acts 20:35; 1 Tim. 6:17). Instead of barn building, be "rich in good works" (1 Tim. 6:18). The ultimate goal of money is that "we pursue a heart that is so satisfied in God and all that he is for us in Christ through the gospel that we are freed from the craving to accumulate. We turn our great earnings, which are not evil, into doing good for others." We may donate a lot. Or we might create industries to employ hundreds of workers and to fund missions.[49]

Cash bonuses motivate my work—is that okay?

To start off, money is a relative thing and "only has value in a culture where it can be exchanged for something else. The paper we call 'bills' or 'money,' or the pieces of metal we call 'coins,' or the checks that stand for money, or the electronic impulses on your phone (that turn into money somehow)—all of that—is relatively worthless." But they have exchange value. So "God gives his people money so that we can use money in a way to show that money is not our God, but that God is our God. That's why we have money. That's why we have everything." But "God does intend for Christians to use money. Money itself is just money. It's not good or bad; it's just stuff: it's paper or coins or potential for value." But it reveals the heart because of what the heart exchanges money for.

The Bible is clear that wages are proper. The laborer is worthy of wages (Luke 10:7). In fact, "it is just to be *paid more* for doing a very good job for your employer. And it's fair to be *paid less* for doing a poor job for your employer." So what might make the desire "defective" for a wage or a bonus or a tax refund?

Seven questions to pose to your heart and work. (1) Is your work virtuous or evil? If you are being rewarded for doing evil, the bonus is tainted. (2) Do you feel the dangers of wealth? There's a "cluster of New Testament texts that wave a big yellow flag in front of the desire for money to say, 'Watch out: this can kill you!'" (Matt. 19:23; 1 Tim. 6:9–10). (3) Are you content with Christ, or are you driven by the idol of wealth? Covetousness is idolatry (Col. 3:5). "Would you still be content in God, happy in God, if the bonus did not come through?" (4) Do you receive the bonus knowing that it is more blessed to give than to receive (Acts 20:35)? (5) Is the desire for the bonus a lost confidence in the presence of God in your life (Heb. 13:5–6)? (6) Do bonuses choke out your joy in God's word (Luke 8:13–14)? "Boy, this is such a good barometer. People start to find the word of God boring when they become more worldly." Or does the bonus drive you into the word as you "contemplate giving or spending or saving or investing the bonus?" (7) Does the abundance of money make you

---

49 APJ 1211: "Does Scripture Forbid Entrepreneurs from Raising Big Money?" (June 15, 2018).

feel more alive than your life in Christ (Luke 12:15)? "That's the bottom line: Will God be more glorious to you? And will he look more glorious through you, because of this bonus and what you do with it?"[50]

The world's wealth will offer you no advantage in the end

What's the bottom line for a man who owns the whole world but forfeits his own soul in the process (Mark 8:36–37)? With this rhetorical question, Jesus interrogates all our possessions—our "money, houses, books, computers, land, businesses." In comparison to the worth of Christ, "suppose your heart is drawn to prefer possessions—which is what is happening to billions of people. Suppose you turn away from Jesus, and you embrace as superior to Jesus all that earthly possessions can give you. And suppose you succeed. All your life you succeed—nothing but success. And by the end of your life, suppose you own everything. The world. Everything. Not just Apple and Google and Mobil Oil—all of it is yours! You call all the shots; you own them all. That's what Jesus envisages, right? 'Gain the whole world.' And then you die. And instantly, you realize it was suicide. It was eternal suicide."

In the presence of Christ, you will want nothing more than to trade all your worldly wealth for your soul. What will Christ say? "He will say, 'You would try to buy your soul with the very possessions that destroyed your soul—the very possessions that you preferred over me?'" That's catastrophic. The "Christ-replacing, Christ-belittling idols" in this life "have no currency in heaven. He will turn his face away, and you will perish forever." Attempting to ransom God with money is vain because only in Christ is our ransom paid.

Despite this stark warning, each of us faces a lifelong battle with our love of this world and all it offers us. "At age seventy-three, there are temptations with *stuff*. I need all the help I can get to be free! You do too!" The calling is to say to our possession-loving selves: "I deny you. I kill you."[51]

To Christians in poverty

To the Christian facing a lifetime of poverty, are there any encouragements?

"Yes, massive encouragements. Frankly, once upon a time, and probably in most places in the world today, that was normal Christianity." Middle-class Americans "are wealthy by all historical standards." For the poor, there is "special help" and grace for them (Luke 6:20). At the same time, the love of wealth is insidious and incredibly dangerous (Luke 18:24; 1 Tim. 6:6–10). "So

---

50 APJ 1527: "Money Motivates Me to Work Hard—Is That Okay?" (September 18, 2020).
51 APJ 1460: "More Precious Than Praise and Possessions" (April 15, 2020).

Paul does not regard riches as a great benefit, but a great danger," and *money* a "much greater danger" than *poverty.*

Here's the greater promise. The godly poor will inherit everything God owns (Rom. 8:17; 1 Cor. 3:21–23). "If you are a Christian and you know Christ—Christ is your treasure, your Savior, your Lord, your friend, your King, your future—then you are richer than the richest billionaire on the planet. That is literally true spiritually *now,* and it is literally true physically, materially, *later.*" For now, realize that "the achievements that count in heaven, that are going to be rewarded by God, are not financial" (Matt. 6:33). "The poor person is at no disadvantage in increasing his reward in heaven. None. Because what is rewarded in heaven is godliness and faithfulness and love and joy and peace and kindness and meekness and self-control. The poor are at no disadvantage—perhaps at an advantage."

Here and now, poor Christians will remain the most compelling models of gospel generosity (2 Cor. 8:1–2). "So take heart. If you are in a situation where your financial resources are pinched, and it looks like they are going to be pinched to the day you die, you are in a position of extraordinary possibility of blessing people and of enjoying Christ."[52]

In sum, "poverty and riches, hunger and fullness, weeping and laughter may be signs of blessedness, or they may be signs of condemnation, depending on how they relate to our devotion to Jesus. If we are utterly devoted to him, no poverty, no hunger, and no weeping can steal our blessedness."[53]

---

[52] APJ 289: "Biblical Hope for Christians Facing Poverty" (March 3, 2014).
[53] APJ 1328: "How Do Christians Survive in Middle-Class America?" (April 10, 2019).

On Gambling, Lotteries, and the Stock Market

Is it sinful to gamble on sports?

Fantasy sports are now a multibillion-dollar gambling industry in the United States thanks to apps like DraftKings and FanDuel, leading a young man to email and ask if a "rather modest" bet of twenty to fifty dollars per week is sinful.

It is, Pastor John replied, but "my words don't make something sinful. God's words make something sinful." Six considerations.

1. We get one life to live for Christ's glory (2 Cor. 5:15). "Then comes eternity." We get no do-overs. "Every day is either invested well or lost forever. Every breath you take, every minute of life you have, is a free gift of God and a trust, a stewardship, which God says should be lived for his glory, for the magnifying of his Son." Innocent games may be a helpful refreshment for the mind and to commune with others, "but in themselves—in a fallen, needy, miserable, tragic, dying, hell-bent world like ours—they have very little significance."

2. We can get disoriented in a fog of unreality if we're not careful. To the degree we get sucked into unreal worlds like *fantasy* football, we must account for how "living in an unreal world" makes our "real-world impact *greater* for the good of people and the glory of God." Sin is fundamentally deceit—a trick to get us to desire what is unreal over what is real (Heb. 3:13). So a nickel bet may be modest, but fifty dollars a week isn't—because "half the world's population lives on $2.50 a day, which is $17.50 a week, which is below what he's gambling. Our friend is throwing to the wind up to fifty dollars a week, calling it *modest* gambling. So there's good evidence he has lost touch with reality, and I would plead with him, 'Wake up, friend. Wake up!'"

3. Beware of loving money. Gambling may enhance the "emotional buzz" of the Sunday game, but it's more likely driven by the desire "to get more money by putting other people's money at risk." An income made apart from

virtuous labor is symptomatic of a love of money that the Bible calls suicidal (1 Tim. 6:9–10).

4. Know that your money is not *your* money. "I would say quite bluntly, forthrightly, and confidently that you have no right to risk God's money this way. Managers don't gamble with their master's money—period." Faithful trustees don't gamble with the trust fund. We all give account for our steward- ship (Matt. 25:14–30). "To gamble with God's money on trivialities like this is a kind of embezzlement."

5. See gambling as a widespread "social sickness," bringing ruin to millions, "especially the poor." It preys on the poor more than anyone else. "The people who can least afford it take the biggest hit. Christians should not participate in lotteries, casinos, or online gambling—an "entire structure of devastation for millions of people."

6. Seek better investments, like stocks that will grow over time. Better, "find gloriously happy, helpful good deeds to do in people's lives. Creatively seek out how to use all that money in an excellent way. Imagine investing fifty dollars a week, two hundred dollars a month, in the causes of justice and gospel- spreading and the relief of the suffering. Oh, my, how much fun that would be. Believe me, friend, it is more blessed to *give* than to *receive*—or to *risk*. It is more blessed to *invest* creatively in the eternal joys of other people than to play with God's money in the dream world of fantasy football."[1]

Speaking of (3) money love, we must free our lives from money fear to live a life of worship. We kill this anxiety by preaching to ourselves regularly. "It ain't automatic for John Piper to be fearless about money, though I get paid plenty, way plenty. It isn't automatic for me. It isn't automatic for you. We are battling fear and anxiety every day, not to mention greed." We do it by af- firming regularly: "He's shepherd to me. He's Father to me. He's King to me" (Luke 12:32–34). And he's not stingy in his care for us. "Preach these things to yourself and attack fear and anxiety in your life with these truths so that when you overcome fear about money, God gets the glory."[2]

Gambling preys on the poor

Later, I asked Piper to elaborate on (5) the effects of gambling on the poor.

Lotteries prey on the poor—especially pull-tabs and scratch tickets whose smaller and more frequent payouts ($10, $100, or $500) "draw in dispropor- tionately more poor people than, say, the $200 million Powerball." As the poor

---

1   APJ 1269: "Is It Sinful to Gamble on Fantasy Sports?" (October 29, 2018).
2   APJ 1820: "How Money Fears Kill Our Worship" (August 10, 2022).

gamble, they redirect their money to local governments. Gambling is a "regressive tax" on the poor, a way of "luring the poor, who pay almost no taxes for social services, to pay a kind of tax in a way that worsens their situation rather than making it better, which is what taxes are supposed to do." And gambling preys on the poor because the poor are more financially hopeless," a feeling that "drives most of the purchases." Buying a scratch ticket won't make a bad situation much worse. When you feel financially hopeless already, "arguments against gambling lose most of their force."

So what's to be done? (1) Consider the poor. We don't dismiss the poor or "stand aloof and roll our eyes at the stupidity of millions of dollars that roll into the state coffers from people who can barely pay their bills." Instead, the Bible calls our minds and hearts to *consider* them (Pss. 41:1; 113:7; Prov. 14:31; 17:5; 31:9). (2) Refuse to financially feed any institution that preys on the poor. (3) Advocate for the poor. "We should give our thinking, praying, advocating, investing, and planning toward the removal of unnecessary barriers to productive work and gainful employment among the poor, the removal of incentives and allurements toward waste and squandering and irresponsibility, and instead seek to put in place encouragements toward deferred gratification, and, finally, the creation of responsibility and hope in people's lives, through the gospel."[3]

Isn't the stock market like gambling?

In truth, money is always risky. "You bury it, and it'll maybe rot. You can hide it in the house, but the house may burn down. You can put it in the bank, and the banks may fail, and the government that insures it may fail. Put it in stocks with differing philosophies of principal protection, and they all may go bankrupt. Yes, there is no escaping risk when it comes to money in this world—or for that matter, doing anything in this world."

So isn't stock market investing as risky as gambling? No, for three reasons. (1) "Investing means letting another person use your money for enterprises that you believe contribute to the common good, while gambling means supporting a system that is counterproductive to the common good, and especially destructive for the poor." (2) Gambling is all or nothing. Stock market investing is rarely a total loss. (3) Gambling rides on high loss-possibility, but the market lets you choose degrees of lesser risk.

The Dow is wiser than gambling, but there's an investment of greater value than both, although it's far riskier because "you might have to lose your life in the process." But this investment is also "foolproof" with guaranteed dividends "greater than any dividends in the universe." It's an investment that cannot be destroyed by bankruptcy, bear markets, rust, age, inflation, robbery, or hackers (Matt. 6:19–21; Luke 2:33; 1 Tim. 6:17–19). In the end, "the main emphasis in the financial life of a Christian should not be how to *minimize risk* and *maximize gain* in the stock market, but rather how to *maximize eternal gain* by *maximizing generosity* for the sake of causes that glorify God and rescue sinners from suffering, especially eternal suffering."

As for corporate corruption, how can we be certain we're not investing in exploitative and evil companies? "As far as I know, you can't. You can't know that. But that's true of every dollar you spend in the marketplace." A local store may be a front for evil. "Any clothing chain where you get your shirt may exploit foreign workers." Do your homework. Never invest in evil. But also know that "you're not responsible for all that somebody might do to misuse your money any more than a salt manufacturer is responsible for high blood pressure."[4]

Are Christians shrewd investors in this age?

No, often not. Jesus uses the parable of the dishonest manager to spotlight how shrewd the world is with money. In this case a manager, about to be fired, barters with others to score points and store favors and win personal influence that he will cash out later (Luke 16:1–13). It's a cunning move. In comparison, Christians are often a lot less shrewd in the world of investing. But Jesus says fiscal cleverness is ultimately insignificant.

Christians eye eternal gains, not quick monetary wins. So "maybe you aren't that shrewd when it comes to the stock market, but guess what? Who cares? You've got a billion years to enjoy your investment." Use your money for eternal gain, because as Jesus says, worldly wealth is destined to "fail" you (Luke 16:9). "Fail" (ἀνέκλειπτος) is a trigger word to remind us that money is temporal and fleeting (Luke 12:33). But "making friends" in the parable translates to using money to meet people's needs. "That's the way to lay up treasure in heaven that does not fail." That's the shrewdest investment. "Here's the basic point: don't worry about being a shrewd investor in this age, where you can provide a future that will only fail." Instead, "use your resources to do as much good as you can for the glory of God and the eternal good of others." This is true financial expertise.[5]

---

4   APJ 1305: "Is Investing in Stocks Any Better Than Gambling?" (January 21, 2019).
5   APJ 1273: "Does Jesus Commend Dishonesty in Luke 16?" (November 7, 2018).

On Pouting, Sulking, and Self-Pity

Self-pity, the destroyer of homes

"Self-pitying woundedness makes for some really sick relationships in the home."[1] The point arose when a listener asked what advice current John Piper would offer newlywed John Piper.

The first bit of advice is to be amazed at marriage. "Lift up your eyes, John Piper—young, newly married John Piper. Lift up your eyes to see what you have gotten yourself into here—an amazing, God-wrought mystery." In marriage, believing couples—and even unbelieving couples—are bound in heaven by God (Mark 10:9). "I would say, 'John, look at the mystery of what this means for your love of this woman. This is a bottomless ocean of wisdom for you. Love her like Christ loves the church'" (Eph. 5:31–32). And draw your life from Christ, not from your spouse, or marriage will "backfire on you, because you will be constantly drawing your strength for love from her lovableness instead of from Christ's love for you and in the gospel."

Then he admonished himself over self-pity using honest words. "John Piper, you are young, and you need to realize that this is going to be a problem for you all your life. Be done with the little-boy need for pity, for mommy to 'kiss the owie' and dote over you till you get better. Be done with that. Be done with pouting and sulking when you don't get what you want, which is so immature and so built into your wiring. You will be regularly disappointed, because you are an intense perfectionist-wanter and, therefore, your wants are not going to be satisfied as often as you would like. Instead of pouting and pitying yourself, draw down strength, John Piper. Draw down strength from Christ to stop being a *reactor* and, instead, be a strong *initiative taker* to this family. Bring strength to this family. Don't *use* this family, and, when they don't meet your needs, go pouting off into a corner. Come out from the

---

1 APJ 1180: "How Do I Show Kindness to My Children and Expect Them to Obey?" (April 4, 2018).

corner, looking to Christ for strength and hope. They need you to be a leader, not to return evil for evil."[2]

Make war on pouting (a lesson from a leave)

Pastor John took a leave of absence in 2010 as a soul check over all the parts of his life: marriage, worship, fathering, pastoring, public life. Three years later I asked if any enduring lessons from the leave remained fresh in his memory.

At the top of his mind was a lesson about attacking the sin of self-pity. "All my adult life I had *ferociously* fought the sin of lust—sexual temptation—and I say *ferociously* or *fiercely* because Jesus said, 'If your right eye causes you to sin, tear it out and throw it away. . . . If your right hand causes you to sin, cut it off and throw it away' (Matt. 5:29–30). I mean, that is really serious." This awakening led to the "huge" and "very important" discovery he never forgot: "I did not attack in the same way, with tearing-out-the-eye and cutting-off-the-hand fierceness, my sins of irritability, frustration, anger, self-pity, sullenness, and pouting." Instead, "I had formed the irrational sense—maybe I didn't articulate it—that, well, those sins are just who I am." The bent toward becoming moody, sullen, easily frustrated, irritable, "or having a hair trigger," were all assumed to be personality. It's wiring, "as if I am *not wired* to have lust. I mean, you see the irrationality of it."

He failed to make war on his self-pity like he did with lust. So he called himself to stop excusing it and to pursue a greater intensity to fight these relationship-damaging sins. "Make war on pouting" may sound like an odd battle cry, but men need it. "We come home, and our wives don't welcome us the way we hoped they would, or they don't want to go where we want to go tonight, or they don't do sex the way we hoped they would do sex, or they don't fix our favorite food, or they criticize us, when we got enough criticism at work today. And we just kind of slink off to the den with our shoulders bent over, licking our wounds, and saying, 'Oh, poor me,' like a little puppy. That is just stupid, evil, wicked, unmanly, unspiritual behavior. And we need to make war on it just as seriously as we make war on lust." Fight porn and fight self-pity with the same "ferociousness and fierceness." That's the enduring lesson.[3]

This sin battle for men refutes the male/female, rational/emotional dichotomy. For example, in 1 Samuel 25, Abigail "is clearly more cool-headed and rational in dealing with David than her idiot husband, Nabal, whose very name means *fool*, and who pouts his way emotionally into the grave." Or take Jezebel,

---

2   APJ 144: "What Advice Would You Give Newly Married John Piper?" (August 6, 2013).
3   APJ 220: "Make War against Pouting" (November 20, 2013).

who "had the ruthless, shrewd, cool rationality to trap the righteous Naboth in a plot to steal his vineyard so that her moping husband could get out of his self-pitying funk because he couldn't have some little property that he wanted."[4]

Seven years after Pastor John's leave, a man asked how to kill this impulse to be angry with his wife. How could he stop responding with shutting down, pouting, sulking, and giving her the silent treatment? These had been familiar patterns for Pastor John earlier in life, and his leave revealed his ongoing sin struggle with "selfishness, anger, self-pity, quickness to blame, and sullenness." The sin of self-pity "comes up when I feel wounded. Others can recognize in me that I want to be admired or pitied for my sense of being wounded or mistreated by someone. I want others to know it, recognize it, and feel sorry for me." Then comes sullenness or sulking, "the sinking discouragement, the moodiness, the hopelessness, the unresponsiveness, the withdrawn deadness of emotion." And "the effect on marriage is that my wife feels *blamed* and *disapproved of* rather than *cherished* and *cared for*. Tender emotions start to die, hope is depleted, strength to carry on in the hardships of ministry wanes. That's my diagnosis."

The sin of sulking must be dealt with. Christ breaks the power of canceled sin, as the old hymn puts it. "The cross cancels sins by faith for all who believe in Jesus." Only in Christ do we have the hope and power to defeat our sin. So we attack it.

Pastor John's war on self-pity took a decisive turn one cold Sunday evening. "It was cozy; and snowy outside. Noël, Talitha, and I were at home alone. I was looking forward to something we could do together. I had this expectation—and you know how discouragements and anger come from shattered expectations. Talitha comes in from the dining room and says, 'Mommy and I are going to watch *Supernanny* on the computer.' They set it up on a stool, and they sit on the love seat together and start watching it. They don't even say anything to me. They don't ask. They don't explain. They don't propose anything else. I feel like poor little John Piper. I feel shut out, ignored. Now, at that moment, the old John Piper feels an enormous temptation to anger, self-pity, blaming, sullenness." Instead, he went upstairs to his study and made war. There "I turned my mind, and my heart—by the power of God in his Spirit—toward the promises of God, and the surety of the cross, and the love of my Father, and the wealth of my inheritance, and the blessing of that Lord's Day, which he had poured out earlier that morning, and the patience of Christ, and the fact that my wife and daughter in their own minds were not snubbing me. I held those truths before my eyes, and I beat down the anger, self-pity, blaming, and sullenness. I beat it down and beat it down until it

---

4 APJ 1181: "Does the Bible Portray Women as Emotional and Men as Rational?" (April 6, 2018).

died. Later that night, I went downstairs, and I mentioned to Noël—in a way I never would've been able to before, without any subtle innuendo and in a noncondemning tone, which was a miracle—that I was surprised we didn't do anything together. We just quietly worked it out. Compared to the way things used to go, it was an amazing victory." When self-pity arises, "reckon your sin canceled," then "carry" the sin "into a room somewhere" and "hammer on it for an hour by the promises of God."[5]

Self-pity—the "desire that others feel my woundedness and admire me for being so mistreated"—must die. And it can die if it's a "canceled sin." Sins canceled at the cross must then "be killed consciously with effort, by faith, in the Spirit—not coddled." In Christ's death, we died to sin (Rom. 6:2). As a result of dying to sin, we now put our sins to death (Rom. 8:13). And in Christ's death, we are forgiven. Now we are to forgive others (Eph. 4:32; Col. 3:13). "In other words, God intends for my sanctification to include conscious, willed opposition to specific sins in my life. I had applied that to sexual temptation, and I think with significant success over the last forty years or so. But for some reason, I failed to apply the same brutal intentionality of sin-killing to my selfishness and anger and self-pity and quickness to blame and sullenness."[6]

When we are hurt, or unappreciated, how do we respond?
Sulking plagues homes when parents don't celebrate the work of their children, when children don't thank mom for her daily sacrifices, when husbands and wives take each other for granted. "It's just a black hole—nobody notices; nobody says anything."

When we feel unappreciated, we need divine awareness (1 Pet. 2:19). We need to know that he knows (Matt. 6:4; Heb. 6:10). Every good thing you do "is kept in a book. It doesn't matter if nobody else in the world—children, spouses, parents, grandparents, colleagues, friends, roommates—never say a word; God writes it down." We can go to our rooms and pray to him, that "of all the audiences in the world that I would like to have, you're the most important. And I want to thank you that you have noticed and that you have approved. And I love you and I need you and I trust you. And would you grant me the grace now to be free from self-pity, to move on, and to love?'"

It boils down to God. "Remember God. Be conscious of God. Trust God. God will *reward you* for all the right things that you have done when nobody else knows them. And God will *avenge you* for all the wrong that has been done

---

5   APJ 1227: "Make War on Your Urge to Sulk" (July 23, 2018).
6   APJ 1501: "How Do I Wage War on My Self-Pity?" (July 20, 2020).

to you when nobody else knows them, so that now, if you believe this God, if he's real to you, if you are conscious of him, if you bank on him, then you can be done with self-pity. And I just invite you—I *plead* with you—leave the yoke and the burden of life-ruining self-pity" behind. "Self-pity ruins life. You can't see anything. You can't see beauty. You can't see people. You can't do anything wholesome or feel large feelings." There's "nothing noble" coming from a life that grumbles and seeks revenge.[7]

God will avenge every wrong done to you. Considering our eternal joy forever, we are called to repay evil with good and blessing (Luke 6:27; 1 Cor. 4:12–13; 1 Pet. 3:9). Where do we find the "emotional resources" for this? "We must have Christ to have resources to respond encouragingly and hopefully and wisely to the one who wronged us, instead of angrily, or with self-pity, or whining, or manipulative moping, or the silent treatment, or solemnness. You can hear my acquaintance with my sin. This is the great miracle that the children of God—John Piper, anyway—want to experience."[8]

Self-pity at work and in the ministry

Self-pity destroys homes. But it rears its head in our jobs too. "Are you ever tempted to feel sorry for yourself at work, to lick your own wounds because someone spoke evil of you, or you got passed over for a promotion? The Bible is shot through with dynamics of life that help us deal with self-pity" (1 Cor. 1:27; 2 Cor. 12:10).[9]

The sin rears its sulking head in ministry too, especially if we feel a lack of gifting. Instead of being insecure about our weaknesses, we should be content with them, because our weaknesses magnify the power of God (2 Cor. 12:7–10). "I quit teaching college in part because I knew I could never be a great scholar. I read too slowly. I remember too little. And I often was sad about that and self-pitying about that, which was sin." But God displays his strength in our weakness. So Piper reminds himself: "Okay, I fail at reading fast. I fail at re-membering a lot. So what should I do? I should ask God to maximize who I am in this weakness for your glory." Instead, he would analyze small portions of Scripture deeply, "dig riches out" from those texts, and proclaim them. "And people have gotten help from my limited ability, because I have made myself look at small chunks of literature instead of big chunks of literature, like whole books that I haven't had time to read."[10]

7 APJ 1520: "I Feel Unappreciated—How Should I Respond?" (September 2, 2020).
8 APJ 1184: "Have I Really Forgiven Someone If I Keep Remembering Their Wrong?" (April 13, 2018).
9 APJ 434: "Should I Read My Bible Daily?" (September 22, 2014).
10 APJ 344: "How Should I Think about My Failures?" (May 19, 2014).

Self-pity also disrupts our communion with God. Jesus warned "against a kind of self-pity when we make sacrifices for him." After Jesus sent off the rich young ruler who loved this world too much, Peter said: "See, we have left everything and followed you" (Mark 10:28). In other words: "Jesus, we have made some sacrifices here." And Jesus's response to Peter is "amazing." He says, "There is no one who has left house or brothers or sisters or mother or father or children or lands, for my sake and for the gospel, who will not receive a *hundredfold* now in this time, houses and brothers and sisters and mothers and children and lands, with persecutions, and in the age to come eternal life" (Mark 10:29–30). The point: "Peter, come on! Do you really think that in the sacrifices you have made, you struck a bad deal that should cause your self-pity? You have exchanged *one house* for *hundreds*." That's not a bad trade. That's "pure Christian Hedonism" on display.[11]

11   APJ 998: "Was Jesus a Christian Hedonist?" (February 3, 2017).

On Cussing, Lying, and Gossip

On cussing

Christians are called to high standards with the words we speak. On the tongue's use and misuse of words, four general principles guide us.

1. Don't misuse weighty words. Weighty words include: *God, Jesus Christ, damn,* and *hell.* Employing God's name in vain is clearly forbidden (Exod. 20:7; Deut. 5:11). "We don't take the words seriously when we use *God* as a throwaway word, or *Jesus Christ* as a word for when I just hit my finger or something terrible just happened, or *damn* as a swear word, or *hell* as a throwaway swear word. The problem with all those words is that they take things that are unbelievably important and serious, and they turn them into moments of smallness." Don't belittle solemn words.

2. Don't use vulgar words. Whole lexicons of "crude, crass, vulgar, and indecent" words don't emerge from nowhere. They're invented because "every culture has something that they view as offensive, off-color, or rude." And Paul tells us that love is not *rude*—it's not *unseemly* (1 Cor. 13:4–5). Paul forbids Christians from using a vocabulary that employs words that the culture would recognize as dishonorable, disgraceful, and indecent. If there was any question, Paul makes the point very clear: "Let there be no filthiness nor foolish talk nor crude joking, which are out of place"—instead, "let there be thanksgiving" (Eph. 5:4).

3. Speak thanks. It's not enough to *not* use crude language. Paul wants us to voice thanks (Eph. 5:4). "Paul thought if your heart is right and brimming with gratitude to God in all things, there will be a monitor on the kind of crudeness that comes out of your mouth. People that tend to use a lot of four-letter words, a lot of scatological talk, a lot of harsh, crude, rough, and crass talk, are generally sounding pretty angry. They are not content. They are not happy in Jesus. Something is out of whack in their heart." Crudeness is the sludge that accrues when the fountain of Godward thanks dries up.

4. Speak grace. Instead of corrupting talk, we speak grace to others (Eph. 4:29). Gratitude works to wash away crude language, but Paul pushes us to consider whether our words are *good* for people. Do my words make others stronger? And do my words "make Christ more beautiful in their eyes?"[1]

Can Christians cuss to prove a point?

In 2009, then Christian and singer-songwriter Derek Webb released a song about the AIDS epidemic with the *s*-word in the lyrics, bait to rile conservative Christians about the cuss word so the conversation could be spun. What makes a Christian angrier? A four-letter word or fifty thousand people dying of AIDS daily? So can Christians cuss to prove a point?

Webb's profanity pioneered nothing. The use of "crude or offensive language to upset an audience and then to spank them that they are more upset by the language than the injustice that was being lamented" is as old as it is "manipulative." To those who use this approach, ask: "'Would you approve of addressing a crowd of liberal-leaning Christians by referring to the sinfulness of being a practicing f*g or q***r?' Then, when they get really furious over that language—which they should—you say, 'See, you are much more worried about being politically correct than you are about the fact that this really is a sin that sends people to hell.'" Equally so, such language "is utterly out of place and unnecessarily demeaning."

On language, the New Testament delivers three important texts, and none condemn specific *words* (1 Cor. 13:4–5; Eph. 4:29; 5:4). They forbid *categories*, including "corrupting talk, filthiness, obscene talk, and rudeness, or unseemly behavior." These terms are used to distinguish acceptable words from words that flaunt a culture's social and moral standards for obscenity. So a Christian ethic of the tongue "is not derived from finding a list of God-*approved* words and God-*unapproved* words." Our speech is governed by these factors: "Does it build up in faith? Does it build a passion for Christ? Does it give grace to those who hear? Our vocabulary is a testimony to this way of thinking about language." And "my guess is that the people that are playing fast and loose with what is offensive, in using obscene or offensive language, would do well to rethink their habits."[2]

Related, Christians should use great discretion with satire and irony. Job, the prophets, Jesus, and Paul all used satire and irony to expose folly in people, who were "hardened" in error to the point that their hearts refused to respond

---

1   APJ 97: "On Cussing" (May 23, 2013).
2   APJ 260: "Can Christians Cuss to Prove a Point?" (January 21, 2014).

to simple exhortation. So "satire and irony are not going to be a Christian's *first* or *main* strategy of correction with people—not people we are trying to win, anyway." The use of sarcasm is blunted by other biblical texts (2 Tim. 2:24–25; James 3:17–18; 1 Pet. 3:8). So "in the rough-and-tumble world of truth-speaking, in a world of evil and folly, there will always be a place for irony and satire to do its work of exposing error and evil and folly. Nevertheless, I think the use of it is very limited in bearing the kind of fruit that love longs to see in transformed lives."[3]

Does profanity make us more culturally relevant?

Profanity doesn't make us more culturally relevant for three reasons.

1. Immorality is a bad strategy for improving the world. "Issues of moral character—that is, issues of biblical uprightness—are being subordinated to our strategies for how to make the world a better place." This principle is true in modern political candidates and true in the language of the church, revealing that "our trust has shifted from the power of God to work through the humility of holiness onto the power of our own cleverness, whether it be political shrewdness or cultural savvy." Such attempts at culture transformation are "hopelessly flawed." No matter how politically shrewd, profane means "will not bring the kingdom. It will not transform culture. It will not convict sinners. It will backfire and destroy the credibility of the Christian church." The strategy has been tried: become like the world to save the world. In the process you lose the gospel. In the church, you lose confidence in God's power, lose confidence in his word, and lose an "authentic thrill that our way is better" than the ways of the world. This vain attempt to appear cool before the world is destined to fail.

2. The world will not be impressed by our crudeness. "According to the New Testament, what will get the attention of the world and penetrate possibly to the inner recesses of their heart is not *cultural similarity with the world* but *sacrificial service to the world*." It isn't "risqué language that will waken the dead, but radical love" (Matt. 5:16).

3. Filthy language is simply unfitting. God doesn't want us to use crude jokes, which are out of place or "unseemly" (ἀνῆκεν; Eph. 5:3–4). So Christians don't simply avoid repeating a list of bleep-able words. No. "We discern what is *suitable* and *fitting* in a hundred situations." The "alternative to the crude, vulgar language that Paul mentions is not *clean language* but *thanksgiving*." Crude language exposes a "gratitude deficiency" in the heart. So Paul's call on

---

3   APJ 1015: "When Should Christians Use Satire?" (March 15, 2017).

the Christian life is not so simple as avoiding vulgar words. Our call is to "fill your mouth with Christ-exalting truth and overflowing, humble thankfulness. Pursue the very good works that Jesus says have a much better chance of impressing the world than if we would just adopt a little bit of their language, which they themselves know is cheap."[4]

But what about soft cussing?
So is it wrong for Christians, even preachers, to use words like: *shoot, crud, dang, crap,* and *friggin'*—softer cuss words?

In defense of strong language, Paul used scatological or garbage language— "dung" (σκύβαλον)—to speak of his former life of legalism (Phil. 3:8). Some Christians would liken this to the *s*-word. And Paul called false teachers "dogs" (Phil. 3:2). To false teachers advocating circumcision, he suggested that they *castrate* themselves (Gal. 5:12). Even Christ called false teachers a "brood of vipers" (Matt. 23:33). There's a category for using "very severe" language "with adversaries of the Christian faith" or false teachers. "So I will not say there is an absolute prohibition of using severe, cutting, aggravating, edgy language in some situations of conflict where huge and deadly things are at stake." But Paul and Jesus used these words seriously, never in a cavalier, joking, trendy, trying-to-be-cool way—unlike how they get used today.

In opposition to strong language in the pulpit, and against pastors "who seem to go out of their way to flaunt coarse, rude, dirty, questionable language," we go to Ephesians 5:3–5. Verses 3 and 5 warn of the physical, sexual sins that condemn. Sandwiched between them is verse 4, a key text on language. So "it is not just what you do with your groin or your heart, but with your tongue or your mouth as well. If it is wrong *to do* sexual things, he is saying, it is wrong to be cavalier and course *in verbalizing* those very things. There are a lot of things people are willing to take on their mouths that they would not take in their hands—and they wouldn't take into their lives." So, for example, "recently I heard a young leader say—and pardon me here—to hundreds of Christians in a joking way about someone who had criticized him the day before: 'Screw you.' And he laughed. I mean everybody laughed. Everybody laughed! Almost everybody. I didn't." Don't say with your mouth what you shouldn't act out physically. "And I would apply the same principle to bathroom language that you would never take in your hand—or *hell* or *damn*, which you would never actually apply to anybody." So "a *pure heart* and *pure hands* should be accompanied by a *pure tongue*. I think that is the point of verse 4."

---

4   APJ 1187: "Will Profanity Make Us More Relevant in Reaching Our Culture?" (April 20, 2018).

The tongue is governed not by compliance with right/wrong and good/bad words. It's governed by categories of what is proper/improper and out of place/ in place. Love is not *unseemly* (ἀσχημονέω; 1 Cor. 13:5). In the world's evil, don't get experienced with it (1 Cor. 14:20). Be a baby in evil. You don't need to adopt the culture's shows, movies, and language. Don't let a fear of prudish puritanism push you into embracing vulgar language. Instead, "honor commonly accepted standards, because it is humble and not self-asserting."[5]

When jokes go crude

Paul contrasts filthiness, foolish talk, and crude joking with thankful speech (Eph. 5:4). "And I think the reason thankfulness is given as an alternative to crude joking and filthiness is a heart that is humble enough to recognize that everything is a gift. And full of thanksgiving to God is the kind of heart that just doesn't get ugly." Humble thanks "cleans up the mouth." We seek to build others up—our "criterion" for everything we say, even our jokes (Eph. 4:29).

So does my wit build up or tear down? Here are five ways that jokes tear down. (1) The joke is corrupting and dirty. (2) The joke is ill-timed and doesn't fit the occasion. (3) The joke is egocentric, trying to be clever and nothing else. (4) The joke is a demeaning put-down, making fun of a group or nationality or ethnicity. (5) The joke is "relentlessly superficial," from a person only trying to be witty.

Yet this list "leaves wide open that there is humor that does none of those negative things, but is full of grace and well-timed and produces a healthy cascade of laughter." There's a laughter that breaks out in sheer joy at God's goodness (Ps. 126:1–2). But there's also a "belly-shaking humor" that "just happens" in life. It happened once in a sermon. "I was using an illustration of, 'Come on, everybody. You want to be a dolphin, right? You want to cut against the currents of culture, and you don't want to be a jellyfish. Who in the world wants to be a jellyfish?!' And a little girl right in the third row raised her hand. 'I want to be a jellyfish!' Everybody simply roared. I could hardly contain myself I was laughing so hard right in the middle of a very important point." Humor just happens.

In the words of Spurgeon: "We must conquer—some of us especially—our tendency to levity. A great distinction exists between holy cheerfulness, which is a virtue, and that general levity, which is a vice. There is a levity which has not enough heart to laugh, but trifles with everything; it is flippant, hollow, unreal. A hearty laugh is no more levity than a hearty cry." So, says Piper, "there is a difference between robust humor in the soul of a saint who is manifestly

5   APJ 640: "What about Soft Cussing?" (July 15, 2015).

taking God with great seriousness and *levity*—that is the negative word—*levity* in the mouth of a resident clown, who can't seem to be serious about anything."

"Humor and laughter in their most natural and healthy forms are spontaneous, not contrived, not planned. Therefore, the challenge in life, as in so many other traits, is to become a joyfully, holy, seriously happy, God-centered, Christ-exalting, Bible-saturated person so that, out of the abundance of the heart, the mouth laughs."[6]

Am I holy or a hypocrite for stopping hurtful words from exiting my mouth?

So out of the abundance of the heart, the mouth speaks (Matt. 12:34). Rude and hurtful words overflow from a rude and hurtful heart. But we're also commanded to *guard* what comes out of our mouths (Ps. 141:3). We face a problem in this pair of texts. "If I am about to say something hurtful, lewd, or unkind because my heart is producing it, and I catch it at my teeth and don't say it"—doesn't that make me a hypocrite? If the heart produced a hurtful thought, isn't stopping the words too late? Hasn't the sin been committed? Or are the hushed words an act of virtue?

Muting the tongue is a virtue of its own. The same heart "is not only *producing that ugly thought* on the way to becoming a word, but that same heart—we have only one heart—is also *producing the hatred* of what it just produced." So we fight for holy tongues on two levels: (1) at the root, with heart transformation, and (2) when that fails, by blocking the hurtful words with zipped lips—a less-than-ideal but still virtuous failsafe.[7]

On gossip

Gossip is ugly for the hurt it inflicts on others, damaging reputations, relationships, and communities. Its ugliness is evident by its companion sins (Rom. 1:29; 2 Cor. 12:20). But gossip is also "the kind of thing that you just fall into when you don't have anything better to do" (1 Tim. 5:12–13).

So what is gossip? (1) It's an unredemptive spirit "more bent on hurting than helping," a pleasure derived from sharing "negative news." (2) It's an intrusion

---

6   APJ 907: "When Does Humor Become Sinful?" (July 28, 2016). For more on the dolphin/jellyfish contrast between those who "cut a path against the current" and those who "float in the current of culture," see APJ 683: "How to Engage Culture and Swim against It" (September 11, 2015) and APJ 1141: "Deep Bible Reading Strategies for the Tired and Busy" (January 3, 2018). Quote from C. H. Spurgeon, *The Sword and Trowel: 1874* (London: Passmore & Alabaster, 1874), 78.

7   APJ 221: "Has My Heart Sinned Even If I Stop Words from Exiting My Mouth?" (November 21, 2013).

into the lives of others. (3) It's motivated by self-promotion. Gossip is a pride that savors knowing something that others don't. "And the remedy for that kind of gossip is *love*—*love* for the person, *love* for the church and her unity, *love* for Jesus whose fellowship is sweet enough. So you don't need to have all the titillation that comes from these unclean pleasures of spreading negative information." Which means that "gossip is not limited to false statements" and can include "spreading true information"—information that is "almost always negative." So "the fact that you are telling the truth doesn't mean you are not gossiping."[8]

When you discover someone's sin, you should make "a real effort not to tell anybody else what you have just seen or found in a person." Go to the person directly (Matt. 18:15).[9]

Show care in how you speak of others (James 4:11) so that gossip and arrogance and conceit do not take root inside the church (2 Cor. 12:20). "I think part of the reason these texts are in the Bible is to warn us that we are so prone to speak about others when *our own attitude* is the real problem. We need to know *ourselves* really well so that we don't even share the things we have permission to share if our motives are impure or if we feel jealousy or undue anger or sinful fear and anxiety or revenge or just the subtle pleasure—we all know this—of sharing news, especially bad news or questionable news, that nobody else knows about but us."[10]

To gossip is to "whisper" (Rom. 1:29; 2 Cor. 12:20). The whisperer's words are like candy—"the person who *speaks them* has eaten them with relish, and now, the person who's *listening* and who's *hearing* is eating them with relish" (Prov. 26:22). Gossip is addictive because we are "one of the first people to hear some juicy piece of news about someone. We can hardly wait to let others know that we're 'in the know.' We've heard the news, and we might be the first one who could tell somebody else about it." *Hard* gossip tears others down by intent. *Soft* gossip tears others down inadvertently. Both are delicious to the sinful heart. The sweetness of gossip is the conceit it expresses, feeding our pride, "which is endlessly hungry." So "in the chain of gossip" you claim "center stage for a moment. *You* got the news. *You* give the news. Aren't *you* something!"

Avoiding gossip calls us to cultivate three spiritual characteristics. (1) Humility that doesn't seek prominence. Cultivate "a deep, humble contentment in God, and you don't need to feed your craving ego with delicious morsels of being the first to hear and the first to tell the juicy bit of gossip." (2) Love that does no harm (Prov. 17:9; 26:20). By dying to "the pride that craves prominence"

---

8   APJ 159: "What Is Gossip?" (August 27, 2013).
9   APJ 642: "Should My Spouse Talk to Others about Our Marriage Struggles?" (July 17, 2015).
10 APJ 873: "How Can I Share Conflicts with My Spouse without Gossiping?" (June 3, 2016).

and dying to "the delicious pleasure of hearing and telling news that may stoke the fires of quarreling or dissension, you are acting in love." (3) A life purpose that is not aimless. Gossipers are idle busybodies who lack vision (1 Tim. 5:13). "Sandwiched between *emptiness* and *aimlessness* on one side (idlers) and *intrusiveness* on the other side (busybodies) is gossip."

So when given the chance to share news about others, ask three questions. (1) Am I motivated by sinful pride? (2) Am I sharing to hurt someone? (3) Is the "sharing of this information part of my large-hearted purposefulness in life, or simply an echo of how empty and aimless I really am?"[11]

On compulsive lying

People lie for many reasons. But like gossip, compulsive lying is an attempt to get attention. We "exaggerate" and serve up "untruths" to impress others. We crave attention to gain human approval. To fight this, start with a foundational truth about who you are in Christ. "You, as a believer, have God's attention, God's adoption, God's delight, God's assistance and promise, God's commitment, and you will one day have his complete acceptance into a flawless heaven. You have that in Jesus Christ, and that is superior in its preciousness to any approval that man could give you." There's no comparison between God's approval and the approval you desire from impressing your peers. In our new birth, the Holy Spirit changes our heart to "love the approval of God" (Rom. 2:29).

The craving for approval led to jealousy among the teachers in Corinth (1 Cor. 3:21–23). And Paul "pulled the plug" on that favoritism by reminding the Christians that everything in the universe is theirs by future inheritance. This is what happens with the fear of being slandered too. Even when people say false things against you, you don't need to self-defend because you have an unspeakably great inheritance (Matt. 5:11–12). So "if God promises to give you all things with Christ, you have no need to fear the slander of men anymore. You should be the freest of all people with your contentment in God." You no longer have to gossip, slander, or lie to make yourself look better.[12]

11   APJ 1119: "Why Does Gossip Feel So Good?" (November 13, 2017).
12   APJ 141: "Help! I'm Addicted to Lying" (August 1, 2013).

On Dating, Romance Idols, and Fornication

Should teens date?

Is it foolish to date in high school? Or could it lead to a satisfying marriage among "high school sweethearts"?

In previous generations, teenagers were expected to marry, and social structures around them anticipated and supported young marriages. Today the social structures are different—but the relational energies remain. "One of the most powerful forces in human life is the awakening of a peculiar happiness and desire that comes from being liked by a person of the opposite sex." This power is strong enough to cause Christians to lose their moral and spiritual grounding. "It's a frightening power to watch because of how blinding it is to wisdom, Scripture, and Christ, and how it has such long-term implications. It's a kind of *moral insanity*, I feel sometimes. This is true for people in their twenties and thirties and forties. So I don't assume that teenagers are any more equipped in their maturity and life experience to encounter that kind of power and risk."

So what's dating for? The practice is included in a stream that is moving toward an end. A man and woman begin hanging out and attending movies and events together. A special commitment to *this* person emerges. Such commitment is "absolutely natural," good, inevitable, and is "how relationships move from *acquaintance* to *dating* to *engagement* to *marriage*. It's normal, not evil." It's like a flowing river. "The question becomes, 'Is it wise for a sixteen-year-old to step into that river that flows toward marriage?' My answer is *no*, I don't think it is wise," with the exception of remarkably mature sixteen-year-olds moving toward a marriage at eighteen. In the end, "it's a wonderful thing to fall in love. What makes it so great is that God has blessed it with an appointed and thrilling consummation called 'marriage.' If you turn that process into a high school pastime with revolving relationships, you are robbing yourself of the very best you can have."[1]

Patience in a culture marrying later

On the other end of the spectrum, Christian adults are waiting for marriage longer than ever before. College and careers are postponing nuptials. What can be said, particularly to women forced to wait longer than expected?

"God is sovereign over your life, and God is good." To his children, "we have it on God's authority that he will withhold from you no good thing" (Ps. 84:11). In the waiting, meditate on two Bible stories. Marriage came to Ruth unexpectedly. And Anna was a woman married for seven years and then widowed for sixty more (Luke 2:36–37). "God is able to stun you with a Boaz out of nowhere, and he is able to keep you chaste and fruitful and happily unmarried until you are eighty-four." For now, focus on four priorities. (1) Don't settle for a non-Christian husband. (2) Stay involved in your local church. (3) "Find your joy in knowing Jesus and serving others. Marriage is not the greatest good. Faithfulness to Christ and his people around you is the greatest good." (4) And then pray. "Tell the Lord your heart's desire," as you make him your supreme treasure.[2]

Is online dating okay?

How you find a spouse is of less importance than *that* you find a quality spouse in the end. "The biblical issue here is not *how you meet*, but *whom you marry*." Refuse to settle for a marriage that is "minimally Christian." Go for the full-blooded model of Christian marriage set out in Ephesians 5:22–24. "What this means is a Christian woman won't look for a man who just has a cross tattooed on his shoulder, but a man who is ready to die daily in the sacrificial calling of leading a home." To find such a spouse, social media and apps can be a great resource. In fact, if you know what you're looking for in a spouse, you can "rule out a lot of losers by using the internet. It won't take long to learn from Facebook and Twitter and blogs if this man or woman is passionate for Jesus or if Jesus is an incidental mark on the shoulder or a trinket around the neck."

Online dating apps are a growing venue for Christians to meet other Christians. "I have recently met numerous couples who said they met online, and they are happily married. They are mature Christians. I have zero problem with that. The great question is this: Are you mature enough to discern a worthy spouse? Put your energies into becoming that kind of person."[3]

---

1   APJ 1101: "Is It Harmful to Date in High School?" (October 2, 2017).
2   APJ 1167: "Christians Are Marrying Later—How Do I Wait in Faith?" (March 5, 2018).
3   APJ 405: "Is Online Dating Good for Christians?" (August 12, 2014).

How do I break free from the buzz of serial dating?

With the arrival of the smartphone, localized online dating has become a primary means for couples to meet. By itself, an online dating app is a useful tool for single Christians (above). But the broader phenomenon also breeds hookup culture, makes local, casual sex more accessible, and feeds the flattery and sinful euphoria of serial dating. Can God's pleasures compete with this buzz?

The Bible doesn't address *serial dating*, but it does address *serial marriage* (John 4:1–45). Jesus meets the woman at the well who is seeking physical water, H_2O. "She knows the pleasure of water when she's physically thirsty. In fact, it would be fair to say that if she had gone without physical water for two or three days, she would have given anything for the physical feel of a cup of water on her tongue." Physical thirst is a potent, "God-given impulse of physical pleasure to keep us alive," akin to how sexual desires serve procreation. "God is very generous with his pleasures."

Yes, but such generosity with our natural appetites and pleasures also creates a problem for sinners like us. Physical pleasures become so potent that they lead us to assume this *one pleasure* is the *only pleasure* I need. And in that situation, unless God disrupts our lives with a divine miracle inside of us, these physical pleasures will make it "impossible" to "taste any kind of pleasure other than natural, physical pleasure." Our physical appetites become so dominant that we find it impossible to believe there are more enduring pleasures than the *one fleeting pleasure* we seek *right now*! Jesus knows it, so he confronts this woman's serial marriage addiction with a "truth bomb" meant to "blow out the walls of her limited pleasure." The woman, on lover number six, has centered her life on the wrong pleasures. She needed an awakened appetite—a new taste—for eternal pleasures.

So, no, Christ cannot match the immediate, sinful ecstasy of serial dating or serial marriage or casual hookup culture. But "what the Bible and Christian Hedonists offer is deeper, better, longer pleasures than the fleeting euphoria of sin." God's joys are future and eternal and superior to every immediate physical comfort in this life (Heb. 10:34). By faith he gives spiritual joys we sample now and the assurance of a feast of spiritual pleasures forevermore (Ps. 16:11; Heb. 11:1).

To serial daters, turn away from the "fleeting pleasures" of Egypt (Heb. 11:26) for the spring of pleasures in Christ that wells up eternally (John 4:14). Replace the subpar, shallow, and fleeting euphoria of serial dating with the pleasures of Jesus that will prove better, deeper, and endless. "Take whatever measure of spiritual pleasure he gives you in this life, and trust him for the rest of it in due time. I don't know how much he will give you in this life. But I do know that serial dating is a dead-end street." Make it your aim to pursue God and to find your eternal fill of joy in his presence (Ps. 16:11).[4]

The danger of idolizing romantic relationships

Given their power over us, romantic relationships can very easily become idols. An idol is "the thing *loved* or the person *loved* more than God—*wanted* more than God, *desired* more than God, *treasured* more than God, *enjoyed* more than God. It could be a girlfriend."[5]

Romantic attachments are potent enough to blind souls to Christ's glory (2 Cor. 4:4). "This is the most terrifying thing in the world to me, that people I love—or I myself—may be so blinded by the devil that they look at Jesus and he is not beautiful. He is not their treasure. Money is their treasure. Videos are their treasure. Making grades is their treasure. Their boyfriend is their treasure. . . . Death is not terrifying. To be so deceived that you can't see Jesus as the treasure of your life, that is the most terrifying thing."[6]

One listener asked about her serious relationship moving toward marriage. She feared that she was idolizing her boyfriend. How can this be avoided?

Instead of trying to define relationship idolatry, consider three constructive questions.

1. Can you say Christ is enough for your joy? In Christ, a Christian woman can say, "'Indeed, I count everything as loss'—boyfriend included—'because of the surpassing worth of knowing Christ Jesus my Lord'" (Phil. 3:8). Can she echo the biblical writer and say: "If I lost everything, even my boyfriend, God is enough for my everlasting joy"?

2. Does your current relationship exemplify Christ? Ephesians 5 sets the stage for our romantic relationships to *reflect* Christ, not *replace* him. "Now *that* deeply changes the way a man and a woman look at their relationship. It is not just about them. It is about *showing him, expressing him* and *his* covenant relationship to *his* bride and the church. Therefore, an intense love for a man by a woman or a woman by a man can and should be transposed into the music of a divine drama so that the intensity of the emotion for the person is not *in contrast* to emotion for Jesus, but *an expression* of emotion for Jesus." Does your romantic relationship drown out Christ or does it express your faith in Christ?

3. Is the relationship deepening your faith in Christ? "Are our lives marked by more passion for holiness because of what we are finding in each other? Is it strengthening or is it weakening our love for Christ?" If all this is true, if

4   APJ 1632: "A Better Promise for Serial Daters" (May 28, 2021).
5   APJ 410: "What Is Idolatry?" (August 19, 2014).
6   APJ 796: "The Christian's Great Vocation" (February 17, 2016).

Christ is enough, if Christ is demonstrated in your relationship, and if your faith is being built up, then "I think the Lord is keeping you from idolatry."[7]

No Christian is immune from this relationship idolatry. We can love a girlfriend or boyfriend too much. And we can love marriage, children, health, reputation, friendship, comfort, and security more than God. We are commanded not to covet (Exod. 20:17). "Covetousness means simply loving something too much, loving it the way you shouldn't love it—like loving a boyfriend, or your husband, or your health, or your life, in such a way that it starts to undermine your love for God."

God cares about us so much that he will use "whatever means" he must "to keep us from loving him less than something else." The point is demonstrated in 1 Peter 1:6–7. The faith of God's children is so precious to him that "he will use fire to refine it so that dross is burned out of it, and it comes through like refined gold to the praise of glory at the end of our lives." Our fight against idols is not purely on us. "God will keep his children absolutely secure" by using "whatever means he must to prevent us from idolatry: from loving anything more than we love him—and thus making shipwreck of our faith—if we are indeed his children." And he gives us means to this end too. God's word exposes our motives as it pierces our hearts (Heb. 4:12). Stay close to the word, and your idols will be made clear. And ask yourself: Does your allegiance to your girlfriend make you a better Christian or a worse Christian? Because in the end, the greatest gift of love you can give your future spouse is to learn to love God above her.[8]

Is jealousy good or bad in dating?

Given the high-strung emotions that accompany dating, jealousy is common. Is it good or bad to have these possessive emotions?

First, we distinguish between *good* jealousy and *bad* jealousy. God himself is jealous (Exod. 20:5; 34:14). Likewise, "there should be a joy within us when affections that belong to God are flowing to God. There should also be indignation in us when affections that belong to God are flowing to something other than God. That's jealousy; that's *good jealousy* that we share with God." We should jealously avoid relationship idolatry. And there's a good jealousy in our relationships too, in a "joyful desire to receive the affections from another person that really belong to you." For example, it would be entirely appropriate for an engaged man to feel jealous if his fiancée decided to date another man.

7 APJ 814: "Is My Dating Relationship Idolatrous?" (March 14, 2016).
8 APJ 1537: "How Can I Love God More Than My Boyfriend?" (October 12, 2020).

But jealousy becomes sinful when it manifests our fear and pride. Bad jealousy "has an inappropriate need for too much attention from the beloved because of an insecurity and fear and unwillingness to trust God to take care of the beloved and provide for our needs." Or jealousy becomes bad when it comes from pride, particularly when "you feel jealous because you want to look like you're the only person the beloved spends time with." You dominate her time, and prevent her from investing in other people, in family, or in friends. Instead, "you want her to act like you are the only thing that matters. Well, that's just sick. That's not healthy." It's an unloving jealousy rooted in self-centered pride.

A healthy relationship will demonstrate "a peaceful confidence in God for your own identity and security so that you have a wonderful, free, loving disposition to allow your beloved to have appropriate relationships besides the one he or she has with you, and to have appropriate emotions toward family and friends that don't at all compromise his or her affections for you."[9]

Speaking of God's good jealousy: "The jealousy of God is the measure of his zeal for our happiness in him. His anger at our spiritual adultery—at our having other lovers besides him—is a reflex of his zeal for his own worth, but also a reflex of his zeal for our joy." Hence, the link with dating. This good jealousy drove Paul "as an apostolic cupid, so to speak, bringing people into this relationship with Jesus" (2 Cor. 11:2).[10]

How do I know if my girlfriend is toxically codependent?

Following up on the jealousy conversation, a boyfriend worries that his girlfriend is becoming too dependent on him. She's obsessive, spending less and less time with family and friends. He's becoming her sole focus in life, and it seems unhealthy. Should he proceed with this relationship?

Ask five honest questions. (1) Is Jesus most precious to your girlfriend? It's the most important question. "Can you detect that you are number two in her life, not number one? Can you discern that she would rejoice to be number two in your life, not number one? If the supremacy of Christ is not firmly in place, nothing else in the relationship will be properly in place" (Phil. 3:7–8). (2) Does Christ steady your girlfriend's life? "Has Christ become so hope-giving and so stabilizing and so satisfying for her that you can see whether he is her strength and her identity and her stability" when life is good and when life is tough (Phil. 4:11–13)? (3) Does your girlfriend *honor* you or *use* you? We were made to need other people. Relational neediness "is not unchristian," but it

9 APJ 1177: "Dating: Good Jealousy and Bad" (March 28, 2018).
10 APJ 1902: "How Could God Be Jealous?" (February 17, 2023).

calls for a weird neediness that seeks to confer honor. So does your girlfriend have the commitment, not to consume you with her neediness, but to honor you in her need? This is the "very unusual kind" of need we should have for others (1 Cor. 12:21–26). (4) Does your girlfriend demonstrate toughness in Christ? Does she have "the inner composure and resilience so that her joy in Christ is not ruined if she is rejected by other people?" Christ's promises deliver this stability (Luke 6:22–23; 1 Cor. 4:12–13). Or, in relational conflict, is she "emotionally incapacitated?" (5) Does your girlfriend rejoice amidst sorrows? Is there any "track record of the paradoxical Christian experience" of being sorrowful and yet rejoicing (2 Cor. 6:10)? Is she composed by God's joy under the waves of sorrow in life?

No sinner satisfies all these questions perfectly, "but a person who is truly born of God knows some measure of these things." In these five questions you can discern "whether the emotional and relational dependence in a dating relationship is dysfunctional or unhealthy or codependent."[11]

Is it sinful to date non-Christians?

First, any relationship that expresses a desire for another person more than God is coveting. "You can date a *Christian* and be sinning. Or you can date a *non-Christian* and be sinning because your affections or your love or your need for that person might reflect that God doesn't have a place in your life nearly as big and powerful and satisfying and beautiful as he ought to have. If you have a felt need for companionship that is greater than your felt need for God, then you are sinning." And "if you are pursuing an unbeliever with a view to awakening, quickening, and deepening a romantic relationship that could lead to marriage, you are compromising your love for Christ, you are going against what the Bible says, and you are doing something wrong." The Bible is very clear: Christians are to marry only in the Lord. "If you are on a trajectory to fall in love with and marry a woman who is outside the Lord, you're on a trajectory to disobey this text" (1 Cor. 7:39). And "there can't be any deep union of soul if two people have different supreme treasures" (2 Cor. 6:14). "So to pursue a dating relationship, cultivating a relationship that would lead to a forbidden marriage, is, I think, forbidden."[12]

Again, the key is to not compromise what you are looking for in a spouse. "What saddens me is how many believers get so entangled emotionally with unbelievers that they either throw away their convictions or they stand on their

---

11 APJ 1647: "On Codependent Dating Relationships" (July 2, 2021).
12 APJ 175: "Is It Sinful to Date a Non-Christian?" (September 17, 2013).

heads to see the other person as a believer when he or she is not." A Christian woman "won't look for a man who just has a cross tattooed on his shoulder, but for a man who is ready to die daily in the sacrificial calling of leading a home." And a Christian man "won't look for a woman who just wears a cross around her neck, but one who is willing to die as she submits to his leadership in reliance upon Christ."[13]

Marriage requires two people with some level of personal assurance. Paul's words are definitive: "in the Lord" (1 Cor. 7:39). To a woman dating a man who lacks any assurance of salvation: "Don't marry him in this condition. You need good assurances that he is your soulmate at the most important level of existence. Is he in Christ like you are in Christ? Is he born again? Is he a child of God? Does he live under God's authority?"[14]

A Christian who deliberately marries a non-Christian does not annul their covenant. The marriage vow holds. But the sinning Christian should be confronted by pastors with the aim of producing "authentic remorse and regret" for this defiance against God (1 Cor. 7:39), an admission that "the heart was not right in putting man above Christ in the affections" and with an apology and "sorrow for spurning the counsel of God's leaders in the church."[15]

Can a White woman marry a Black man?

One of the earliest viral episodes in the history of the podcast came as a shock over a question I assumed was long ago settled. Can a White woman date and marry a Black man? The question came from the woman.

In sum, Christian women are given "two basic restrictions" on marriage: marry a man, and a man who loves Christ (1 Cor. 7:39). Interracial marriage was largely forbidden in the Old Testament, a stipulation that was "religiously motivated, not racially motivated." But interracial marriage is also evident in the Old Testament. Moses, for example, married a Cushite, "and everybody agrees that the Cushites are black Africans" (Num. 12:1). Now, in Christ, God's people are comprised of Jew and Gentile and every ethnicity on the planet. That's our new tribe. "Marry in your tribe, namely, the tribe *Christian*—across any ethnic or racial lines—but marry in the tribe of this new tribe" headed by Christ.

This point was made memorable for the Pipers at Urbana in 1967, where they heard a missionary get asked on stage, "Aren't you worried if you minister in Pakistan for many years that your daughters will end up marring Pakistani

---

13 APJ 405: "Is Online Dating Good for Christians?" (August 12, 2014).

14 APJ 909: "Should I Pursue Marriage If I Doubt My Salvation?" (August 1, 2016).

15 APJ 1560: "Christian Marries Non-Christian—How Does a Church Respond?" (December 11, 2020).

men?" To which the missionary responded: "Better a believing Pakistani farmer than a rich, unbelieving, American banker." Decades later, Piper recalled this moment. "It sank into me that, *yes*, that's exactly the right answer. Of course it matters who she marries. She must marry a Christ-lover, a Christ-follower. And if it's a Pakistani, praise God. But don't marry a rich, White, American banker if he's not a believer." And don't settle for "a marginally Christian man." And whoever you marry, expect challenges and stresses because "every marriage is a cross-cultural marriage."[16]

In a later question over interracial marriage, this time from a man, it became clear that Piper's position was long in developing. His opposition to interracial marriage as a teenager was the "conscious foundation" of his opposition to integration in South Carolina. "And I think it was the origin of most of my deplorable attitudes toward other races in those days. I wasn't just *taught* that it was a sin; I *believed* it was a sin. So I don't take this struggle lightly, and I very much would love to persuade this young man that, biblically, his conscience should be clear in marrying a godly, Christ-exalting, otherwise compatible woman—whatever race she is."

Consciences are cleared by four biblical observations. (1) Everyone's heritage traces back to Adam and Eve, and we all belong to a single human race (Gen. 1:27; Acts 17:26). "Being human, in God's image, compared to any racial distinction, is ten million to one in terms of importance." (2) Christ is creating a new humanity, the Christian race (1 Pet. 2:9–10). Ethnic background is no impediment (Col. 3:11). "So in the old humanity, the decisive factor in human unity was being created in the image of God. In the new humanity, the decisive factor in human unity is that Christ is all and in all." (3) The Bible forbids Christians from marrying non-Christians but makes no such prohibition with different ethnic groups (1 Cor. 7:39). Paul here echoes the core concern in the Old Testament. "The issue back then was not race. The issue was faith, religion, and allegiance to the true God, Yahweh" (Deut. 7:3–4). (4) Again, Moses's marriage to a Cushite woman is illustrative. When Moses's sister Miriam took issue with the marriage, she was struck with leprosy, and her hand became bleach-white, which seems to carry stark connotations of skin tone. "God is not pleased with Miriam's criticism of Moses's marriage to a Black woman, and there is no other criticism of it."

For these reasons, and many others, "it is right to not simply *permit* or *tolerate*, but to *celebrate* the marriage of a godly, Christ-exalting man and woman who are marrying in the Lord across racial lines."[17]

16 APJ 98: "Can a White Woman Marry a Black Man?" (May 24, 2013).
17 APJ 966: "Should We Encourage Interracial Marriage?" (November 21, 2016).

Should we marry *before* or *after* we reach financial stability?
Among a couple who loves Christ, in a relationship applauded by family and the local church, and who are honoring sexual boundaries, should they wait to marry until the man provides financial support?

In general, take the risk and trust God. But two cautions. Is the man on a trajectory to eventually support his wife even if she works for a season? And, related, is he plagued by personal weaknesses that will undermine him when it's time to lead in making the income? The woman can ask, "Does my fiancé have character traits that are holding him back from finding the kind of employment that can support us? Is he lazy? Is he fearful? Is he distracted? Is he totally into sports and not yet grown up? Is he irresponsible with money?" These patterns would call for maturity and growth first. On the other hand, "if there is maturity, if there is deep love, if there is a community and family support, I would probably say, 'Go for it.' Two can live more cheaply together than apart. Marriage, at its best, is to help us through tough times, not something to be rejected because there are tough times."[18]

Simply put: "I am not a believer in long engagements. It seems to me that there is something, especially in our culture, that is unnatural and unwise when a couple knows that they are heading for marriage—and others have confirmed that wisdom—to keep putting it off for various practical reasons. It seems to me that, in general, if two single people can make a living and get along *on their own*, then they can probably make a living and get along *together*." In John's own engagement and marriage to Noël, they didn't have all the practical details worked out on the front end. "We decided that we would rather starve together than be comfortable alone."

So get practical, use a budget, and find ways to lower your living costs. "Your food is not going to cost any more than when you live together, depending on where you live now. You might be able to find a rental situation that is just as cheap as what you both are doing now, and so on." But the larger question: Is it God's time for us to move forward into marriage? "I know that is subjective and difficult to tell. But is it God's time? And if you sense that it is, as Noël and I did, then expect God to do wonderful things to make life together possible. And as part of that, pray together. Pray earnestly together that the Lord would open the door for this good thing in your life called 'marriage.'"[19]

Should we share details about our sexual history?
Especially when it comes to the sexual history of young men and women before coming to Christ, how should couples be open and clear about their past?

---

18   APJ 295: "Are We Too Financially Unstable to Get Married?" (March 11, 2014).
19   APJ 880: "Should I Finish School before I Marry? Six Options to Consider" (June 14, 2016).

If you have been sexually active in the past, "virginity is a precious gift that you cannot give to your fiancée, nor she to you. That is a great sadness and a great loss." Later, you will want to train your children on how precious this gift is, to be protected for marriage. But as a relationship moves toward marriage, there are gifts that you can give your fiancée, even if virginity is lost. "You can look your fiancée in the eye and say, 'I failed you. I failed God and I am deeply, deeply sorry. I hate what I did. I hate the hurt it caused you and me. I hate the dishonor that I brought upon the Lord. I hate the disrespect I showed you in not caring for you better. And I repent. I turn away from that sin and sinful forces that drove it. I renounce them. And I turn to Jesus Christ my Lord and my Redeemer, and I receive from him his full and blood-bought forgiveness, and I cherish it with all my heart. I tremble at the thought of despising his blood now. And by the Spirit that he has given me, I resolve in his strength never, never, never, never to betray him or to give my body to any woman but to my wife. I offer you my forgiven, redeemed, cleansed soul and body in marriage to cherish you and honor you and be faithful to you. I invite you into this new forgiven, redeemed, cleansed union with me. I know there will always be scars and memories. But God is merciful, and in his time and his wisdom and his way, he will make these scars of sin the emblem of his mercy and the signs of his cross.'"[20]

How far is too far before marriage?

Sexual temptations are all around us. Sex is good, not ugly (Prov. 5:18–19; 1 Tim. 4:3). Sex is designed particularly "for Christians" (1 Tim. 4:5). And sex is for pleasure, not just for making children (1 Cor. 7:5). But sex is reserved for the marriage covenant. "There is illicit sex in marriage; it is called 'adultery.' And there is illicit sex before marriage; it is called 'fornication.' Don't go there. Flee them both, says Paul" (1 Cor. 6:18).

Dating moves toward consummation, but "physical union of sexual intercourse is meant to be the physical capstone of an emotional, spiritual union in a lasting covenant. We are not animals. Sex has roots and branches penetrating all our being, and it affects all our being" because "sexual touching is designed by God and experienced by most healthy people as a prelude to sexual intercourse. That is what it is for. It is extremely frustrating to start touching sexually and have to break it off as the passions become strong. Those touchings and that passion is meant to take you all the way. God designed it that way." So avoid all situations where you experience "an awakening of the desire to go further and

20 APJ 336: "When Past Sexual Sin Haunts Your Wedding" (May 7, 2014).

further." In serious dating relationships, couples need boundaries. Men—initiate the boundaries. And women—"don't entice a man to touch you, thinking that this is the way to keep a man. He is not worth keeping if that is the way he is kept." In the end, sexual purity is about God. "Blessed are the pure in heart, for they shall see God" (Matt. 5:8).[21]

The theme of dampening premature intimacy brought up another topic. How far is too far for couples in matters of spirituality and emotions? Is praying and reading Scripture together too intimate?

These spiritual practices, too, are part of the natural trajectory (the river). "Sexual intercourse is the natural, appropriate, and longed-for completion and consummation of *emotional* and *spiritual* union. I am starting with that conviction. That is why it is so wounding and tragic for men and women to have purely physical one-night stands, experimental sexual encounters, or serial relationships." The more seriously a relationship moves toward marriage, the deeper the emotions will become. Men especially must be alert. If the relationship is *not* moving toward marriage, the relationships should *not* be moving into deeper spiritual and emotional intimacy. "Be alert that every step deeper into emotional and spiritual union with a woman's soul is a step toward physical union—that is, toward marriage. Don't take her there. Don't go with her there if this is not moving toward a marriage relationship. It will deeply wound her—and you—if you awaken depths of oneness in each other emotionally and then try to just walk away from it. Those depths are meant to lead somewhere, namely, sexual intercourse in marriage." In the end: "No, I don't think there are emotional, spiritual limits, provided a couple is on their way in growing commitment toward a wedding and a physical union." However, "they need to know the limits of where they can go with themselves before the emotion takes control" and they find themselves tempted to sin sexually.[22]

If our relationship is moving toward marriage, why wait?

If the stream of a dating relationship is moving toward marriage and that is the intention, why save sex for later? This question came first from a *dating couple* and later from an *engaged couple*. First, a boyfriend wrote in about this logic presented to him from his girlfriend.

Quite bluntly, "If she *does not* think it is a sin to have sex outside marriage, then you have a very ignorant and very foolish girl on your hands. . . . If she *does* think that it is sin, then you have a very selfish, and even cruel, girl on

---

21 APJ 73: "How Far Is Too Far Before Marriage?" (April 19, 2013).
22 APJ 84: "How Far Is Too Far Before Marriage, Spiritually and Emotionally?" (May 6, 2013).

your hands. She not only is willing to sin herself and put her own soul at risk, but is trying to get you not only into bed, but into hell with her, and so put your soul at risk." Don't give in to the temptations of the seductive woman (Prov. 7:21). "We save sex for marriage precisely because it is natural and normal and beautiful—so that we can keep it that way. So that it does not become common and sordid and manipulative and diseased and cheap, but remains precious and personal and clean and sacred. You don't put fences around weeds. You put fences around gardens." Withholding sex until the wedding night "doesn't make it unnatural. It makes it priceless."[23]

The same question arrived later from an *engaged couple*. If the wedding date is set, why save sex for later? Such logic is a flesh-driven, "worldly prag-matism"—acting like "an *intention* to get married is the same as being mar-ried. They're not the same." The union is solemnized in the wedding vow (Mark 10:9). "It happens in the formation of a decisive covenant vow which is permanent—'for better or for worse' and 'till death do us part.' Those are not empty, meaningless words tacked on to sleeping together for six months." We see this in the awkwardness induced by Mary's pregnancy, proving that "you don't sleep together when you're betrothed and trying to live in God's way." It is true in the Old Testament and the New (Matt. 1:18–22). Paul's "remedy" for a couple's sexual desire is marriage (1 Cor. 7:2). So what is human sexual-ity for? "Sex is, by God's design, the consummation of the sacred covenant of God in marriage. All other sex is a prostitution of God's creation." An engaged, godly couple "will treat every act of sexual self-control before marriage as an exaltation of the preciousness and the beauty and the meaning of this act as the consummation of covenant commitment in marriage."[24]

A couple moving toward marriage but also living in sin must immediately stop sleeping together, stop living together, repent of their sin against one another, and (if wise) proceed with the wedding in a spirit of sobered sorrow. If the couple "sees the wrong of what they are doing and repent and bear the fruit of purity and public display of the lordship of Jesus in their lives, then I would move forward with their wedding plan, all other things being in proper order." If they won't stop or repent? "No, I won't do the wedding. And if they are members of my church, they would be disciplined for that kind of willful sin."[25]

Paul weaves together five interrelated arguments for celibacy before mar-riage (1 Cor. 6:18–20). Sexual sin is a violation against your own body. And your body is a temple of the Holy Spirit. You have been bought with a price.

23 APJ 445: "Why Save Sex for Marriage?" (October 7, 2014).
24 APJ 1080: "Our Wedding Date Is Set—Why Not Have Sex Now?" (August 14, 2017).
25 APJ 365: "Will You Marry a Couple Already Living Together?" (June 17, 2014).

Therefore, you are not your own. So glorify God in your body. As a model of all ethics, without serious meditation on Paul's logic you'll be more easily swept away in the moment of temptation.[26]

Should dating couples travel together in overnight contexts?

No, this seems unwise. Unfortunately, such trips are now culturally accepted. Western societies do not stigmatize such trips, just as they have normalized sexual sin. But Christian men and women must swim against the cultural tides of what is popularly accepted and celebrated today. Every couple must be aware that "God has created the human body and mind in such a way that those who are in love desire very strongly to touch each other and move toward sexual climax together. That's normal; it's inevitable that that desire would happen. God has made provision for the joy of that relationship and satisfaction in marriage and nowhere else." But before marriage, couples are to make no provision for the flesh, meaning, "don't put yourself in an unnecessary position that will likely stir up desires that you cannot control" (Rom. 13:14).

If you choose to travel, and even if you book two rooms, "most of the world will assume you're sleeping together." Non-Christians will think you *cultured*, Christians will think you *careless*, and everyone will assume you're sleeping together. This matters because we are called to guard our testimony very closely (Rom. 12:17; 2 Cor. 8:21; 1 Thess. 4:12). Carelessness here—even if only in appearance—may end up leading younger Christians into sin because "by taking this trip or not taking it, you weaken or strengthen the standards of other Christians, especially younger ones who may be even weaker than you are and are looking for more justification to do what you're about to do."

So do you have the liberty in Christ to take such a trip? "Probably." But don't use your liberty to cause others to stumble (2 Cor. 6:3). "For Paul, this meant not doing things that he had every right to do. The issue is not rights. The issue is love and purity and whether you will participate in a cultural pattern that is destruction in the long run."[27]

On sending nude selfies

A troubling trend was seen in the rise of nude selfies, made possible by the ubiquity of cameras and the mobile web encroaching life's most private spaces. This phenomenon emerged especially among teen boys who began to send unsolicited nude pictures of themselves to girls, as an initiative act to show

---

26 APJ 900: "Can We Overthink the Christian Life?" (July 19, 2016).
27 APJ 1355: "Should My Boyfriend and I Travel Alone?" (June 12, 2019).

interest, with the corresponding assumption that the girls would reciprocate with nude images in return. The practice became common in high schools and then among dating adults.

"I think I have good biblical authority in saying on behalf of God to every one of his children, male and female, don't ever ask to see anyone naked except your spouse and don't ever offer to show yourself to someone naked for erotic or sexual reasons, except your spouse." Fundamentally, nakedness is a form of divine judgment, an embarrassment of bitter shame felt acutely in the fallout of Adam and Eve's first sin, in the new awareness of their nakedness (Gen. 2:25; 3:7). The shame of nakedness is "lifted" only in "the sacred relationship of marriage." Not on a movie set, not in a striptease joint, not in porn, not before a boyfriend or girlfriend, and not in front of our phone camera. The holiness of nakedness is preserved for "the profound respect and love and security of a covenant relationship called *marriage*."

Outside of that covenant, how we clothe ourselves speaks to what we think about God. In Paul's words to women about dressing modestly, he calls them to dress *respectably, modestly*, and in *self-control* (1 Tim. 2:9–10). And "all three of those words, interestingly, have the connotation of thoughtful, serious use of a woman's mind as to how to make her clothing speak about her godliness." "Clothing is not a matter of indifference in God's economy. It speaks about a woman's (and a man's) view of God and her own commitments to God and joy in God and her freedom from the manipulative maneuvers of men to get what they want."

Paul simply assumes that our most "unpresentable parts" will be treated with greater modesty (1 Cor. 12:23). And he commands Christian men to treat "younger women as sisters, in all purity" (1 Tim. 5:2), meaning that "until a man is married, he should let his proper treatment of his sister, his real sister, dictate the purity of his behavior with his girlfriend."

So if a Christian man asks his girlfriend for nude images of herself, the man is, by definition, "unworthy of her—unworthy of her trust, her affection, and her covenant. That request that he is making, in itself, should be enough for the woman to say, 'Goodbye.' I mean this. I really mean this. Come on, women. If any woman thinks that is normal male-Christian behavior, it is not. It is sick. It means he is clueless as to godliness. It means that when he gets tired of you before or after marriage, he will feel free to ask someone else to take off her clothes. If he can't get it in person, he will get it from the internet."

Until the marriage covenant, sexual love is not to be awakened (Song 2:7; 3:5; 8:4). Erotic pictures "stir up desire that cannot be lawfully satisfied," meaning they will lead either to masturbation or to fornication. "I don't know what goes on inside a woman's head. But I can only think that it is a deformed sense of sexuality if a woman gets pleasure out of helping a man act like a thirteen-year-old boy with his masturbation. Is that really the kind of man she wants?"

Finally, imagine the liability involved in pictures you send that can be shared with others or online when the relationship ends, and then "you will discover what God meant by bringing judgment on yourself" (Isa. 47:3; Lam. 1:8; Ezek. 16:37).[28]

We sinned and had sex. Now what?

It is not uncommon to hear from couples who intended to remain pure until their wedding day but failed. One Christian couple sexually sinned and now they feel "dirty, cheap, and ashamed." Now what? asked the man. Can we become pure again?

The feeling of brokenness is appropriate because he knows that "something has been irrevocably lost. He and his girlfriend will never be able to go behind this sexual encounter and undo it. They have lost something very precious." It is a harsh word but called for, "because I feel a tender and jealous concern for those who are listening who have not lost their virginity. It is a very precious thing for men and women. The world views it as weakness—silly, in fact. God views it as a very great strength and beauty beyond compare." But in this case, a beautiful thing has been lost.

The brokenness is appropriate. And yet this is why Christ was crucified. "Those who take their sins lightly and treat the blood of Jesus as a kind of quick fix have never seen the true costliness of what Jesus did to purchase their purity." God commands us to flee from sexual sin (1 Cor. 6:18). And yet all our past sins can be forgiven (Mark 3:28; 1 John 1:9). "In other words, there is no specific, single sin—or *kind* of sin—that is so ugly, so gross, so offensive to God that it cannot be forgiven by the blood of Jesus."

This couple's great challenge is repenting for a sin they led each other into. The guilt is mutual, and they will need to forgive one another (Eph. 4:32). The natural impulse will be to shift blame. The man who feels shame that "he did not take more responsibility for chastity as the masculine leader and initiator" may begin to shift blame on her seduction, that "she could have helped him stop, and she didn't." And then she "may feel shame and conviction that she was too compliant, or maybe even seductive." She "might begin to shift more blame onto him and find fault that he didn't protect her in that moment of temptation." Both were wrong, and both must admit their culpability. The sin may end the relationship. If there is any hope of moving forward, it will require

28 APJ 1000: "Never Send Nude Selfies: Seven Reasons" (February 8, 2017).

forgiveness and forbearance to rebuild broken trust. "So be patient with one another, and be honest about this. It is very painful to look a person in the eye and say, 'I don't know if I can fully trust you yet.' That is enough to destroy a relationship, but being dishonest to try to preserve the relationship will wreak havoc in the long run."

In all things, reclaim the glorious, forgiving grace of the gospel in 1 Corinthians 6:9–11. In Christ, this couple can inherit heaven, as redeemed children of God, with the sin of fornication solely in their past.[29]

In another scenario, a young woman was led away from Christ and her local church by a foolish boyfriend. To appease and keep him, she gave in to sexual temptation. She now sees her recklessness. The boyfriend is gone, and she's left feeling distant from the church and alienated from God. She once felt spiritually vibrant. That's gone.

First, perhaps it's worth asking whether the earlier spiritual vibrancy was a mirage. The spiritual high was there, but the heartfelt obedience was missing. "If you loved Jesus so little that a boyfriend was more important than Jesus, you did not have a close walk with God." These hard words make way for something greater ahead. "I'm suggesting that the Lord is not, in these years, allowing you to lose a close walk with God but rescuing you from a phony walk with God." He's not going to allow for a return to "the old religious *you* that sells Jesus like Judas for a thirty-pieces-of-silver boyfriend." Perhaps now, through "the miseries of that wreckage" of the past relationship, God is awakening new, authentic desires for him. "He's not calling you back to the kind of faith that concealed a heart that was ready to commit idolatry as soon as the boyfriend came along. He's got something way better planned for you than that."

There is gospel hope for her future. Meditate on God's faithfulness in the harsh chapter of Ezekiel 16, particularly the final five verses (Ezek. 16:59–63). And ponder the grace given to Paul, the "Christian-killer" (1 Tim. 1:16). "I want you to be tough, unshakable, and unbendable in your allegiance to Jesus as your supreme treasure. No loosey-goosey, churchy, emotional stuff anymore. I'm talking major, deep-down, unshakable, authentic allegiance to your King and supreme treasure." Tough words, spoken with grace-filled intent.[30]

Is pregnancy before marriage a sin?

Sex belongs "only in the safe, holy, beautiful sanctuary of a marriage covenant between one man and one woman while they both live." Fornication is

---

29 APJ 827: "I Slept with My Girlfriend—Now What?" (March 31, 2016).
30 APJ 1171: "When God Feels Distant, He May Want Us to Grow Up" (March 14, 2018).

forbidden (1 Cor. 6:18; 7:2). And the presence of a child outside of marriage is the result of sin. Either the woman sinned, or she was sinned against. So is the pregnancy itself sin, if it was the result of sin?

No. Historically, a cultural stigmatism stained pregnancies outside of marriage, and this was good and helpful to some degree. But that stigmatism is vanishing, due to the "normalization of sexual immorality and because of putting people's feelings above a call to holiness." But any shame for sin should "only attach to the *previous sin*, not the *present pregnancy*." The sin can be forgiven and cleansed, and the shame taken away in Christ. But "if the shame attaches to the *pregnancy* or the *child* itself, then there is no overcoming it." That's a problem because the child does not carry shame for the sin! God's grace and blessing shine through children born in any situation. "No one needs to feel—no woman needs to feel, no family needs to feel—that because the child originated in a sinful act, if it did, God cannot make this child great. He can."[31] (A similar hope for anyone raised in a dysfunctional home.[32])

We're pregnant. Should we marry?

First, the question is from a pregnant couple comprised of one believer and one nonbeliever. Does premarital pregnancy override the unequally yoked command? Is it better to marry a child's father, even if he is not a believer, than to wait and marry a Christian man later?

Christians must marry in Christ, as Paul makes abundantly clear (1 Cor. 7:39; 2 Cor. 6:14). In Paul's mind, "behind these two commands for believers to marry only believers is the wisdom that marriage ought to be built on the foundation of faith in Christ with all the challenges and goals of marriage shaped by the lordship of Jesus Christ." These commands stand as a "perpetual guide," and premarital sex and premarital pregnancy don't change them. Sex does not make a marriage covenant, a surprising point made by Paul (1 Cor. 6:15–18). Even "one-flesh" sex with a prostitute does not inaugurate a marriage covenant.

But here's the pressing challenge for a pregnant woman in relation to the father, who is not a believer. Can you "see twenty or thirty years into the future and what a twenty- or thirty-year marriage with an unbeliever will be like? Whether the marriage will even survive?" The present situation looms larger than the long-term impact of marrying a non-Christian man. "It is very difficult, probably, for this Christian young woman to imagine two or three years from now falling in love with a different man who's a Christian and having a fifty-year marriage of

31 APJ 976: "Is It Sinful to Be Pregnant before Marriage?" (December 14, 2016).

32 APJ 720: "Can My Life Be Plagued by Generational Sins, Hexes, or Curses?" (November 3, 2015) and APJ 1612: "Hope for Children from Dysfunctional Families" (April 12, 2021).

unity and common faith with him. But that is what she should dream about—or if not, then waiting prayerfully for the Lord to give new life to this child's father."[33]

But what changes if the pregnant couple *is* Christian? A fearful Christian couple finding themselves in this situation write in after having entertained the unthinkable: abortion. They sinned, they're pregnant, and now they're afraid of what's next. Should this scenario hasten marriage?

The question came from the man. He took the initiative, and there appears to be genuine repentance over the sin. For such a Christian, "do not entertain any thoughts that you have sinned your way *out of Christ* or *out of heaven*. Those would be thoughts of the devil and his accusation. If you confess your sins, and humble yourself before Christ as your Lord and Savior and treasure, you will be forgiven."

But there are consequences to work through. As the man, take the lead. This situation is a failure of leadership. "I'm not at all denying that your girlfriend bears responsibility and complicity in the sin. She should've said *no* and kicked you out. But I am saying that the man—you—bears a greater responsibility and is charged by God to protect and care for and lead her." But since that calling was "misused" and the stewardship failed, "You have a chance in this terrible situation to redeem at least your role as a courageous, initiative-taking, humble leader in doing what is right, which will be very difficult."

This includes saving the child. "You are the one who will say, 'We will not kill this baby. We brought this baby unlawfully into the world, and we will not add to the unlawfulness of our creation the unlawfulness of its destruction. No, we won't.'" And you will lead in confessing your sin and the situation to her parents and your own parents, in person. And you will serve your girlfriend who bears the immediate, life-altering weight of your sin. "This is why we have so many abortions, because mothers and fathers put their own plans ahead of the life of the child. As a mature Christian man, you will realize your girlfriend's heavy load in all of this, and you will do everything in your power to lighten her load. Killing children doesn't lighten her load. It doesn't."

Own the consequences of your sin. Trust Christ. Trust that he is working all things for good (Rom. 8:28). Protect your child's life. Serve the mother. But don't rush into the marriage covenant. "You need time to know each other and whether a lifetime commitment would be advisable." In the end: "This will be the hardest season of your life, so far at least. It will be a huge test of your faith and your manhood, and you will discover that Jesus is a great Savior and a great friend and a sufficient counselor."[34]

33 APJ 1264: "Does Premarital Pregnancy Nullify 'Unequally Yoked'?" (October 17, 2018).
34 APJ 1265: "My Girlfriend Is Pregnant—What Do I Do Next?" (October 19, 2018).

Is my boyfriend's porn a marriage deal-breaker?

Pornography is unloving, adulterous, love-destroying, and soul-ravaging. (1) It's unloving because it doesn't care for the woman presented and the brokenness of her life. It simply uses others as objects of pleasure with zero concern that the misuse of her body corrupts her own relationships and eternal destiny before God. (2) Porn "cultivates and pursues mental and physical pleasures that are made by God to flourish in marriage" but pursued by women who are not our wives. (3) "Porn is destructive to a man's capacities to love a woman purely for herself. When he needs increasingly different, strange, erotic situations and bodies, he is training himself and his body." He's rewiring his desires toward what can only corrupt and destroy the affection meant to be solely for his wife. And if a man fails to cultivate a "kind of pure love for his wife," for who *she is*, "then his eyes are going to be cruising continually beyond what she has to offer him at forty and fifty and sixty."

As a truism, "the soul tends to shrink to the size and the quality of its pleasures." The human soul form-fits to the size and shape of what it most treasures. And when a soul shrinks down around the pleasures of porn, "it won't be able to make much of God, won't be able to see God, won't be able to delight in God anywhere near like God should be delighted in, in the glorious pleasures that he offers us in his word and in his world."

Can a Christian man defeat his addiction to porn? Yes. "If Jesus is not just a doctrine, but is Lord and friend and Savior and supreme treasure of our lives, the way he should be, then we won't be continually hating women with our choices to demean them and confirm their destruction. We won't be continually committing adultery in our hearts with those women. We won't be continually defiling our capacity to love our present or future wives. We won't be continually shrinking our soul's ability to savor the glories of God. We won't, because Jesus is so utterly different than that." There's hope for victory. But, yes, porn addiction is a marriage deal-breaker. Women, don't lower your standards.[35]

Has my past porn already doomed my future marriage?

A young man has used porn for seven years. Now he seeks marriage. But has his past sin already doomed any hope for holy intimacy with his future bride?

---

35   APJ 122: "Is My Boyfriend's Porn a Marriage Deal-Breaker?" (June 28, 2013). On replacing the term "addiction" with "sinful excess," see APJ 530: "The Real Cost of Pornography" (February 11, 2015) (on porn addiction), APJ 657: "How Do I Choose between Two Good Things?" (August 7, 2015) (on digital media and smartphone addiction), APJ 1314: "How Do I Break My Entertainment Addiction?" (February 18, 2019) (on gaming and video entertainment addiction), and APJ 1702: "On Cigarettes, Vaping, and Nicotine" (November 8, 2021) (on nicotine, vaping, and smoking addictions).

No, it has not. "There is hope for a loving, godly, healthy intimacy in marriage—if, in God's mercy, a cluster of miracles happens in you and in your future wife." But this won't be automatic as a Christian. "You must pursue these miracles." Here are two ways.

1. Seek full victory immediately and walk in holiness. Admit that "seven years of poisoning your mind are going to have consequences that you are responsible for and that will require unusual self-abasement in relation to your sexual expectations and your wife." But also see that in Christ, your body, its desires, and your future marriage are not vulgar but holy. Your redeemed body is now a temple (1 Cor. 6:18–20). Sex in marriage is pure in Christ (1 Cor. 7:3). Know that God bought you as you are—broken and distorted by lust. "He knew what he was buying. He bought you, body and soul, by his blood. You are not your own. He bought you so that he could indwell you. And the one who indwells you is explicitly called 'holy.' And that is your calling—be holy—because you are bought to be holy and indwelt by the Holy One." You are now learning to live holy in all of life.

2. Admit that sex was distorted in your mind for years, and for years you will be unlearning what you've seen. Don't assume you will know what Christ-honoring intimacy looks like in the bedroom. A potential fiancée will need to hear your history. She will need to be alerted that you are haunted by a false picture of sex. And as you move into marriage, you will learn through communication, learning "an unspoken language, a kind of delicate signaling, so that there emerges over time a natural rhythm of intimacy that both of you find sweetly and deeply satisfying." You will be learning to express your desires in *selfless love* not *selfish lust* (1 Cor. 7:3–4). "A woman will feel properly enjoyed by her husband, rather than used, if she can tell that he is delighting in her body and her person as one." This is learned, and it will take time because your past porn use has assaulted God's holistic vision of love in marriage.[36]

Is my boyfriend's spiritual laziness a marriage deal-breaker?

A woman in a relationship headed toward marriage is dissatisfied by how casually her boyfriend takes Christ. The woman knows that she needs to marry a believer (1 Cor. 7:39). Now she's trying to figure out if a *serious* Christian woman can marry a *lackadaisical* Christian man.

The short and "blunt" answer is *no*. Not yet.

Paul says to avoid idle Christians (2 Thess. 3:6). The idle Christian violates several commands to be spiritually, wholeheartedly earnest and engaged and

---

36 APJ 1582: "Has Porn Already Broken My Future Marriage?" (February 1, 2021).

growing (Ps. 100:2; Luke 10:27; Rom. 12:11; Eph. 6:10; 2 Pet. 3:18; Rev. 3:16). Avoid such a man, Paul says. "So you need to spend some serious time and see whether or not some changes come about to prove another kind of character." More on that later.

Marriage is a "one flesh" union (Gen. 2:24). "That bodily union in sexual intercourse is the physical expression of a much deeper union of heart and soul, pointing to the covenant relationship between Christ and the church" (Eph. 5:32). That means marriage is "the profoundest of human relationships" at both the physical and spiritual levels. Anyone contemplating it must ask: "Will I be able to pursue such a profound union of heart and mind and body with this other person?"

This man's trajectory is unsettling. "Christian women are not called in marriage to lead their poor, benighted husbands. The Bible says that the husband is to be the head of his wife and their family. There is a spiritual maturity, a strength of character, that precedes this leadership. That's what she should be looking for."

But give him time. Maybe he's a new believer and hasn't been discipled or taught well. Point him to resources, encourage his discipleship, and watch for "emerging character traits of leadership and maturity and wisdom and humility and grace and strength." If he's eager and receptive, "she may be encouraged to keep moving forward." If not—if he remains unresponsive and lazy or even resistant and defensive to suggestions—"it seems to me she would be asking for a lifetime of frustration to move forward."

"If you should think it wise to put the brakes on this relationship, don't doubt God's good and wise and loving providence in your life. God is for you as you walk in his will." There's grace for a delay in marriage, even for a life of singleness. In the end, it's "better to remain unmarried than to marry a nominal, spiritually lethargic man."[37]

Is video-game addiction a marriage deal-breaker?

To a woman expressing concern over her fiancé's overuse of video games, Pastor John laid out some principles of interpreting the behavior. (1) All things are lawful, but not all things are helpful, and we are not to be "dominated" by anything (1 Cor. 6:12). "Nothing is to be enslaving, even the subtlest temptations of video games." Christ breaks all our slavery (Gal. 5:1). (2) "What does the fact that your fiancé is enslaved by something as trivial and banal as games say about his elevation of mind?" (3) If he lacks control with video games, what will he be unable to control in other more important areas of life?

37 APJ 1683: "My Boyfriend Is Spiritually Lethargic—Should I Still Marry Him?" (September 24, 2021).

Will such a man lead you well? "Headship always involves doing hard things. That means denying immediate gratification. It means pursuing the desire of long-term joy in obedience, love, sacrifice, and helpfulness. If he cannot deny himself a video game, will he be able to deny himself things for the good of the family? Will he be able to get up from the television? Will he be able to leave his hobby in the garage? Will he be able to put his book down? Will he be able to leave his computer and lead the family in Bible reading and prayer? Or will he just be stuck?" Will it matter to him if his "family is perishing in the living room" because he lacks self-denial and self-control to engage with those challenges? Without "significant character growth and freedom for greater things than games, I would not move forward in that relationship."[38]

Is feminism a marriage deal-breaker?
A complementarian man is dating an evangelical feminist and thinking about marriage. Is this wise?

The discord is stark. "Which of you—you or your future wife—will choose to sacrifice your conscience and, with it, your integrity to make the marriage work?" You enter the marriage "believing that it is God's will for you to fulfill the role of head as you see it laid out in Ephesians 5:22–33." But she enters the marriage "believing that it is God's will that you *not assume* a special role as leader or head." You enter it "believing that God calls you to raise your children in the instruction of the Lord, including his instruction that your sons should be husbands who lead out in marriage and your daughters should be wives who submit gladly to their husbands. And she will enter the marriage believing that God calls you to raise your children to be egalitarians." Husbands and wives will disagree about many things. "But in matters of biblically informed conscience that affect the dynamic of the relationship at every turn, disagreement of that sort is unworkable."[39]

Is a gay-affirming girlfriend a deal-breaker?
A girlfriend says that homosexual sex is holy. The boyfriend calls it sin. Is that a deal-breaker for marriage?

"Yes, it is a deal-breaker." *Engagements* can be broken over this scenario, but *marriages* cannot. "Once you are married, what she believes can't end the marriage. You're not free to put asunder what God has joined together" (Mark 10:9). "For better or worse" includes better-or-worse *beliefs*. "She may cease

---

38 APJ 486: "Is My Boyfriend's Video-Game Addiction a Marriage Deal-Breaker?" (December 5, 2014).
39 APJ 798: "Could a Complementarian/Egalitarian Marriage Work?" (February 19, 2016).

to believe in Jesus at all after you're married. She may become a satanist. She may become a witch, a real witch. But she's your wife by sacred covenant before God. And he's the one who created the union, not you. What God has joined together, let no one put asunder."

Prior to marriage, imagine how this stark convictional difference will emerge in how you raise kids. A mother and father may disagree about many things in life, but for a mother to say two men kissing and having sex is *holy*, and for a father to say that this behavior is *unholy*, is a root difference that will manifest in many other ways later. "The fact that she can affirm homosexual activity— and you can't—signals deep, deep differences in what your most basic moral and spiritual instincts are." These conflicting dispositions are sure to emerge in many other disagreements down the road. "When the *roots* of spiritual instincts and inclinations are different, there is no predicting what the *fruit* differences might be."

Scripture is clear that homosexual sin brings eternal destruction (1 Cor. 6:9–11). "To approve of the very pattern of life that the gospel is designed to save you from is to oppose the gospel and promote destruction. I don't see how you can believe this and move forward with the deepest and most precious union of souls and bodies that exists on the planet among human beings. It's a deal-breaker."[40]

Hope for breakups

The pain of rejection, especially in dating, leads to various human responses— ranging from anger, thoughts of suicide, acts of self-harm, substance abuse, overeating, workaholism, or redirecting personal focus to new diets and crafting the physique to return to the "market" of attracting a mate. Responses like these mask the aftermath of a painful breakup.

When our relationship status changes, God's character remains the same. He created us, loves us, satisfies us, and strengthens us. The human approval of a boyfriend or girlfriend does not establish our worth. God does. In all our flaws, "God accepts us and forgives us and loves us, in spite of all the effects or defects that may push others away." We are loved, not because of an absence of personal flaws, but because of the perfection of Christ.

God's love to us in Christ never wanes. So our greatest joy is not bound to impressing ourselves in the mirror, or impressing the opposite sex, or even impressing God. "The supreme satisfaction of our souls is that we stand in front of God and are thrilled by the beauty of God outside of us. He is *all* at

40 APJ 1317: "My Girlfriend Affirms Homosexual Love—Is This a Deal-Breaker?" (February 25, 2019).

ON DATING, ROMANCE IDOLS, AND FORNICATION 165

that moment, and he is our highest joy. The highest joys are self-forgetful joys in the presence of infinite beauty."

Even with these glorious truths in mind, the rejection is real. It really hurts. But when God is the highest beauty we see, we find the inner strength we need to move on from the breakup. "In Christ we have all we need to live useful and joyful lives through that kind of rejection and pain."[41]

One final word of caution: be careful. Breakups breed grudges. The deeper the wrong, the deeper the resentment. We begin to think that no one knows the depth of our pain. But God knows all our wrongs, and he offers us liberty in the "laid-down grudge." Until we lay down our grudges, we are not free to love as we ought. "You've been wondering, 'Why can't I love like I ought to love? There seems to be a blockage to my love.' And one of the answers is that you keep holding on to that wrong." Perhaps you got pregnant, and as a result, an old boyfriend "picked you up and dropped you like a stone." You can lay down this wound because God has promised to take it up himself (Rom. 12:19). Because of him, you can drop the grudge, lose the burden, and learn to love again.[42]

41 APJ 656: "Biblical Hope for Breakups" (August 6, 2015).
42 APJ 1433: "How Do I Let Go of Anger over Past Wrongs?" (February 12, 2020).

On Married Sex, Bedroom Taboos, and Fading Attraction

Sex is good, sex is for Christians, sex is for marriage

Four key points frame sex in marriage.

1. Sex is good (1 Cor. 7:1–5; 1 Tim. 4:1–5). Scripture celebrates marital intimacy as a good gift. Sex is for more than baby-making; it's a good gift for pleasure and to help us resist Satan's temptations.

2. Sex is for Christians (1 Tim. 4:1–5), "for people who will give thanks for it." Faith unlocks the true purpose of sexual intimacy, in evoking our Godward worship.

3. Sex is for marriage. "There is illicit sex in marriage; it is called *adultery* (μοιχεία). And there is illicit sex before marriage; it is called *fornication* (πορνείαν)." Flee from them both, says Paul (1 Cor. 6:18). Sex is reserved for marriage because "the physical union of sexual intercourse is meant to be the physical capstone of an emotional, spiritual union in a lasting covenant. We are not animals. Sex has roots and branches penetrating all our being, and it affects all our being. We have tried to abstract sex from the covenantal, deep, personal, emotional, spiritual union of a man and a woman in our movies and in our literature and our advertising. It is wreaking havoc all over the world." So God created marriage—"that beautiful, whole commitment and covenantal, deep, personal, spiritual, reality with a capstone of sexual intercourse."

4. Mental sex is for marriage (Matt. 5:28). Outside of marriage, imagined sex is fornication or adultery in the heart. But in covenant marriage, "you are supposed to have mental sex in marriage as well as physical sex."[1]

Regarding point 4, among a couple where each is a servant "of the other's maximum pleasure," a husband cannot lust after his wife (1 Cor. 7:3). So it's not

---

1 APJ 73: "How Far Is Too Far Before Marriage?" (April 19, 2013).

wrong "for a husband to want his wife sexually and to think about having her and to hold her in his mind the way he would hold her in bed." For you, "there is no sin in your mind that wouldn't be sin in your bed." But it would be sin if he "imagined sin or desired sin or took on attitudes to his wife in his heart that would be wrong in the bedroom."[2] For Christian couples, fantasized sin in the mind and "playacted sin" in the bedroom are always forbidden.[3]

How is sex made holy?

Sex is "*made holy* by the word of God and prayer" (1 Tim. 4:5). Meaning "good sex"—like good food—is designed for Christians who "give thanks for it."[4] The Creator's full design for human sexuality can only be realized in spiritual realities and by Christians who honor his glory in the gift.[5]

1. How do Christian couples sanctify sex *by prayer*? Through gratefulness. "Thanksgiving is the dethroning of a god and turning it into a gift." This holds true as we find a healthy balance for sex in married life. "Sex is starting to get this power over us, it's starting to exert an enslaving, godlike force on our life. And thanksgiving humbly says, 'You are not a god. You are a gift from God. And I will let him determine how this gift is to be used, and I will be filled with humble thanksgiving."

2. How is sex made holy *by Scripture*? In the same way. When we look to the word, we see that "the earth is the LORD's and the fullness thereof" (Ps. 24:1). True of food and sex, "we prevent them from having undue control or an undue place in our lives by bringing them both under the word," particularly in texts that generate thanks in us for the gifts. By prayer and the word, we thank the Creator, thereby "dethroning *a god* and making it *a gift*."[6]

How does sex glorify God?

Animals mate through instincts and rituals, "amazing" revelations of the Creator's glory. "So it is with human sexuality. We have instincts and desires and understandings that cause us to make love and reproduce the race. But without eyes to see the goodness and the glory of God in our sexuality, we are more like animals than we are like God." So we open the Bible to be "thrown into a world of divine glory," a world only visible to reborn eyes (1 Cor. 2:14). "Without spiritual life, without the awakening of our spirit by the Spirit of God,

2   APJ 278: "Can a Husband Lust after His Wife?" (February 14, 2014).
3   APJ 1684: "Should Couples Use Role-Play in the Bedroom?" (September 27, 2021).
4   APJ 73: "How Far Is Too Far Before Marriage?" (April 19, 2013).
5   APJ 712: "Everything about God Is about Everything" (October 22, 2015).
6   APJ 123: "How Food and Sex Are Made Holy" (July 1, 2013).

the reality of God, the glory of God in all things, we may have intense feelings and poetic thoughts about sex—even far above the animals—but we will never see the goodness and the glory that God reveals of himself in and through our sexuality." Without spiritual vision, we will never see that sex "has to do with the glorious reality for which we are made, Jesus Christ."

Three texts demonstrate these divine glories. (1) Sex demonstrates Christ's relationship to his bride (Eph. 5:25–27). "The whole drama of marriage, including sex, is a drama about the glories of Christ's covenant relation to his bride, the church. None of this reality is visible or enjoyable for the person without spiritual discernment." (2) The married couple's one-flesh sexual union illustrates our union to Christ (1 Cor. 6:15–17). Only Paul could weave together "the most nitty-gritty physical reality, like prostitution, with the most spiritual reality of our oneness with Christ." Prostitution is a *prostitution* of our union with Christ. (3) The sexual union is how God binds a couple, in heaven, in a lifelong covenant (Mark 10:7–9). Thus "the *goodness* and the *glory* of sexuality is for those with eyes to see."[7]

Without new eyes, we mishandle precious texts like the Song of Solomon. Blind to the beauty of allegorical realities, readers "stomp all over this beautiful poem," like with spikes on, not slippers. This book "is not for men and women for whom sexual intercourse is merely a one-dimensional flight of passion" but for those who see in covenant sex a glorious "parable" about Christ and his church. The "literary sex" in Solomon's song is allegorical. So too is the "real sex" in the marriage bedroom. Indeed, all physical life "points to something spiritual." Glorifying God in sex requires spiritual eyes to make this connection. Our new eyes don't make our physical lives less physical. They properly connect physical joys to eternal glories, our physical joys to our joy in Christ.[8] So Solomon speaks of sexual pleasure "with such remarkable graphicness" because God is setting the stage for us to understand the union of Christ to his bride. If such connections embarrass us, our eyes need adjusting.[9]

Does marriage cure lust?

Marriage does not cure lust. Marriage is a "God-designed *help* in dealing with the overpowering passions of sexual desire" (1 Cor. 7:2–9). "But there's nothing here that I see about a *total cure.*" God certainly designed marriage to weaken satanic temptations toward lust and adultery. But assuming marriage will be a full fix for lust is a wrong way to think about it.

7 APJ 615b: "Blind to the Glory of Sex" (June 11, 2015).
8 APJ 285: "Is Song of Solomon an Allegory?" (February 25, 2014).
9 APJ 760: "Why Sexual Metaphors of Jesus and His Bride Embarrass Us" (December 29, 2015).

Most of all, marriage displays the glorious vision of Christ's love to the church (Eph. 5:22–33). Only within this exalted vision do we find the "nitty-gritty, practical sexual effects of marriage." Again, marriage is not a *cure* for lust but a physical *help* to defeat the sin of lust, much like adequate sleep is *a help* to defeat the sin of impatience, exercise *a help* to defeat the sin of melancholy, or walking outside *a help* to defeat the sin of discouragement. In these ways "sexual relations in marriage is *a great help* in the spiritual battle against lust and adultery, but not *an absolute cure*." Sex is not simply a mechanical, "pressure-valve" release. "That's a truth, but it's not the totality of what's going on when Paul says that sexual relations are a firewall. There's more to it than that. I think in our culture, which has so prostituted sex into a hookup, weekend sport, it's very hard for them to grasp what I'm about to say. God intends, in the intimacy of physical union in marriage, that something amazing, glorious, beautiful, and spiritual takes place. Depths of affection, covenant intensification, and spiritual union—and unfathomable personal bonding—take place. As these grow, these depths of union make pornography and adultery more and more unthinkable. That's the real glory of sexual relations in marriage."[10]

Appropriate, frequent, satisfying sexual intimacy in marriage serves as "a protection" to "lessen the likelihood" of lust, fornication, and adultery in the future (1 Cor. 7:1–5).[11]

Is sexual attraction or sexual pleasure essential for marriage?

A Christian woman wrote in because she felt emotionally attracted to a Christian man but not physically attracted to him. Should she consider him for marriage? Is sexual attraction essential for marriage?

It's a tough dilemma. On the one hand, *no*, sexual attraction itself "does not belong to the *essence* of marriage." But sexual relations do. "The essence of marriage is the making and keeping of a covenant between a man and a woman to be husband and wife to each other as long as they both shall live. That is the essence of a marriage: covenant-making, covenant-keeping—to be a husband and a wife. And to be sure, that covenant includes the promise to give one's self to the other in sexual relations" (1 Cor. 7:3).

The Bible mandates *sexual relations* but not *sexual pleasure*. This is true for two other reasons. (1) "Throughout most of history, I think, and in most cultures, marriages have been arranged by parents. Couples did not look around to see who made them sexually aroused." This means that "most mar-

---

10 APJ 1345: "Will Marriage Cure My Lust?" (May 20, 2019).
11 APJ 1887: "When Does Despondency Become Sin?" (January 13, 2023).

riages in history have not started based on a sense of sexual attraction. That had to come later, if it came at all. And those were real, essential marriages." (2) Lifelong marriages experience cycles of more and less physical pleasure. This can be due to high-pressure seasons of life, demands of young children, aging, conflict, and wayward children. "And if you said that sexual attraction were of the *essence*, then aging would be the gradual *end* of marriage when, in fact, the glories of marriage may increase with aging and with the waning of sexual pleasures."

So sexual attraction is not *the essence* of marriage. That's "the easy part of the answer." But is it *important* to marriage? Men tend to be attracted to women sexually "minus emotion" and "animal-like." Men must be intentional to experience sex emotionally, as a "person-to-person, eye-to-eye, heart-to-heart, not just body-to-body" dynamic. But women seem to be more generally integrated, with emotions "much more closely connected to their sexual pleasures."

So to the potential wife in this scenario, "can you see yourself gladly yielding this emotional intimacy to your husband's desires for physical intimacy so that it becomes part of the emotional intimacy?" If she sees intimacy as painful or unpleasant, "this could be a serious problem" that should caution proceeding with marriage. "Sexual pleasure is not essential to marriage, but the absence of the desire for it at the beginning could signal deeper problems of distaste for sex or resistance to the male desire. And I would try to see that changed before moving ahead."[12]

The Bible mandates sexual relations (1 Cor. 7:3). "But even lengthy interruptions do not turn marriage into something other than marriage, as when a husband or wife is in prison for ten or twenty years, or when seafarers go on a two-year whaling expedition." A real and happy marriage "can exist when those pleasures are not part of the joy." So "I am not in any way commending pleasure-absent sexual relations. I regard such experiences as a very sad reality that some must live with. The loss of sexual pleasure in marriage is not the ideal; it is not the goal."

So why does the Bible celebrate sexual pleasure if it's not essential? The Song of Solomon is "an utterly sensual song" of the "lavish celebration of God's gift of sexual pleasure in marriage. I am glad it is in the Bible." The song is a celebration of sex because "it completes the picture of how intense the pleasures of knowing Christ will be forever." Such pleasure is "not essential" but "staggeringly important and wonderful" in marriage.[13]

---

12 APJ 475: "Is Sexual Attraction Essential for Marriage?" (November 18, 2014).
13 APJ 516: "Is Sexual Pleasure Essential for Marriage?" (January 22, 2015).

If I feel no sexual attraction, should I pursue marriage?

Does the Bible applaud asexuality in 1 Corinthians 7:6–11? And how should a currently asexual young woman proceed in thinking about singleness and marriage? Should she consider the possibility of a future marriage?

First, "my guess" is that a woman with little sexual attraction is "closer to the norm of how women feel about sex, in general, than the sexually spring-loaded and predacious women glorified as normative in the entertainment industry." In fact, "the vast majority of marriages in the history of the world have not been based on romantic sexual attraction," a standard that "has skyrocketed to preeminence in the last couple of centuries in the West." Instead, most marriages in history were "arranged by family" or "dictated by other relational and social circumstances." So we live in a "weird time" where "personal romantic affection" has become "the be-all and end-all of how you form lifelong relationships of commitment." If sexual attraction is *not* the historic norm, it means that "millions of human beings have been born into the world having been conceived in moments *not* of mutual sexual passion."

Biblical passages about sex do not seem to imply that the only "valid" or "beautiful" sexual relations are those done in "mutual passion." Each husband, each wife, and each season of their lives will see different levels of passion. So passion cannot be the *essence* of marriage. "There are far bigger issues at stake in marriage than *being* or *staying* in love. Marriage is about the cove-nant-keeping love between Christ and the church, and displaying that can happen profoundly, even where romantic affections rise and fall—maybe especially when romantic affections fall."

When considering future marriage, ask three questions. (1) "Can you imagine yourself spending the rest of your life living with a caring, mature, responsible Christian man? And do you have any desire for that to happen?" (2) At any point in life, did you dream of having a husband? (3) Does the thought of sex with a man seem gross? Does it seem frightening, or beautiful, or godly, or a "necessary evil for making babies?" There's a huge difference between thinking sex is a *dirty act* and thinking of sex as a "*godly way* to bless your husband, even though you yourself haven't had any passionate pursuit of it." The former is a warning flag against marriage. The latter isn't.

So "accept your present indifference to sexual desires." And "seek to love and serve people with all your gifts, be joyful in the Lord, and be mature and wise and strong and humble and honest. In other words, be a great, mature, deep sage of a woman. Don't go out of your way to make relationships happen, but if a worthy man shows an interest in you, go with it—in all purity—until it's plain that there is or there isn't a sense of desire or a sense of calling to spend your life with him in a growing intimacy of every kind."[14]

My spouse doesn't enjoy sex

Finding little pleasure in sex—this "quite common" challenge plagues couples who "seldom have the same level of interest and passion about sexual relations," including "frequency, location, timing, methods, privacy, kinds of touch." Simply put, "no couple has the same comfort level with all these variables." So this challenge is "virtually common to every couple: how to live sexually when desires in all of these areas are often significantly different—or, at least, in some of them."

Our sex lives fall short of God's mutual design. "God made sexual relations to be profoundly mutual in marriage; each *gives*, each *receives*, each feels the act as the consummation of a wider and deeper spiritual and personal union for which sex is only one of the capstones—but an important one." Lacking this mutual pleasure leads to a "dismay and sadness" in any marriage.

The key text is 1 Corinthians 7:3–5, set in the context of intimacy. Married couples are called to share their bodies. The text says, "Wife, accede to your husband's desires," and, "Husband, accede to your wife's desires." The husband can do what he pleases; the wife what she pleases. So what's to be done when the desires differ? "I don't think Paul slipped up here." No, "he knew exactly what he was doing" in "dealing with one of the deepest, most complex emotional moments in human life. Which means that any simple formula—for *who* gets to do *what* and *when* and *where* and *how*—will not fit reality." This formula would lead to "a total stalemate." Meaning, what happens in the marriage bed must fulfill Romans 12:10: "Outdo one another in showing honor." A competition of self-giving. "*She* will want to honor *him* by giving him *what he desires*. And *he* will want to honor *her* by giving her *what she desires*—which may be *less of his desire*." This honor principle prevents a total stalemate due to 1 Corinthians 7:3–5.

To the uninterested wife: "Don't say *yes* to your husband's desire tonight by complying, and then in a half-dozen ways communicate, 'I wish I weren't here.'" Take joy in that "you can give him pleasure," that "he only wants it from you," and that he trusts you "with his naked, emotional, physical, ridiculous abandon, which he would be embarrassed in any other context to display." So "a mature, growing, gracious wife who does not find physical pleasure in sexual relations can find lots of pleasures in the event because of the way God set it up to be."

14   APJ 1393: "I Feel No Sexual Attraction—Should I Still Pursue Marriage?" (November 11, 2019).

To the husband: "Don't assume the worst about her. Assume that even without sexual desires, she has other good desires to please you, and that is a kind of love that you can receive and enjoy. Yes, you wish she were more passionate, more there, more engaged. Yes, you do. That is normal. That is good."[15]

Paul's paradox for resolving bedroom disputes

Although just mentioned (above), and coming up again (later), it may be worthwhile to isolate the pair of texts Piper draws in to just about all marital disputes in the bedroom. One creates deadlock (1 Cor. 7:4). The other breaks the deadlock (Rom. 12:10).

Any "logic-chopper" who reads Paul's words about sex in 1 Corinthians 7:4, will see that his reasoning ends in a "total stalemate."[16] On the surface, Paul's "law" for resolving bedroom disputes doesn't resolve anything. The husband can do whatever he wants. The wife can do whatever she wants. Paul puts the focus on the wants.[17] "She gets to call the shots. And he gets to call the shots." It's a tie. So what happens when they disagree? Did Paul mess this up by creating a draw? No. "He knew exactly what he was doing" in dealing delicately "with one of the deepest, most complex emotional moments in human life." A "simple formula" will not resolve the challenges.[18] At first it looks like a "total stalemate" because no sex dispute in marriage can be resolved "by authority." The husband and wife have equal say. It's "a draw." The tie-breaker resolution must be found in Paul's "principle of love" (Rom. 12:10).[19] Bedroom disputes are resolved by self-sacrificing love and honor. Put these texts together (Rom. 12:10; 1 Cor. 7:4) to discover Paul's point. "Each of you strives to find your greatest sexual pleasure in the greatest sexual pleasure of your spouse."[20]

How do I stay physically attracted to my aging spouse?

First, "we live in a sex-crazed culture. Concepts of beauty are exaggerated, distorted, artificial, and disconnected from the reality of true, inner beauty. Anyone who watches television or movies will almost certainly have a distorted view of beauty and sexuality in our age." Sex is "vastly overrated" because even "in our own bodies the voice of sexual desire is very loud." The culture "creates an echo chamber where that loudness is so great it virtually drowns out

15 APJ 517: "My Spouse Doesn't Enjoy Sex" (January 23, 2015).
16 APJ 760: "Why Sexual Metaphors of Jesus and His Bride Embarrass Us" (December 29, 2015).
17 APJ 1582: "Has Porn Already Broken My Future Marriage?" (February 1, 2021).
18 APJ 517: "My Spouse Doesn't Enjoy Sex" (January 23, 2015).
19 APJ 1662: "Is Sex during Menstruation Sinful?" (August 6, 2021).
20 APJ 1582: "Has Porn Already Broken My Future Marriage?" (February 1, 2021).

other wonderful voices that are much more important, more precious, more lasting, and more essential to our humanity and God's glory than the voice of sexual desire."

In contrast, "Jesus Christ was the fullest, richest, deepest, most complete human being who ever existed, and he never had sexual relations with anyone. There are other dimensions to our nature that are infinitely more precious and more crucial to our humanity than the screaming force of sexual impulses, which silence other voices and deceive us into thinking that this impulse must be gratified." In other words, "modern men and women almost inevitably have absorbed distorted, deceptive, disproportionate views of sexuality" that influence marriage over the years.

The Bible says, rejoice in the wife of your *youth* (Prov. 5:18–20). And that's because "sexual desire is a good thing. God made it. It belongs in the covenant of marriage. And in that place of God-sealed commitment, it can be fully enjoyed for his glory." But the Bible also says, rejoice in the wife of your *aging* (Mal. 2:13–14). In this text, as time passed, "these men said, 'I'm going to get another woman—younger, better skin, better breasts, better legs, more desire.'" God hates this. It's evil because (1) your wife is your companion, (2) your wife is your covenant partner, and (3) God is the witness to your covenant. These three factors carry "explosively powerful, beautiful implications for affection and attraction as we grow old together, if those realities sink into us as they ought."

Youth and age carry their own splendors (Prov. 20:29). But in aging, we put more and more emphasis on the true splendor of internal beauty (2 Cor. 4:16–18). "Our focus is not on the wasting away of our outer beauty and strength. Our focus is on the unseen." This is true of your wife's current glory (on the inside) and her future glory (on the outside). She will be a queen of heaven! In this life, external beauty is *perishable*; inner beauty is *imperishable* (1 Pet. 3:3–4). The world gets this reversed. But "if women are to prioritize inner beauty over outer beauty, then we men, we husbands, should grow in our capacities to see and cherish and be moved by—deeply moved by, *physically moved by*—that inner beauty. . . . And I would put *no limits* on what those affections or desires might be." Perceived inner beauties can become physical turn-ons.

"So, out of this aged mouth, face-to-face with this once-glamorous, now-glorious companion, come these words: 'I love you. You are my treasure, my crown, my life companion. I cherish you. I have no eyes, no heart, for any other, old or young. Of all the women in the world, I chose you. I choose you still. I want you. You are precious to me. I want to be with you, near you. I want to touch you and hold you. You give me pleasure. God has been very, very good to me that I could call you mine.' If that comes from the heart, I don't think a woman would want you to say any more about her looks."[21]

As my body ages, how do I compete with other women for my husband's eyes?

The question came from an older woman in her seventies, a wife who noticed her husband checking out the body of an attractive, younger woman while shopping. It was more than a glance. So what should be done?

To the husband: Jesus said if your eye or hand cause you to sin, cut it off, gouge it out (Matt. 5:29–30). "Like a man in a nursing home that reaches out and pets the behind of a nurse, put the desire for the flesh of another woman—in sight or in hand—put that to death, man." Kill it. Or it will kill you. This is immature. "You are old enough, fella, to know that there are deeper, wider, longer, greater pleasures in life than the titillation of skin (Ps. 16:11). Come on, this is adolescent of you. It is mere animal. A seventy-year-old man acting like a dog in heat is not only silly; it's tragic."

In contrast, a wise older man will treasure his wife and say, "This is my woman—saggy, blotchy skin, gray hair, wrinkled face, decreased or absent libido. This is my woman, my treasure, my jewel, my gift from heaven, my covenant one, my intimate flesh, my own body, myself. To be faithful to her with my eyes and my hands is a satisfaction deeper and higher and sweeter than any glimpse or any touch of any other woman in the world."

To the wife who sent the question: (1) When you have time alone with him, talk with your husband about the episode at the store and how it made you "feel less loved, less valued." (2) Know that the wandering eye of a husband is "not inevitable" in old age. "No, a man can mature and love his wife for all that she has been, and is, and will be, including delicious memories of young bodies and deep pleasures of present and seasoned faithfulness. If a man insists on being a playboy at age seventy, he should realize that he is playing the part of a boy and not a man. And he should be ashamed." (3) Don't dwell on this and let the devil "sow seeds of distrust and anger." (4) Delight in God. "He delights in the inner beauty of your faith and fearlessness and humility and quiet peaceful-ness, and God gives himself to you for your fellowship and your enjoyment." He is with you and will never forsake you (Deut. 31:6; Isa. 41:10; Heb. 13:5). He can satisfy you forever (Ps. 16:11). (5) "Give your husband as much joy as you can every day," and know that as you do, "you are serving your heavenly

---

21   APJ 1396: "How Do I Stay Attracted to My Aging Spouse?" (November 18, 2019).

husband who is infinitely worthy, even when your earthly husband, at any given moment, may not be."[22]

Is oral sex okay?

The question about oral sex led to our most popular episode (now closing in on three million plays). Such a sensitive question must be handled with "verbal modesty, rather than shocking or crass words." But it should be handled, because it's a "real concern" and "people want biblical guidance. So here is my effort at biblical wisdom."

That wisdom is found by answering four questions.

1. Is it forbidden? No, oral sex isn't forbidden by Scripture.

2. Is it unnatural or unfitting? This answer is less overt. "The male and female genitals are so clearly made for each other that there is a natural fitness or beauty to it." So with oral sex we might "jump to the conclusion" that this is unnatural. "But I'm slow to go there because of what the proverbs and the Song of Solomon say about a wife's breasts." Breasts have a function, to feed babies. "So is there anything physically *natural* about a husband's fascination with his wife's breasts? Well, you might say *no*, that is not what breasts are for." But Scripture says the opposite. They *do* capture a husband's attention (Prov. 5:19; Song 7:7–8). So "though there is very little anatomical correlation between a man's hands, or his lips, and his wife's breasts, it surely seems to be 'natural' in another way—namely, built-in delight and desire that God, in his word, seems to commend for our marital enjoyment." This applies to other variables in sex. "So I doubt that we should put a limit on a married couple based on the claim of it being unnatural. That is risky, but that is where I come down on the naturalness of it."

3. Is it unhealthy or harmful? Maybe. In the presence of STDs, yes, it could be, so "the couple needs to be very honest and caring by not taking risks that would be unloving."

4. Is it unkind? This fourth question is the one "that touches the rawest nerve and the one that has the greatest impact." If you pressure a spouse for oral sex when "he or she finds it unpleasant," then you're being *unkind*, and that is a sin (Eph. 4:32). In the context of sex, the wife does not have authority over her body, nor the husband over his (1 Cor. 7:4). Practically speaking, this means that "both the husband and the wife have the right to say to the other, 'I would like to [fill in the blank].' And both of them have the right to say, 'I would rather

22 APJ 412: "I Caught My Husband Checking Out Another Woman" (August 21, 2014). "My favorite verse in the psalms is Psalm 16:11" (APJ 545: "Finding the Courage to Be Christian" [March 4, 2015]).

not [fill in the blank]." It's a stalemate. A beautiful, biblical marriage can only answer the question in seeking to outdo one another in love (Rom. 12:10).[23]

Is role-play okay in the bedroom?

Consider five warnings.

1. Sinful, fantasized pleasures are evil. If it would be a sin to act out what you desire, that desire is sinful. Jesus makes this clear (Matt. 5:27–29). He sets the standard of holiness for both "bodily deeds" *and* for "mental delights." So, for example, for a couple to agree to pretend to commit fictional fornication is a sin because "play-acted sin is sin."

2. Fantasized pleasures expected from an *unwilling* spouse is mistreatment (Rom. 12:10; 1 Cor. 6:19–20; Phil. 2:3). It is a "failure to honor, a failure to count the other more significant, a failure to glorify God with your body, and a failure to show you are not your own but bought with a price, belonging to Jesus."

3. Sinful, fantasized pleasures are bondage (Prov. 9:16–17; Rom. 7:7–8). "In the marriage bed, to the degree that you pursue some act as more pleasurable because it is illicit, you are in a fool's bondage to a sinful impulse."

4. Sinful, fantasized pleasures are a failure of purpose. "Sexual urges become too big when we lose big purposes for our lives." Our lives are about beholding Christ's glory (2 Cor. 3:18). "We need a big, beautiful, glorious, transcendent, majestic vision of God and his purpose for our lives if sex is to stay in its pleasurable, small place."

5. Fantasized pleasures fail. To men especially, "if you hope to have a thrilling, joyful, mutually satisfying sexual relationship with your wife for the next fifty years, you absolutely will not have it by demanding or expecting ever more bizarre exploits. Rather, you will have it by devoting 99 percent of your effort to loving your wife well outside the bedroom so that she finds you somebody she really desires." There's too much brokenness in this world to promise paradise in the bedroom for godly Christian couples. "But I do promise you, you will not find fifty years of mutual pleasure on the path of playacted perversion."[24]

Likewise, it is "adultery" for a man to fantasize in his mind about other women when in bed with his wife.[25]

Is sex during menstruation still prohibited?

Sex during menstruation was banned by law (Lev. 18:1–30; 20:10–21), and universally forbidden, since the practice would get even non-Jewish nations

---

23 APJ 400: "Is Oral Sex Okay?" (August 5, 2014).
24 APJ 1684: "Should Couples Use Role-Play in the Bedroom?" (September 27, 2021).
25 APJ 149: "My Husband Is Okay with Racy Scenes—I Hate It" (August 13, 2013).

divinely evicted from their lands (Lev. 18:24; 20:22–23). Is it taboo for Christian couples?

Several guidelines help us determine which Old Testament laws were fulfilled in Christ and which ones endure with varying levels of ethical relevance today. But in this case, there are no abiding commands against sex during menstruation for Christian couples. Without this "absolute prohibition," what now guides the decision?

Consider two roots to the Old Testament prohibition.

First, menstruation in the Old Testament made a woman unclean (Lev. 18:19) and potentially her husband too (Lev. 20:18). It was *not* "sinful impurity," because it required no sacrifice, only washing (Lev. 15:19–24). Though not a sin issue, menstruation was a "tremendous burden" for ancient women as a matter of ritual purity and community hygiene, challenging enough without intercourse factored in.

Second, the act of sex during menstruation "uncovered the fountain of her blood" (Lev. 20:18). This verse is likely a reference to the "sacred and profound" reality that the woman's monthly cycle "is a constant testimony" of her glory in being designed to bear and nurture new life in her womb. Her potential is manifested every month. Life is in the blood (Lev. 17:11). So we're speaking of a sacred, "life-giving spring or fountain. And during the menstrual flow of blood, there is the reminder that a life did not happen this month, though it might have." That sacred reality and monthly reminder should be protected and covered.

So what approach do Christian couples take? (1) Absent a prohibition, a couple may decide to refrain from sex briefly, "not because they have to, but because they choose to." (2) Absent a prohibition, a divided couple— whose *desires* are divided—must learn from the "total stalemate" dynamic of the new covenant (1 Cor. 7:4). The wife doesn't have authority over her own body. The husband does not have authority over his own body. "Which means that *he* has authority to have sexual intercourse with his wife during menstruation. And *she* has authority not to have sexual intercourse with her husband during menstruation. Which means this issue is not going to be resolved by authority. It's a draw. It's going to be resolved by love." And so, "if she finds sexual relations during menstruation offensive (or he does), his inclination will be to exercise self-control and love for her sacrificially, like Christ—for her sake, and really, thus, for his. And if she finds his desire for her to be very strong, she may give him that gift, or she may surprise him with some other pleasure. But I would say, especially to husbands: as the leader, you should take the lead in exercising self-control, and so bless her and win her affections, which I don't doubt will pay dividends in the rest of the month."[26]

Is sex the root of sexual sin?

David's sin against Bathsheba is solemnly instructive on many levels. It was malicious. David "raped" her.[27] A bold charge justified by the text.[28]

In Psalm 51 we read of David's later contrition and sincere repentance. He had raped Bathsheba, a married woman, got her pregnant, and attempted to cover it all up by murdering her husband, Uriah. But the adultery and murder are never mentioned in Psalm 51. "There is not a word about sex in this psalm, nor is there a word about murder, nor is there a word about lying. And it all started with sex. Or did it?" Sigmund Freud imagined all our problems are rooted in sexual problems, but "the Bible doesn't see it that way." Contra Freud, misusing God's beautiful gift of sex is a "symptom of a disease, not the disease."

So David pleads with God: "Restore to me *the joy of your salvation*" (Ps. 51:12). This is his "main issue" because "when that joy fades, I click on pornography. When that joy fades, I start cruising the neighborhood. When that joy fades, I get an itch for another woman." So "every sin on the outside is symptomatic of the absence" of joy in God. David knows how to fight lust with superior pleasures. "I don't have any problem doing all kinds of things to surround men and women with protections against sexual sin. In fact, I think that is a very good idea. It is just not the main point. If that is where you fight the battle continually, you will never get to the root of the issue. The root of the issue here is this renewed heart—this joy and gladness that the bones that God has broken, he has healed with the joy of our salvation."[29]

How our sex lives manifest our soul health

In Romans 1, Paul connects sexual dysfunction to the sinner's God dysfunction. And he does it in four ways. (1) Sinners exchange God's glory for idols, "*therefore* God gave them up in the lusts of their hearts to impurity" (Rom. 1:23–24). (2) Sinners are given over to sexual lust "*because* they exchanged the truth about God for a lie and worshiped and served the creature rather than the Creator" (Rom. 1:24–25). So "the cause of lust and impurity and the dishonoring of the body is the embrace of a lie about God." We wrongly believe that "sexual pleasure is more valuable to us than God. We have exchanged him

26 APJ 1662: "Is Sex during Menstruation Sinful?" (August 6, 2021).
27 APJ 234: "Muslims vs. Christians on the Sovereignty of God" (December 11, 2013).
28 APJ 1735: "Did Bathsheba Sin with David?" (January 24, 2022).
29 APJ 396: "Why Sex Is Not the Root of Sexual Sins" (July 30, 2014).

for a lie, and God hands us over." (3) Sinners exchange God for a lie; *therefore* God gives them up to dishonorable sexual passions (Rom. 1:25–26). "Three times so far he has said that the cause, the reason for God handing us over to the dishonoring of our own good, God-given passions, is that *we traded God. We traded* his truth and *we traded* his glory for other things, though they are not preferable." (4) "They did not approve of having God in their knowledge," *so* "God gave them up to a debased mind to do what ought not to be done" (Rom. 1:28).

Sex problems are not ignorance problems. Sex problems are preference problems—the fondness for a life without God. Sex dysfunctions are rooted in this attitude: "'I don't want you in my head. I don't want you in my heart. I don't want you to be supremely valuable. I will not have a God in my life who is supremely valuable. I just won't.'" Sinners *don't want* God, so God gives them up to do what ought not to be done (Rom. 1:28). So "it just could not be clearer—repetitively clearer." The root issue of sexual distortions—"homosexual and heterosexual"—are in this exchange. "God, I don't want you here." And when this is out of place, everything goes wrong.[30]

New passions prevent adultery. New passions drive our holy conduct. "And if you try to turn it around, you don't have Christianity anymore. I am a Christian Hedonist for theological reasons. I am after people's affections—their hearts, their emotions, their feelings—because all of our behaviors come from this. There may be a few behaviors that you do by dint of willpower against your passions. Very few. Ninety-nine percent of what you do is 'out of the abundance of the heart the mouth speaks,' and the arms move, and you live" (Matt. 12:34). So pursuing sexual holiness in marriage is all about "having new passions." Thus, we must not conform to the passions of our preconverted selves (1 Pet. 1:14).

Peter drives holiness and purity not merely by making claims on our holiness. He does it by revealing to us the glories of the gospel (1 Pet. 1:1–12). He first says, "Do you see the hope that you have? Do you see the inheritance? Do you see how it is imperishable and undefiled? Do you see how God is keeping you for it? Do you see how he is putting you through fire in order to make it precious so that you receive glory and praise and honor? Do you see that? Do you have knowledge now? If you do, you have got some new passions. And these old ones are not going to govern you anymore. Therefore, your conduct will be holy. Holiness is three steps out." Step 1: see the world as it really is and see eternity and see the value of your eternal hope. Step 2: "feel new passions." Step 3: do obedience. "That's Christianity."[31]

30 APJ 871: "How Our Sex Life Manifests Our Soul Health" (June 1, 2016).
31 APJ SE07: "The Passions That Prevent Adultery" (September 4, 2015).

How do our sex lives affect our prayer lives?

The apostle Paul says that a husband and wife should not deprive one another of sex, except for a brief season of prayer (1 Cor. 7:5). So how do our sex lives interfere with our prayer lives? And when should couples abstain for the sake of prayer? Is this like the principle of fasting, where the desire for sexual relations is meant to put our focus back on the Lord, to remind us that he is our ultimate joy and satisfaction above all else?

"Paradoxically," Paul sees this "suspension of sexual relations as a means of intensified devotion to prayer, presumably because the couple wants a breakthrough and some answer to prayer, because the devil is doing something they don't want him to do. They want to resist the devil—resist the unrighteousness that he's promoting. Abstaining from sexual relations for prayer is a way of making war on Satan." But not for too long, because "regular relations in marriage is a weapon against satanic triumphs. So abstaining from sexual relations for prayer is a weapon against Satan, and carrying on regular sexual relations is a weapon against Satan." That's "the paradox."

Take three principles from the text. (1) God designed physical life so that "ordinary things like sleeping, exercising, eating, and sexual relations in marriage all have their place in maintaining the appropriate spiritual equilibrium that keeps us from being knocked off balance by Satan." Go without sleep and you'll be more vulnerable to Satan's attack of depression and impatience. Go without food and you'll be more vulnerable to sins of irritability and of gorging later. (2) Our sex lives don't directly interfere with our prayer lives, "but they may provide protection from satanic attack against our prayer lives." A satisfying sex life "may free the mind for prayer and triumph over temptations to adultery or other kinds of sexual sin." But temporary abstinence from sex is a way to "show with our body's denial" how desperate we are for answered prayers. (3) But "the abstinence may be less planned than that and simply a response to some terrible news that we got. For example, you and your spouse may be planning a special evening that might climax in sexual relations. You're looking forward to it." But that evening you get a call about one of your children, injured in another state. Instead, you "give yourself to prayer." But either way, "planned or unplanned, the point is not that sex is *evil* or that it is a *hindrance* to the ordinary life of prayer. The point is that every legitimate pleasure we enjoy may be given up for a season to underline our intensity or desire for answered prayer or to show our emotional empathy for someone who is suffering."[32]

---

32 APJ 1068: "Does My Sex Life Affect My Prayer Life?" (July 17, 2017).

On Barrenness, Conception, and Birth Control

Do children burden the planet?

When the Pipers started their own family in 1972, large families were discouraged. Overpopulation was the concern. Children are a detriment to the health of the planet. So it was said. But our children will not burden the planet if we raise them to be burden lifters. "They are in the world to lift the world, to save the world, to love the world. You are not just adding dead weight to the world when you bring a child up in the kingdom. You are bringing up lovers of people and servants of the world." Parents shape the world changers of the future in ways convictional DINKs (double income, no kids) cannot imagine.[1]

Why have children, when there are so many orphans?

The "modern resistance to having children, as though they get in the way and are a pain in the neck, is a sign of cultural corruption and selfishness." Biological children are a blessing from the Lord (Ps. 127:4–5). And adoption is a wonderful way to love another, like God adopted us. But these two realities, the goodness of biological children and the goodness of adoption, are not mutually exclusive. "The vast majority of adoptive parents also have children biologically," and "I have never met anybody who has *not* adopted because they have had children of their own." By the same logic, it's "permissible and good" for us to eat food even if someone in the world needs food more than we do. Wear clothes even though others need clothes more than us. Live in houses when others live in tents. In other words, "our having is usually not the reason others don't have. It is not a zero-sum game in this world of resources."[2]

---

1   APJ 230: "Should Christians Use the Pill?" (December 5, 2013).
2   APJ 202: "With So Many Orphans, Why Have Children?" (October 25, 2013).

On birth control pills (and their alternatives)

"Abortion is *birth control*."[3] *Birth control* is the wrong term for *conception control*. All Christian couples "should operate on this principle: I am not going to destroy a fertilized egg." Tragically, the so-called birth control pill seems to be designed to do this. So "do your best, by whatever research and consultation you can, to decide what means of *conception control* you should use."[4] Not killing a conceived child is "a top-level Christian commitment." This raises issues with so-called birth control pills, because "most oral contraceptives run the risk of functioning as abortive agents," designed (at least in part) to abort fertilized eggs, "which have become human beings." This issue is worth a lot more critical thinking in the church. "I think one of the things I most tremble about from forty-five years ago is whether Noël and I may have inadvertently aborted a baby because of a pill. I wasn't even thinking in those terms—that some of these pills worked that way."[5] The blatant goal of inducing an abortion is more clearly stated in the morning-after pill and other chemical abortifacients of the past, present, and future.[6]

Before deciding on contraception, consider these five principles. (1) Sex is to be celebrated for its most common function—pleasure, not procreation. (2) Commit to never use abortifacient contraceptives that destroy a fertilized egg, which is a human being. (3) Be cautious with all permanent contraception decisions like vasectomies or tubal ligations. What if your spouse dies and you remarry? You will have made a final decision without your future spouse's consent. (4) Don't use selfish excuses to intrude on God's will for how many children you bear. (5) "Don't decide against children because they are a burden to your lifestyle of travel and free evenings. In other words, everything I have been saying assumes a radical commitment to kingdom purposes, not worldly conveniences. If we decide to have children or not to have children, let it be worshipfully—because we have said *yes* to God's radical call on our lives—not selfishly, because it spares us some discomfort."[7]

On permanent birth control

A middle-aged couple asked a follow-up question to (3) above. They've had children. Now in their late thirties and forties, is it okay for a monogamous husband and father of two, who seems to be done having children, to get a vasectomy?

---

3   APJ 552: "Is Permanent Birth Control a Sin?" (March 13, 2015).
4   APJ 230: "Should Christians Use the Pill?" (December 5, 2013).
5   APJ 552: "Is Permanent Birth Control a Sin?" (March 13, 2015).
6   APJ SE31: "*Roe v. Wade* Has Ended—Our Pro-Life Work Has Not" (June 30, 2022).
7   APJ 552: "Is Permanent Birth Control a Sin?" (March 13, 2015).

1. Hear a cultural caution. "The older I get, the more suspicious I become that I am more a child of my historical and cultural circumstances than I once thought I was." We have been—"almost certainly"—"deeply infected" by a culture that has twisted our understanding of marriage and children and sex and personal comforts and freedoms. We are "profoundly shaped by the cultural air we breathe." This cultural air refuses to "rejoice at the blessing of children. It does not gladly embrace the enormous cost and effort of raising children in the nurture and admonition of the Lord. It does not see marriage as forming a beautiful, meaningful, lifelong, faith-building, character-forming matrix for growing the next generation." Our culture doesn't value "covenant commitments" to spouses and children, and instead it "justifies every possible means of minimizing our own personal frustration and pleasure and maximizing personal freedom, whether through postponing marriage, or not having children, or avoiding any kind of commitment, or divorcing in order to get out of an uncomfortable marriage, or neglect of children, sticking them in some institution while we go about our careers."

2. Set this decision in a biblical framework. Rehearse six convictions. (i) Marriage is normative. It's not good for a man to be unmarried (Gen. 2:18). (ii) Within the normative marriage covenant, making and raising children is also normative. (iii) Conception control is not prohibited and may be used by couples seasonally. (iv) Singleness remains an option for any Christian who refuses marriage for "God-centered, Christ-exalting, mission-advancing, church-building, soul-saving, sanctifying purposes" (1 Cor. 7:7–9, 32–35). (v) If singleness remains an option for kingdom-minded Christians, it is also analogously true that a married couple may decide to *not* have children for the sake of kingdom work. Both decisions—singleness and childlessness—are made from a "self-denying, Christ-exalting, mission-advancing motivation." (vi) It's "a sin" for couples to reject the gift of children for the sake of worldly gain and personal comfort.

3. Get honest with your motives and plead for help. Determining *why* we choose what we do is a "huge burden." Our culture's media warp us, our sinful hearts shroud our true motives, and we are "prone to come up with a theology and an ethical framework that justifies our desires." So plead for God to search your heart (Ps. 139:23–24). Beware of the culture, beware your feelings, and don't presume upon the future. As a couple, ask for God's guidance by pleading Psalm 25, because "I don't know any other passage of Scripture that is better for putting into words our cry for guidance and wisdom from God."[8]

---

8   APJ 1761: "On Permanent Birth Control" (March 25, 2022).

Can couples go childless on purpose?

Yes, there are "kingdom reasons" for going childless. But "the modern resistance to having children—as though they get in the way and are a pain in the neck—is a sign of cultural corruption and selfishness. And so if that is your motive for not having kids—*no*, you are not obeying Jesus. If you are viewing children as that kind of pain in the rear end, and you want to go on and do your thing without the encumbrance of having to care for kids, then you have an attitude that isn't biblical. I would never commend childlessness the way the world commends childlessness."[9]

So "don't decide against children because they burden your lifestyle of travel and free evenings." Instead, consider selflessness. The selflessness of missions is one kingdom reason for childlessness. Think of it this way. Marriage and children were normative and good, even before sin entered the picture (Gen. 1:28; 2:18). A world without sin is a world without need for world missions, gospel-suffering, or martyrdom. So prior to the fall, marriage and children were "virtually an absolute" reality. No longer. Now that global missions is essential, marriage and children are not (1 Cor. 7:7, 32–35).[10]

Paul's counsel to singles on forgoing marriage (1 Cor. 7:7–9, 32–35) also applies to couples who forgo children, because "the principles relating to spouselessness and childlessness are the same." Missionaries headed to hard places may forgo marriage, and married couples are "free to forgo the normal, wonderful blessing of children." Yet that may not mean *never* having children. Perhaps you will welcome children in the future. Children or no children, make it your mission to make all the children on this planet into glad worshipers of God.[11]

A quiver full of children is a blessing from the Lord (Ps. 127:4–5). "And yet, by the same logic, it may be wise to have two or three or four, not ten, if you are going to go to Guinea." Marriage is a good "creation ordinance," but Paul qualifies it with a "redemption ordinance." In this gospel age, it is both *not good* for man to be unmarried (Gen. 2:18), and also *good* for a man to be unmarried on mission (1 Cor. 7:7).[12]

Can nonmissionary families "simply choose" to go childless?

Missionary families may limit their quiver on purpose. But what about nonmissionary families? A childless couple in Finland wants to know if it's permissible for an ordinary Christian couple to "simply choose" to not have children.

---

9   APJ 202: "With So Many Orphans, Why Have Children?" (October 25, 2013).
10   APJ 552: "Is Permanent Birth Control a Sin?" (March 13, 2015).
11   APJ 286: "Childless Missionaries by Design?" (February 26, 2014).
12   APJ 230: "Should Christians Use the Pill?" (December 5, 2013).

To start, "I don't think there is any such thing as 'simply choose.'" To "simply choose" would mean "'without any struggles or conflicts or reasonings, but just because we feel like it.' And my first response to this is to say that there is no such thing." Whatever we *say*—still more, whatever we *choose*—is spillover from our heart's abundant desires (Matt. 12:34). So choosing to not have kids is a choosing from "deep realities that have shaped our hearts, our preferences, our desires, our wants, our inclinations." Five things will reveal the heart in this decision.

1. Children are a precious gift and normative for couples. Bearing children is the pattern for couples, prefall (Gen. 1:28) and postfall (Gen. 9:7). "It is normal, beautiful, fitting, natural, and normative, according to Scripture," explicitly and implicitly, "for a married couple to have children." Children are a great gift (Ps. 127:3–5), a glory to a father (Prov. 17:6), and a blessing to a mother (Prov. 31:28). "What a sadness when many modern women—shortsightedly, I think—choose to forgo that blessing, while millions would literally give their right arm to have it."

2. God knows all families will struggle. The parent-child relationship can go very badly in this world (2 Sam. 18:33; Prov. 30:11; Matt. 26:24; Luke 12:52). "The Bible is not a Pollyanna tale of happy families. Almost all of them in the Bible are broken, one way or the other. But none of this—none of it—hinders the ongoing reality that conceiving and raising children is normal, beautiful, fitting, natural, normative."

3. The goal of life is not to avoid "hardship or heartache or suffering." We will never know if our future child will be born disabled or "break our heart with unbelief." We don't know if our children will outlive us or not. And healthy, godly children will demand all sorts of sacrifices from parents. But in all of this, the Bible assumes that we are saved *in* and *through* (not *in spite of*) life's struggles (Acts 14:22; 20:35; James 1:3).

4. We cannot predict our children's influence. None of us can predict if our child "will be a *debit* or a *credit* to the human race, a *curse* or a *blessing*, a *taker* or a *giver*." Maybe a son will become "a freeloader with a big carbon footprint, or he may be a genius who invents the very means of saving millions of lives." Parents are called to raise their children to bless the world as they glorify God.

5. God has made the path to childbearing clear in his pattern of fertility. Scripture (and nature) point to childbearing as normative for couples, "unless God himself makes it crystal clear that the self-denying path of Christ-exalting obedience is childlessness."[13]

A couple wants to pray against pregnancy for a season. Is this acceptable?

---

13 APJ 1507: "Are Christian Couples Required to Have Kids?" (August 3, 2020).

This question is answered by balancing the same two text-groups. In Genesis, God says "it is *not good*" that a man remains alone—he should add a wife to his life (Gen. 2:18). And they should bear fruit and multiply and fill the earth with children (Gen. 1:28). So it's "right, normal, and proper to want and pursue a family in the world as God created it," and to "raise up lots of lovers of God who fill the earth with his glory." But then Paul steps in and says "it is *good*" for a single man to remain alone—he doesn't need to add a wife to his life (1 Cor. 7:26–27). Paul claims that singleness is "preferable to marriage" when it comes to our devotion to Christ. This claim is "astonishing" in view of Genesis 2:18, "that Paul would say there are times when it would be better to be alone and not to marry."

Here's the point: "while it is normal and right and proper in the ordinary order of creation for marriage to be pursued, nevertheless, now that Christ has come into the world, there are redemptive priorities—saving priorities—where it's right, for redemptive and saving purposes, for a person to forgo marriage. This means that Christ-exalting kingdom principles and kingdom values on this side of the cross *relativize* the mandate for marriage in the order of creation." The "goodness" of the creation mandate is relative to "the glorification of Christ and the advance of his kingdom." If so, this applies to marriage and, by extension, to children. "In other words, this is the normal, right, good pattern for all people in the order of creation. But there may be situations in life when, for Christ-exalting, God-centered, kingdom-advancing reasons, restricting the number of children that we have may be appropriate."

So the question over quiver size is made more challenging, not less, because it's not a question about the size of the family but about whether or not our priorities are driven by "Christ-exalting, God-centered, kingdom-advancing motives" or by "fear or unbelief or selfishness or worldliness." God knows our hearts. "He's a merciful Father, and he loves children. But our having children is not his highest priority. His highest priority for his children is Christ-exalting faith and Christ-magnifying joy that overflow in meeting the needs of others. That's his highest priority. He loves big families with lots and lots of children— not for their own sake, but for Christ's sake. The issue is: how do our lives, with *many* or *few* children, magnify the greatness of Christ?"[14]

Should young couples postpone children?

Many young couples seek to postpone children as they finish school and establish careers. Is this a good idea?

---

14 APJ 1176: "Is It Sinful for My Husband and Me to Pray against Pregnancy?" (March 26, 2018).

Married right after college, Pastor John faced six more years of school (three years of seminary and three years of doctoral work). With prayer and a season of searching Scripture, Noël became the temporary breadwinner. "So we took steps to avoid pregnancy—I hope without any abortifacients. The reason I say *I hope* is that I was so ignorant in the late sixties and early seventies that we may not have taken all the necessary precautions that we should have to make sure the way we were avoiding conception was in fact nonabortive. I tremble at what we may have unknowingly done. But nobody needs to make that mistake in ignorance today."

After four years, they stopped using the pill and embraced the financial risk of children. Noël looked at her season of working outside the home as a temporary diversion from her calling and desire to manage a home, the wife's normative calling. She saw these four years as "part of the overall united effort that we were making together to create a home . . . with me as the main breadwinner," the normative calling of the husband.[15]

I want kids, but my husband doesn't

The question is from the wife. The episode is for the husband. "I know his heart can change, because my heart changed." The Pipers had four boys, and "I loved them" and "thought we were done." Then came the opportunity to adopt Talitha. Piper was fifty. "And I thought, 'Oh, my goodness. I am too old. This will never work.'" But "God did a great work in my heart." So here are ten reasons why "a man, a husband, should want to be a father."

(1) The mandate. God calls men to multiply and bear fruit (Gen. 1:28). It's not absolute, but it's the norm. "God's plan is to fill the earth with image bearers of his glory, and it is a glorious thing to participate in that." (2) The heritage. Children are an inheritance (Ps. 127:3). And "even if every one of your children breaks your heart," this truth holds. Some rewards come only through "fatherly sorrow." (3) The glory. Fathering children and welcoming grandchildren is "a glorious affair in both directions" (Prov. 17:6). (4) The divine link. "God, the Creator of the universe, has revealed himself as a heavenly Father," creating the world "with fatherhood in it" from the beginning, before there were human fathers, "so that we would experience what he is like in his fatherhood-ness." (5) The fruit-giving potential. One of fatherhood's most compelling motivations is that it makes a woman into a mother. "In having children, a man discovers he is married to a mother, which he wasn't before." In this new glory, "you now get to be married not only to a wife but to a life bearer, a mother with all of her

---

15 APJ 1347: "Should We Postpone Children While I Finish My Degree?" (May 24, 2019).

years of motherhood in front of her. If motherhood is a beautiful thing—and it is—how beautiful it is to participate in the making of a mother." (6) The love. To be married to "a woman who deeply longs to have children" is to see "a God-blessed, natural, beautiful, longing in her heart." Love her as you would love your own body (Eph. 5:28–30). This is neighbor love, but with a neighbor "who sleeps with you every night" (Matt. 7:12; 19:19). To love her is to love yourself. You are one flesh. And "when she becomes joyful in motherhood, this joy will be your joy, because she is you. Her joy is your joy." (7) The gift. You give children to her, children who will eventually honor and love her back (Prov. 31:28). When they leave home, and "write home from college, having awakened to the reality of all of those years of sacrifice and gifting"—this is the gift of future honor "every husband should be happily willing to give his wife." (8) The wonder. Pregnancy is a miracle, a process whereby "human life has come into being that never existed before and now will live forever. And we—this woman and I—we were God's instruments of creation. God just created an everlasting human being by our seed. What a wonder. What a calling. What an honor." (9) The blessing to the world. Children are not simply a detriment to the planet and a cause of overpopulation. No, they can be raised as burden lifters who shape the world. (10) The communion. "In having children, expect to know God as you never knew him before. And expect to be made more humble, more holy, more mature, more loving, more alive, more far-seeing, more seriously joyful than you could be any other way."[16]

On the fear that God maybe didn't elect our future children

The arguments for not having kids extends beyond personal comfort to matters of theology. If there's a chance that our future children are not elect, and they will suffer eternally, isn't this risk high enough for Christian parents to simply never have children?

No, the risk is not too high, for at least five reasons. (1) God's call to obedience is not ignorant. God commands us to multiply (Gen. 1:28), and he gave us this command in full knowledge of the fall to come. "He knew what the fall would mean for perishing and suffering, misery, relational horror, and catastrophe. Nothing took God off guard." The fall does not change his command. Nor does election. "God created the doctrine of election and commanded us to have children." He commanded us to bear children in full awareness of the fall and election. (2) We can trust him. God is infinitely wise and good. "He knows what he's doing. He has good reasons for why one person is shown mercy

16 APJ 908: "'I Want Kids. My Husband Doesn't'" (July 29, 2016).

and another is passed over in their rebellion and unbelief. We must be very, very careful lest we think in a way that implies that God's ways are foolish or unwise or cruel." (3) The calling to parenthood is a high and holy calling, even if it brings pain and uncertainty. "All the risks and all the sorrows that it brings are part of a high and holy and precious and honorable calling and purpose of God." (4) God's plan for his glory and the joy of the elect remains incomplete. Christ's return to earth has been delayed for two millennia so that "all of the elect will repent and be saved and have the experience of eternal joy in the presence of God" (2 Pet. 3:8–9). The elect are still being born today, and time must be allowed for their full number to arrive. God set the timeline, aware "that thousands, indeed millions, of others will be born during that delay of Christ—others who will not believe but will perish." (5) The second coming is delayed for the sake of the joy of the elect. "He does not let the fact that many will become rebellious and reject his love compel him to withhold from his elect their eternal joy." This is the mindset of parents for their children. "We will pray, work, agonize, weep, and maybe even die so that Christ would be formed in them. But we will not let the possible misery of some prevent us from pursuing and hoping for the eternal joy of all [the elect]."[17]

On the fear of childbirth
The fear of giving birth (*tokophobia*) is not irrational. The curse in Genesis 3:16 "brought pain and risks into the act of childbirth," including death to child and mother. "It is understandable that a woman would look with some circumspect seriousness and hesitation about whether to marry at all, and whether to risk the pain of childbirth in marriage. I get it." Yet these exact fears are met with the triumphant promise of 1 Timothy 2:15, paraphrased like this: "Even though a woman may need to *pass through* the painful remnants of the curse that came on childbearing in Genesis 3, nevertheless, she should not see this pain as God's curse in Christ but rather press on by faith, with love and holiness and self-control, and thus experience God's complete salvation." Christ has overcome every possible tragedy in the delivery room. The upshot: "While childbearing is still hard, nevertheless, you will *come through it* in Christ." Guaranteed. The same promise echoes in John 16:21—"the pain of childbirth is not an end in itself. By God's grace in Christ, it leads to great joy, just like the resurrection brings joy after the sufferings of Jesus."[18]

17 APJ 1326: "Why Have Kids If They Might End Up in Hell?" (April 5, 2019).
18 APJ 1366: "I'm Terrified of Giving Birth—Should I Still Pursue Marriage?" (July 8, 2019). See also, John Piper, "How Are Women Saved through Childbearing? A Careful Study of 1 Timothy 2:15," Desiring God, June 10, 2014, https://www.desiringgod.org/.

On the fear of messing up our kids

Another young woman is afraid of childbirth but even more afraid of corrupt-ing her children and perpetuating her own dysfunction and sins into them. She doesn't want to "ruin their hearts." Any advice?

A lot can be said, but there are five glories to motherhood.

1. The glorious body. The child originates inside the mother's womb and is sustained for nine months, and then, "in most cultures, is sustained at her breasts for another year or two." A mother should be "continually amazed" by God's design for herself and her child. These are "fallen glories, imperfect glories, corrupted glories because both our souls and all of nature have fallen under the judgment of God because of sin. But the glories still shine through, and in Christ we are meant to embrace them and free them as much as we can from the contamination of the fall." Not until after the fall was the first woman—Eve, the mother of all living—"the source of all human life" (Gen. 3:20). God could have done this differently. He didn't. And Paul echoes its significance in 1 Corinthians 11:11–12 to prove that "every man who has ever lived, however small or great, owes his life to a woman, his mother."

2. The glorious workmanship. Psalms describes the glories of pregnancy to reveal "that her womb is no mere natural cocoon, but the sacred place of God's own personal handiwork" (Ps. 139:13–14). He's there "forming an ever-lasting human being just as closely as if he were using his fingers and knitting needles—and that is a great glory."

3. The glorious shaping influence. A mother shares life-giving teaching with her children over the years (Prov. 1:8–9). "The most influential people in the world are mothers. Thousands of men may rise up to positions of power all over the world. All of them come from the womb and the influence of mothers, even kings and presidents."

4. The glorious honor. Rightly, children are called to glorify their moth-ers for all the honorable and glorious things they have done in birthing and influencing them (Eph. 6:1–2).

5. The glorious sorrows. The "sorrows that every mother will experience in giving birth and raising her children will be glorious sorrows. And what I mean is that when a mother has sorrows—even over the forsaking of God, the forsaking of a family, by a child—when a mother has such sorrows, it is a glorious sorrow because it is a partaking in the very sorrows that Jesus him-self experienced at the one point where he compared himself to mothering" (Matt. 23:37).

So "take heart" for the future and trust God's promises for motherhood. God will supply all your mothering needs in Christ (Phil. 4:9). And he will make his grace abound to you as a mother for all the good deeds you will be called to achieve (2 Cor. 9:8).[19]

Additionally, there's hope for young parents seeking a break with the broken homes of their own childhood. To those raised in dysfunctional homes, your past doesn't condemn your future.[20] And to those conceived out of wedlock, you can "become great" in Christ.[21]

On infertility

The pain of infertility is deep and real, but God is sovereign and "infinitely wise" and "his timing, his giving, and his withholding are all done in an infinite wisdom as he shapes and guides our lives for our ultimate good and for the glory of his name." Pray for a miracle. And if he does not answer, it's no violation of the promises to the righteous in Psalm 84:11. While you wait, seek first the kingdom. Trust that God's work is good even in this pain. He comforts the barren with the promises in Isaiah 56:3–5. "Faith takes a verse like that and says, 'Okay, you have withheld from me my desired son or daughter. And you are going to give me a monument and a name better than sons and daughters.' That is simply amazing. And I think we ought to hold fast to it. Jesus never had children, and Paul never had children, and I am sure they looked at little children and thought, 'Now that is a joy that I would love to have.' But God withheld marriage and children from those two men and gave them, instead, a monument and a name both in this life and in the life to come that are superior."[22]

Isaiah 56:3–5 is a profound promise for singles who will never marry, and for married couples who will never conceive. God has for you a name and eternal legacy superior to marriage and sons and daughters of your own.[23]

Should Christians conceive via IVF?

Traditional in vitro fertilization (IVF) practices are abortive and more destructive than childlessness. "I don't think childlessness leads to the kinds of harmful effects that have come from the massive move toward various types of surrogacy and reproductive artificiality outside the womb. These have resulted, for example, in three quarters of a million 'frozen babies' whose natural parents do not want them, not to mention other harmful effects. Childlessness is painful,

19 APJ 993: "What If I Ruin My Kids?" (January 23, 2017).
20 APJ 720: "Can My Life Be Plagued by Generational Sins, Hexes, or Curses?" (November 3, 2015) and APJ 1612: "Hope for Children from Dysfunctional Families" (April 12, 2021).
21 APJ 976: "Is It Sinful to Be Pregnant before Marriage?" (December 14, 2016).
22 APJ 46: "Care for Couples Struggling with Infertility" (March 13, 2013).
23 APJ 984: "Will I Be Single for the Rest of My Life?" (January 2, 2017).

but it is not sinful. It is not destructive of human life, and there is great grace that God has for the childless."[24]

These types of procedures—IVF, egg donation, sperm donation, and surrogacy ("renting a womb")—call for the utmost caution. They have resulted in "an entire global industry of baby-making which is shot through with unanswered ethical and medical questions." Left in the wake are abortifacient procedures and frozen embryos ("frozen babies") discarded or awaiting adoption. And yet, no matter the means, "creating human babies is decisively God's work, not man's. No baby decides if he or she is human. No parents decide if their baby is human. No sperm donor, egg donor, or womb host decides if the baby is human. No doctor, who's putting all the pieces together, decides if this baby is human. So who does? *God does*" (Job 10:11–12; 31:13–15; Pss. 71:6; 139:13–14; Eccl. 11:5; Jer. 1:5). God's sovereignty over the cross is the same sovereignty that brings about new human life, even via unnatural means. "If God can orchestrate Herod, Pilate, brutal Roman soldiers, and unbelieving Jews to bring about the greatest life-giving event that ever was—the death and resurrection of Jesus—then making a human baby with sinful humans is not a problem." Only God makes human life, no matter the means. And "God often uses foolishness, and even evil, to bring beauty into being."[25]

Considering the tragedy of discarded embryos, embryo adoption is a legitimate choice for pro-life Christians.[26] But it's a grave decision. The existence of "750,000 frozen children" in America who will mostly be discarded one day is a "tragedy" resulting from the "unwise and sometimes sinful" desires and practices of reckless couples abusing IVF solutions. We must (1) confront the upstream causes of discarded embryos, while (2) mitigating the tragedy's downstream effects through adoption.[27]

To a young woman conceived via IVF by a biological father she will never meet because he never intended to be a part of her life, know that many children are conceived in ways that are less than ideal. Some are made through reproductive technology with a donor who has no interest in a future child. And many others are conceived by "accidents" of rape, casual sex, or from couples not intending (or wanting) to get pregnant. Children are put up for adoption for all sorts of good and bad reasons, and many children will never meet their biological parents. Whatever your origin story looks like, we are all conceived in sin, a product of other sinners (Ps. 51:5). We all share this fundamental

24 APJ 1165: "Do Reproductive Technologies Oppose God's Design?" (February 28, 2018).
25 APJ 1450: "Are IVF Babies Knit Together by God Too?" (March 23, 2020).
26 APJ 1450: "Are IVF Babies Knit Together by God Too?" (March 23, 2020).
27 APJ 1768: "Should Pro-Lifers Embrace Embryo Adoption?" (April 11, 2022).

problem. And yet, by grace, "God is eager to adopt us, to make us his children and heirs with his eternal Son, Jesus Christ." His adopting grace is offered to us all (Rom. 8:16–17; Eph. 1:4–7). "This is the rock-solid, unshakable, always-valid, always-reliable truth about you. Compared to the sorrow of thinking that biological parents treated you as a commodity, which is a sorrow—compared to the sorrow of that thought and that reality, the fact that God has desired you as a daughter and bought you at the cost of his Son's life is ten thousand times more precious and more important."[28]

Did my sin cause our miscarriage?

A man gave in to lust and now wonders if his porn use caused his wife's miscarriage. Four questions must be answered.

1. Does God discipline his children? Yes, God disciplines the children he loves (Heb. 12:5–6). And God also looks on his children as perfect (Heb. 10:14). So "God can view his children both as *perfected* by Christ and still *in need of perfecting* in this life. And we should take tremendous heart from his painful, perfecting work as evidence that we are perfected."

2. Does God's discipline include physical death? Yes, in his final work of perfecting us he may cut our physical life short (1 Cor. 11:29–32). In this case, the premature death of a justified Christian "is the discipline of deliverance from condemnation. God takes him out so that he will not be taken out by the devil and by sin and go to hell." So God's ways "are not to be trifled with or made little of."

3. Could God's discipline of us lead to the death of a loved one? Yes, as seen in the fallout of David's sin with Bathsheba and the death of their newborn son (2 Sam. 12:14). "I would certainly say in my own life the most painful and humbling disciplining from the Lord has regularly been through the pain and suffering—and sometimes death—of those I love, rather than through any blows against my own body." But it remains deeply difficult to discern God's purposes. "I don't know whether our friend who wrote this question lost his child in miscarriage as a *direct* discipline from God because of his pornography. I do not know. This man does not know. I do know that in the loss of the child, God wills a new humility and a new submission and a new faith and new purity through the pain of this loss."

4. Now what does he do? This situation holds many uncertainties, "but the path of gospel obedience is not uncertain. The glorious truth of the gospel is that we never need to be sure whether *a specific suffering* is owing to *a specific*

28 APJ 1165: "Do Reproductive Technologies Oppose God's Design?" (February 28, 2018).

disobedience." We're not left to figure this out. "I have dealt with so many people over the years who come into my office longing to know whether there is some connection between *some pain* and *some sin*. And I always start and end with the fact that you don't need to know that. And the reason we don't need to be sure about that is that the gospel forgiveness and gospel righteousness imputed through faith in Christ does not depend on that certainty of understanding."

So this man should "stop fretting about whether his pornography was the *direct cause* of this miscarriage" because he cannot expect a "sure answer" to that question, "short of some direct revelation." But in either case, the conclusion is the same. "The Lord gives and the Lord has taken away. And God's merciful design for our friend is that he worship. Blessed be the Lord (Job 1:21). Worship more deeply, the way Job did."[29]

---

29 APJ 963: "Did My Lust Cause Our Miscarriage?" (November 14, 2016). On replacing the term "addiction" for "sinful excess," see APJ 530: "The Real Cost of Pornography" (February 11, 2015) (on porn addiction), APJ 657: "How Do I Choose between Two Good Things?" (August 7, 2015) (on digital media and smartphone addiction), APJ 1314: "How Do I Break My Entertainment Addiction?" (February 18, 2019) (on gaming and video entertainment addiction), and APJ 1702: "On Cigarettes, Vaping, and Nicotine" (November 8, 2021) (on nicotine, vaping, and smoking addictions).

On Hard Marriages, Divorce, and Abuse

Is marriage worth the trouble?

Paul says, "Be married, mourn, rejoice, buy, and deal with the world with a certain detachment, because this is a fragile, short-lived world" (1 Cor. 7:29–31). So "don't sink your roots too deep here in this world, whether it is happy or whether it is sad." Into this context, Paul speaks of marriage. Paul himself "loves being single for ministry" and commends it (1 Cor. 7:26–28). He affirms that marriage pleases God, but the married will have added tribulations. This point raises a curious dilemma. Paul was *single* and had all sorts of *tribulations* added to his life, so "he clearly does not mean singleness is free from tribulation," because "he was in prison every other week," shipwrecked—an unmarried life that was "tremendously burdened." Paul wants Christians freed from worldly anxieties but anxious for the things of God (1 Cor. 7:32). So Paul employs three jarring contrasts that end up *not meaning* what we think they mean. Things of the Lord (single life); things of the world (married life). Please the Lord (single); please the wife (married). Seek to be holy in body and spirit (single); please the husband (married). These three contrasts "are so contrary to what Paul teaches elsewhere, even in this letter, that we know they don't mean what they seem to mean at first." Marriage is not vain worldliness. The husband does not stop pleasing God when he pleases his wife. And the wife does not become unholy by pleasing her husband. So what's his point?

In the end, Paul is "recruiting radical devotion to the Lord that is uncomplicated by the practical demands of marriage." So Paul wants "a lot of people to be single because of the nature of the demands of ministry and the press of time." But for those who choose to marry, Paul has another magnificent text—not here in 1 Corinthians 7. "You have got to go to Ephesians 5 for that. And when you go there, it is glorious."[1]

---

1   APJ 584: "Is Marriage Eternally Futile?" (April 28, 2015).

Does my spouse's sin terminate our marriage?

The question came from a wife, married to a porn-abusing husband.

"My answer is *no*. Your husband's struggle or compromise with pornography is not a marriage deal-breaker. And I would also say that a wife's compromise with pornography is not a deal-breaker for her husband." Why not? Four reasons. (1) Marriage is a covenant union (Gen. 2:24; Eph. 5:32). It is "covenantal to the max," a "model of how Christ is bound to his church in the new-covenant relationship. And he is *really, really* bound to his church." (2) Marriage is God-bound in heaven (Mark 10:9). In the wedding vows, something beyond human activity is happening. "God is creating a marriage," bound in the courts of heaven. (3) The covenant bond holds until physical death (Rom. 7:2–3). (4) "Marriage is consummated in sexual union," in the two becoming one flesh (Gen. 1:28; 4:1; Matt. 19:5; 1 Cor. 7:2–3).

With those four points in place, a couple should remain married "through hell and high water." Man must not separate what God has united (Mark 10:9). Divorce is prohibited (Mark 10:11–12; 1 Cor. 7:10–11). So "when we make the vow—'for better or for worse'—we don't mean, 'for better or for worse *unless* there is pornography.' We don't mean, 'for better or for worse *unless* you turn out to be somebody I never dreamed you were.' That, by the way, happens to pretty much everybody. Wives and husbands do not stay the same. Marriage is risky business, which is why I think the disciples said, 'If such is the case of a man with his wife, it is better *not to marry*'" (Matt. 19:10).

But the porn-compromised husband is "committing a grave sin against God and his wife," and he needs the rebuke of the men in the church. A wife should never feel entrapped or isolated by her husband's sin. "Marriage is not a trap."[2]

To a spouse considering divorce

"Not many things are heavier on the heart than long-term marital disappointment."[3] But sadly, the world's pain seems to concentrate in families. It is "the cost of covenant-making and covenant-keeping love. It cost Jesus his life to be in that kind of relationship. So I am not ever making light of the kind of pain that can be sustained in a parenting or marriage relationship." But "the path to hope is not the path of divorce." The marriage vow is unbreakable because "marriage was created by God from the beginning as a picture or an expression of the covenant-keeping love of Christ and his church" (Eph. 5:22–33).

---

2   APJ 165: "Is My Husband's Porn a Marriage Deal-Breaker?" (September 4, 2013).

3   APJ 1830: "How Do I Address My Spouse's Ongoing Sin?" (September 2, 2022).

John Piper's plea, given "countless times" to women and men over the years: "Put divorce out of your mind as a remedy. Don't consider it. Say to yourself, in the truth of Christ, by the power of the Holy Spirit: 'This is not an option. I am not going to pursue this. It may be forced upon me, but I am not going to pursue it.' Don't want it. Pray and work in the other direction."

You may have married an immature spouse, and in your immature decision you "sinned your way into this marriage." That may be true, "but now that you are married, this man is God's man for you." Don't look back with regret; "look to Jesus as the one who satisfies in measure now and immeasurably later. Believe that the path of lost dreams in this life is the path of greatest joy overall." Marriage is not for maxing out *earthly happiness* but for maxing out *eternal happiness*. We rejoice, even amid life's pain, because those tribulations represent God's work inside of us, bringing about our eternal good. So "marriage may disappoint with a thousand tribulations, but hope-filled obedience to God will never, never disappoint us" (Rom. 5:3–5).

A wife dedicated to changing her husband isn't misguided. This is Peter's direction to the believing wife married to an unbelieving man (1 Pet. 3:1–6). Aim for it, but don't major on the transformation. Work and pray for it, "but don't stake your greatest happiness on his change." Focusing on our spouse's failures will make us "demanding and nagging and angry, all of which will be self-defeating. So focus your main heart energies not on fixing his failures, but on deepening your own godly responses to those failures." God doesn't hold you accountable for your spouse's sins, but "he does hold you accountable for the godliness of your responses to those sins." God will see and reward your private obedience, even if those acts escape the notice of your spouse (Matt. 6:3–4).

Who knows? "When the decades have gone by, God might work a miracle in that man, and your life might end in a way that you never dreamed." About three decades into his ministry, a woman approached Pastor John on a Sunday morning. "I remember it so clearly. She reminded me that when she was about to leave her husband twenty years ago, she came to talk to me. And I pleaded with her: 'Don't do it.'" Her husband was "unresponsive, unaffectionate, traveled all the time, didn't pay any attention, didn't care for the kids," etc. But she stuck it out, and twenty years later, he "had become a kind and thoughtful and very different man."[4]

But didn't Moses permit divorce?

Yes, he did—a temporary allowance that would later mark a "dramatic alteration" between the Old and New Testaments. When the Pharisees asked Jesus

4   APJ 397: "To a Spouse Considering Divorce" (July 31, 2014).

this question, he replied: "Because of your hardness of heart, Moses allowed you to divorce your wives, but from the beginning it was not so" (Matt. 19:8; see vv. 1–12; Mark 10:1–12). In other words, Christ says, "even though Moses made this provision, I don't anymore." Thus, "you can see change is coming to the world with Jesus, in the moral expectations upon the people of God."[5]

So the Pharisees were getting and giving divorces "when they shouldn't— even though it was permitted in the Old Testament." And "the reason Jesus *did not any longer permit* what *had been permitted* is that he chalked it up in the Old Testament to tolerance of the expressions of the *hardness of the heart*." Christ raised the moral standard—a "tolerance" in the Mosaic law now "forbidden."[6]

Moses's allowance for divorce ended with Christ. In "the coming of Jesus Christ into the world, and the revelation of the love of God in the sacrifice of his Son, and the pattern of suffering and self-denial set by Jesus, and the outpouring of the Holy Spirit as the Spirit of the risen Christ, and the vivid clarification of the riches of the Christian inheritance beyond death, and the radical, countercultural teachings of Jesus on how Christians are to live, and the establishment of the new covenant in which the law is written on our hearts—I start with the conviction that all of these and more mean that the standards of behavior for God's people now are higher than they were in the Old Testament. Jesus raised the bar." Christ's arrival and his own unbreakable covenant with his bride now call for married couples to "rise up above the Mosaic compromise with sin."[7]

To couples considering divorce because they're no longer in love

In addressing a man considering divorce because he's no longer "in love," Pastor John called three words to mind: *joy, significance,* and *ownership.*

1. Joy—"Oh, what joy lies ahead for those who do not break their covenant, even when their hearts are broken." Over the decades, most couples "fall in and out of love numerous times." In fact, it's "almost ludicrous to think that we experience 'being in love' the same way for the entire sixty years, just like we felt at the beginning of that relationship." Thus, it's "naive and immature to think that *staying married* is mainly about *staying in love.*" We cannot imagine that every season of life "will be one of warmth and sweetness and sexual romance." That's "contrary to almost the entire history of the world and contrary to every makeup of fallen human nature." Staying married is "not first" about staying in

---

5   APJ 795: "Doesn't the Bible Tell Christians to Put Homosexuals to Death?" (February 16, 2016).
6   APJ 860: "'May I Have Two Wives?' Six Vetoes" (May 17, 2016).
7   APJ 1539: "Are Our Standards for Sexual Purity Too High for Pastors?" (October 16, 2020).

love but about covenant faithfulness. "The modern world of self-centeredness and self-exaltation and self-expression has taken the normal, fifty-year process of falling in and out of love and turned it into a fifty-year process of multiple divorces and remarriages. That pattern has not and will not bear the fruit of joy. It leaves a trail of misery in soul and misery along the generations. Marriage is the hardest relationship to stay in and the one that promises glorious, unique, durable joys for those who have the character to keep their covenant. That's what I mean by joy."

2. Significance—"God offers to husbands and wives the highest possible significance for their marriage relationship by showing them what its greatest and most glorious meaning is—namely, the replication in the world of the covenant relationship between Christ and his bride, the church." Ephesians 5:22–33 is the pinnacle text, "the highest meaning of marriage," and "a parable of the greatest, strongest, deepest, sweetest, richest relationship in the universe—the blood-bought union between Christ, the Son of God, and his bride, the church." Christ makes marriage profound. To get divorced because you don't *feel loved* is to have a very low view of marriage. What if Christ divorced his church because he felt unloved by her? It would defy the very nature of his eternal covenant.

3. Ownership—"The union between a man and a woman isn't theirs to break. They didn't create it. They can't break it." God bound you (Mark 10:9). It's a sure sign of the "man-centeredness and contemporary self-centeredness" inside the church "that a young couple would have the mindset that *they created* the union called 'marriage' and, therefore, *they can break it.* They *didn't* create it. They *can't* break it. God made it. God breaks it with death." Or, as Paul's theology implies, "you are free to break your marriage covenant when Christ breaks his covenant with his bride."

So "for the sake of maximum, long-term *joy,* for the sake of the deepest and highest *significance,* and for the sake of the maker and *owner* of your union, keep your covenant. Oh, what joy lies ahead beyond anything you can presently imagine for those who keep their covenant, even when their hearts are broken."[8]

Can I divorce my unbelieving spouse?

The marriage of a Christian to a non-Christian can be the result of many scenarios. A Christian may sin and knowingly marry a non-Christian.[9] Or two non-Christians marry, and one eventually gets saved.[10] Or two professing

---

8   APJ 1142: "Why 'Falling Out of Love' Never Justifies Divorce" (January 5, 2018).
9   APJ 1560: "Christian Marries Non-Christian—How Does a Church Respond?" (December 11, 2020).
10 APJ 1029: "How Do I Love My Unbelieving Spouse?" (April 17, 2017).

Christians get married, one proves faithful over the years, or is genuinely converted, and the other falls away over time.[11]

All couples change. Over time, a wife senses that her husband is no longer a Christian. And she wants to know if the no-divorce rule for the unequally yoked is God's *verdict* or Paul's *opinion*, because it really appears to be Paul's opinion (1 Cor. 7:10, 12).

Here are four reasons why Paul's words carry the weight of God's authority. (1) Paul spoke on behalf of the risen Christ as an "authorized apostle." (2) All that he wrote was via the Holy Spirit (1 Cor. 7:40). (3) Paul claims divine authority on ethical issues to which the church's prophets must submit (1 Cor. 14:37–38). (4) Paul makes a distinction between what he got from Christ's teaching and what goes beyond it. Christ, not Paul, said don't divorce (1 Cor. 7:10–11; see Mark 10:11–12). But Paul, not Christ, said don't divorce *an unbelieving spouse* (1 Cor. 7:12–13). So "in the one case he has an actual explicit teaching from the historical Jesus as we have it in the Gospels, whereas in the second case, when he is talking about marriage to an unbeliever, he doesn't." So Paul says, "I am rendering my apostolic, authoritative judgment on that."[12]

Is my second marriage illegitimate?

To a man or woman considering divorce to marry someone else, Jesus's warning is stark and stern. You contemplate adultery. Don't do it (Matt. 5:32; Mark 10:11–12).[13] But many Christians have already divorced and remarried (with living exes). What now? Is this second marriage legitimate?

The remarried couple is in a complicated place, according to Jesus (Luke 16:18). Twice Jesus calls the remarriage *adulterous* (μοιχεύω). And twice he calls the remarriage a *marriage* (γαμέω). "There's no escaping that Jesus uses the word *marry* for what ought not to happen. But it does happen." And when it does, "it is what it is"—a "real marriage."[14] Similarly, Jesus said the woman at the well had five former husbands, distinguishing them from the unmarried man she was now sleeping with (John 4:17–18).

So while this second marriage is "an adulterous act," nevertheless Jesus still calls it a *marriage*—"a matter of covenant faithfulness between a man and a woman." To a couple in this remarriage (that "should not have happened"),

---

11 APJ 680: "Hope for Hard Marriages" (September 8, 2015), APJ 1690: "Are Non-Christian Marriages Valid in God's Eyes?" (October 11, 2021), and APJ 1839: "I Want to Be Baptized— My Husband Opposes It" (September 23, 2022).

12 APJ 680: "Hope for Hard Marriages" (September 8, 2015).

13 APJ 920: "Divorce, Remarriage, and Honoring God" (August 16, 2016).

14 APJ 1690: "Are Non-Christian Marriages Valid in God's Eyes?" (October 11, 2021).

repent and "consecrate your union." By the blood of Christ, this new marriage can be made holy.[15] But the "unholy relationship involves unholy sex until that relationship is newly consecrated to God through repentance and forgiveness."[16]

How do I change my unbelieving spouse?

A wife's Christian faith is driving her unbelieving husband (and kids) away. What can she do?

"Well, there aren't going to be pains in life greater than the pain of family pain and children pain and marriage pain. In the ministry, I have often said to Noël, 'If you are happy at home, I can endure anything at church.' And I think that is the way a lot of spouses feel, like if work or society is bringing them misery and they have a place to go at home where there is peace and harmony, they can almost stand anything. But if the home is broken, then where do you turn? So I totally resonate with the urgency and the pain of these kinds of situations."

In the pain, consider four points. (1) Jesus said that the gospel would divide households (Matt. 10:34–36). That's a reality to expect in this world. "As the gospel enters into the world, it doesn't always neatly save couples," sometimes only "half of the couple." (2) Paul calls women to win their unbelieving husbands (1 Pet. 3:1–3). And you're not going to win him by "hoping in flirting or hoping in fixing your hair a certain way or hoping in being sexy enough for a husband." No, she wins her husband by her hope in God. "And I don't think that means she should let herself go and *not* be pretty and *not* be attractive, but rather it says focus your attention on hoping in God." If she does, she will be gentle, not anxious, panicked, manipulative, forceful, or demanding. "The family won't experience her as a tyrant. They will think, 'Mom seems quietly content in her spirit. She seems to have a sweet peace over her.'" (3) Do good (1 Pet. 3:6a). Keep serving your husband and your home. (4) Be strong (1 Pet. 3:6b). Moms who hope in God are fearless, laughing at the future (Prov. 31:25). Her husbands and kids will eventually ask about her hope, "because they have seen a kind of quiet, gentle, serving, fearless strength in this mom." She can articulate her hope (1 Pet. 3:15). She's brokenhearted and yet pressing on in strong, selfless ways that are attractive.[17]

Wives, be careful not to say: "'It's *not* my job to change him.'" Actually, it is. Peter calls women to win over their unbelieving husbands. That's the job (1 Pet. 3:1–2). "Of course, that does not mean that it lies within a wife's power ultimately or decisively to convert her husband. But Peter isn't talking about

15 APJ 1343: "Should a Gay Couple, Once Converted, Stay 'Married'?" (May 15, 2019).
16 APJ 920: "Divorce, Remarriage, and Honoring God" (August 16, 2016).
17 APJ 51: "My Faith Is Driving My Family Away—What Do I Do?" (March 20, 2013).

what's *ultimate* and *decisive*. He's talking about what's *secondary* and *possible*—causes that really matter. God may use a wife's humble, godly, loving, supportive behavior to change a husband's willingness to hear the gospel and be saved."[18]

In another episode, Pastor John gave five more encouragements to a wife with an unbelieving husband. (1) First Peter 3:1–2 addresses this situation "exactly," though it doesn't give us all the details. Take heart that the situation is addressed in the Bible so directly. (2) We know that the Lord promises to "give *you* all the grace *you* need to be pleasing to him" (2 Cor. 9:8). "Whatever your husband does, thinks, or feels, God looks to you alone for whether you are walking in sin—not your husband." (3) "Marriage is a parable of covenant *faithfulness*, not covenant *bliss*. Your faithfulness to your vows is pleasing to the Lord, no matter how much sadness is in your heart or in his heart." Covenant-keeping marriage "is telling the truth about Christ and his church as a covenant-keeping Christ and church." (4) God can change your marriage, even after years of sorrow (Eph. 3:20). "So don't make your faithfulness depend on your husband's change, but do keep hoping and praying for it. Keep knocking on the door of heaven." (5) "Even if your marriage falls short of your hopes to the end—and what marriage doesn't?—God will reward your faithfulness in the age to come a thousandfold" (Eph. 6:8). "Your husband and your friends may have no idea how many sacrifices you have made in order to love your husband as well as you can. But God knows every single one of them, and he says you will be repaid. All our trials are working for us an eternal weight of glory" (2 Cor. 4:17).[19]

Seven years later, Pastor John detailed the biblical priorities that can sustain a wife who for years has been praying for the salvation of her husband.[20]

Must I submit to my husband's sin?

Wives with unbelieving husbands should memorize 1 Peter 3:1–6. Win him without a word. Obviously, that doesn't mean you *never* talk to him about Christ. You will. You must. But "don't harangue him. Don't nag him. Don't preach at him. In all humility and all lowliness, somewhere along the way, lay your heart bare before this man, as to where you stand and why you're there." Give him your testimony. Say: "This is why I love Jesus. I believe that loving Jesus will help me love you better. So please don't think that when I put him first, I'm loving you worse." He may find that unintelligible, so you'll need to bear this out over time in your actions, that loving Christ *most* makes you a better wife.

18 APJ 1315: "My Husband Is Passive—What Can I Do?" (February 20, 2019).
19 APJ 680: "Hope for Hard Marriages" (September 8, 2015).
20 APJ 1843: "How Do I Pray for My Husband's Salvation?" (October 3, 2022).

All submission for a wife is qualified because it's a kind of submission "that does not make your husband your absolute lord." In fact, Peter "makes no sense unless Jesus is your Lord *above your husband*, because you're aiming to convert the husband to the Lord that's above you both. And if you're aiming to convert your husband, clearly you have not submitted to his wrong ideas." So submission does not mean that a wife submits her brain to an unbeliever's thinking. She stands her ground in biblical conviction. "You have an independent relationship with the Lord that's authentic and unshakable." No matter what the husband says or does, "Jesus is your Lord," which is "remarkably independent—in a sense, you might say, nonsubmissive."

So Jesus is the absolute Lord over this woman's life. "But, oh my, once you have rested in Jesus and longed to show *this man* [your husband] as a leader—that is, honor his leadership, though he may not even be a leader—you're going to do everything you can to honor that leadership and call out of him all the *initiatives*, all the *protection*, all the *provision*." That's the leadership of a husband: protecting, providing, and initiating.

So how does a submissive wife say *no* when he wants to lead her into sin, like in sexual sin? She says, "'I can't. I love you, but I think this is bad for you, bad for us. I can't do that because of Jesus.'" And in the end, with all that the Bible says about subordination—"children to parents, wives to husbands, citizens to governments, and church members to elders, those four groups—all of them are qualified." Because "the absoluteness of Jesus relativizes, qualifies, the subordination of a child, a wife, a citizen, and a church member."[21]

Second, to believing couples, a godly wife is permitted to speak up and confront her husband's sin patterns because the mutual accountability dynamic is already in their marriage. "The Christian husband is not a free-standing moral agent, doing whatever he pleases in this marriage." He's accountable to his local church (Heb. 13:17). So is the wife. They're "not an isolated couple with no accountable relationships." Spouses "have recourse" to seek help from the church. In light of these accountabilities, there remains for a wife a posture of submissive confrontation. "A mature, godly, Bible-saturated woman knows the difference between nagging a husband in a pushy or insubordinate way, on the one hand, and humbly and wisely bringing to the husband her concerns and seeking with him a way forward toward relational health that would make both of them and the children holier and happier."[22]

21 APJ 1376: "How Do I Submit to My Unbelieving Husband?" (October 2, 2019).
22 APJ 1830: "How Do I Address My Spouse's Ongoing Sin?" (September 2, 2022).

Marriage challenges in ministry

"I think the biggest challenges you will face in ministry will very likely relate to your family—your marriage and your children. That certainly has been true for me. I have told my wife, Noël, though we have been married forty-five years, 'All I need in the ministry from you is for you to be happy, because if momma ain't happy . . . !'" But Pastor John confessed, "We have gone through really hard times." During one season, they spent three years in counseling trying to answer, "'Why do we hurt each other like this? Why do our mouths do this to each other?' Then we get along for ten years, and then we need to work on it again." Even within a "pretty embattled relationship," . . . "I love her like crazy, and she me." Yet at sixty-eight, he remained "baffled as to why we have some of the issues we do." Family struggles are "the greatest anvil of sanctification in the world. And that is no accident. Nothing has shown me my sin like marriage. Nothing has given me opportunities for grace like marriage. While it has been for me one of the hardest things, it has also been one of the most glorious things."

This great anvil of sanctifying grace exists alongside the work of ministry. "We got a phone call one time from *Christianity Today*. They had a magazine called *Partnership*. I don't think it exists anymore. They always featured a smiley pastoral couple on the cover. They called one time and said, 'We would like to put you and Noël on the front and do a special article on you.' I said, 'You would? Well, look, we're barely talking right now. So I think you had better come back later.' They never called back."[23]

Should my spouse talk to her friends about our marriage struggles?

A season of struggle in any marriage requires close friends who are informed and engaged.[24] But a husband caught his wife messaging her best friend about their personal marriage challenges. He was heartbroken. So if not behind one another's backs, how should couples invite others into their struggles when they need help?

Five guidelines, with the important disclaimer that we are talking here of "normal hardships" in the "frequent disappointments in life," not in illegal or life-threatening abuse situations calling for immediate police involvement. (1) Don't gossip. Go to your spouse first, privately. This is a general principle of Scripture whenever we have interpersonal struggles (Matt. 18:15). Deal privately "before these other principles kick in to play." (2) Do unto others. Treat your

23   APJ 313: "Marriage Challenges and Christian Ministry" (April 4, 2014).
24   APJ 1794: "Counsel for Wives with Harsh Husbands" (June 10, 2022).

spouse like you want to be treated (Matt. 7:12). Love your spouse as you love yourself (Eph. 5:28). In the one-flesh union, the Golden Rule blesses you both because "we are doing something really good for ourselves not to betray each other's trust." (3) Honor and respect your spouse. Wives revere their husbands (Eph. 5:33). "Similarly, husbands should think long and hard whether what they are saying about their wives in private or in public honors them as a fellow heir of the grace of life, the way Peter says in 1 Peter 3:7." It's a principle of respect and reverence and honor. (4) Ask permission. Get your spouse's permission for you to share marriage struggles "with one or two very trusted couples or friends." Agree on who they are. "So Noël can say whatever she wants to X. And I can say whatever I want to Y. We have entrusted each other to those friends. It is a huge thing, right? You don't do that unless you have got some very close friends." Find friends you can trust with your most sensitive struggles and get permission from each other to speak with these select friends when needed. (5) Speak cautiously. Even with these trusted friends in place, speak "with the greatest of care," because such conversations "easily degenerate into simply venting our frustrations." A wise friend will call you out here.

And whenever sharing sensitive details, consider how much you share, the tone you use, and the medium you share it (in person, via text, or in messaging apps). "Any kind of media that would run the risk of someone else listening in on what is meant for one person should be avoided at all costs." All this dialogue should be done "in a context of praying *for* and *with* our spouses and reading Scripture *with* our spouses so that we seek help from God who alone can keep us married and bring this relationship to a God-honoring, satisfying situation." These lessons were hard-learned. But there's always hope, because "if some breach of trust has happened, there is a way forward. There can be repentance and forgiveness. I know that from personal experience. Noël and I are in a really good place after forty-six years, and we have really blown it more than once."[25]

How can my hard marriage glorify Christ?

A husband who walked away from Christ and sinfully neglected his wife for many years is now in a better place, back with Christ and rededicated to his marriage. But the marriage is strained from neglect. Can this hard marriage still model Christ's relationship to his church?

The question assumes a Christ-church dynamic (Eph. 5:22–33). And the answer is *yes*. "Whether a marriage is *easy* or *hard* is not what undermines the testimony to the world about Christ and his church." When the Christ-church relationship is stressful, it is entirely the fault of the church. "What communicates something *false* about Christ and his church is when a marriage covenant is treated as broken, because the covenant between Christ and his church is never broken." Hard marriages glorify God in perseverance. They testify that this "blood-bought new covenant will never be broken—ever." This is what's *new* in the *new* covenant. Christ "secures its permanence by his blood." And that's why "Jesus raised the standards of faithfulness in marriage above the standards of the Old Testament law."

But there are other ways to magnify Christ in hard marriages. "A believer whose marriage is destroyed and no longer presents a parable of covenant love, that believer can show the worth of Christ in dozens of other ways that God has appointed. And one of those ways is how he or she treats people in that horrific process of dissolution." Glorifying Christ is not determined by perfect scenarios. "It is possible to have failed to glorify Christ in one area and yet, in the very ruins of that failure, to glorify Christ in different ways. In fact, we are all in that situation, aren't we? Don't all of us bear the scars of some past failure that we wish we could undo? We can't. And yet this is the very life with all of its scars, all of its ruins, that Christ intends to redeem and in which he intends to be glorified."

Think of Paul, murderer of Christians, who lived with lifelong regret (1 Tim. 1:13, 15). He glorified God in his remaining days. "So my answer is that a hard marriage can, indeed, display the covenant-keeping love of Christ. Not only that, a faithful, covenant-keeping spouse after a failed marriage can display the truth of that covenant. And if it looks like there has been complete failure in regard to marriage, God can yet so transform you that, in the ruins of it, he gets glory."[26]

My husband is spiritually passive—what do I do?

A wife in a fourteen-year marriage has spiritual goals. She wants to pray and study the Bible together with her husband, but he is spiritually passive. He prefers television and sports. It's not the wife's job to change him, right? So what does she do?

Actually, *yes*, changing a husband is part of a wife's calling. Of course, "only God can go deep with her husband and awaken the kinds of longings and passions that she is eager to see." But on the other hand, "it's not quite right to say: 'It's not my job to change him.'" Peter makes this point (1 Pet. 3:1–6). Wives

26 APJ 1017: "How Can My Difficult Marriage Glorify Christ?" (March 20, 2017).

can, and should, aim to change their husbands—from *unbeliever* to *believer* and from *spiritually passive* to *spiritually active*. God uses *means* to convert and sanctify husbands, "and one of the means to wake him up is how a wife lives and believes and loves."

But the wife is mainly right "to be very cautious about thinking of her relationship to her husband as primarily calculated to change him. Her position is analogous, I would say, to a single woman who would like to be married. Her focus in life should be on living a productive, Christ-honoring single life rather than turning every situation into an effort to win a man. That backfires, and so do marriages where the spouse thinks of every situation as calculated to bring about change in the other spouse." So in Paul's famous love chapter, he mentions fifteen things that love *is* and *does*—and *changing others* isn't one of them (1 Cor. 13:4–7).

So what happens if, after one or two or three decades of marriage, you realize that the marriage is not living up to the dream that you had at the beginning? "That is where most marriages are." It means that God is working on you. "God's purpose for you is to refine and deepen *your faith* and *your holiness* through the disappointing parts of your spouse's personality. The fight of faith is to treat your spouse better and better out of the resources that you find in Christ."

Marriages will struggle because the *idle*, the *fainthearted*, and the *weak* populate churches—and marriages too (1 Thess. 5:14). The *idle* are "undisciplined, disorderly, and lazy." The *fainthearted* are "small-souled, incapable of feeling large and great things with any attraction, easily discouraged, and content with insignificant experiences." And the *weak* are "vulnerable to something incapacitating—some debilitating limitation that could be physical or mental." These people will always be in churches, and likely in marriages. So we pray, hope for growth, and show patience with them all. "Love suffers long and is kind. How long? Well, the marriage vow that says 'for better or for worse' is 'as long as we both shall live.' God will provide every grace you need to make your marriage the most fruitful place for growing in godliness."[27]

A word to husbands of unbelieving wives

A man converted by the gospel feels like he's experienced a spiritual divorce, but he's committed to not legally divorcing his unbelieving wife. How can he persevere?

Six encouragements. (1) Be in the word daily (Rom. 10:17). Sustained faith requires "God to speak to us every day." (2) Don't just read, but pray that God

---

27 APJ 1315: "My Husband Is Passive—What Can I Do?" (February 20, 2019).

will direct your heart to see his love and Christ's faithfulness. In the prayer of Paul, "May the Lord direct your hearts to the love of God and to the steadfastness of Christ" (2 Thess. 3:5). Become convinced of God's love and Christ's steadfastness because this is "essential for being steadfast in marriage," any marriage. (3) Look to God for harmony with your wife. Paul says that we can persevere in harmonious living because we worship the "God of endurance" (Rom. 15:4–6). It's "a beautiful passage that, without any twisting, can be applied to marriage." (4) Live from joy, and model joy in Christ before your wife and kids. "May God strengthen you according to his glorious might for all endurance and patience with joy (Col. 1:9–11). Nobody but God can do that in a difficult marriage." Don't just endure and persevere, "but do so with joy." *Show* your family that Jesus satisfies and that within this life "with all of its sorrows, there is profound joy." (5) Remember that marriage isn't a sprint; it's a marathon. "And some marathons have more hills, more heat, more obstacles." So look to Christ's example—he anticipated eternal joy and lived and served from that joy. "Don't be ashamed of looking forward to your future joy to experience portions of it in the present to sustain you in your marathon of marriage" (Heb. 12:1–2). (6) See your endurance *in your hardship*. Our suffering produces endurance, and this perseverance produces character, and this "approvedness" produces hope (Rom. 5:3–5). By God's grace, our sufferings in this life "are meant to help us persevere" to the end.[28]

On living with a quarrelsome wife

Proverbs issues several warnings about the quarrelsome wife (Prov. 19:13; 21:9, 19; 25:24; 27:15). Don't these texts encourage a husband to separate from her?

No. Any man who reads these texts "and concludes in his heart that divorce and remarriage are being commended here, we know that he is in the power of a *hardened* heart, which God disapproves of" (Mark 10:2–7). As Jesus said about Moses's allowances for divorce in the Old Testament, the desire to divorce originates in a hard heart. And Jesus died to give us soft hearts.

So how does a soft heart respond to the quarrelsome wife? Four thoughts. (1) Be selective. Many proverbs are advice from parents to their children, instructing the unmarried. "Don't marry a quarrelsome woman. Live in a desert if you have to. Live in a tiny room on your roof with your parents if you have to before you do that." In other words, wait patiently for the right wife (Prov. 18:22). (2) Be agreeable. These texts warn women—and men— from becoming a quarrelsome spouse. "It's a lesson: don't marry quarrelsome

---

28 APJ 1029: "How Do I Love My Unbelieving Spouse?" (April 17, 2017).

people. And if you're married, women, do your best not to be quarrelsome and contentious." (3) Be patient. God changes hearts. A prudent wife is a gift from the Lord (Prov. 19:14). And if that is true, "then God is able to make out of a *quarrelsome* wife a *helpful* and *prudent* wife. If he sovereignly gives the gift, he can give it before marriage, and he can give it after marriage by changing the wife." (4) Be loving. Never repay evil for evil (Rom. 12:17; 1 Thess. 5:15; 1 Pet. 3:9). Love your wife better than she deserves. "It's easier, it's more comfortable, it's more peaceful to just go up on the roof and get away from this nagging and quarreling wife, from this contention." Yes, but escape is not to be favored "over the path of love." Seek reconciliation and love with your covenant partner for life.[29]

How do I care for my depressed wife?

"As I thought and prayed over this situation—and I know several marriages like this, *long marriages* like this, even marriages where there's been hospitalization over and over again for a depressed spouse—I thought of ten words of counsel that I would share with this anonymous husband."

(1) Give thanks for grace. Praise God for the years of this marriage, an amazing gift of God's keeping grace. (2) Be done with the doubts. You didn't marry the wrong person. (3) Be patient with her limits. Every Christian must reckon with limits to personal holiness, because we will "never in this life grow beyond certain limitations" (1 Thess. 5:14). Within a "diversity of weakness among believers," God alone "assigns faith and growth according to his own inscrutable wisdom" (Rom. 12:3). "In other words, it may be God's plan for you to shepherd your wife, not *out of her depression*, but *with her depression*, to the end." (4) Influence with patience and gentleness. Under God's sovereignty over all things is a principle from Paul that can apply to marriage, the principle that "kindness, patience, gentleness, and willingness to endure sorrow might bring about change" in another. "Whether it does or not, it's our calling to be that way" (2 Tim. 2:24–25). (5) Commit to your calling. Never be harsh with your wife (Col. 3:19). Love her like Christ loves his bride (Eph. 5:25). "Let this sink in: Christ is married to a wife, the church," and she (us) "falls far shorter of the command to love him with all our hearts than our wives fall short of any expectations we have. In other words, we fall shorter of what Christ deserves from us than our wives fall short of what we deserve or hope for." And our calling holds whatever the circumstances, because "no husband is promised a cheerful wife." (6) Lead in the habits of grace. No matter

29   APJ 1356: "How Should a Husband Treat His Quarrelsome Wife?" (June 14, 2019).

where she is emotionally, lead her into the word and "speak promises from God to her every day—not criticisms, but promises." Pray with her. Pray for her. Take her to church. Point to texts about believers enduring the darkness (like Micah 7:8). "You have no idea what the long-term effects of steady-state spiritual disciplines of grace may accomplish." (7) Feed your own soul and find friends who can help carry your burden. (8) Seek counsel from wise Christians. (9) Embrace what God has given you. Study hard marriages in history, like that of Abraham and Mary Lincoln. "It was not a happy marriage." They both brought their flaws. Mary "often flew into rages" and lashed out against others, including her husband. In this crucible, Abraham embraced the pain, learned patience for leadership, and was made stronger in the "refining fire" of his marriage. (10) Remember the coming joy. "Picture the thankfulness of your wife in the resurrection, when she has been set free and thinks back over the remarkable patience and kindness that you showed her for decades. Right now, she does not even have the emotional wherewithal to respond to you as she should and as you desire that she would. But one day, in the resurrection, she will have that capacity, and her memory of your patience will be part of your joy."[30]

Marriage recovery after adultery

Infidelity is not a "biblical pass" for divorce. Christians are taught to forgive a mountain of sins against us (Matt. 18:21–22). A forgiving spirit keeps us out of court (1 Cor. 6:7). God's covenant faithfulness to his people is not broken by spiritual adultery (Isa. 54:6–7; Jer. 3:8, 12), a point modeled in Hosea's marriage to an adulterous wife (Hos. 1:2; 2:14–15). God's long history with Israel shows us that "she was never deserving of his faithfulness to her—ever." And eventually, "with unspeakable longsuffering, by the power of the new covenant and the blood of Jesus," the bride would be made beautiful (Eph. 5:25–27). God makes spiritual adulterers into a radiant, holy, and unblemished bride for his Son. This is the work of the gospel.

Any hope of preserving a marriage in the fallout of adultery calls on two divine miracles.

Miracle 1: offering forgiveness (Eph. 4:32). "Only by being overwhelmed—and I mean *stunned*—with our own forgiveness from Jesus, at the cost of his infinitely valuable life, will we be able to forgive such a horrible and painful betrayal as adultery." Jesus teaches us that "every husband and every wife who is a Christian has been forgiven thousands of adulteries against God" (Matt.

---

30 APJ 1441: "How Do I Care for My Depressed Wife?" (March 2, 2020).

18:23–35). Understanding this becomes the basis for the miracle of forgiving a spouse who has so deeply sinned.

Miracle 2: rebuilding trust. "Being forgiven is not a *right* to be demanded, but a gift of *grace* to be received with humility and thankfulness and tears." Then comes the long process of rebuilding trust. This trust, "coming from the spouse who has been betrayed, is not like a stake you drive in the ground and walk past; it's like an acorn you plant in the ground. And some day, God willing, it may be an unshakable oak tree of trust. But it will grow through tender stages by patient protection and watering and nurturing through storms that will threaten to kill the little sapling of trust."

Both miracles must be lived out "by faith in the promises of God." He will never leave you, forsake you, or divorce you—neither of you (Josh. 1:5; Heb. 13:5). Only by clinging to these promises can you endure to the end, when, "sitting across from each other, holding your wrinkled hands, and with tears and smiles, you say: 'We made it! We made it!'"[31]

Anger, the great relationship killer

One sin ends more marriages than adultery. Anger is "the great killer." In the context of a question about the difference between holy anger and unholy anger: "I was much more optimistic about a righteous place for anger when I was thirty than I am now. I have seen the destructive power of anger in relationships, especially marriage, to such a degree over the last forty to fifty years that I am far less sanguine about so-called righteous anger than I once was."

Anger is a vicious destroyer. "Anger is not just a relationship destroyer; it's a self-destroyer. It eats up all other wholesome emotions. Not dealt with, it consumes everything in its path and leaves the woman or man with nothing but bitterness and anger, incapable of any other emotion. It's either silence or anger. And it's a horrible development."[32]

Colossians 3:19 calls husbands to love their wives and to not be harsh with them. The Greek word for *harsh* (πικραίνεσθε) carries the same root as *bitterness* (πικρία) in Ephesians 4:31. "That word means, 'Don't become deep, long-term embittered and angry with a spouse.' Anger kills a marriage way more often than sexual misconduct." So the message of the New Testament is put away anger (Eph. 4:31–32; Col. 3:8). "What a miracle that would be! What a world changer. What a marriage changer!"[33]

31 APJ 1440: "How Can Couples Heal after Adultery?" (February 28, 2020).
32 APJ 1711: "Does Righteous Anger Kill Our Joy?" (November 29, 2021).
33 APJ 1100: "The Great Marriage Killer" (September 29, 2017).

What your spouse needs most from you

"I think the biggest investment that husbands and wives can make in their spouse is the investment they make *in their own souls*. Here's what I mean: If you do get married, all's rosy and great. You love each other." But as time passes you may begin to treat marriage as a project, calling for reading new books, attending another seminar, and adopting the right love languages. All that can be helpful. "But far more important is: Do I go to the Lord and invest in him and say, 'God, make me a new person'? That's not just what you pray at the beginning of your Christian life. Those of us who have lived long enough know that we're still sinners today. And I've got soul work to do so that when I open my mouth with my wife, I'm not only investing in her, but I'm a new person who loves better than I did yesterday." At age seventy-three, "I'm fighting for my marriage every day by fighting for *my holiness*. I'm going to the Bible and asking not to be unkind, not to be critical. I'm asking for love, joy, peace, patience, goodness, kindness, meekness, faithfulness, self-control (Gal. 5:22–23). That's a happy marriage. And the main battle is *here*, inside *me*."

Bear with your wife and forgive her—a "massively important text" for marriage (Col. 3:13). "Forgiveness is an awesome and wonderful thing. Every spouse needs to make a vocation out of asking forgiveness and giving forgiveness." But "here's the rub that I learned really quick. *She* doesn't think that what bothers *me* is a sin. She's got nothing to repent of. And, therefore, I've got nothing to forgive. And I'm ticked off." So where do you put the unresolved disagreements? You put them in the compost pile. Every marriage needs one. "It means you've got a really nice green backyard. It's wonderful. It's a great place to hang out. And the relationship has pukey, dirty, lousy, no-good stuff in it that neither of you considers to be sin. And you could be wrong on that. But you build a compost pile way off in the corner, and you throw that habit of your spouse in the compost pile. Now, you can camp out by a compost pile and smell the stinky stuff all night long. Or you can pull a curtain around it and have a picnic at the picnic table on the green grass with the woman you married. While all your junk and all her junk is in the compost pile, you both know they're there, but the smell is bracketed—it's just cut off. And you both are looking in each other's eyes and you know very honestly there's a compost pile back there. 'We're not going to talk about it right now. We're going to enjoy these grandkids, and we're going to do this barbecue.'"

Our behaviors are "late things" compared with the "early things" of "attitudes, feelings, angers, and joys." And this is where the battle is fought. "You get up in the morning and go down to the breakfast table after a half an hour with

Jesus, coming to terms with your own sin and confessing. Then you are able to speak upbuilding things."[34]

On Abuse
Some core principles need to be sketched out whenever dealing with emotional, verbal, or physical abuse of women by men (points to be filled out in later sections).

Through life, a woman will experience various relationships with men: her husband, her husband's friends, her pastors, her colleagues at school or work, even delivery drivers, plumbers, and mechanics. "The dynamic and the dance of gender relations are different for every relationship," but what unites them all is that God has called all men to protect women, and women to love and delight in that protection.[35]

This theme returned in a question about whether complementarity applies beyond marriage, particularly in the lives of singles. Yes, because "gender alone—that is, our sexual maleness or femaleness alone—is an essential part of our God-given identity, whether we're married or not. You are who you are everywhere you are, and with whomever you are." Thus, "there is nothing magical about a wedding ceremony that turns a man into a man or a woman into a woman. What a woman has been becoming all her life is what she will be in marriage. What a man has been becoming all his life is what he will be in marriage." We don't activate manhood or womanhood for the first time on our honeymoon.

These gendered roles have implications. For example, a woman doesn't date men blindfolded. She's watching for "evidences of whether a man's instincts and inclinations reveal a deep-seated sense of benevolent responsibility to *lead* and *provide for* and *protect* women in ways appropriate to his different relationships." She studies the trajectory of his life to predict "what kind of *leader* and *provider* and *protector* he will be in marriage."[36]

This point is drawn from a core reality in the male-female relationships. Woman is "the weaker vessel"—which "is not a value judgment; that is just a statement of fact. Physically weaker" (1 Pet. 3:7).[37] God's normative design is for men to be stronger. It's no "fluke of nature" or "a random effect of natural selection or evolution. It's the way God designed it. And when you pause and think about that, it carries enormous implications for men." Especially on the abuse topic.

34 APJ 1418: "What Every Marriage Needs Most" (January 8, 2020).
35 APJ 42: "Biblical Womanhood in Five Minutes" (March 7, 2013).
36 APJ 1271: "Do Gender Roles Apply beyond Marriage?" (November 2, 2018).
37 APJ 587: "Does God Favor Boys over Girls?" (May 1, 2015).

But this *weaker* designation doesn't diminish women or create a superiority structure. The same text says, "You are *fellow heirs* of the grace of life" (1 Pet. 3:7). Every woman in Christ will radiantly shine as a "breathtakingly glorious human being" (Matt. 13:43). The wife *does not share* her husband's physical strength; she *does share* in the glory of being an heir of God. Treat her as such. Men: "mingle your caring, protecting, leading strength with a sense of wonder and awe that you get to live temporarily with an heiress of God."[38] And if you are married to her, know that "you live with a woman who is destined to inherit the world, because that is what you are promised in Christ. She will be a queen of the universe, and you sleep in the same bed with this stunning being. So wake up to the reality of what you are dealing with here."[39]

Physical abuse

In the summer of 2014, disturbing video surfaced of NFL football All-Star Ray Rice knocking his fiancée unconscious in a casino elevator with punches to her face. An earlier video showed Rice dragging her unconscious body out of the elevator. At first, he claimed that he slapped her, and she fell back and hit her head accidentally. But the later video, which showed him knocking her out with his fists, exposed his lie and unleashed a chorus of public outrage. Rice was suspended indefinitely from the NFL and never played in the league again. So what do complementarians say in such a situation?

First some background. Complementarity means that men and women relate in ways that are not the same, but different. They complement one another, not unlike doubles figure skating. Together man and woman "make something beautiful to watch that is more than just each of them excelling on their own." In other words, God designed biological sex to determine certain roles not based on culture or competencies. It's not simply a question of who is more intelligent, more articulate, or more physically strong. The question is whether or not "the man, as man, created by God with a built-in deep sense," is given "an inclination, a disposition—something deeper than cultural, deeper than societal, deeper than upbringing—a sense of responsibility deep in his soul to nurture and provide for and protect and take life-giving initiatives with the women in his life." And the answer to that question, for complementarians, is *yes*.

God created man with a sense, "deep in his masculine soul," that he's been given a "special responsibility to show special care for and provide for and

---

38 APJ 1614: "What Makes Women the 'Weaker Vessel'?" (April 16, 2021).
39 APJ 587: "Does God Favor Boys over Girls?" (May 1, 2015).

protect and be hope-giving and life-enhancing and woman-ennobling in the initiatives that he takes in relation to the women in his life." It will look different in the home, church, work, school, and society in general, but this pattern of complementarity is relevant for all of life and society.

God calls men to protect women. And we see this pattern for society modeled specifically in marriage (Eph. 5:23, 25, 29; Col. 3:19; 1 Pet. 3:7). But again, "men don't become men on their wedding day." All the "beautiful burdens and responsibilities" put on men in marriage hold true *outside of* marriage and *before* marriage. Marriage simply concentrates the dynamic that is at work in all male-female relationships. This protective role will play out differently in each relationship, but the principle is "always relevant, whether the issue is women in combat, or women in an elevator alone with a man."

Pastor John's word to Rice is relevant to all men: "Your manhood—as God designed you, and as Jesus Christ the Son of God can remake you through a faith relationship with him—means conquering your selfish impulses with the realization that *real men* don't hit women. *Real men* protect women. *Real men* don't use women to provide for their appetites. *Real men* use their strength to provide for a woman's good. *Real men* are not led by the leash of their own temper, hooked by their nose. *Real men* master their temper and lead women out of harm, not into it. And where men cease to be such men, *real men* step in and do what needs to be done."[40]

Sexual abuse

The #MeToo movement sought to expose a long list of powerful men, each accused of making unwanted sexual advances on women. Allegations were made against Harvey Weinstein, Kevin Spacey, Louis C.K., Al Franken, Roger Ailes, Roy Moore, Matt Lauer, Charlie Rose, Bill O'Reilly, and Garrison Keillor. Men on the left and the right. Liberals and conservatives. Politicians and entertainers. The movement targeted Hollywood, Minneapolis, DC, and New York City. So how does this situation relate to fifty years of our society's denial that men's and women's roles complement each other?

The problem is that "egalitarian assumptions in our culture, and to a huge degree in the church, have muted—silenced, nullified—one of the means that God has designed for the protection and the flourishing of women. It has silenced the idea that men as men—by virtue of their created, God-given maleness, apart from any practical competencies that they have or don't have—have special responsibilities to care for and protect and honor women. This call is

40 APJ SE05: "John Piper's Message to Ray Rice" (September 11, 2014).

different from the care and protection and honor that women owe men. That's my thesis. That's my point."

Egalitarian ideology claims that the roles and responsibilities of men and women in the home and in the church, and even in broader culture, should all emerge "only from competencies rather than from a deeper reality rooted in who we are differently as male and female." The result is "a firm conviction of most of our egalitarian culture, that men as men *do not owe* women a special kind of care and protection and honor that women do not owe men." And fifty years of "denying" this special care and protection is bearing its rotten fruit of men misusing women.

There will always be situations where women are called to care for, protect, and honor men. But as a normative pattern, the Bible shows that "men— *as men*—have special, God-intended, God-designed responsibilities for care and protection and honor toward women that women do not have toward men." All the way back in Genesis, Adam failed to lead and protect Eve from Satan (Gen. 3:6). This failure led to the need for Jesus, the second Adam, who entered the world as a man, "to destroy that failure, and cause Adam to own up to the fact that he's got a special burden, a special responsibility, to bear in protecting and caring for and honoring this woman."

Following Christ, husbands are called to gentleness toward women (Col. 3:19). Paul calls husbands not to be harsh with their wives. This is particularly a call to men's misuse of women, offering "a special restraint on typical sinful male harshness and roughness and cruelty that's gone on for thousands of years," particularly in the harshness of attempting to take advantage of women sexually. Instead, men should use their strength to serve women, the weaker vessel (1 Pet. 3:7). Men are called to honor women "precisely *because* he's a man and, in general, men are in the position of physical power and strength over women." This relative physical weakness of the woman calls forth a special *honor* (τιμή) from the man. True inside the home. True outside the home.

The sad fact is that "millions of people in our day would sacrifice this peculiar biblical mandate given for the good of women" rather than "betray any hint of compromise with egalitarian assumptions." The result: "we have forfeited both a great, God-ordained restraint upon male vice and male power and a great, God-ordained incentive for male valor, because we refuse to even think in terms of *maleness* and *femaleness* as they are created by God, carrying distinct and unique responsibilities and burdens." Instead of honoring these created distinctions, "we have put our hope in the myth that the summons to generic human virtue, with no attention to the peculiar virtues required of manhood and womanhood, would be sufficient to create a beautiful society of mutual respect. It isn't working. Men need to be taught from the time they are little boys that part of their manhood is to feel a special responsibility for the care and protection and honoring of women, just because they are men."[41]

On demeaning, verbal abuse

The same marriage intended to protect women and children can become a prison of anger and verbal abuse. One wife wrote in to share that she was being demeaned by her husband. He treated her as inferior. He was deluded into thinking that women are subservient to men.

First, this man is not a complementarian; he's a narcissist, "so fixated on himself, and his pleasures, and his privileges, and his rights, that counting another person more significant than himself is literally inconceivable" (Phil. 2:3). For a man like this, God will have to do a miracle of humbling repentance in his life. Likely he needs to be saved.

That husband is wrong on many accounts. Women are not inferior to men, but equal image bearers (Gen. 1:27; 2:18). "Man and woman are deeply alike and yet so wonderfully different. Woman is called 'a helper fit for him'—that is, suitable, completing, complementing." This is the origin of the term *complementarian*. But when the tempter arrived on the scene in Genesis 3, "the man failed to take the responsibility God had given him." Watching passively, Adam failed to lead and protect Eve. Instead, he fell "right into line with the devil's assault on God's wise and good order, by being silent when the enemy was attacking his wife" (Gen. 3:6). Then Adam had the audacity to *blame* his wife (Gen. 3:12). Sin feeds this type of harsh blame-shifting, ravaging horizontal and vertical relationships.

The husband is "designed to be thrilled by his partner-helper," his "glory" (1 Cor. 11:7). "The man gladly bears a unique responsibility to take a special initiative to protect her. Who is superior to whom, and on what counts, is irrelevant for the central issue of love and protection. They were in God's image and perfectly suited to each other's fruitfulness and joy. They were naked and not ashamed. They did not shame each other."

Man and *woman* do not relate as *superior* and *inferior*. Men and women are given equal value by their Creator, an equality not tied to personal competencies. Again, 1 Peter 3:7 factors in here. Any comparable weakness in the woman (say, physically) never justifies the *demeaning* of women, but invites the *honoring* of women. That's Peter's profound logic. "Whether you focus on any particular weakness, or on the fact that both men and women are destined for glory, the

---

41 APJ 1172: "Sex-Abuse Allegations and the Egalitarian Myth" (March 16, 2018).

call is the same: honor, honor, honor—not shame, shame, shame." The verbally abusive husband is blind to Peter's profound logic.

The anger and aggressiveness that creates a prison for his wife is really the man's own "prison cell." It will destroy his marriage. It will destroy him. The "quick-to-hear, slow-to-speak, slow-to-anger" paradigm is especially important for marriage (James 1:19–20). Angry and harsh men become prisoners of their own sin. And they will treat others like prisoners. Harsh men become "childish bullies . . . like a child throwing a tantrum. Only he's bigger now, so instead of running into his bedroom and slamming the door against his parents, he can run in and lock her out."

This wife needs help on the ground. This childish bully of a husband needs men from the church to step in, particularly elders—all under the caveat that this is only dealing with *verbal* abuse. The counsel would immediately change in the case of *physical* abuse, in which this wife would be "obliged—rightly and legally—to go to the police and to the ways that the arm of our government has set for helping women or men deal with that kind of brutality."[42]

Confronting the emotionally abusive husband

Another wife wrote in, discouraged from putdowns from her husband that are aimed at her and her children. His behavior includes anger and cussing to force his opinion on the home, all done in a consistent and unrepentant pattern. Now what?

This is emotional abuse—a "cruel use of power," and it will result in "long-term damage." To affirm the sinfulness of such behavior, the New Testament is clear. This emotional abuse is unacceptable. Put away bitterness, anger, wrath, malice, clamor, slander, and obscene talk (Eph. 4:31–32; Col. 3:8). Be tender-hearted, upbuilding, and forgiving (Eph. 4:29, 31–32; 1 Pet. 3:8–9). Particularly to husbands: be loving, gentle, and not harsh (Eph. 5:25, 28–30; Col. 3:19). Emotional abuse is serious—whether done by a husband or by a wife. This wife should turn to the church's elders for help, to initiate a process that, depending on the husband's response, may lead to his excommunication by the church.

But an important point to add applies to every marriage. Around every Christian marriage "there should be a web of relationships which should exert correcting and rebuking and healing influences *before* there is the need for official involvement of the elders." The epistles are "shot through with commands to ordinary laypeople to exhort each other, rebuke each other, correct each other, and pray for each other regularly. It's amazing how many marriages

---

42 APJ 1449: "A Word to Men Who Demean Their Wives" (March 20, 2020).

painfully limp along with nobody able to do that. That's tragic." Guard against this from the start of marriage. To every young couple: "Immerse yourselves in a web of relationships, a small group, a set of friends, who are close enough to you that they can know when problems are happening in your marriage."

Have one or two friends who know "absolutely everything" happening in your marriage. It requires enormous trust between the couple and their friends, and "a great deal of courage for friends to then turn around and confront the husband or the wife. But that's the kind of web of relationships I'm talking about." And if these relationships cannot resolve the sin issues, "then the involvement of the elders will not at all seem precipitous. All things will be established in the mouth of two or three witnesses."[43]

Marriage meant as a protective shield

In a question over whether traditional wedding ceremonies are important, there's something to be said for the formalities of marriage licenses and rings and customs. "Virtually all cultures have thought it important for the functioning of the family life, and the protection of women and children, and the civic order, and the social stability, that there be public ways of confirming the difference between marriage and serial sexual liaisons." Wedding formalities are meant to serve the good of women and children. Of course, the Bible doesn't legislate any of these customs today, and they will change with cultures, but the Bible does clearly assume that some formal practices will be in place to "establish public recognition that two people have entered a lifelong marriage covenant with each other before God," because marriage is not a private act—neither private to the government nor to the church. Marriage is necessarily a public union of accountability meant to protect women and children.[44]

---

43 APJ 1102: "Confronting Emotional and Verbal Abuse in the Home" (October 4, 2017).
44 APJ 474: "Must My Wedding Be in a Church?" (November 17, 2014).

On Male Headship, Guns, and the Midlife Crisis

The cultural challenge

In our most popular television and movies, "scene after scene portrays a God-ignoring, man-exalting, sin-condoning, sex-distorting, marriage-weakening, maleness-mocking, femaleness-trivializing, righteousness-ridiculing, arrogance-admiring worldview." This godless worldview of Hollywood undermines true masculinity.[1] So what is it?

Male leadership

At its most basic definition, "leadership is acting and speaking so as to create a following toward a goal." Leadership is particularly Christian when its final goal is defined by the Bible, "to move people toward godliness, toward worship, toward honoring Jesus, toward loving people." To that end, it's self-giving. Leadership has a "servant quality about it, a humble quality about it. It is going to be trying to get *under people* and lift them up to something good as their servant, rather than getting *over people* and oppressing and manipulating and using them to accomplish your private ends."[2]

Specifically, men are created to bear the burden of leadership in the home, church, and society. Men lead, protect, and provide, something "God has put into men." And he "put into women to love that, delight in that, honor that, come alongside that, and use all their manifold gifts to advance the cause of Christ through that, so that when they are together they are complementing each other, and the beauty of God is displayed more fully."[3] So in the home, the husband's leadership or headship is "a sense of benevolent responsibility

1 APJ 1398: "Is It Sinful to Watch Sin on a Screen?" (November 22, 2019).
2 APJ 25: "What Is Leadership?" (February 12, 2013).
3 APJ 42: "Biblical Womanhood in Five Minutes" (March 7, 2013).

to lead, protect, and provide for his wife." The important qualifier is "a sense of benevolent responsibility." Even if the man is disabled, preventing him from being the breadwinner, "that disability does not keep him from feeling a benevolent responsibility that the family's needs are met."[4]

Whether in business, church, politics, or the home, a man leads by vision, not by micromanaging every detail. "Leadership is initiative and planning. Inside that big picture exist all kinds of delegation and decision sharing. I think a godly wife wants leadership, not micromanagement." A competent woman wants the man "to get off his duff and plan something" while she herself is standing by, "happy to bear significant decision-making responsibility inside that big picture as she and her husband work out the details."[5] So "leadership means sitting down at the table and taking the initiative to put things in motion that solve problems. Women love to have their husbands take initiative to put things in motion to get problems solved." And "they *want* to be part of the solution—and *ought* to be a part of the solution."[6]

So where did this male-female model of complementarity originate? Many people today wrongly assume that "men should lead their families on the basis of the fact that men should lead their families." Or they say, "'God says in the Bible that men should lead their families because men should lead their families.' I want to discourage you from thinking that God flipped a coin in the garden of Eden when he was deciding about leadership in the home." Male headship is not arbitrary but designed.[7] Yet others will confuse masculinity with athletic "physical brawn." But true masculinity is "protective initiative with courage and strength" and may come in the form of "a guy who is into art and has a more sensitive spirit. Don't let him think he is less of a man. Don't give the impression: 'Oh, you are not really a man if you don't hunt, carry a gun, and play tackle football.' No, no, no, no."[8]

Again, where does the male-female relationship originate? A longer answer came in an episode to explain why women should take their husband's name. God created headship, and he intentionally appointed man to be the head. Men are called by God to *lead, protect,* and *provide*—a trio of components pulled directly from Ephesians 5:22–23. (1) In *leadership*—the husband is the head, like Christ is the head of the church. (2) In *protection*—the husband loves and gives his life, a costly call. The husband is "not a Christ in the full sense, but he is *a christ*—in a

---

4   APJ 769: "What Does It Mean for a Man to Lead His Family Spiritually?" (January 11, 2016).
5   APJ 348: "Vision for Your Family Vacation" (May 23, 2014).
6   APJ 495: "What Will Submission to My Husband Look Like?" (December 18, 2014).
7   APJ 1549: "My Wife Is More Spiritual—How Do I Lead Her?" (November 9, 2020).
8   APJ 90: "A Mother's Role in Raising Boys" (May 14, 2013).

mini sense—for his wife in that he saves her from any danger that is encroaching on her." (3) In *provision*—or nourishing, the man loves his wife as himself. This role is "a very costly burden. Many men have lost their lives fulfilling this role."[9]

Men don't lead from superior competencies

This male-female relationship dynamic is never based on *superiority* or *inferiority*. It's not about competence. Men don't lead because they're more reasonable or rational. (In fact, the sexes don't render easily into the rational/emotional dichotomy.[10]) Such a competency standard would perpetually undermine male leaders. For men, what makes your leadership "fitting and beautiful" is precisely that it doesn't ride on competence. It's set by divine design (Eph. 5:22–33). So, men, headship is not rooted in "your superior knowledge, or your superior wisdom, or your superior insight, or your superior language skills." Women can (and will) exceed you in all these areas, "and yet the fitness of your leadership is still firmly in place." Intelligence, articulation, and wisdom are real competencies that will help you lead, "but they're not the essence" of leadership. "No, no, no, no, they're not. Nor are they the essence of what a godly woman hopes for in her husband's leadership. The essence of this God-given call on your life as husband is a mature, loving sense that you bear a primary responsibility for the relationship."[11]

On the other side, egalitarians argue from the assumption that "peculiar roles and responsibilities among men and women in the home, in the church, and in the culture should emerge *only from competencies*—rather than from a deeper reality rooted in who we are differently as male and female." So we need to ask: Does the New Testament call out "built-in responsibilities" based on sex? The answer is *yes*. It stands in Scripture that "men have a special, God-given responsibility that comes with being a man," and not rooted in "practical competency."[12]

In the home, "God never said that the man is appointed to be head because he is *more competent* or that the woman is appointed to submission because she is *less competent*. Competence is not the issue in whether a man is head and a woman is submitting." A husband with an eighth-grade education is qualified to lead his wife who has a college degree "because the issue is not competency."[13] In headship, competencies are "irrelevant."[14] Indeed, "a good wife, a submissive

---

9   APJ 222: "Must a Wife Take Her Husband's Last Name?" (November 22, 2013).

10   APJ 1181: "Does the Bible Portray Women as Emotional and Men as Rational?" (April 6, 2018).

11   APJ 1549: "My Wife Is More Spiritual—How Do I Lead Her?" (November 9, 2020).

12   APJ 1172: "Sex-Abuse Allegations and the Egalitarian Myth" (March 16, 2018).

13   APJ 769: "What Does It Mean for a Man to Lead His Family Spiritually?" (January 11, 2016).

14   APJ 940: "Is Christian Hedonism Only for Complementarians?" (September 21, 2016).

wife, may have more competency than her husband in lots of areas."[15] Within God's good design, such competencies are never a threat. The wife's skills are an asset to the marriage.

Likewise, inside the church, male-only preaching isn't a claim of superior masculine aptitude.[16] Women should aspire to becoming gifted teachers (Titus 2:3). So "don't ever make the mistake of thinking, 'Oh, a woman is not permitted to do this kind of authoritative teaching because she is incompetent.' That is not the issue."[17] Thus, the call for "the authoritative leaders and teachers of the church to be spiritual, Christlike men is not random or arbitrary or merely competency-based or cultural."[18] In male-female relationships, "the issue, as always, is not the competence of women teachers or intelligence or knowledge or pedagogical skill. It's never competence! That's not the issue in the home or in leadership. It's not the issue in church leadership."[19]

Take the prevailing assumption that men lead just because they're men (detached from God's intentional design and Christ's relationship to his bride), separate it from the idea that men owe women a special kind of care, and then add in egalitarian assumptions that leadership means superior competency, and you have a recipe for disaster in society and in marriage, of men who become misogynists, falsely assuming men are superior to women. That's not complementarity.[20] It's arrogant narcissism.[21]

Complementarity: a dialogue between husband and wife

In the home, husband and wife "enact the magnificent drama of Christ and the church in Ephesians 5:24–25."[22] And as they enact this drama—not begrudgingly, but willingly—they co-appreciate and co-encourage God's design for one another.

Men honor their wives as "the weaker vessel," which is not a statement of value but a statement of fact. She's physically weaker (1 Pet. 3:7). Very carefully, *weaker* does not diminish women, nor does it create a superiority structure that favors men—because the same text says, "'you are *fellow heirs* of the grace of life.'" This text, applied to a man, says: "'Mr. Husband, you live with a woman

---

15 APJ 495: "What Will Submission to My Husband Look Like?" (December 18, 2014).

16 APJ 56: "Do You Use Bible Commentaries Written by Women?" (March 27, 2013).

17 APJ 533: "Can a Woman Preach If Elders Affirm It?" (February 16, 2015).

18 APJ 1030: "Is Male Headship a Lost Cause?" (April 19, 2017).

19 APJ 1149: "Is There a Place for Female Professors at Seminary?" (January 22, 2018).

20 APJ SE05: "John Piper's Message to Ray Rice" (September 11, 2014) and APJ 1172: "Sex-Abuse Allegations and the Egalitarian Myth" (March 16, 2018).

21 APJ 1449: "A Word to Men Who Demean Their Wives" (March 20, 2020).

22 APJ 67: "The Parent's Role in a Child's Gender Development" (April 11, 2013).

who is destined to inherit the world, because that is what you are promised in Christ. She will be a queen of the universe, and you sleep in the same bed with this stunning being. So wake up to the reality of what you are dealing with here."²³ Husbands "honor" their wives on the very basis that she is a "weaker vessel." The differences, here in physical strength, generate "a peculiar, special honor—a kind of honor God has built into the man as the stronger one. This is not merely mutual honor; this is a *special honor* flowing from the stronger to the weaker." A "special duty" and "special responsibility" given to men.²⁴

The dialogue works in the other direction too. As a man bears his responsibility to *lead*, *protect*, and *provide* for his wife, his wife takes note. Wives, "with their God-given strength and wisdom, come alongside their husbands and support that leadership. That is what submission means. They help their husbands *carry it through*." A wife *helps* her husband carry out his leadership role (Gen. 2:18–20).²⁵ So a woman, "assured of her feminine identity in such a deep and powerful way," who knows that she is man's equal in the kingdom of God and in eternal joy, is thereby "poised and free to affirm the manhood" of her husband.²⁶ She will honor the leadership and protective "instincts" of her husband.²⁷ She will find creative ways to encourage his leadership of the family spiritually.²⁸

A woman who is married to a non-Christian husband who is a weak leader can still honor and celebrate the glimmers of leadership she perceives in him. This will encourage more of it. Indeed, "do everything you can to honor that leadership and call out of him all the initiatives, all the protection, all the provision."²⁹ Believing husband or not, "a wife's basic disposition toward her husband should be: 'I love it when you lead.'"³⁰

On leading a family

Headship and submission are rooted in the Christ-bride drama of Ephesians 5:21–25. "The wife takes her cues from the church as the church is called to follow Christ as its leader. The husband takes his cues from Christ as the head of the church who gave himself up for her." The human drama is *similar* and *dissimilar*, and "both the *similarities* and the *differences* shape the way we flesh out this drama of Christ and the church."

23 APJ 587: "Does God Favor Boys over Girls?" (May 1, 2015).
24 APJ 1172: "Sex-Abuse Allegations and the Egalitarian Myth" (March 16, 2018).
25 APJ 940: "Is Christian Hedonism Only for Complementarians?" (September 21, 2016).
26 APJ 65: "What Is 'Strong Feminine Womanhood?'" (April 9, 2013).
27 APJ 90: "A Mother's Role in Raising Boys" (May 14, 2013).
28 APJ 1301: "How Can We Prioritize Our Marriage over Work and Kids?" (January 11, 2019).
29 APJ 1376: "How Do I Submit to My Unbelieving Husband?" (October 2, 2019).
30 APJ 94: "Do Online Sermons Undermine Local Churches?" (May 20, 2013).

Again, one *similarity* is that "Christ wants the submission of the church to be free and joyful, with a full understanding of who he is and what he stands for and why he is doing what he is doing. Christ does not want slavish obedience or joyless compliance or mindless submissiveness from the church." Like a good husband, Christ "wants his wife to be full of intelligence and understanding and wisdom and joy and freedom when she commits herself to following him."

But the Christ-bride drama comes with plenty of *dissimilarities*. (1) Husbands are "fallible and sinful, but Christ is not. Therefore, you can never draw a straight line from the way *Christ* leads his church to the way the *husband* leads his wife without taking into account this distinction, this difference. The husband's finiteness and his sin have to come into the picture." (2) Wives hold to an allegiance that is higher than their husbands. The wife's first allegiance is not to her husband, but always to her Lord. For the husband and the wife alike, Christ is "their supreme master" (Eph. 5:21–33; Col. 3:17–25; 1 Pet. 2:13–17). Christ commissions us into "the institutions of the world, like marriage" to live out a free submission, "because our supreme and primary Lord has said to. The submission, therefore, that a woman offers to her husband is done so freely, at the bidding of her Lord Jesus." Christ sets the standards. The wife submits to honor Christ. And that same wife will refuse to follow her husband into sin because it would dishonor Christ. Only Christ gets our unqualified allegiance. "Jesus is always wiser than the church. Husbands are not always wiser than their wives." So "a mature Christian husband will not express his leadership with childish, proud bullying or one-sided decision-making, but he will always seek out both the wisdom and desires of his wife. This is what good, fallen—fallible yet Christlike—leadership does." (3) Unlike the Christ-bride roles, the husband-wife roles are rooted in the Creator's design, not in a superiority-inferiority hierarchy (above).

Within this relationship, taking his cues from Christ, the man takes responsibility that will "move him to take *initiatives* with his wife and children to see to it that the family is cared for." In male leadership, this is "the main issue" to ensure "that God's will is done as much as possible by every member of the family." The man initiates the family vision, ministry involvement, financial planning, insurance coverage, and retirement funding. He initiates the "moral vision" and expectations for the children—their discipline, media use, involvement in youth sports, and how to redeem leisure time. The wife "is going to have superior wisdom on many of these things." But the wife "longs for a husband to take initiative to put processes in motion by which these things can be worked out, problems can be solved, and plans can be made." And "most importantly," the man will "feel a special responsibility to lead the family in a pattern of prayer and Bible reading and worship."[31]

Husbands, make Ephesians 5:25–33 "your lifelong charter" in living out your covenant marriage. This "inexhaustible passage" will "break you down and then build you back up again and again as you discover more and more deeply the wonders of the mystery of marriage. Very few people in our day— even in the church—think of marriage as deeply and seriously and gloriously as God intends." And add 1 Peter 3:7 into your charter too. You're married to a fellow child of God and a future queen of heaven.

Ephesians 5:25–33 functions to restore what was destroyed by the first couple's sin in Genesis 3:1–13, particularly in three ways. (1) The shame of nakedness gets removed between husband and wife. (2) The vertical rupture with God is restored in Christ. (3) The "shame, fear, blame, guilt-shifting" between man and woman is healed in Christ. So Christ entered this fallen world "to save people from all that relational destruction. That's why he came. His central, all-important way of saving us from shame and fear and blame and guilt-shifting is to die—to die in our place and on our behalf, rise from the dead, and give us eternal hope. In other words, Jesus deals with our sin in such a way that fear and shame and blame and guilt-shifting are destroyed in his redeemed family. He does it by dying—dying."

Within this drama, the man feels "a special responsibility to take initiatives for creating an atmosphere and putting in place the means of grace that replace shame with honor and fear with joyful confidence, and to endure blame or guilt-shifting with forbearance and forgiveness." Husbands, "first receive the redeeming work of Christ in your own brokenness and sinfulness, and then bend it outward after the model of Christ to show it to your wife and your children." You live with them as fellow heirs of glory (1 Pet. 3:7). The wife, too, experiences the same redemption in the same way—by faith in Christ. Then she takes that grace and also bends it outward to her husband and children.

But it all comes back to initiative. As the head, husband, you "must take initiatives for creating and sustaining a spiritual and emotional and physical atmosphere where your wife feels protected and safe. She needs a place safe from verbal putdowns and other wounding that might come from you or the children. She needs a place where she feels provided for and where she feels that she doesn't have to push because you're already moving in the direction of establishing a gracious and godly atmosphere in the home." Get practical and ask: Who in this marriage is the initiator? The husband or wife? "The husband

31   APJ 769: "What Does It Mean for a Man to Lead His Family Spiritually?" (January 11, 2016).

needs to establish a healthy family pattern of life—prayer patterns, Bible reading patterns, church attendance patterns, patterns of moral guidance for the children, patterns of pace and schedule, patterns of how you handle iPhones, patterns of financial responsibility in living within the budget, and on and on." He initiates and facilitates decisions, not "one-sided decision-making." The husband leads with "Let's . . . ," not with "unilateral commands, because you're not Christ."

Christ is sinless and superior to his bride. The human husband is not. But even as fallible sinners, the drama of Ephesians 5:25–33 remains intact as the charter for a fallen marriage. The husband loves and leads his wife "as Christ loved the church. That means you take into full account your own sinfulness and finitude and how a sinful, finite leader creates the fullest joy and fruitfulness in the family. You may find in any of these cases that your wife has greater wisdom than you do. That doesn't mean she suddenly becomes the leader. She will be thrilled that in your initiative-taking leadership you are humble enough to receive a wise word when you hear it. No worthy leader—whether the president of the United States or the general of an army—no worthy leader assumes that he has all the wisdom he needs."[32]

My wife is more spiritual than me—how do I lead in the home?

The husband is the head of the wife, and husbands are to love their wives like Christ loves his church. Wives submit to their husbands (Eph. 5:23–25). "Now that's all very, very radical in every culture on planet earth. It is a restoration of what God established in the garden of Eden and a transformation of the mess that the relationship became after the fall. It recaptures what God originally designed, and it redeems what was ruined in that design by sin. That's the point of Ephesians. It restores headship or leadership, and it transforms that leadership by modeling it on the self-giving love of Christ for his church."

God's full design for marriage in Eden would only make sense in Christ's relationship to his bride. God's ultimate meaning of marriage was kept a secret for thousands of years (Eph. 5:23–25). So "when God created man as male and female, he already had in view Jesus Christ and his church as the model for Adam and Eve and all marriages to follow." And from the very beginning, God's plan "included this glorious destiny of the man echoing Christ in his role as husband, and the woman echoing the church in her role as wife." In due time, the plan would be revealed to us.

So how does this work out in a marriage, when the husband does not look "especially fitted for leadership" nor the wife "especially fitted for submission"?

32 APJ 1113: "How Do I Know If I'm Loving My Wife Well?" (October 30, 2017).

And how does this work when the wife seems to be more spiritually mature? (1) Be thankful for her maturity. "That's your first job: confident, Christ-exalting thankfulness that you have such a wife." Don't be "intimidated or resentful" of her maturity. (2) See skills and competencies as secondary. A husband's leadership in the home is "fitting and beautiful," not because the man is more competent and gifted in all areas. Despite your limitations, you bear the primary responsibility, and "you should feel a uniquely masculine burden that the buck stops with you for making this relationship work. When anything is not working in this relationship, you feel the primary responsibility to get it fixed."[33]

Who disciplines the kids—mom or dad?

Discipline is ordained by God in many spheres. The state can avenge evildoers (Rom. 13:4). Employers can withhold wages from those who refuse to work (2 Thess. 3:10). The church disciplines the unrepentant (1 Cor. 5:5). And parents discipline children (Eph. 6:4).[34]

In some countries, corporal punishment of children (spanking) is illegal. So this discussion requires nuance.[35] But especially where it is legal, a lack of parental discipline is likened to nothing short of child hate (Prov. 13:24). The terms are so stark because "coddling children with no physical repercussions for their defiant behavior is preparing them to be unable to recognize the discipline of God in their lives when it comes in physical forms. And it will come in physical forms. And we are doing them a great disservice if we haven't shown them how a loving parent can lovingly spank a disobedient child."[36]

The goal of discipline in the home is a positive action meant to result in a restoration "laden with grace." Discipline is not damage. "If you damage, you are not disciplining; you are abusing." But within this conviction of the goodness of discipline, the main principle in the Piper home was that "the parent whose word is most immediately disobeyed does the discipline, whether verbal or physical, except when both parents are present; then the father steps in and does it." So disobeying mom brings mom's discipline. "You disobey daddy, daddy is going to call you to account." But "if you disobey mommy or daddy when daddy is around, daddy is going to call you to account." Dads are not the sole discipliners and should not be made out to be the home's "bogeyman" who does it all. But he can certainly be called on by mom to handle things when he returns home from work, particularly in situations when things have "gotten

33 APJ 1549: "My Wife Is More Spiritual—How Do I Lead Her?" (November 9, 2020).
34 APJ 318: "Should Christians Be Cops and Soldiers?" (April 11, 2014).
35 APJ 879: "Spanking Is Illegal in My Country—Now What?" (June 13, 2016).
36 APJ 948: "How Do We Prepare Our Children for Suffering?" (October 10, 2016).

out of hand." As a norm, moms and dads are codiscipliners (Deut. 21:18). And yet when mom and dad are together, dad steps in.

Four reasons. (1) Dad leads the family. Scripture teaches that the husband is "the head, the leader, and the normal initiative taker, which would include being the vision caster for the moral life of the family" and thereby "the most natural person for taking the initiative in discipline." He is not passive, not "waiting to see if mom acts." In him, the children learn that dad is "not waiting around for mom to deal with things." But the kids also know mom is no "pushover" either. (2) Dad protects his family. Ephesians 5 presents Christ as a bride rescuer. In this way, husbands protect their wives and kids, and "discipline is mainly protection—protection from a kid's own selfishness, and protection from future tragedies and lawlessness that is going to get the kid in trouble if he lives a life of insubordination and selfishness." (3) Dad supports and nurtures mom. Christ nurtures his bride, so too the husband nurtures his wife. Especially in homes when mom "has been with these kids hours on end carrying the burden of discipline," the husband brings a reprieve to her, and the kids know that when dad is present, he's the "buck stopper." (4) Dad "most immediately" images the Father, who disciplines the children he loves (Heb. 12:6). "God is not male. And so women and men together are displaying things about God the kids need to know. But God is revealed in the Bible mainly as a father, not a mother. This means that a father's role is centrally important in giving a child a sense of what good fatherhood is like. And that includes fatherly discipline."

In the end, "both parents discipline kids." Mom, when she's alone with them. And, normally, "dad steps up when both parents are present."[37]

Dad, don't exasperate your children

Dad carries the lead burden in disciplining, and he must do it in ways that don't damage and don't provoke, embitter, or exasperate the kids (Col. 3:21). A "daunting" and "impossible" task, really. But godly fathers will do their best to lead and discipline their children in ways that don't belittle, put down, nag, demand, or expect the impossible. He will aspire to discipline without anger, and without being too quick to discipline or too slow to forgive. The balance is challenging. But the calling is dad's.[38]

Angry dads make angry kids (Eph. 6:4). And the cure for angry dads is not simply a list of commands, but a list of commands—to be kind, tenderhearted, and quick to forgive—topped off with a glorious gospel reminder (Eph. 4:31–32).

---

37 APJ 267: "Who Should Discipline the Kids—Mom or Dad?" (January 30, 2014).
38 APJ 1785: "How Do I Not Provoke My Children?" (May 20, 2022).

Dads, "the gospel is our only hope for child-rearing. The main issue in making kids mad is that we're mad. And if we're going to pull the plug on our anger, this is it. I don't know any other Christ-exalting answer to how to overcome anger than the way Paul says here." Dads need perpetual reminders that all their sins have been forgiven.[39] Instead, dads bear the "joyful, weighty responsibility" of "cultivating joy as the indomitable atmosphere" of the home, rooted in "the gospel and the sovereignty of God."[40]

Doesn't male leadership in the home call for gun ownership?

No, it doesn't—and this answer provoked one of our most controversial episodes. Pastor John does not own a gun. For four reasons.

1. The anger factor. In heated moments, vengeance and anger can dominate the emotions. This anger must be subdued (James 1:19). "I am really quick to think *payback*, and that is unbiblical and unchristian, and I have to subdue it. And I don't want a gun in my hand while I am engaging in that battle."

2. The arrogance factor. The culture's media bombardment daily is to glorify "cool, hard, tough-talking, tough-acting women and men who have a kind of unflappable, cocky swagger that gets the last word and has the last shot." And "when that is the attitude breaking in on my soul every day, the last thing I need is a gun in my hand."

3. The repaying evil-with-evil factor (Matt. 5:39–41; 10:16; Rom. 12:17; 1 Thess. 5:15; 1 Pet. 3:9). "These texts describe a real way of loving people and glorifying the all-satisfying, all-sufficient Christ. They are one form that love takes—a very powerful form, a form that Jesus chose, almost all the time, a form of love that we don't have enough of—that I don't have enough of in my heart, and we don't have enough of in the world." So then does a man have no justifiable defense to employ in protecting his wife and family and home? No, there are other defenses (fists for example). These texts don't suggest "an arming spirit," and they "disincline" us from choosing "the quickest and most deadly harm in self-defense."

4. The protection-of-God factor. Pulling a gun does not invite the protection of God. "When Peter pulled 'his gun' on the high priest in the garden of Gethsemane and 'shot off' the ear of the high priest's servant, Jesus picked up the ear and put it back on" (Matt. 16:23; Mark 8:33). And then he told a parable: "All who take the sword will perish by the sword." Meaning this: "the mindset that plans to save its life by killing is not inviting the protection of God, but the violence of man."

---

39 APJ 1829: "Overcoming Anger in the Home" (August 31, 2022).
40 APJ 255: "Dad's Role in Homemaking" (January 14, 2014).

"So, my response—for what it is worth, and this is *testimony*, not *prescription*—has been to live in the inner city in Minneapolis for thirty-three years, raise five children there, surrounded by petty crimes and some gunshots and a little bit of a break-in, and never to possess a firearm. Nor do I ever intend to. God has protected us, and I believe he will. But as I see it now, I would rather be killed than to kill. For me, that would mean instant joy. But if I killed him, it might be instant hell [for him]. I am ready, and he may not be."[41]

That controversial gun episode, and particularly this last point, led to a follow-up. If a man isn't ready to die and face God, doesn't this logically prevent his execution by the state too?

No. "When I said that I would rather be killed than kill, and then I mentioned that my assailant may not be ready to face eternity and I am, I didn't mean that was my *primary* reason for not killing him." It would equally apply "if I knew that my assailant was heaven-bound as a Christian." Instead, gun ownership (or nonownership) is principally governed by what Jesus said about not returning evil for evil. Jesus's main point "is not that our adversary will benefit from our behavior. He may, or he may not. Jesus doesn't make that the issue. The main way Jesus argues is that when we sacrifice ourselves and our goods for others, we show the value of God himself as our reward." This is true whether facing a believing or unbelieving assailant (Matt. 5:11–12, 46; Luke 6:35). "So I didn't mean to argue that I would rather *be killed* than *kill* because it is always wrong to take the life of a person who may go to hell. I didn't mean to do that. If I gave that impression, I gave a misimpression." Instead, the Bible is clear that there are situations where a life must be taken irrespective of one's spiritual state, particularly for those in law enforcement and the military. God has ordained the state "to take the life of murderers" (Rom. 13:1–4).[42]

Can Christian men become cops and soldiers?
This was another follow-up theme arising from the controversial 2014 episode, where Pastor John explained why he refuses to arm his home with a gun, owing to the retaliatory bent of the sinful heart and the vengefulness of our culture's media.[43]

So can Christian men serve in law enforcement or the military?

Yes—on the condition of serious heart work. When soldiers came to John the Baptist, they were not told to quit the military, but to focus on their hearts to become more holy soldiers (Luke 3:14). Believers-as-soldiers is a legitimate

41 APJ 306: "God, Guns, and Biblical Manhood" (March 26, 2014).
42 APJ 317: "More on Guns and Self-Defense" (April 10, 2014).
43 APJ 306: "God, Guns, and Biblical Manhood" (March 26, 2014).

profession. At the civic level, God has designed the enforcement of retributive justice (Rom. 13:1–4). "So the sword bearers, the billy-club bearers, the gun bearers are servants of God, an avenger who carries out God's wrath on the wrongdoer." Nothing in the New Testament overturns Genesis 9:6. So God is manifested to the world through Christian mercy and state justice. "Christian-enemy love that *sacrifices itself* and official, state-enemy punishment that *protects citizens* both declare truths about God. Christian self-sacrifice declares that our God is all-satisfying. He is our treasure. He is our reward. He will fully satisfy us in the end. He will settle all accounts in the age to come. And state punishment declares God is a God of justice. He ordains that there is a limit to evil even in this world. He will not tolerate it to go beyond certain means, and he is a God of justice, now and in the world to come. Both are true. And Christians are involved in saying both with their lives in the way that the New Testament prescribes."[44]

Pastor John carries "a lot of sympathy" with pacifist convictions (Matt. 5:38–41; 10:16; Rom. 12:17; 1 Thess. 5:15; 1 Pet. 3:9). Such texts "should probably have a greater effect on our attitudes than they do." Because, again, we Christians are naturally (and sinfully) quick to seek vengeance instead of mercy. "But I can't go all the way with the Christian pacifist when he tells us that retributive justice should have no place in the Christian life." Retributive justice has a God-designed place in the realms of military and police (Rom. 13:4; 1 Pet. 2:14), in the workplace (2 Thess. 3:10), in parenting (Eph. 6:4; Heb. 12:5–11), and in the church (1 Cor. 5:1–13). This mercy/justice dynamic adds very real tensions to the Christian life. "I admit very freely that the mingling of mercy toward our enemies and the application of justice is not easy. We are supposed to love our enemies and return good for evil."[45]

Christian cops and soldiers will live inside the tension of a world that exists to display (1) God's mercy *and* (2) his justice. These two principles will "collide" in the heart and mind of the Christian soldier or police officer because a Christian continues to be a Christian in uniform. This tension will not go away in this life. "And that is just the way it has to be, it seems to me, in a partially redeemed world."[46]

The Christian cop or soldier—as one who learns to deal out mercy *and* justice—will need incredible wisdom when his finger is on the trigger, a wisdom requiring personal holiness. And it will require death to the retaliatory bent of the sinful heart inside of us and resistance to the vengeful media surrounding us.

44 APJ 317: "More on Guns and Self-Defense" (April 10, 2014).
45 APJ 1635: "Should Christian Jurors Show Mercy to the Guilty?" (June 4, 2021).
46 APJ 318: "Should Christians Be Cops and Soldiers?" (April 11, 2014).

On the midlife crisis

The midlife crisis theme was introduced to the podcast by a question from a pastor who felt depressed after preaching. His Mondays got predictably dark. To him, Pastor John first shared with listeners about "a period of deep discouragement," one he experienced at age forty. The discouragement was "so deep my mind could scarcely recall my children's names." It's not uncommon for many men. The age of forty, or right before or after, "can be a crisis for men for reasons I don't think we fully understand physically and psychologically. It certainly was for me." It can hit with surprise. "So beware all you men between thirty-five and forty-five. You are in a season that you will get through. Don't leave your wife and buy a sailboat or a motorcycle and find another woman. That is a stupid way to solve a problem. Stay faithful to your ministry. Stay faithful to your wife."[47]

This counsel emerged from personal experience. And when another pastor wrote in to say he wanted to quit the ministry, it reminded Pastor John of this season when he nearly walked away from pastoring at the age of forty, an age that marks an "emotionally vulnerable place for a man to be." He didn't quit but remained in the pastorate for another twenty-seven years, "a warning against precipitous resignations when God may have something wonderful in store by persevering through seasons of blankness. He certainly did for me, and I'm so thankful he didn't let me go, in both senses. He didn't let me leave the church, and he didn't let go of me."[48]

Those two episodes for pastors opened the door for me to ask Pastor John to explain more about this midlife challenge, which he did. It hit him while vacationing in California. There in his vacation home, Piper sat down on the stairs and broke down in tears. "My wife found me and was startled because that's not typical. She asked me, 'What's wrong?' And I simply said, 'I don't have any idea.'" He pressed on and preached as a guest at a local church. Afterward, a man perceptive to the midlife crisis approached and asked Piper's age. "I said, 'Forty.' He smiled and said, 'You got a year and a half.' He meant the average age for men to pass through midlife crisis." It was news to Pastor John, who rarely trusts generalized diagnoses. In this case, the evidence seemed clear. "Something happens for many men as they move into their forties, and not all of it is pretty."

Here are five warning flags that the midlife experience is brewing. (1) Unseen physical and hormonal changes may lurk behind it all—a sort of "male menopause" to be factored in. (2) The career has peaked, and disillusionment

---

47 APJ 429: "Handling Post-Sermon Blues" (September 15, 2014).
48 APJ 1143: "To Discouraged Pastors and Their Wives" (January 8, 2018).

sets in. Maybe the vocational dreams didn't materialize, or the job failed to deliver the fulfillment expected. The thought of doing the same work for a few more decades becomes "really oppressive." (3) Physical health declines for the couple. Maybe he fails to get sleep and exercise and has become an "overweight, bedraggled, average, run-of-the-mill, paunchy man. He may feel lousy about it but physically too tired to do anything about it." (4) Marriage becomes dull. It's easy for a couple to no longer enjoy a joyful partnership working toward goals and personal holiness and instead settle into a "twenty-year-old coexistence," ignoring simmering tensions under a mutual truce. (5) Parenting gets hardest. Kids become teens and then adults. In the transition to adulthood they force on dad the hardest questions of life, leading to a "never-ending pressure and confusion for which there are just no simple answers."

So what can be done?

1. Keep hoping. "Looking back now from age seventy-one, I am overflowing with thankfulness for the mercy and the power of God to hold on to me during those years." Preserve your daily communion with Christ and lay hold of him because he has laid hold of you (Phil. 3:12). Practically, find time to get away for half a day. "Take a Bible and a notepad and wrestle with God for three hours until you get fresh clarity for why you are on planet earth." Not just your job, but your purpose over all of life (something like Paul did in Acts 20:24 and Phil. 1:20).

2. Keep seeking God's face. "I have no doubt, brothers, that if you will take the time to seek his face and know him and love him, you will mount up with wings like eagles. You will run and not be weary; you will walk and not faint. It's true. I know it's true. I have tasted it in the impossible moments—in the moments when you don't think you could do another thing. In those moments, you lay hold on Isaiah 40" (especially Isa. 40:31).[49]

3. Keep fighting to be kept. God holds us fast in the midlife years. "The older I get, the more I want to give God public, heartfelt, explicit credit and praise for keeping me through every kind of distress that I have experienced," and "give God glory for being a keeping, holding God." But that does not mean that the *way* God preserves us through this darkness is unimportant. God's keeping grace "is manifest, shown, evident—precisely through our fighting to be kept." In other words, "God moves us to fight to be kept, and thus he keeps us." God is the one who keeps us (Jude 24–25). And God keeps those whom he calls (1 Cor. 1:8–9; 10:13; Phil. 1:6). "If you don't feel amazed that you woke up a Christian this morning, you don't get it. You just don't get it. Because if God

---

49 APJ 1173: "My Midlife Crisis—and Counsel for Yours" (March 19, 2018).

hadn't kept you at 3:00 a.m., you'd wake up at 6:00 a.m. and be an unbeliever. That's stupendous!" We are kept by a power that "works by awakening in us faith every morning" (1 Pet. 1:5). And God's keeping grace is manifested in our fighting to be kept. "I'm going to say it again because this is just so perplexing why people have a hard time getting this, yet they do. God's keeping—God's decisive, sovereign keeping of his own, his children—is manifested, works itself out, is shown, is evident in our lives—precisely *through* our fighting to be kept." Let your guard down, and sin will knock you out (1 Cor. 9:26–27). God kept Paul by making him a fighter. Press on *because* you are held by God (Phil. 3:12).

"As I look back over my life, I have never stopped fighting to tremble at God's severity. I have never stopped fighting to rejoice at God's kindness. I cannot remember missing a day that I was not in God's word and in prayer. I suspect there were some. I'm not claiming any perfection. I just can't remember any. It's that much a part of my life. Every day is a day of pleading over the word that I would be kept and shaped according to the God I see in the Bible." Be careful not to isolate yourself from others. Depend on God's means to cling to him in this dark midlife season. And keep fighting to be kept.[50]

---

50 APJ 1365: "How Do I Survive This Midlife Crisis?" (July 5, 2019).

On Fearless Women, Feminine Beauty, and Modesty

Backbones of stainless steel

At one of his major conference messages in 2008, Piper reiterated his love for strong women (maybe too strongly). From the pulpit he sent out a clarion call: "Where are the women, the single women and the married women and the pastors' wives"—who will say with Esther, I will do what needs to be done, "and if I perish, I perish" (Est. 4:12–17)? "Where are those women? Our church is crawling with them. I could marry all of them!" To which the audience broke out in laughter. "I'm too old." Another laugh. "And I'm married." The most laughter. "And I married one of them." A great save.[1]

A little later in a Q&A panel, he reiterated the point. "We've got a lot of strong women at our church. They bear a lot of things. They endure pain through marriages and through kids that are disabled in other ways. . . . I love strong women. I think they are magnificent testimonies to Christ." As complementarians, "they're combining things the world can't explain—a sweet, tender, kind, loving, submissive, feminine beauty with this massive steel in their backs and theology in their brains!"[2]

Five years after the conference, I asked him to expand on what he said about strong women. For example, the valiant woman of Proverbs 31 has strong arms (Prov. 31:17). Yes, Piper said, but her strength is most obvious in that "she laughs at the time to come" (Prov. 31:25). "A woman laughing at the time to come is not a woman who is looking at her biceps and getting encouragement. She is looking at her God and getting encouragement." She knows a foreign invasion

---

1   John Piper, "How the Supremacy of Christ Creates Radical Christian Sacrifice," Desiring God, April 17, 2008, https://www.desiringgod.org/.

2   John Piper, "T4G 2008 Panel Discussion," Desiring God, April 17, 2008, https://www.desiring god.org/.

could happen in an instant. A deadly plague could sweep over her village. Her God, not her biceps, will be decisive. Peter's powerful text is important here (1 Pet. 3:1–6). The godly woman displays a "gentle and quiet spirit" in a vessel intentionally designed to be physically weaker than a man (1 Pet. 3:4, 7). And yet she remains fearless (1 Pet. 3:6). "Now that is what I mean by a *strong woman*. I mean a woman who can lose a child, lose a husband, lose her health, face a family crisis, see the world becoming anti-Christian all around her and wonder about raising children in this world. Women who go to a dangerous place on the mission field, women who return good for evil over and over again, women who get up a thousand times with a sick or disabled child at night—all of it in the strength that God supplies, because God is her hope. God is her rock." That is feminine strength.

A worldview gulf separates that *strong woman*—strong in her womanhood—from a woman trying to prove her strength by *becoming man-like*. This theme infects Hollywood action films in which "women are constantly being portrayed, not as *strong women*, but as *imitation men*. And it is absolutely hopeless." On screen, women kick, punch, and kill like men—even take down whole rooms full of men by their strength. In contrast, a truly strong woman "knows she is a man's equal" in God's sight, kingdom, and eternal joy. She has nothing to prove. Eternity's joys are equally hers. If she tries to prove her strength by adopting male standards, she's doomed to be stuck perpetuating the world's male-versus-female war. But in true feminine vigor, with her strength long settled, she's now "poised and free to affirm the manhood of the men around her and come alongside them and help them in every way they can in their unique calling. In this way, the dance and the rhythm and the choreography of man and woman become a beautiful partnership."[3]

With backbones of steel, women also need deep doctrine in the brain—a deep knowledge of God. Or to say it another way: wimpy theology makes wimpy women. "During my thirty-two years of preaching at Bethlehem, one of the deeply gratifying things for me is that alongside a spiritually mature, biblically informed, humble, Christlike male eldership, there has risen an army of intelligent, articulate, mature, Bible-saturated, God-centered, Christ-exalting, strong women who partner with the men of the church. They work to get the ministry of family and society done."

Women need deep theology, and they can handle it. "Women's brains are usually sharper than men's brains, at least in my experience." His mother outsmarted his dad. In high school, Piper graduated nineteenth in his class.

---

3   APJ 65: "What Is 'Strong Feminine Womanhood?'" (April 9, 2013).

Above him were eighteen more intelligent girls. In college, at Wheaton, women outsmarted men. "As far as mental capacity for grasping theology, there is zero reason why we shouldn't seek for the women of our church to be as fully taught and as articulate and intelligent in their grasp of God's glory as the men."[4]

The world needs her. We need more, not fewer, women in ministry.[5]

A primer on biblical womanhood

1. Biblical womanhood begins in the "immeasurably massive" truth that she is "created in the image of the Creator of the universe." It means that "every woman you pass on the street or every woman you relate to in any way is a potential queen of heaven because she is created in the *imago Dei*. She is in the image of God in the same way that the man is in the image of God, having a human nature which mirrors the very nature of God."

2. Women are equal in dignity and worth to men. Woman is made of the same nature as a man, and together they display a "fuller revelation of God's glory" than man alone.

3. She's unique, with "special capacities physically, mentally, and emotionally that are different from men."

4. She is called to honor and celebrate and support the "leadership and the protection and the provision of godly men appropriately according to their different roles." This applies broadly in culture to her husband, pastors, her husband's male friends, the husbands of her female friends, male colleagues, mailmen, and mechanics. "The dynamic and the dance of gender relations are different for every relationship, but there is something that God has put into men to be leaders and protectors and providers, and something that God has put into women to love that, delight in that, honor that, come alongside that, and use all their manifold gifts to advance the cause of Christ through that—so that when they are together, they are complementing each other, and the beauty of God is displayed more fully."

5. These glorious gender distinctions will echo eternally, even after marriage has ended. This is because "our gender is wrapped around our personhood, that if we were stripped of our maleness or femaleness, we would be unrecognizable." So Jesus is (right now) a man, not an androgynous being. Heaven will be beautifully gendered as a place where all the sin that inhibits men and women in this life will be done away, and true manhood and womanhood will image God in its full splendor.[6]

---

4 APJ 66: "Wimpy Theology Makes Wimpy Women" (April 10, 2013).
5 APJ 388: "The World Needs Women Ministers" (July 18, 2014).
6 APJ 42: "Biblical Womanhood in Five Minutes" (March 7, 2013).

What's wrong with dressing sexy for attention?

A twenty-two-year-old woman wrote in to admit that she cares too much about physical attraction and getting noticed. She uses her sex appeal, in skimpy clothing, to attract the eyes of a future husband. But this approach to life seems like bondage, analogous to the women of Isaiah 3:16–26.

Four considerations for this woman, and others like her. (1) Guard your eyes. "If you are spending hour after hour watching television, movies, and videos, there's little hope that you will be set free from the bondage of wanting to look sexy." So locate the "streams" of content feeding in you this "river of sensual desire" and "cut them off." (2) Don't use sex as a power play. Looking sexy to find a husband is likely not the root issue with immodesty. Some married women who intend to remain married also try to look sexy for everyone else to see. And many single women, with no intent to marry anytime soon, try to look sexy for everyone else to see. Revealed skin is a power grab. And "of course there's more power in sexiness if you want to pull a man by his hormones and not his heart." To be frank about it, "there's more power in sexiness if your aim is to hook a man in his groin and not his godliness. Of course. This is not rocket science. That's not the way you want to find a husband. Please, it's not. Trust me, twenty-two-year-old—you're my daughter's age." The guy you're trying to allure by dressing sexy is not the guy you will marry, because the guy you want to marry is the guy averting his eyes from your immodesty, as Jesus commanded him. The strategy is futile. (3) Don't feed your ego. All of us seek to attract human approval, and such a desire severs us "from what it means to embrace Jesus as Savior and Lord and treasure" (John 5:44). (4) Let your adornment be internal so that you will not be bound by the culture or by the need for approval but will instead live fearless in God (1 Pet. 3:3–7). "Fearless hope in God—that's the great need of men and women. God is ten thousand times greater than any husband. *His* look of approval and favor is ten thousand times more valuable than the glance of any hormone-heated man in an airport or any woman who says, 'Cute outfit.' Oh, how wonderful and satisfying and significant is the identity that God offers us in Jesus."[7]

About three years later, a nineteen-year-old woman wrote in to say that she too was obsessed with her self-image.

First, Pastor John shared a story. Evelyn Brand (1879–1974) was born in England into a wealthy family. She was well-educated. Upon marriage, she and her husband became missionaries to the mountains of India. Just ten years later, she was widowed. She kept up the work, living in a portable hut as

---

7   APJ 1144: "What's Wrong with Dressing Immodestly for Attention?" (January 10, 2018).

she "poured her life into the hill people: nursing the sick, teaching farming, lecturing about guinea worms, rearing orphans, clearing jungle land, pulling teeth, establishing schools, spreading the gospel." As she aged, she faced personal injuries but refused to leave the work. She died at ninety-five and was buried in the mountains by the villagers she spent her life serving. "Now here's the great part: for the last twenty years of her life, she refused to have a mirror in her house. I love this. She was consumed with ministry—not mirrors, not self." By contrast, we live in a world that is "spending billions of dollars and endless media time to persuade women that life consists in their looks: their skin, their shape, their hair. The scam is as old as history. At the center of it is the attempt to trick women into the habit of comparing themselves with other women." The Old Testament pleads with women not to buy the scam (Prov. 31:30). So does the New Testament, in the writings of Peter (1 Pet. 3:3–4) and of Paul (1 Tim. 2:9–10). The main point in appearance is that "outward beauty is insignificant compared to the inward beauty of humility and wisdom and love—a life lived for others."

From Pastor John's own life, "testifying as a man now who has been a teenager, a twenty-year-old, a thirty-year-old, a forty-year-old, a fifty-year-old, and a sixty-year-old—I can testify without any doubt that at every age of my life, my masculine life, women's sexy dressing is less attractive than modest beauty."[8] Excessive time spent before a mirror is wasted effort. "Simple hair, simple makeup, or none, and simple clothing are generally more attractive than heavily made-up faces and hair."[9] It is something "that will encourage a few thousand women and offend a few million—maybe. I don't speak for all men, but I do speak for, I don't know, a few thousand, when I say that we don't find makeup attractive. Lipstick, eye shadow, facial colors, nail coloring—they're off-putting. We love natural, authentic faces. Now, if that sounds liberating to you, I'm glad." If not, "don't worry. It's just John Piper's weird opinion."[10]

On bikinis and modesty

Modesty rules alone cannot fix a church, youth ministry, or Christian school that is "permeated with immodesty." Of course, "rules have a place," but they cannot accomplish "a Christ-exalting, gospel-rooted, Spirit-empowered, faith-sustained, Bible-informed, joyful, free culture of modesty." True modesty requires heart change. "Deep things must happen in a woman's or man's soul before they have any chance of thinking and feeling about these things in a way that honors God."

8   APJ 342: "Bikinis and Modesty" (May 15, 2014).
9   APJ 268: "Feminine Beauty in God's Eyes" (January 31, 2014).
10 APJ 1540: "I'm Obsessed with My Appearance—How Can I Stop?" (October 19, 2020).

To women (and men) who dress immodestly, "I say this: until God has become your treasure, until your own sin has become the thing you hate most, until the word of God is your supreme authority that you feel to be more precious than gold and sweeter than honey, until the gospel of Christ's death in your place is the most precious news in the world to you, until you have learned to deny yourself short-term pleasures for the sake of long-term joy and holiness, until you have grown to love the Holy Spirit and long for his fruit more than man's praise, until you count everything as loss compared to the supreme value of knowing Christ, your attitude toward your clothing and your appearance will be controlled by forces that don't honor Christ."

So Christian leaders and preachers, spend 99 percent of your time stressing divine glories (not human guidelines). Without these divine glories, a church splits into "two kinds of carnal people." One will "bristle at every mention of modesty," and the other will put all the emphasis on outward conformity "with little sense of the heart." Both fail because neither group is "deeply transformed by the gospel."

Addressing modesty means addressing the pride of licentiousness, self-will, externalism, and formalism. "Preach and pray for a gospel culture where men and women have a sweet submission to Christ, a saturation with the word of God, a humble attentiveness to the wisdom of others, a desire to grow and learn, a deep suspicion of the power of worldliness to control our habits, and a loving consideration of others when choosing what to wear." Then when the time is right, preach a text like 1 Timothy 2:8–9 to show that the Bible "really does want us to dress in a way rooted in humble, joyful, Christ-exalting, others-serving, gospel faith." In everything, "cultivate the joyful sense that modesty is beautiful. Renounce any mindset that *modest* means *frumpy*."[11]

Feminine beauty in God's eyes

Exposed skin is a powerful sex magnet. But exposed skin doesn't increase feminine beauty.[12] The world will not understand this. Pop media infects our ideas of female body image via "endless" ads and TV shows and movies "where women are presented with amazingly consistent expectations that external savvy, external strength, external cool, external beauty, and external sexiness are the norm." But the key is beauty—true beauty—the inner beauty of 1 Peter 3:3–6. Clothing and hairstyles are not unimportant, but they pale to the value of inner beauty, Peter says. "Don't put your main energy there on the clothing. Put your main energy inside. I would love to free women from this. It seems to

---

11 APJ 342: "Bikinis and Modesty" (May 15, 2014) (repeated in APJ 886: "Bikinis and Modesty" [June 22, 2016]).

12 APJ 1834: "How Much Jewelry Is Too Much Jewelry?" (September 12, 2022).

me that some put so much energy and so much time into their hair and their eyes and their clothes, and it seems very sad to me."

Draw six points from 1 Peter 3:4. (1) Be most concerned with how God sees you. Let your adorning be the hidden part of you. The part only God can fully see. (2) Know that the inner you *is the real you*. We don't live from behind a mask. "The *real you* is not your face. The *real you* is the hidden person," a person made in God's image, not a dressed-up mannequin or a clothing model. You are a person, "not a doll." This inner you *is the you that matters*. (3) Cultivate your heart. "The heart is the seat of the affections and the will. That is who you are most deeply." The body simply projects outwardly the person of the heart inwardly. So cultivate the heart. (4) Heart beauty is forever. Physical beauty perishes. Inner beauty never does. "Outward beauty is going to fade away, whereas the heart can get more and more beautiful. And God delights in it because it lasts forever." (5) Rest in God. Gentleness and quietness reveal a heart that trusts God. To trust in God "is why we have peace, and we can be meek and tranquil and quiet and not troubled or anxious, not fretful or frantic. When a woman has a peaceful soul—not fretting about how she looks—it shows that God is her portion and she is banking on God." It's the attractive beauty God finds precious. (6) Live with quiet fearlessness. All this inner beauty, meekness, quietness, and tranquility in the "weaker vessel" does not produce "pansy" women. "These women are lionhearted, because that is what it says. 'You are [Sarah's] children, if you do good and do not fear anything that is frightening' (1 Pet. 3:6). I mean, that is the kind of woman you want, right? A kind of woman who is quiet, peaceful, serene, meek, fearless, bold, not frightened in anything. My guess is that the woman who gets up in the morning and spends endless hours on her face and worries about her figure is frightened all the time. She is very insecure. But we want mighty women of the word, mighty women of God who are fearless. And that comes from hoping in God and cultivating this inner beauty."[13]

The faith-filled woman's fearlessness

Biblical womanhood is defined by a woman's faith in God and her resulting fearlessness at whatever life throws at her (1 Pet. 3:6). (1) Fearless of the future. Like the Proverbs 31 woman, "she laughs at the time to come" (Prov. 31:25).[14] "That has got to be one of my favorite verses in all the Bible."[15] (2) Fearless before her

13 APJ 268: "Feminine Beauty in God's Eyes" (January 31, 2014).
14 APJ 51: "My Faith Is Driving My Family Away—What Do I Do?" (March 20, 2013) and APJ 65: "What Is 'Strong Feminine Womanhood?'" (April 9, 2013).
15 APJ 65: "What Is 'Strong Feminine Womanhood?'" (April 9, 2013).

kids. "A son should see his mother not as a weak woman who is always anxious about tomorrow, but like an oak of stable righteousness who laughs at the time to come. She communicates that when you have God, you can be strong and laugh in the face of uncertain futures."[16] (3) Fearless of her husband. The wife's relationship to her husband "is not governed by fear," even if he's not a Christian (1 Pet. 3:1).[17] And her fearlessness also means she will refuse to follow him into sin.[18] (4) Fearless in confessing Christ. Note the close context that draws together a woman's fearlessness (1 Pet. 3:6) and bold witness (1 Pet. 3:15).[19]

A book titled *The Insanity of God: A True Story of Faith Resurrected* tells the story of a twenty-four-year-old widow, Aisha, a former Muslim who was arrested for her outspoken witness for Christ in a large Islamic country and held in the basement of a local police station. As recounted in the book, in her moment of deepest terror, "she intended to scream out to God that she couldn't take any more. But when she opened her mouth in protest and de-spair, a melody of praise rose out of her soul instead. She sang. Surprised and strengthened by the sound of her own voice and overwhelmed by the renewed sense of God's presence beside and within her, she began to sing her praise and worship to Jesus even more loudly." The police upstairs stopped moving and shuffling and listened. She could tell. Later that night, the powerful police chief returned, bewildered, and released her. "'I don't understand,' he admitted. 'You are not afraid of anything!' He sighed and shook his head again. 'My wife, my daughters, and all the women in my family are afraid of everything. But you are not afraid of anything. I want you to come to my house so that you can tell everyone in my family why you are not afraid. And I want you to sing that song.'" The fearless woman of faith is not impervious to anxiety, but her faith-filled fearlessness wins out in the end.[20]

16 APJ 90: "A Mother's Role in Raising Boys" (May 14, 2013).

17 APJ 740: "Is God Directing My Life through My Anxieties?" (December 1, 2015).

18 APJ 680: "Hope for Hard Marriages" (September 8, 2015).

19 APJ 51: "My Faith Is Driving My Family Away—What Do I Do?" (March 20, 2013).

20 APJ 844: "What Is the Line between Courage and Foolishness?" (April 25, 2016). Quotes from Nik Ripken and Gregg Lewis, *The Insanity of God: A True Story of Faith Resurrected* (Nashville, TN: B&H, 2013), 294–95.

On Gyms, Exercise, and Body Image

Personal practices

To stay fit, Pastor John jogs, a discipline he began at age twenty-two.[1] A "really slow" jog, he admits, at about a thirteen-minute-mile pace. For most of the year he runs outside through his neighborhood in Minneapolis.[2] During the winter months he jogs on a treadmill in his attic.[3] His present routine has not changed much in several years: three days of jogging (Monday, Wednesday, and Saturday), mixed with two days of weight training and calisthenics (Tuesday and Thursday), leaving two days off (Friday and Sunday).[4]

Is my body my enemy or my friend?

It's both. As *friend*, our body is the platform we use to live and experience pleasure. It will be resurrected one day, a future anticipation that gives present value to our bodies. But as *foe*, sin turns our flesh into a "base of operations for much enemy activity," a base that's "complicit in that attack of the evil one on us." Our fallen bodies are a "body of death" (Rom. 7:24). So Paul maintains "an ambivalent view of the body. He doesn't want to throw it away in suicide or mutilate it in some unhealthy way." He doesn't want his body to be annihilated. And he longs for his future resurrection. "He knows God gave us a body for a reason. Yet, while he's here on the earth, the enemy has made Paul's body complicit in his destruction. He hates it in that sense, so he opposes it and will not let the body destroy him." We don't hate our bodies for their shape or flaws or skin color. We hate our bodies when they work as agents of sin against God. So learn to "cherish your body as the vehicle of God-given earthly life that will one day be made a glorious body in the resurrection, when you will shine like the sun."

1 APJ 1042: "Is Body Image My Idol?" (May 17, 2017).
2 APJ 1310: "Is Street Evangelism Better Than Building Relationships?" (February 1, 2019).
3 APJ SE17: "How Do I Fight My Coronavirus Fears?" (March 26, 2020).
4 John Piper, email to author, October 1, 2022.

Obsessive concern with body image is a big problem of small things. Our "absolutely crucial need is to set our minds on things different and greater than ourselves." Namely, on Christ (Col. 3:2–3). Learn to "set your mind on things that are above, not on your body." Self-obsession is too narrow of a world for us to live inside. "The walls in this little room, this world that you live in, are all made out of mirrors." The "confined, cramped, smallness of the world" in which you live must get "blown up" by the "majesty and greatness and unimaginable expansiveness of God. Many of the problems that we try to deal with are absolutely unsolvable because the solution lies not in adjusting things in the little room where we live, but in blowing out all the walls of the room where we live so that we suddenly find ourselves staggered by the grandeur of God and his creation." Delighting in God's majesty frees us from self-obsession—a "glorious freedom!"[5]

Will asceticism make me holy?

Metaphorically speaking, in his battle for holiness, the apostle Paul self-punished—pummeling (ὑπωπιάζω) his own body with punches to his face to gain self-control over his selfish desires (1 Cor. 9:26–27).[6] So does Paul mean we can make ourselves more holy if we treat our bodies more harshly? Because in another place, Paul defines asceticism as a "severity to the body" and says it holds "no value in stopping the indulgence of the flesh" (Col. 2:23).

The false teaching in Colossae needs to be more broadly understood as including "the worship of angels, visions, severity to the body by abstaining from certain foods and drinks, keeping certain religious holidays, following these elemental principles and rules—'Do not handle,' 'Do not taste,' 'Do not touch.'" These three prohibitions failed in two ways. They didn't glorify Christ. And they didn't defeat sin. They fed the flesh and produced arrogant, Christ-less, self-sufficient religious people.

So *fasting* and *feasting* have their own place in the Christian life. And they have their own challenges. "Asceticism has a legitimate place in the Christian life, as does the thankful enjoyment of food and drink that God gives us. Eating and drinking can become gluttony with a loss of self-control, and not eating and drinking can become boastful and Christ-diminishing." Thus, "the question is not simply, do you eat or not? Do you drink or not? Do you sleep or not? Do you deny yourself certain legitimate pleasures or not? That's not the main question. The main question is: Is Christ being exalted

5   APJ 1194: "My Body: Friend or Foe?" (May 7, 2018).
6   APJ 60: "How Can We Serve One Another in Battling Lust?" (April 2, 2013).

or is self being exalted?" So while you "crucify the sin of gluttony, are you feeding the sin of pride?" Does your asceticism help kill your sin, or does it feed your vanity?

However, the self-defeating misuse of asceticism doesn't render all asceticism pointless. Asceticism is self-denial. Paul used it. He correlated his own regimen to that of an athlete, one who *disciplines* his body—literally, *pummels* his body (1 Cor. 9:25–27). Earlier, Paul said, "I will not be *dominated* [or *controlled* or *enslaved*] by anything" (1 Cor. 6:12). "In other words, Paul is hard on his body when he needs to be hard on his body in order to protect himself against sin and unbelief." Self-denial remains central to Christian discipleship (Luke 9:23).

So "we dare not treat all asceticism as bad." And "we should not treat God's *good* gifts—of food and drink and friendship and marriage and hundreds of other delights in this life—as *evil*" (1 Tim. 4:4). "We glorify Christ if we receive his good gifts with thankfulness, which shows that he's the good and generous Savior. And we glorify Christ by strategically denying ourselves some of his good gifts in order to show that he is our greatest treasure—not his gifts."[7]

Asceticism's spiritual benefits are found only in Christ. To prove the point, Paul employs the identical Greek term (ταπεινοφροσύνην) *positively* for genuine Christian humility or lowliness (Col. 3:12) and *negatively* for powerless, non-Christian asceticism (Col. 2:18, 23). The "non-Christian use of a Christian virtue," like asceticism, has only the appearance of wisdom. Such physical deprivation—apart from Christ's forgiveness and the power of his Spirit—is not only powerless to stop the flesh; it feeds the flesh's bondage to self-righteousness. No matter how harsh, Christ-less asceticism can only feed a sinner's soul-damning spiritual arrogance before God.[8]

God is pro-body and pro-workouts

We are gloriously woven from physical and spiritual realities. "We know that our spiritual responses in life—our treating people with grace, for example—are affected by sleep, food, drink, coffee, or alcohol. All of those affect us." Exercise affects our minds with brain chemicals. Weather affects our emotions with changing sunshine and barometric pressure. In sum: "We are affected by the physical strategies and physical remedies that we embrace."[9]

So Paul reminds us that bodily training is "of some value" (1 Tim. 4:8). If you must choose between the two, choose spiritual training. But do both if

7   APJ 1752: "Is There a Place for Asceticism in the Christian Life?" (March 4, 2022).
8   APJ 1884: "Is Intermittent Fasting Sacrilegious?" (January 6, 2023).
9   APJ 283: "Antidepressants, Sleep, Diet, and Exercise" (February 21, 2014).

you can. God is *for* the body" (1 Cor. 6:13). "God is very pro-body. He is not a Platonist. He created the body, and he is going to raise the body from the dead. He wants us, therefore, to take care of the body."

Again, our physical body is inseparably connected to our spiritual life. "When I was in Germany, between twenty-five and twenty-eight years old, I realized for the first time that when I lack sleep, I get irritable and impatient; and with enough sleep, I am less irritable and more patient. This was theologically problematic for me, because the Bible says that patience is a fruit of the Holy Spirit, not a fruit of sleep." And yet it became "crystal clear that my sanctification level rises and falls with eight hours of sleep versus five hours of sleep." Likewise, proper sleep patterns are impossible without addressing sins of anxiety and pride. Our physical and spiritual lives are interlaced.

With a tendency to depression and discouragement, "I have discovered that if I go to the gym three times a week and hammer my body, I simply don't get depressed as often. Now, I am sure there are physiological reasons for that. But whatever those are, I know that they work. I know depression hurts my ministry, my marriage, and my parenting. So for the sake of kingdom purposes, I am off to the gym."[10]

Ministry burnout and postsermon blues

One of the keys to longevity in ministry is regular exercise. "Beat your body. Hammer it three times a week. Make it sweat and be exhausted. It will reap mental benefits you cannot measure. I mean that. There is something going on with exercise that God knows about and some psychiatrists know about, but few people know about. And it makes a difference."[11]

On Monday, when the postsermon depression settles down on a preacher, what can he do? Get after it again. "Hammer your body with whatever exercise works for you. Don't become a couch potato. It is deadly. God made muscles for work, and he made the heart to sustain it. He made the brain to produce antidepressants in response to vigorous exercise. Don't spare yourself in this. Get a bike. Ride twenty miles as hard as you can on Monday morning or run or swim or do weights or dig in the garden. But don't fool yourself that you are exercising when you are not panting. I mean, a lot of people think, 'I am exercising.' You are not exercising. You are lolling. Make it happen. You will be surprised how closely connected are the body and the soul."[12]

10 APJ 12: "Exercising the Body (for the Sake of the Soul)" (January 25, 2013).
11 APJ 142: "Avoiding Ministry Burnout" (August 2, 2013).
12 APJ 429: "Handling Post-Sermon Blues" (September 15, 2014).

When has my body become my idol?

Physical fitness is helpful, but it "becomes sinful self-glorification" when it is pursued for ends other than overcoming personal sin, serving others, and magnifying Christ. The idolatrous temptations we face here are especially strong because "hour after hour, every day, through advertising and other media, we are being told that to be successful and happy, our bodies must have a certain appearance." Contrary to pop gym culture, Scripture commends physical exertion for three glorious ends.

1. Work out to overcome sin. Paul *beat* or *pummeled* his body to keep his own sin in check (ὑπωπιάζω; 1 Cor. 9:26–27). This included the sin of sloth. "It is a good thing to exercise and eat and sleep in a healthy way so as to subdue the enslaving impulses of the body, including laziness." But as we resist sin with physical exertion, we must not flaunt our self-discipline. This was Jesus's caution with fasting (Matt. 6:16–18). Fasters, like gym rats, can use their bodies to broadcast their discipline. If your physical appearance is what you are going for, don't check your appearance in a mirror—check your heart motives.

2. Work out to serve others. Jesus said, "Whoever would be great among you must be your servant" (Mark 10:43). "In other words, instead of mirrors in the gym, there should be big signs on the wall: 'Whoever would be great among you must be your servant' (Mark 10:43). You want to be strong? You want to be fit? You want to be buff? Are you going to use it to be a more faithful servant of people, or are you out to be seen by others?"

3. Work out to magnify the worth of Christ. Our strength is Christ (Eph. 6:10). "In other words, it's true strength when we are seeking to be strong in the strength of Christ, not strong in ourselves." We aim to become strong to make Christ look stronger. "We've got to figure that out or we're going to be idolaters. We're going to be vainglorious." We must work out in a way that acknowledges that our physical strength is fleeting and destined to wither and fade (1 Pet. 1:24–25). "Believe me. I am seventy, and I have been jogging regularly since I was twenty-two. It is not a fountain of youth, folks. You're going to sag. You're going to be wrinkled. You're going to be splotchy. You're going to be scaly. You're not going to be pretty or cool. And if you have invested your life in that, oh, you will look pathetic—like all those older folks in Phoenix with their ridiculous tans and their sagging, wrinkled skin." So set a gym routine to (1) defeat sin in your life, (2) become useful in serving others for their eternal good, and (3) "show that Christ is more valuable, more precious to you, than your looks or your health or your reputation for being so disciplined."[13]

---

13 APJ 1042: "Is Body Image My Idol?" (May 17, 2017).

The man everyone avoided

In a 2008 sermon, Piper recounted seeing a disfigured man. The man bicycled through his neighborhood at odd hours to avoid others, shrouded in a hat and dark glasses. Even so, seen from 30 feet away, he had "the most hideous face I've ever seen in my life." But Pastor John had a conviction to meet the man and to share with him "the best news in the world."[14]

In 2020 Pastor John recounted the meeting. "I don't know where he came from or where he went. He was only here for a short time, as far as I could tell." He only appeared at dusk to avoid people and to not draw attention to the "massive purple birthmark" that covered "most of his face." He was discolored and disfigured to a degree that "would have frightened virtually any child that saw him and probably cause most people to cross the street." So one evening Piper timed his walk. "As we passed, I greeted him and asked if I could say a word to him. Now, this is hugely risky, what I'm about to do. I don't necessarily recommend it, but it's what I felt led to do. He stopped, and I just cut straight to the chase. I said, 'My name is John. I live down the street, over there at that red house [pointing]. I'm a pastor at the church over there [pointing]. I just want you to know that I know you're here, and I don't want to avoid you. I realize life must be hard for you, but I want you to know two things that are true because of Jesus. One is that I care about you and am not put off by your looks.'" There's the risk. Will this offend him or make him angry? "'Second, I have spectacular news for people with every kind of disability—namely, everyone who trusts in Jesus will be completely healed in the resurrection. We will have brand-new bodies, new faces, new legs, new arms, but we'll still be ourselves.' He actually thanked me, and then went on his way." It was their first and only meeting.[15]

Why did God make me ugly?

The Bible is not beauty blind. It celebrates physical attractiveness (Exod. 2:2; 1 Sam. 17:42; 2 Sam. 14:25; Est. 2:7; Song; Heb. 11:23). So why did God make me ugly? An honest question from a struggling listener.

Such natural ugliness is only "the tip of the iceberg" of broader human suffering that includes "horrific deformities" and "dreadful disfigurements" and diseases that cause "hideous malformations and growths and cankerous, open, unhealable flesh" and "ghastly wounds that leave people in pain the rest of their lives—disabled, unsightly." Unattractiveness is part of a much larger

---

14 John Piper, "Treasuring Christ and the Call to Suffer: Part 1," Desiring God, April 8, 2008, https://www.desiringgod.org/.

15 APJ 1540: "I'm Obsessed with My Appearance—How Can I Stop?" (October 19, 2020).

conversation on disfigurement, disease, deformity, and injury. For some, this topic is relevant from birth. For others, it becomes increasingly relevant in old age.

There are no "more helpful or important or profound" texts to explain why physical ugliness and deformity exist than Romans 8:18–23. Because of Adam's sin, God subjected the world to the curse, but he did so in light of a future hope (Rom. 8:20). But it means the fall into sin in Genesis 3 ushered in "all the horrific consequences of sin, including every disfigurement, every injury, every disability, every catastrophe." In the fall, God syncs our physical, bodily world to the realities of our moral world. "He made physical ugliness and misery correspond to moral ugliness and misery, even in some of the most godly people on the planet. Every bodily or material burden in the world should point us to the burden of sin. Every ugliness should point to the ugliness of sin and Satan."

Now, two points of clarity. (1) Your unattractiveness or deformity or sickness is the consequence of human sin but not necessarily the direct result of a sin—yours or your parents' (John 9:2–3). Physical brokenness is fundamentally the consequence of Adam and Eve's sin, "which infected the whole human race." (2) Yes, Satan causes physical deformity (Luke 13:11–16). But more fundamentally, "all physical ugliness and deformity and misery point to the moral ugliness and deformity of sin and Satan."

But in all the pain of our fallen world, God left us with a hope—a groaning hope. "It's as if the creation is pregnant, and all the pain and misery and disfigurement are like cosmic birth pangs—of a mother crying out in pain, a world in labor." The joy of the reborn creation in resurrection is coming. Our bodies will be redeemed. And this promise "covers the whole waterfront of aging miseries, disease miseries, disability miseries, ugliness miseries. In other words, he makes explicit that the horrors of groaning and corruption and futility include Spirit-filled Christians. Our bodies desperately need now, or will need soon, redemption. We feel it in disease, we feel it in aging, and we see it in the mirror—some early, some late."

Here's the good news to the unattractive. A Savior has come, an unattractive Savior, who "had no form or majesty that we should look at him, and no beauty that we should desire him" (Isa. 53:2). He took on himself the ugliness and deformity and sickness of our sin. "He died to put an end to all ugliness and all misery for everyone who trusts him and treasures him more than we treasure human beauty. And then, in his precious blood-bought people, he makes all physical ugliness serve to show his own worth, because he satisfies the soul so completely and promises a future so glorious that he makes his homely family happy. And in spite of all earthly rejection, all that happiness bears witness to the all-satisfying moral beauty of Christ and the confidence we will share in it. Christ is most glorified in us when we are most satisfied in him, especially in our temporary ugliness."[16]

Temporary ugliness is a key point. What you now see in the mirror "is not glorious." But after the resurrection, what you see in the mirror will tempt you to self-worship (1 Cor. 15:42–44). ("But you won't, because you'll be perfected.")[17] In the resurrection we are given what Paul calls a "spiritual body"—perhaps one like Christ's after Easter morning, a new body that "transcends the ordinary experience of space."[18] Christ ate fish "to prove to his disciples that he was not a ghost or a spirit," and yet he also "came and went in ways that defy ordinary categories of space and time" (Luke 24:36–43).[19]

Aim for undistracting attractiveness

To the degree that we control our appearance, we shape our bodies for gospel purposes. The apostle Paul said, "It is my eager expectation and hope that I will not be at all ashamed, but that with full courage now as always Christ will be honored *in my body*, whether by life or by death" (Phil. 1:20). Here, in one of Pastor John's "favorite texts"—the foundational text for Christian Hedonism— Paul "wants his body to be an instrument of magnifying God, and when he dies, he wants to die well with his body so that people can see that his treasure is Christ and not his body or its health or its life. So we need to give enough attention, I think, to our bodies so we keep them fit for Christ and serviceable in his cause. And we may need to give our bodies to imprisonment or whipping or execution or death to show that Christ is more precious than the body. So there is a middle way of eating and exercise that doesn't fall off the horse on the side of *neglect* of the body as though it were *worthless*, or the side of *idolizing* the body as though it were a *god*. It just keeps us healthy with a kind of, what I would call, *undistracting attractiveness*."[20]

16 APJ 1699: "Why Did God Make Me Unattractive?" (November 1, 2021).

17 APJ 1650: "Will God Really Praise Us?" (July 9, 2021).

18 APJ 1138: "Where Is Heaven Right Now?" (December 27, 2017).

19 APJ 1516: "Will the New Creation Look Like This One?" (August 24, 2020).

20 APJ 185: "Botox, Dieting, and Plastic Surgery" (October 2, 2013).

On Food, Fasting, and Feasting

Food is for worship

God's creation is good. And since God's creation is good, we are free to feast to God's glory, right?

Well, it's not quite that simple, because there's more to proper God-centered eating than acknowledging the goodness of creation. Food is about worship, as Paul explains in 1 Timothy 4:1–5. True use of food requires three actions and none of them "an act of the stomach or the taste buds." They are actions of mind and heart—*thanking, believing,* and *knowing.* Each act is God-centered, turning our bread-eating into a higher purpose: an act of worship.

So Paul didn't argue that since creation is good, eating is good and God-honoring. Nor did he argue that since God created food, God is glorified in all enjoyment of food. Instead, Paul argues that everything God created is good, and out of that goodness "nothing is to be rejected if it is received with thanksgiving" (1 Tim. 4:4). "What makes eating good, what makes food good, or at least one essential part of what makes it good—essential, not optional—is the thankfulness of our hearts." We sanctify a good gift of creation, like food, by setting it apart for God as a means of expressing the infinite worth of God.[1]

A bite-sized theology of food

The Bible offers five key texts, five ingredients, to properly understanding the place of food in our lives.

1. Food is a gift to be sanctified (1 Tim. 4:4–5). God designed food—both its nutritional value and its taste—"for believers, not just the world in general." Food must *become* something else for it to be lawfully enjoyed, namely, it must be converted from a commodity into a gift that has been sanctified by the word and prayer. Non-Christians cannot do this. Those without faith can only eat food

---

1 APJ 1400: "How Do We Feast to the Glory of God?" (November 27, 2019).

unlawfully. Food is not some ultimate or final good in itself. "You have to do something with it in order to experience it as part of the final good. You have to turn it into something holy by prayer and the word, then enjoy it with gratitude."

2. Food puts words to our appetite for God (Ps. 34:8). Food gives us language of taste, and language of taste helps us articulate how satisfying God is to us. Food is "a type or shadow or pointer or parable," as we see when the psalmist exclaims: "Oh, taste and see that the LORD is good!" (Ps. 34:8). "I have tasted bread, and I can know what it means that *he is the bread of life*. I have tasted water, and I can know what it means that *he satisfies my thirst*. What we enjoy in food we should find in God. In fact, we should find God in the very enjoyment of our food."

3. Food is not God (1 Cor. 6:12–13). God will destroy (καταργέω) food and the stomach eventually. "So don't treat them as your idols. If you treat them as gods, your gods are going to perish. Food is lawful, but not as a master." When food no longer can "send you with a thrill of thanksgiving to God," it has become your master. Don't be mastered by anything, including food.

4. Food is for sacrifice (Matt. 6:17). Jesus assumes that we will fast. So "why would God build fasting into this age? Why would he have us abstain from something he created which is perfectly good? I think he did because fasting is a way of saying that I am not mastered by my delight in my food. I am mastered by my delight in God." Indeed, our delight in God is *intensified* "by abstaining from alternative pleasures, so that, without calling them evil at all, I can say: 'God is better.'" By fasting we declare, "I love you, God. I love you more than I love food. I need you more than I need food. I want you more than I want food. You taste better to me spiritually than food tastes to me physically."

5. Food is insufficient (Matt. 4:3–4). Jesus says we need God's word "vastly more" than a meal. Pressed for time, anyone who chooses breakfast instead of morning devotions hasn't reckoned with Christ's words. "The word that mediates the love of God is more important than life-sustaining food."

Our appetites control our behavior, and either our appetites glorify God by showing that he is our "supreme satisfaction," or our appetites show that we have a stronger appetite for food, which is idolatry. What most satisfies you? "Let's cultivate a taste for God, an appetite for God and his word, that out-satisfies everything."[2]

Ingredients for a theology of feasting
Both feasting and fasting are worship for the Christian. So what should we know about *feasting*?

2   APJ 321: "A Bite-Sized Theology of Food" (April 16, 2014).

First a rough definition: "Feasting is the enjoyment of abundance." The Old Testament prescribed a lot of feasts, beginning in Leviticus 23. But the problem is that not every feast in the Old Testament signifies *material* abundance. So maybe a better definition would be: "Feasting is a communal sharing of a celebrated meal with a focus on some remembrance and thankfulness of some event of God's mercy." A very simple "feast" of unleavened bread is nothing like the "big Thanksgiving dinner" we might have in mind. So to balance our expectations with what Scripture says, here are four ingredients to a theology of feasting.

1. Feasting may be good or bad (Prov. 17:1). "The mere abundance of food and drink does not make for a happy family or happy community. There must be more to it." (i) Our *timing* may be off. It's wrong to feast when you should be working (Eccl. 10:16–17). (ii) The *season* may be off. A season of mourning is more instructive than a season of feasting (Eccl. 7:2). (iii) Our *heart* may be off. God hates feasting when the act conceals sinful and loveless lives (Amos 5:21–24).

2. When done right, feasting echoes the worship of our hearts. All things we enjoy are richly provided to us by him (1 Tim. 6:17). "The sights and sounds and smells and tastes and touch of good things that God has made are not mainly tests to see if we will make them our god and become idolaters, but, rather, they are mainly pleasures to send our hearts joyful and thankful back to God." We receive these gifts and sanctify them by the word and prayer (1 Tim. 4:4–5). "So the difference between unholy feasting and holy feasting is not what's on the table, but what's in the mind and in the heart. Is the mind grasping the God-centered meaning of these things from the word of God, and is the heart sending up joyful prayers of thanksgiving as we taste more of the goodness of God in the very things we're eating?"

3. Feasting is our culinary future (Isa. 25:6; Matt. 22:2–10; Luke 22:29–30; Rev. 19:9).

4. Feasting is the metaphor of our eternal delights (Ps. 36:7–8). "In some measure now, and then perfectly at the last day, God himself will be our feast."

These four ingredients help us to "move wisely between *fasting* and *feasting*, between *the joy of self-denial* and *the joy of abundance*, in a way that shows the supreme value of Christ in our lives."[3]

On overcoming food idolatry

When Paul talks about not being dominated by any desire, he speaks of food desires in the same context as sexual desires (1 Cor. 6:12–13). "So clearly these two huge appetites that human beings have, created by God—the sex

3 APJ 1687: "Ingredients for a Theology of Feasting" (October 4, 2021).

appetite and the hunger appetite—can become idolatrous." False teachers met these idolatrous tendencies with the "pea-shooter" of asceticism by simply forbidding marriage and certain foods. Paul responded to these restrictions by saying that marriage and food are "made holy" by the word of God and prayer (1 Tim. 4:3–4).

1. Food is made holy by prayerful thanksgiving. "Thanksgiving is the de-throning of a god and turning it into a gift." So praying over food is how we say, "I am thanking God for *you*, food, and, therefore, *you* are not going to compete with God. *You* are going to be a means of my worship rather than a competition with my worship."

2. Food is made holy by faith. Paul said that God created sex and food "to be received with thanksgiving by those who believe and know the truth" (1 Tim. 4:3). Only regenerated Christians rightly use God's good gifts by faith, seeing that all our food is a gift from him. This is like Paul's words to Christians who were eating meat sacrificed to pagan idols. Why? Because "the earth is the Lord's, and the fullness thereof" (1 Cor. 10:25–26). Paul cites God's governance over the world to sanctify the food we eat in faith and thankfulness (Ps. 24:1).

Sex and food will not wield "undue control" over us when we keep them under the word of God. "You don't need to worry that you are eating this meat that was offered to an idol. It belongs to God. He is offering it to you as a gift." As we thank God for the gifts, we dethrone a potential idol. "So I would have everybody put all the gifts of God—not just sex and food, but all the gifts of God—in the context of his word. Let his word define their place, and then be filled with thanksgiving, and let it overflow in prayers of gratitude."[4]

When has food become my idol?

Food idolatry is called "gluttony," and gluttony resembles a lot of sins. For ex-ample, sexual desires are not evil, but lust is. Enjoying praise from others is not sin, but vainglory is. Resting is not sinful, but sloth is. The desire for possessions is not sinful, but covetousness is. And the desire for food is not sin, but gluttony is. In the hands of a sinner, good gifts become idolatrous obsessions. "One of the historical ways of talking about those sins is that they are *disordered loves* or, another way to say it, *inordinate loves*. They start with legitimate love—proper and proportional and Christ-exalting and God-rooted—for something innocent that God has given for our enjoyment. But then they become improper and disproportionate. They cease to exalt Christ. They cease to have their root in God" (Phil. 3:8; 4:11–13; 1 Tim. 6:6–10).

---

4   APJ 123: "How Food and Sex Are Made Holy" (July 1, 2013).

In a financial example, a healthy desire for money can degenerate into a twisted and perverse love of money (1 Tim. 6:10). What happened? "The use of money governed by a sweet, deep, pervasive contentment in God has been replaced by the loss of that contentment and the emergence of a powerful love for money and *craving* for money, as Paul calls it." Without contentment, a legitimate desire turns self-destructive. Without God-centered contentment, gifts become idols. And when our "supreme contentment or happiness or joy or satisfaction in God ceases to be the great guide or ballast or moderator or regulator of our souls," then "everything goes bad."

Paul's "secret of a godly Christian life" is contentment. Godly contentment says: "I count everything as loss because of the surpassing worth of knowing Christ Jesus my Lord. For his sake I have suffered the loss of all things and count them as rubbish, in order that I may gain Christ and be found in him, not having a righteousness of my own that comes from the law, but that which comes through faith in Christ, the righteousness from God that depends on faith—that I may know him and the power of his resurrection, and may share his sufferings, becoming like him in his death, that by any means possible I may attain the resurrection from the dead" (Phil. 3:8–11). No loss of money or sex or food can rob us of this promise.

In contrast to contentment, gluttony is displayed in four ways. (1) "We become indifferent to the harmful effects that the food is having on the temple of the Holy Spirit, our body." (2) "We become indifferent to the way we are stewarding our money as we spend unwisely on wrong foods." (3) "We start using food as an escape from our problems and a medication for our sadness, misery, or discomfort." (4) "We stop enjoying food as a way of enjoying God. We stop *tasting* the goodness of God in the goodness of the food, and we start *replacing* the goodness of God with the goodness of the food. This is gluttony." These are the four warning signs of gluttony. "The way back may involve many external controls and disciplines outside. But in the end, the only way out will be when God himself through Jesus Christ becomes our satisfying soul food, and contentment in him becomes the regulator of all our appetites and desires."[5]

Declare war on sinful appetites

"There is a mean, violent streak to the true Christian life." Against whom or what? *Not* people. *Not* violence against Muslims or Hindus or Buddhists or atheists or secularists or nominal Christians. But a violence against the cravings

5   APJ 752: "Four Signs Food Has Become an Idol" (December 17, 2015).

within us. We make war against "all enslaving desires for food, caffeine, sugar, chocolate, alcohol, pornography, money, the praise of man, approval of others, power, fame. This is our enemy. This is where we make war."[6]

What's fasting for?

We learn about fasting as we discover why Jesus's disciples *didn't* fast. Followers of John the Baptist came to Jesus to ask him why not (Matt. 9:14–17). The text teaches us that fasting is for two clear purposes.

1. Fasting gives urgency to our desire for Christ's return. "While he was here, they didn't fast, because the bridegroom was present. But when the bridegroom was taken away, to come a second time, there is this ache in the heart of God's people. Fasting is a physical exclamation point at the end of the sentences 'I need you! I want you! I long for you! You are my treasure! I want more of you! Oh, for the day when you would return! Maranatha! Come, Lord Jesus!'" For a season, we turn from our stomach to give wholehearted "intensity and expressiveness to our ache for Jesus." We want to see him move to heal the sick, save the lost, and fix broken marriages.

2. Fasting exposes our latent idolatries. "When I am not being medicated by food, what comes out of my heart? Anger? Lust? The need for television—more and more of it? People need to know what is at the bottom." So "if I go without food for twenty-four hours—from supper to supper or breakfast to breakfast—my, oh, my, what is exposed of my heart toward my wife and my daughter! Fasting is a very good discipline. Not only as a positive expression of longing in prayer, but also as a negative exposure of the heart—so I can deal with these things as they come up."[7]

Fasting is valuable but not commanded. It "doesn't have the same place in Christianity that it does, for example, in Islam." Although the New Testament doesn't command fasting, Scripture indicates that fasting "was *normal* and that Jesus *expected* it would happen among his followers." Jesus assumed it: "*when* you fast" (in Matt. 6:16). We don't fast to impress others. Instead, we "go out of our way" to "keep other people from knowing that we are fasting." Such a secret fast takes on "a radically Godward focus." Fasting serves as a "great test and confirmation that God is real to us," since only he knows the secret.

Again, the presence of Jesus changes fasting in the new covenant (Matt. 9:14–17). Fasting was inappropriate while Christ was with his disciples. Rather,

6 APJ 489: "Declare War on Sin" (December 10, 2014).
7 APJ 72: "What Is the Purpose of Fasting?" (April 18, 2013).

fasting is called for when Christ's physical presence is absent from us. The King came and died and rose and ascended, and now "we long and we hunger for the consummation of the day of his return, his coming and reigning."

Among church leaders, fasting displays a need for missional breakthrough (Acts 13:1–3).

In the end, fasting is the "handmaid of faith," not its replacement. "Fasting is a way of saying with our stomach and our whole body how much we need and want and trust Jesus. It is a way of saying that we are not going to be enslaved by food as the source of our satisfaction. We will use the renunciation of food from time to time to express that Jesus is better than food. Jesus is more needful than food."

So food is a wonderful gift, and we use it to glorify God in two ways. We glorify God with food when we *feast* in thankfulness to his goodness. And we glorify God with food when we *fast* and forfeit food out of a hunger for him. "When we *feast*, we gladly taste the emblem of our heavenly food: the bread of life, Jesus himself. And when we *fast*, we say, 'I love the reality more than I love the emblem.' Both feasting and fasting are worship for the Christian. Both magnify Christ." And both are dangerous. "The danger of feasting is that we fall in love with the gift, and the danger of fasting is that we belittle the gift and boast in our willpower, our discipline. At its best, Christian fasting is not a belittling of the good gift of food. It is simply a heartfelt, body-felt exclamation point at the end of the sentence, 'I love you, God! I need you more than I need food—more than I need life.'"[8]

Intermittent fasting purely for its physical benefits does not prostitute a Christian spiritual discipline. Fasting didn't originate in the church, or in ancient Israel, and it can be found "in most other religions" (Dan. 6:18; Jonah 3:5). Like all asceticism, the practice is physically useful but spiritually perilous whenever non-Christians ascribe life-changing power to it (Col. 2:16–23). Concurrently, fasting can benefit the body and stoke pride in the heart. All forms of Christless asceticism can feed the flesh, that "proud, self-reliant, self-exalting aspect of human nature." So to use "secular fasting" for "physical benefits" isn't a problem. It's a problem when the practice "slides" into "spiritual expectations" that such a discipline will "make me a better person" or "more pleasing to God." There's the danger. Christians will labor to help others distinguish "gospel self-denial" from "worldly self-betterment through asceticism."[9]

---

8   APJ 789: "Why Do Christians Fast?" (February 8, 2016).
9   APJ 1884: "Is Intermittent Fasting Sacrilegious?" (January 6, 2023).

Should we pray before meals even when we're not *feeling* it?
Yes, we should, but not with the *should* of duty or obligation. Mealtime prayers don't have to wait until we *feel* like praying. "A lot of people think that it is a spiritual and life-giving thing if habits of the soul give spontaneous rise to acts of the body, and that is right. They do. That is wonderful. That is life-giving. That feels free. But in the real world where we live, it works the other way too." So "habits of the body, like praying at mealtimes—which sometimes are enlivened by the spontaneous delights of the soul in God and in his goodness, and sometimes are at 50 percent, and sometimes at 10 percent, and sometimes we are just doing it—should be preserved for the sake of the soul, for the sake of the spontaneity, for the sake of the joy."

Mealtime prayers are life patterns set in place that don't fluctuate with our feelings. They reserve the time and preserve the habit for when we *do have* an authentic and warm prayer to offer. So we preserve "a pattern of life that has value not only to express the affection when it *is there*, but to tip me off when it *is not there*, and to *be there* when the affection returns." Such is the practice of mealtime prayers.

This prayer is an act of obedience to the command of "giving thanks always and for everything to God the Father in the name of our Lord Jesus Christ" (Eph. 5:20). "What better time to build obedience into our lives than at a very moment when God is freely giving us something we need for our very lives?" It's particularly powerful in training children who are watching and listening. So given what mealtime prayers represent in the lives of Christians around the world and throughout the centuries, and for what it can mean for our own lives, why would we *not* pray before meals?[10]

Should we use impromptu prayers or memorized prayers? "Mix it up. If the only prayers that children hear their parents pray are memorized prayers, it will probably communicate to them that this is the only way you can pray to God, at least at mealtimes. And yet, I don't want to discount memorized and well-thought-through prayers, because they have a blessing too." For his family, Piper wrote three prayers: one each for breakfast, lunch, and dinner.[11]

Can we pray over junk food?
Can we honor and thank God for junk food—fast food, fried food, snack foods? Or would this be hypocritical?

In sum, to the degree that you are justified to eat something, you are justified in giving thanks for it. To the degree that your conscience is clear, you can thank

10 APJ 124: "Mealtime Prayers: Necessary or Optional?" (July 2, 2013).
11 APJ 126: "Mealtime Prayers: Impromptu or Memorized?" (July 5, 2013).

God with a clear conscience. But if your heart is divided, "partially approving and partially disapproving when you eat something," then you'll be left with a divided heart when you try to thank God.

But not everything *good* is *wise*. Being able to *thank God* for something as simple as bread does not mean that you are *always justified in eating it* (Matt. 4:1–11). For Christ, on his way to the cross, bread was "off-limits because of the path assigned to Jesus. I commend that we reflect on that—in relation to what's permitted in one sense but may be not advisable for other reasons."

Perhaps a clearer answer is deduced from 1 Corinthians 10:23–33. Paul reminds us that all food is the Lord's, and food is a good gift, even if it has questions attached to it—like, was it offered to idols? In this context, Paul makes it clear that "if you regard something as *questionable*—not *certainly evil* or *certainly good*—but something where true believers may disagree with each other, then the issue of genuine thankfulness becomes relevant." Here's an example. "Here is my brother doing something that seems questionable to me—like eating something I regard as less than healthy—and he has a genuine, heartfelt thankfulness to God for what he's eating. Therefore, my attitude should be to *rejoice* that his heart is good toward God and leave to God and his conscience whether eating the questionable food is sinful or not."

Thankfulness is decisive. So when you eat—and *whatever you eat*—do it all to the glory of God (1 Cor. 10:31). "This is Paul's final criterion for eating every kind of food. Is my eating of this food an expression for how much I value the glory of God? Am I content in the glory of God? Do I esteem the glory of God?" The famous text "speaks to the one who is watching the person eat as well as the eater himself. If the eater is supposed to eat and drink in a way that gives glory to God, then the watching person is also supposed to assess his eating and drinking in a way that glorifies God. Now, this raises the difficult issue—not only of what is in the eater's heart, but also what food is really off-limits for one who would eat to the glory of God."

In the end, "I am highly skeptical that we can judge with confidence what foods are certainly *junk* and what are not. That may be heresy to some people, but that's my skepticism. What foods *damage health*, and what foods *serve health*? What foods are more or less neutral? My guess is that when it comes to eating *this* food or *that*, we are in greater spiritual danger of *judging people* where we shouldn't than we are in physical danger of *eating* what we shouldn't." So Jesus shows, "Just because you give thanks for a divine gift doesn't mean you should take it." But Paul shows, "If you can give thanks for something that is not clearly wrong, then it is better to rejoice in the thanks than to condemn the wrong."[12]

Are energy drinks useful?

Should Christians rely on energy drinks to get them through their days?

God is pro-body. Our bodies are united to Christ, and they will be resurrected (1 Cor. 6:13–15). Paul shows that "the Lord is *for* the body; the body is *for* the Lord." We must make wise food choices based on three factors. Does it help, enslave, or edify?

Paul leads us in this direction in 1 Corinthians 6:12–13—"the pivotal text" for a discussion over food. A specific food may be lawful for us to eat, but lawfulness is not enough. We must ask three other questions. (1) Is it useful? (2) Is it enslaving? (3) Will it edify others? Our dietary decisions must answer these three questions (1 Cor. 6:12; 10:23).

(1) Energy drinks are lawful for me; but do they help me? "This is really part of a much bigger issue of the proper use of not just caffeine, but other stimulants: medications, Ritalin, Adderall, antidepressants, and so on." Do they work for my "deepest advantage"? Or do these stimulants mask problems in my life? (2) Energy drinks are lawful for me; but do they enslave me? In Christ we have been freed from slavery to sin. "Anyone who uses coffee or soda or energy drinks or other kinds of stimulants or medication should ask, 'Am I dominated by this? Am I mastered by this? Am I controlled by this? Am I living consciously as Christ's freed man?'" (3) Energy drinks are lawful for me; but do they edify others? This question is "huge," because in "deciding what is right and wrong about energy drinks" you could "obey a law without love—without giving a hoot about whether you are building anybody's faith." In this case, "be sure that your heart is set on the good of others and that your example to them and your choices are aiming to build people up in faith, that is, helping them trust Jesus and treasure Jesus and honor Jesus above all things."

So does Piper use energy drinks? Yes, on occasion. He keeps a box of them in his office. "If I have a pressing task and I cannot stay awake, yes, I will go there." But a question lingers for him. Does he default to this "artificial stimulant" because he is too proud to get enough sleep? "See, in other words, that is what I mean by *masking*. If my real problem is that John Piper doesn't have the discipline to go to bed at night and therefore gets six hours instead of eight hours of sleep, and therefore he is always falling asleep at his tasks, and, thus, he

---

12 APJ 1335: "Does Junk Food Dishonor God?" (April 26, 2019).

resorts to an artificial stimulant, that is *masking*. That is hiding." That's running away from God in pride. An abuse of energy drinks.[13]

Can Christians eat halal meat?

A listener in North Africa was cooking dinner with halal meat, meat slaughtered by praying Allah's name while the animal was faced toward Mecca. Is such meat forbidden for Christians? And are Christians forbidden from eating this meat with their Muslim neighbors?

No, not necessarily, primarily because the label seems to signify only to Muslims that the meat has been made permissible to eat. If that is correct, this label "*doesn't* make the eating of it when it gets to your table an act of *worship*." That's a big caveat, and the remaining response assumes this is the case.

Christians should think through this question with 1 Corinthians 10:18–28. Christians are forbidden from participating in false worship. As Paul says, "You cannot drink the cup of the Lord and the cup of demons. You cannot partake of the table of the Lord and the table of demons" (1 Cor. 10:21). But whatever meat is sold in the market, eat with a free conscience (1 Cor. 10:25). The hinge is whether someone raises the topic that the meat was used in a religious sacrifice. If not, eat. If so, don't eat (1 Cor. 10:28). "If your guest turns the supper that you are now going to share with him into a worship service, expecting you to participate in the meaning that he is now attaching to the meat that was offered, then you politely decline."

In general, Christians can buy, serve, and eat halal meat for two reasons. (1) "The slaughter does not seem to be a formal worship event that turns the eating of the meat into a participation in worship." Thus, "joining with a Muslim in eating halal foods is not joining in an act of worship to Allah." (2) "Even if they were offered in an act of worship to Allah, this would only be a hindrance to Christians eating it if the Muslim hosts at the supper made it clear that the sharing in this food is a sharing in the worship of Allah." Otherwise, the Christian is "free to eat halal foods at home, and you are free to have Muslims over and serve it, and you are free to go to their house and eat it, because, I think, Paul has addressed a situation incredibly similar to yours and solved it that way."[14]

Are God's People impervious to famine and starvation?

No, they're not. In meditating on Habakkuk 3:17–18, the Pipers' wedding text, we find a purpose in seasons of lack. "This is why famine exists, among other

13 APJ 679: "Should Energy Drinks Fuel the Christian Life?" (September 7, 2015).
14 APJ 444: "Should I Eat Halal Meat?" (October 6, 2014).

reasons: so that Christians who are swept away in the famine will bear witness: 'God is better than food. God is all-satisfying to my soul as I die of starvation.' Yes, he is. And what a tribute you pay to him when that happens."[15]

Okay, but didn't Jesus tell us not to worry because God would always feed and clothe his children? He did (Matt. 6:25–34). So aren't Christians impervious to famine, starvation, and exposure?

Again, no, because "several things should give us pause before we think that Jesus is naive or simplistic or false" in his promises. Factor in these three points. (1) Christians will be martyred—perhaps through exposure or starvation. If you are decapitated in Christ's name, not a single strand of your hair will perish (Luke 21:16–18). "Now, that should give us pause if Jesus can say, 'Not a hair of your head is going to perish,' right after he says, 'They are going to kill you.' We had better be slow to say that 'all your needs are going to be met' means 'you can't die of hunger.'" (2) Christians learn contentment in Christ even through deprivation (Phil. 4:11–13). This was Paul's testimony as a specially chosen apostle. He faced hunger, but in that hunger he was sustained by a greater contentment. "God's promise to meet every need does not mean providing all the food and clothing we think we need." (3) God will in fact give us all that we need, and the blood of Christ proves it (Rom. 8:32). Within that promise, we are told that experiencing famine and nakedness will not separate us from God's love (Rom. 8:35).

Combine the texts and we learn that "everything will be given to us that we need in order to do God's will, in order to glorify God most fully, even if it means death. Jesus isn't promising all the food, all the clothing, all the housing, all the health care, all the protection that we need to be comfortable, or even to stay alive. He says we are going to die in his service. He is promising that we will have every single one of those things in exactly the right measure for doing his will and glorifying his name, even if it means perishing from exposure or starvation in the path of obedience."[16]

Related, see the story of Piper reciting Psalm 34:20 one Sunday morning, about how God "keeps" all our bones, and "not one of them is broken," then noticing a nine-year-old boy in the third row with a broken arm in a cast.[17]

Isn't veganism closer to God's original design?

Ever since a tablecloth of animals descended in Peter's vision, the menu for God's children has been wide open to all sorts of delicacies—bacon, lobster,

15 APJ 625: "God Takes Away to Display Christ's Beauty" (June 24, 2015).
16 APJ 971: "Does God Promise to Feed and Clothe Christians?" (December 2, 2016).
17 APJ 1885: "Getting the Tone Right on Sunday Morning" (January 9, 2023).

coconut shrimp, and sushi (Acts 11:4–10). But if we reverted to veganism, wouldn't we more closely reflect God's original dietary design for humanity?

No, that's not how it works. (1) No one in the New Testament "argued from a prefall eating pattern forward—or a future eschatological eating pattern backward—to the way we should eat today." Neither view will instruct us. (2) Animals do not belong to themselves. They don't belong to the earth. "They belong to the Lord, who provides his people with their needs for food. So eat them" (Ps. 24:1). This was Paul's argument for eating meat (1 Cor. 10:23–26). He was following Christ, who declared all foods clean (Mark 7:19).

In the light of these new-covenant realities, Paul wrote Romans 14:13–21 "to deal explicitly with the conflict between vegetarians and meat eaters." Other issues are included, "but vegetarianism and meat-eating are front and center." Meat eaters and vegetarians must not pass judgment on one another. "In Paul's mind, the issue of vegetarian versus meat-eater is not an issue of health. It's not an issue of attaining the ideal of prefall or post-sin eschatological conditions. It is an issue of love. In that sense, it's a great issue, but only in that sense. It's not a great issue in and of itself. Hear me on this. This is going to shock some. What we eat here is of almost zero significance compared to righteousness, peace, and joy in the Holy Spirit, which are the manifestations of the saving reign of God among his people. Let's keep things in perspective. Manifest the reign of God and love one another."[18]

Animals are edible. The Old Testament affirms the point. After Noah's ark landed on dry ground, God reaffirmed that man was made in God's image (Gen. 9:6). And for that image bearer all green plants and "every moving thing that lives shall be food for you" (Gen. 9:3). It's clear. "Humans and animals are in two absolutely distinct categories. One is in the image of God, and the other is eaten by things that are in the image of God."[19]

Any Old Testament food law was "a temporary part of God's way of making Israel distant or distinct from the nations of the world. With the coming of Christ, dramatic changes take place in the way God governs his people, because we are no longer a political-ethnic people like the Jews were, but a global people from every tribe and language and ethnicity and race."[20] So those laws are lifted by Christ (Mark 7:18–20). The "laws which once defined Israel as a people of ethnic, religious, and political distinction from the world don't function that way anymore."[21]

18 APJ 1160: "Isn't Veganism Closer to God's Original Design?" (February 16, 2018).
19 APJ 537: "Do Pets Go to Heaven?" (February 20, 2015).
20 APJ 962: "Should We Obey Old Testament Law?" (November 11, 2016).
21 APJ 632: "Why Are Old Testament Commands No Longer Binding?" (July 3, 2015).

So today, "if a person chooses not to eat pork for various nutritional reasons or preference, that is no big deal. You are free to eat or not to eat." But as soon as this abstinence is invested with biblical authority as the only sure path of Christian obedience or even salvation, a line has been crossed that contradicts Christ and the gospel. Instead, "when you have Christ as your treasure and your all-satisfying food, you are free to eat pork. Or not" (Col. 2:16–17).[22]

Don't miss the beauty for the food

We eat and drink to the glory of God, and that means the pleasure of food does not compete with the glory of God; it communicates it (1 Cor. 10:31). God is communicating himself "in the good creation that he has made."[23] Food is not ultimately about food. Food is for worship. So when hungry crowds chased Christ down and requested another free meal, he became angry at them (John 6:26). "Can you imagine Jesus being angry that somebody is seeking him? Why would he get upset if you sought him? It's because they were seeking him as useful—useful for the bread, the money, the health, the prosperity. 'He's useful to my stuff.' They didn't let their eyes run up the beam and say, 'There he is. That's my treasure!'"[24] Don't miss the giver of food in the gift of food.

22 APJ 962: "Should We Obey Old Testament Law?" (November 11, 2016).
23 APJ 1020: "What's the Appeal of Heavenly Rewards Other Than Getting Christ?" (March 27, 2017).
24 APJ 1448: "Jesus Didn't Die for Our Present Prosperity" (March 18, 2020).

On Alcohol, Tobacco, and Pot

On smoking, vaping, and nicotine addiction
The topic was raised by concerned parents watching their teens get drawn into vaping.

Cigarette smoking is dangerous, and the consequences of nicotine are well-known and published by the FDA. "It's not a debate anymore whether nicotine is a harmful drug and whether smoking causes numerous diseases. That includes nicotine in cigarettes, cigars, e-cigarettes (vaping), and chewing tobacco. Nicotine is harmful—whatever form you choose to put in your mouth or lungs."

The Bible is clear that "taking deadly risks" can be "noble and beautiful" if you are "entrusting your soul to Jesus and for the purpose of rescuing other people, especially people in eternal danger." But the Bible offers "no praise for those who risk their lives or health for private pleasure." This is a deceitful misuse of God's design for your body (1 Cor. 6:19–20; Eph. 4:22).

Enslavement to nicotine arrives in seven stages that can begin early. It may begin when a teen takes up smoking (or vaping) to be cool. Coolness is the desire to be liberated from authority, to appear more attractive, and to belong to a certain peer group. In these early years, the potency of this coolness factor overrides concerns over bodily harm. First comes "the initial nausea or coughing or dizziness." If that's endured, then comes the "nicotine buzz," a buzz that grows from a "chosen pleasure" to a "perceived need." An addiction. The habit grows, and so grows a "sense of indifference as to how it negatively affects others, whether at home or in public." In due time, over the years, serious physical problems arise, threatening a premature death.

This plunge into self-destruction violates Scripture at every stage. Coolness—the desire to be liberated from authority and to belong to a chosen peer group—becomes a heart-enrapturing idol. "This is the main root that parents should address as soon as their children can talk: What will be their treasure and their guide—Christ or the crowd?" To choose the crowd, and to ignore the physical consequences, is self-deception (John 8:32). This new appetite for a physical buzz sparks an internal war against personal holiness (1 Pet. 2:11). The desired buzz becomes enslaving (1 Cor. 6:12). The habit harms others (Phil. 2:4). And premature death devalues the precious gift of life.

"I would say to parents: from the earliest years—with prayer and a thoughtful use of the Bible—build into your children a freedom from the herd mentality of needing to be cool." Instead, build into them "a love of the truth; a passion for self-control and self-denial for the greater joys of righteousness; a deep commitment never to be enslaved by anything in this world; a strong concern for the interests of others, not just our own; a proper stewardship of the gift of health and life; and a fearlessness in the face of death, but a refusal to risk it for the sake of personal pleasure."[1]

Is marijuana useful?

No and *yes*. Marijuana is a "mood-altering drug that creates a kind of pleasant euphoria. It is not generally thought of as making one more attentive to reality but more oblivious of reality." It's not caffeine, which works to make us more alert to reality. Blunts blunt. "I don't think marijuana is generally thought of as an empowering drug that enables you to be a more competent dad, a more competent mother, a more competent employee, or a more competent citizen." It's a "recreational escape" that leads to "lasting negative effects on the mind's ability to do what God created it to do." Avoid pot and keep your body pure and your mind sharp (1 Cor. 6:13; 14:20).

"The root here is that God gave us minds to know him, and he gave us hearts to love him." So the Christian will reject anything that would "numb, dull, or distract our mind away from the growing capacities to know him better and love him more." Caffeine is the contrast. Drunkenness is the parallel, which also "leads away from the kind of sober, self-controlled use of the mind for the glory of God" (Prov. 23:32–33).

But *yes*, marijuana's pain-killing power is medically useful if governed by prescriptions and appropriate physician oversight. "We have lots of drugs that are sold by prescription that, if they were abused, would be as destructive or even more destructive than marijuana."[2]

That previous episode was recorded when recreational marijuana use was illegal in all but two states (2013). Since then, twenty states have legalized it. Many others have decriminalized possession, showing where the cultural trajectory is headed. So how does the church respond?

---

1   APJ 1702: "On Cigarettes, Vaping, and Nicotine" (November 8, 2021).
2   APJ 77: "Christians and Marijuana" (April 25, 2013).

Legalization pushes the challenges back into the spiritual realm. Laws can hold back rivers of sin, but laws cannot change the heart's desires. In fact, laws will eventually succumb to any culture's widespread cravings. So our "primary focus" is to do "what *only* the Bible and *only* the gospel and *only* the Holy Spirit and the truth and Jesus can do in transforming human beings into the kind of Christ-exalting, Spirit-dependent, God-glorifying people who freely choose not to use drugs— whether caffeine or alcohol or cannabis or cocaine or meth or heroin—to escape into a world where Christ is less clearly perceived, scriptures are less understood and precious, the Spirit is less personal, the glory of God is less satisfying, the way of righteousness is less defined, and the path of obedience is less compelling."

Such a radical life change, in Christ, will require new focus from pastors and parents to bring about a generation of youth "who are joyfully willing to be out of step with the world. That's the message, I think, God is sending us in the destigmatization and normalization and legalization of behaviors and attitudes and drugs that we think are out of step with the gospel. It's a call to be the church, and to be the home." A call to disciple the desires of the heart.[3]

Is drinking alcohol a sin?

No, not explicitly. "I'm a default teetotaler. What that means is if I have my choice, I don't drink alcohol. But I might, to be a good guest." The decision is driven by love. Love can lead to drinking to honor a host, but mostly "love inclines me *away* from alcohol."

Any drink can be sin, even drinking water, if your neighbor needs the water more than you. So wine itself is not condemned. Jesus made it (John 2:1–11). God gifts it (Ps. 104:14–15). Paul prescribed it (1 Tim. 5:23). But church leaders must not get enslaved to it (1 Tim. 3:8). "So I don't think anyone can make a case from Scripture that teetotalism is required. If you choose not to drink alcohol, like I do, as a kind of default way of life, it needs to be based on some principle other than what the Bible requires."

Scripture is abundantly clear on the dangers of drunkenness (Deut. 29:6; Prov. 20:1; 21:17; 23:30–35; 31:4–5; Ezek. 44:21; Rom. 14:21; Eph. 5:18). So "even though wine was permitted and was a blessing, it was fraught with dangers." Culturally today, drunkenness destroys lives, tears apart families, is a leading cause of driving fatalities, and burdens America's health-care industry.

But doesn't the Lord's Table presume that all Christians will consume alcohol?

No, the New Testament's Communion was "probably" wine, but the text stops short here, calling it "the cup" or "the fruit of the vine"—juice at least,

---

3 APJ 1698: "The Church's Calling in an Age of Recreational Pot" (October 29, 2021).

but not prescribed alcohol. Thus, "nobody can insist that we are commanded to drink wine" in the Lord's Supper. Alcohol is eschatological, reminding us to anticipate the new-creation feast to come. "I am saving the best for last. I am saving the best for when I can handle it—and I know I am a man with an addictive personality. I buy a pack of gum, and I chew the whole thing in five minutes. So knowing myself, knowing this culture that is being destroyed in measure by it, I find little incentive myself for pursuing something I have no desire to pursue." And yet "I do not condemn those who make other choices. It is just not on my agenda to go on a crusade to get other people to join me in this. I am just explaining where I am coming from."[4]

Are painkillers forbidden?

If God is sovereign over all our suffering, isn't it sinful to seek medical relief from pain?

No, not necessarily. Paul prescribed wine to Timothy (1 Tim. 5:23). Without embarrassment, Paul traveled with a physician at his side (Col. 4:14) and picked up some therapies along the way, to the point that he could recommend wine for Timothy's "chronic stomach problems." The medical application of wine did not oppose faith and prayer. And it parallels our age of synthetic medical advances. "The line between natural remedies and less-natural remedies is not all that clear. And when you think about it, those lines become very blurry."[5]

This same text encourages us to help one another. Timothy suffered from "frequent ailments," that is, *chronic* ailments that were at least "distracting discomfort, if not real pain." The text "is a clear illustration of using God-given natural means, even medical means, of eliminating as much discomfort and pain as we can." When it comes to pain, "we should help each other get rid of it if we can."[6]

Does the Bible prescribe alcohol to the depressed?

A listener who struggled with depression wrote in about Proverbs 31:6–7, a text that apparently prescribes alcohol to numb the pain of depression.

No, it's making the opposite point. "Lemuel's mother is picking up on a theme that runs through the Old Testament about alcohol and how it distorts reality and unfits the mind for responsible action and therefore should be used with the greatest caution" (1 Kings 16:9–10; 20:16; Prov. 20:1; 23:31–33; 31:6–7; Eccl. 10:17; Isa. 28:7; Hos. 4:10–11). Lemuel's mother is stressing that "your heart

4   APJ 200: "Is Drinking Alcohol a Sin?" (October 23, 2013).
5   APJ 890: "Does Medicine Impede God's Plan for My Suffering?" (June 28, 2016).
6   APJ 922: "Prepare for Suffering Now" (August 18, 2016).

must stay clear, your eyes must be open, your mind must be sharp so that you can utter just and wise things."

Particularly, the alcohol reference in Proverbs 31:6–7 can be interpreted in one of two ways.

1. Strong drink was primitive morphine. "Every TV Western I've ever seen, when they're going to cut off the guy's finger, they give him whiskey, right? Well, so would I! I'm so thankful today for pain medication." Alcohol dulls pain (1 Tim. 5:23). But "I don't think that justifies us in using alcohol to escape our sorrows or our mental miseries."

2. The text may be sarcastic. "Lemuel's mother has just told her son that the king should beware of strong drink. And then she says, 'Give it to the miserable.'" That would be irony to say, "'Go ahead and give it to them to do with it what they do, but you're the king and you don't use alcohol that way.'" Both interpretations are legitimate, and neither encourage the depressed toward alcohol.[7]

Substance abuse demands physical restraint

"Drug addicts don't fondle needles. Alcoholics don't keep stashes of brandy. Sexually supercharged eyes put safeguards on their computers. And smartphone junkies who are throwing away their lives or wasting money or becoming irritable and angry and impatient may go back to a flip phone. This is not unbiblical. This is not legalism. This is wisdom. This is fighting on all fronts for holiness in the power of the Holy Spirit for the sake of the heart, for the sake of the Lord, for the sake of the family."[8]

Can Alcoholics Anonymous (AA) break a Christian's addictions?

A Christian woman was delivered from alcohol addiction through the help of AA. But should social programs wield such delivering power in the Christian life?

AA was born from a Christian worldview, so it's no surprise that meetings help. The "Twelve Steps" echo Christian truth but in themselves end up lacking, containing a "shell" of Christianity after "the nut of Christ" is removed. But even limited to this "shell," limited to an "outward similarity to the way Christians overcome sin, it's not surprising to me that the 'Twelve Steps' have, and can be, amazingly helpful for those moving out of addiction to alcohol."

Christians prone to alcoholism may not need fewer AA meetings, but they will need more than AA meetings. "Go deep with Scripture, probably with the help of a good older woman who knows her Scripture well, and a good solid

7 APJ 1031: "Does the Bible Prescribe Alcohol to the Depressed?" (April 21, 2017).
8 APJ 670: "When Should I Get Rid of My Smartphone?" (August 25, 2015).

church, to see the full picture of how God provides for our warfare with sin, including alcoholism." In the battle against sin, be involved in a local church, a "camaraderie in warfare against sin," a spiritual family fighting all sorts of sins together (not just drunkenness).

But here's the main concern. The glaring omission "is not that the 'higher power' is unnamed." No, "the most glaring omission is the entire transaction between God and man in Christ Jesus at the cross—*the cross*—is missing. The *atonement for sin* is missing. And that is because *the greatest problem of human-kind* is missing—namely, not alcoholism, not the hurt we have done others, but sin against God, and the outrage it is in dishonoring God. The greatest problem that has to be solved in every human life everywhere on this planet—no matter what tribe, language, or culture it is—is the just and holy wrath of God against us because of our dishonoring God in our sins against him. Without this grasp of this vertical alienation between us and God and the price paid on the cross to overcome that alienation—even adding the name *God* or *Jesus* to the 'higher power'—will become a religious technique rather than an act of redemption or ransom by means of the death of Jesus paying for our sins and providing our perfect righteousness and acceptance with God."

Victory over sin is only for justified sinners. If it helps, "give thanks to God for his great grace in using AA." But then press into the gospel, because "Jesus shed his blood to deliver alcoholics and the rest of us from whatever bondage holds us fast" (Titus 2:14). Press on to "glorify Christ and his cross by defeating our sins with the power of that blood and righteousness."[9]

The only sin we can purge from our lives

That last point on gospel holiness is crucial. The point is made in seven key Bible texts that have arisen nearly two hundred times on APJ. The only sin I can defeat in my life is the sin Christ has already canceled for me on the cross (Rom. 7:6; 8:13; Gal. 2:20; Phil. 2:12–13; Col. 1:20–23; Titus 2:14; 1 Pet. 2:24–25). Justification precedes sanctification. "The only sin that we can defeat is a forgiven sin. That's the way I like to say it." But if you begin to say, "I have got to kill this sin, or I can't get right with God," you've embraced "the opposite of Christianity."[10]

As the old hymn put it, Christ "breaks the power of canceled sin" (Charles Wesley). "The cross *cancels* sins by faith for all who believe in Jesus. Then— on the basis of that *cancellation* of our sins—the *power* of our actual sinning is broken. It's not the other way around. There would be no gospel and no

9 APJ 1435: "Should Christians Attend Alcoholics Anonymous?" (February 17, 2020).
10 APJ 18: "Fighting Porn Addiction with Grudem's Systematic Theology" (February 1, 2013).

hymns if we tried to sing, 'He cancels the guilt of our conquered sins.' That's not gospel. First the *cancellation*, then the *conquering*. Which means that the link between the cross and my conquered sin is a Holy Spirit–empowered willing. It works a willing in me."[11] Justified Christians fight for holiness because their "canceled sins"—their "blood-covered sins"—must be "killed consciously with effort, by faith, in the Spirit. Not coddled."[12] The sin-canceling power of Christ's blood provides us the basis, power, means, and motivation to purge sin from our lives. Our only hope of expunging sin from our lives is to fight that sin "as blood-bought, justified, forgiven children of God."[13]

Christless attempts at killing sin through worldly philosophies or self-help books or the "pea-shooter" of asceticism will prove to be, says Paul, "of no value in stopping the indulgence of the flesh" (Col. 2:20–23).[14]

Are both the junkie and the Christian Hedonist just chasing their next joy hit?

It's true that both junkies and Christian Hedonists chase joy. And "the intensity of our pleasure in *physical experiences* and the intensity of our pleasure in the *spiritual experience* of fellowship with Jesus both rise and fall." So there's a "superficial parallel." But nothing more.

The two pursuits of pleasure are fundamentally dissimilar in five ways. (1) Christ is the encounter of a person, not a substance. He gives to us the satisfying bread and water of life (John 6:35). "*He is* the bread. *He is* the water. We're not comparing substance and substance. We are comparing *a created substance* with the *person* who created it. That's the first difference. It's a massive and infinite difference." We get *him*. (2) Christ makes us new (2 Cor. 5:17; Eph. 4:23). United to Christ, "you become a new kind of being forever and ever and ever." On the contrary, "you're not born again by using drugs. You do not have a new nature by using drugs." (3) Christ woos us back. We press on toward the resurrection of the body, and we press forward to our perfection, because Christ made us his own (Phil. 3:12). He initiated our relationship, and he sustains it. So "the reason we keep returning to Christ is that *he himself*, as a person who loves us, has chosen to make sure that we return. We're not being

---

11 APJ 1227: "Make War on Your Urge to Sulk" (July 23, 2018).

12 APJ 1501: "How Do I Wage War on My Self-Pity?" (July 20, 2020).

13 APJ 1435: "Should Christians Attend Alcoholics Anonymous?" (February 17, 2020).

14 APJ 123: "How Food and Sex Are Made Holy" (July 1, 2013), APJ 1749: "How Can I Avoid Worldly Thinking in My Studies?" (February 25, 2022), APJ 1752: "Is There a Place for Asceticism in the Christian Life?" (March 4, 2022), and APJ 1884: "Is Intermittent Fasting Sacrilegious?" (January 6, 2023).

sucked back by addiction; we are being drawn back by a Savior." (4) Christ's beauty transforms us (2 Cor. 3:18). "The more we return to him, the more we fully become whole and rational and free and joyful. But the more we return to substances, the more we become broken, irrational, enslaved, and miserable." For the Christian, the all-sufficiency of Christ overflows in and through us (John 4:14; 7:37–38). (5) Christ is our good physician. In the "spiking and falling of pleasure"—compared to drugs and Christ—they result in two totally different ends. For the Christian, these affection variations are experienced along the pathway to total healing in Christ. "It is the ups and downs of our experience in Christ that mean we are on the way to an everlasting, uninterrupted joy."[15]

---

15 APJ 1205: "Drug Users and Christian Hedonists—Aren't Both Just Chasing the Next High?" (June 1, 2018).

On Smartphones, Social Media, and Selfie Sticks

Tweeting to the glory of God

In everything we say or do—including our Twitter feeds—we aim to honor God (1 Cor. 10:31). "God is a planning God. He is a purposeful God. And he calls us to do things purposefully." We plan. We purpose. And we "let the *why* govern the *how*," not the other way around. Before we set parameters on social media, we resolve our aims.

On the use (and misuse) of Twitter, we must first use the platform to build up, not to tear down (Eph. 4:29). Self-critique the motives that drive you online. Are you praise-*giving* or praise-*seeking*? When it comes to social media, this is "probably the biggest thing I do. I ask: 'All right, beware, Piper. Am I seeking the praise and attention of people?'" All of us face "a deep, fallen, and human craving to be seen, known, liked, and praised. Oh, Jesus had strong words for that!" (Matt. 6:1, 16; Luke 20:45–47). Instead, we look to John the Baptist's resolve that he decrease as Christ increases (John 3:29–30). "And I just want that to fly as a banner over every tweet: 'Jesus up; Piper down.' But I will tell you, that is really, really tricky. It makes all of us distinguish between self-promotion and truth promotion—self-promotion and Christ promotion."

Another trap is the humble brag. "It goes something like this: 'Humbled to be invited by the most famous person in the world to their super important event.' This is using humble language to quote a tribute to yourself. I see this all over Twitter. Everybody talks as if they are self-conscious about repeating something somebody said about them, and yet I see this everywhere. There is something inside of me that cringes when I see that." We post to influence. But we don't seek attention for ourselves, we seek to share the truth we love. And, as a final note, don't scold in public when it would be more productive to talk in private.[1]

---

1 APJ 61: "Twitter Goals and 'Humble Brags'" (April 3, 2013).

Is it wrong to seek online fame?

Influence is not wrong. Seeking to influence others is very Christian. But many Christians now set out to become social-media "influencers." When does this become fame seeking?

The desire *to be famous* is a sin. But the desire *to be influential* isn't, not inherently. "And the problem arises when the pleasure sought in *being made much of* is greater than the pleasure sought in *being of service*. So, there is the rub. It is not a sin to desire that those who know us think well of us, provided that our hope and our prayer and our effort is that they will see the grace of God in us and give glory to God and, in that sense, make much of us or think rightly or well of us." This goes back to our calling. We exist to make much of Christ, to find God to be all-satisfying, to find his promises completely trustworthy, and overall to be a person "whose joy is overflowing, even in suffering, in the pursuit of other people's joy in God." That's why we exist.

But religious acts done in the pursuit of self-glorification are insidiously wicked, and Jesus gives us all sorts of warnings to check our vainglory (Matt. 5:16; 6:1–6, 16–18; 23:5). "So all those warnings, it seems to me, are meant to give us tests to see if God is our true reward. All of them say, 'If you seek satisfaction in man's praise, you will not have your Father's reward.' The whole focus is on: Where is your heart? Where is your treasure? Is it in fame, or is it in God?"

Our motive for influence reveals what we treasure. It's not a sin to seek to become an influencer. In fact, "it may be a sin *not to want to be influential*. We should want to win more and more people to Christ. It is a sin not to want our lives to count for winning more and more people to Christ. We should want to do more and more good, to relieve suffering, especially eternal suffering." This is influence in service of others.

In the end, "let's all admit how deadly difficult this distinction is"—the desire to bless others and not self-glorify. It's the ongoing battle inside us, between the Spirit and the flesh (Rom. 8:5–7).[2]

Self-absorption and selfie sticks

Paul tells us that in the end times we can expect to see a spike in "lovers of self" (2 Tim. 3:1–2). So are vlogs, selfies, and self-focused social media proof of this end-time self-love?

Yes (and *no*).

2   APJ 983: "Is It Sinful to Seek Fame Online?" (December 30, 2016). For more on the virtue of influence, see "On Writing, Grammar, and Poetry" later in this book.

"*Yes*, vlogs, selfies, and self-focused social media are often (not always) an expression of the self-exaltation, self-preoccupation, and self-fascination of these last days. But *no*, these new technologies are not the emerging of such final experiences of sin. They've always been there. The new technologies are giving new ways to express old sins."

"*Yes*, these are the last days, and we should be looking keenly and expectantly and hopefully and joyfully for the coming of our precious, longed-for, all-satisfying Lord Jesus. But *no*, these are not yet the very last days. But they are very much like the last days that began two thousand years ago in the first century." Paul says that "in the last days" there will come people who are self-lovers, and we ought to "avoid such people" right now (2 Tim. 3:1–5). Because they were already here.

But the larger question is about why we have "selves" to begin with. "God gave us a self, not so that we would have something to *exalt in*, but something to *exalt with*. He gave us a self, not to be the *object* of our joy, but the *subject* of joy. That is, not to be the *focus* of happiness in front of the mirror or the selfie, but the *furnace* of happiness in front of Jesus. He gave us a self not as an instrument of self-worth but as an instrument of worship." Indeed, God intended for the self to be "a desire factory," producing "endless desires" that push us to seek after "a joy outside ourselves." Endless desires are never satisfied by the self. Those desires are given "to lead us outside our self—indeed, outside the world, because nothing in this world finally satisfies." Our desires are meant to lead us to God, in whose presence is fullness of joy and at whose right hand are pleasures forevermore (Ps. 16:11). "That's what I'd say to the self-absorbed user of social media. The self was never meant to satisfy us. The self was never meant to find satisfaction in the perception or promotion of self. The self was made for God."[3]

Should I Instagram my good works to magnify Christ?

Like the humble brag, social media gives us new opportunities to broadcast our good works to the world. So how do we let our light shine before others so that they may see our good works and give glory to our Father who is in heaven (Jesus's command in Matthew 5:16) but also not practice our righteousness before other people in order to be seen by them (Jesus's command in Matthew 6:1)?

Jesus motivates our modesty with future rewards (Matt. 6:1). To desire that our virtue be rewarded now by our peers is evil—because "it signals you are not content with your Father's reward. You need to add to it. You crave human

---

3 APJ 1158: "Avoiding Pride in a World of Selfie Sticks and Social-Media Platforms" (February 12, 2018).

praise, and so God's reward is not sufficient for you. You need to supplement it by a little human adulation, and that's what makes it so evil."

So don't blow a trumpet and bring attention to your good works done in private (Matt. 6:2–4). When you give to the needy, "don't tweet your soup kitchen picture." Do righteous deeds "so quietly that your *right hand* is able to make the gift to the needy and your *left hand* was hanging out on the other side and didn't even know what happened." Don't aim for self-praise. For example, it's one thing to encourage others to pray for victims of a tragedy. It's another thing to say that *you did pray* for a certain situation. Know this difference. Jesus calls us "to make a concerted effort" to keep our prayers, deeds, and generosity to the poor unseen by others (Matt. 6:5–6).

But there remains "a real problem." How do we also allow our deeds to be so seen that others praise God for them (Matt. 5:14–16)? We should aim to serve in secret, but often we cannot. Three suggestions.

1. Many practical deeds of love "simply cannot be hidden, especially from those for whom you're doing the deeds. You can't stop and help somebody change a tire without them watching you do it. You can't risk your life during a public act of terrorism to rescue a child without the crowd seeing what you're doing." Many good deeds can't be hidden. But most can. Imagine going online to donate to a cause and right there you see "a little button that says, 'Give anonymously.' A real test, right?" Will you donate anonymously? Or put your name on it?

2. Jesus recalibrates the goal and end of our love. Good works are not for the public theater of self-aggrandizement. We do good deeds so that more and more people will be pulled into worship of the living God. "Christians are never merely public do-gooders. We want people to know God, love God, serve God, glorify God, be saved, and be with God forever. This is the great passion of mercy ministries and justice ministries. If it's not, we are probably being politically correct in order to win the praise of whatever group we happen to prize at the time."

3. We are all acquainted with the insidious desire to be worshiped. "We all know that there is a way to act publicly that gives the impression that you crave the approval and the praise of other people. This certainly comes to the fore in Twitter and Instagram and other social-media outlets." It's fleshly, not holy. Works of self-aggrandizement are a turnoff. It deters others; it doesn't win them.

Jesus's profound words in Matthew 5–6 tell us that we should be "deeply content with the reward of God—knowing him, loving him, treasuring him as supremely satisfying and glorious." We should not crave the praise of man as if the praise of God is insufficient for us, "which is what craving signifies." We should love genuinely, driven by the goal that others "would come to worship God and give glory to him." And to that end we pray, "Fill us with spiritual desires, not vain, egoistic desires."[4]

Social-media superficiality

Our social-media posts will be superficial if our feed is full of frivolous voices. "Do not be deceived: 'Bad company ruins good morals'" (1 Cor. 15:33). "Superficiality is a very, very, very contagious disease. If you only hang out with superficial people, you will almost certainly be a superficial person. If you only hang out with superficial social media and TV programs, you will almost certainly be a superficial person." On the flip side, walking with the wise—following the wise—will make you wise (Ps. 119:63; Prov. 13:20; Heb. 10:24).[5]

Yet on social media, "everybody talks incessantly. Most of the talking is clever. It's repartee. It's banter. All of these together produce a life that results in a superficial, trivial, clever Christian banter, shaped for the Twittersphere and crafted for spreading on Facebook. I don't think we can do real evangelism on the basis of this kind of ubiquitous levity."[6]

Setting goals for social media

So how do we use our phones and our social media influence for eternal purpose—to evangelize and edify? Social media is a potent power for good. Before Twitter, we could hand out tracts, distribute doorknob hangers, rent billboards, buy newspaper ads, slap on bumper stickers, write letters to the editor, publish articles and books. Today we go directly to Facebook, Twitter, Instagram, YouTube, and blogs. "Now the possibility exists that something you say might reach thousands, even millions, besides the little cluster of friends you have. Now, that's a new situation, and for Christians it's another stewardship that God has given us to manage. He will call us to account for every careless word we utter (Matt. 12:36). This includes careless words on Twitter or Facebook or in blogs."

A few principles for tweeting to edify others online.

1. Proclaim Christ. Every Christian aims to "proclaim the excellencies of him who called you out of darkness into his marvelous light" (1 Pet. 2:9). If you choose to be on social media, your "mandate" is to proclaim "the excellencies of Jesus." The major note of our social media is broadcasting—scattering truth like seed, to declare God's glory to the nations (Pss. 40:10; 96:3; Prov. 15:7; Acts 5:28). "So pray over your tweets, pray over your blogging and your Facebook.

---

4 APJ 1151: "'Let Your Light Shine'—Should I Instagram My Good Works?" (January 26, 2018).
5 APJ 1033: "Three Strategies for Overcoming the Superficial Life" (April 26, 2017).
6 APJ 1234: "Three Threats to the Joy of This Generation" (August 8, 2018).

Pray over it that God would breathe on it and send it by his appointed means to somebody who has exactly a need for what you have said. That's the way I do it. I put tweets in my scheduler almost every day, and they come from the Bible—almost 90 percent of them. I'm saying, 'God, do something extraordinary with this verse. Make it be timed perfectly for somebody's need.'"

2. Confront evil (Eph. 5:11; 1 Pet. 3:15). "I don't think the dominant tone of your life on the internet should be exposing darkness. You're going to get your hands and your heart dirty that way. But periodically, God's going to burden you with something you saw that needs to be set right, and you're going to expose some sin."

3. Edify others (John 8:32; 17:17; Rom. 14:19; Eph. 4:29). "So we fill our mouths, our Twitter feed, our Facebook page with Scripture accurately cited and wisely interpreted. This is the safest way to do good. Minimize yourself. Maximize God in his word." Offer life-giving, love-offering, grace-filled words (Prov. 10:11; 15:4; 16:21, 24; 25:11; 1 Cor. 16:14; Eph. 4:15; Col. 3:16; 4:6).

4. Be exposed. Social media is an exposé of what lies within us (Matt. 12:34). "You may not know it, but you are revealing yourself all day long. What kind of person are you based on your use of social media? Is this a feisty person, an angry person, a cynical person, a mean person, a gentle person, a kind person, a loving person, a whole person, a broken person?" Social-media you is your heart revealed to the world.

5. Focus on the cumulative effect. "Sometimes [my tweets] are very severe in pointing out the judgment of God. Sometimes they're very tender in reaching out to the brokenhearted. What I do is look not only at each tweet, but at the overall effect of thousands of tweets over the years. I think I've maybe sent seventeen thousand tweets so far" (to 2018). The investment is made with the hope that my "overall impact will be for the magnifying of Christ, the winning of the lost, the everlasting holy joy of God's people, and the glory of God."[7]

Before you criticize on social media

Social media can quickly flame into an inferno of angry insults. Even professing Christians can add to the rage without considering the foolishness of spewing verbal abuses. We need to do better.

Here are seven questions to ask before you post. (1) Is it true? Publish only what is true, self-evidently true if possible. Biblically verifiable truth is best. Always avoid publishing falsehood. (2) Is it well-timed? Even if what you have to say is true, Job's friends remind us that "truth can be used unrighteously" if

---

7   APJ 1204: "How Can We Tweet to the Glory of God?" (May 30, 2018).

we misjudge the timing. Fools wield proverbs wrongly (Prov. 26:7, 9). (3) Is it edifying? "Am I aiming in my social-media posts to help the person that I'm talking to or talking about know God better, trust God more, love people better, walk in less sin and more holiness?" (Eph. 4:29). That still leaves room for corrective criticism when necessary. (4) Is it right for this audience? Is social media the right occasion for those to hear what you are about to say (Eph. 4:29)? Social media lacks context for hard conversations that are better done privately, one on one. "In fact, one of my biggest complaints about the way people use Twitter, for example, is that lots of what is said publicly for ten thousand people to read should be said privately to the person, not publicly. So many things are said to an individual for a grandstand of people to watch you say it. And I don't get that." (5) Is it aimed at future unity? If you criticize others online, is it centered on a falsehood or is it a personal attack? Is it dismissive? Or do you critique with the heartfelt desire for peace among believers (Eph. 4:1–3)? (6) Is it angry? We are so easily provoked to respond in sinful anger that we must show caution any time we seek to communicate angrily (James 1:19–20). "Be slow to anger, slow to speak, because it's very, very, very likely that your anger is not righteous—and mine isn't either—and it will not produce the good you think it might." (7) Will it magnify Christ? "Can people detect that your heart is deeply content in and satisfied by the beauty and worth and greatness of Jesus? That's why we exist: to display Jesus Christ as the supreme treasure of the world. Do they taste that?"[8]

On political Twitter

John Piper's social-media activity includes very little about politics, breaking news, hashtags, or viral trends. And he knows it. "When Twitter is ablaze with some new controversy, where is Piper? He's over there quoting Bible verses, like he doesn't even know what's going on. 'Don't you know we're about to lose the Supreme Court nominee? Come on! Do something!'"

Piper is slow to address political topics. In the summer of 2018, newcomer-progressive Alexandria Ocasio-Cortez won the Democratic primary in New York's fourteenth congressional district, hailed as the biggest election upset of 2018. She went on to win the seat in November. She is "to the left of [Bernie] Sanders on socialism," Piper said, and yet he hesitated to address her socialism in public. Why? Three reasons.

1. It's about authority. "Most of the macro and international, political, economic issues are too complicated for me to figure out." He's a Bible expert. "I want them to

8   APJ 1581: "Before You Tweet Criticism: Six Considerations" (January 29, 2021).

hear my perspective on the Bible. But seldom do I come to the point where I feel like, with some complex issue out there, I've risen to the level of knowledge that would warrant my voice to be authoritative." In sum: "I deal with the Bible pretty far upstream from the flow down into the nitty-gritties of political realization."

2. It's about the church. "I am one hundred times" or "two hundred times . . . more passionate about creating the kind of Christians and the kind of churches that stand with unshaken, faithful, biblical, countercultural spiritual-mindedness in a socialist America than I am in *preventing* a socialist America. I'm one hundred times more passionate about creating Christians and churches that will be faithful, biblical, countercultural, and spiritually minded in a socialist America, in a Muslim America, in a communist America, than I am in *preventing* a Muslim America or a communist America. That puts me in a very different ballpark than many public voices. My main calling is not to help America be anything, but to help the church be the church" as the "radical outpost of the kingdom of Christ, no matter what kind of America it happens to be in or any other people group or country in the world." But he's not normalizing his approach. "I will say again that I am glad—glad, glad, glad—that there are Christians who are politically more active than I am in trying to shape laws that are just and wise."

3. It's about expositional impact. "I do feel that the greater, long-term impact for the glory of Christ and for the good of the nations and for the purity and strengthening of the church will come not through the politicizing of my voice, but through a more penetrating, personal, eternal focus on the human soul and how it can be most effectively conformed to Christ." Pastors shouldn't feel pressure "to become experts on every issue that faces the local, state, and national legislature" but should feed Christians (even Christians in politics) a "steady stream of exposition of what biblical texts actually mean, with whatever measure of application the pastors can bring."[9] Speak biblical truth, and "call your people to radical allegiance to King Jesus. Set them on a quest of lifelong learning, and trust the Spirit of God in their lives."[10]

That said, in full disclosure, exactly three years earlier, Piper did confront socialism on the podcast, well-prefaced by reservations, disclaimers, and misgivings.[11]

Keep the phone off in the morning

We impulsively reach for our phones immediately in the morning when we wake up. But should we?

---

9 APJ 1263: "Why Does Piper Avoid Politics and What's Trending?" (October 15, 2018).
10 APJ 1804: "Politics, Patriotism, and the Pulpit" (July 4, 2022).
11 APJ 710: "How Should Christians Think about Socialism?" (October 20, 2015).

Some cautions are in order. First, we never wake up apart from our calling. "We are to love God with all of our heart, soul, mind, and strength when we wake up in the morning. And we are to prepare ourselves to love our neighbor and to serve our neighbor as ourselves." And yet, "given how sinful John Piper is—and I presume others are like me—very few of us wake up with our whole soul spring-loaded to love God and love people. This process takes some refocusing, to put it mildly."

After "analyzing John Piper's soul and his temptations," here are six heart problems we all wake up with. First, three candies, three attractions that immediately push us to our phones. (1) Novelty candy. We want to get caught up. "Most of us like to be the first one to know something, and then we don't have to assume the humble posture of being told something that smart and savvy and on-the-ball people already know." (2) Ego candy. We want to see that we have been seen. We open our phones to look for mentions or retweets. "In our fallen, sinful condition there is an inordinate enjoyment of the human ego being attended to. Some of us are weak enough, wounded enough, fragile enough, insecure enough that any little mention of us just feels so good. It is like somebody kissed us." (3) Entertainment candy. We want to be entertained for a moment. So we open social media where we can find "an endless stream of fascinating, weird, strange, wonderful, shocking, spell-binding, cute pictures and quotes and videos and stories and links. And many of us have gotten to the point where we are almost addicted to the need for something striking and bizarre and extraordinary and amazing." Even in bed.

Beyond these candied promises, there are three repellants—three avoidance motives that push us to postpone our day for another thirty minutes. (4) Avoiding boredom. When our day ahead looks boring, we find "little incentive to get out of bed." So we turn to our phones to fill a hole in our heart. (5) Avoiding responsibility. We don't want to face the weighty responsibilities we have ahead. Maybe we are afraid of them. Maybe we feel incompetent for the day's tasks. We feel the pressure, so we grab the phone, flick our thumbs, and delay the day. (6) Avoiding hardship. We turn to our phones in the morning when we want to put off the "megarelational conflict or issues of disease or disability in the home, or friends who are against you, or pain in your own body so that you can barely get out of bed because it hurts so bad. It is just easier to lie there a little longer, and the phone adds to the escape."[12]

But what if in our search for novelty candy we are met with horrific news? And what if, in looking for ego candy, you wake up to being hated online? And

12 APJ 636: "Why Not to Check Your Phone in the Morning" (July 9, 2015).

what if you feed on entertainment candy immediately, rather than facing your responsibilities, "only to find, at the end of those five minutes of avoidance, that you are spiritually, morally, and emotionally less able to cope with reality in the day than you were before?" Then what?

There's a better way to start our day. We can resolve to have our audio Bible be the first thing we turn on in the morning. "What we want in the morning routine is to be filled with the Holy Spirit. We want something that gives us a zeal for the glory of Christ for the day's work. We want to be strengthened to face whatever the day may bring. We want something that gives us joyful courage and the resolve to count others better than ourselves, something that helps us to pursue true greatness by becoming the servant of all, just as Jesus said (Mark 9:35). That is the real agenda in the morning." In the morning we wake up desperate for God to act (Pss. 5:3; 90:14; 143:8), and we should turn immediately to his word. But this must be planned. The morning's first decision must be made the night before.[13]

How to break an internet addiction

An internet addict wrote in, a young man not addicted to internet porn or video games, but to consuming solid Christian content. The content itself is virtuous, although it is impeding his relationships and misdirecting him from the needs of others. How do we address the overuse of a good gift?

First, "addiction" is a label we should use less frequently. In this case, it would be more helpful to say, "I read Twitter, Facebook, blogs, news (or whatever) *to sinful excess.*" Because now we can more clearly see "an intensity of desire that is out of proportion, perhaps sinfully out of proportion, to the value of what I am doing and the value of other things I may not be doing." Reframed as a "sinful disproportion of desire," the moral problem becomes stark—a "giving in to an intensity of desire against my best judgment." In this case, "it names the problem of *sinful excess.* It names the problem of *disproportion of desire.* It names the problem of contradicting our own best judgment. It doesn't use this almost therapeutic or medical word of *addiction* which kind of, in a vague way, covers all these specific sins."

So, again, we're talking about good content consumed *in excess* (not an inherently sinful compulsion). The question is *not,* Is this wrong? The question is, Is it wrong to do so much of this? "In other words, a God-pleasing life of faith and love and holiness is a life not just of avoiding bad things and doing good things. It is a life of doing good things with good motives in proper proportion to other good things."

13 APJ 637: "Don't Waste Your Mornings" (July 10, 2015).

Four responses. (1) Soak in Scripture until "God's revealed proportionality becomes instinctual" in shaping how you decide what habits are helpful and what habits obstruct your obedience. (2) Pray for God to show you where you are wasting time and cannot see it. (3) Seek to "bring the intensity of your desires into balance with the diversity of good things God gives us to do—relationships at home and work and church as well as all these other good things that we discover through the Bible reading that we are doing." (4) Surround yourself with Christian friends who will help you discern when you lose your balance.[14]

With others, put the phone away

A wife is frustrated that her husband spends most of mealtimes on his phone, largely ignoring her.

Here are five reasons the husband should put his phone away at dinnertime. (1) Your wife is a coheir of eternity, and she is not honored by being ignored (1 Pet. 3:7). (2) Your face represents your benevolent attention. God gives us his attention (Num. 6:24–26). And we can give our attention to love others too. It's a high honor to know that "God would turn away from his iPhone and look at us with favor. He is not more interested in something else." (3) Like Christ, seek the interests of others (Phil. 2:3–4). Pay attention to your own interests (screen on). And attend to the interests of your wife (screen off). (4) Don't act from what *you feel*; act from what *you ought to feel* (Mark 8:34). Maybe there's disharmony in the home driving the inattention. Don't act on this; instead "act the way you ought to feel." (5) Like Christ, love your bride (Eph. 5:25). "You are called to treat her not the way she deserves, but the way that will show how Christ loves his church." Die to yourself to make this happen, because "any husband that ignores his wife and sinks away into his social media when she is longing for his attention and engagement is displeasing the Lord and walking in sin."

How can the wife respond? She can consider six actions, contingent on his spiritual condition. (1) Address the concern at a good time, not necessarily in the moment. (2) Don't accuse. Instead, tell him what you miss from him, a lost opportunity. (3) Tell him that you love talking together at the dinner

---

14 APJ 657: "How Do I Choose between Two Good Things?" (August 7, 2015). On replacing the term "addiction" for "sinful excess," see APJ 530: "The Real Cost of Pornography" (February 11, 2015) (on porn addiction), APJ 657: "How Do I Choose between Two Good Things?" (August 7, 2015) (on digital media and smartphone addiction), APJ 1314: "How Do I Break My Entertainment Addiction?" (February 18, 2019) (on gaming and video entertainment addiction), and APJ 1702: "On Cigarettes, Vaping, and Nicotine" (November 8, 2021) (on nicotine, vaping, and smoking addictions).

table. (4) Call on your circle of Christian friends for prayer. (5) If all this leads to heightened tension in the marriage, draw in another couple to help. (6) In all things, seek to "win him with the greatest respect and helpfulness" so his heart doesn't harden toward you. Pray. And seek that the mind of Christ will win out in the marriage.[15]

Getting rid of the smartphone

One listener asked a sobering question: Could my iPhone be the reason I eventually fall away from Christ?

The New Testament story of Demas is a stern warning to us all. He was a fellow worker with the apostle Paul, but a man who eventually fell in love with this present world (2 Tim. 4:10). In fact, "*the world* did not destroy Demas; his *love for the world* destroyed Demas, it seems." Thus, "*an iPhone* does not, will not, destroy a marriage or a mom or a soul. But *love for what is on the iPhone* can." So in light of this danger, Jesus says if your eye causes you to sin, tear it out (Matt. 5:29). Reverting from a smartphone to an old flip phone is less radical than removing an eye. But be willing to "take radical steps against something that is intrinsically neutral or good in order to fight what in our hearts is bad."

Our war for personal purity is battled on two fronts—the *internal* and *external*. "We are fighting on the *internal front* of the heart—the heart front to be so satisfied in Jesus—to see him so clearly and love him so dearly and follow him so nearly—that nothing, not even a smartphone, can control us." This is "the main battlefront." So "love Jesus more, and you won't be enslaved by your smartphone." But on the other hand, "we are also fighting on the *external front* to remove or avoid stumbling blocks to our faith" (Rom. 13:14). "Drug addicts don't fondle needles. Alcoholics don't keep stashes of brandy. Sexually supercharged eyes put safeguards on their computers. And smartphone junkies who are throwing away their lives or wasting money or becoming irritable and angry and impatient may go back to a flip phone. This is not unbiblical. This is not legalism. This is wisdom. This is fighting on all fronts for holiness in the power of the Holy Spirit for the sake of the heart, for the sake of the Lord, for the sake of the family."

Guard your digital diet so you can fill your life with more of Christ. "Getting rid of bad influences doesn't make anybody love Christ in and of itself. True freedom from the bondage of technology comes not mainly from throwing it away, but from filling the void with the glories of Jesus that you are trying to fill with the pleasures of the smartphone. Fight the deceitful, fleeting pleasures

---

15   APJ 633: "Put Your Phones Away at the Dinner Table" (July 6, 2015).

of the iPhone with the true, lasting pleasures of knowing and being cared for by Christ."[16]

Social-media fasting

Another helpful discipline in the Christian life is to fast from social media. To do it, "pick a period of time. A week, for example—or like I did two years ago, eight months with no Twitter and zero blogging—and see what happens to your soul. See if your soul has become addicted to being known, being followed, and being read. Don't post on or read Facebook or Twitter for X amount of time. That is a Twitter fast or a blogging fast."[17]

Do you read comments?

"Sometimes I do. And I don't find it helpful, because for every person who says, 'Thank you, it was a great help,' somebody else has given me the f-word." So "I don't think I can look enough at comments to draw any valid conclusions. I would have to do some sophisticated analysis to say, 'Okay, 70 percent of the people said they got help, and 30 percent thought it was hogwash. Surely the 70 percent are right.' Even then, maybe that's true, or maybe not." Better than weighing public responses, get feedback from friends and pray over every post.[18]

John Piper's last tweet

In the era of the 140-character tweet (2006–2017), what would John Piper post as his capstone and final tweet to the world? This: "Jesus, God's Son, died in the place of sinners and rose so that all who love him supremely might be forgiven all and have eternal joy in God." The sentence is modeled from Paul's concise statement of "first importance" (1 Cor. 15:3–4).

It's a gospel tweet of what's most important. "The most controversial thing in my sentence, I think, is that I said the beneficiaries of this death are 'all who *love him* supremely' rather than saying, 'all who *trust him*' or, 'all who *believe in him.*' And I certainly don't mean to set this up as a way everybody should always present the gospel. I might be wrong in choosing to emphasize *loving* Christ supremely instead of *believing* Christ." Inarguably, the affections are essential to the genuine Christian life because "in view of two thousand years of church history and millions and millions of nominal Christians who would

---

16 APJ 670: "When Should I Get Rid of My Smartphone?" (August 25, 2015). On fighting pleasure with pleasure (a.k.a., the expulsive power of a new affection) see APJ 850: "Can Pleasure in God Really Compete with the Pleasures of Porn?" (May 3, 2016).

17 APJ 62: "Fasting from Twitter and Facebook" (April 4, 2013).

18 APJ 62: "Fasting from Twitter and Facebook" (April 4, 2013).

say they believe in him and have not experienced the slightest heart change, or the slightest change in their lives and are lost, I wanted to stress the necessity of the kind of faith that really transforms people at the level of our deepest affection—so that Christ is our supreme treasure, not just a belief-ticket out of hell, which he is for so many people who think they're believing."[19]

---

19 APJ 1026: "What's the Last Thing You Would Tweet?" (April 10, 2017). Five years later he published his case for the affections within justifying faith in John Piper, *What Is Saving Faith?: Reflections on Receiving Christ as a Treasure* (Wheaton, IL: Crossway, 2022).

On Television, Movies, and Fun

Far too easily bored

The mobile screen in our pocket offers us "an endless stream of fascinating, weird, strange, wonderful, shocking, spellbinding, cute pictures and quotes and videos and stories and links—and many of us have gotten to the point where we are almost addicted to the need for something striking and bizarre and extraordinary and amazing."[1]

The pattern was true before smartphones. Generations have turned to illuminated displays to find glory because the fallen human heart grows quickly bored with God's revealed glories in creation. "We go to the Alps, see them for the first time, and are stunned speechless. We rent a little chalet at the foot of the mountains, and for three mornings we get up amazed. And by the fourth morning we are watching television." This is the result of the fall. "And won't that be wonderful in the age to come where we never get tired of anything?" For now, we need cultivated powers of imagination, "not just to think of things that are not, but to look at the things that are and see them for what they are."[2]

The world needs you to be uncool

Televised glory substitutes lose their power the closer we get to eternity. "I want to invite, frankly, all Christians to join me in this pursuit of greater purity of heart and mind. In our day, when entertainment media is virtually the lingua franca of the world, this is an invitation to be an alien. And I believe with all my heart that what the world needs is radically bold, sacrificially loving, God-besotted freaks—aliens. In other words, I am inviting you to say *no* to the world for the sake of the world. The world does not need more cool, hip, culturally savvy, irrelevant copies of itself. That is a hoax that

---

1   APJ 636: "Why Not to Check Your Phone in the Morning" (July 9, 2015).
2   APJ 195: "How Your Imagination Helps You See" (October 16, 2013).

292 ON TELEVISION, MOVIES, AND FUN

thousands of young Christians have been duped by." You don't reach the world by being worldly.

Popular shows and movies are "shot through" with "the commendation and exaltation of attitudes and actions that are utterly out of step with the death to self and the exaltation of Christ." What keeps Christians coming back to them "is the fear that if they took Christ at his word and made holiness as serious as I am saying it is, they would have to stop seeing so many TV shows and so many movies. They would be viewed as freakish. And that, today, is the worst evil of all. To be seen as *freakish* is a much greater evil than to be *unholy*."[3]

How do I overcome the trivial life?

Superficiality is a cultural "epidemic," the "tragic loss of wonder and amazement" of the created beauties and glories, like ourselves—image bearers of God (Gen. 1:26–27). Our glory is that we are "full of potential to know God, and to know things the way God knows them, and feel with the affections that even God has in his own heart." But we sinned, becoming "glorious ruins," falling so far short of our potential that "we are so easily bored with glorious reality. We go to visit the magnificent Rockies, or Alps, or Himalayas, and, for a day or two, we are breathless with amazement. By the end of the week, we're sitting in front of the television in our chalet on top of the mountain, watching pitiful, human, cinematic efforts to create amazement. That's just who we are. It's tragic. It's the great, tragic effect of the fall: superficiality in a world of wonder, easy boredom, loving something for two, three repetitions, and then after that, 'ho hum.'"

We trade our capacity for glory to consume trifling and trivial substitutes. So how do we escape the triviality trap? Five practical responses. (1) Repent. Confess to God all the sin that has led you here. "Cry out to God for help that he would wake you up from the slumbers of emptiness and meaninglessness and boredom in the endless quest to be titillated in body while the soul is languishing and starving for greatness." (2) Engage. "Set yourself on a conscious quest to obey God's strategy for cultivating a spiritual mind that is fully alert to the glories of God, radiant *in the world*, and radiant *in the word*." Take Paul's commission in Colossians 3:1–3 as "your marching orders." Set your mind on eternal glories. Focus on what is excellent, "on things that are worthy and that have the potential to deepen and strengthen and purify our souls" (Phil. 4:8). (3) Find a local church "where the preaching is blood earnest and serious, where God-besought joy, and not flippant silliness, marks the wonders of the word of God." (4) Find eternally minded friends (1 Cor. 15:55). "Superficiality

3 APJ 368: "Should Christians Watch *Game of Thrones*?" (June 20, 2014).

is a very, very, very contagious disease. If you only hang out with superficial people, you will almost certainly become superficial. If you only hang out with superficial social media and TV programs, you will almost certainly be a superficial person." (5) Read the great Puritan authors whose books are "unlike anything you will find in the twentieth and twenty-first century, because they are so nonsuperficial, nonsilly, nontrivial, non-man-centered."[4]

When cultural trivialities abound, sovereign glories stabilize our souls. "I have felt over the years that the greatest threat to my soul is not committing adultery against my wife, or embezzling money from some ministry, or even suddenly throwing away my faith and becoming an advocate for atheism, or being overtaken by some terrible fit of rage and killing somebody. None of those things has seemed to me to be nearly as threatening to my soul as the creeping effect of *pettiness*—the loss of all capacity to feel greatness, and beauty, and magnificence, and depth, and wonder, and awe, and reverence, and weightiness. My fear has not been that I will make shipwreck of my life through some dramatic, egregious sin, but through the steady drip from the faucet of silliness." We must get "in touch" with "the greatest realities in the universe." And that means seeing and savoring and grasping and cherishing "God's all-pervading, all-embracing providence" over everything. With our heart awakened, providence "goes a long way to protecting us from the trivializing effects of contemporary culture and from the widespread habit of trifling with great things, even divine things." (1) God's providence protects our own souls from triviality. "I dread, from my heart, being shrunk down in heart to the level where my heart's capacities for happiness consist only in silly TV jingles and empty-headed slapstick. That's what I fear. In my life, it is seeing and savoring the all-pervasive providence of God that has protected me from the shrinking of my soul." (2) God's providence protects us from sliding into the "banality, triviality, silliness, superficiality, and an eerie addiction to flippancy and levity" that "has permeated the church and most Christian communication." Embrace providence and be done with the trivial life.[5]

Should we "recharge" or self-medicate with entertainment?
We must recharge. "The mind—John Piper's mind, anyway—cannot always be wound tightly for the sake of maximum rigor in analysis and synthesis. There is a place for more relaxed, passive entertainment. But I personally believe that the Christian should not be entertained by things that require a spiritual bath

4 APJ 1033: "Three Strategies for Overcoming the Superficial Life" (April 26, 2017).
5 APJ 1583: "Escaping the Fog of Triviality" (February 3, 2021).

to cleanse the mind when you are done. That is not a good way to get entertained." Don't violate your conscience in the name of entertainment. Instead, consider audiobooks.[6]

It's when we feel tired, depressed, or discouraged that we are most susceptible to vain media. "Don't medicate your sadness and weariness with television. There are some things, I don't doubt, that may provide innocent and wholesome recreation for your mind. But they are so few and so far between. Most television and most advertisements on television drag your soul away from Christ. They don't promote holiness and purity and heavenly mindedness and nobility of soul. They make you feel small and stupid and silly and childish. Don't join the millions of old people who simply vegetate in front of animated worldliness." Instead, again, consider audiobooks.[7]

What's wrong with watching sitcoms like *Seinfeld* or *Friends*?

The "what's wrong with it?" question comes from a heart "that is basically governed by a desire to *minimize* wrong rather than *maximize* holiness or faith or spiritual power or worship or zeal for the lost or missions or justice." So we could address specific media sins: obscene talk, filthiness, foolishness, and crude joking (Eph. 5:4; Col. 3:8). But the deeper problem is a lack of longing. "I think most Christians are so in the grip of the spirit of the age and in the grip of popular culture and popular entertainments that the kind of radical reorientation I'm talking about is almost unthinkable for them. For me to pitch into that mindset a few little warnings from Bible verses that disapprove of certain things seems to me almost useless." It calls for a more radical reorientation, a "miracle" and "a great work of God, not me."

Does your heart long for more? Do you long for more intimacy with Christ, more spiritual power, to hear God's voice more clearly, to follow his will more closely, to see his "smile of favor" more than his "frowns of discipline"? Do you think in these terms? "Do you go to bed with these longings? Do you wake up with these longings governing your life? Do you devote time, perhaps on the Lord's Day, to seek his face in intensifying these longings? If not, *that's* the issue. *This* is ten thousand times more important than what particular shows you click on. *This* will govern that. But if *this* is missing—if *the growing intensification of these longings in your relationship with Jesus* is missing—no answers will make any difference about your entertainment habits." Only with this "new passion" can we move from "being a nominal, minimalist, 'get-by,' cultural

6   APJ 828: "How Do You Use Your iPhone and iPad in Christian Growth?" (April 1, 2016).
7   APJ 1069: "'My Life Feels Pointless'" (July 19, 2017).

Christian to an authentic, passionate, earnest, God-centered, Christ-exalting, Bible-saturated lover of Jesus." *Then* you can ask: "Does this show build up my faith? Does it weaken my faith?"

It's about becoming the kind of person who lives for eternal realities, and then making life decisions based on that passion. "'Spread a passion for the supremacy of God'—that's what I'm after. I'm after the kind of passion for his supremacy in everything that functions as a radical litmus test on what we find amusing and entertaining in media."[8]

Do I love God more than entertainment?

Our entertainment appetites expose our desires, or at least expose our lacking longings. So what if my desires for entertainment are stronger than my desires for God? Can communion with God win my attention in this age of entertainment?

These questions are serious. Asking them is not legalistic. "I don't think the New Testament ever says, 'Lighten up.' It says, 'Fight to the end.'" Our culture will tell you to relax your entertainment standards. Don't. "Modern-day antinomians, who use their own unbiblical brains to describe the indiscriminate lifestyle of justification, are leading many people astray." In reality, justification doesn't excuse our entertainment decisions. Justification "unleashes a power for holiness which we in fact experience through major spiritual warfare against the world, the flesh, and the devil."

So what do we do when God seems boring compared to our entertainment? Tremble. "And the reason we should tremble is because that preference for the world is the condition of the whole world. The natural man cannot receive or enjoy or be satisfied or find supremely interesting the things of the Spirit. They are foolishness to him (1 Cor. 2:14). That's the mark of the natural man. Therefore, if we feel that way, we should *tremble* because we're acting like mere men—not like children of God." Christ is beautiful and glorious (2 Cor. 3:18). By growing bored with Christ, "something is hindering you from seeing and tasting the totally beautiful, totally interesting, totally satisfying God in Christ and all that he is for us." Here's the battle—that we will desire a greater glory than what's pixelated on our screens.

So how do we fight? Four tangible suggestions. (1) Find a nonbeliever or a new Christian and share your love of Christ. This may feel counterintuitive for a Christian struggling with a dull soul, but "when I am thrown into a situation where my own love for God is tested by my love for people and my desire for them to know God and enjoy eternal life, barriers come down between me and God." (2) Redeem your downtime. We all need downtime. But we need to redeem all our time and not compromise ourselves with worldly entertainment (Eph. 5:15–17). (3) Find good authors to edify your soul, living or dead, an author "who speaks or writes about God as one who has really tasted and seen that God is glorious and beautiful and satisfying and who writes about it in such a way that when you read it, you taste it." (4) In all things, keep up the good fight and battle to the end (2 Tim. 4:7).[9]

What do my entertainment habits say about my own soul?

The question came in during the 2020 coronavirus quarantine. In the stress of being stuck inside, a female listener spent far more time on screens than in communion with God. She asked, What does this reveal about the state of my soul?

Loving God "means that God holds a place of value in our heart that makes us want to know him better, and enjoy him more, and be near him in friendship and fellowship. Movies are not well designed to do that. In fact, most of them are well designed to hinder that and to undermine the very thing that the love of God implies—namely, a passion to know him, a passion to enjoy him and be close to him. Movies do not have that effect. Therefore, defaulting to movies day after day is at least a sign that love for God is weak, and probably growing weaker."

The woman's greatest fear is that she does not love and trust God. But Scripture shows that those two actions will come together, both loving him and trusting him (1 John 5:3–4). "Love for God delights so much in pleasing God and being close to God that obedience to his commandments is not burdensome. And then he attributes that sense of burden-lifted enjoyment of God to the fact that we have overcome the world. In other words, worldliness is not the dominant, controlling force in our lives anymore; it has been broken and overcome" by faith. "Faith receives God, receives all that God is for us in Christ, receives him as such a precious deliverance and help and treasure that the world loses its power to be the most attractive thing in our lives. So, love for God and faith in God are, in the apostle John's mind, overlapping or interlocking realities." By them, "the power of the world to be our controlling treasure is broken, overcome, and obedience has ceased to be burdensome."

Compulsion to the world's entertainment, at the expense of communion with God, at least signals a "defect of faith and love." But what if it's worse? What if our media intake exposes that we are not actually regenerated? "I would not

---

9   APJ 1116: "How Do I Love God More Than My Entertainment?" (November 6, 2017).

spend much time analyzing the failures of the past two months or even a more distant memory of conversion and whether it was real or not. I think that kind of introspection and past-experience analysis, by and large, does not produce the hoped-for outcome—namely, assurance of salvation and peace of mind. Our hearts are simply too deceptive. Our memories and our powers of assessment about the past experiences are too limited to see what we need to see." Repent of the problems you see now. Turn from the sin. And turn to 2 Peter 1:10–11. "The confirmation that we are truly called and truly elect, truly the children of God, truly Christian, happens—the confirmation happens—by stepping into the future with faith and obedience. Assurance of salvation does not primarily come from the analysis of the past but from the God-given earnestness of present and future faith and obedience."[10]

How do I break an entertainment addiction?
The accessibility to entertainment is problematic. "Today we carry radio, television, internet, games, and anything that will be titillating—fun—in our pockets." So how does one break this overdependence on entertainment? (1) See the problem. This is step one. (2) "Pray like crazy that God would open your eyes to see wondrous things out of his *law*"—to see and delight in his *torah* (תּוֹרָה), all of his *teachings* (Ps. 119:18). (3) Soak in Scripture, "even when you don't feel like it. Plead with God to open your eyes to see what is really there." (4) Find friends who love eternal things. (5) Share your faith with others. "One of the reasons we are not as moved by our own faith as we should be is that we almost never talk about it to any unbeliever." When we don't talk about our faith, it begins to "have a feeling of unreality about it, and then the powers of entertainment have more sway in our life." Of course, it's ultimately "a gift of grace to feel the glory of God." (6) Consider death "a lot." What are you going to be doing "in the season of life or hours or days leading up to meeting Christ?" Will he find you serving and delighting in the eternal or passing the time with vanities?[11]

How do I break my addiction to gaming?
A gamer at the console for three hours a day says that he "cannot break" his "addiction to entertainment."

But this is fundamentally untrue. "By labeling this *habit* an *addiction*, you might be giving yourself a partial pass. Whatever you think *addiction* means, it's probably not what you think it is. When you waste three hours of your

10 APJ 1522: "What Do My Entertainment Habits Reveal about My Soul?" (September 7, 2020).
11 APJ 328: "Breaking My Addiction to Entertainment" (April 25, 2014).

precious life playing a video game over and over, this is *not* something you *can't* stop doing."

Two illustrations to reframe the discussion. (1) A negative motivator. "If a man walked up to you while you were playing a video game and lit a blowtorch, and said, 'If you don't stop playing this video game, I will burn your eyeballs out with this blowtorch,' you'd stop—done. Of course you would. It's ludicrous to say you can't stop. You *can* stop." (2) A positive motivator. "If a man walked up to you with a million dollars in cash and convinced you that it was his to give to whomever he pleased, and he offered it to you, all of it, if you would just stop playing that game, it's ludicrous to say you wouldn't stop. You'd stop. Of course you would stop! You're not in bondage to that game. You *can* stop. You *can* walk away from it. I promise you. With a blowtorch in your face or a million dollars in your pocket, it would be easy."

So you *can* stop playing video games for three hours a day, with ample threat or promise. Either way, our natural desires must be dethroned (Rom. 6:12). So to the man who wrote in, who may now feel beat up, "I'm showing him that he is being beaten up by these two-bit pleasures called video games. Two-bit, no-count, low-grade, wasteful video games are beating him up, deceiving him, making him a lackey and a slave." So tear out your eye and cut off your hand (Matt. 5:29). "That is, get rid of all the apps that suck you in and make a slave of you. Just tear them right off your phone. Tear them right off. I mean, tearing out your eye surely has an application to your devices. Say with Paul in 1 Corinthians 7:23, 'My body is not my own. I've been bought with a price—the blood of Jesus. I will not be enslaved to anyone else. He is my master.' Then turn away from the games and receive the million-dollar gift from Jesus. No, no, no, no—that was an understatement. Billions, billions, and billions of dollars' worth of reward! Better than anything else!"[12]

This same argument—overcoming sin with ample warnings or promised rewards—can be applied to the war against lust and pornography.[13]

Avoid a few scenes, or avoid the whole movie?

Scenes ruin movies. "I am appalled at what Christians do for entertainment—by taking it for granted that if it is in the theater, it should be watched. I am appalled, not because I am a prude—I have my favorite movies—but because I am ruined by certain *scenes*. I won't watch certain good movies because of *that scene*. I will not, because Christ is dishonored in my soul, and my mind is

12 APJ 1314: "How Do I Break My Entertainment Addiction?" (February 18, 2019).
13 APJ 530: "The Real Cost of Pornography" (February 11, 2015).

contaminated for months—and he is more precious than the pleasure of the other 124 minutes. Come on. Let's be Christian through and through. Let's get ready to suffer." If we cannot deny ourselves "a little bit of entertainment," how will we ever endure persecution? Christ is our standard. "Use everything to enhance your enjoyment of Jesus. And if it doesn't enhance it, don't do it."[14]

Can we watch sin celebrated on a screen if we're personally revolted by the sin?

A listener wrote in with a question about media that takes the Lord's name in vain. But the answer applies to all media that refuses to show the sinfulness of sin.

"This train left the station sixty years ago, and it's roaring down the track about 250 miles an hour. And I don't simply mean the obvious fact that movies and TV shows long ago forsook the God of the Ten Commandments and the God of the New Testament—who didn't just say, 'Don't take the Lord's name in vain' (Exod. 20:7)." It also abandoned Paul's commands to Christians against filthiness, crude joking, and foolish and corrupting and obscene talk (Eph. 4:29; 5:4; Col. 3:8). "So, that train left the station. I'm not just talking about the train of forsaking such a God at the station; I'm talking about the fact that Christians are on the train."

Little effect will be made to stop the train. But here's a word to a few passengers that might have ears to hear. "The enjoyment of being entertained by sin is the issue. Whether it's the sin of taking the Lord's name in vain; or the sin of cocky, self-exalting arrogance, which seems to permeate everything; or the sin of lust and fornication and adultery and indecency and immodesty, which is virtually ubiquitous; or the sin of distortions of womanhood and manhood; or the sin of disrespecting parents; or the sins of drunkenness; or the sin of desiring to be rich, which Paul said we ought not to do; or the sin of dishonesty; or the sin of slandering with stereotypes; or the sin of simply, profoundly, ubiquitously ignoring and thus not glorifying or thanking God— whatever the sin, the issue is, what does it say about our souls that we enjoy being entertained by them?"

If a Christian viewer says that he is saddened by the on-screen sin: "Well, I'm certainly glad about that." You are "an amazing person, with capacities for purity and holiness far greater than mine. If you can, over and over again, be entertained in your relaxed, amused, pleased state by the enacting of sins that are not treated as sins—they're glorified, they're not treated as sins in the shows, but

---

14 APJ 696: "Does Netflix Make Christ More Precious to You?" (September 30, 2015). For his favorite movies, see APJ 1882: "John Piper's Favorite Things" (January 2, 2023).

as acceptable and often preferable to righteousness—while not being defiled or shaped by those sins, you are an amazing person. I could wish for such holiness."

But for most Christians, who are "tired and want to unwind from a good day's work, we settle in with some series or movie that we hope will be minimally offensive or crass or obscene, and then we're drawn into a suspenseful or interesting plot. And then scene after scene portrays a God-ignoring, man-exalting, sin-condoning, sex-distorting, marriage-weakening, maleness-mocking, femaleness-trivializing, righteousness-ridiculing, arrogance-admiring worldview. We ordinary, struggling saints who long for purity of heart and holiness and all the fruits of the Holy Spirit simply won't be able *not to be* entertained by sin and shaped in our minds and hearts by that very entertaining worldview."[15]

Screen idols

Sinners exchange the glory of God for *images* (Rom. 1:18). "When the real God is rejected, images are embraced" because sin "loves God-substituting images. And we, more than any culture in the history of the world, live in an age of images. We spend almost all our leisure time looking at images. It's quite irrelevant, I think, for Paul, that those images were stone or wood alongside of an Athenian road, and ours are on our phone or television or computer—that's irrelevant! The issue is substitution: we exchange the infinitely valuable glory of God for the glory of that show of images coming off the screen."[16]

So can Christians watch any television or movies at all?

One Christian feels guilty for watching a movie because that time could have been spent in more edifying ways like prayer and Bible reading. Isn't the time spent on television and movies basically out for Christians?

The answer here is analogous to wealth. A rich man accumulated capital by building bigger and bigger barns. His sin was not in laboring or in saving, but in the aim of his saving. He was effectively replacing God with his own wealth and ease and self-security. This was the sin (Luke 12:16–21). The rich man "was planning to play, play, play," and "he was about to lose his soul." This foolish, wealthy man felt no spiritual struggle with wealth. But we should. Most prosperous people in the West "are not being too self-denying, not too ascetic." But this is the Christian's struggle.

Money can become an idol, but we are all commanded to work (Eph. 4:28). "For most people around the world, work has always involved eight to twelve

---

15 APJ 1398: "Is It Sinful to Watch Sin on a Screen?" (November 22, 2019).
16 APJ 560: "The Heart of Screen Addiction" (March 25, 2015).

hours a day of doing things with their hands or feet or backs or brains that are not simply Bible reading and prayer. And that's commanded of us." But after working hard, we are called to rest and to feast (Mark 6:31; 1 Cor. 10:27). So it is "not a sin to take time away from Bible reading and praying and do the more ordinary things that the world does—working, resting, going to dinner, and so on."

When it comes to entertainment, "seek to bring every act into connection with the Lord." Use a fivefold grid for all activities. (1) Do all things for God's glory (1 Cor. 10:31). (2) Do all in the name of Christ (Col. 3:17). (3) Do all things to love others (1 Cor. 16:14). (4) Don't set your hopes on wealth or what wealth can buy, like video games and entertainment (1 Tim. 6:17). (5) Receive all good gifts from God with Godward gratitude to him (1 Tim. 4:4–5). "Paul assumes that there is a way, a necessary way, for Christians to transpose the enjoyments of good things in this world—God-given, good gifts—into worshipful acts that are holy, Christ honoring, and people loving. Those very acts of food and sex make music. You transpose that music into Christ-honoring music by the word of God and prayer—by bringing them into connection with the glory of God, the name of Jesus, and love for people." So gifts are not idols if those gifts become "avenues of knowing God better, enjoying him more, and being a greater blessing to other people." The more challenging you find thankfulness for anything, the more likely that thing "should be replaced with something more fruitful."[17]

What is entertainment doing to me?

Each of us, and pastors especially, need to take our spiritual pulse. What is entertainment doing to my soul? "We must be honest with our hearts here." The hot new movie release, the viral television series, the new video game everyone is playing—do they "leave us refined and intensified in our capacities to revel in the unsearchable riches of Christ in the Scriptures?" Or not? Again, recharging in edifying ways puts audiobooks front and center. "All of us know that there are great books, both fiction and nonfiction, that are a hundred times superior to what is on TV or the trending movies, and which we have always wanted to read anyway. Listening to a great book may not provide the same exactness as reading it. But we are not comparing listening to reading. We are comparing listening to a great book on the one hand to groveling in the world's sensual entertainment on the other hand." So when you need to recharge, and are tempted toward the screen, consider "great and edifying" audiobooks instead.[18]

---

17 APJ 1313: "How Much Entertainment Is Too Much?" (February 15, 2019).
18 APJ 988: "I'm Exhausted—How Do I Recharge My Body without Neglecting My Soul?" (January 11, 2017).

The potency of worldly entertainment to capture the heart should haunt us. "I really felt that the continual danger of drying up spiritually was huge—of waking up some morning and being bored with the Bible and wanting to watch sports on TV instead of studying my Bible. And fortunately, by God's amazing grace, that never happened. 'Take care, brothers, lest there be in any of you an evil, unbelieving heart, leading you to fall away' (Heb. 3:12). But the fear of it happening kept me praying over the word with tremendous pleas for light: 'Lord, please don't let that happen to me. Give me light.' So that is one effect of that pressure. It forced me over the text, into it every day for my soul."[19]

We need personal awakening and global revival, and the world's entertainment won't bring them

We become like what we watch. The dominant object of our attention is our trajectory (2 Cor. 3:12–4:6). We are designed so that "if you behold the glory of God and hold it in fixed view, you will become like him in your mind. You will *think* the way God thinks, *see* the way God sees, *feel* the way God feels, *be repelled by* the things that repel God." It's a lifelong, progressive holiness of degrees (2 Cor. 3:18). Do you desire this? If so, "stop watching the world. Which very practically comes down to television. Why would we want to be entertained so much by unbelievers? Why are we so hooked on music and videos and television and movies? 'World: Tell me! Show me! Feed me! Shape me! Make me!'" And it does. The world shapes us into its own image as we feast on its entertainment. "Compare in your life the degree to which you behold the Lord Jesus and the glory of our God to the degree to which you behold the world. How do they compare?" Maybe this explains our spiritual weakness, susceptibility to temptation, ineffectiveness to change the world, and succumbing to broken relationships we never fix. We watch the world until we "ooze" the world. "Do you want to become holy? Do you want to become new so that you *see* like Jesus, *think* like Jesus, *feel* like Jesus, *love* like Jesus, *care* like Jesus, *judge* like Jesus? If you do, there's the agenda. Watch Jesus. A lot!"[20]

Deprioritizing the world's entertainment will require a generational revolt. "The pursuit of purity of heart (1 Tim. 1:5), possessing the mind of Christ (1 Cor. 2:16), setting our affections on things that are above (Col. 3:1–2),

---

19 APJ 218: "Busy Pastors and Biblical Encounters, Part 1" (November 18, 2013).
20 APJ 1673: "We Become Like the Videos We Behold" (September 1, 2021). On what it looks like to "watch Jesus," see APJ 304: "Visualizing Christ to Battle Lust?" (March 24, 2014), APJ 1886: "How Do I Push Truth from My Head to My Heart?" (January 11, 2023), and APJ 1895: "How to Keep Your Eyes on Christ" (February 1, 2023).

being renewed in the spirit of our thoughts (Eph. 4:23), being transformed in our emotions, keeping our lives unstained from the sinfulness of the world (James 1:27), laying up treasures in heaven and not on earth (Matt. 6:19–20), keeping a clear vision of the light of the gospel of the glory of Christ (2 Cor. 4:4), enjoying the daily fellowship of the Son of God (1 John 1:3), having the eyes of our hearts enlightened to know what is the hope of our calling, and the riches of the glory of our inheritance, and the immeasurable greatness of God's power toward believers (Eph. 1:18–19), the taste of the age to come (Heb. 6:5), freedom from the desires of the eyes and the desires of the flesh and the pride of life (1 John 2:16), the power of the Spirit in our inner being (Eph. 3:16), a clear sight of the breadth and length and height and depth of the love of Christ (Eph. 3:17–18), and the enjoyment of all the fullness of God (Eph. 3:19)—all these precious marks of what it means to be real Christians will require a kind of radical recovery of the ancient early-church commitment to being more intentionally detached from the patterns of the world, especially the patterns of entertainment, for the sake of the everlasting enjoyment of the greatness of Christ." Such a revolt is coming. "I do believe that God will raise up a generation who are so thrilled with what they gain in God and Christ and salvation and the way of righteousness and the sacrifices of love that they will not be intimidated by the accusations that they are a new kind of fundamentalist." They will embrace a countercultural separation from the world's dominant media (2 Cor. 6:16–18).[21]

The church's task in the entertainment age

"The goal of life, worship, and preaching is a people alive to God—knowing God truly, loving him duly." This is the end goal of the preacher. "My people need to know God, and my people need to have passions for God so that they have more satisfaction in God than food or sex or money or sports or media. They're idolaters if they don't." So if that's the pastor's job, how does he do it? Both aims are humanly impossible. "The devil is blinding their minds, and their hearts are as hard as stone. You can't do anything about that in yourself. Preaching is an impossible task; it has an impossible goal. Miracles have to abound in this room [the sanctuary] if anything eternal is going to happen. So what do you do? Those two words: *expository* and *exultation*—with a *u*, not an *a*. Not ex*a*ltation, but ex*u*ltation."

Expository, the first half, "means my job is to see what God has revealed of himself in this book [in Scripture], to see how he revealed it in the very words,

21 APJ 1654: "How Much Media Is Too Much Media?" (July 19, 2021).

phrases, sentences, and paragraphs, and then to find words and structures of thought to teach it." Paul says that elders must be proven "able to teach" (διδακτικόν; 1 Tim. 3:2). That means when the pastor is done, "understanding has happened, light has gone on in the mind," and the hearers are "better aware of the reality of God."

Exultation is the other half, because if the pastor is "not responding with his heart to what he's seen, he's not preaching, and he's not worshiping. There must be evidences in that man's voice, in that man's eyes, in that man's demeanor that he believes this. He *loves* this. He's *afraid* of this. He's *amazed* at this. Whatever the proper emotions are for this particular psalm or text in Romans—whatever those particular, appropriate responses of the heart are—he should have them. That's *exultation*—expository *exultation*."[22]

This visible worship of the preacher—and his flock—is one reason why children belong in the worship gathering. "Long before children fully understand the words said and sung in the service, they are absorbing tremendous amounts of valuable experience. This remains true even if they say that they are bored. Over time, music and words become familiar. The message of the music starts to sink in. The form of the service starts to feel natural. Even if most of the sermon goes right over their heads, experience shows that children hear and remember remarkable things. The content of the prayers, the songs, and the sermon gives parents an unparalleled opportunity to teach their children the great truths of the faith. If parents would only learn to query their children after the service and explain things to them, they would sow enormously valuable seeds for their children's long-term growth in the knowledge of God." This is because "there is a sense of solemnity and awe which children should experience in the presence of God. They should sense the sacred moment, the sacred place. This likely will not happen in children's church. Unfortunately, it is also not likely to happen in many adult services that put a high premium on horizontal chatter rather than vertical joy. We should aim to awaken our children to the greatness and majesty of God, not just his tenderness and familiarity."[23]

Does John Piper hate fun?

Entertainment culture seeps into the church and shows itself in chipper, playful, and "fun" talk. It's out of place. "My lament is with a spirit of flippancy, jokingness, silliness, playfulness—a spirit that is manifestly uncomfortable with serious joy—and only comfortable with chipper, upbeat, jolly feelings of

---

22   APJ 1385: "What Makes a Sermon Good?" (October 23, 2019).
23   APJ 919: "Should Children Sit through 'Big Church'?" (August 15, 2016).

joy language." Churches need more "serious joy—not somber joy, but serious joy. I fear there are so many people who don't have a clue what I am talking about. All they can do is put this into the categories of glum." Churches need pastors who are earnest about life and worship and ministry, happy to be God's children, happy to be called into his service, "and gloriously able to show that and express that without borrowing from the same demeanor and the same vocabulary of a carnival or a talk show."

Pastors are called to deal seriously with God, to see the effects of sin on this world, and to see the local and global effects of suffering. They are called to proclaim the realities of heaven, hell, "the slaughter of Jesus on the cross," his resurrection, the binding power of sin, the blinding power of Satan, the precious gift of the Spirit, the glory of forgiveness, our call to suffer, our hope of eternal glory, "the sweetness of Christian camaraderie," the privilege of ministry, the miracle of new birth, and the gifts of the Holy Spirit. "How in the world does the word *fun* or the phrase *having a blast* fit emotionally with those realities?" It doesn't. Levity here conforms to a culture "infected" with the vocabulary of entertainment and amusement—our "default vocabulary resource" and the "native air" we breathe. "The vocabulary of *earnestness* and *gravity* and *depth* and *weightiness* and *substance*, these are foreign. They make us feel awkward. They are not natural to us. And that is my lament. It is not about words. We have borrowed the language of entertainment to describe sacred, weighty, serious, holy joys. And the best thing we can say to being an ambassador of the King of kings is, 'It is a blast!'"

But Scripture calls us to live with "an intermingling of *gladness* and *gravity*, woven together in the life and preaching of a pastor—or anybody—in such a way that sobers careless people and sweetens the burdens of the saints. I want careless people to be wakened by the sobriety of joy, and I want burdened saints to come in on Sunday morning to have their burdens sweetened and lightened." The language of *fun* and *blast* does neither.

Fun is contextual. "Unbroken seriousness of a melodramatic or somber kind will inevitably communicate a sickness of soul to the great mass of people, and rightly so." Think of a child who simply wants dad to get on the floor and play. "The daddy who cannot do this with abandon and joy and fun and 'having a blast' doing it will not understand the true seriousness of sin because he is not capable of enjoying what God has preserved from its ravages, the ravages of sin. He is really sick. He is a man unfit to lead others to health. In the end, he is earnest about being earnest. He is not earnest about being joyful."

"So my lament is not a lament about the word *fun*. It is a lament about the loss of the capacity to feel and express the *fun* of cotton candy and roller coasters at the fair with our kids and the *tear-stained joy* of soul-saving ministry in the service of a crucified, triumphant King. There is a difference, brothers. There is a difference. And it would be a good thing to use words that help people feel the difference."[24]

Is John Piper happy?

"I have asked this question of myself many, many times—not only because I have written so much about the importance, indeed, indispensability of being happy in God, but also because the Bible simply says, 'Rejoice in the Lord, John Piper!' (Phil. 4:4). So I take up the question, not because I feel any external constraint coming from one of our listeners, but because I live with the question all the time—because I live with the Bible all the time."

Four biblical factors add complexity to the question. (1) Christians are obligated to express *genuine joy* and obligated to express *genuine sadness* (Rom. 9:2–3; 12:15; 2 Cor. 6:10; 1 Pet. 1:6). Christians remain "sensitive to the sorrows of the world," so our happiness "will always be intermingled with sorrow." Each person will handle this differently, but "in this fallen world, true spiritual happiness—that is, Holy Spirit–given happiness—will always be experienced as conflicted and not perfectly harmonious. That's certainly true for me, anyway." (2) Sadness is designed to deepen our joy (Rom. 5:3–4). Tribulation combats our joy, yes, but it also serves our hope and joy in the end. "This tension between sorrow and joy is not merely a tension, but a design by God to make our happiness deeper and purer." (3) The fight *for faith* is the fight *for joy*. (4) Hence, pastors labor for the joy of others (2 Cor. 1:24) and for their own "progress and joy in the faith" (Phil. 1:25).

So is John Piper happy? "*Yes*, I am happy. And, *yes*, a huge component of this happiness is what Paul calls in Romans 5:2, 'Rejoicing in hope.' In other words, looking beyond the present reasons for sadness" that are "sometimes overwhelming," and seeing into "the future reasons for joy, where all the sad things will be set right. God intends for the promises of that future joy to penetrate back into the present and sustain us with measures of joy now in the midst of sorrow."

He is happy, but fallibly unhappy. His failures in personal evangelism are driven by a fearful "*failure to rejoice* in the promises of God and his care for

---

24 APJ 905: "Does John Piper Hate Fun?" (July 26, 2016). Variations of Piper's catchphrase ("joyful seriousness" or "serious joy") made thirty-five appearances in the first decade of the podcast. Most fully here in APJ 905: "Does John Piper Hate Fun?" (July 26, 2016). See also APJ 1234: "Three Threats to the Joy of This Generation" (August 8, 2018) and APJ 1374: "John Piper's Most Bizarre Moment in Preaching" (September 27, 2019).

me and his promise to work with me and through me." His failures in anger, "which have probably cost me more than I know, are owing to *failures to rejoice* in the providence and grace and goodness of God." His failures of lust "are owing to *failures of joy* that come through the pure-eyed sight of God's all-satisfying glory."

And yet "God is the lodestar of my sky. He's the true north of my life compass. He is the blazing sun at the center of my emotional solar system, and he is the unerasable home setting on the GPS of my life." So for seventy years now, when his heart "begins to wander toward another competing satisfaction," God "has always exerted a Holy Spirit gravitational pull on me that has brought the planets of my life back into their God-treasuring orbits around his glory. I very much look forward to the day when I'm with Jesus, when I will be free from warfare and free from sinning." So is John Piper happy? His answer today is complex. But "I think if you ask me the same question in fifty years, I will answer from heaven with a simple yes!"[25]

25 APJ 1034: "Is John Piper Happy?" (April 28, 2017).

On Lust, Porn, and TV Nudity

Watching sex scenes

A husband is comfortable with racy sex scenes in movies; his wife isn't. And she's right. The sin of playacting sin on a screen to stimulate lust in viewers is a sin that Christ died for. Sin is not a toy. And watching sex as entertainment is the opposite of loving the actors.

A man enjoying a topless woman on screen is unloving, "because watching these scenes, buying these movies, and paying to go see them endorses—de facto—the behaviors and desires in those scenes and those women that are going to destroy them." The viewer is complicit in how sinful scenes will corrode the marriage or future marriage of an actress who "has stripped herself bare for so many men and has been touched in so many ways that nothing seems sacred and pure and precious anymore for her husband." It also ignores the heartbreak of her parents and family.

Such lust for nudity on a screen is "just plain adulterous. This wife is naive, I think, if she thinks that these scenes in her husband's head have no relationship to how he relates to her. That's crazy. That means every time he is lying with her, he has competitors in his brain. He does. And the more he has watched, the more competitors he has." And when the wife seems less attractive, "he will just switch gears and go into one of those scenes, and that is the way he will have his stimulation. That's adultery."

Lust distorts the soul. "Our souls shrink to the kind of pleasures we are indulging in." Such sin-laced media damages our communion with God. It blinds us to natural glories in sunsets. The costs are so high, the husband is a "jerk" to not respect his wife's conscience in this scenario. Sex is not made to be prostituted on the screen. Sex "is not a spectator's sport."[1]

To sharpen the point of the question, we targeted *Game of Thrones* (2011–2019), a popular television series rated TV-MA, infamous for explicit nudity

[1] APJ 149: "My Husband Is Okay with Racy Scenes—I Hate It" (August 13, 2013).

and sex scenes, and even graphic scenes of rape and sexual violence against women. Can Christians, in good conscience, enjoy such a show?

"The closer I get to death, and meeting Jesus personally face-to-face, and giving an account for my life and for the careless words that I have spoken—and how much more for intentional stares—the surer I am of my resolve never intentionally to look at a TV show or a movie or a website or a magazine where I know I will see photos or films of nudity. Never. That is my resolve." Such a conviction runs against the culture where "entertainment media is virtually the lingua franca of the world." Instead, Christians accept the "invitation to be an alien. And I believe with all my heart that what the world needs is radically bold, sacrificially loving, God-besotted freaks—aliens. In other words, I am inviting you to say *no* to the world *for the sake of the world*. The world does not need more cool, hip, culturally savvy, irrelevant copies of itself. That is a hoax that thousands of young Christians have been duped by. They have got to be hip, cool, savvy, culturally aware, watching everything in order not to be freakish. And that is undoing them morally and, I think, diminishing their witness."

There are twelve good reasons to say no to *Game of Thrones* and any popular entertainment featuring nudity. (1) Realize that Christ died to forgive your past lust and to break the power of your present lust. "It is an absolute travesty of the cross to treat it as though Jesus died only to forgive us for the sin of watching nudity and not to purify us for the power not to watch it." He died to forgive us *and* to purify us (Titus 2:14). "If we choose to endorse or embrace or enjoy or pursue impurity, we take a spear and ram it into Jesus's side every time we do." Live free from the bondage of lust. (2) Radical holiness is the expectation for our redeemed lives (2 Cor. 7:1; 1 Pet. 1:15). Televised nudity cannot advance our calling to purity. (3) Imagined lust is real sin (Matt. 5:28–29). "If Jesus told us to guard our hearts by gouging out our eyes to prevent lust, how much more would he say, 'Don't watch it'?" (4) Use your freedom for holiness and love, not for distorted selfishness (Gal. 5:13; Phil. 4:8). (5) Aspire to see God (Matt. 5:8). Pure eyes are the mark of one who wants more of God. "The defilement of the mind and heart by watching nudity dulls the heart's ability to see and enjoy God. I dare anyone to watch nudity and turn straight to God and give him thanks and enjoy him more because of what you just experienced." (6) Value modesty (1 Tim. 2:9). Televised nudity celebrates its opposite. (7) Imagine the pain. Would you want the world to see your wife or daughter nude on television? You are watching someone's child, spouse, or future spouse. (8) Televised nudity is real. On-screen murder is pretend, with fake blood and painted-on bruises and scars. "But nudity is not make-believe. These actresses are really naked in front of the camera, doing exactly what the director says to do with their legs and their hands and their breasts," in front of "millions of people for the world to see." (9) On-screen nudity is perversion. Sex is for covenant marriage. Actors and actresses "who want to be watched in their nudity are in the category of exhibitionists who pull down their pants at the top of escalators." (10) Great films don't need nakedness. "It is not art that puts nudity in film. It is the appeal of prurience. It sells." (11) The pressure of the world keeps Christians coming back to the screen. "If they took Christ at his word and made holiness as serious as I am saying it is, they would have to stop seeing so many TV shows and movies. They would be viewed as freakish. And, today, that is the worst evil of all. To be seen as freakish is a much greater evil than to be unholy." (12) Listen to your doubts (Rom. 14:23). If you doubt, don't watch. This point alone "would alter the viewing habits of millions. And, oh, how sweetly they would sleep with their conscience."[2]

Is it sinful to watch porn with a spouse?

Yes, watching porn together is "a revolting sin," a twisted distortion of marriage and of Christ's love to the church. "It is inconceivable that the pleasures Christ has in the church would be awakened and stimulated by his imagining a prostitute." In the Bible, the pleasures of Christ in his church represent the pleasures of a husband in his wife. The intimacy of married sex is how you say to your spouse: "You have I chosen above all others. You alone are the one in whom I feast with pure and unsullied pleasure. I have eyes for no one but you. I do not run after other women in my mind or in my body. I am utterly devoted to you with my mind, with my eyes, with my body. You alone are my pleasure." So "what does it say about Christ and his love to his church if you feed the moment of sweetest, purest union with the poison of putrid food from pornographic sexual sin?"

To the man who suggested that his wife watch porn with him: "This is a great insult to your wife. Husband, if you have tempted your wife, cajoled her, lured her, persuaded her, seduced her into this pornographic delusion of marital love, you should be ashamed. You should repent now to God, and you should tell her how sorry you are for contaminating something so pure, so tender, so deep, so holy with something so vile. And yes, you should say *vile*. You need to have a word like *vile* in your vocabulary. She is not honored by this practice. She is debased. And a husband who insists on this is acting like an animal, not a husband." This "revolting sin" blasphemes Christ, celebrates a sin-sick porn industry, and insults the wife you are called to cherish and nourish.[3]

2 APJ 368: "Should Christians Watch *Game of Thrones*?" (June 20, 2014).
3 APJ 955: "Is It Sinful to Watch Porn with My Spouse?" (October 26, 2016).

More generally, wives are forbidden from joining in a husband's sin. "A wife never follows her husband into sin" because Christ is her "ultimate head"— an authority that always trumps her husband.[4] Peter applies this point to wives of unbelieving husbands (1 Pet. 3:1–6). Wives submit to their husbands, but not absolutely. "The whole point of that passage is that a woman has a new Lord, Jesus, above her husband—and she is trying to win her husband to join her in that allegiance to Jesus."[5]

Pornography's evil

Pornography, the use of explicit images and videos for self-stimulation and masturbation, is a dominant issue for men (and women). It includes an image or video used to sexually fantasize about someone who is not your spouse.

In the context of men, porn is evil in four ways. (1) Porn use is unloving. Men and women who sell their naked bodies for money or attention are engaged in practices that will condemn them eternally if they don't repent. At the same time, these actions erode the potential of fulfillment with a future spouse. Such viewing is unloving to the heartbroken parents of this naked actor. It is the opposite of love for a man to enjoy watching a woman break her parents' hearts, weaken her hope for future marriage, and flaunt nudity or engage in fornication that could condemn her eternally. (2) Porn use is adultery. Porn "cultivates and pursues mental and physical pleasures that are made by God to flourish in marriage" (Matt. 5:27–30). (3) Porn use destroys the viewer's marriage, as a power "destructive to a man's capacities to love a woman purely for herself." Instead he's "training himself and his body, when he engages in pornography, to need increasingly different, strange, erotic situations and bodies." Men who fail to cultivate a "pure love" for a wife will have eyes "cruising continually beyond what she has to offer him at forty and fifty and sixty. A woman needs to be able to trust a man. She needs to be able to believe he is okay when she says, 'I am what you have. I am what you need. You don't have to have eyes for another woman.' A woman feels profoundly compromised when a man says to her, 'No, I really need more than you can offer me.'" Porn destroys a man's capacity to love his wife for who she is. (4) Porn use ravages souls. Porn destroys a man's capacity to see the purity and the greatness of God's glory. "The soul tends to shrink to the size and the quality of its pleasures. A man may say to his soul, 'Adapt yourself now to this low, brief, unclean, selfish pleasure. Adapt yourself to this, soul. Get yourself around this, soul. Form yourself around this,

4   APJ 495: "What Will Submission to My Husband Look Like?" (December 18, 2014).
5   APJ 680: "Hope for Hard Marriages" (September 8, 2015).

soul?' And if he does, it will become that small. When a soul shrinks like that, it won't be able to make much of God, won't be able to see God, won't be able to delight in God anywhere near like God should be delighted in, in the glorious pleasures that he offers us in his word and in his world."

These four arguments are strong deterrents for any Christian man who seeks to treasure Christ above all else. "If Jesus is not just a doctrine but is Lord and friend and Savior and supreme treasure of our lives, the way he should be, then we won't be continually hating women with our choices to demean them and confirm their destruction. We won't be continually committing adultery in our hearts with those women. We won't be continually defiling our capacity to love our present or future wives. We won't be continually shrinking our soul's ability to savor the glories of God. We won't, because Jesus is so utterly different than that."

The Bible leaves no excuses for men addicted to porn. "We have treated men like dogs in heat rather than men who are created in the image of God and who have the Holy Spirit, whose fruit is love, joy, and self-control. That last one, self-control, is usually used in relation to sexuality. Men are not victims, and women have a right to expect more from us."[6]

Killing the lust for porn inside us

In the realm of temptations, porn is a "monster." Lust must be killed immediately, given the urgency of what the Bible says is at stake.

1. Get the gospel first. "The first thing you need to establish is that getting right with God precedes getting our pornography issues fixed. That is, justification precedes, and is the foundation for, sanctification. The only sin that we can defeat is a forgiven sin." Try to kill your porn-driven lust *in order to get right with God*, and you have "the opposite of Christianity."

2. Feel the urgency of the lostness at stake. As Jesus warns: "If your right eye causes you to sin, tear it out and throw it away. For it is better that you lose one of your members than that your whole body be thrown into hell" (Matt. 5:29).

3. Count the cost. Porn kills our delight in God, a terrible trade for a lesser pleasure. "I know from my own experience, the times when I give way to any

---

6 APJ 122: "Is My Boyfriend's Porn a Marriage Deal-Breaker?" (June 28, 2013). On replacing the term "addiction" for "sinful excess," see APJ 530: "The Real Cost of Pornography" (February 11, 2015) (on porn addiction), APJ 657: "How Do I Choose between Two Good Things?" (August 7, 2015) (on digital media and smartphone addiction), APJ 1314: "How Do I Break My Entertainment Addiction?" (February 18, 2019) (on gaming and video entertainment addiction), and APJ 1702: "On Cigarettes, Vaping, and Nicotine" (November 8, 2021) (on nicotine, vaping, and smoking addictions).

kind of sensuality, my capacities for spiritual delight in God diminish, and I know that the tradeoff is always lousy. So for the sake of greater joy in a greater pleasure, we fight against temptation."

4. Subdue lust with theology. Paul tells Christians to abstain from sexual sin and not to be guided by "the passion of lust like the Gentiles *who do not know God*" (1 Thess. 4:5). In the battle against porn, feed yourself on great theology. Push yourself to know God more deeply. Because when Satan tempts us to lust, we tend to rely on our "little pea-shooter, Sunday school–level knowledge of God to try to defeat Satan's attack. There are such vast, deep, glorious, beautiful, strong, wonderful things about God, and when you are grasped by them, there is a powerful effect of making sensuality less attractive in your life." Robust theology "is an indirect way of undermining the powerful effects of sexual temptation." Seek divine glories that can outshine the false, flashy bait of lust.

5. Read great books on the art of sin-killing, like John Owen's *Mortification of Sin.*

6. Respond to temptations with ANTHEM, an acronym coined for every battle with lust. It stands for immediately (*A*) *avoiding* giving in to the temptation, consciously saying (*N*) *no* to the temptation within five seconds, (*T*) *turning* your mind and heart to something greater, like the glory of Christ crucified, (*H*) *holding* in view this beautiful vision of Christ in your consciousness "until it triumphs over the other sensual vision," (*E*) *enjoying* Christ and his blood-bought promises, and finally (*M*) *moving* to an activity that honors Christ. "I wrote that [acronym] not as some theoretical proposal of how to fight temptation. I wrote it because in the backyard one day, I was pushing my lawn mower after my wife had just told me the night before that some people were fooling around behind our garage. And as I passed by pushing my lawn mower, my mind immediately created that scene and became lustful at that moment. I had to fight back just to get this thing out of my head."[7]

Defeating porn with warnings and rewards

Anyone can overcome a moment of sin—even lust and porn—with ample warnings or promised rewards. "Lust is a sexual desire that dishonors its object and disregards God. Lust disregards the promises and the warnings of having or losing the beauties of Christ." It treats nudity on the screen (or lust in the imagination) as something less than the body-objectifying and belittling activity that it truly is.

---

7   APJ 18: "Fighting Porn Addiction with Grudem's Systematic Theology" (February 1, 2013). For more on ANTHEM, see John Piper, *Collected Works*, ed. Justin Taylor and David Mathis (Wheaton, IL: Crossway, 2017), 11:89–91.

The term *addiction* is "relative" because no man or woman is "absolutely addicted to pornography or any sexual sin." Indeed, "if the stakes are high enough and sure enough, you will have all the self-control you need to conquer any sexual temptation." Take the examples of warning and reward. (1) Imagine a moment when you are totally fallen into the "sway of a sexual desire—more blazing, more powerful than you have ever felt it in your life," and in that moment you think you cannot resist online porn. But suddenly an ISIS terrorist barges in the room, pulling your best friend or spouse in front of you to say, "'If you click on the porn, their throat will be slit.'" In that moment, "you will have self-control. You are not addicted. You won't click." (2) Or imagine a reward. Someone walks in with a duffle bag stuffed with a million dollars. All you must do is resist the porn. Same result—"total self-control." In the end, "99 percent of those who give way to lust in pornography or fornication or adultery are not decisively controlled by their *sexual desire*; they are decisively controlled by what they *believe*, what they *believe* will happen if they act on the lust or don't." And compulsive porn habits can be stopped if the warnings or promises are strong enough.

But neither this warning nor this reward is expressly Christian. The gospel reminds us that we have Christ and his Spirit in the battle. "The blood of Christ was the price of our self-control, and the beauty of Christ is the mission of the Spirit in us. The blood of Christ purchases the presence of the Christ-exalting Spirit, and the Spirit is there to exalt Christ in all that we do, including self-control" (Ezek. 36:27). In Christ, we see that the stakes are far higher than an ISIS execution or a million-dollar reward. The Spirit reveals, through the word, "that the all-satisfying beauties of Christ can be lost forever in the bondage of lust, or they can be enjoyed forever in the purity of heart (Matt. 5:8, 29). That is what he shows us. That is how he works the miracle in us." The stakes with lust couldn't be higher. Do we believe it?[8]

Did Jesus advocate for castration to break lust addictions?
Porn is eternally perilous (Mark 9:43). In such light, a man who struggles greatly with pornography use asks if Jesus advocated for man-made eunuchs—what today amounts to surgical or chemical castration (Matt. 19:12).

This extreme response is doubtful, for four reasons. (1) The option is not prescribed. Even if Jesus was talking about "physical castration literally," it doesn't mean he's offering it up as an option. "It's not a mandate, and it's not a prohibition." (2) If you lust, Jesus says to gouge out *one eye*, not both (Matt. 5:29). But if you only gouge out the right eye, that means the left eye is "perfectly free to

---

8   APJ 530: "The Real Cost of Pornography" (February 11, 2015).

continue with lust." So it's highly doubtful that Jesus was speaking literally here because jamming a screwdriver into your right eye won't remedy the problem. "The left eye will pick up right where the right eye left off." So *yes*, this remains a deadly serious call to mortify lust. But *no*, it's not a call for literal self-mutilation. (3) Jesus's words seem to refer "to a radical call to chaste celibacy—like Paul in 1 Corinthians 7—rather than physical castration." (4) But don't rule out "physical steps to dampen one's sexual drive if the aim is spiritual victory over sin." There are other ways to weaken the potency of all sorts of personal temptations by working out and going for walks. In the end, take "physical steps to mute the power of lust or of whatever impulse it is that is leading us into sin. But I would beware of procedures that have permanent and unknown personal effects."[9]

Does porn disqualify a pastor from ministry?

Any episode of porn use by a pastor should jumpstart Matthew 18 by a church's leadership team. "Go with the informant to talk to him personally, privately." Disqualification will depend. Is this "an isolated incident or a pattern?" If it was a nonrepeated stumble, an "aberration of his consistent purity of heart, purity of eyes, purity of relationships, then I would try to resolve it privately with his wife and the other elders." But if the incident is part of an ongoing habit, "I do regard him as unqualified for the pastoral ministry, the eldership." Here are nine priciples why. (1) He doesn't conform to the high moral standards held for leaders in the Pastoral Epistles. (2) He has disrespected and possibly proven himself unfaithful to his wife. (3) His heart is impure, and he cannot see God clearly (Matt. 5:8). "How can you lead a people if you can't see God for who he really is and are constantly defiling your ability to see the Lord?" (4) He lacks the sexual purity demanded of him in dealing with women in his church. (5) He lacks self-control, an explicit elder qualification. (6) He would lose the respect of outsiders who learned of this behavior. (7) He's analogous to an elder with a sinful love of alcohol or money, both forbidden (1 Tim. 3:3). Because "if money and wine knock you out of the ministry, how much more the inability to overcome the temptation to pornography?" (8) He dishonors eternal beings. The nude women on screen "are real women" with souls who are headed to heaven or hell. Of all people, he should know the cost of their decisions on their soul and on their future marriages. (9) He has undermined the credibility he needs to call his church to holiness and purity. "So, the fact that the New Testament elevates the qualifications for leadership in the church above what is expected of all Christians—and even those are high—makes it

9   APJ 1157: "Did Jesus Advocate Castration to Break Sex Addiction?" (February 9, 2018).

ON LUST, PORN, AND TV NUDITY 317

difficult to imagine how a pastor in a pattern of pornography could be qualified to lead the flock of God into a more holy and pure walk with God, which is what his job is at its heart."

Of course, there's blood-bought forgiveness for all sin, even a pastor's sin. Grace is powerful for us all. But the same grace that is *forgiving grace* is also *protective grace*, guarding the church so she can maintain "godly examples in leadership." In the end, "I would encourage pastors who are in a pattern of pornography to step down."[10]

Killing lust by desiring God

Paul calls Christians to "abstain from sexual immorality" and to live self-controlled, honorable lives, "not in the passion of lust like the Gentiles *who do not know God*" (1 Thess. 4:3–5). This text is foundational to every podcast episode on the fight against lust. To *not* know God is to be enslaved by the flesh. "Lust comes from not knowing God, having no regard for God, not holding him as the supremely holy and important one in your life." Thus, disregarding what Scripture says about sex does not disregard man, but disregards God (1 Thess. 4:8). Lust fills a theological vacuum. "Lust is taking a perfectly good thing that God created—namely, sexual desire—and abstracting it or stripping it off from an honor toward a person and stripping it off from a supreme regard for God's holiness. You take God away, and you take the honor of man away, and what you have left in sexual desire is lust."[11] By implication, however, "knowing God has a powerful effect on subduing passions" when we see and learn and love that "there are such vast, deep, glorious, beautiful, strong, and wonderful things about God. And when you are *grasped* by them, there is a powerful effect of making sensuality less attractive in your life."[12]

The point becomes a sin-fighting strategy. Shameful embarrassment does not kill lust. But the presence of God's glory does. Lust's great tragedy is that it undermines what we need most, which is deep intimacy with God (Matt. 5:8). So "the way to fight lust is by feeding faith with the knowledge of an irresistibly glorious God." If you want to defeat sexual sin, ask: "Do you know God? Are you engaged in week-by-week growth in knowing God? Do you meditate on God's word day and night? Do you spend time focusing on the snapshots of the image of God, in his Son, in the Gospels? Do you read great, solid books that describe the character and the ways of God? Do you associate with people who are God-besotted and God-saturated? Are you praying daily, sometimes with

10 APJ 946: "Does Porn Use Disqualify a Pastor?" (October 5, 2016).
11 APJ 426: "Lust Defined" (September 10, 2014).
12 APJ 18: "Fighting Porn Addiction with Grudem's Systematic Theology" (February 1, 2013).

fasting, that God would so waken and quicken your heart that you would have the capacity to be ravished by the irresistible glory of God—with emotion, and a movement, and a joy overpowering all the passions that can go out toward pornography? Are you engaged in the warfare at that level?" Expel the "junk" of lust from your heart by "knowing God in all his irresistible glory." Become "greedy for God" to escape the bondage of porn.[13]

You can't fight lust with only an academic knowledge of theology. A head knowledge of God cannot repel the potency of sexual lust. We must get greedy for a heart-enrapturing experience of "God's greatness, his grandeur, his glory, his beauty, his power, his wisdom, his justice, his goodness, his truth. It is a knowledge that *humbles you* and *wins you* and *holds you*."[14] In such a context, where sexual passions control and ruin lives, Paul explains that slaves of lust "don't see, don't meditate on, don't know, don't absorb, don't receive the knowledge of God (1 Thess. 4:3–5). In other words, they haven't been 'renewed in knowledge' (Col. 3:10). They haven't 'set their minds' to behold the glory of Jesus day and night so that they become *like* what they admire (2 Cor. 4:6; Col. 3:2). They are at the mercy of their sinful passions because they haven't been transformed by putting on the new self, renewed in knowledge. That's the biblical pattern of transforming our minds and our hearts so that we are less vulnerable to sexual temptation. It's both *resistance* against unbelief and temptation and doubt and Satan, and it is the sweet and enjoyable *reception*, through God's word, of the preciousness and the beauty and the greatness of Jesus."[15]

Freud got it backward. Lust is a symptom, not the root problem. In Psalm 51, David repents of his grievous sin against Bathsheba. But he doesn't dwell on lust—in fact, he never mentions it. Instead, his confession is a prayer: "Restore to me the joy of your salvation" (Ps. 51:12). The takeaway: "The misuse of the beautiful gift of sex is a symptom of a disease, not the disease." Lust is not the main issue. Here's the main issue: "'Restore to me the joy of your salvation.' Because when that joy fades, I click on pornography. When that joy fades, I start cruising the neighborhood. When that joy fades, I get an itch for another woman."[16]

So in this fallen world, lust bondage is the consequence of a broken exchange (Rom. 1:22–28). Sinners exchange God's beauty for created things. And when sinners give up God, God gives sinners over to lust, to dishonor themselves sexually. It all begins with a trade. These sinners did not "*acknowledge* God"

13 APJ 456: "Winning the War against Lust" (October 22, 2014).
14 APJ 436: "The High Cost of Sexual Sin" (September 24, 2014).
15 APJ 1153: "Two Strategies to Win the War on Lust" (January 31, 2018).
16 APJ 396: "Why Sex Is Not the Root of Sexual Sins" (July 30, 2014).

(Rom. 1:28). Or, using Piper's own translation, these sinners "did not *approve* (δοκιμάζω) of having God in their knowledge." Replace *acknowledge* with *approve* to "feel the horror of it."[17] They don't *want* God.[18] So "nobody's main problem is an *ignorance problem*" but a "*preference problem*" with God: "'I don't want you in my head. I don't want you in my heart. I don't want you to be supremely valuable. I will not have a God in my life who is supremely valuable. I just won't.'" Sinners who don't *desire God* are given over to a debased mind, to *desire sin*. The absence of desire for God is the vertical root of all other horizontal social chaos.[19]

Without a new desire for God, the heart will go on lusting. "One of the main reasons that we are drowning today in America, and in the church, in an ocean of lust and pornography—men and women committing fornication, adultery, masturbation, exhibitionism, homosexuality, bestiality, rape, and sexual innuendo on every screen—is that we are intellectually and emotionally disconnected from infinite, soul-staggering, divine grandeur. And instead we are drowning in a sea of triviality, pettiness, banality, and silliness. We have lost, by and large, our capacity for being staggered by divine grandeur, and we live at a low dog-in-heat level. Television is trivial. Music is trivial. Conversation is trivial. Education is trivial. Christian books are pressed by publishers to be trivial. Worship styles become increasingly trivial. We trifle with our little jokey ways so if everybody feels comfortable in our jokey churches, they might come back. We have lost our capacity to be staggered by the terrifyingly joyous dread and peace of an infinitely untouchable, embracing God. Life is just boring, humdrum. And when a creature—created by God to live in the presence of God and to be staggered by the glory of his infinite power and justice and wisdom and truth and grace—swims in an ocean of triviality, it must be that he will embrace the best buzz available. And it is sex."

Mental strategies like ANTHEM (see under "Killing the lust for porn inside us") are valuable tools. But God must resuscitate the heart. He must awaken in us new desires for him. Indeed, "sex is one of a hundred issues that will overwhelm you and debase you if your life is out of touch with the magnificence of God." If all the trivial things of this world only feed our bondage to lust, our only hope is to become "intellectually and emotionally staggered by God."[20]

"I know without the shadow of a doubt, on biblical authority, that the little spaceships of our moral regimes—our little tactics to fight lust [like ANTHEM],

17 APJ 871: "How Our Sex Life Manifests Our Soul Health" (June 1, 2016).
18 APJ 181: "How Do We Know God's Will?" (September 26, 2013).
19 APJ 871: "How Our Sex Life Manifests Our Soul Health" (June 1, 2016).
20 APJ 1610: "Escape the World's Infatuation with Sex" (April 7, 2021).

our little spaceships to nudge the planet of our sexuality back into orbit—are absolutely futile if the supremacy of Christ is not the sun at the center of the solar system of our life. I know that. I don't know many things, but I know that beyond the shadow of a doubt." So "when you're not reading substantial theology, how do you think you're fighting lust? We are made to know Christ. We are not made to do little diddly things. We're made to know this massive Christ. This world is a little two-second slice, and then we are with him—or not—forever."[21]

Visualizing Christ to beat porn

The *H* in ANTHEM (see under "Killing the lust for porn inside us," above) stands for "holding a beautiful vision of Jesus in your mind until it triumphs over the other sensual vision." So how exactly does this work in practice?

To begin, visualization has challenges. We're not visualizing a gentle, soft, and warm version of Jesus but the violence of the crucifixion through revealed words like: "cross, blood, nails, spear, side of body, hands, feet, thorns, beard, spit, rod, sun-darkened hill." These words form sights and sounds of the cross that are meant to be heard and seen and felt by us today. "I fight nudity in my mind with Christ's misery on the cross." There "Christ died to make me pure. This lustful thought is not pure." So in that moment of temptation, picture Christ dying for your sin, proclaiming his love to you as he dies to break your sin bondage. It's not a photo-realistic image, but a "word-created" image, one Paul clearly lived by (Gal. 2:20). Yet Paul really saw people crucified with his own eyes. So "when he said, Christ 'gave himself for me,' I can't believe that he didn't have some picture—if not photographic—in his mind of Christ suffering profoundly for his purity, and, thus, his faith was empowered to defeat lust." We who have never seen a crucifixion have the same power available to us in the gospel, as we behold the crucifixion in our imagination.[22]

Don't fight alone

Figuratively speaking, in the battle for holiness, the apostle Paul self-punished. He landed punches to his own face, giving himself a black eye (ὑπωπιάζω) for the purpose of gaining self-control over his selfish desires (1 Cor. 9:26–27). This is the vigilance we need to battle porn. Our most potent sins can only be "punched out" by a radical self-denial and severe "self-opposition" (Matt. 5:29). Jesus's words are clearly figurative, because by saying to tear out your

---

21 APJ 1628: "The Key to Killing Lust" (May 19, 2021).
22 APJ 304: "Visualizing Christ to Battle Lust?" (March 24, 2014). To see this practice demonstrated, see APJ 1886: "How Do I Push Truth from My Head to My Heart?" (January 11, 2023) and APJ 1895: "How to Keep Your Eyes on Christ" (February 1, 2023).

right eye, you still have the left eye, "and you can seek the naked woman just as well with your left eye as your right eye. So we know that the literal tearing out of the right eye wouldn't solve the problem. He means that you should be as vigilant and as forceful in your opposition to sin as you need to be in order to kill it in your life."

Our approach requires such force because porn taps into a "psycho-erotic euphoria," drawing us to click "or to linger over some bathing-suit issue of *Sports Illustrated*, or to linger over some ad for a movie." This euphoria is not localized but wields a power that can consume the entire body, "that makes you so pleased by the erotic, by the visual, that you are moving toward it visually with such a force that it starts to nullify moral conviction."

Lust is like drunkenness. Imagine your friend is out and gets drunk and plans to drive home. You block his plans and drive him home instead. Lust is likewise an intoxication that requires "personal accountability where we have some kind of connection, some kind of special number on our cell phone, a way to call up a friend" in moments of temptation. When lust temptations hit, reach out to a friend who can point you to greater truths. Take strong action. Call on friends to help prevent you from being "hardened by the deceitfulness of sin" (Heb. 3:13). Set in place a drastic protocol. Because no action you take can exceed the radical call of Jesus in these moments (Matt. 5:27–30).[23]

The power of porn is most felt by those who resist it

A man who continues to give himself to porn, enjoys it and then feels guilty later is not *struggling* with porn. "Calling it a *struggle* is a little less damning than what it really is, namely, *capitulation* and *participation*." Better to reserve the word *struggle* for the man who "conquers the temptation ninety-nine times out of a hundred, and in a moment of weakness gives in, but quickly turns away and repents." That's truer to a *struggle*. In both cases, sin is sin.[24] With pornography just a click away, must a man give in to the sin to know its true power? No! Men who repeatedly give in to lust should not call it a *struggle*. It's not a struggle to give yourself over and over to sin. It's to be a "wimp" who gives in too easily. The one who best *struggles* against the power of lust is the man who resists porn to the point of bloodshed, a point made by a graphic parable.[25]

The power of lust is most deeply felt by the man who always resisted giving in to temptation—Christ. No one can better sympathize with us in our weaknesses. He was truly tempted by sin "in every respect" (Heb. 4:15). In the words

23 APJ 60: "How Can We Serve One Another in Battling Lust?" (April 2, 2013).
24 APJ 963: "Did My Lust Cause Our Miscarriage?" (November 14, 2016).
25 APJ 291: "Pornography and Resisting the Power of Temptation" (March 5, 2014).

of C. S. Lewis, "a man who gives in to temptation after five minutes simply does not know what it would have been like an hour later." Hence, bad people "know very little about badness" because they simply give in to their desires. "We never find out the strength of the evil impulse inside us until we try to fight it, and Christ, because he was the only man who never yielded to temptation, is also the only man who knows to the full what temptation means—the only complete realist."[26]

The Christian *struggle* with porn is refusing to succumb to the temptation. Such a Christlike realist "should shout at the top of his lungs, with clenched fists and gritted teeth, in the face of Satan's lie: 'I am not helpless! God did not make me to drift. I am not a jellyfish in the currents of lust. That is not what God created human beings to be. That is not why Christ died for me. That is not why I have the Holy Spirit. That is not why I am a new creature in Christ. I am not helpless. I have Christ. I have the Holy Spirit. I have the blood of the cross of the Son of God. I have the hope of glory. I have the entire word of God. I have the promises of grace. I am not helpless! God, get that lie out of my life.' As long as men and women play the victim—as if lust is an omnipotent enemy, and they are helpless—they are done for." We all have a choice: "the enjoyment of God forever" or "the rush" of porn right now. The stakes are sky-high.[27]

Mental sex is for marriage

Looking at a woman with lustful intent is analogous to having sex with her mentally. And for anyone who is not your spouse, it is forbidden (Matt. 5:28). "This means that doing sex in your mind—looking at a woman and thinking through some fantasy where you get into bed with her or take off her clothes— is *not* supposed to happen. You are supposed to gouge out your eye rather than let that happen," because this is meant for marriage. But on the flip side, it also means that "you *are* supposed to have mental sex in marriage as well as physical sex."[28] Within the context of marriage where a couple each serve to "the other's maximum pleasure," a husband cannot lust after his wife (1 Cor. 7:3). Indeed, it's not wrong for "a husband to want his wife sexually and to think about having her and to hold her in his mind the way he would hold her in bed." For him, "there

---

26 APJ 1706: "Only Jesus Knows the Full Force of Temptation" (November 17, 2021). Quote from C. S. Lewis, *Mere Christianity* (New York: HarperOne, 2001), 142.

27 APJ 804: "Has My Sexual Sin Made Me Unsavable?" (February 29, 2016). For the dolphin/jel-lyfish contrast between those who "cut a path against the current" and those who "float in the current of culture," see APJ 683: "How to Engage Culture and Swim against It" (September 11, 2015) and APJ 1141: "Deep Bible Reading Strategies for the Tired and Busy" (January 3, 2018).

28 APJ 73: "How Far Is Too Far Before Marriage?" (April 19, 2013).

is no sin in your mind that wouldn't be sin in your bed. What would be sin is if a husband imagined sin or desired sin or took on attitudes to his wife in his heart that would be wrong in the bedroom. I think it is right for a husband to enjoy his wife any way in the mind that would be right to enjoy her in the bed."[29]

Is divorce justified for a porn-addicted husband?

No. Porn is not a marriage breaker. Marriage is "covenantal to the max" (Gen. 2:24; Eph. 5:32), bound in the courts of heaven (Mark 10:9), for life (Rom. 7:2–3), and consummated in the sexual union (Gen. 1:28; 4:1; Matt. 19:5; 1 Cor. 7:2–3). All of which implies that you should stay together "through hell and high water" (Mark 10:9–12; 1 Cor. 7:10–11).

The marriage covenant still holds when your spouse turns out to be what you didn't expect. "That, by the way, happens to pretty much everybody. Wives and husbands do not stay the same. Marriage is risky business, which is why I think the disciples said, 'If such is the case of a man with his wife, it is better not to marry' (Matt. 19:10). And Jesus replied that it is given to some but not others. It is given to Christians. It is our privilege and right to commit in this way."

So a husband sinning regularly with porn is "committing a grave sin against God and his wife." But the marriage covenant is greater than any sin, because marriage is "a picture of Christ and the church. In that stunning framework, you can go to Christ and plead with him for the power, grace, and wisdom to move toward repentance." The cross can free sinners from their strongest chains. Nevertheless, a wife may need to call on the men of her church to intervene. "Marriage is not a trap." She can call for help.[30]

Is porn an unpardonable sin?

According to Scripture, "the only sin that cannot be pardoned is the sin that cannot be repented of." Sins that *can be repented of* share four characteristics. (1) We must be genuinely sorry to God for the *guilt* of the sin, not simply sorry for the *consequence* of the sin. (2) We must put the sin under the blood of Christ, by faith. (3) We must then resist the sin by the power of the Spirit. (4) And we must renounce the sin "with a genuine embrace of Christ as our superior treasure." Any sin handled in these four ways is a sin that can be forgiven.

But, yes, there is "an extent of sinning" that leads to a place where "the sinner can't repent anymore." Esau proves it, the figurehead of a haunting warning against sexual bondage, even if his struggle wasn't sexual in nature

---

29 APJ 278: "Can a Husband Lust after His Wife?" (February 14, 2014).
30 APJ 165: "Is My Husband's Porn a Marriage Deal-Breaker?" (September 4, 2013).

(Heb. 12:15–17). The text says he "found no *chance* (τόπος) to repent, though he sought it with tears" (Heb. 12:17). There was *no chance*, or *no place*, for repentance in Esau's heart. He couldn't bring himself to repent even though he lamented his loss. "The remorse has to be more than just remorse for the loss of punishment. There's a 'too late' in our compromise with sin. God does, at times, withdraw his patient protection from final destruction and hand us over."

But this means hope for all repenting sinners. "Don't assume it is too late. Assume that God's mercy is still leading you to repentance (Rom. 2:4). Assume that he is still at work in your life." A porn addiction "is not unforgivable" if the sin can be repented of. But never assume any ability to repent will continue forever. It won't. It may soon end, "and I don't know how long it might last. God alone knows how long it would go on." God is "very, very patient," but don't presume on his patience (Rom. 2:4). His patience is calling forth our repentance. Repent and make war on this potent sin now. Porn is a "very resilient foe." Don't give up, don't give in, and don't settle. Because as soon as you "make peace" with this sin, you've entered the "big trouble" of Esau's plight. Don't settle! Fight on! And find friends for the battle.[31]

Esau made seventy appearances in the first decade of the podcast, and for good reason. He's a stark lesson on the eternal dangers of toying with sexual sins like porn (Heb. 12:15–17). In Esau we see that a man can "backslide" to a place of "no return,"[32] to a place where we "sin so long" that God finally gives us up and gives us over to our sin with no hope of repentance.[33] It's an alarming hardness of heart. Esau's nightmare was that he was "no longer *capable* of repenting," not that "he repented and repented and cried over his repentance, and God wouldn't forgive him. No, no, no. *He could not repent.* He had sinned to a depth or a degree that God had given him up."[34] Esau sold his soul for porridge, a prime text "for a man to go to when he is about to sell his soul again to lust."[35]

Esau warns us of a "final shipwreck from which there is no salvation. We sin *so long* or *so deeply* that we can't repent. We can't. Our hearts have become too hard." The sin will not be forsaken. But for every living sinner, there is hope. Hear the glorious call. Repent. Come back to Christ. "If you can come, he will have you" (1 John 1:9; 2:1).[36]

31 APJ 273: "Is Porn the Unforgivable Sin?" (February 7, 2014).
32 APJ 391: "Is God Fed Up with Me?" (July 23, 2014).
33 APJ 206: "The Danger of Deserting Community" (October 31, 2013).
34 APJ 1131: "What Is the 'Sin Not Leading to Death' in 1 John 5?" (December 11, 2017).
35 APJ 804: "Has My Sexual Sin Made Me Unsavable?" (February 29, 2016).
36 APJ 1900: "I Shipwrecked My Faith—Am I Doomed?" (February 13, 2023). Pastor John weds this frightening warning about Esau (Heb. 12:17) to the glorious promise of forgiveness to the repentant (in 1 John 1:9) in APJ 110: "Why Eternal Security Needs Community" (June 12,

Is serial adultery or seeking out a prostitute an unpardonable sin?
Esau came to center stage in a question from a man asking about Proverbs 2:19.
Does this mean that after seeking out a prostitute, he's now permanently lost?
Has he committed an unforgiveable sin?

"My answer, very simply, is that I do not know if [he] has crossed a line from
which he cannot return. But I can say to him that having sex with a prostitute,
or intending to and paying for it, is not beyond God's forgiveness, if there is
genuine repentance—that is, an authentic repudiation of the ugliness of that
sin, and a turning to Christ for mercy, and for the power of reformation, and
for the enjoyment of Christ himself as a superior pleasure to all such sins."

All sins can be forgiven—even "big" sins. The challenge is determining
whether this sin crossed a line of no return in this man's life. Esau is a fitting
example (Heb. 12:15–17). "Notice it does not say that he genuinely repented
and sought forgiveness, but couldn't find it though he repented. That's not what
it says. What it says is that *he was not able to repent*. That's the line that you
can cross. His sin had brought such bondage and deception and distortion on
his soul. This is what happens in sexual sin. Oh, my goodness, it's horrific how
insane sexual sin makes people."

But if we confess our sins, God forgives us (1 John 1:9). The text doesn't
exclude forgiveness for prostitution, adultery, rape, or some other "really outrageous sins." No. "If we confess our sins—if we agree with God all the way
down that we are hopeless; and that he is merciful, powerful, and worthy, and
that Christ is enough in his death and resurrection and as a treasure for our
lives—if we confess, he forgives all of it." So the line that can be crossed is not
tied to a particular sin's grossness or duration or frequency. The line is crossed
in the "hardness that one reaches in sinning from which he cannot repent: you
can't bring yourself to be set free from your love of sin."

So, yes, "be *that fearful* of the insanity of uniting your body to a prostitute"
(Prov. 2:19). But also realize that any sexual sin can be forgiven, *if* it can be
genuinely repented of (1 Cor. 5:1–5).[37]

To a professing Christian man who turned away from Christ to live in
a season of serial adultery, but who now regrets it, does Hebrews say he's
eternally lost and without hope (Heb. 6:4–6; 12:15–17)? Again, the answer
is uncertain—an uncertainty that is equally *sobering* and *hopeful*. "*Sobering*,
because it is possible to sin oneself into a condition of being unable to repent.

2013), APJ 206: "The Danger of Deserting Community" (October 31, 2013), APJ 1131: "What
Is the 'Sin Not Leading to Death' in 1 John 5?" (December 11, 2017), and APJ 1546: "I Sought
a Prostitute—Am I Doomed?" (November 2, 2020).

37 APJ 1546: "I Sought a Prostitute—Am I Doomed?" (November 2, 2020).

But *hopeful*, because in Christ Jesus, the worst of sins will be forgiven if there is authentic repentance and faith in Jesus Christ."[38]

Is fornication worse than porn?

Yes and *no*. Both are sinful. "Both displease the Lord. Both reveal a heart of rebellion against God and a heart willing to belittle God, because in our sin we say that he is insufficient for our satisfaction."

Yes, fornication is worse in the sense that a man "violates a woman" physically. "Yes, a woman who is not your wife is *violated* when you use her body sinfully online in a picture or in video to gratify your desires simply in those pictures or videos. But the violation goes far deeper, to another level, when her actual, physical self is compromised." In the same way, anger is a type of murder, but actual murder is worse (Matt. 5:21–22). So in fornication a man violates a woman, a consenting woman, because "God holds men uniquely responsible for protecting her from this violation, and he is guilty of violation even if she would never call it that." Physical, sexual sin is a holistic, entire-bodied sin that proves "uniquely damaging" (1 Cor. 6:18).

But *no*, porn may turn out to be worse. Imagine one night of fornication "leading to the most profound remorse and contrition and repentance and forgiveness, followed by a life of chastity that never falls again." Compare that to "year after year after year of increasingly crude and violent pornography, resisting all calls to repentance, and being indifferent to the women in your life—even your wife—and hardening yourself more and more to the calls of purity and repentance." This sin pattern is "ugliness," and the ongoing unrepentance is worse than the one-night stand. But never live to merely avoid "worse sins." Instead, live for "maximal holiness and purity." Flee from all sexual sin and instead "pursue righteousness, godliness, faith, love, steadfastness, gentleness" (1 Tim. 6:11).[39]

Can spiritual pleasures really compete with physical pleasures?

Speaking to a doubter who doesn't believe that the pleasures of God are stronger than the allures of porn, Pastor John said: "I realize that this is a battle not between two pleasures measured on the same scale." One pleasure is dominantly *physical*. The other pleasure is dominantly *spiritual*. So we fight for greater pleasures over time, a product of long discipline, and we do it by focusing our attention on how Christ handled sex and lust. In Scripture, we behold Christ

---

38 APJ 1274: "Does My Sexual Past Make Me Unsavable?" (November 9, 2018).
39 APJ 329: "Is Fornication Worse than Porn?" (April 28, 2014).

so we can be transformed by his glory (2 Cor. 3:18). How this works, very practically, is that we consider that Christ himself experienced fifteen to twenty years "of masculine virility, yet not one single millisecond of a sinful thought or feeling or immoral act. Women were hanging on his words, following him around. Former prostitutes wept over him and wiped his bare feet with their hair." His life was "supercharged with sexual temptation—and he never sinned. He never once committed any lustful thought or act. He denied himself perfectly without denying the goodness of sexuality. I watch him. And as I watch him, I love him. I admire him." His sexual purity is "contagious."

"But I would plead with you to believe and to pursue the Christ who has depths and heights and unexpected dimensions of pleasure for you" (Ps. 16:11). Because if you do, his spiritual joys "will transform your life and pull the power plug on those sinful temptations."[40]

Killing soft porn

The battle against porn appears in subtler forms, like when suggestive images appear online or in commercials, or when swimsuit issues or lingerie catalogs appear in the mailbox. A male listener wrote in about battling these craftier forms of lust.

"I know exactly what he's talking about," Piper said. "I dumped three [women's catalogs] in the garbage yesterday." And yet even in these subtler forms, in these catalogs, "the male eye is like a magnet in its attraction to excessive female skin, or tantalizing gaps in clothing, or featured bodily shapes through tight clothing. God cares about these magnet impulses of the male eye and what we do with them."

Five guidelines compel the ongoing fight for purity, even after the battles against blatant porn have been won. (1) Be faithful in these little decisions to dump catalogs (Luke 16:10). (2) Be urgent in the war (Matt. 5:27–29). Heaven and hell hang in the balance of what our magnetized eyes and imaginative fantasies do, even with fully clothed women. (3) Fight like a dead man (Col. 3:2–6). "Here's the uniquely Christian paradox: you *have died*, so *put to death*. 'You have died' means that, by faith alone, you really have, through identification with Jesus, died and risen and passed from death to life. Your life is hidden with Christ in God: sins forgiven, eternity secured. Now, fight! Kill sin." The first four sins Paul mentions are connected to our sexual desires. "Go figure. There's nothing new under the sun." (4) Make covenants, and make them specific (Job 31:1). Say it out loud: "I will not crack open a single women's magazine that comes in the mail.

---

40 APJ 850: "Can Pleasure in God Really Compete with the Pleasures of Porn?" (May 3, 2016). "My favorite verse in the psalms is Psalm 16:11" (APJ 545: "Finding the Courage to Be Christian" [March 4, 2015]).

Not one page. Period." Leave no exceptions, because "if you leave your hormones wiggle room, which is what lifelong, *general commitments* do without *very specific commitments* or *covenants* with your eyes, your hormones will almost inevitably convince your mind that this little exception is okay. 'They're just bathing suits.'" (5) Be pleading for God to turn your eyes from worthless things (Ps. 119:37). "Depersonalized female skin is a worthless thing. Now, women as persons are of infinite worth in relation to God. But lust depersonalizes skin and turns it into a worthless thing. It's demeaning to women. It's deadly for men."[41]

How do I respond to sexually sinful dreams?

A man is winning his war with porn but now struggles with lucid sexual dreams of women who are not his wife. He feels powerless to stop them.

A few things about dreams.

1. Dreams can lie and give us false messages (Zech. 10:2). Or dreams can terrify us in order to test us (Deut. 13:1–3). In this case you can say: "'Dreams—Satan, brain, hormones—whatever you are, I won't be sucked in by this. I see how my faith is being tested here. Do I love my wife? Do I love purity? Do I love holiness? Do I love Christ, who died to make me pure? Yes, I do. I will not be undone by this test. I will pass it by faith in the blood of Jesus to cover all my sins, to empower me to walk in the truth.'"

2. Dreams can reveal our physical desires, according to a text that "comes as close as anything as far as I can see in the Bible to a Freudian view of dreams—namely, that they signal deep needs or desires, even sexual ones" (Isa. 29:7–8). Real thirst makes people dream of drinking. Real hunger causes people to dream of eating. "I would say that in the same way, sexual hormones, desires, impulses, born of nature, might make a person dream he's having sex, and he wakes up and he didn't have sex. Now, that does not explain why you would dream about women who are not your wife. That may be traced to old patterns of fantasies that go back thirty years, twenty years, fifteen years, and need to be broken. But the point here is there is nothing remarkable when a physical craving like hunger or thirst or sexuality causes a dream that the craving is being satisfied when it isn't." The main concern isn't over the dream happening, but what you do with that dream in your waking life.

3. Dreams can warn us, terrify us, and humble our pride to keep us from sinning (Job 33:14–18). "One way to look at sexually illicit dreams—dreams when you're doing illicit things in the dream—is that God is terrifying us in our dreams of the horror of this prospect in real life so that we won't do it."

---

41 APJ 1408: "How Do I Battle Subtle Temptations to Lust?" (December 16, 2019).

Here are five practical responses. (1) Pray, and find friends to pray, that you would be delivered from these dreams. (2) Read your Bible for ten minutes before bed, and particularly texts on the value of Christ (Phil. 3:8; Col. 1:15–18; Heb. 1:1–3). (3) Rid your screen habits of sexually stimulating content—"not just porn, but worldly sexuality. Now that's just about all TV shows and all movies. Sorry about that. You don't need it." (4) Consider a sleep study and find physical irregularities. (5) Stand in the promise of Psalm 25:15, "and say with confidence: 'My eyes are ever toward the LORD, for he will pluck my feet out of the net.'"[42]

Winning the war on lust

Winning the war against lust is analogous to physical fitness. We use (1) *resistance* and (2) *reception*.

1. *Resistance* is like weight training. We push against a resisting force to grow our muscles. So, too, we learn to push against lust temptations. When temptations arrive, "you've got about five seconds to decide whether you're going to let it take over or whether you're going to push on it with, 'No—you're out of here. In Jesus's name, you're out of here!' You must direct your attention to some superior promise: 'Jesus is better. Jesus is enough. He said this. You're out of here.' And you keep pushing until [the temptation] is gone." These tests build our spiritual muscles to meet greater temptations in the future. But resistance isn't enough, because "so many Christians try to solve the problems of their temptations and their defeats only by the resistance half of sanctification. It just won't work in the long run."

2. We must also have the right *reception*, or diet. We behold Christ's glory to be changed into his likeness (2 Cor. 3:18; Col. 3:10). "We linger over the sweet and beautiful descriptions of the person and the work of Jesus Christ. We marinate our minds receptively by faith in the Crock-Pot of God's word. We fix our eyes, the eyes of our hearts, on Jesus." Sexual passions control those who do not see, know, meditate on, or absorb the knowledge of God (1 Thess. 4:3–5). "In other words, they haven't been renewed in knowledge. They haven't set their minds to behold the glory of Jesus day and night so that they become like what they admire. They are at the mercy of their sinful passions because they haven't been transformed by putting on the new self, renewed in knowledge." The glory and beauty of Christ transform us.

Learn to use both—*resistance* and *reception*—to win the long war against lust.[43]

---

42 APJ 1417: "How Do I Respond to Sexual Dreams?" (January 6, 2020).
43 APJ 1153: "Two Strategies to Win the War on Lust" (January 31, 2018).

On Satan, Demons, and
the Unforgivable Sin

Is Satan real?

Yes, "Satan and his demons are real and massively influential." Satan is a super-natural being "stronger than any mere human power," and "a monster in terrible ways." He's no local, tribal deity, but a global force (John 12:31; 14:30; 2 Cor. 4:4; Gal. 1:4; Col. 1:13; 1 John 5:19). The devil is a "monster who sweeps down a third of the stars, wants to eat the Son of God, and, failing that, wants to eat us," the church (Rev. 12:4, 9, 17). He's "marauding through the world for those who bear the testimony of Jesus" and makes war "by delusion and murder." He's a liar and a murderer (John 8:44; 1 Pet. 5:8), destined for destruction (Rev. 20:10).

For now, Satan "is on a long chain and loose in the world. He is the god of this world and the whole world lies under him." Our sworn enemy (Eph. 6:12). And he is active throughout the world, "wreaking havoc in families and churches and cultures and nations. He is behind the bloody carnage of abortion. He is behind the destructive insanity of so-called same-sex marriage. And he is behind the intractable racial, ethnic hatreds in the world. He is behind the industrial and political structures of corruption that fatten the pockets of the rich and powerful with no concern for the poor and the weak. He is behind the horrors of Islamic terrorism and the blows that they wreak against innocent people almost every day." He is behind suicide bombings, human trafficking, and "the multibillion-dollar porn industry that rips souls to shreds and ruins families." Satan's carnage "is literally indescribable."

But Satan is also a fool. "He brought Jesus to the cross through Judas." It was "his suicide" and his "undoing," because at the cross he was disarmed (Col. 2:15). There Christ stripped Satan and disarmed him from his one "eternally lethal weapon" and "the only thing that can condemn us in God's courtroom at the end of the age." Unforgiven sin. But in Christ, we have no unforgiven sin, so

"Satan's accusations against Christians come to nothing" (Rom. 8:33). On the flip side, this means (put bluntly), "you don't have a snowball's chance in hell of resisting Satan outside of Jesus. But Christ has conquered him, and in Christ there is light and freedom and life and joy forever."[1]

Why does God allow Satan to roam now?

God could take Satan out at any moment. And he will eventually toss him into the lake of fire. So, God, why didn't you do this yesterday? You have the *right* and the *power* to take him out. "You are doing nobody wrong when you take him out." So why not do it now?

These questions are given no direct answer in the Bible, "so we go on inferences." One summary answer is this: "God has ordained that Satan have a long leash, with God holding onto the leash, because he knows that when we walk in and out of those temptations—struggling both with the physical effects that they bring and the moral effects that they bring—more of God's glory will shine in that battle than if he took him out yesterday. There will be evidences of God's patience with us as we struggle with sin, evidences of his mercy to us as we struggle with sin, evidences of his sustaining grace through horrific physical suffering that Satan was the immediate cause of." Satan is allowed to harass people for many years "in order that the glory of God, his mercy, his justice, his grace, and his wisdom would shine more brightly" (Luke 13:10–17).

We can disagree with God's handling of the world, but that is ultimately a rejection of God himself. So "I choose to trust him, that his way of managing the devil, and managing evil that comes at me, is wiser than the way I might choose to manage it." Most notably, God "sent his Son right into the middle of this satanic warfare. It was Satan that put it in the heart of Judas to betray Jesus." Jesus exposed himself to the horrors of Satan's deceit and lies and murder. Satan was a murderer from the beginning and a liar (John 8:44). But Jesus died to make a public display of the principalities and powers in his defeat of them (Col. 2:15). So it must be true that "there is *more glory* that will come to Jesus Christ by suffering to destroy Satan than by powerfully shooting Satan in the head," like a sniper. "And there is more glory that will come to Jesus Christ by our sharing in the sufferings of Christ and holding on to his supreme value than if we had been able to say, 'Satan, depart!' and never have another problem." In the end, "the glory of God shines most brightly, and the glory of Christ shines most brightly, when we are seen to be supremely satisfied in Christ in spite of Satan's torments."[2]

1   APJ 668: "The Case for Satan" (August 21, 2015).
2   APJ 408: "Why Does God Allow Satan to Live?" (August 15, 2014).

How much authority does Satan have?

In one of the desert temptations, the devil offered authority to Christ on the condition that Christ would worship him (Matt. 4:9; Luke 4:6). So how much legitimate authority does Satan hold in the world today?

"My first answer is that if Jesus had worshiped Satan, of course Jesus would have abdicated his divine authority. He would have ceased to be God. If he were worshiping the devil, he wouldn't be God. The devil would be God. Satan would then give him the whole world and still control the world because Jesus would not be God. He'd be Satan's lackey. All of this, of course, did not, and could not, happen. Satan, as usual, was a fool to suggest it. He's an idiot. He's always saying stupid, half-true things."

But Satan is not the world's "ultimate authority." Whatever authority the devil has was given to him from another—namely, God himself (Luke 4:6). "In his sovereignty, God considered it wise, as part of his curse on the world after the fall of Adam and Eve, to give Satan huge power in this world." But not ultimate power. "We're not dualists. We don't think there's God and Satan duking it out for power in the universe." Satan has "no autonomy to do anything that God does not permit for infinitely wise purposes." So "all his acts of opposition to God and God's people are part of God's plan, as God gives Satan permission to exercise tremendous power in this world." Satan does wield tremendous power (Eph. 2:1–2). He afflicted Job greatly (Job 1:12). Indeed, "the whole world lies in the power of the evil one" (1 John 5:19). He's "the ruler of this world" (John 14:30).

At the cross, Satan got his hour of glory (Luke 22:53). But that's it. That same cross *evicted* the "ruler of the world" (John 12:31; 16:11). Christ defeats Satan by forgiving our sin (Col. 2:13–15). "So, in dying for your sins, in nailing your record of debt to the cross, he disarmed the rulers and authorities and put them to open shame by triumphing over them in him." Satan's power is in his accusations. So "if he has nothing in his court folder as he stands before the bar to accuse us, what's he going to do?" In Christ, Satan is rendered powerless over us because we have no unforgiven sin (Rom. 8:38–39). We are united to Christ and indwelt by the Spirit. Now, "he who is in you greater than he who is in the world," namely, the devil (1 John 4:4).[3]

But Satan's extensive authority over this world remains, and that is why we feel like exiles. "That's what makes us feel so alien here: the god of this world is Satan. He holds such extensive sway. The world is permeated with sin. It makes us feel like we're not at home—and we're not, in a very real sense, while that

---

3   APJ 1349: "How Much Authority Does Satan Have in the World?" (May 29, 2019).

334 ON SATAN, DEMONS, AND THE UNFORGIVABLE SIN

kind of sinfulness permeates the world. We are just aching to be done with sin, mainly our sin, not just the grossness and godlessness that we see in the world. We long to be holy and to be in the presence of Holiness himself."[4]

Our citizenship is in heaven. We are now "sojourners and exiles" on earth (1 Pet. 2:11). We feel out of place here, "owing to the fact that this world is *fallen*, not the fact that it is *created*. We are going to spend eternity in a *created* world. But Satan won't be the god of that world anymore." The alienation we feel now is due to the reality that "the god of this world" holds such an extensive sway over this planet. "The world is permeated with sin. It makes us feel like we are not at home. We are just aching to be done with sin and be in the presence of holiness." To that end, Satan will not rule the new creation. "So when I say that we are aliens and exiles and sojourners and pilgrims, I don't mean that the earth is a place we despise. I mean that the structures we find ourselves in are so permeated with sin. We want something new." We long to live in a place where Satan has been truly banished.[5]

Satan lost two weapons over us

The work of Christ is glorious as we see in Colossians 2:13–15. "The riches of these verses are infinite." And they teach us five glorious realities about our redemption. (1) We were legally condemned for our long list of sins. (2) The long list of sins was put into Christ's hand and a spike was driven through his hand, into the record, and into the cross. (3) Our sin debt was canceled, and the record of charges against us went missing. It was "taken out of the midst" (Col. 2:14), "a very unusual thing to say. In the courtroom of heaven, where our record of debt guarantees our condemnation, nobody can find it. It's been taken." The docket of charges against us has disappeared. (4) We are forgiven. (5) We are made alive in Christ.

As a result of this precious gospel, Satan (and his demonic forces) were stripped of two powers.

1. Satan's power to condemn Christians is stripped. He is the great accuser (Rev. 12:10). "Satan can do a lot of damage to us physically, emotionally, and relationally in this world." But he can only condemn as a persistent prosecutor by "valid accusation of our sins before a holy God. If he can do that, we're done for. If he can make our sins stick in the courtroom of heaven, as he accuses us before the judge of the universe, we're doomed; we're hopeless." But our record of debt was canceled when it got nailed to the cross. "The one damning weapon

4   APJ 1494: "How Much Patriotism Is Too Much Patriotism?" (July 3, 2020).
5   APJ 125: "Patriotism and the Christian" (July 4, 2013).

that he has—namely, unforgiven sin, with which he could accuse us—has been stripped out of his hands." No charge can be brought against us (Rom. 8:33–34). The docket of charges is nowhere to be found.

2. Satan's power to terrify Christians with death is stripped. Our fear of death is ended. Satan torments sinners with death's reality (Heb. 2:14–15). But it was through Christ's death that he abolished the one who held the power of death—the devil. "When Christ died in our place, he took the sting out of death because he took sin out of death. He took condemnation out of death. And so he took fear out of death." Death is no longer our enemy. We are free from what was a lifelong slavery to the fear of eternal judgment.[6]

Satan's two strategies to ruin our joy in God

Satan seeks to diminish the glory we give to God in our lives in two ways. "One of those is *pain*, and the other is *pleasure*."

1. *Pain* can cause us to value something else more than God—by making us angry at God that we have this pain, and making us want to be done with it more than we want to embrace God. In this suffering is a golden opportunity for us to glorify God—when we show how much more we value him than we value comfort or freedom from the pain.

2. *Pleasure* can also cause us to cherish something else more than God—"not by making us angry at God, but by making us forget God, because we're so satisfied in the pleasures that his gifts give us" (Ezek. 16:14–15). "God gave Israel the great gift of beauty, and instead of leading them to glorify God for the gift, they fell in love with the gift. They preferred the gift over the giver; they dishonored God by not being satisfied in God, but fell in love with God's good gift."

So "*pain* and *pleasure* are Satan's strategies to undermine our glorification of God. *Withholding good things* can ruin us. *Giving us good things* can ruin us. Both can be an occasion for dishonoring God and not glorifying him—or for glorifying him."[7]

Speaking of pain, Satan wants to turn our suffering into resentment toward God. But "it is never right, never good, never virtuous—never merely neutral—to feel anger at God. Never."[8] Biblical lament is godly, the act of telling God how much he has hurt us, "without feeling anger at him." But of course, we sin here. Christians can get angry at God. "Good grief, of course they do. They shouldn't. But they do. And if they do get angry at God, they should tell him so." God can handle it. We can repent—we must repent—because "anger

6   APJ 1750: "How Did the Cross Disarm the Devil?" (February 28, 2022).
7   APJ 1504: "How Do I Glorify God in My Daily Life?" (July 27, 2020).
8   APJ 1828: "Can I Be Angry with God and Be Holy?" (August 29, 2022).

at God is not godly lament."[9] Job modeled godly lament for us (at the start) but then fell into sinful anger toward God (later).[10] Our Savior on the cross remains our perfect model of suffering without anger.[11] So we follow Christ's lead to manifest his worth to the world. This gets to the very design of this fallen existence. This "world of loss exists so that you and I, by not murmuring or complaining or getting angry at God, but rather resting in him and trusting in him, can show the world that God is more precious to us than everything we just lost."[12] Satan is out to stop that.

Satan's most terrible work

Satan remains powerful in this world. He's behind "much" sickness (Luke 13:11) and the thorn of physical pain that punctured Paul's life (2 Cor. 12:7). Satan can throw Christians in prison (Rev. 2:10). And Satan got Jesus arrested, beaten, and thrown on a cross (John 13:2, 27). The devil's aim is to destroy our faith (1 Pet. 5:8–9), and he's very powerful. But not all-powerful. Satan's work is allowed by divine "permission" and never because he has "ultimate control." Nevertheless, he's real, he's strong, he's evil—and he's on "a long leash." Even on that leash of God's providence, he can do "terrible damage" to us.[13]

But Paul exposes Satan's greater work in the world. "The god of this world has blinded the minds of the unbelievers, to keep them from seeing the light of the gospel of the glory of Christ, who is the image of God" (2 Cor. 4:4). "This is the most terrifying thing in the world to me, that people I love (or I myself) may be so blinded by the devil that they look at Jesus and he is *not* beautiful. He is *not* their treasure. Money is their treasure. Videos are their treasure. Making grades is their treasure. Their boyfriend is their treasure. . . . Death is not terrifying. To be so deceived that you can't see Jesus as the treasure of your life, that is the most terrifying thing."[14]

Among Christians, "the devil is in the business of killing our enjoyment of the beauty of Christ in the gospel."[15] In the broader world, call it "Satan's blinding"[16] or "satanic blinding"[17] or "satanic blindness"[18] or "demonic blindness"—it's a

9   APJ 931: "How Do You Pray in Public, without Performing?" (August 31, 2016).
10   APJ 1695: "Is Stress Making Me More Holy or More Sinful?" (October 22, 2021).
11   APJ 1515: "Is Angry Prayer Okay?" (August 21, 2020).
12   APJ 625: "God Takes Away to Display Christ's Beauty" (June 24, 2015).
13   APJ 1869: "How Can Satan Harm Christians?" (December 2, 2022).
14   APJ 796: "The Christian's Great Vocation" (February 17, 2016).
15   APJ 128: "How Do I Delight Myself in the Lord?" (July 9, 2013).
16   APJ 583: "The New Book John Piper Wrote" (April 27, 2015).
17   APJ 1638: "Are Our Enemies Spiritual, Human, or Both?" (June 11, 2021).
18   APJ 1357: "Does God Ever Soften a Heart He Has Hardened?" (June 17, 2019).

terrifying force that screens eyes and veils hearts to "the glory and beauty and excellence and worth of Christ" in the gospel (2 Cor. 4:4).[19]

So although Satan is a "supernatural being," he wields "remarkable power" in the material realm—"he can make people sick, he can throw them in prison, and he can even kill them." But "his main way of opposing God and destroying God's people is not in the *physical* or *material* realm but in the *mental* or *intellectual* or *moral* realm. In other words, the best way to think about his power is not in terms of physical strength, but of moral deception."

Satan is "the deceiver of the whole world," working to deceive the nations (Rev. 12:9; 20:8). "He destroys, not mainly by the sword or disease or killing, but mainly by lying." He's "the father of lies" (John 8:44). "He lies mainly about God, about Jesus, about the gospel, and about sin." He blinds sinners' minds to Christ's radiant beauty (2 Cor. 4:4). Thus, today, "wherever saving truth is hated and resisted and distorted and muted, Satan is at work so that people are kept from being saved by the truth of the gospel" (2 Thess. 2:9–10). Right now, "Satan is mainly bent on preventing the message of the cross from being spread, from being understood, and from being believed. And he does everything in his power to distort and silence the saving message of the cross." Like a bird grabbing seed off a path, Satan tries to "snatch away" the gospel after it has been preached (Matt. 13:19). But once Christ is embraced and sins are forgiven, Satan's accusations become baseless.

Against the elect, Satan "can oppress us, he can distress us, he can tempt us, he can make us sick, he can kill us. But he cannot damn us—ever." In the cross, "the satanic rulers and authorities are decisively defeated. They are undone. Their one condemning, damning weapon has been taken out of their hands—namely, unforgiven sin" (Col. 2:13–15). "Who shall bring any charge against God's elect?" (Rom. 8:33). No one. Scripture puts this statement right "in Satan's face." Who can justify? Who can condemn? "It is Christ Jesus who died, Mr. Satan. You couldn't stop it. More than that, Jesus was raised from the dead, and he is at the right hand of God. He indeed intercedes for us, Mr. Accuser. So I am sure that neither death nor life, nor angels nor rulers—nor Satan—nor anything else in all creation can separate us from the love of God in Christ Jesus" (Rom. 8:38–39).[20]

On the unpardonable sin

As you see throughout this book, many listeners have written us in fear that they have crossed a line, committed the unforgivable sin, fallen under the

---

19 APJ 1266: "I Didn't Treasure Christ When I First Believed—Was I Unsaved?" (October 22, 2018).
20 APJ 1209: "Where Is Satan Most Visibly Active Today?" (June 11, 2018).

damning sway of Satan, and disqualified themselves from God's forgiveness. The question is often worded generally, on whether or not a born-again Christian *could* commit the unpardonable sin,[21] and whether a season of unrepentant sin is enough to violate it.[22] More often, the question asks whether this grave sin is committed by premarital sex,[23] prostitute-seeking,[24] porn-viewing,[25] a season of serial adultery,[26] or by a "really gross"[27] or "particularly ugly act" of sin,[28] even the act of suicide itself.[29]

But the unpardonable sin is none of these. The unpardonable sin is classified in two ways: (1) the final rejection of Christ, and (2) the condition of becoming unable to repent over sin.

1. Rejecting Christ. The unpardonable sin is a blasphemy against the Holy Spirit (Matt. 12:31). That sin, Jesus says, will not be forgiven. So what is this sin? It comes in a context where people were saying that Jesus was empowered by the devil. "They were saying that he cast out demons by the power of Beelzebul and, therefore, they had turned the world on its head (Matt. 12:24). They were seeing Jesus as demonic, and they were no longer able to see Jesus as who he really was." They rejected Christ. If you have not finally rejected Christ, you have not committed the unpardonable sin.[30]

2. Refusing repentance. In this case, the "unforgivable sin" is not a "particularly ugly act," but sinning to "a particular depth or degree or aggravation or persistence in sin" to where "authentic confession and repentance have become impossible."[31] This is the embodied tragedy of Esau (Heb. 12:15–17). If you can repent of your sin, "there is hope." If you can repent of your sin, you have not committed the unpardonable sin.[32]

So, first, the unpardonable sin is "attributing Jesus's deeds to the devil instead of God" (Mark 3:28–30). This is the blasphemy of the Holy Spirit, which will not be forgiven (Luke 12:10). "Over the span of my ministry, there have been several people . . . deeply convinced they had committed the sin against the Holy

21 APJ 902: "Can a Christian Blaspheme the Holy Spirit?" (July 21, 2016).
22 APJ 168: "Have I Exhausted God's Patience with My Sin?" (September 9, 2013).
23 APJ 365: "Will You Marry a Couple Already Living Together?" (June 17, 2014).
24 APJ 1546: "I Sought a Prostitute—Am I Doomed?" (November 2, 2020).
25 APJ 273: "Is Porn the Unforgivable Sin?" (February 7, 2014).
26 APJ 1274: "Does My Sexual Past Make Me Unsavable?" (November 9, 2018).
27 APJ 1546: "I Sought a Prostitute—Am I Doomed?" (November 2, 2020).
28 APJ 1131: "What Is the 'Sin Not Leading to Death' in 1 John 5?" (December 11, 2017).
29 APJ 352: "Suicide and Salvation" (May 29, 2014).
30 APJ 168: "Have I Exhausted God's Patience with My Sin?" (September 9, 2013).
31 APJ 1131: "What Is the 'Sin Not Leading to Death' in 1 John 5?" (December 11, 2017).
32 APJ 168: "Have I Exhausted God's Patience with My Sin?" (September 9, 2013).

Spirit and were therefore beyond forgiveness. They were terrified, as you can imagine." Faced with this question, it's always helpful to be clear that "everyone who calls on the name of the Lord will be saved" (Rom. 10:13). Or, in Paul's words to a convicted man, "believe in the Lord Jesus, and you will be saved" (Acts 16:31). Or in the promise of Christ: "For this is the will of my Father, that everyone who looks on the Son and believes in him should have eternal life, and I will raise him up on the last day" (John 6:40). These are open offers of the gospel, none of them negated by some particularly "bad" sin.

Second, the unforgivable sin is a *condition* in which people are "sinning in such a way that they are unwilling and unable to repent and believe." Esau is the prime example—a man who literally had "no place of repentance" (Heb. 12:17). He couldn't repent. "He had come to such hardness of heart against God, such love for the world . . . he couldn't stop loving the world. He could find no genuine repentance. And so he perished. His tears were not tears of repentance. They were tears of remorse that he couldn't repent." So, *yes*, "there is a kind of willful, determined, settled opposition to God and his Spirit," a kind of sinning, leading to death, that is beyond prayer (1 John 5:16).

True Christians cannot commit the unpardonable sin because (1) they *cannot* blaspheme the Spirit, because this "willful, determined opposition to the present power of the Holy Spirit" is something Christians cannot commit. And (2) while "Christians can commit all kinds of sin," Christian's hearts are marked by genuine, ongoing repentance. They hate their sin. So *blaspheming* the Spirit is very different from *grieving* the Spirit. The Christian *can* "grieve the Holy Spirit of God, *by whom you were sealed for the day of redemption*" (Eph. 4:29–31). And yet in grieving the Spirit, as we see in this text, final salvation is never in question.[33]

Can Satan "touch" or "devour" a Christian?

Satan is our sworn enemy, who right now "prowls around like a roaring lion, seeking someone to *devour*" (1 Pet. 5:8). So can a genuine Christian get *devoured*?

The word picture reminds us of Jonah swallowed whole. Satan wants to devour us and snatch us away with himself into the lake of fire. "That is what *devour* means. Now the question is, can that happen to me and you?" Note that in the next verse Peter commands us to "resist" the devil (1 Pet. 5:9). Is this command of resistance a "charade" or "war game," like playing make-believe war with plastic guns? Will *nothing* happen to Christians if we *don't* resist? Well,

---

33 APJ 902: "Can a Christian Blaspheme the Holy Spirit?" (July 21, 2016).

given the urgency of Peter in this text, "it doesn't sound like a game. It sounds like heaven and hell are at stake."

So, again, can a genuine Christian be devoured by Satan? No, "because true, born-again Christians *always fight*. They fight back. That is what it means to be a true, born-again Christian. True, born-again Christians have the Holy Spirit within them so that when they see the lion coming, they don't say, 'Ah, nothing is at stake here. I don't need to fight. I don't need to stir up my faith. I don't need to read the Bible. I don't need to pray. I don't need to be with other believers. I don't have to be vigilant over my eyes and make sure that flesh doesn't get the upper hand—because nothing is at stake here.'" No. True, born-again believers hear the urgent word, resist Satan, and fight because their lives depend on it. "If you don't fight, you are probably not born again."

Earlier in his epistle, Peter makes a similar claim about true believers, those who "*by God's power* are being guarded *through faith* for a salvation ready to be revealed in the last time" (1 Pet. 1:5). "God says, 'I am going to keep you by *my power* through *your faith* against the devil.'" God guards us from destruction and keeps us safe from Satan, not *despite* our faith and resistance, but *in and through* our faith and resistance.[34]

Likewise, to those who are born again, the Bible promises that "the evil one does not *touch* him" (1 John 5:18). Christ "intercedes for us, and he is with us to the end of the age, helping us. And his blood covers us and keeps us safe from Satan's accusations—because none of them can hold, because Christ has died for us." The devil's "accusations and temptations and harassments can hurt us terribly, but they can never destroy us. There is no *deadly touch*. There is no poisonous bite. His fangs were removed at the cross, and his lethal poison is taken away from believers. He cannot destroy us." Satan can "hurt us terribly," and "I don't want to minimize Satan's realty in this world. He can throw us in prison, and he can move others to kill us. But he can't hurt us ultimately. He can't touch us with the touch of destruction and damnation." That power was ripped from his hands by Christ's blood (Col. 2:13–15).[35]

Can a Christian get handed over to Satan?
Yes. When two professing Christians shipwrecked their faith, Paul handed them over to Satan with the hope they would be disciplined and "learn" a sanctifying lesson (1 Tim. 1:19–20). To "learn" (παιδεύω) is to be instructed. Paul handed Hymenaeus and Alexander to Satan for discipline, instruction, and training. In

---

34   APJ 896: "Can Satan 'Devour' True Christians?" (July 13, 2016).
35   APJ 700: "Does the Bible Say True Christians Never Sin?" (October 6, 2015).

a related scenario, with a professing Christian man caught in egregious sexual sin with his stepmother, Paul called the church "to deliver this man to Satan for the destruction of the flesh, so that his spirit may be saved in the day of the Lord" (1 Cor. 5:5). All three men were handed over to Satan for "remediation" and "improvement" in the hope of restoration. "The aim of handing him over to Satan is salvation, not damnation." Which means that shipwrecked faith "need not be final loss. There's hope for a turnaround." Shipwrecks are not final, as Paul knew firsthand as the survivor of at least four real shipwrecks.[36] So Paul's prayer for the man who sinned sexually "was that suffering and impending death would shake the disciplined person out of his spiritual stupor and bring him to faith and life," even if that discipline eventually ended his physical life.[37]

God makes use of Satan in our suffering

"Every loss that we endure as sinful children of God has two designs: one from Satan, one from God. Satan designs our unbelief and rebellion and renunciation and guilt and paralysis and loss of faith. God designs our purification and that we would hope less in this world and more in God who raises the dead."[38]

"God never lets Satan out of his control and often uses him to accomplish his purposes. This was true for Job—Satan had to get permission to go hammer Job, and then Job said it was the Lord who had 'taken away.' The writer says that Job 'did not sin or charge God with wrong,' even though Satan was more immediately involved in the wind that blew down the house that killed the kids" (Job 1:18–22).

Paul said he was tormented by Satan to further his own humility (2 Cor. 12:7). "Really? *Satan* wants you not to be conceited? No, no, no. *God* wants him not to be conceited. And Satan happens to be the instrument that God is using in this thorn to keep Paul from sinning. I am sure that Satan did not appreciate that use, because that is exactly the opposite of what Satan designs in the thorn! If you have a thorn, Satan is designing your sin. But God is designing your sanctification. So Satan is one of God's instruments in causality."[39] To build in Paul a Christlike humility, Satan became God's tool for his holiness. "That must gall Satan!"[40]

So God permitted Satan to afflict Job "with horrific boils—fibromyalgia, perhaps." And although we don't know how long they lasted, they brought him "to the brink of unbelief." But "God showed up just in the nick of time in those later chapters to keep Job back from despair." Job forces us to see two things.

36 APJ 1900: "I Shipwrecked My Faith—Am I Doomed?" (February 13, 2023).
37 APJ 1666: "Is Death Past, Present, or Future?" (August 16, 2021).
38 APJ 963: "Did My Lust Cause Our Miscarriage?" (November 14, 2016).
39 APJ 280: "Does God Cause All Sickness?" (February 18, 2014).
40 APJ 481: "Doesn't Prosperity Preaching Glorify Jesus?" (November 26, 2014).

(1) "It forces us to come to terms with the fact of God's absolute sovereignty over our suffering, even though Satan had a hand in it." The Lord brought it (Job 42:11). (2) "Even though Satan was the immediate cause of Job's horrible sickness, and it's right and good to resist the devil always and to pray for relief from his attacks always, nevertheless, we always submit to the fact that God is sovereign over Satan."[41]

"God's permission for Satan or man to act is part of God's ultimate design and final control." Satan demanded to sift Peter like wheat (Luke 22:31). And God will allow it (Luke 22:34). "In other words, 'Yes, I'm going to give Satan permission to sift you like wheat, and I know it's going to involve three denials. I know you're going to turn, and I know that the purpose of bringing you back according to my prayer is that you might strengthen your brothers.' Even in situations where God is permitting, he is permitting by design. When you permit something and you know what it's going to do and you know all of its outcomes and you go ahead and permit it, you permit it wisely if you're God—and then it wisely fits into the overall pattern of what you are planning and doing." God's sovereign reign here "does not diminish human accountability." But the question remains: "Which world would you rather live in? One where *humans* or *Satan* or *chance* govern what happens to you? Or one where an infinitely good, infinitely wise, infinitely powerful *God* works everything together for the good of those who trust him and for his glory?" (Rom. 8:28).[42]

All our suffering accords with God's will, "even when Satan may be the immediate cause of it." We know this from the lives of Job and Paul (2 Cor. 12:7–10). Paul's "thorn in the flesh" was a "minister of Satan" used to humble Paul and make him more holy "so that he would love the glory of Jesus Christ." So it's clear from this case that God reigns over Satan and over all our suffering. "And therefore, it's okay to *resist* your suffering in prayer and pray against it and ask God to remove it, like Paul did. And sometimes he *does*, miraculously and wonderfully. And sometimes he *doesn't*, for holy and wise purposes because he loves us. But his sovereignty is not called into question by the immediate causality of sin and Satan. So many passages of Scripture show that God is overruling these things constantly for our great good."[43]

Satan wants you to give up

"When the storms come, don't quit. Satan wants you to quit. He is as active as anybody in this thing, and he wants you out of the ministry—or at least

41 APJ 1055: "What Can We Say to Friends Facing Suffering?" (June 16, 2017).
42 APJ 1094: "Does God Control All Things All the Time?" (September 15, 2017).
43 APJ 1523: "What Is God Accomplishing in My Suffering?" (September 9, 2020).

out of fruitfulness. He wants you paralyzed with discouragement. Tell him to go to hell, which is where he belongs, and then bank on the promises of God that 'he who is in you is greater than he who is in the world' (1 John 4:4). That promise has been very precious over the years as I have gotten in Satan's face about his temptations."[44]

Satan is not your greatest enemy

Living in victory over Satan and his hosts is not about technique. "We tend to think of spiritual warfare as this little thing where you find *some way* to pray or *some way* to lay hands on or *some way* to do a Satan thing. Well, that is important. Believe me. That is important, because 'we do not wrestle against flesh and blood, but against the rulers, against the authorities, against the cosmic powers over this present darkness, against the spiritual forces of evil in the heavenly places'" (Eph. 6:12). But there's an even greater consideration. "The only foothold Satan has in your life is your flesh and your sin. Nobody goes to hell because of Satan. The only reason we go to hell is sin. Much more important than fighting Satan is fighting sin. . . . My biggest enemy is not Satan. My biggest enemy is John Piper. Fallen, fleshly, rebellious, hostile, selfish, lusting, power-grabbing, fame-loving John Piper is my biggest enemy, and he is the only reason I will go to hell, not Satan." So "Christianity is not a settle-in, live-at-peace-with-the-world-the-way-it-is religion like most Christians live their daily lives."

Paul makes this blunt and clear. "For if you live according to the flesh you will die, but if by the Spirit you put to death the deeds of the body, you will live" (Rom. 8:13). "There is a *mean streak* in Christianity, and it is not against anybody else but ourselves. In fact, it is against the meanness of ourselves against other people. If you feel like you are a mean person against others, a harsh person, a critical person, you know your problem? You haven't learned to make war. You haven't learned to be *mean*. You haven't learned to get violent against *your* violence, against *your* meanness, against *your* critical spirit. And you complain of it, talk about it, but have you made war 24/7 against it?"[45]

Therefore, the world lives in bondage and calls it freedom, "acting in lockstep with the prince of the power of the air." Satan hooks unbelievers in the nose and leads them around by their own passions (Eph. 2:2–3). "So the prince of the power of the air and the passions of our heart are in sync with each other, and any time we let our passions lead us into sin, we are not acting in freedom. We are in lockstep with the devil."[46]

44 APJ 256: "What Steals Your Joy?" (January 15, 2014).
45 APJ 489: "Declare War on Sin" (December 10, 2014).
46 APJ 725: "Nine Forceful Warnings to Confront Your Friend's Adultery" (November 10, 2015).

"There's only one lethal weapon in the artillery of Satan. You know what it is? Your sin! Nobody goes to hell because of being *harassed* by the devil. Nobody goes to hell because of being *possessed* by the devil. Nobody goes to hell because of being *oppressed* by the devil. Nobody goes to hell because of seeing green apparitions on their ceiling at night and hearing weird noises under the bed. People go to hell for one reason. *Unforgiven sin.* Period! That's all. Satan has *one way* to get you to hell and keep you from a savior." But if your sins are canceled in that Savior, "get rid" of your fear of the devil.[47]

Where did Satan's first inclination to sin come from?

Where did the universe's first sin come from? "How could a perfectly good being—with a perfectly good will and a perfectly good heart—ever experience any imperfect impulse that would cause the will to move in the direction of sin?"

Apparently, Satan is counted as one of the perfect angels "who did not stay within their own position of authority" (Jude 6). Ever since, God and evil are *not* rival powers. "I am not a dualist: God and his goodness and wisdom and power are the only ultimate, eternal realities. Evil is somehow derivative. It is secondary, without God being a sinner." And granting Satan "free will" doesn't answer the question. So ultimately we don't know. "For as many years as I can remember, I have said that this is among the mysteries in my theology for which I do not have an adequate answer." The Bible opens, not with the beginning of evil, "but with the presence of unexplained evil. Man is created innocent, and the serpent is already there."

"Here is what I do know. God is sovereign. Nothing comes to pass apart from his plan, which includes things he more or less *causes directly*—and things he more or less *permits indirectly*. There is no doubt in my mind that Satan's fall and all the redemptive plan of God for the glory of his grace afterward were according to God's eternal plan." This is because God can "see to it that something comes to pass which he hates." The supreme display of evil in the cross was preplanned by God (Acts 4:27–28). It is a great mystery, but God is both "sovereign over all sin" and "he never sins."

Regarding Satan, no single text settles the matter. But consider two lines of thought. (1) Consider God's active role in the people's wandering (Isa. 63:17). (2) Also consider that sin most grips the soul that cannot see God's glory, especially when God hides that glory (Isa. 64:7). "I am not saying this is a foolproof explanation of sin, but somehow God cloaked his glory from Lucifer, and in the cloaking of his glory—somehow still inexplicable to me—there rises a prefer-

---

47 APJ 1871: "Satan Cannot Scare You into Hell" (December 7, 2022).

ence in Lucifer's heart for himself over God." Perhaps God governs the presence or absence of sin by revealing or concealing his own majesty to creatures. But in the end, "how the very first sin in the universe came about is a mystery to me. I do not know how. What I am taught in the Bible is that God is sovereign over all things, including sin, and he himself is never a sinner."[48]

Isaiah delivers "the highest testimony of God's holiness and spotless sinlessness" (Isa. 6:3), and "one of the clearest statements of how God wills that sin happen in certain situations" (Isa. 64:7). Both are true.[49]

If Satan (and Adam) fell from perfection, can we sin in heaven?

No, we will not sin in heaven.

"We are not going to fall like Satan did or like Adam did. One of the marks of the new covenant is not only that God gives us eternal life, but also that God commits himself, because of Christ, to keep us from doing anything that jeopardizes our eternal life. In other words, the *newness* of the new covenant is precisely that God is committed to keeping us from falling away the way Satan did or Adam and Eve did in their days of innocence. They were not the beneficiaries of the blood-bought new covenant. We are." And this blood-bought covenant comes packaged with tremendous promises of our eternal flourishing (Jer. 31:31–34; 32:40; Ezek. 11:19–20; Luke 22:20). Notably, in the new covenant, the Spirit implants the fear of God in our hearts so that we will never turn away from him (Jer. 32:40). "In other words, the glory of the new covenant is that God will never find himself in the position where his redeemed people turn against him, because the very heart of the new covenant is that he won't let it happen." And it is "precisely this keeping power of God, this keeping commitment of God, which Jude sees as the mark of God's majesty and dominion and authority," because God "devoted his entire being to keeping his children" (Jude 24–25).

We will not fail in eternity because Christ will continue interceding for us (Heb. 7:25). Christ did not die and get resurrected to go "on a vacation forever." No. "The resurrection of Christ led to his new role as the Redeemer in heaven who continually intercedes on behalf of the saints." Like he prayed for Peter, Christ prays for our endurance (Luke 22:31–32). In the glorification, this "eternal intercession of Jesus will keep us from any sinning. This is what he bought for us in the blood forever."[50]

---

48 APJ 749: "Where Did Satan's First Desire for Evil Come From?" (December 14, 2015).
49 APJ 809: "Does Sin Have a Necessary Place in God's Plan for the Universe?" (March 7, 2016).
50 APJ 777: "How Do We Know We Cannot Sin in Heaven?" (January 21, 2016).

On exorcisms

As a young pastor in 1981, John Piper's phone rang at ten thirty one night. The caller was distressed about a woman in an apartment, apparently demon possessed. Would he come over? He agreed, called his fellow pastor, Tom Steller, and together they arrived at an apartment where one man and five women were barricaded inside the apartment with another woman—bitter, threatening, eyes glazed over, holding "a little penknife in her hand." They talked for two hours. "I read Scripture and read prayers of deliverance." But the evening came to a head when the woman turned violent. "She knocks the Bible out of my hand, she rips the paper out of my hand, she pounds on my back. About one in the morning, when the word of God and the force of evil were at their fever pitch, one of the young women started to sing." They simply sang "Alleluia." And with this song, the violent woman "became vicious, threatened everyone if we wouldn't stop singing. She fell on the ground, screamed for Satan not to leave her, went into convulsions, and then went limp. When she came to, she didn't have any idea what had happened. She was willing to take the Bible, read Romans 8, and pray with us." Just ten minutes of song "banishes Satan. It has great power." So march off to spiritual war with Scripture. And armed with a song (2 Chron. 20:21–22).[51]

Such experiences are exceedingly rare in the West. "People sometimes ask, 'If Satan is real, why don't we see more demon possession and exorcisms in America? How come we just hear about that from Indonesia?' I've got an idea. Satan holds American Christianity so tightly in the vise grip of comfort and wealth that he's not about to tip his hand with too much demonic tomfoolery."[52]

When spiritual encounters occur, the power to cast out demons doesn't equate to personal spiritual authenticity. Think of Judas, a disciple who knew Christ and who healed the sick and cast out demons. "And he was not saved. He was not born again. He was not elect. He was, Jesus said, 'a son of perdition'" (John 17:12). Jesus knew this was going to happen; it was not going to surprise him, and yet "he chose to have Judas in his band and to give him unusual power." Prophecy and exorcisms will be done by those who do not know Christ (Matt. 7:22–23). Today these "Judas-type people" have been in the church for a long time. "They have benefited in all kinds of ways from their walk with Christian people and their external connection with Jesus Christ, and they are performing certain kinds of wondrous works. And they are not saved." Instead, the true mark of personal, spiritual authenticity "is not an attachment to Jesus *who can do miracles*," even exorcisms, "but rather an attachment to Jesus *who loves*" (1 Cor. 13:2).[53]

51 APJ 1532: "Dismiss the Devil with a Song" (September 30, 2020).
52 APJ 1466: "What Are the Spiritual Dangers of Technology?" (April 29, 2020).
53 APJ 223: "Does John 15 Defy Calvinism?" (November 25, 2013).

On divination, necromancy, mediums, witches, sorcerers, charmers, fortune tellers, and palm readers; the use of signs, omens, séances, and Ouija boards; and talking to angels, demons, the dead, and the recently returned from the dead

If someone dies on the operating table, goes to heaven, gets sent back to earth, comes back to life, and writes a best-selling book about what he saw in heaven, should we read it?

No. The Bible forbids communicating with the dead, and the prohibition applies here. In principle, there's no difference between calling up the dead in a séance, as the witch of Endor did (1 Sam. 28:1–25), and someone coming back to life on the operating table. God's "beef" with both is the same: "It belittles the sufficiency of God's communication" (Isa. 8:19). Seeking to hear from the dead means you don't trust God and what he has spoken. When it comes to heaven, meditate on the banquet feast of revelation God has given us already.[54]

Speaking of Saul seeking out the witch of Endor (1 Sam. 28:1–25), what should we draw from the story? Does it mean speaking to the dead is possible?

At this point in the story, King Saul and David were enemies. David was rising in the ranks, and would soon become the replacement king. Saul hated this and grew more blatantly disobedient to God. Saul's rejection as Israel's king was bad news delivered by the great prophet Samuel. And Samuel told Saul that his personal rebellion against God amounted to "the sin of divination, and presumption is as iniquity and idolatry. Because you have rejected the word of the LORD, he has also rejected you from being king" (1 Sam. 15:23). Divination is idolatry. Divination amounts to rejecting God. But the story continues. The great prophet Samuel dies (1 Sam. 25:1; 28:3). And in a wise act, Saul purges from the land all its mediums and necromancers (1 Sam. 28:3). But Saul can't help but want to hear from Samuel again, so he seeks out a witch. He knows this is wrong because he shrouds his identity and goes out in the darkness. The witch he finds also knows it's illegal (1 Sam. 28:8–10). But it works. The witch of Endor connects him with Samuel—and Samuel is angry. The prophet confronts Saul and "predicts he's going to die in the battle because he's broken the law of God at every level and sunk to the degradation now of using an illegal medium. This is the bottom of Saul's degradation." It's the point of the story. "In his next battle with the Philistines, Saul is a dead man."

So the point is not that "necromancy and divination or the work of mediums is *impossible*, but that it is to be *avoided* at all costs by God's people because it is an assault on God's wisdom and authority and love—and is therefore in the

54 APJ 302: "How Real Is the Book *Heaven Is for Real*?" (March 20, 2014).

category of idolatry and rebellion and abomination." We're not secularists. We believe in the supernatural. So "the point is not that they're unreal, but that you should not, in any case, participate in them."[55]

Yes, we believe in the supernatural. So what about angels? Angels are God's servants, here to help us. They surround us. So can we speak with them? Or is it more likely that those who claim to converse with angels are really conversing with demons?

A person claiming to speak with angels may be "simply conversing with images or voices in his own head that are not in fact either demons or angels." Or, yes, he could be conversing with demons (2 Cor. 11:14). But the main concern is that people seeking to speak to angels are wrongly directed. Consider four points. (1) Seeking to communicate with the supernatural realm, but not with God, is pagan idolatry (Deut. 18:10–12). This practice gives the impression "that God's not real, or that he's begrudging in telling us what we need, or that he's insufficient in himself to provide the truth we need to live by." (2) The New Testament doesn't tell us to speak to angels. And no Christian or apostle is described as speaking with angels. (3) The New Testament warns us to never replace Christ with angels (Col. 2:18–19). "Paul is concerned not simply with people who are worshiping angels, but they're replacing Jesus as the head, esteeming angels more significant than the paths of nourishment and strength and help and encouragement that God has appointed through the head, Jesus Christ." (4) Related, our solidarity with Christ is better than what angels offer (Heb. 4:14–16). We come directly to Christ, not to angels, when we need help. "So, for those reasons, I would strongly discourage anyone from seeking to communicate with angels. I would regard the claim that one does such a thing to be a mark not of maturity but of immaturity in thinking that something more glorious, more satisfying, more amazing, more helpful, could be found through angel conversations than through the glory of God's word and prayer by the Spirit in the fellowship of God's church."[56]

So we should say no to conversations with angels. But what about something subtler, like "signs" from God? If God rules over all things by his providence, shouldn't we expect our lives to be filled with little "messages" we can decode?

This question can be answered wrongly and rightly. First, the *wrong answer*. We try to read providence "as if the hundreds of events that befall us each day had messages in them that we're supposed to decipher," codes to "show us how to think and how to feel and which way to go." But here's the *right answer*. "We

---

55   APJ 1052: "Did Israel's King Consult with a Witch?" (June 9, 2017).
56   APJ 1744: "Can We Speak with Angels?" (February 14, 2022).

live in the slipstream of God's merciful, all-governing providence by orienting our entire life toward understanding the revealed will of God in his word—not a secret, hidden will in the coding of clouds and coincidences. And by availing ourselves of all the biblically appointed means of grace, like corporate worship and pastoral teaching and brotherly correction, and by being transformed in the spirit of our minds, like Ephesians 4:23 says, so as to discern, moment by moment, the way of truth and love."

God's all-governing providence bolsters our confidence in his word. So here are four reasons that we don't attempt to read the tea leaves of providence. (1) We simply don't have the wisdom to interpret a hundred experiences every day. (2) We don't root our faith in "providential circumstances." Whenever we meet uncertainties, we turn to faith and the means of grace and to fellowship (Rom. 10:17; Eph. 1:18). (3) We reject desires for special knowledge. "Very often, the desire to find coded meaning in natural phenomena or circumstantial coincidences is a desire that flows from the pride of possessing private knowledge that others don't have." Instead ask: "Am I dissatisfied with the word of God, the Bible—which everybody has access to—because I don't want to be lost in the crowd of just any old, ordinary Bible reader? I want to have my own special, private source of revelation so that I can feel set apart and special." (4) We should cherish the ways God reveals himself to us. "I think one of the main reasons that the Bible is so adamant in rejecting omens and sorcery and fortune-telling and mediums and divination is that all of these ways of trying to read providence fail to do precisely what the prophets and apostles made central. Namely, the prophets and apostles revealed God and his ways by relating everything to the character of God, the nature of God, the personhood of God, the wisdom of God, the justice of God, the love of God." We treasure his revelation. "So, I would plead with all the lovers of the all-pervasive, all-embracing, all-governing providence of God: don't replace the infinitely precious word of God with your puny, fallible capacities to decode the infinitely complex providence of God. While this age lasts, the paths of providence will be a mystery, but his word will be a lamp to our feet and a light to our path" (Ps. 119:105).[57]

Avoiding false gods and demon worship

False gods represent real beings, not fictional phantoms. The gods of the nations were "real, supernatural beings" and their worship was strictly forbidden (Deut. 29:18; Josh. 23:7–8). God makes it clear that "his people were not to assume that these gods were simply manifestations of his own true being—as if

---

57 APJ 1645: "Should We Watch for Signs from God?" (June 28, 2021).

the same god were behind every religion. They were different. They were competitors. They were enemies. They were demonic. They were not God. They were contenders for deity—real, supernatural, demonic realities" (1 Cor. 10:19–20).[58]

In this world of spiritual rivalry, we participate in Christ together in the Lord's Supper (1 Cor. 10:16–22). The meal is exclusively for those who have renounced the gods of the world (1 Cor. 10:21–22). The elements are for Christians only, not to be distributed to non-Christians in attendance to some evangelistic end. Pagan idolaters held feasts of unbelief, paramount to sharing the table and drink of demons.[59] But Christians hold a feast of faith. The feast is not for the unbelieving (1 Cor. 11:27–28). It would be "a tragic misunderstanding of the glorious transaction between Christ and his people at the Lord's Supper if pastors tried to reinterpret this supper [in its practice] as an evangelistic tool to point unbelievers to Jesus." The feast is exclusive in its participation, yet evangelistic in its plea. It tells non-Christians, what you cannot have now can be yours. Turn from the world's idols and embrace Christ.[60]

Should we love, hate, or pray for Satan?

As for *prayer*, no, "I don't pray for the devil or angels. I don't see any reason for doing that in the Bible."[61] As for *love*, no. We are never commanded to love the devil. "God never gives any evidence of loving the devil. He is beyond all redemption and, therefore, he has been handed over to his rebellion."[62]

As for *hate*, it's the opposite of *love*. And love carries two displays: (1) a love for what is lovely and pleasing, and (2) a love that seeks the welfare of a person "regardless of whether the object is lovely or pleasing." Likewise, hate has two displays: (1) an "intense disapproval or dislike for what is evil or ugly or distasteful," and (2) "an intense desire or choice that someone would suffer, would be judged, or that they be ruined or destroyed."

Regarding Satan, yes, "it is right to say that we should *hate* Satan in both of these senses and that God himself *hates* Satan in both of these senses." In both senses, God hates sin and hates the impenitent, and wills their judgment. This is especially true of Satan, as one "beyond repentance." The Bible never explicitly tells us that God hates Satan, but it's a conclusion implied by several texts. God and the Son, together, hate wickedness (Heb. 1:8–9). And those who fear God hate evil too (Prov. 8:13; Rom. 12:9). But God not only *hates wickedness*;

58 APJ 1076: "Do All Religions Lead to God?" (August 4, 2017).
59 APJ 444: "Should I Eat Halal Meat?" (October 6, 2014).
60 APJ 1561: "What Happens to Non-Christians Who Take the Lord's Supper?" (December 14, 2020).
61 APJ 1439: "How Can I Jumpstart My Prayer Life?" (February 26, 2020).
62 APJ 936: "Does God Love His Enemies?" (September 12, 2016).

he likewise *hates the wicked* (Pss. 2:4; 5:4–5; 11:5; Rom. 9:13). Likewise, the psalmist *hates wickedness* and *hates the wicked* (Pss. 31:6; 119:113; 139:21–22).

"So in the light of all these texts and others, I say, since Satan is the source and embodiment of all wickedness, God and the godly should, indeed, hate him—meaning both in a sense of *intense disapproval* and in the sense of *intense desire for his judgment* and dispatching out of history and out of influence into the lake of fire." Such a conclusion is "confirmed by the fact that Satan is beyond repentance, and never in the Bible is any thought of praying for Satan or wishing for Satan's conversion mentioned or considered virtuous." So in order for us to *love good*, we must also *hate evil* (Rom. 12:9). Thus, a failure to hate this "impenitent fountain of evil" is to fail to love the good. So, yes, "I think God hates Satan in both of those senses, and I think we should too."[63]

Don't read the Bible like the devil does

Satan "knows more truth than most theologians"—but "hates" what he knows. Demons know many facts about God, but they're not saved "because they *hate* those facts" (James 2:19). So affirming the Bible as true and reliable is no evidence of spiritual transformation, because the Bible is not merely full of facts but also "statements about the *worth* and the *beauty* and the *desirability* of those facts."[64] Unbelievers, like the demons, refuse to *love* the truth (2 Thess. 2:10), and this is their eternal catastrophe.[65]

So don't read the Bible like the devil. "The devil owns that God is true and probably knows more true things about God than we do. But the devil will not own that God is supremely valuable and supremely satisfying. The devil values himself above God. God's presence gives no joy and no satisfaction to the devil whatsoever. Therefore, our aim in reading the Bible should not be demonic, to rise just to the level of the devil. Our aim is, of course, to see what is really there, what is true about God—but always more, always more; namely, with a view to *feeling* what is valuable about God, *treasuring* the treasure that God is. Our aim is to see the millions of reasons why God is a treasure, not just the millions of evidences that God exists or has certain attributes." All our Bible and theology reading is for "doxological embrace and enjoyment. This affects the way you read. This is what I try to do. I try to read. You read on the lookout for evidences of value, evidences of preciousness, evidences that he is beautiful and sweet and satisfying."[66]

63 APJ 750: "Should I Hate Satan?" (December 15, 2015).
64 APJ 346: "Can I Believe the Whole Bible and Not Be Elect?" (May 21, 2014).
65 APJ 1194: "My Body: Friend or Foe?" (May 7, 2018).
66 APJ 939: "Five Strategies for Avoiding Intellectualism" (September 19, 2016).

Did Christ's death ransom the devil?

"No way" is Christ's death "a negotiation with Satan or a payment to Satan." When Christ met demonic forces in his ministry, he didn't barter. "He commands, and they go. No negotiations. When Paul describes what happened to Christ on the cross in Colossians 2:15, he says, 'He disarmed the rulers and authorities and put them to open shame, by triumphing over them in him.' This is a total defeat, not a negotiation. In my mind, there's just no thought in the Bible about God paying the devil a ransom."[67]

Why did the demons ask Jesus for pigs?

Jesus doesn't barter with demons. But in one of our most viral episodes (garnering 1.5 million views on YouTube alone in its first twelve months), we addressed Matthew 8:28–34. So why did the demons request to be sent into pigs, to be immediately drowned? Jesus conceded to them. But why?

A few things are very clear in the story. The demons know Christ; "they know that he has absolute power over them and can choose either to cast them out or not, and to decide where they go." Thus, "there's no negotiation here, as if they were equal partners at the negotiating table—Jesus is superior, and they know it." They know that their future is eternal torment. We know that there were "about two thousand" pigs (Mark 5:13). So the story is set in an unclean, Gentile land, a "pointer" that Christ's ministry "is going to result in a global mission to all the peoples of the world" (Matt. 28:19–20). That the demons asked for pigs "shows how much they hated roaming about in the world without any habitation." And yet "demons could not have seen that their new habitation, the pigs, would suddenly run down the hill and all drown—because if, in fact, they saw that coming, they wouldn't have asked for it."

But the pigs aren't the main point of the story. Foregrounded is the deliverance of two demon-possessed men. The pigs here serve to remind us of another place in the Bible "where Satan attempted to negotiate with God—namely, in the first two chapters of Job." It was a test of Job. "Job would face the choice: you can love God and trust him, or you can love your possessions and your family and your health more, and curse God for taking them away. In other words, God used Satan to test Job." This is what Jesus is doing here. "Jesus comes into this Gentile world. He conquers the devil. He sets the prisoner free. He presents himself as a great deliverer, able to restore life and hope. But he also takes away a herd of pigs—the livelihood, the wealth, from some in the community. He forces a choice: prosperity *over* love, money *over* Jesus, human resources *over*

67   APJ 1126: "To Whom Did Jesus Pay Our Ransom?" (November 29, 2017).

divine power—the power and grace of Jesus to give life and hope, or the love of possessions and wealth to be had from these pigs. And to our utter amazement, the people beg Jesus—the life giver, the devil defeater, the hope maker and hope giver—to leave their region."

Jesus is God. He defeats demons. He liberates the bound. And he's seeking worshipers from among non-Jewish, pig-raising people. "But Jesus demands a choice: love him and his salvation, or love your prosperity and your wealth—namely, your pigs. They failed the test. Matthew reports it, I think, in the hopes that we will not fail that test."[68]

---

68 APJ 1534: "Why Did Demons Ask Jesus for Pigs?" (October 5, 2020). Other episodes on consumerism, materialism, and the love of possessions include APJ 345: "Do I Love God or Just Love Loving Him?" (May 20, 2014), APJ 419: "What Luxuries in My Life Are Sinful?" (September 1, 2014), APJ 743: "Counsel for Online Shopping Addicts?" (December 4, 2015), APJ 1185: "Do the Biblical Warnings against Riches Apply to Most Americans?" (April 16, 2018), APJ 1460: "More Precious Than Praise and Possessions" (April 15, 2020), and APJ 1493: "How Can I Be Free from Materialism?" (July 1, 2020).

On the Reprobate, Capriciousness, and Divine Unfairness

Is God capricious?

After a three-week trip to Ethiopia and the United Arab Emirates in 2013, Pastor John returned home with a "significant theological, missiological insight" about divine impulsiveness.

After Piper delivered a lecture on God's sovereignty over all things, one listener raised his hand and noted that it "sounds a lot like the Muslim view of God's sovereignty—God does whatever he wants." Later in the same trip, said Piper, "I was standing in the second biggest mosque in the world, in front of the biggest wall of the one hundred names of God, under the biggest chandelier of its kind, standing on the biggest handwoven carpet. These are all the ways they describe it [the chandelier and carpet] when you are there. And my friend Mike was there explaining the names to me. He was just pointing out name after name written in Arabic. And he said, 'That one up there is usually translated *Capricious*, which means God is free; he can do anything he wants.'" There were other names on the wall—*Wise, Just, Kind, Compassionate*—but "*Capricious* virtually cancels those out, because if God can do anything he wants—meaning if you are standing before him, and he can just flick you off to hell or flick you off to heaven capriciously, without reference to his kindness, without reference to his justice, without reference to his compassion—then what good are those names?" In the end, Muslims must come to terms with a God who will do with them as he pleases—send them to heaven or hell as he chooses in the moment. Therefore, que será, será—whatever will be, will be.

So what distinguishes Allah's capriciousness from the Lord's sovereignty? Romans 3:25. "God put [Christ] forward as a propitiation by his blood, to be received by faith. This was to show God's righteousness [or justice], because in his divine forbearance he had passed over former sins." This is the heart of our faith. "God loved us by removing his own wrath from us by having Jesus, in his blood, absorb the wrath which was owing to our sin." For millennia, God had been passing over sins, as if "the belittling and the dishonoring of his glory didn't matter" (Rom. 3:25). And that's "unjust" and "unrighteous" of him, "to treat the infinitely valuable glory of God as though it were not valuable. And therefore, God, in order to vindicate his righteousness and demonstrate his just allegiance to the value of his glory, sends his Son to fix that." But this dilemma is a nonissue in Islam, "because God doesn't have to *do* anything to fix anything. God is free to take up a person like David and say, 'I will just let your murder of Uriah and your rape of Bathsheba go. I am free to do that.'"

Here was Piper's discovery. God's sovereignty exists only from within "the constellation of other attributes of God—his *justice* and his *mercy* and his *grace* and his *wisdom*, so that when God passes over a rape and a murder, something has got to give." God cannot simply let our sin "be swept under the rug of the universe." So he sent his Son to the cross to "vindicate" his own divine righteousness (Rom. 3:25). "So the upshot is that Christian views of God's sovereignty and Muslim views of God's sovereignty are profoundly different, because in the Christian view, his sovereignty is being guided or shaped by the other attributes from within God. Muslims tend to feel like if God has to yield to some sense of justice or some sense of righteousness or mercy or compassion, then he is limited." But God is not limited, "because those attributes are not *outside* of him, governing him like controllers from another source. They are *inside* of him. They are *who he is.*"[1]

Was God unjust to kill his son?

At first glance, the answer appears to be *yes*. Justice for sin calls for punishment on the wrongdoer alone (Deut. 24:16). The sinner must die, not the sinless one. "That is why the cross is an offense to the Jews." So the question is, "Did God break God's law in presuming to cause Christ to be a substitute?" The answer is "the very heart of the gospel," because the one who *did not* commit the sin was the one condemned for the sin (Isa. 53:4–5; 1 Cor. 15:3; 1 Pet. 3:18).

So how is the cross just? Three responses. (1) The cross is fair by union. "God has the right and the ability to constitute, to make, a union between Adam and humanity so that when Adam fell, we all fell in him, so that the punishment that came on Adam also came on us because we were in union with Adam." Thus,

---

1   APJ 234: "Muslims vs. Christians on the Sovereignty of God" (December 11, 2013). If forced to choose only one, Romans 3:25 is "the most important verse in the Bible" (APJ 272: "The Bible's Most Important Verse" [February 6, 2014]).

Adam's sin condemns all sinners of the old humanity (Rom. 5:17–18). In turn, it means that the second Adam can die for his people, his "new humanity" (Rom. 5:19; 2 Cor. 5:21). These two spiritual unions are unique, God-given, and not replicated in, for example, the natural parent-child relationships. (2) Considering the gravity of sin and its due penalty, the cross is fair. A mother cannot enter prison to pay the penalty of her son's sin against the state. But Christ is different. "Christ *did* come to vindicate the righteousness of God" and to repair the injury to his Father's glory brought about by our sin (John 12:27–28; Rom. 3:25). Christ alone can atone for and fix the wrongs done. (3) The cross is powerful to convert convicts. The mother could not change her son by this act. "This mother's desire for her son to go free provides no guarantee that this will not release a criminal onto the community or make him law-abiding. There is nothing certain about that at all. It looks like we are playing fast and loose with whether criminals go free. That is not the case with Christ. And this is unique to Christ. Everyone whom he saves by dying for them, he sanctifies" (Rom. 6:1–23). In his death, we died. "Our old self was killed, was dead, and therefore substitution is always transformation. That is just not true in ordinary jurisprudence." So, no, the cross was not unjust.[2]

In a later episode, the justice of the cross was made even clearer. First, the Bible contains several "glorious" texts on substitution (like Isa. 53:5; Gal. 3:13; Col. 2:14; 1 Pet. 2:24). Those texts will either change us, or we will manipulate or dismiss them. "And I grieve. I grieve that there are people who turn away from those truths as inconceivable or unjust." We must receive truth as it is revealed because "if people today are unwilling to have their way of thinking about the world changed, then either we will twist the Bible to fit our preconceptions or we will reject the Bible, because the Bible is resolute in insisting that Christ died in the place of sinners so that the justice of God is satisfied and sinners escape punishment."

At root is the derisive power of sin. Sin "dishonors God," "detracts from his glory," and "belittles him." We treat *what is not God* as valuable to us as *God* is meant to be. Thus, sin "is an effort to rob God of his glory" (Rom. 1:23; 3:23). "God's creatures have gone on record as devaluing the glory of God. It's as if the image of the Roman Caesar was ripped off the wall and trampled underfoot by mobs. Treason like that has always been a capital crime everywhere in the world. Trampling the glory of the most glorious being is the most serious crime in the universe. How then is this situation to be remedied justly?" God's glory must get "restored to its rightful place of exaltation and admiration. This

2   APJ 271: "Was God Unfair at the Cross?" (February 5, 2014).

justice happens by stripping glory from the perpetrators in proportion to the way they have stripped it from God. That is the meaning of hell. It will take an eternity to strip sufficient glory from finite creatures. They don't have infinite glory." Thus, "the enormity of defacing the glory of an infinite being" calls for eternal punishment.

So can Christ fix this? Yes! Christ arrived specifically "to repair, to vindicate the glory of God" (John 12:27–29). So "he emptied himself. He endured utter humiliation, not in a random way but precisely *for the glory of the Father*. Christ's whole incarnation was a reversal of our attack on the glory of God. Since he is infinitely valuable, his loss of glory in his humiliation and death can cover all our God-diminishing, God-dishonoring, God-defaming sins" (Phil. 2:1–11). In the cross of Christ, God's glory is vindicated to the degree that it was insulted.[3]

So is the brutality of the cross and the inferno of hell "overkill" for sin? No. "The essence of evil is loving and preferring and desiring and treasuring and enjoying anything above God." Sin is cosmic treason. "And since God is of infinite worth and beauty and greatness and honor—infinite—the failure to love and treasure and enjoy him above all things is an *infinite outrage*, worthy of *infinite punishment*. This will make no sense where God is small and man is big. It will only make sense where people see God as great as he really is, and see man, see ourselves, and see our outrageous God-belittling self-centeredness for what it is." Thus, it is "the most appalling reality in the world," that humans "turned from God as the all-satisfying fountain of life and joy and tried to find it, not in God, but in what he made. It is high treason and worthy of eternal punishment" (Jer. 2:12–13).[4]

Does God predestine people to hell?

Reprobation (or double predestination) is a tricky topic that must be handled with great pastoral care. But it must be handled, with attention to four considerations.

1. Proceed cautiously. If a *yes* answer to this question will undermine your faith and confidence in God, slow down. If a God who predestines whom he saves and who perishes can only mean to you "that he is unrighteous or unjust or not good," then "you shouldn't believe, even if it is true. I know that sounds strange. Only believe it if you see it taught in the Bible, *and* if it does not undermine other true and important things taught about God in the Bible." The answer to this question must come in due time, not hastily. "I am not eager to undermine

---

3   APJ 729: "Articulating the Glorious Cross to an Atonement-Rejecting Culture" (November 16, 2015).
4   APJ 1420: "Are Hell and the Cross Overkill for Sin?" (January 13, 2020).

anyone's confidence in the goodness and the justice of God." Piper's patience draws from personal experience. "I have wept—I mean, my early twenties was a season of great torment mentally and emotionally over theological issues like this. I have tasted what it means to put my head on my desk, face in my hands, and cry out to God: 'I don't get this.' So I want to be patient with people."

2. Know that all God's judgments are just. "No one will ever be in hell who does not deserve to be there. And this fact, that they deserve to be there, will be open and plain in all the universe in that day."

3. Know that God's actions are beyond our immediate comprehension. This means, "if God ordains ahead of time that anyone will perish, he does it in a way which is probably inscrutable to us and beyond our understanding. He does it in a way that the person is *really* responsible, *really* accountable for his choices, *really* guilty, *really* deserving of punishment."

4. Beware of cultural biases. "We live in a time where it is very difficult for people to let God be God. Even to conceive of a God with this much authority, this much complexity, this much power, is almost impossible for many modern people." Don't fail to understand and believe in the God of the Bible because you choose to be "a child of your time."

In the end, the final answer is affirmed implicitly or explicitly in at least seven key texts (Prov. 16:4; Rom. 9:11, 22; Eph. 1:11; 1 Pet. 2:7–8; 2 Pet. 2:3; Jude 4). "My answer is *yes*, God does determine from eternity who will be saved, who will be lost. But he does it in ways that are mysterious to us—so that on that day, no one will find any legitimate fault with God. No. The redeemed will know that they are saved utterly by grace while deserving hell, and the rest will know that they suppressed much knowledge of God's grace—and they deserve to perish."[5]

God does all things *well*, and as the judge of the universe he does all things *justly* (Gen. 18:25; Mark 7:37). This means that "no one will perish who does not justly deserve to perish. In heaven there will not be the slightest suspicion that God has acted unjustly, and all who are saved will know they deserve to be in hell—we know this—and the fact that we are not in hell, and some are justly in hell while we are in heaven, will not make us doubt God but will make us amazed with thankfulness of this utterly undeserved grace."[6]

If these answers make it appear that election is unconditional (prior to sin) and reprobation is conditional (because of sin), that would be a false deduction.[7]

---

5   APJ 450: "Does God Predestine People to Hell?" (October 14, 2014). See also APJ 1827: "Is Double Predestination Biblical?" (August 26, 2022).
6   APJ 547: "If God Is So Happy, Why Did He Create the Nonelect?" (March 6, 2015).
7   APJ 1302: "Are Calvinists Inconsistent with Romans 9?" (January 14, 2019).

Isn't this life too short to determine our eternal destiny?

Purgatory is fiction.[8] Our eternal fate is sealed at death (Luke 16:19–31; Heb. 9:27).[9] So a listener asks if it is "silly" for the soul's eternal destiny to be irreversibly determined by the eye blink of seventy years of life in this world.

No, it's *not silly*. It's *"perfectly just* for God to condemn a person to eternal suffering, not just on the basis of seventy years of sinning, but on five seconds of sinning." Three reasons. (1) One five-second sin condemned all men in sin (Rom. 5:18). Five seconds—"that's how long it took Adam and Eve to be condemned, along with the whole human race. Treason against the all-wise God—the all-powerful Creator, the sustainer of the universe—brought condemnation." (2) One sin violates the entire law (James 2:10–11). Judgment is not based on how many sins we amass. "The issue is the vast difference between us as sinners and the infinite greatness of the person we're sinning against." (3) The law obligates us to *complete obedience* or *utter failure* (Gal. 3:10).

So "any offense, any dishonor against an *infinitely worthy*, an *infinitely valuable*, an *infinitely dignified*, an *infinitely beautiful* being is an *infinite sin* and deserves an *infinite punishment*. If the only way to measure the seriousness of sin and the seriousness of punishment was the time it took to sin and the time it took to punish, then maybe eternal hell would be an overreaction. But neither human nor divine justice operates that way."

In just five seconds, you can kill a man. Imagine a twenty-year-old murderer who gets fifty years in jail—"378 billion times more punishment than the five seconds it took to murder." The heinousness of evil is punished by disproportionate time. "We all know that *time* is not what measures the grievousness of a sin. Otherwise, the five seconds it takes to kill means you'd be in jail for five seconds." And "everybody knows" that five seconds in prison wouldn't serve justice. The dishonor is proportionate to the one dishonored. To dishonor an image bearer of God is serious. But "if you dishonor a toad, you're not very guilty. I stomped on a toad when I was a teenager, and I felt a little bad, but not much. If you dishonor a man, you're very guilty. If you dishonor God, you are infinitely guilty because he's infinitely worthy of every millisecond of worship in your life. If you don't give him worship, you multiply

8 APJ 179: "Can a Sinner Be Saved after Death?" (September 23, 2013), APJ 832: "Does My Soul Sleep after Death?" (April 7, 2016), APJ 1162: "Can a Devout Roman Catholic Be Genuinely Born Again?" (February 21, 2018), and APJ 1290: "How Will Christ 'Reconcile' Unbelievers to Himself?" (December 17, 2018).

9 APJ 179: "Can a Sinner Be Saved after Death?" (September 23, 2013), APJ 1267: "How Do I Question Someone's Salvation at the End of His Life?" (October 24, 2018), and APJ 1863: "Do Unbelievers Get a Second Chance after Death?" (November 18, 2022).

the storehouse of wrath. And who can measure such an offense? Well, God can, and he is just."[10]

God made me—doesn't he owe me eternity?

We don't self-create. We don't choose to exist. God made us by his will, not by our permission. So wouldn't it be fairer for us all to be saved in the end? By making us, doesn't the Creator owe us eternity?

No—just the opposite. Paul answers why *we owe God everything*, and *he owes us nothing* (Rom. 11:34–36). God knows all things, so we don't counsel him. Indeed "we have never given anything to God that would put him in our debt as one who should pay us back, because everything is his already." That means "since all things come from God and are sustained through God, they exist to call attention to his glory, not our glory. That's the root issue of proud people. They don't like everything existing for God's glory." Paul makes this point in his potter/pot metaphor (Rom. 9:20–21). The pot does not answer back to the potter because "the creation has no right to tell the Creator how he should have done his work." In a parable, Jesus clarifies how a spirit of entitlement feeds pride (Matt. 18:21–35). A servant owed the king "zillions of dollars," and the gracious king canceled this unpayable debt. In return, the forgiven—but arrogant—servant demanded tiny sums of debt from his own debtors. The assumption that God *should* forgive me leads me to take an abusive posture toward others. "The mindset of being owed—'You owe me, God!'—is the essence of pride, and that leads to the destruction of others. You can see it in history, but the mindset of owing God everything—being a debtor to mercy, expecting nothing because of our merits but only freely in mercy, and deserving nothing good from God at all—that leads to a life of brokenhearted humility and service." This is exactly how Paul put it (Eph. 4:32). "If you are treated better than you deserve, then you have the mindset to treat others better than they deserve."[11]

Isn't election divine favoritism?

God shows no partiality. But he seems partial in election. "Jacob I loved, but Esau I hated" (Rom. 9:13). So is God impartial or partial? Isn't election divine favoritism?

(1) It's true that God is impartial (προσωπολημψία; Rom. 2:11; Eph. 6:9; Col. 3:25). But "impartiality does not mean treating everyone the same. It means basing your treatment of others on the right kind of considerations: Did the defendant actually

---

10 APJ 1150: "Is This Life Too Short to Determine Our Eternal Destiny?" (January 24, 2018).
11 APJ 1032: "God Made Me—So Doesn't He Owe Me Salvation?" (April 24, 2017).

kill the man? If he did, then he goes to jail. Is the kid a really good ball player? Then he should be on the team." That's impartiality. (2) But God's impartiality means that he never elects by "irrelevant considerations" like personal holiness, wealth, wisdom, power, or pedigree (1 Cor. 1:26–30). (3) God's electing choice is "based on his own hidden wisdom" (Eph. 1:11). From "the counsel of his will" he chooses some because he's after a remnant (Rom. 11:5). By doing it this way, showing no favoritism, he maintains an awe-inspired humility in his elect (1 Cor. 1:26–30).[12]

Wouldn't God have been more loving to not create anyone?

Why create humans at all if a majority of them will spend eternity in hell?

1. Paul cautions us in Romans 9:20. Who are we to advise God? "God is not taking a vote on what he should or shouldn't do. And I guess that leaves us to simply trust and believe that his foreknowledge of most of humanity's future eternal damnation doesn't compromise his character in creating them anyway." In that light, God has secrets he doesn't reveal to us (Deut. 29:29; 1 Cor. 13:9–10, 12).

2. It's a problem for us all. Why would God create a world that could potentially lead to so many people suffering eternally in hell? That's a problem for Calvinists, Arminians, and open theists alike. Calvinists ask the question because we believe that God planned all things that come to pass, including eternal judgment. Arminians have the question because God can foresee the fall of man and decides to create humans anyway. Open theists have the question because God knows that one possible future would be a world where sinful creatures are condemned, yet he proceeds to create within this risk.

3. Consider the available responses. You can become an atheist, a universalist, or an annihilationist; or you can believe that God is evil; but in the end, "none of these is a very happy solution." The response boils down to Scripture and "whether you have seen the compelling, self-authenticating signs of God's glory and truth in the Scriptures, and in its center, Jesus Christ, winning you over to the trustworthiness of God's word. All these worldviews stand or fall, not finally by whether we can think up enough negative or positive consequences for each worldview to arbitrate between them, but rather which of them accords with the word of God, the Bible."

In the end, God's glory "includes his wrath and his power and his mercy, in proportions that are just and right and good, even if we can't see it perfectly now" (Rom. 9:22–23). So we should be amazed that we are saved and eager to reach the lost. We should be deeply humbled, "with our hands on our mouths and our knees on the ground and our heads bowed before the wisdom and

12   APJ 399: "Is Election Divine Favoritism?" (August 4, 2014).

holiness and righteousness and goodness of God in choosing to create a world in which he knew that millions of people would reject him and suffer eternally because of it."[13]

Why are the rewards of heaven unevenly distributed?

Listeners ask about God's fairness in heaven too. In a previous episode (APJ 417), Pastor John suggested that eternal rewards are based on the level of our faith. So does God show an eternal bias toward those with greater faith?

It's true. There *are* distinctions in eternal rewards. This conclusion is built on three pillars. (1) No one in heaven will live with regret or sorrow (Rev. 21:4). (2) In eternity, every believer's heart will be filled to the brim with God's joy (Ps. 16:11). (3) Yet within this regretless eternity of full joy, the Bible says that we can expect to see rewards distributed at differing levels, based on our earthly lives (Matt. 10:41; Luke 19:17–19; 2 Cor. 5:10; Eph. 6:5–8; Rev. 2:23). Any eternal reward is a gracious gift. "We don't deserve them. And they will be evidences that God looks with favor upon his own work of grace in our lives, working through us." So our rewards, and the rewards of others, can only prove to be "occasions for happiness in heaven" and never reasons for regret or "disappointment."

So how do we resolve (3) in light of (1) and (2)? Jesus says that generous people in this life will get more reward, a point made with the image of measuring cups (Luke 6:37–38). In effect, we measure our eternal reward by the measure we use in our cheerful giving here. "So will those who give God a small ladle be defective or lacking in fullness of joy? No, they won't, because Jesus says, 'Good measure, pressed down, shaken together, running over, will be put into your lap.' You will be full, more than full. It is all grace. But your *capacity for fullness* has been determined, it seems—this is my interpretation—by your generosity to others."[14]

Distinctions in eternity aren't toxic and will never lead to eternal envy, resentment, or regret. How is that possible? Is it because we will be oblivious to the distinctions? No. It's possible because heaven is a place of perfect fellowship and complete joy. The fullness is based on the differing capacities we each will have to hold that joy. The difference in our rewards comes from the difference in our capacities. We will all be full of joy, but our volume of joy

---

13 APJ 1489: "Would God Have Been More Loving Not to Create Anyone?" (June 22, 2020). In the first decade of emails to the podcast, Romans 9:22 is by far the most mentioned Bible text. See APJ 1720: "Do the Nonelect Have a Chance to Repent?" (December 20, 2021) and APJ 1827: "Is Double Predestination Biblical?" (August 26, 2022).

14 APJ 996: "Will Some People in Heaven Have More Joy Than Others?" (January 30, 2017).

will differ. And it will be no secret. Those who perceive a *fuller* volume of happiness in others will rejoice for them genuinely and without envy. And those who perceive a *lesser* volume of happiness in others will not be made arrogant by the difference but be further motivated to share their own joy. Our eternal fellowship will become a perfectly designed cosharing, even as our rewards differ (1 Cor. 12:26).[15]

So, yes, the deeds we do now correlate to our future, eternal rewards (Eph. 6:8; 1 Cor. 3:14–15; 2 Cor. 5:10). In eternity there will be "different degrees of glory—not that there are unholy people in heaven, or inglorious people in heaven, or unhappy people in heaven, but that everybody's capacities will be full, but the capacities are different." There will be a perception of difference, but no envy and no boasting in the distinctions, only perfect humility. Heaven's differing rewards will be visible to all, within a sinless hierarchy of perfect humility.[16]

15 APJ 1188: "Why Will Some of Us Get Fewer Rewards in Heaven?" (April 23, 2018).
16 APJ 549: "Will Some Saints Be Happier in Heaven?" (March 10, 2015).

On Trials, Sorrow, and Chronic Pain

Suffering, sacrifice, and Christian Hedonism

Pastor John's signature book, *Desiring God*, was published in 1986. When it released, one missionary gave it a scathing critique, calling it "warmed over, middle-class American, feel-good Christianity." Do what makes you happy, or you're sinning, the critique claimed. The criticism came from a misreading, but it motivated Piper to better develop his theology of suffering. As he did so, Paul's "sorrowful, yet always rejoicing" phrase became "a mantra" for him (2 Cor. 6:10). "There is sorrow at every turn of the road in this fallen life, not only because things go hard for us, but now in this modern world [of media] we can watch people suffer everywhere all the time." The Christian life is 24/7 rejoicing, but we have causes to be weeping 24/7 too (Rom. 12:15). Sorrow never abates in this life. So "if Christian Hedonism can't create a people who can cry and rejoice at the same time, let's just close up shop, because *you should always be crying*, and *you should always be rejoicing*, and there is *always reason* to do both in your life." We always carry within us, simultaneously, sorrow and joy. So suffering became an essential part of the theology of Christian Hedonism to combat the assumption that Christian Hedonism is just "'another one of those American, middle-class, feel-good theologies,' when in fact my whole purpose was to destroy and attack a comfortable settling-in with the American way, which I think finds its pleasure in stuff, not God."[1]

Will God give me more than I can handle?

This question boils down to two sets of questions and four possible answers.

First question: (A) How does *handle* relate to our capacities? (A1) Does it mean that God "takes into account our independent possibilities based on our track record of *handling* trouble" and then "measures out that trouble to us so

---

1 APJ 121: "Suffering, Sacrifice, and Christian Hedonism" (June 27, 2013).

that it doesn't go beyond what we—independently, by our own resources—can *handle*"? Or (A2) does *handle* mean things that we *can handle* "if we receive them by faith in divine assistance?"

Second question: (B) How does *handle* relate to personal failure? (B1) You will *handle* everything—meaning you will never fail, only succeed. Or (B2) you will fail, but never so badly "that you never recover or repent or restore reconciliation, and that you are never finally lost because you failed."

Paul promises that no temptation (or test) will "overtake" you, because God "will not let you be tempted beyond your ability" (1 Cor. 10:13). That means "God won't give you what is beyond what you are able," meaning "not beyond what you are able with God's help." In the testing, there will be grace for you (2 Cor. 9:8). Surviving trials—*handling* them—magnifies God's work in us, not in our self-sufficient handling power (1 Cor. 15:10).

And *handle* doesn't imply that we never fail. No, we will stumble, but God will bring his work in us to completion as he guards us from ultimate spiritual failure (Luke 22:31–32; Rom. 8:30; 1 Cor. 1:8; Phil. 1:6; 1 Pet. 1:5). "God will never let us *so stumble* or *so fail* that we don't recover and repent and are restored. In other words, he will never let us sin our way into apostasy and damnation. He will enable us to bear the fruits of genuine faith and perseverance to the end." So the final answer is *no* to A1 and B1, and *yes* to A2 and B2.[2]

Cancer blinded me—and I'm only twenty

"I feel about the prospect of blindness the way I feel about suffering at the end of my life or being persecuted or tortured," Pastor John admitted. "I sometimes wonder if today's grace will be there for that trial. And I know that is not the way it works—that if I am going to be able to meet the trial of going blind or suffering or being tortured at the end of life, I am going to need a special grace, a specific grace, in the moment for that very specific trial that I face."

To the blind, four suggestions. (1) Take it day by day. Pray for "a special grace, a specific, precise, tailor-made grace for this particular burden of blindness." But know that we cannot live off future mercies, because "there is a new, special mercy from God for every new, special trouble that each day brings" (Lam. 3:22–23; Matt. 6:34). (2) Study the life and testimony of quadriplegic Joni Eareckson Tada. (3) Without pretending, romanticizing, or dreaming, but in utter realism, know that this life is "very, very short" (2 Cor. 4:17). Our afflictions are *momentary*—and by *momentary*, Paul meant *only a lifetime.* So our trials can only last "a little while" (1 Pet. 1:6). A lifespan is a vapor

---

2   APJ 694: "Will God Ever Give Us More Than We Can Handle?" (September 28, 2015).

(James 4:14). So it becomes "a wonderful, God-given miracle" to live in the "joyful confidence" that in the time of a vapor's breath I will see again! (4) In a world blinded to eternity, ask God to open your eyes to your eternal hope (Eph. 1:18). To the blind, consider that "millions of people use their *good eyes* and look at the natural world and do not see the glory of God." Even during Jesus's life on earth, "thousands of people used their *good eyes* and looked at the very Son of God in the flesh and did not see the glory of the only begotten from the Father" (Matt. 13:10–17). Today, "millions of people hear the gospel with their *good ears* and read the precious pages of the Bible with their *good eyes* and do not see the light of the gospel of the glory of Christ." *That* blindness is "the greatest tragedy in the world."[3]

Prepare for suffering before the suffering arrives
Testifying to forty-five years of ministry experience, "a biblical orientation on suffering" has profoundly served many people in making their hardships more bearable and more meaningful.

The Bible offers two guidelines on suffering. (1) Relieve as much suffering as you can in this life, and (2) "squeeze as much Christ-exalting significance" from your pain as possible. On (1), love your neighbors by relieving their pain. As an example, Timothy faced chronic ailments that were clearly painful and disabling. So Paul prescribed wine, an ancient medicine (1 Tim. 5:23). On (2), four key points. (i) Pain is necessary (1 Pet. 1:6–7). "Only God knows when our pain is *necessary* (δεῖ)," and only he "knows how to test us with fire so that our gold—our faith—will be purified and not destroyed." So we cling to the promise that suffering may be needed, but "it is ultimately going to result in praise and glory and honor at the revelation of Jesus." (ii) Suffering throws us into the unseen arms of God (2 Cor. 1:8–9). (iii) Suffering produces an eternal weight of glory to come (2 Cor. 4:16–18). (iv) Hope in God protects us from bitterness (Rom. 8:22–23). "None of the promises of God keep us from groaning in our pain, but they do keep our groaning from becoming bitterness and despair. They turn meaninglessness and misery into waiting for glory."[4]

Essential to this prep work is 1 Peter, which, "more than any other book in the New Testament, is pervasive with suffering. It focuses on, teaches about, and prepares people for suffering."[5] The theme has become the particular calling of John Piper and the ministry of Desiring God—to "help people prepare to suffer" as we are taught in 1 Peter 4:12–19, although "all of 1 Peter is designed

3   APJ 834: "My Young Life Has Been Physically Ruined—Now What?" (April 11, 2016).
4   APJ 922: "Prepare for Suffering Now" (August 18, 2016).
5   APJ 628: "How Should We Respond to Calamity in the News?" (June 29, 2015).

to help people get ready to suffer." For a man and a ministry that so stresses God's sovereignty, "there is a certain burden you feel—at least I feel—to help people understand how this sovereignty is good news in suffering, and not just in easy times."[6]

To prepare to suffer, consider four things preemptively. (1) Consciously choose Christ over all else. (2) Use all the gifts God gives to draw you nearer to Christ. (3) Make it clear in life that the world is not your treasure (1 Cor. 7:29–31). (4) And be willing to renounce and lose everything in Christ (Luke 14:33; Phil. 3:8).[7]

The first step in preparing to suffer is to run a ledger. In one column, count every present possession as *loss*. In a second column, count Christ as *gain* (Phil. 3:1–11). "This is how you prepare to suffer. You turn upside down your value system." You get up every morning and consciously count (ἡγέομαι) and settle this ledger in your mind.[8] The prosperity gospel has no loss ledger, proving itself powerless to prepare Christians to suffer well.[9]

How do we prepare our children for suffering?

Pastors are faced with the challenge (and opportunity) to prepare others for suffering. Parents, too, face the prospect of raising children in a world where they will suffer. How can those children be prepared for future suffering? Three considerations guide parents in this solemn task: worldview, discipline, and model.

1. Worldview. Teach them that the world was created good but got broken by sin (Rom. 3:23). Things are no longer the way they are supposed to be. Sin introduced death, and death means suffering (Rom. 5:12; 8:20). The whole creation groans to be freed from this pain (Rom. 8:22–23). But God remains sovereign over all things, and his purposes never fail (Isa. 46:9–10). He's stronger than weather, storms, floods, lightning, dangerous animals, and killer viruses. "He is stronger than everything. Children need to hear this. They get it. They will embrace it more quickly than we do. And they can handle the mysteries." Never "give the impression to your children that suffering exists because God is helpless." Also, make the gospel clear. Christ bore all the suffering our sin deserves. "All the suffering, therefore, that comes into the life of a Christian is not because God is punishing him in his wrath—oh, let children understand this! But, rather, it is God's fatherly discipline for the sake of holiness" (Heb.

6   APJ 682: "Are Comfortable Christians Compromisers?" (September 10, 2015).
7   APJ 696: "Does Netflix Make Christ More Precious to You?" (September 30, 2015).
8   APJ 1853: "Step One in Preparing to Suffer" (October 26, 2022).
9   APJ 689: "How to Help Friends Escape the Prosperity Gospel" (September 20, 2015).

12:3–11; 1 Pet. 1:5). In all painful suffering, God is good and wise and loving and has a good purpose for us (Rom. 8:28). We will not understand everything about suffering, but "we do understand what God has taught us; namely, that he is sovereign, that he is good, and that he always has purposes for our everlasting joy." He will set everything right in the end (Luke 14:14; Rom. 12:19). "Saturate your child with this worldview."

2. Discipline. Discipline children with "appropriate firmness" (Prov. 13:24; Eph. 6:4). Discipline helps children learn to say no to selfish desires (Gal. 5:22–23; Col. 3:5). Without this, they will be "destroyed" by their own desires. By "coddling children, with no physical repercussions for their defiant behavior," you fail to train them to see God's discipline when it arrives in future, physical form.

3. Model. Of the three points, "this may be the most important: We should model for our children trust and joy in the midst of *our own* suffering and sorrows. They are watching." Let us apply our obedience to Christ before their eyes (Rom. 5:3; James 1:2). The parent's "greatest challenge" is "not primarily remembering all the things that should be taught in the catechism, but primarily being a parent growing in grace and humility and trust and joy in all the ups and downs of life." Because "few things will have a greater power in our children's lives to help them suffer as Christians" than to see mom and dad's suffering endured in humble faith.[10]

How do I find meaning in life as I suffer?

When life gets especially painful, and those pains bring questions about the meaning of life to our minds, where do we find meaning?

1. The problem. "Does the world, with all of its beauty and ugliness, gladness and groaning, love and hate, pleasure and pain, nobility and vulgarity, kindness and abuse, selfishness and sacrifice—does such a world as ours have a wise, good, just, satisfying purpose under the providence of an all-wise, all-powerful God?" Satan wants you to say no! He wants to steal from you "every vestige of confidence that God is wise and good and just and holy, and that God is working everything together for a great purpose." He wants you to think this world is meaningless and pointless (1 Cor. 15:32).

2. The response. You must take the sword of the Spirit and fight back. Open Scripture to see that the meaning of life "is to know God, and to enjoy God, and to reflect some of the beauty of God as we know him in Christ, and one day to see him perfectly and unendingly enjoy him." The meaning of this life "is not

10 APJ 948: "How Do We Prepare Our Children for Suffering?" (October 10, 2016).

comfort in this world now, nor escape from suffering now, nor the avoidance of loss now, nor the maximizing of physical pleasures now, nor the amassing of riches now, nor the achievement of any fame now, nor the right to any health now, nor that we would be treated with respect and justice now."

Sin corrupted all things. And into this corruption, God came to save us through his Son. So we can rejoice in the gospel and rejoice in the hope of what's to come (Rom. 5:2). The suffering will end. In light of that hope, for now, our faith is being tested and refined (1 Pet. 1:3–9). God means to test us. "The meaning of suffering in this life is the refinement of faith by the fires of various trials, that we might know God, love God, and show God as more precious than everything that the fires consume. Jesus Christ suffered precisely to bring us through these fiery trials, refined and purified, into the very presence of God for our eternal joy" (1 Pet. 3:18). In other words, these light and momentary afflictions are preparing for us an eternal weight of glory beyond all comparison (2 Cor. 4:17).[11]

God *tests* us; he does not *tempt* us. That the same Greek word is used for *trial* and *temptation* (πειράζω; James 1:2, 13) requires careful explanation.[12]

How do my sufferings complete Christ's sufferings?

The apostle Paul boldly rejoiced in his missionary sufferings, because in them, he said, "I am filling up what is lacking in Christ's afflictions for the sake of his body, that is, the church" (Col. 1:24). So what did Christ's work lack? And how do we complete it?

On the surface, this verse sounds heretical. "Surely it does not mean that anything is lacking in the atoning effect, the atoning sufficiency, of those afflictions." Jesus said that his work was finished (John 19:30). His "atoning price was paid in full." He bore "the whole curse" and paid "the whole ransom." So what's lacking? A parallel text brings clarity. For Paul, it seems that "to fill up what is lacking" means to *bring* or *carry* something, something that is, in itself, complete. So the church in Philippi gathered a big gift to give to Paul, and Epaphroditus "completed" the gift by carrying it hundreds of miles to Paul, thereby filling what was lacking in the gift (Phil. 2:30; 4:10, 18). "The way Epaphroditus *completed* or *filled up* what was lacking in their service was not by *adding* to it, but by *bringing* it."

So "Paul completed Jesus's afflictions by *transmitting* them. They have zero effect on lost people until they are known, until they are seen, believed, and

11 APJ 1590: "What Is the Meaning of Life?" (February 19, 2021).
12 APJ 1815: "Does God Ever Tempt Us to Sin?" (July 29, 2022).

loved. Here is the shocking implication for missions that I have discovered: Paul really does mean that his own sufferings are the means by which people taste and see the sufferings of Christ. This is a sober word to missionaries, because it says: Not only will you speak about the sufferings of Christ; you will live the sufferings of Christ. In both of those ways, you will bring people into contact with those sufferings so that they can be saved. In that sense, you will complete the afflictions of Christ."[13]

Suffering missionaries

So the shocking implication for missions is that the message of a suffering Messiah is *completed* by suffering messengers. The cruciform medium conveys the cruciform message. This is God's good design. "Paul's very bodily existence as a suffering apostle was a presentation in the flesh of the sufferings and death of Christ so that people could actually see in Paul—by his suffering—how much they are loved by Christ" (Col. 1:24–29).[14]

"The purpose of God in creating the universe is to display the greatness of the glory of his grace supremely in the suffering of his Son. Will you join the Son in displaying the supreme satisfaction of the glory of grace, in joining him on the Calvary road of suffering? Because there's no other way the world is going to see the supreme glory of Christ today except that we break free from the Disneyland of America and begin to live lifestyles of missionary sacrifice that look to the world like our treasure is in heaven and not on the earth. It's the only way."

The prosperity gospel can only distort the true gospel—its message and medium. Promises of wealth cannot gain "praise for the suffering Christ." The apostle Paul suffered regularly for Christ. "I die every day!" he said (1 Cor. 15:30–31). In his own suffering body, Paul *completed* Christ's suffering (Col. 1:24). He didn't *add* to Christ's finished work. He *extended* Christ's suffering "to those for whom he died." True for us today. We extend the gospel by our words and in our "own body and suffering."

So in a sermon, Piper pleaded with thousands of college students: "Christ died for millions of people all over the world—people on your campus, people in the unreached peoples of the world. Their debt has been paid, and they don't know it—they can't taste it; they can't feel it." And Paul isn't simply suggesting that the message of the gospel needs to be retold. He's also saying: "'It is through my body and my sufferings that the sufferings of Christ arrive in the unreached peoples of the world or on your campus.' How do the sufferings of

13 APJ 355: "Do My Sufferings Complete Christ's?" (June 3, 2014).
14 APJ 1666: "Is Death Past, Present, or Future?" (August 16, 2021).

Jesus arrive on your campus? They arrive *through your sufferings*. That's the meaning of Colossians 1:24." Gospel breakthroughs—whether among the nations or on your local college campus—come through suffering messengers. Your personal suffering, not your social-media appeal, is how the message will spread. "If you're going to be a missionary, mark it down: pain, loss of a child, malaria, marital strife, tensions on the team, demonic opposition, martyrdom. It's going to come. Don't think it's strange when it comes. It's the price. Jesus paid his life for our salvation. We join him in that suffering to display the nature of it."[15] Not *despite* our suffering, but *through* our suffering, we *complete* Christ's afflictions and reach the world (Col. 1:24–29). A cruciform message extended to the world through a cruciform medium.

Are we rewarded only for persecution or for all of life's pains?

What's included in the "various trials" or "fiery trials" of life (James 1:2–4; 1 Pet. 4:12)? Are these trials limited to direct persecution (Phil. 1:29)? Or do these trials include other forms of pain?

While most New Testament texts on trials focus on persecution, those same texts deliver principles that apply to "*all suffering in the path of obedience*—including disease or calamity, natural disaster or whatever." A simple hypothetical illustration: Imagine that, in your obedience to Christ, you set out to visit a sick person to encourage them. On your way, a persecutor of the church shoots you and injures your arm. You're brought to the ER, unable to finish your mission. In such a case you're "in a similar position" as you would be if you failed to get to the sick friend because you got into a car accident on the way and broke your arm and were brought to the ER. The same basic truths "guide" both cases—the intentional and the inadvertent injuries that stopped you.

How so? Romans 8:16–23. First, we will be glorified in Christ for the "sufferings of this present time" (8:18). In the context, these "present-time" sufferings clearly include the sufferings due to the fall's curse (8:23). So "Paul explains the sufferings with Christ in verse 17 as the sufferings of this fallen world. And then he says that they include groanings that come from these bodies that need resurrection." So in the path to serve a sick person, we could get shot, get in an accident, get sick ourselves, or get grounded by a natural disaster. In each scenario, "God is testing you. Will you trust him? Satan is tempting you. Will you doubt God?" So "it doesn't matter whether you have got cancer or whether you have just been put in jail by people hostile to Christians—both of those situations are covered by the principles of how to deal with suffering."

15 APJ 1442: "Will Suffering Weaken My Ministry?" (March 4, 2020).

Finally, it proves "impossible to draw a clear line between suffering that comes from *persecution* and suffering that comes from *disease*. If you are flogged for Jesus's sake and your back is ripped open—like Paul's was five times—suppose a week later, infection sets in. You thought you were done with that persecution, and weeks later, when you are almost healed, you get this residual infection, a fever comes, and death threatens because of the fever. Now are you dying because of a disease, or are you dying because of persecution?" The answer: *yes*. Or what if you get malaria on the mission field? Same dilemma. "And there are countless such ambiguities. We just can't make that distinction hard and fast. And thank God we don't have to." In persecution and in cancer—God is testing you in both. "He wants you to trust him in both. He is sovereign in both. He is good in both. The devil is wicked in both, and you need to resist him in both."[16]

So not only persecution suffering, "but body-wasting-away, disease-type suffering" is covered by Romans 8:23.[17] Including the taxing burdens and pains we endure daily.[18]

My sports team lost the championship.
Is this pain part of my eternal reward?
It's a threefold question. When God rewards us in heaven for our suffering, is this only for (1) the suffering of persecutors intentionally inflicted on us? Or does it include (2) the suffering our own sin caused us? And could it possibly include more trivial things like (3) our disappointment over a sports loss? Category 3 may sound silly at first, but it's not, because this is where we live—in a world filled with relative disappointments, like sports losses. Paul tells us that "this light momentary affliction is preparing for us an eternal weight of glory beyond all comparison" (2 Cor. 4:17). So are sports losses included here?

First, three observations about (2), suffering because of our sin. (i) God can use our sins to make us depend on him. In a context not about sin, Paul tells us that coming to the end of ourselves can cause us to throw ourselves on God (2 Cor. 1:8–9). In this way our sin can add to our eternal glory, if it throws us on God. (ii) But sin diminishes the believer's weight of glory. "It would be terribly misleading to say that our sins work for us an eternal weight of glory. In fact, sin in the Christian life is precisely what diminishes the weight of glory for the believer." But sin diminishes our eternal reward (2 Cor. 5:10). "So, if we go on sinning, that is like building with wood, hay and stubble, and it is not going to become a weight of glory for us. It is going to diminish our weight

16 APJ 518: "What Parts of My Suffering Are 'Trials'?" (January 26, 2015).
17 APJ 689: "How to Help Friends Escape the Prosperity Gospel" (September 20, 2015).
18 APJ 1401: "My Life Is Endless Drudgery—How Do I Find Joy in Christ?" (November 29, 2019).

of glory" (1 Cor. 3:12–15). More holiness means more glory beheld and more joy experienced (Matt. 5:5, 8). But sin diminishes this future glory. (iii) Sin causes lifelong damage to us and others (2 Sam. 12:1–23). "You might have a car wreck when you are going 60 miles an hour in a 45-mile-per-hour zone. That is sin, and you will be paralyzed the rest of your life because you broke your neck sinning. Now, will that affliction caused by sin function to bring you to a greater weight of glory? And my answer is, it can indeed!"

So what about: (3) suffering in the form of sports team losses? "You just lost your ball game, missed your field goal, and you were the kicker. Or you miss an airplane, and you are going on vacation. You miss your flight. Or it is prom night, and you wake up, and you have a pimple right in the middle of your forehead. Do those qualify as afflictions suffered for Christ, working for an eternal weight of glory? And before we laugh, think of it this way: All our troubles—*all of them*—are on a continuum from *easy* to *horrible*." And each hold potential "to make us sin by grumbling and not trusting the goodness and wisdom of God, whether it is a pimple on prom night or the loss of a child." There's the resolution. Does affliction—no matter how slight or tragic—cast us on God as our only *help* and *hope* and *treasure* and *joy*? "The girl that laughs at her pimple the night of the prom and sees it as a small thing compared to belonging to the King of the universe, and the boy who springs back quickly after the high school football loss because his identity and his joy is in Jesus, have both just experienced tiny afflictions that have produced big fruits of holiness. And that will be part of their reward."[19]

How do I honor God in my chronic pain?

Chronic pain is a serious trial for the believer. Magnifying God in chronic pain raises questions in two directions: (1) How do I maintain my own faith and joy? And (2) How do I help others enjoy God? Because (2) won't happen without (1).

Regarding (1), four considerations. (i) All the promises of God to us are "yes" in Christ (2 Cor. 1:20). (ii) "Every horrible thing that comes into our life is meant to cause us to fall on Christ, who raises the dead; increase our confidence that we will be raised; and rely on nothing but him" (2 Cor. 1:8–9). (iii) All our suffering is preparing for us "an eternal weight of glory beyond all comparison" (2 Cor. 4:16–18). Take heart. Every pain is "increasing a weight of glory in the age to come for us." (iv) Plead for relief. And if that relief does not come, glory in "the all-sufficiency of the grace of Christ" to sustain you in the pain (2 Cor. 12:8–10).

Regarding (2), helping others magnify God through your testimony in the pain, three thoughts. As seen in the last reference (2 Cor. 12:8–10), in pain "we

---

19 APJ 199: "What Pains Here Bring Greater Reward in Heaven?" (October 22, 2013).

should exult in Christ in our weaknesses." And your testimony here is critical. (i) "Don't murmur against God." To *not grumble* in hard times is to shine in a dark world like the noonday sun (Phil. 2:14–15). (ii) Within the pain that others witness, testify to the goodness of God. (iii) See your testimony as serving the good of others (Phil. 2:4–5). Even when "everything in you may be crying out, 'I hurt—pity me,'" testify of God's grace in the pain.[20]

As a related question, a listener asked: How does unalleviated nerve pain glorify God?

Look to Peter's life for a lesson. Peter's life was a yo-yo of faith and faithlessness. Without reserve he committed his life to Christ (John 13:37). But he soon denied even knowing Christ (John 13:38). The denial would break him to tears. But after Christ rose, Peter was restored (John 21:15–17). So what was Peter's reward for following Christ in his newfound maturity? His pains would increase. And he would be murdered like Christ was murdered (John 21:18–19). Christians all over the world experience this same reality. In youth—pain free. In maturity, after your faith has been tested and tried and proven authentic—chronic pain, with the last years of life spent "in unremitting pain, to the glory of God." This depth of pain does not correlate to a lack of maturity. Quite the opposite. So we must be assured that pain, no matter its form, will not separate us from God's love (Rom. 8:35).

So why do faithful saints suffer so deeply?

1. To testify that Christ is better than painlessness. "When we suffer without cursing God, without forsaking Christ, declaring ourselves to be his friend and servant and disciple and follower and a great lover of his glory and faithfulness, we make plain to others that having Christ is more precious to us than having freedom from pain. The pain, in fact, becomes a suffering with Christ because we are walking with him, we are holding fast to him in the midst of our suffering, rather than throwing him away because of our pain." Christ is greater than either a pain-free or pain-filled life (Phil. 1:20–21).

2. To accumulate more future glory. The light and momentary sufferings are *producing* (κατεργάζομαι) for us an eternal weight of glory beyond all comparison (2 Cor. 4:17). To *die* is gain, yes (Phil. 1:21). But "the long, drawn-out *pain of dying* is producing greater gain." So "with every bolt of pain, we can say—if we have the consciousness to do it—'God will make it up to us. He will make it up to me. It will not be wasted.' In heaven we will look back on all those years of seemingly meaningless sorrows and pains and say, 'It was worth it. He has made it worth it.'"[21]

20 APJ 548: "How Do I Honor God in Chronic Pain?" (March 9, 2015).
21 APJ 1611: "How Does Chronic Pain Glorify God?" (April 9, 2021).

So "not only is all your affliction *momentary*, not only is all your affliction *light* in comparison to eternity and the glory there (2 Cor. 4:17a), but all of it is totally meaningful!" (2 Cor. 4:17b).[22] "Every hour that you hand over your suffering to Jesus and bear it in the strength that he supplies and for the glory of his name, your reward is increasing in heaven. There is meaning to what looks to the world like absolutely meaningless suffering."[23]

I have chronic fatigue—how do I not waste my life?

A female missionary to Haiti became sick and is now stuck in bed with debilitating chronic fatigue, exhausted of the energy she needs to minister. How can she not waste what remains of her life?

The key is understanding the race of the Christian life. God calls us to run the race in a spiritual Olympics (1 Tim. 6:12). We all must run, "whether old or young, whether sick or healthy, whether blind or seeing. This Olympic spirituality is possible for the sick and senile because the race is against unbelief, not against sickness or senility." The race is a fight against lost hope and lost faith, "not against lost health." As Paul's life came to an end, he exemplified that this race "can and may be run *flat out* on your back" (2 Tim. 4:7). "Finishing the race means keeping faith. It's a race against unbelief, not against aging or physical deterioration." So "what gets us across the finish line with the saints cheering and the crown of life is not legs, and it's not hands—it's faith and hope." In the end, we cross the finish line "not by a burst of human energy, but by collapsing into the arms of God." In this fight for faith, we encourage and help one another (1 Thess. 5:14).[24]

How does a disabled mom achieve Proverbs 31 productivity?

A wife and mom of two young children struggles with chronic fatigue. She reads Proverbs 31, the model of a vigorous, valiant, and strong woman—up early, late to bed, endlessly busy inside and outside the house. How on earth does this model apply to her broken life?

Physical strength is a wonderful gift, but it pales in significance to God's grace in the heart. God doesn't delight in strong legs; he delights in those who fear him (Ps. 147:10–11). God wants faithfulness, and the faithfulness he wants from us is tailored to our capabilities.

So Proverbs 31 must be tailored. In this text we are witnessing "faithfulness in the life of an ancient woman in the full bloom of her health and strength. It

22 APJ 741: "Your Suffering Is Working for You" (December 2, 2015).
23 APJ 1605: "How Can I Serve the Dying?" (March 26, 2021).
24 APJ 1243: "I Have Chronic Fatigue—How Do I Not Waste My Life?" (August 29, 2018).

doesn't describe the form of faithfulness for a woman who is deaf and blind in her eighties or a woman who's recently married at age sixteen, just beginning to discover what wisdom is. And it doesn't describe the form of the faithfulness of a woman with disabilities that might keep her from planting a vineyard or putting her hand to the spindle or rising while it is still dark or even clothing herself." So take stock of what *does* transfer from the Proverbs 31 woman's life. She's trusted by her husband (Prov. 31:11). She's sharp with the finances (Prov. 31:16). She's generous to the poor (Prov. 31:20). She laughs at the future because "her faith is unshakable in the goodness and sovereignty of God" (Prov. 31:25). She speaks wisdom and kindness (Prov. 31:26). She demonstrates true beauty. Above all, she fears God (Prov. 31:30).

When you feel handcuffed by the limitations to your fruitfulness, look to Paul. Paul experienced this very thing (2 Cor. 12:7–10). When he met unproductivity, he embraced contentment. "God does not put as high a premium on productivity as we think he does. He puts a much higher premium on the qualities of character, the fruits of the Spirit, that you can exercise flat on your back in a hospital bed. I don't say it's easy. I do say it's possible. The form of faithfulness for a paraplegic, for example, is different than the form of faithfulness for an Olympic athlete. One person is given ten talents; another person is given five. The form of their faithfulness is not measured by the same set of achievements." So stop measuring yourself by the abilities of the ancient woman in Proverbs 31 or the healthy supermom you see today. God looks at your heart (1 Sam. 16:7). "There is a kind of mothering that God has designed for every disabled mom who will look to Christ and trust him.[25]

Your suffering is working for you

Jeremiah 32:40–41 made fifteen appearances in the first decade of the podcast. It's one of Pastor John's favorite Bible texts,[26] and his favorite promise that God will not leave us.[27] The text abounds with love. "What more can God say than that he rejoices to do good to us with all his heart and all his soul?"[28] So if God loves us this much and is sovereign over everything that happens to us, couldn't he simply make it so that his children never suffer?

Yes, he could. And no, he doesn't. In a sermon on Jeremiah 32:36–42 on the theme of purposeful suffering, preached in 1996 on the 125th anniversary of Bethlehem Baptist Church, Piper delivered this four-line poem. "Not grace to

25 APJ 1639: "The Disabled Wife and the Proverbs 31 Woman" (June 14, 2021).
26 APJ 1148: "Does God's Happiness Depend on Mine?" (January 19, 2018).
27 APJ 338: "If God Never Leaves Me, Why Does He Withdraw?" (May 9, 2014).
28 APJ 1798: "Crucial Texts for Our Hardest Battles" (June 20, 2022).

bar what is not bliss, / Nor flight from all distress, but this: / The grace that orders our trouble and pain, / And then, in the darkness, is there to sustain." Then he offered two real-life illustrations of how suffering works for a greater good.[29]

So in your God-appointed suffering, don't lose heart. And don't fixate on your circumstances.[30] To those ends, Paul writes to sufferers in 2 Corinthians 4:16–18 (a text that has come up in this section a few times already). In suffering, don't lose heart (2 Cor. 4:16). Why not? "Because"—the main argument—your suffering is *working* for you (2 Cor. 4:17). Our suffering is not meaning*less*. In Christ, it's made meaning*ful*. A "very controversial statement" today. Paul doesn't say that suffering *will be followed by* an eternal weight of glory. "That would be good enough." No, he says that the suffering *is producing* (κατεργάζομαι) an eternal weight. Meaning, "every millisecond of your pain from the fallen nature or fallen man, every millisecond of your misery in the path of obedience, *is producing* a peculiar glory you will get because of that." But in the moment of tragedy, "if anybody says to me that a believer's suffering was *meaningless*, I will be quiet, probably, because he is probably hurting really bad right now." But when the time is right, "I am going to come back eventually and say it *wasn't meaningless*. I don't care if it was cancer or criticism. I don't care if it was slander or sickness. It wasn't meaningless, because verse 17 says, 'My light, momentary, lifelong, total affliction is *doing* something.' It is *doing* something. It is not meaningless!" Therefore, don't look to what is seen and don't lose heart.[31]

The content of this compelling episode was later incorporated into what became an incredibly popular version of Shane & Shane's song "Though You Slay Me."[32] The song is derived from Job 13:15, a text Pastor John rarely ever mentions (intentionally).[33]

Doesn't medicine impede God's plan for my pain?

If our sovereign God ordains cancer for his glory and a Christian's good (Rom. 8:28), why is it *not sinful* to use chemotherapy and other modern medicine?

The answer: "It may be sin *to pursue* chemotherapy, and it may be sin *not to pursue* chemotherapy." It's not a question of human medical technology, because "if God ordains that I get prostate cancer, which I believe that he did, then I could ask in relation to prayer and supernatural healing the same thing that [was] asked about chemotherapy." Both medical technology and prayer

29 APJ 1715: "God's Plan When Our Plans Fail" (December 8, 2021).
30 APJ 1538: "My Suffering Feels Meaningless—What Can I Do?" (October 14, 2020).
31 APJ 741: "Your Suffering Is Working for You" (December 2, 2015).
32 APJ 639: "A Song for Sufferers" (July 14, 2015).
33 APJ 1876: "'Though He Slay Me'—Why the Silence on This Verse?" (December 19, 2022).

raise the same dilemma: "Why interfere *by prayer* with the natural progression of a disease that God ordains for his glory?" Because both *prayer and medicine* seek to impede sickness.

Take note of five key texts. (1) Three times Paul pleaded with God for pain relief (2 Cor. 12:7–9). God "doesn't treat prayer as an intrusion upon his sovereignty. He invites it as part of his sovereignty." God can magnify his *healing grace* in us, or his *sustaining grace* in us. Either way, we are invited to pray. (2) Whether God alleviates our pain or not, he designs disease to drive us back to himself (2 Chron. 16:12). "Asa proved to be so indifferent to his relation to God, and so saturated with a 'this-worldly' mindset and all of the resources of the world, that it didn't even seem important to him at all to seek God's help. He went straight to doctors without consulting God at all. And he was clearly wrong to do it." It's right to seek healing via medicine. It's wrong to seek medicine and ignore God. "If you fly to chemotherapy with no reference to God, no love for God, no dependence on God, no prayer to God, you are in the same situation as Asa." (3) Paul traveled with his physician (Col. 4:14), and he wasn't embarrassed to say it. "Rather, it seems as though he regarded Luke's skill as a physician as a gift from God." (4) Paul valued early medical therapies, like wine (1 Tim. 5:23). (5) Adam and Eve were called to cultivate creation (Gen. 1:28). "So you might cut down a tree. Cut it into boards and build a house to keep the sun off and the rain off. Or you might pick grapes and crush them under your feet and store them in a cool place and make wine out of them, which, in some cases would be called medicine. Or you might take the flight of electrons around the nucleus and so alter them that you create a beam that kills cancer cells."

Do we trust and depend on God? That's the issue. "Are we praying, trusting, loving, and seeking to submit ourselves deeply to his sovereign will? For there is no doubt—his sovereign will will be done. It will be done through *prayer* and through *miracles* and through *medical intervention*. And what God is looking for is not the least intrusive strategy of dealing with disease. He is looking for the deepest, most joyful submission to his sovereign will, however we deal with our suffering."[34]

Did my sin cause my suffering?

Sometimes our most painful suffering is directly caused by our sin (1 Cor. 11:30–32). But often our suffering isn't directly caused by our sin (John 9:3; 2 Cor. 12:8–9). So how do I know if my suffering should be met (1) with *patient endurance* or (2) with *immediate repentance*?

34 APJ 890: "Does Medicine Impede God's Plan for My Suffering?" (June 28, 2016).

Both categories are true. (2) God sends some suffering for us to *evaluate* our lives (Heb. 12:6). And (1) God sends some suffering for us to magnify God as we endure it in faith and patience (John 9:3). So how do we know which pain has come into our lives? "God may make it plain. He may. But he may not." Normally, these categories are "permeable" and "overlapping." So we should respond to all our suffering with self-evaluation *and* patient hope.

James calls us to meet all the various trials of life with "all joy" so that those trials can build "steadfastness" in us (James 1:2–4). And "he doesn't distinguish whether they are coming in response to specific sins we've committed or not. What he says is that in every kind of trial—every kind—faith is being tested. And the aim in every trial is a kind of steadfastness that shows that God is trustworthy, and wise, and good, and valuable, and all-sufficient for our situation." So whether or not we can tell that a certain sin has caused our suffering, we respond the same. So "let every trial have its sanctifying effect of killing sin, and furthering faith, and furthering patience, and furthering love. If the sin is known, kill it. If it is unknown, ask the Lord to protect you, to cleanse you from hidden faults, and to advance your capacities for faith and patience" (Pss. 19:12; 139:23–24).

Note that Job's suffering began when he was a blameless man (Job 1:1). But over time, Job's sufferings stirred up in him "the sediment of remaining sinfulness," which he repented of later (Job 42:5–6). "Whether the suffering in our lives is chastisement for some specific sin, or whether the suffering is an opportunity to glorify God through faith and patience—in both cases, we're going to discover remnants of sinfulness in our lives, which we should repent of and move beyond. Which is why I said there's always room for self-evaluation." So when suffering hits, *evaluate* and *endure*. Don't *ignore it* or *fear it* as a sign of God's condemnation—both of those responses are wrong (Rom. 8:16–17).[35]

In reckoning with the pain inflicted on Job's life, we must be aware of his sin. And our own. Each of us is worthy of God's judgment as "children of wrath" (Eph. 2:3). So anything and everything we are given that's *not judgment* is "undeserved." Every breath we take, any moment we *don't* suffer—it's all "undeserved" grace to sinners. Aware of this, we can be assured that "no injustice from God is ever done to any human. On the earth, everyone is treated by God better than we deserve—*everyone*." When it comes to the justice of the global flood, "until we feel the depth and horror of sin like this, much of the Bible will simply make no sense to us at all." Global tragedies remind us of the horror of sin against God. But redemption doesn't end our suffering in this life. Christians suffer (1 Thess.

35 APJ 1536: "Is My Suffering a Correction for Sin?" (October 9, 2020).

3:3; 2 Thess. 1:5). But we suffer in the comfort that our pains are "in the hands of our all-wise, all-powerful, all-good Father." Not in the hands of Satan, fate, or a god who is self-amused by our pain. Every sting in life is appointed and managed by a loving Father toward our final good (Rom. 8:28). So we can draw comfort from the fact that (1) God appoints our pain, (2) for our ultimate good, (3) to advance his wise purposes. Through it all, he will hold us fast.[36]

On this topic, redemption matters. Never confuse *judgment* and *discipline*. Between them is "an *infinite* difference." (1) God *judges his enemies*—the "misery" he brings on those without "any purifying or restoring or rehabilitating purposes, but solely to express his holy justice, his retribution," not restitution (Rev. 16:5–6). This is made especially clear in his coming eternal judgment (Rev. 19:1–3). (2) But God *disciplines his children*—a stark contrast. Discipline is "not retribution" for God's enemies; it's reserved for the sons "he loves and means to improve, even though it involves God's displeasure," all to our final good, "that we may share God's holiness as loved children" (Heb. 12:5–11).

The sobering truth is that "many of the painful things in the Christian's life are owing to our own sins: some that we committed before we were Christians, and some that we have committed since we have been Christians." Our sin can even warrant physical death, as we will see in a moment (1 Cor. 11:30). But in such extreme situations, this discipline prevents something worse (1 Cor. 11:31–32). It's "a stunning example of God's disciplinary judgment that goes so far as to bring about the death of his child. And that death is the disciplinary effect of sin in the child's life because it keeps him from going to hell." So "there is an infinite and precious difference between God's *retributive justice* in punishment and God's *purifying discipline* in our pain. And that difference does not lie in the origin—the human origin—of the pain, whether good or evil. It lies in the purpose and the design of God in our suffering."[37]

Can God kill his children?

Yes, he can. God brings discipline only to the children he loves (Heb. 12:6). But this may include the discipline of physical death (1 Cor. 11:27–32). "If he makes us weak, he's loving us. If he makes us ill, he's loving us. If he takes our life, he's loving us." He knows best how "to bring about in his children (1) love for his absolute holiness, (2) hatred of our bent to sinning, (3) gratitude for his amazing grace and patience in our lives, and (4) passion to trust him in every circumstance of life." But only "he knows best how to produce these great

---

36 APJ 1693: "Reckoning with the Message of Job" (October 18, 2021).
37 APJ 1002: "Is Pain Punishment for My Sin?" (February 13, 2017).

wonders in his church." We should not "second-guess" his means, even when they include the drastic discipline of physical death.[38]

So God can discipline through weakness, illness, and even death (1 Cor. 11:30)—the very same things Christ healed in his earthly ministry (Matt. 4:23; 8:17; 14:14). By death, God brings his children to heaven swiftly "because of the trajectory of their sin that he was cutting off and saving them from. Not to punish them, but to save them."[39] So God can protect his work of eternal salvation in his child through early mortality.[40] This "breathtaking" reality reminds us that "the death of a saint" whom God loves may be "the discipline of deliverance from condemnation. God takes him out so that he will not be taken out by the devil and by sin and go to hell."[41] Obviously, only God has the right to prematurely take the life of his child.[42]

Why is my child disabled?

A young couple, eager to start a family, has been told that their firstborn child in the womb likely has Down syndrome. How do they respond to such shocking sadness at having their joy stolen?

"One of the things that makes all sorrows even more sorrowful is that they are often such opposites of what we hoped for, prayed for, and expected." So it's not only "the painful fact that their whole life is now changed by the prospect of parenting a disabled child, but that this comes as a crowning response to their prayers for the opposite." The disappointment calls for three struggles for faith.

1. The struggle to see God's goodness. He remains good even as the most painful circumstances press us to see and live by faith—with hope in eternity, not with despair for our immediate circumstances (Pss. 27:13–14; 34:8; Matt. 5:8; 1 Cor. 13:12; 2 Cor. 5:7).

2. The struggle to see God's gift. "It's not wrong *to rejoice in* the gift of a healthy child, but it is wrong *not to rejoice in* the gift of a child with a disability. Both of these acts of joy are miracles." Christian parents must pray for God's help to change the object of their joy from *expected hope* to *given gift.* "The transition from the *hoped-for joy* in a healthy child to the *painful joy* in the disabled child is a huge transition. The first joy dies. It's a real death, and that death is painful. That wonderful joy disappears. It's gone. All that is happening

---

38 APJ 1352: "Why Does God Discipline Some Christians with Death?" (June 5, 2019).

39 APJ SE16: "How Do We Make Sense of the Coronavirus?" (February 28, 2020).

40 APJ 1561: "What Happens to Non-Christians Who Take the Lord's Supper?" (December 14, 2020).

41 APJ 963: "Did My Lust Cause Our Miscarriage?" (November 14, 2016).

42 APJ 684: "If Babies Go to Heaven, Why Oppose Abortion?" (September 14, 2015) and APJ 857: "Why Can't God Eternally Love Those Who Don't Believe in Him?" (May 12, 2016).

while the new joy is struggling like a little seed to push its way up through the rocks of disappointment and fear and sorrow. There are days, and weeks, and maybe months of transition from the death of one joy to the full flower of another joy, and those are not easy days." But it's a miraculous joy. In the end, God is not stealing your joy but "replacing one joy with another, one you did not ask for, and perhaps one you just now are not able to embrace with joy. It will come." Be encouraged by the testimony of many parents who have children with Down syndrome who can now say, "Every trial is a cause for joy" (Rom. 5:3; James 1:2).

3. The struggle to see God's plan. Isn't a child's disability a cruel way to confront parents' sin or to sanctify them? Four considerations. (i) God has ten thousand purposes here, so "life is never simply 'one thing causes another thing.' There are always thousands and thousands of things God is doing that we cannot see, like in the birth of a child with Down syndrome." (ii) The world is broken. The pain and brokenness of our lives "are part of the vast fallenness of creation, and not explainable only in the immediate terms of how we experience them" (Rom. 8:18–25). (iii) Christ was afflicted to make us whole. It cost a Son. This is not "cosmic child abuse." Don't call God cruel for afflicting Jesus so that you might be saved. "The Bible says this was the greatest act of love ever performed, even though it cost Jesus his life." (iv) Suffering is the means of gospel spread. Why some suffer and others don't is a mystery, but undeniable "benefits come from the suffering of others."[43]

A word to strengthen parents of disabled children

First, to the mom who cares for an adult son. Thousands of moms (and dads) bear the burden of caring for a disabled child, a disabled adult child, or a disabled elderly family member. "I am sure that they often feel like this is one of the loneliest jobs in the world, with little or no public recognition or reward. How do you laugh? How do you keep on, so quietly and out of the way, bearing so much weight? How do you press on?" The Bible foretells of a day when the Redeemer will arrive to "snatch futility and death out of the hands of Satan" (Isa. 53:6). A Redeemer will "cover all our sins, and we will obtain grace that is so powerful and so pervasive that it turns every disappointment and every frustration and every pain in the path of obedience to Jesus into a final triumph." This Redeemer "will pay the price to purchase for us the reality that it will all work for good" (Rom. 8:28). This includes the fact that no good deed done to your disabled family member will go unnoticed or unrewarded (1 Cor. 15:58;

---

43 APJ 1235: "Why Is My Child Disabled?" (August 19, 2018).

Eph. 6:8). Your disabled adult child cannot repay your service now. But you will be amply rewarded for your service in the resurrection (Luke 14:12–14).[44]

Second, to a burned-out dad of three special-needs kids under the age of ten, Pastor John shared eight profoundly beautiful truths to help this dad endure the burdens at home, to see that "inside these protective, life-giving walls, where you live and struggle and feel beaten down with weariness and discouragement, that's where God Almighty has worked, is working, and promises to work for his trusting children."[45]

How can God be sovereign and good and allow so much suffering in the world?

A respiratory therapist who works with brain-dead patients wrote in because she wrestles with the goodness of God in the severe suffering she sees daily.

The question of why suffering exists can be asked and addressed from (1) the *micro* level and (2) the *macro* level. (1) On the micro level we ask: "Why *this* particular suffering? Why *this* particular person? Why *this* particular time? Why *this* particular intensity? Why *these* peculiar complications? Why in all *these* particular relationships? Why *this* particular duration? When we're talking about those micro reasons, we usually don't know exactly why." Answers at this level are very hard to read. But suffering is not a mystery, because (2) "when it comes to *macro* reasons for why there is suffering in the world, the Bible is rich with helpfulness." The Bible tells us that suffering is helpful: (i) for repentance (Luke 13:4–5); (ii) for reliance (2 Cor. 1:8–9); (iii) for righteousness (Heb. 12:6, 10–11); (iv) for reward (2 Cor. 4:17); and (v) for reminder (Phil. 3:10).

But there's another topic to consider: how suffering exists for the sake of others. "Paul the sufferer turns his pain into a Christ-exalting experience by showing Christ's all-sufficiency in his weakness" (2 Cor. 12:8–9). Paul understood that his weakness was for onlookers. God was using his suffering to work a deeper love of Christ in others.

In more mundane terms, God could simply make every Christian industrious, lionhearted, and strong. Instead, he calls church leaders to admonish the idle, encourage the fainthearted, and help the weak (1 Thess. 5:14). Weaknesses in others "draw out" evidence of God's grace in other more mature believers. The weak exist to be honored and served by the strong. "This is service that can never be paid back in this world. Their suffering is not about *their* sanctification. It's about *your* sanctification" (1 Cor. 12:21–26). Your reward for serving the

44 APJ 1208: "A Word to Strengthen Parents of Disabled Children" (June 8, 2018).
45 APJ 1401: "My Life Is Endless Drudgery—How Do I Find Joy in Christ?" (November 29, 2019).

disabled is a future reward (Luke 14:13–14). "God's ways are not our ways. He has purposes with our weaknesses, even those massive disabilities that leave us unable to do anything for ourselves. This is not about sanctifying the helpless in this world. It's about sanctifying the strong."[46]

A similar question came from a struggling dad who was witnessing the world's suffering, inner-city violence, and a disabled son enduring mistreatment at school. How can God be all-sovereign and all-good in the face of the world's pain? In other words, what sustains John Piper's faith, knowing God is sovereign even though there's so much suffering? Three realities sustain him.

1. The Bible never whitewashes God's governance over human suffering (Deut. 28:15–57). We have questions about God's sovereignty over the world's sufferings, but not because "we have seen things more clearly or honestly than the Bible sees them." The Bible is raw and honest and real on this very point, and it never "shrinks back from any horror or injustice in this world." So "I can't throw away the Bible because it's naive or deceptive or a whitewash of the miseries that God himself ordains." The Bible is honest with us.

2. The Bible uses physical pain to demonstrate spiritual estrangement. "The physical horrors of suffering in this world can make sense to us—and have meaning and eventual righteous resolution—only if we come to embrace the biblical reality that sin against an infinitely wise and just and good God is a moral outrage greater than the physical outrage of centuries of global suffering." And we can only hope to know and embrace this truth by the Spirit's power. God is the sovereign king of the universe. So to see the goodness of God and the evil of sin, "we have to undergo such a profound mental and spiritual Copernican Revolution of mind and heart so that God ceases to be a planet circling the sun of humanity and he becomes the massive, blazing, glorious sun at the center of the solar system of all things." We must see him as a "supreme reality" of "supreme worth" and the "treasure of the universe." Only when we see the true majesty of God can we feel the true horrors of our sins against him. And only then can we affirm that "all human suffering is a screaming witness to the greater horror of human sin."

3. The Bible gives us a Savior who was intentionally sent to suffer. "God sent *his Son* into this world—sent *his very self*—to suffer a moral outrage greater than the outrage against his Father by all his people in their sin" (Rom. 5:8). The cross is the highest sin and the harshest suffering ever to occur. And it was all divinely designed. "The infinitely pure and good and wise and strong and holy Son of God" descended into this broken world to subject himself to

46 APJ 1272: "How Can God Be Sovereign and Good and Allow Suffering?" (November 5, 2018).

the "degradation and torture of a Roman crucifixion" and to suffer "enough indignity" that his atoning act would cover over the injustices and the cosmic outrage for our sins against God.[47]

Suffering's "screaming witness" to the cosmic rupture of our sin

Regarding this "screaming witness" of pain to demonstrate the moral rupture of our relationship to God (2), in every loss we feel, we are meant to feel "the horrors of sin."[48]

The horrific judgments of God in the Bible are "stunningly graphic" to the point that "you will want to throw up if you have any kind of sympathetic engagement" with what "God ordains against sin in this world."[49] But we feel this same rupture all around us in this world. Every pinch of pain in this life is fallout from Adam and Eve's sin (Gen. 3:1–24; Rom. 8:20). More personally, in this groaning world we *feel* our sin against God. "Why did God do that? Why did he ordain that the effect of moral evil would be displayed in the horrors of physical evil—earthquakes, floods, famines, pandemics, wars, and every manner of horrible mistreatment of man on man? Oh, my. He did it because he knew that people who are dead in their trespasses and sins would never comprehend the moral outrage of treason against God unless they saw it reflected in the physical outrage of violence against men." Sinners don't "lose sleep over their treason against God. But let their physical body be touched with cancer, and then their emotions rise up with moral indignation." Piper (a survivor of prostate cancer) says that cancer exists "as a divine witness to the meaning and the seriousness and the outrage of sin against God."[50]

All human "ugliness and disfigurement" exist because of *sin*. Though not on *a particular person* due to *a particular sin* (John 9:2–3). "Horrific deformities" and "dreadful disfigurements" and "hideous malformations" and "open, unhealable flesh" (of some) exist to declare the deformity of our broken relationships with God (of all). "God brought the physical world and the bodily world into sync, into correspondence, with the moral world" (Rom. 8:18–23). "God decreed that there would be physical manifestations of the horrors and outrage of sin against God."[51] In other words, all suffering is "a trumpet blast" to all humanity, pronouncing sin's "outrage against God's character and glory." But the blast is a mere "echo" of the outrage of "belittling God" by our sin and

---

47 APJ 1753: "If God Is Sovereign, Why Is His World Full of Suffering?" (March 7, 2022).
48 APJ 625: "God Takes Away to Display Christ's Beauty" (June 24, 2015).
49 APJ 1416: "What Should I Expect My First Time through the Bible?" (January 3, 2020).
50 APJ 1530: "Why Is the Bible So Violent?" (September 24, 2020).
51 APJ 1699: "Why Did God Make Me Unattractive?" (November 1, 2021).

unbelief.[52] Belittling God is the greater moral outrage. So while we all respond with indignation at the pain inside our bodies, for us to see and feel the greater outrage of our sin against God requires a "Copernican Revolution" of mind and heart.[53] Or this "screaming witness" falls on deaf ears.

Doesn't the Old Testament alienate the disabled?

Jesus approaches, touches, and heals the lame. But in the Old Testament, the disabled were shunned from God's holy places (Lev. 21:16–21). Why did the Old Testament alienate the disabled like this?

In particular, this text deals with blemished priests. God "insists that there be a correlation between the perfections of those who approach the sanctuary and the perfection of the sanctuary itself, which is a reflection of his own perfection." This requirement is true for all time. God is unapproachably holy. "Nothing imperfect can approach God without being destroyed." Throughout the Old Testament, we are reminded that no moral, spiritual, or physical imperfection can dwell in God's presence. In other words, those laws were foundations for what was to come in justification, sanctification, glorification, and the re-creation of the entire material universe. "That's how holy he is. He would one day not only justify the ungodly and be willing to touch lepers—God himself touching lepers in the flesh—but he would also utterly transform the ungodly into sinless, godly people and take away every leprosy, every disease, every disability, and every deformity."

"The Old Testament is, as it were, standing on tiptoes, looking over the horizon of the future, waiting and wondering how God could ever create a people who could come boldly into his presence." In the New Testament, this "glorious" new reality dawns in history. "The reality is that God has provided a way by Jesus Christ, the very perfection that we must have to approach him now. He has provided by his Spirit the sanctification and resurrection and perfection of bodily and spiritual newness in the age to come so that we can be in his presence forever." So "we need the Old Testament to sober us about how holy God is, and we need the New Testament lest we despair of any hope that we could survive in the presence of such a holy God—let alone enjoy him forever."[54]

What do I say to my Christian friend who suffers every day?

Remain faithful to your friend in four ways.

1. Don't let the suffering push you away. "It is easy to become weary when sharing in someone's suffering." Endure and bear with your friend (Gal. 6:2).

52 APJ 1707: "Is Violent Crime under God's Providence?" (November 19, 2021).
53 APJ 1753: "If God Is Sovereign, Why Is His World Full of Suffering?" (March 7, 2022).
54 APJ 1321: "Does the Old Testament Alienate the Disabled?" (March 25, 2019).

2. Don't empathize as if you know what it's like. All suffering is unique. Instead, your compassion "will be seen and known by your presence and your patience and your mercy."

3. Don't give up on "praying patiently for relief and healing. Sometimes we just settle in with sickness, and we've prayed so long that we've given up on hoping for healing." Unless you get a "pretty clear word from the Lord" to halt, don't stop praying for healing. Over time, pray for the effects or specific parts of the suffering. "There's always some measure of relief that they could use, even if the whole disease isn't taken away."

4. Remind your Christian friend that his suffering is not retribution. When the time is right, speak of the righteous who suffer. "Remind your friend and his family that suffering, while owing to the universal sin of mankind, is not always owing to a specific sinfulness in the one who suffers. Therefore, this suffering need not be an indictment of some particular flaw in your friend." Go to Hebrews 11 to see the triumphs of the righteous (Heb. 11:33–35a) and the suffering of the righteous (Heb. 11:35b–37) side by side. *By faith* the faithful *triumphed*, and *by faith* the righteous *endured* unspeakable pain. Remind your friend of the "whole stream of Scripture about the suffering of the righteous, not just the suffering of those who need chastisement." This can change everything. Job is a prime example, a suffering man who was "blameless and upright" (Job 1:1). "Yet God permitted Satan to afflict him with horrific boils—fibromyalgia, perhaps—without even knowing it. We don't know how long these boils lasted, but Job was brought to the brink of unbelief by them, and God showed up just in the nick of time in those latter chapters to keep Job back from despair." Going deeper, Job forces us to embrace two things. (i) God is sovereign over Satan and all our suffering (Job 42:11). (ii) God's plans for us are wise and good and compassionate and merciful, even when the means are painful (James 5:10–11).

(5) So pray for two miracles: the miracle of physical healing, and the miracle of "actually seeing and feeling the hand of God as compassionate and merciful. That's a miracle of equal standing with healing."[55]

Are faith healers legit?

Should a sick Christian attend a healing crusade led by a faith healer? First answer these five questions.

1. What does the healer believe? Who does he say God is? Who is Christ? What is the gospel? Theological convictions are essential to our spiritual af-

55 APJ 1055: "What Can We Say to Friends Facing Suffering?" (June 16, 2017).

filiations. Be warned about any faith healer or ministry "hesitant" to answer for their theological commitments. "Lots of people want spiritual power these days—and they always have—without loving biblical truth" (Luke 23:8). But a power demonstration "without truth" is certain to "damage the cause of Christ in the end." We know this because unbelievers will wield more and more miracle-working power at the end of the age (2 Thess. 2:9–10). And they will do it for the cause of falsehood.

2. What is the healer's aim? Is healing the goal, or is healing the means to the goal of "glorifying Christ and sanctifying human life and building up the local church?" The Bible is not a prelude or a "priming of the pump" for a power encounter. The spread of God's word is the point of physical healing. "All the physical miracles of the New Testament serve to confirm the word of truth and the glory of the saving word of God. If these get turned around, the long-term effect is going to be unhealthy."

3. Does the healer claim healing is always God's will? Any faith healer claiming that God wants every Christian healed in this life is lying. It's not for a lack of faith that some Christians are sick. God's promise of our total healing is tied to the resurrection (Rom. 8:23–24). Until then, "God *can heal*—and he *does heal*. And we should pray for healing always when we get sick or somebody we love is sick." But we are not God. And the Bible doesn't lead us to believe that healing is always in our hands "if we can just muster enough of this so-called faith."

4. Is your healing more precious to you than Christ? "Do these faith healers rank physical wholeness above treasuring Christ through pain? That is, do they think that the miracle of physical healing is a greater miracle than the miracle of strong, joyful, unwavering faith *through* sickness and pain? Do they see that both are wonderful miracles? Do they see that the miracle of faith in the face of suffering may be a *greater miracle* than the removal of suffering?"

5. Have you pursued your healing locally? God gives us local leaders in our churches to minister in times of suffering (James 5:14–15). God may heal you through them. And he may also lead them to consider whether a healing gathering is wise for you (or not). But whether it comes through your elders or friends, it remains true today that God gives "gifts" of healing—plural (χαρίσματα; 1 Cor. 12:9). Don't misassume that this gift has been "locked into" a specific person, like a self-proclaimed "faith healer." No. "It doesn't say that. You don't know through whom you might receive healing when a person prays for you. Anybody may be given a gift of healing." Your elders. A friend. These "gifts of healing" can flow through any Christian God chooses to use.[56]

---

56 APJ 1758: "What Should We Make of Healing Ministries?" (March 18, 2022).

Are we called to thank God for our severest suffering?

A fourteen-year-old boy died of bone cancer. He was a believer in Christ, with a firm faith in the face of death. His mother wrote in as she was processing the grief. She asked, should she be *thankful* to God for such a devastating loss?

Piper offered six responses. (1) This teen boy had the faith to face death, and that faith is "a staggering miracle" itself. "Few things, if any, cause me to stand in awe of the grace of God more than a fourteen-year-old with genuine faith—real, authentic faith that gives him peace in the hour of death. That is glory upon glory upon glory, and I say it not oblivious of the horror upon horror upon horror of the process of dying—and perhaps a worse experience for a mom, watching a child die." (2) This mom's trust in God's goodness in such a loss is another evidence of grace. The testimony of this mom and her family, shared now on the podcast, will lead others to praise the glory of the grace of God. (3) We don't grieve like the world grieves, without hope (1 Thess. 4:13). And grief is rarely experienced in a mere moment. Paul's word for *grieve* (λυπέω) is in the present tense, ongoingly, "which implies that grieving is not a moment" or "an event" but a "continuing activity." So to say of a son's death two years later that the loss feels unbearable and comes crashing in waves that at times feel impossible to withstand, "Paul would know exactly what you mean." Such a stinging loss will grieve you for life, but that pain does not exclude thankfulness. (4) Be thankful *in suffering*; and be thankful *for suffering*. Paul says it both ways. Be thankful *in all circumstances* (1 Thess. 5:18). And be thankful *for all circumstances* (Eph. 5:20). So how do we work toward thankfulness for the pain? (5) Know that God knows your pain. He didn't spare his Son but gave him from his heart to suffer and die (Rom. 8:32). Christ embraced the cross to love us (Rom. 5:8). Combine the texts, and "the love of God for us is magnified both by the immeasurable cost in God losing his Son in death and by the fact that he embraced this loss for people who didn't deserve it." In the loss of his Son, God knows what you are feeling in the loss of your son. (6) Gratitude will come in due time. We often learn to be thankful for the hardest pain only after we have some distance from those circumstances. God "will show you little by little, though not entirely in this life, what he's doing."[57]

What is God accomplishing in my suffering?

In our suffering, God is doing his sovereign work in and through us. "If I may bear witness, from fifty years of ministering the word of God like this to many, many suffering people, here's what I would say. For every one person whom

57 APJ 1092: "Are We Called to Thank God for Our Severest Suffering?" (September 11, 2017).

I have heard or seen forsaking the truth of God's all-pervasive providence because of suffering, I have seen ten others bear witness that the biblical truth of God's absolute sovereignty, in and over their suffering and loss, saved their faith. And some have said, saved their sanity." God's providence "assures us that the so-called *problem* of God's sovereignty in suffering is more than relieved by the sustaining *purpose* and *power* of his sovereignty through suffering."[58]

Peter commands us to "rejoice insofar as you share Christ's sufferings, that you may also rejoice and be glad when his glory is revealed" (1 Pet. 4:13). "This text doesn't just say rejoice *in spite* of but *because of* suffering." It's not a quote from self-help or a jolt of positive thinking: "'Let's make the best of it.' 'Let's rise above it.' 'Let's be heroic.' 'Let's have some mind over matter here.' That's not the point. The point is, you're being called to do something that is so abnormal and so countercultural and so against human nature—it is supernatural, and you can't do it." It's nothing short of a divine miracle to count it "all joy" to suffer with Christ on the path of obedience (James 1:2). Such a response to suffering is not stupid or foolish—for one reason. God is sovereign, "and if he's sovereign, and if he rules Satan and suffering and me, and causes kingdoms to go up and go down, and if he reigns over all the nations, and over all circumstances, and over my cars, and my children, and my wife, and my marriage, and my job, and my sickness, and this church—and he's good—then it's not stupid to say, 'Count it all joy; he loves you.'" It's not foolish. Not easy, but true. "Keep on rejoicing because the suffering is not a surprise, but a plan."[59]

Such a perspective on suffering produces endurance (Rom. 5:3). "Endurance of what? Faith. How does that work? Every hardship, from the tiniest stubbed toe to the loss of a spouse or the loss of a child—from the smallest to the biggest— every hardship in your life is the kicking out from under you of a prop that was supporting your happiness. You can either curse God or fall on God—and God is kicking them for you to fall on him because that's what makes you strong." So our "pathway to glory" includes suffering as a means to transfer our allegiance from self to God (2 Cor. 1:8–9). "Faith is the only way to heaven, and tribulations serve our faith—if the Holy Spirit is testifying that God is your Father."[60]

Joy in the mourning or joy in the morning?

David said joy comes *after* the suffering (Ps. 30:5). Paul says joy comes *inside* the suffering (2 Cor. 6:10). So are sorrow and joy *sequential* or *simultaneous* in the believer's life?

---

58 APJ 1589: "Sustained through the Hardest Suffering" (February 17, 2021).
59 APJ 1523: "What Is God Accomplishing in My Suffering?" (September 9, 2020).
60 APJ 1544: "God's Good Design in Our Suffering" (October 28, 2020).

The question is not theoretical for Piper. "My mother was killed in a bus accident in Israel in 1974. I was twenty-eight years old. My brother-in-law called me and told me that my mother was dead, and my father was seriously injured and might not make it. That's all he knew. He would keep me posted. I hung up the phone, and I told Noël what he told me. I went to the bedroom, knelt by the bed, and wept for a long time. And in my weeping—*in my weeping, simultaneous*, not *sequential*—I was rejoicing. The weeping was owing to, of course, the overwhelming pain of sorrow and loss—massive loss of one whom I so, so cherished. The joy was this: 'Thank you that I had such an amazing mom. Thank you that you gave her to me for twenty-eight years. Thank you that, evidently, she didn't suffer very much. Thank you that she is in heaven and not in hell. Thank you for countless kindnesses she showed me growing up. Thank you that my father is still alive; please save him [physically]. Thank you that I will see her again. Thank you, Jesus, for dying for us and covering her sin and my sin and his sin.' Every sweet memory that tumbled to my mind made tears flow more and joy taste sweeter."

And yet "it is just as true that my night of weeping would give way, in due time, to a tearless joy. That's what I think the psalmist means when he says that joy follows sorrow" (Pss. 30:5; 126:5–6). David shows us "tears followed by shouts of joy" (a *sequential* joy). So does Jesus (John 16:20–21). And so does Paul (2 Cor. 4:17). And yet other key texts highlight a *simultaneous* joy (Rom. 5:2–3; 12:12; 2 Cor. 6:10). So "beyond any shadow of a doubt in my mind, it is not double-talk" for Paul to say "sorrowful, yet always—in the very sorrow—rejoicing" (2 Cor. 6:10). That's not contradictory, it's "simultaneous reality. I've tasted it." In the end, sorrow and joy are both sequential and simultaneous, acute pain coexisting with real hope for a day when pain is erased (Rev. 21:4).[61]

How should we respond to the suffering we see in our community and on the news? To be completely *insensitive* to the world's suffering is to be a sociopath. To be entirely *sensitive* to the world's suffering is to be crushed by its collective pain. So for the sake of our joy, should we ignore it all?

No, we don't ignore it. But as we sense more of the world's suffering, we must draw from a larger vision of God—one that will rejuvenate our joy even amid the increased perception of suffering. Even in our relations to others, we are rejoicing and weeping in the same day (Rom. 12:15). "Christians are always sorrowful at one level and happy at another level. And we give expression to the one or the other, according to whether we are at a wedding or at a funeral—even

61 APJ 1563: "Does Joy Come after Suffering, Or in It?" (December 18, 2020). See also APJ 387: "The Mystery of Sorrowful Rejoicing" (July 17, 2014). He detailed the circumstances of his mother's death more fully in APJ 1433: "How Do I Let Go of Anger over Past Wrongs?" (February 12, 2020).

though we know at the wedding that another family is at the hospital right now with a dying wife and mother. We will be there in a few hours probably. But we are not going to ruin the wedding." So we carry in us a joy that never goes away and a sorrow that never goes away (2 Cor. 6:10). As we see more and more suffering in the world, "the other Godlike attributes have to increase, lest we be crushed under the weight of simultaneous, multiplied empathies, or hardened with self-protecting indifference. These other attributes that I am thinking about are things like greater capacities for mercy, greater capacities for compassion, a growing grasp—this one is really essential—of biblical truth that gives some meaning to the suffering of the world, even the suffering we can't reach, and what is happening to people out there and what meaning that might have. If these other Godlike attributes don't increase in us in proportion to our awareness and our experience of suffering, we are going to be overwhelmed."[62]

Christian Hedonists don't pursue joy *after* sorrow. We seek joy *in* the sorrow. Our watchword is from Paul: "sorrowful, yet always rejoicing" (2 Cor. 6:10). The text means five things are true. (1) You'll never have to fake your emotions. "Your sorrow will be real. Your joy will be real." Your emotions are always authentic because one doesn't "contradict or exclude" the authenticity of the other. (2) Your sorrows will never crush you. Joy will not make the sorrows lighter in our lives, but it will make the sorrows "less destructive" to our lives. (3) You will enter the sorrows and joys of others authentically. "Your sorrow will not ruin the joy of others. And your joy will not offend the sorrow of others." This is "delicate," but important to get right. "You will enter in and out of relationships that are either sorrowing or rejoicing. And you don't want to ruin either of them. You don't want to offend the sorrowing [with your joy]. And you don't want to rain on the party [with your sorrow]." You can be authentic with each group. Jesus can sustain you for an hour at a wedding with a smile on your face even if you return home to cry in sorrow. "That's not hypocrisy—that's love. The sorrow that's being interpenetrated with simultaneous joy is of a different kind than worldly sorrow." It becomes a selfless sorrow, not the self-centered sorrow of the world. (4) Christ is reflected. He wept and he rejoiced (Luke 10:21; 19:42). We need churches marked by "serious joy." For decades, week after week, Pastor John opened Sunday morning church gatherings to "welcome people in such a way that those who are coming out of the funeral and out of the wedding feel good about this moment." (5) Christ is exalted. Christ is exalted in our joy as we rejoice in him. And Christ is exalted in the sorrows that come when we see and feel the ugliness of sin in this world and the horrors of its

62 APJ 479: "Does Happiness Require Apathy to Others' Sorrows?" (November 24, 2014).

effects in human life. "When you get that in one person—the joy reflecting the infinite worth of Jesus *and* the sorrow reflecting the ugliness and the horrors of sin—you meet somebody more like Jesus, and you want to be like him." So "sorrowful, yet always rejoicing" is our watchword (2 Cor. 6:10). "May the Lord work this paradox, this miracle. I speak as one trying to understand and do this as a dad, as a husband, as a pastor right now. I'm speaking over my head. I'm saying words that I wish were truer for me."[63]

---

63 APJ 1664: "Living the Mystery of Joy in Suffering" (August 11, 2021). Variations of Piper's catchphrase ("joyful seriousness" or "serious joy") made thirty-five appearances in the first decade of the podcast. Most fully in APJ 905: "Does John Piper Hate Fun?" (July 26, 2016), APJ 1234: "Three Threats to the Joy of This Generation" (August 8, 2018), and APJ 1374: "John Piper's Most Bizarre Moment in Preaching" (September 27, 2019).

On Deadness, Depression, and Desertion

I feel zero motivation to get out of bed. Is this depression?
The question was from a college-age woman. "Oh, how I feel empathy for this, because I've tasted these kinds of seasons many times: don't want to get out of bed, dread doing the things we have to do, no motivation for anything, don't feel like fighting the fight, loss of joy in what we thought God had called us to do, oppressed by what feels like demonic darkness."

So is this depression? "I don't know." She may need a checkup with a doctor to rule out physical causes, because "our bodies can play tricks on us and wreak havoc with our minds and our spirits." Sleep, exercise, and eating habits should be reviewed too—because "there are so many ways that we can be depleted, and it feels *spiritual* when it has *physical* roots as well." But here are seven "wonderful, spiritual, biblical, God-given truths that he means for your help and strength right now."

(1) Endure well. Don't merely look for escape. For Paul, the escape from trials is the capacity to endure the trial. Endurance *is the escape* (1 Cor. 10:13). (2) Know that God tests our endurance because he loves us. He delights in the children whom he disciplines (Heb. 12:6). "Don't let the devil convince you that this season of testing is because God is against you. That's hellish. That's not from heaven." (3) Await God's timing (Ps. 40:1–3). "I just want to testify that much Christian obedience consists in waiting for God to do what we need him to do when the timing seems very slow to us." (4) Read and reread Scripture. Everything we find in the Bible is there, says Paul, "for our instruction, that through endurance and through the encouragement of the Scriptures we might have hope" (Rom. 15:4). When you need endurance most, don't ignore the Bible. Maybe you can only get into a few verses. Fine. But be in the word, and "give yourself that medicine every day." (5) Affirm that only God's power

396 ON DEADNESS, DEPRESSION, AND DESERTION

can sustain. Through times of testing, our need for endurance and patience and joy all calls forth omnipotent power (Col. 1:11). (6) Know that God knows you. He knows that you are dust (Ps. 103:13). "Isn't that amazing that God takes into account the fragile frame that we have as humans?" (7) Practically, write down a few promises on index cards or Post-it notes and take them into your day. Start with Psalm 139:11–12 and Isaiah 43:2–3.[1]

Should a lack of joy make us feel guilty?

Are there times in the Christian life when God chooses to withhold his presence from us, thus nullifying the hope that we experience Godward affections? If so, and God withdraws from the Christian at times, does this make our joy in him impossible? In that case, would Christian Hedonism—the call to always be happy in God—just heap more guilt on such a person?

"I do believe that God will sometimes lift his hand from his children" or "cover us with darkness at times. Nevertheless, I don't think Christian Hedonism *adds guilt*. I think Christian Hedonism *names guilt*. In other words, it is proper to feel bad that we are not rejoicing in the Lord. That is part of what darkness is. We feel we can't rejoice, and we feel bad because we know we should." So even in our darkness, the divine commands to delight in God remain unchanged (2 Cor. 6:10; Phil. 4:4; 1 Thess. 5:16). Christian Hedonism is not a "naive view of joy." There will be "seasons of horrible darkness." So what do we do?

We name guilt. "My favorite passage of Scripture regarding darkness and seasons of desertion is Micah 7:8–9." It teaches us "gutsy guilt." In the darkness we embrace our guilt and await our return to the light. Or as David puts it, in the pit we wait for God to put a new song in our mouth (Ps. 40:1–3). Christian Hedonism affirms that "we ought to be happy," yet we are not. So we *own* this lack. "We acknowledge it is bad" but not to the point of self-centered despair. And then we look away from ourselves in the darkness. We look to Christ and await God's timing to restore the joy of our salvation.[2]

In this "gutsy guilt" theme, a third text emerged, Psalm 119:7–12. There the psalmist is preaching to himself in the darkness. He's saying, "'Darkness is all over me. It is just covering me. I don't see any light.' [And in this moment,] "feeling all of that desertion, all of that darkness," [he says to himself:] 'This darkness is not dark to my God. He sees me. He knows me. He is with me. And though I can't see him, he can see me.'" So we preach these truths to ourselves, "even if, in the very moment of preaching, there is almost no feeling of them.

1 APJ 1046: "God's Work in Your Depression" (May 26, 2017). Speaking of Psalm 103, it's Pastor John's "favorite gospel psalm" (APJ 1361: "Is God Angry at Me When I Sin?" [June 26, 2019]).
2 APJ 19: "Does God Ever Withdraw His Presence from His Children?" (February 2, 2013).

We assert them as true. We throw them in the devil's face. We stick him with the sword of the Spirit." And we wait for the Lord to move.

This holds for the deepest darkness to come at the end of life. Pastor John testified of the final minutes of a forty-year-old woman as she died of cancer, horribly and graphically. In such darkness and pain, the miracle was that she refused to curse God. She held on to the end. "So I think there are some moments of darkness where the most beautiful triumph is when Satan is screaming in your ear: 'This is your God! So much for your merciful God!' And you just look back at him and say, 'I am not going to curse my God.' I think that was basically Job's response to his wife when she said, 'Curse God and die.' He just said, 'Look, we are going to receive evil and good at the hand of the Lord. I am not going to curse him'" (Job 2:9–10).[3]

Gutsy guilt

As his favorite text for dark seasons of life, Piper applies "gutsy guilt" to so many assorted situations that it's worth isolating the text in a synthesis. The text (Micah 7:8–9) is diversely applicable to any situation where we face the guilt of our sin and bring it to God. Gutsy guilt is the testimony of Micah, a prophet of God, who sinned against God. Adam sinned and *ran from* God (Gen. 3:8). Micah did the opposite. He sinned and *ran to* God. He was enduring spiritual darkness, a darkness he fully deserved. So how did he respond? He owned his sin and awaited God's vindication and restoration. That's "gutsy guilt," and it applies to our lives in five scenarios.

1. Gutsy guilt in seasons when we fail to delight in God. We "embrace our guilt" when our affections feel dead toward God. Such a state is a sinful violation of Scripture (2 Cor. 6:10; Phil. 4:4; 1 Thess. 5:16). It will do no good to blame-shift this drought of affection. We're spiritually numb (directly or indirectly) because we sin. So our response to the darkness—"even lengthy darkness"—remains the same: "Keep holding on to the hope that God is going to vindicate you and bring you out to the light." This principle remains "one of the most magnificent and realistic statements of what it means to be a justified sinner in darkness," the "unbelievably gutsy experience of guilt." A guilt that turns us toward God.[4]

2. Gutsy guilt in seasons of depression. A step further than spiritual deadness, depression can be the direct consequence of sin. But often not. In either case "we've all sinned, and therefore there's no point in trying to play

3 APJ 21: "What Does Christian Hedonism Offer the Depressed?" (February 6, 2013).
4 APJ 19: "Does God Ever Withdraw His Presence from His Children?" (February 2, 2013).

goody-goody while we're under the darkness." In any experienced darkness, we feel our sinfulness. "We do not despair, and we do not feel presumptuous. Our confidence is in God and his vindication."[5]

3. Gutsy guilt when the pain of suffering hits hard. Judgment for sin begins with the church (1 Pet. 4:17), not because God hates us, but because he loves us so much that he "will not spare us anything to get out of us what he hates." God purifies sin from his people through suffering. And in all the suffering we endure—"under the ashes, under the shadow, under the frown—we count it joy." In God's purifying flame we hope in God, evidenced in Micah's gutsy testimony.[6]

4. Gutsy guilt when others sin against us. Micah is a sinner, but apparently he's been *sinned against* too (Mic. 7:5–6). His society is "in chaos." Families are "in crisis." Sin is everywhere. Despite the social and relational ruptures, Micah is *most broken* over his own sin. It's a "miracle" of the Spirit, that "in the midst of being sinned against, we own our sin against God." Two truths require one another. (i) "*My sin* is my biggest problem. *My sin* is our marriage problem. *My sin* is my parenting problem. *My sin* is my work problem. *My sin* is the church's problem." The pain of being sinned against never shrouds the fact that we are sinners. (ii) "There is no God like our God." He's eager to pardon us. "I want you to be just as deeply convinced of that as that you are a sinner." To taste the gloriousness of his forgiveness (ii), you must be really convinced of your guilt (i). "I'm a sinner, and he's a great Savior." Especially now, after the cross, these truths make us gutsy with our guilt.[7]

5. Gutsy guilt to face the fallout of our most egregious sins. A woman looking back on her abortion wrote with a question "filled with self-recrimination, doubt, fear, and guilt." She needs Micah's testimony. "Micah owns his sin. He owns his guilt. He's in darkness, sitting there under the Lord, and the Lord is disciplining him." Micah makes no excuses. He doesn't call it spiritual warfare. "He knows this is from the Lord, and it's awful." It hurts. But his only hope is in God. "That's the only way I know how to survive as a saved sinner—real guilt, real sorrow, real pain, real darkness under God's discipline, and real gutsy faith. Gutsy faith that the very God who is disciplining me and displeased with me is on my side and will vindicate me."[8]

---

5   APJ 1248: "What Hope Does God Offer in My Depression?" (September 10, 2018), APJ 1441: "How Do I Care for My Depressed Wife?" (March 2, 2020), and APJ 1506: "Can a Christian Hedonist Get Depressed?" (July 31, 2020).

6   APJ 1523: "What Is God Accomplishing in My Suffering?" (September 9, 2020).

7   APJ 1688: "Parenting through a Family Crisis" (October 6, 2021).

8   APJ 1067: "'I Had an Abortion'" (July 14, 2017).

For a related text—on foolish sinners, suffering for their sins, owning their guilt, and calling out to God for deliverance—see also Psalm 107:17–22.[9]

Why does God withdraw from us if he promised to never leave or forsake us?

We can be content with our material possessions because God promised to never leave or forsake us (Heb. 13:5). But doesn't this contradict the fact that God withdraws his presence from believers on purpose?

Three realities can be confirmed from Scripture. (1) God is omnipresent. "There is no place where he is not" (Jer. 23:24; Acts 17:28). (2) "God is never, ever going to abandon or leave his people" (Jer. 32:40; Matt. 28:20; 2 Cor. 4:9; Heb. 13:5). (3) And yet God's *presence* can be withdrawn from his people (Pss. 69:17; 143:7; Isa. 64:7). But we can ask, since these desertion texts are limited to the Old Testament, is this dilemma resolved by the new covenant and the coming of Christ?

No, it's not that simple, since the New Testament promise of Hebrews 13:5 is just a quote from the Old Testament promise in Joshua 1:5. So this dynamic—combining points (1), (2), and (3)—has always been in play. And God's never-leaving presence was affirmed for Old Testament believers as well (1 Sam. 12:22; Pss. 23:4; 37:28).

In the end, "the old Puritans put it all together by talking about the *manifest presence* of God. And they were using that phrase—*manifest, experienced, known, tasted* presence of God—to distinguish it from the omnipresence of God and from the covenant-keeping of God, which may or may not be experienced intensely from time to time. And I think this is really, really helpful. In other words, sometimes God withdraws his *presence* from us," but that doesn't mean "we are *forsaken* by our covenant God." Instead, it means "*the manifestations of his presence* are limited. He doesn't withdraw his covenant commitment to us or his sustaining grace from us. What he withdraws is *the sweetness of his fellowship* from time to time or the conscious sense of his power. And he has his reasons for doing this—I think maybe there would be another time for us to talk about that—but surely one of them is to make us feel our desperate need for him so that we fly to Christ and to the cross where we hear the covenant promise afresh."[10]

So when God *feels* distant, he's not (Ps. 44:20–22; Rom. 8:35–38). "God's face is hidden only in the sense that outward physical blessings are being withheld." Withheld so that we will eventually see God more clearly. "The thorns of life,

---

9 APJ 130: "I've Sinned Horribly—Is There Any Hope?" (July 12, 2013).
10 APJ 338: "If God Never Leaves Me, Why Does He Withdraw?" (May 9, 2014).

which we think are God's desertion, are in fact designed to pin back the veil of worldliness that hides God's loving face." How we experience the Christian life is variable. But whether we feel it or not, Christ is always present (Matt. 28:20; Heb. 1:3). "Therefore, my experience is not of God's *absence* but of *my* absence, *my* dullness, *my* faithlessness, *my* disobedience. I don't fight to get God's *objective presence*. It's there. I fight to get his *manifest presence*, his *experienced presence*. My faith, my sanctification, is the issue. And that's the battle of my life every day."[11]

But these previous episodes skirted the main question. Why? Why does God give over his children "to seasons of perplexity, confusion, and darkness"? Three reasons. (1) To resweeten his presence (Eph. 1:18). He teaches us "the value of his precious presence by withdrawing it for a season." So Paul asks "that fresh glimpses of the worth and beauty and greatness of God would be given to us, and that we would cherish him more because of having lost sight for a season." (2) To remind us that we are weak (Jude 24–25). "From time to time he allows us to slip into darkness so that we realize how desperately dependent we are on his grace for seeing him, which Jude so powerfully celebrates." (3) To resweeten our deliverance (Eph. 2:12). "He never wants us to forget what a wonder it is that God has revealed his beautiful face to us, removed separation, stepped in, lifted the veil, and made his face bright to us in the gospel. So from time to time he allows us to taste that former darkness so that we will come trembling back to the word and prayer and the cross, and lay hold on God in a fresh way and to love our salvation more than ever."

As we endure the darkness, we walk in trust (Isa. 50:10) and with eager expectation that he will again shower us with the blessings of his felt presence (Hos. 6:3).[12]

Can Christian Hedonists get depressed?

We aspire to glorify God by delighting in him every moment of every day. So is it possible to live out a *flourishing* Christian Hedonism while enduring a season of dark depression? Or is that a stark contradiction of terms?

Thankfully we have the Psalms, a "very realistic" book that describes "the ups and downs of human emotion in relation to God." The Psalms encourage us, "because there is nothing about Christian Hedonism that claims anything different than ups and downs in the Christian life, nor does it deny that the downs can last a long time." The complicating factor in the question is the word "flourishing." Christian Hedonism *can coexist* with seasons of dark depression. But it *cannot flourish* when depression dominates. Perhaps a better question

---

11 APJ 1689: "Has God Abandoned Me?" (October 8, 2021).
12 APJ 1728: "Why Does God Hide Himself from Christians?" (January 7, 2022).

is, Can "*rugged, solid, unbroken* Christian Hedonism" coexist with seasons of dark depression? "And my answer is *yes.*"

Depression is not like "ordinary kinds of *disappointment* or sadness or frustration or anger or discouragement, say, that we have when we lose something of value." The Christian's battle against idolatry calls for a reset on our life's priorities but doesn't usher in "unlifted darkness." So *depression* is more complex, with "physical components, perhaps genetic tendencies, perhaps satanic oppression. And the darkness is not necessarily because the depressed person is cherishing some idol more than God. Depression is when the capacity to cherish *at all* has dried up, and there is a deep, dark numbness of soul. So the battle in depression is not primarily to persuade the soul that *Christ is more precious* than, say, money or family; the battle is to persuade the soul that *Christ is worth waiting for* in the darkness and that his beauty will dawn again, not just on the mind *as a truth*, but on the soul *as a treasure.*"

Five key texts are "kindling for the fire of joy." Keep piling these texts like logs for a bonfire, and "God will set the match in due time." (1) Learn the secret of gutsy guilt (Mic. 7:8–9). Not all depression is brought on "by particular sins," but in this text it has been. Even so, the justified saint can own the sin with "gutsy guilt" and say to the enemy: "'Don't rejoice over me that I'm down; I will rise. Until he raises me up, I will wait.'" (2) Know that God is never far away (Ps. 139:7, 11–12). Say with your soul, "My darkness is not dark to God, and he is not far from me." (3) Preach truth to your soul (Ps. 42:5–6). "That text served me for years in a struggle with discouragement—so much so that we put it as a big sign on the side of the church building: 'Hope in God.'" As the church's depressed preacher was walking from his house to his church, he would see this huge banner, and "he'd be reminded in all of his doldrums: 'Hope in God; you're going to praise him again.'" (4) Keep desiring God (1 Pet. 2:2–3). All Christians "have tasted the truth and the kindness of the Lord." Something has awakened in us. "We have tasted it, and we know there's nothing better. He is our fountain. He is our life, our joy, our final joy." From that memory, and that inborn impulse, desire God. (5) Hold on because Christ holds you (Phil. 3:12). "In other words, we press in, we press on to know, to taste, to feel, to love, to delight in, to own Christ, because we know we've been owned; we've been known. God holds us decisively—not the other way around. We reach out because we are in his arms."[13]

---

13 APJ 1506: "Can a Christian Hedonist Get Depressed?" (July 31, 2020). On the "hope in God" sign hanging on the church building ("because they have a depressed pastor who needs encouragement as he walks to church"), see APJ 1334: "I Want Jesus to Be My Treasure—Is the Wanting Enough?" (April 24, 2019), APJ 1506: "Can a Christian Hedonist Get Depressed?" (July 31, 2020), and APJ 1798: "Crucial Texts for Our Hardest Battles" (June 20, 2022).

Isn't God most glorified in us when we *desire* him?

Don't we glorify God in our *desire to enjoy him* even when we don't *feel* the joy itself? Would it be more accurate to say: God is *most glorified* in us when we *desire* to be most satisfied in him?

No, to the wording change. *Yes*, to glorifying God in the *desire* to enjoy him, even when I don't feel it. "This might seem to contradict Christian Hedonism, but it doesn't." We can honor God in three different levels of emotional capacity. (1) In our white-hot affection for God. In this rare intensity, "we are free, we are unhindered, we are rooted in the truth, and our emotions are free." We are "all there" in total love and service. And "clearly" God is *most* honored when "our emotions are 'all there' and we are enjoying him." (2) In our lack of intense affection for God. This is "where we live most of our life," in a state where we *feel sorrow* for the fact that we *don't feel more intensely*. This sorrow and regret is not the best way we honor God, as in (1), our white-hot affection, but (2) our regret does honor God as "an echo of the joy, the seed of which is still in us." In this desire we find a leftover, a remnant, a memory that "we have tasted and seen that the Lord is good. That taste has become temporarily dull." (3) In seasons of deep depression. In this season, the affections are so numb that we scarcely have a memory, echo, remnant, or leftover of a previous joy. "We can't even function. This is depression at its worst." In this state, we honor God by *waiting* and not cursing him, because even the "ability to wait for him, feeling virtually nothing but numbness in our soul, is rooted in something real and authentic that God has done in us."

"God wants us to be hot, not lukewarm" (Matt. 22:37). "So we *glorify* God in sorrow, and we *glorify* God in waiting in the dark seasons. But God is *most glorified* in us when we experience wholesale—mind, body, soul—joy. Yes. And I assume that this is the case, because God does away with depression in heaven. If he were most glorified by us hanging on by our fingernails while we are in a season of darkness, I would think that heaven would be a season of darkness, and we would all be hanging on by our fingernails in heaven, because that is the way God gets most glory for eternity. But that is not the case."[14]

As an aside, this gradation of *more/most* glorifying God is central to the slogan of Christian Hedonism: "God is *most glorified* in us when we are *most satisfied* in him." And it applies to many situations beyond the vibrance of personal affection.[15] For example, God gets more glory in our struggle with

14 APJ 30: "Three Levels of God-Glorifying Emotion" (February 19, 2013).
15 APJ 30: "Three Levels of God-Glorifying Emotion" (February 19, 2013).

sin than if we were made sinless immediately.[16] And God gets more glory in the harmony of diversity—in the male/female genders and in the plethora of races—than he would get if we were all the same.[17] Christ gets more glory by being honored by a diversity of tongues and nations than he would be in a single race.[18] Christ receives more glory in the atonement than if he didn't take up the cross.[19] Christ is more glorified by living out his perfect life and dying in public than if he lived out his perfect life and died in private obscurity.[20] Christ gets more glory by defeating Satan at the cross than if he took Satan out at a distance, like a sniper.[21] And God gets more glory from our willing service than if he forced and coerced labor from "a tireless slave-labor force."[22] Later, we directly addressed why this more/most glory-grade is biblically warranted.[23]

What do I do when God feels distant?
In the darkest season of life, the psalmist preached to himself (Ps. 42:5). We should follow this model and preach the gospel to our hearts. "On this side of the cross, we know the greatest ground for our hope: Jesus Christ crucified for our sins and triumphant over death. So the main thing we must learn is to preach the gospel to ourselves." We say to ourselves: "'Listen, self: If God is for you, who can be against you? He who did not spare his own Son but gave him up for you, how will he not also with him graciously give you all things? Who shall bring any charge against you as God's elect? It is God who justifies. Who is to condemn? Christ Jesus is the one who died—more than that, who was raised—who is at the right hand of God, who indeed is interceding for you. Who shall separate you from the love of Christ?'" That's Romans 8:31–35, paraphrased.[24]

This *felt distance* from God is "common to God's people." In response, rest in the gospel. Christ "died for sinners like us. He absorbed the wrath of God against his people. He covered our sins by paying the price of the suffering and death we deserved. He rose from the dead to give invincible hope. He purchased a new-covenant promise never to let his people fall away into destruction. And

16 APJ 33: "The Spirit Lives in Me, So Why Do My Affections Waver?" (February 22, 2013).
17 APJ 169: "Why Adam's Singleness Was Not Good" (September 10, 2013).
18 APJ 927: "Red, Yellow, Black, and White—Could Every Race Come from Adam, Eve, and Noah?" (August 25, 2016).
19 APJ 265: "Why Is Jesus My Advocate If I'm Already Justified?" (January 28, 2014).
20 APJ 1816: "Why Did Jesus Need to Suffer and Die Publicly?" (August 1, 2022).
21 APJ 408: "Why Does God Allow Satan to Live?" (August 15, 2014).
22 APJ 1432: "Would God Be Just as Glorified If We Were His Slaves?" (February 10, 2020).
23 APJ 1717: "Can We Really Give God More or Less Glory?" (December 13, 2021).
24 APJ 711: "When Depression Descends, Do the Next Thing" (October 21, 2015).

he makes all of this available to us by faith alone, by seeing ourselves as helpless and receiving—receiving like a little child—all that God is for us in Christ and embracing him as our supreme treasure. That is the gospel." We rest in this gospel, even when God feels distant.

The psalmist gives us a twofold approach to this darkness: (1) seek him, and (2) don't stop waiting for him (Ps. 27:8–9). First, seek him. The psalmist himself models this seeking in his language (Pss. 6:2–3; 13:1–2; 90:13–14). And "don't stop seeking because it has been a long time." Wait, and don't fret (Pss. 27:14; 37:7). Psalm 40 is a great help. The psalmist waited, he was delivered, and his joy was restored—and all so that others would see this process in his life. "It is a strange kind of evangelism." But maybe this is the purpose, to serve others. "The world needs people who have walked through darkness and come out at the other end in some measure and can empathize with what they are going through."

In the end, seasons of distance from God "have made me a better pastor—a more effective pastor, not a less effective pastor." God is at work. "If you ask, 'How long?' I don't know. I just know you mustn't let go. Don't let go. I had a friend who was seriously depressed for eight years, almost to the point of immobilization." But then, after years of Bible memory, God-seeking, holding on, and waiting, something happened. "God broke in, and broke my friend out of his depression. I knew him till the day he died, and he never went back into it. He always chalked it up to the fact that he continued in the word, even when he didn't feel much and could barely function. He continued in the word and sought the Lord."[25]

Did my sin bring this darkness on me?

A young woman wrote in with a heartbreaking story. She had been involved in the church, was experiencing joy in her walk, but was eventually led away by an unbelieving boyfriend. They sinned sexually. Now the boyfriend is gone. She's broken, but back in church. Her life seems dark now, and she's scared that she lost something forever that cannot be reclaimed.

She needs these hard words: "Consider the possibility, which I think is probably the case, that your spiritual condition in those good years was not as good as you think it was. You were having many religious experiences—church, joy, gifts, and singing. But when it came to the actual obedience, where you had to choose the value of Christ over a boyfriend leading you away from Christ, you chose the boyfriend." But these hard words are good news for her: "I am suggesting that the Lord may be doing in your life something very different.

25 APJ 542: "What to Do When God Feels Distant" (February 27, 2015).

I'm suggesting the Lord is not, in these years, allowing you to lose a close walk with God but rescuing you from a phony walk with God."

The previous walk was "very religious but not real. If you loved Jesus so little that a boyfriend was more important than Jesus, you did not have a close walk with God. Whatever it was, God wrecked it, right? He wrecked it. Now, through the miseries of that wreckage, he has awakened in your heart a new desire for him. He's not inviting you back to the old kind of joy and singing and church life. No. He's not calling you back to the kind of faith that concealed a heart that was ready to commit idolatry as soon as the boyfriend came along." Now he's "aiming at a deep, strong, doctrinally sound, Christ-exalting, Bible-saturated, unshakable *new you*. Not a return to the old religious *you* that sells Jesus like Judas did for a thirty-pieces-of-silver boyfriend." Pointed words to make a strong woman. "I want you to be tough, unshakable, unbendable in your allegiance to Jesus as your supreme treasure. No loosey-goosey, churchy, emotional stuff anymore. I'm talking major, deep-down, unshakable, authentic allegiance to your King and supreme treasure. I'm not interested in making you feel soft right now. I want you to be tough."

To that end, study the entirety of Ezekiel 16, "a horrible depiction of un-faithfulness between Israel and her husband, God." God gave Israel over to horrible judgments. Then read to the last five verses, "a staggering, absolutely astonishing act of gracious forgiveness." And meditate on Paul, who was saved from deep sin to display God's patience (1 Tim. 1:16). "God saved Paul from being the worst example of a legalistic, hateful Christian-killer so that you would feel Christ's perfect patience and take heart to believe on him for eternal life. I will pray with you that God grants you to see this and feel this and happily come home."[26]

Scripture texts for when your heart feels dead
"To be sure, there are many dimensions to depression—from genetic, to dietary, to exercise, to trauma, to demonic harassment, to relational stress, to financial burdens, to weather conditions, to sinful entanglements, to sleeplessness, and on and on. I don't want to give the impression that I am oversimplifying the complexities of what might trigger a season of darkness, or depression." But the accumulated causes of the darkness do not make Scripture irrelevant, because "under and over and through all these issues" is the key question: "What has God said to me?" That is, "What does the Scripture say?" Depression weakens our faith and hope, the very things reclaimed through Scripture (Rom. 10:17).

26 APJ 1171: "When God Feels Distant, He May Want Us to Grow Up" (March 14, 2018).

406 ON DEADNESS, DEPRESSION, AND DESERTION

Without the Bible, "there's no hope of a Christ-exalting turnaround of our emotions." So medication "might turn us around emotionally, but by itself, without the word of God, it won't put us on a right footing with Jesus Christ. It may feel good, but without the word of God, it may not have done you any long-term good." Consider these five groups of key texts when darkness comes.

(1) Wait-and-pray texts (Pss. 30:5; 40:1–2; 56:8). "We feed in green pastures, yes. *And* we walk through the valley of death. We experience the shining of his face, and we experience the hiding of his face. So in the scriptural prescription, what we find is that when his face is hidden, we are to wait and pray. That's the first group." (2) Gutsy-guilt texts (Mic. 7:8–9). "I'm not saying every darkness is a specific punishment for sin. I'm just saying we've all sinned, and therefore there's no point in trying to play goody-goody while we're under the darkness." Yet, "we do not despair, and we do not feel presumptuous. Our confidence is in God and his vindication." (3) Canceled-sin texts (Isa. 53:4–6; Rom. 5:6–8; 8:3; 2 Cor. 5:21; Gal. 3:13; Phil. 1:6; 3:12; 1 Pet. 2:24–25). Perhaps most importantly of all, "fix your attention especially on the passages that describe the stunning work of Christ on the cross. The work that was outside yourself, to provide your vindication as a justified sinner before an all-holy, all-loving God." (4) Thanks-and-praise texts (Ps. 86:10–13). It's important to "recite scriptures of thanksgiving and praise, even though you do not feel them." (5) Seed-of-joy texts (Pss. 51:12; 85:6). These are "texts that cry out to God for the restoration of life and joy." These longings for joy are evidence "that the seed of joy in God is still alive in your soul."

In the seasons when you feel like you cannot possibly be a Christian because your heart is so blank, be encouraged as you look for three "evidences that the seed of joy in God is still alive in your soul." (1) "You can still see, objectively, that God is the supreme treasure of the universe, even if your feelings about him are very flat." (2) "You can cry out for the restoration of true joy, and that very cry is the seed sown by the taste of the joy." (3) "You can refuse to turn away from God and embrace idols."[27]

On antidepressants

All things are lawful, but not all things build up (1 Cor. 6:12; 10:23). So are medications like Ritalin, Adderall, and antidepressants helpful to me? "Do they help me go after my deepest advantage?" Or do I take them to mask deeper problems? "I think that is the crucial question when it comes to the kinds of medications or stimulants that we take. Are we hiding from our hearts? Are

---

27 APJ 1248: "What Hope Does God Offer in My Depression?" (September 10, 2018).

we hiding from sins? Are we hiding things that ought to be dealt with, and this is just a superficial overlay?"[28]

Likewise, complicating matters further, our spiritual and physical lives are deeply interwoven with our environment "in ways that are complex and inevitable. God made us that way. We are souls with bodies. We always will be souls with bodies. We are not platonic—trying to slough off our body. We are going to be raised as bodies and souls in the last day." As people "who are affected by the physical strategies and physical remedies that we embrace," how do we turn natural gifts "into something spiritual or holy?" Five steps, serving as "my best shot at trying to help a person practically to think about sleep, or antidepressants, or the whole range of everything else in between that affects our moods and our spiritual condition." (1) Acknowledge the gift. Every beneficial thing to us is a divine gift (1 Cor. 4:7). (2) Admit dependence. We can do nothing apart from him (John 15:5). (3) Pray for help (Phil. 4:6–7). (4) Trust God (Isa. 41:10). (5) Thank God for what he does in you (1 Thess. 5:18). "Whether it is sleep, or coffee, or exercise, or antidepressants, this is how we take the gifts of God in the physical world and sanctify them for the sake of our souls."[29]

Doesn't the Bible prescribe alcohol for the depressed?

Speaking of antidepressants, does the Bible prescribe alcohol to the depressed in Proverbs 31:6–7? This seems to be exactly what a depressed person *doesn't* need.

The context makes clear that alcohol is not for a king who needs a clear head to rule (Prov. 31:4–5). Alcohol "unfits the mind for the kind of thinking that leaders have to do in order to do justice." Leaders who do not abuse alcohol bring happiness (Eccl. 10:17). Leaders who abuse alcohol are a disgrace (1 Kings 16:9–10; 20:16; Isa. 28:7). Wine corrupts and leads astray (Prov. 20:1; 23:31–33; Hos. 4:10–11). "This is not what kings should do, Lemuel's mother is saying. Your heart must stay clear, your eyes must be open, your mind must be sharp so that you can utter just and wise things." So why does she commend alcohol to the depressed to forget their poverty and misery? Two possible interpretations.

(1) She's commending alcohol as morphine. Deaden the pains of death with alcohol. Though "I don't think that justifies us in using alcohol to escape our sorrows or our mental miseries." Such a move cannot relieve the symptoms of sorrow, and it would simply "cut us off from the real remedy—namely, knowing clearly the truth of God in Christ." (2) She's using irony. Give to the miserable alcohol, a fitting use for it, as a way of saying that the king should never

---

28 APJ 679: "Should Energy Drinks Fuel the Christian Life?" (September 7, 2015).
29 APJ 283: "Antidepressants, Sleep, Diet, and Exercise" (February 21, 2014).

consider this approach. Both interpretations are legitimate. "In either case, she's not teaching her son, or us, in our very low and discouraging moments, to damage our ability to see the truth that can heal us deeply. Don't open your mouth [and drink] to obscure reality. Open your mouth [and speak] to make right judgments. In other words, don't open your mouth to take in the very thing that would make you blind to the truth that could heal you. Open your mouth as a king to speak right things, and open your ears to hear right things that would deliver you from misjudgment."[30]

At what point is the joyless pastor disqualified from ministry?

First, yes, "there is a point at which joylessness does disqualify an elder. A lot of people don't think of that." Here are four reasons why. (1) Pastors are called to pastor in joy (Heb. 13:17). So "a chronically joyless pastor is of no advantage, no benefit, to his people," and would call for a step back or step down. (2) Pastors are called to lead others into joy (2 Cor. 1:24; Phil. 1:25). "That was Paul's apostolic mission—to seek the joy of other people. I think it's the calling on every pastor and every elder, to work for the joy of their people. If their own inability to rejoice in the Lord hinders that, there may come a time when they are not able to fulfill that calling." (3) Pastors are examples of joy in suffering (Rom. 5:3–5). But "if we can't rejoice in our own sufferings, how are we going to help our people obey the Scriptures?" (4) Pastors exemplify the overflow of joy, even in suffering (2 Cor. 8:1–2). "An elder who wants his people to love other people—that is, to overflow in joy for them in the midst of affliction, in the midst of poverty—has to be able to set the example for that himself."

Considering these convictions, a joyless pastor should ask five questions. (1) Is it dullness or bitterness? Distinguish between "a temporary dullness of spirit and a growing bitterness of spirit. Both dullness and bitterness can rob us of joy, but there is a world of difference between the two." A joyless, desperate, brokenhearted pastor "will cry out to God affectionately" for mercy, and his people will "deeply appreciate" and "resonate with it." His desperation can serve others. But the "pastor who is giving into joylessness out of anger and bitterness" serves nobody. (2) Have you asked for help? Hidden sins kill joy. Ask fellow elders if they see concerning patterns of sin in your life. (3) Can you preach the text? Preaching calls for appropriate emotions that resonate with the text. Can you preach with emotional authenticity? "I found, over the decades of preaching—even though my private life at times was filled with sorrow, real heartache, and I had to preach the next Sunday—the text really did, in that mo-

---

30 APJ 1031: "Does the Bible Prescribe Alcohol to the Depressed?" (April 21, 2017).

ment, create its own emotions in me that were real and authentic." (4) Do you love your church? "Are you able still to feel sweet affection for your people? Do they sense that?" (5) Do you need to rest or resign? "How long has the struggle of seeming darkness—or dullness, or heaviness, or joylessness—gone on? That matters." Take a sabbatical and consider resignation as "a last resort," especially if it would greatly disrupt the church.[31]

Depression is a ministry killer. So as one "prone to depression and discouragement," Pastor John exercises regularly to "hammer" his body, resulting in less frequent depression. "I know that depression hurts my ministry, my marriage, and my parenting. So for the sake of kingdom purposes, I am off to the gym."[32] And particularly when the Monday morning blues hit, "hammer your body with whatever exercise works for you. Don't become a couch potato. It is deadly. God made muscles for work, and he made the heart to sustain the workload. He made the brain to produce antidepressants in response to vigorous exercise. Don't spare yourself in this. Get a bike. Ride twenty miles as hard as you can on Monday morning, or run or swim or do weights or dig in the garden." Work hard, and "you will be surprised how closely connected are the body and the soul."[33]

31 APJ 1261: "Does Depression Disqualify a Pastor?" (October 10, 2018).
32 APJ 12: "Exercising the Body (for the Sake of the Soul)" (January 25, 2013).
33 APJ 429: "Handling Post-Sermon Blues" (September 15, 2014).

On Writing, Grammar, and Poetry

On writing

In our very first APJ episode, we spoke about writing. Pastor John admitted that he was not much of a reader or writer until he turned sixteen. "And suddenly, Mrs. Clanton—I do not know what she did in the eleventh-grade literature class, but, wow, something just locked in on me for poetry and writing and reading."[1]

Since those formative teen years, he's learned that writing is key to learning and discovery, especially when we are seeking to understand a biblical truth. "Be writing, writing, writing, either in a file on your computer or, like I do often, with a folded half-sheet of paper. I'm doodling and I'm constantly writing because, when I write, I'm able to hold more things in my head. Without writing, everything tends to be a muddle. It's just so complex." Writing helps us see. "People that aren't writing really aren't going to go very far in bringing a coherent picture of some reality."[2] This is because "writing does not just record what you see; it increases what you see."[3]

Think of the transcendent importance of writing. God chose to communicate to us by words on paper, "and that way is not less direct than if he spoke by some other agency." God could speak to us regularly by audible words. He doesn't. We hear his voice in Scripture. He speaks to us in a book. "If you read the Bible out loud, you are hearing the voice of God—just as much as if he made some bush rattle and a voice come out of it" (Exod. 3:2–4).[4]

On the writer's calling (and influence)

A published writer, or an *aspiring* writer, should aim to influence. Why? "If you are not praying that what you write would influence people, is it because you

---

1 APJ 1: "Reflections from John Piper on His Birthday" (January 11, 2013).
2 APJ 1058: "How Do I Study a Specific Topic in the Bible?" (June 23, 2017).
3 APJ 1414: "I Have a New Journaling Bible—How Should I Mark It Up?" (December 30, 2019).
4 APJ 299: "God Has No Vocal Chords" (March 17, 2014).

412 ON WRITING, GRAMMAR, AND POETRY

do not believe *what you say and think* matters, or is it because you think *people do not matter?*" The writer is called to deploy gifts for both purposes—to celebrate truth and to influence; to glorify God and to love (1 Cor. 10:31; 16:14). These ends are united because "the way you love people is by influencing them, persuading them, winning them, and awakening them to delight in God above all things. This means that whenever you write, you should be writing in such a way as to make God look better than anything else in the world, to make the path of sin look worse than anything else in the world, and to make the path of righteousness look beautiful in spite of all the difficulties that the path of obedience might bring." In light of this aim, a *calling* emerges. So you as a writer, called to glorify God and love others, "cannot be indifferent to whether you want people to be affected by your writing." A true influencer.

So is Pastor John conscious of his audience as he writes? Not necessarily. He's more self-conscious, immediately focused on writing from self-awareness. "The way I have gotten to know humans mainly is by knowing John Piper—*my* sins, *my* worries, *my* longings. I am so introspectively driven on these things, and so second-guessing about everything I do, that I think I have gotten to know *this* human pretty well. And then I try to read and watch, being aware of the effects of what I write." His writing aims to self-teach, self-reprove, self-correct, self-train, and self-edify, with the hope that this influence will translate to readers. So the writing is never first about the byline. "This is why I would write quite apart from any publishing. If the Lord said, 'No more publishing,' goodness, I would not stop writing." Why? "Because writing, for me, has become a way of seeing and a way of feeling."[5]

A writer's influence on others is decisive. So how do I know if God has called me to be an author? The calling to write is "a recurrent, not temporary, long-term, not short-lived, compelling, not merely interesting, benevolent, not selfish, Christ-exalting, not self-exalting desire to write, which proves fruitful in the lives of others." Discerning this call comes in three stages. (1) Write to see. This level of writing is personal and wonderfully self-edifying but not yet a calling. (2) Write to create. But even here, creating beautiful prose is not yet a calling either. (3) Write to serve. "A divine calling to write is a calling from God, through God, and for God. Until the writing is *for God*, it is not a calling *from God*. So we move from *truth discovery* through writing, to *creative expression* through writing, to the role of a *servant* in writing—the impulse to instruct and awaken and delight and transform people into obedient worshipers of Christ." The Christian writer discerns his gift in his effective discipleship.[6]

5   APJ 3: "How Important Is a Christian Writer's Influence?" (January 13, 2013).
6   APJ 614: "Has God Called Me to Write?" (June 9, 2015).

On planning and writing books

How does Piper, a best-selling author of over fifty books, set out to write a new one? It requires several steps of preparation. (1) Schedule your time. Make time and block the time you need from your calendar. (2) Narrow down your topic. (3) Pray earnestly to God for "perseverance and for insight and creativity, and ask him for competence and truthfulness and faithfulness to the Scriptures." Pray for him to "make the book a great honor to Christ and good for the church and an advancement to the global mission of the people of God." (4) Draw in what you've written previously in your journals and files. (5) Think about what you want to include in the book. (6) Print out all your ideas and scribble your notes and try to connect all the ideas you want to include into some organization. (7) Of all your ideas and subcategories, decide on one idea and begin working on it. Don't be overwhelmed by the whole project. Simply start with one subtopic that you can develop immediately. The underlying takeaway in these steps of preparation is that any aspiring book author should already be writing content to return to later.[7]

Once the prep work is done, how is the book written? (8) Start writing. On the subtopic of the last step, begin writing and don't wait too long. "You discover by writing. You see by writing. You understand by writing. You conceptualize the structure of what you are going to do by writing. One of the biggest mistakes people make at every stage is when they think that discovery, seeing, understanding, [and] conceptualizing must come before the writing. That is paralyzing. And it fails to see that writing is a revelatory act. It doesn't just record what you have thought; it is thinking." (9) Write down newly inspired ideas and connections because "when I write, my mind just becomes fertile. And until I write, it is one big mess." (10) Read your sentences aloud to self-edit as you go. (11) Move to another subtopic. (12) Plod along until the book becomes clearer. (13) Research sources, but don't pause too long to research. (14) Keep plodding along in the writing process. (15) Expect God to hear and answer your prayers as you go.[8]

Three years later, Piper repackaged his entire book-writing process into six steps. (1) Get a seed idea. A "seed idea is sown in my mind, usually by something I'm reading or something I'm hearing. This happens either positively, because I so want to dig into that seed and flesh it out, or negatively, because I hear something or I read something I so dislike that I want to give a beautiful alternative view of reality." (2) Gather existing material. "Here, I simply throw

7   APJ 581: "How John Piper Prepares to Write Books" (April 23, 2015).
8   APJ 582: "How John Piper Writes Books" (April 24, 2015).

things into a big electronic file. I just gather and gather and gather, and just throw whatever I find in there." No sequence or order is necessary at this point; just compile what you've written in the past. (3) Structure all your material. "Frankly, I think this is, at least for me, the hardest step in writing" and "the step that kills most writing projects and kills most writers. It simply looks impossible. It looks too big, too complex, too confusing. The reason for that is that we are staring at something that doesn't exist. It's like a painter staring at a palette of colors and a blank sheet of paper with a view to creating a scene. He hasn't even made up his mind whether it's going to be a scene of an ocean or a mountain or a meadow or an urban scene." In the chaos of possible material and directions you could develop, pray for clarity. "I think God has to break through, or we just give up." (4) Then begin writing. "Just start writing anywhere. It may be the middle of the book. It may be the conclusion. It may be the introduction." Just get writing on one theme. (5) Be original. "Avoid falling into worn-out jargon and into familiar ways of saying things. I am always trying to describe and explain glorious reality in fresh and compelling ways." (6) Watch the book come alive. Watching a book take its own form is "the most mysterious and wonderful part" of authorship.[9]

On ghostwriting

Every author needs editors, but not ghostwriters. "I think putting your name on a book you didn't write is a lie." If you wrote it, your name must be on the cover. And if the editing process reaches a point where the book becomes substantially the editor's work, the editor's name goes on the cover.[10] Ghostwriting "comes from the love of money over truth. Big names sell books. Ghostwriters don't sell. So to sell books and make money, you *conceal* the *real* writer. Believe me, if books sold more copies by putting the name of the ghostwriter on the cover, it would be on the cover. Nobody doubts that." In practice, ghostwriting cloaks the author's weaknesses. But in Christ, the Spirit "makes us happy to be dependent people. He makes us eager to magnify him by exposing our dependence, not our independence, not our self-sufficiency, not our super-giftedness. He makes us humble. He makes us eager to take less credit, to give more credit." We boast in our weaknesses when we celebrate others' gifts (2 Cor. 12:9). "Ghostwriting is the opposite of boasting in weakness." Indeed, the practice reveals "the love of money more than the magnifying of Christ through the exposure of our weakness. That is my take on what is going on here."[11]

9   APJ 1196: "Piper's Six-Stage Process for Writing Books" (May 11, 2018).
10   APJ 129: "On Ghostwriters" (July 11, 2013).
11   APJ 245: "Ghostwriting and Research Assistants" (December 30, 2013).

On the place of grammar and need for commas

When it comes to grammatical rules and punctuation, Pastor John once tweeted: "I love commas. No punctuation mark is more useful in helping a reader know how you want your sentences to be read."[12] Later asked to expand on his (comma-less) tweet, he said, "grammatical rules and punctuation rules are practical ways of helping us love people. So grammar has a moral dimension to it." Grammar helps us carry our meaning to others with less obstacles in the way. "It is unloving to cultivate patterns of grammar or punctuation that make communication harder." In particular, the comma is "a friend indeed," and it "signifies a pause in thought so as to avoid confusion." When speaking, our pauses are naturally given. But not in writing. "So any place I think people might miss my cadence, and could get help from a comma, I am going to stick in a comma, just to help them keep going with me as if they are listening to me talk into their ear. So, for love's sake, and for understanding's sake, and for beauty's sake, I love this little servant, the comma."[13]

On writing short biographies

It's important to write devotional biographies. "I really would like to encourage others to do what I have done in those little biographical talks that I give; namely, tell the life story of some Christian in a way that inspires others to love Christ and gives them insight into perplexing aspects of the Christian life and motivates them to follow Jesus no matter what the cost." Pastors should think of ways to lead a church through biographies. Imitation is biblical (Phil. 3:17; Heb. 6:12; 13:7). Biography is a profitable and compelling way to blend history, theology, psychology, counseling, politics, economics, geography, and devotion. Pick a subject, read a couple of biographies—one scholarly, one inspirational. Read lots of primary sources written by your subject. Choose a point of emphasis and a thematic focus to tell the life story. Biography, in Piper's case, is basically a biblical sermon with 95 percent of the message comprised of illustration drawn from the life of his subject.[14]

On writing poems

Poetry plays a key role in the development of the writer. "I grew up in a home where my dad read poetry to us, and it was always of the simplest kind—I think that is what families need. Families don't need really obscure poetry. Families need birthday poems, anniversary poems, Christmas poems, and thanksgiving

12 John Piper (@JohnPiper), Twitter, January 24, 2013.
13 APJ 404: "Use Commas to Love Your Reader" (August 11, 2014).
14 APJ 1041: "Will You Write More Biographies?" (May 15, 2017).

poems from dad or mom or children. Just write something sweet and beautiful from the heart for God," and don't sweat its artistic quality. To improve as a poet, read lots of great poetry, memorize the psalms and other poems, and consider a course on poetry at a local community college.[15]

On the writer's hazard

The art, craft, and discipline of writing comes with a warning. To the new Calvinists he said: "You might love *thinking about God* more than you love God, or *arguing for God* more than you love God, or *defending God* more than you love God, or *writing about God* more than you love God, or *preaching* more than you love God, or *evangelizing* more than you love God."[16] Mere theological intellectualism is death. "John Piper must be totally persuaded that knowing God truly without loving him duly is eternally deadly. Deadly. I must be persuaded of that. So I am trembling at the thought that I could go about my academic work or my scholarly work or my writing work or preaching work or study work in some kind of cold frame with no awakened love for God, affection for God." Writers must guard their own emotional lives—not merely typing creatively about God, but living out an authentic love for him. This is the writer's "life-and-death battle."[17]

15   APJ 24: "Writing Poetry: Where Do I Start?" (February 11, 2013).
16   APJ 326: "Cautions for New Calvinists" (April 23, 2014).
17   APJ 939: "Five Strategies for Avoiding Intellectualism" (September 19, 2016).

On Joining, Leaving, and
Finding a Church

How do I find a good local church?

When looking for a healthy church in your area, consider twelve suggestions.

Before Sunday morning, four suggestions will guide your research. (1) Look to God and start your search with prayer. He loves to lead the humble (Ps. 25:4–9). (2) Define your convictions. Before you look, write out your definition of a biblical church. What nonnegotiables do you seek? (3) Ask for suggestions. Talk to your Christian friends about the options in your area. Reliable people are "more trustworthy" than even "quick impressions from a one-Sunday visit to the church." (4) Search the web. Run a Google search: "Churches in [a locale] that believe the doctrines of grace." That's a start, although one "liable to serious error" and not immune from some "wacko results." Better, find a trustworthy church-locator map and zoom in to your region (like the one at the 9Marks website).

On Sunday morning, five suggestions will help you evaluate each church. (5) Look for humble leaders. Seek out leaders who love to serve, who don't love money, and who live simply (1 Pet. 5:2–4). Watch for leaders who are "not coercive and demanding." Look for humble leaders who lead by example, lead by serving, demonstrate self-giving, and do not feed themselves on power (Mark 9:35). (6) Look for authentic love. Yes, *study the leaders*, Peter says (1 Pet. 5:2–4). Then Peter says, *study the congregation* for humility, faith, and an impulse to cast their anxieties on God (1 Pet. 5:5–7). Watch for signs of love, the mark of authenticity (1 John 3:14). And beware of cliques. "Do you smell any kind of exclusiveness that pushes away believers of different races, believers of different economic levels, believers of different education? Do you smell a kind of exclusionary attitude that's foreign to born-again love?" (7) Look at the teaching. Is the church ashamed of what the Bible says, or not? Biblical manhood and womanhood is a good litmus test "because that's such a hot, controverted issue in our day." The point: "Don't go to a church that is fearful of displeasing people who are more shaped by the culture than the Scripture." (8) Look to serve. You're not a "pew-sitter." You need motivation for ministry and equipment for the work (Eph. 4:12). Will *this* church motivate and equip you? (9) Look for serious joy. "Are they people who have learned to suffer by the grace of God, and have not become embittered? Do they know how to be 'sorrowful, yet always rejoicing' (2 Cor. 6:10)? Are they real with their problems and with their suffering?"

Factor in personal taste last. (10) Look to your preferences if multiple churches meet the previous criteria. These preferences have no biblical mandate but "can be a legitimate part of your decision to the degree that they are shaped and formed by the word of God, even if not mandated, and to the degree that they don't take precedence over more important things." Preferences include church size (small or large), worship mood (reflective or expressive), dress (formal or casual), vibe (traditional or contemporary), music (organ or band), setting (pews or folding chairs), and time (early morning or late morning), and whether or not Sunday school or Sunday evening meetings are offered.[1]

Finally, consider two additional factors. (11) The content of musical worship. "Find a good church where they put together beautiful, Christ-exalting, gospel-saturated songs that heal you every Sunday."[2] And (12) look for a church fighting together for holiness, all members with their own battles, but in combat together—a "camaraderie in warfare against sin."[3]

When should I leave my church?

This question is common in the inbox, but foreign to the New Testament. The early believers had one church per city, and church shopping wasn't an option. For us, we begin by determining what a church *is*. Then we can ask: "Is the church being the church here, or is it defective to a degree that I should go to another one?"

Here are four nonnegotiable marks of a healthy church. (1) The church's leaders (its elders or pastors) preach the word faithfully. (2) They celebrate the Lord's Supper and baptism. (3) The church exercises church discipline, "excluding from membership those who walk in a way that contradicts the gospel or brings reproach upon the Lord." (4) The church loves—loves one another and seeks to reach the lost, both locally and globally. Any one of these missing could prompt you to find a new church.

In practice, this decision will be rarely made because of one Sunday. More likely you will leave a church after you sense all four traits are fading to the

1 APJ 1431: "How Do I Find a Good Church?" (February 7, 2020).
2 APJ 894: "How Do I Survey All the Deep Wonders of the Cross?" (July 11, 2016).
3 APJ 1435: "Should Christians Attend Alcoholics Anonymous?" (February 17, 2020).

point that it becomes clear to you that "your faith and obedience would be damaged if you stayed" and that your own "usefulness there doesn't outweigh the pitfalls." Then you are *free* to leave and find another church, *free* to go to another church. But *"not free* to go nowhere. *Not being in a church* is not a New Testament option." You *must* belong to a church. And there are no perfect churches. So you'll need to find another defective one (a less defective one). If you live in a city, this may be easy. If you live in a rural area with no alternatives, you may be forced to start your own little church. "But you never leave hastily. You never leave without serious prayer or consulting with other believers—mature, spiritual believers. You never leave without talking to the leaders about why you are considering leaving and taking your time and praying about it with them. And you always strive for peace, even when you must go."[4]

Preaching is a major factor in your decision. Essential to your own growth in Bible knowledge throughout the week is to find a church that preaches the word faithfully on Sunday. "If your pastor doesn't preach Bible texts and explain to you what they mean, please try to find another church. Because the decades of your life will be gloriously transformed if you sit under the healthy preaching of the word for a long, long time."[5]

Compared to preaching, the excessive expression of emotion in a church should be a lesser factor. Piper guesses "millions more people perish in dead, emotionless churches than in churches that are excessively emotional." So he doesn't aim to dampen emotion in a church "even if I find it excessive." Instead, the goal would be to ramp up the preaching and to lift up "a clear, robust, intellectually responsible, biblical vision of the sovereignty of the grace of God with all of its radical implications of God's absolute control." The substance of the preaching, not the expressive emotion, is what defines the authenticity of a church. Focus on the pulpit's content, and let expressiveness be secondary.[6]

Can I attend multiple churches?

Is it okay to hop from church to church without belonging to one?

No, it's not. Here are five reasons to become a member of one church.

1. The church is the final appeal to unrepentant sinners (Matt. 18:15–17). The church brings discipline to unrepentant sinners in the church, and removes them from the community when necessary. For discipline to work, there must be a community determined by covenant membership.

---

4 APJ 187: "When Should I Leave My Church?" (October 4, 2013).
5 APJ 1296: "How Do I Make the Most of Daily Bible Reading?" (December 31, 2018).
6 APJ 239: "Why Stoicism Is Toxic" (December 18, 2013).

2. The church removes unrepentant sinners from membership (1 Cor. 5:12–13). This text implies that "there is an in-the-church group and an outside-the-church group." Being *in the church* equates to a formal membership accountability. Being *out of the church* means being removed from a formal accountability status.

3. God commands submission to church leaders (Heb. 13:17). "We have to know who our leaders are if we are going to submit to them. But if we are jumping from church to church, we are not likely to come under that kind of leadership and give ourselves to that kind of submission."

4. Church leaders bear responsibility over a community (Acts 20:28). "This is one of the biggest struggles for me in all my years at Bethlehem. For whom am I accountable at the last day when the Lord says to me, 'Did you keep watch over your flock?'" Many people came in and out of Bethlehem over the decades, "and there is no way I could fulfill this command for the thousands of people who rotated through those doors. But I think there was a body of believers who said, 'We are here. We belong. You are our shepherd. We are your people. We expect you to hold us accountable. We are going to hold you accountable to be a faithful shepherd.'"

5. Believers find a home in the local church body (1 Cor. 12:21). In Christ, we are part of a universal church. And this universal church finds expression in the local church, a place of accountability, belonging, and service. "So I don't think Jesus died to create unattached, free-floating Christians. I think he died to create the church where the real, true individuality of every believer comes into its own. The more disconnected we are from a local church, the more confused we will be about who we are and who God made us to be. We find our true individual selves in relationship to others."[7]

I will not leave Jesus—but I'm done with the local church

In 2014, prominent Christian author Donald Miller admitted that he rarely attended church. He said he felt closer to God while working on a weekday than he ever did worshiping on Sunday morning. And he never connected with God through singing. For him and for many evangelicals—both young and old—they say that the local church "doesn't work." Besides, they say, no local church looks like the churches in Acts. So why pretend that modern churches are of equal value to those in the first century?

In response, Pastor John gave four reasons why church membership is expected for Christians. First, a definition. A church is "a group of Christians who are covenanted together to gather regularly for corporate worship, celebration

---

7   APJ 433: "Should I Commit to One Church?" (September 19, 2014).

of the ordinances, and ministry of the word of God under the leadership of biblically qualified elders, and who are submissive to the discipline of the body, on mission for Christ and the world. That is a church." (1) Jesus expected membership. When a Christian is "out of step with his brother," there's a church "that can love him and pursue him and, if necessary, discipline him" (Matt. 18:15–17). (2) Paul assumed membership. Every person on the planet is either *inside* the church or *outside* the church. You can be added or removed from a church (1 Cor. 5:12–13). Paul assumed that each Christian is added to a local church and lives under its association. (3) Christ's appointment assumes membership. Christians are church members who are submitted to the leadership of qualified men who watch over and will give an account for their leadership (1 Thess. 5:12; Heb. 13:17). (4) Elder responsibilities assume membership. Elders oversee a particular congregation (Acts 20:28). So "how can they be responsible to their flock if the members of the flock consider it optional whether they stay or go, or whether they are accountable or not accountable? The whole structure of Paul's understanding of how eldership and church works presumes that people have belonging—*serious* belonging—to a flock."

And what if I don't like to sing on Sunday mornings? (1) There are seasons in life when singing is hard (Ps. 32:3–4). (2) Whether we emotionally connect with singing is a secondary question to the fact that singing is a means of mutual upbuilding in the gathered people of God (Eph. 5:18–19). "If we are not inclined to sing—and there are lots of people who are not wired to sing—I think we should do the best we can as the Spirit enables us to sing, and we should look forward to the day when our musical brokenness is healed." (3) Acknowledge that a failure to connect in singing is owing to the brokenness inside of us (Ps. 51:10–15), not a flaw in the design of the church.

In the end, "the New Testament doesn't know any Christians who are *not* accountable members of local churches." Independent, "Lone-Ranger" Christians are fallacies. We are united to Christ, and that means united to one another. We belong to one another. We need each other (1 Cor. 12:21). To belong to a healthy local church is a deep privilege. "It is sad when people say, 'Do I *have to* do church?' And Paul, I think, would throw up his hands and say, 'Have to?! This is one of the most precious gifts in the world!'"[8]

I will not leave Jesus—but I'm done with church leaders
What do we say to someone who says, "I will never leave Jesus, but I'm done with the local church because of the sins and scandals of its leaders"?

8 APJ 287: "Giving up on Church" (February 27, 2014).

"If you do that, you are walking away from Jesus." And here's why. To say that you love Jesus but you will not submit to his word is a lie. To love Jesus is to obey his word (John 14:23). "Jesus founded the church. I didn't. Paul didn't. Jesus founded the church. He established apostles to be—according to Ephesians 2:20—the foundation of the church. And then he built it with prophets and teachers and pastors and ordained that there be a structure of local churches in the body of Christ called the church." And yet many "young, cool, hip, and leftward-leaning" evangelicals think they can substitute it for something else. "Well, I would have to look at what they are substituting and say: Are you really just trying to create *church*? If you are trying to create church, just create it biblically. Start a biblical church. And that means listening to your Master and his word and his apostles." In the end, "the choice of Jesus over church implies a choice of your opinion over the Bible, because the Bible is where we meet Jesus. You can't make Jesus up. He is the Jesus of the Bible or he is the Jesus of your imagination. If he is the Jesus of the Bible, you take the whole Jesus. You can't carve him up in pieces. And the whole Jesus is the Jesus who loves the church. He died for the church."[9]

When do I unfollow my pastor?

Our loyalty *to the people of God* is universal and absolute in the broadest sense (Rom. 12:5; 1 Pet. 2:4–5). Our loyalty to God "necessarily includes loyalty of love to his people," to the universal church, to Christians, "wherever you find them."

But our loyalty *to a local church* is not absolute. "We know this because there are New Testament instructions which imply that a church leadership can be unworthy of being followed, which would imply no longer putting yourself under the ministry of that leadership." This example is shown in two cases.

1. Unfollow an unrepentant pastor (1 Tim. 5:19). Any pastor who is "sleeping around, guilty of greed, an embezzler, idolater, reviler, drunkard, swindler," who refuses to repent, is unqualified. This is also true if other elders are complicit in a cover-up. It is still true if a denomination isn't willing to address it. Don't associate with such a pastor (1 Cor. 5:11). "So you clearly wouldn't sit under his ministry anymore." Elder qualifications serve as elder disqualifications too.

2. Unfollow a false teacher (2 John 10–11). Unfollow any pastor who will not deliver the apostles' gospel. The text says don't even greet him. If you're not supposed to greet him, how much more would you not attend his church? In sum, our "allegiance to any specific local church depends on the leadership fulfilling its moral and spiritual and doctrinal responsibilities."[10]

---

9 APJ 751: "I Will Not Leave Jesus—but I'm Done with the Church" (December 16, 2015).
10 APJ 1051: "When Do I Unfollow My Pastor?" (June 7, 2017).

When church leaders fall into scandalous sin

We should pause for a moment to praise and thank God for holy men—nameless pastors, forgotten missionaries, and tireless evangelists—who gave their lives to ministry and never fell into scandalous sin. This includes heroes like Billy Graham.[11] Nevertheless, the podcast features cautionary tales of men who did fail.

Longtime apologist, evangelist, and preacher Ravi Zacharias died of cancer in 2020. Months after his death, a chorus of allegations arose and ignited a posthumous sex scandal that rocked the evangelical world. How do we process scandalous sins in our heroes?

We should be reminded of a category of gospel ministers who, "for a season, spoke the truth in useful ways, and then made shipwreck of their lives—indeed, their faith." Namely in the examples of Judas, Demas, and Hymenaeus.

Judas—the son of destruction. For three years, Judas covertly stole money from the ministry of Jesus (John 12:4–8), stole it so well that "none of the other twelve even suspected him of sedition and betrayal" (Matt. 26:21). Judas was one of the disciples—preaching, healing, casting out demons. But for all his apparent ministry power, he was lost (Matt. 7:22–23). He loved money. He was a "son of destruction" (John 17:12).

Demas—the man infatuated with the world. A once-trusted partner of Paul's (Col. 4:14; Philem. 23–24), Demas fell in love with the world (2 Tim. 4:10). Like Judas, during those years of ministry, "there's no reason to think that he didn't preach the gospel truly and that people came to faith, along with coming to faith through Paul's preaching." But in due time, "Demas's true colors were revealed—namely, what he really loved: things like association with notable people, access to money, experiences of power, accolades for eloquence, commendations for courage. There are plenty of worldly pleasures to be had doing so-called otherworldly work. But Demas decided to stop playing the game." He abandoned Paul. And he abandoned the gospel.

Hymenaeus—the man hardened by sin. This Bible teacher shipwrecked his faith by sinning against his conscience and not repenting (1 Tim. 1:18–20). Failing to heed our conscience, failing to repent of our sin, proves deeply dangerous over the years. A "bad conscience," or a hard conscience, leads to an Esau-like, unrepentant life.

We get three lessons from these lives. (1) "Soul-saving, Christ-exalting truth may be spoken by hypocrites." (2) "Forsaking a good conscience is prelude to moral disaster." (3) "The amassing of money and the pursuit of lavish lifestyles in ministry are the alarm bells of the love of this age."

---

11 APJ SE14: "On the Day Billy Graham Died" (February 21, 2018).

From the allegations around Ravi's life come two lessons. (1) Be honest and truthful before others. (2) Never use "excuses," like the fatigue of a demanding ministry, to solicit sin from others. Christian leaders should be given only "tethered sympathy," sympathy chained to truth and holiness. "How did Ravi manipulate people into sinfully sending him nude pictures? How did he manipulate people into sinfully providing him with sexual stimulation? He did it by demanding untethered sympathy. He portrayed himself as an embattled, burdened, wounded warrior in the righteous cause of the gospel." Deny the advances of any leader who seeks sinful favors in the name of gospel entitlement.

As for those who came to faith under his ministry: "Don't let the imperfections and failures of men turn you away from the perfections and the triumphs of Christ, who will never, never fail you."[12]

The Judas-like desire for wealth has taken down many pastors. One casualty was the founder of the largest megachurch in the world, David Yonggi Cho, a South Korean convicted and sent to prison in 2014 at the age of seventy-eight for embezzling twelve million dollars. "Every public dishonoring of Christ and every public dishonoring of his word and his gospel and his church makes me angry and makes me sorrowful."

To block the love of wealth, leaders need five guardrails. (1) Pastor, "kill every desire to be rich in the ministry" (Matt. 19:23–24; 1 Tim. 6:10). (2) Pastor, donate more. As earnings rise, don't simply raise the *sum* of your own giving; raise the *percentage* of it. (3) Pastor, let your elders see your full income. "Secrecy around money is deadly. It is a sign that something is not right. So work to give your ministry the flavor that we are not like peddlers of God's word" (2 Cor. 2:17). (4) Pastor, live simply. Don't live like a pauper, but live modestly. Prove by your buying that you are not in ministry for wealth (1 Pet. 5:2). Use your money to "show the world that Christ is your supreme treasure." (5) Pastor, don't lead alone. Raise up fellow elders and empower them to veto you for the good of the church.[13]

How to keep the faith when you lose confidence in the church
How do we enjoy the blessings of a healthy church while safeguarding ourselves against rooting our salvation (or feelings of salvation) in the health of our local church and leaders—both of which may disappoint us in the future? Especially for new believers, how do we guard ourselves from equating a sense

12   APJ SE28: "How Have You Processed the Sin of Ravi Zacharias?" (April 29, 2021).
13   APJ 290: "Pastor of World's Largest Church Convicted of Embezzlement" (March 4, 2014).

of belonging to our church community with genuine belonging to God? This will become a crisis of faith when the community proves fallible.

Here are three ways to guard the stability of your faith from the instability of man.

1. Christ will never disappoint you. Certainly we strive for church unity (Eph. 4:3). And "right at the heart of how to do that will be the steadfast effort to make Jesus obviously more precious than the community. In other words, what holds the community together is that Jesus is more important than the community." For the entire lifespan of a local church, to old and new believers, we must reiterate: "Jesus is better than the community of Jesus. Jesus will be there when the community of Jesus lets you down. Part of keeping the community real is focusing on Jesus with that supreme value."

2. The local church will disappoint you. While striving for unity, the "realistic biblical picture" we get is that the local church remains "very imperfect." We make it imperfect. We sin against one another, and therefore we need to forgive one another (Eph. 4:32). And forgive often (Matt. 18:21–22). We must learn to forebear and endure those who are annoying (Col. 3:13). Some members will disrupt community life with serious sin (Matt. 18:15–20). But lesser sins will need to be addressed all the time (Gal. 6:1; 1 Thess. 5:14). People in the church may fall away (2 Tim. 4:10). Wolves will threaten the church with twisted teachings (Acts 20:29–30). And even beloved Christians will disagree strongly with one another (Acts 15:39), which "must have crushed some new believers" to see that Paul and Barnabas couldn't work out their differences. Let the word prepare you to be disappointed with the local church.

3. Recenter your life on Christ, not the church. "Show the new believer who came in because of the sweetness of the community that the community is precious, not as a god or a savior, but as something that helps us know and enjoy our God and our Savior." Whoever loves a church community more than Christ is not worthy of Christ (Matt. 10:37). Learn to count everything—even the local church—as loss compared to the worth of Jesus Christ (Phil. 3:8).[14]

Turnover in my church has left me relationally jaded

Like a turnstile, people rotate in and out of local churches. Relational depth suffers. Just when relationships deepen, people leave, and the process starts all over. Committed, longtime members try hard not to get stuck inside a clique of longstanding members. Is relational depth worth the investment in the age of turnover?

---

14   APJ 1192: "How to Keep Your Faith When You Lose Confidence in a Local Church" (May 2, 2018).

Yes, it is. Here are five reasons to keep investing.

1. Be patient. Expect disappointment in all areas of life. "We expect a *better* church, a *better* marriage, *better* kids, *better* government, *better* health, *better* friends. The reality falls short. The more it falls short of these expectations, the more it will make us cynical and bitter." And we fall short of our own ideals for ourselves too. "Therefore, we need a mindset about this age that is sober and marked by the long view of patient waiting." Be patient until Christ returns (James 5:7–11). "That's a long, long patience."

2. See Christ's relational disappointment. Jesus expressed "holy frustration" with his disciples (Matt. 17:17). "It helps me to know that there is a kind of godly frustration with the imperfections of this age, including the imperfections of God's people and including the imperfections of the whole system that keeps people moving around—coming in or moving out of God's church." Jesus felt it.

3. Live and give from Christ's fullness. The point is analogous to forgiveness. We forgive others, Paul says, because we were first chosen, set apart, and loved by God (Col. 3:12–13). From the amazing grace received, we forgive. Likewise, all our sustained self-giving must pour from our joyful confidence in God and eternal standing in him. God's grace to us is what makes us a fountain of grace to others "so that we can keep on giving ourselves in friendship," and never stop flowing, even "when people drink and leave." In this spring of self-giving, we offer the world "a beautiful witness to the all-sufficiency of Christ." Christ is our source (John 4:14; 7:38).

4. Stay in touch when people move away. Keep investing in Christian friends outside your local church.

5. Rest in the Friend who never leaves. "There is a friend who sticks closer than a brother, closer than a sister, closer than a spouse. And he has promised never to leave you, and he will always be with you to the end of the age" (Matt. 28:20; Heb. 13:5).[15]

Should we meet in house churches?

In rural areas, if you cannot find a faithful church, you may need to gather your own.[16] But the challenge is faced by urban Christians too, raising a broader question. Should we just meet in small house churches?

Seven considerations. (1) The church is *always* about a people, *never* about a place. Don't get hung up on building sizes and styles. Mentions of the church in the New Testament are "always—without exception—people, not places."

15 APJ 1112: "Church Membership Has Left Me Relationally Jaded" (October 27, 2017).
16 APJ 187: "When Should I Leave My Church?" (October 4, 2013).

(2) Don't underappreciate house churches. Even small house churches served to express the universal church on earth (1 Cor. 16:19; Col. 4:15; Philem. 2). (3) Don't idealize house churches. It's clear that some of the early Christians were leaving their homes and gathering at a large venue in Corinth, something other than a house (1 Cor. 11:17–22). (4) The Bible doesn't command house churches. "This is not something God thought it wise to regulate. No doubt, I think, in part because of the incredibly diverse cultural situations the church would find itself in for the next two thousand years: under trees, in garages, in stores, in cellars, in caves, in cathedrals, in homes." (5) Make the decision based on your church's goals. Every location and meeting space has advantages and disadvantages. "And we should be really slow to judge the decisions that are made here since God, it seems to me, has been pleased to bring great awakenings and massive church growth during times with and without church buildings. He is not limited in that way, and woe to the denomination or movement that presumes to say architecture, buildings, or location is the key to the dynamic of the almighty spread of God's kingdom." (6) Make the decision based on your church's finances. A meeting space in the downtown of a major urban area may prove too expensive. (7) Appreciate the value of large and small venues. The early church gathered and preached in large venues, in the temple, in small areas, and in homes (Acts 5:42). Appreciate all these places.[17]

College ministry and the local church—can they work together?

Christian college students who leave home for school tend to church hop, not taking membership seriously during the school year.[18] Can local churches and campus ministries work together?

They can (and do), once certain assumptions are changed. "I'm not on a crusade here against parachurch campus ministries. I think they have done great good for hundreds of thousands of students and that many churches have benefited greatly from the ripple effect of those evangelistic and discipling efforts. Nevertheless, I think that the relationship between the local church and campus ministries should be different than it often is." Envision how the leadership within the local church can oversee a campus group. In this case, the campus ministry is "an extension of the ministry of a particular local church." It both honors God's design for the local church and "benefits from the special focus and training and strategy and funding that is explicitly target-ing the special challenges of young people at the university." Build an organic

17 APJ 932: "Should We Meet in House Churches?" (September 2, 2016).
18 APJ 433: "Should I Commit to One Church?" (September 19, 2014).

relationship between church and parachurch and use the campus outreach to build students into a particular local congregation. Done right, it's a win-win for church and outreach.[19]

To college students: "Belong to a Bible-saturated, Christ-exalting, God-centered church that preaches the whole counsel of God. And be connected there with God's people. Don't wait till *after* college to be a mature, responsible church member. Break the mold of late-adolescents who think that life is just play and school. It is not. Life is responsible membership in a local church relating to people of all kinds and all ages." Demonstrate a maturity beyond what is often expected of college students.[20] And never forget that "the university is an institution created by *man*. The local church is an institution created by *God*. If you prioritize allegiance to university over allegiance to church, you are prioritizing man over God."[21]

19 APJ 1025: "Campus Ministry and the Local Church—Do They Work Together?" (April 7, 2017).
20 APJ 690: "Seven Tips for College Students" (September 22, 2015).
21 APJ 1081: "How to Stay Christian in College" (August 16, 2017).

On Retirement, Snowbirding, and Finishing Well

Don't waste your retirement

The title was splashed on the *Reader's Digest* cover and set off in bold font: "Start Now—Retire Early." Catchy. Piper doesn't remember where he saw the 1998 issue, but it caught his eye. Maybe in a dentist's office or some other waiting room. He picked it up, opened to the article, and read the first paragraph about a resourceful couple—Bob and Penny—who "took early retirement from their jobs in the Northeast five years ago when he was fifty-nine and she was fifty-one. Now they live in Punta Gorda, Florida, where they cruise on their thirty-foot trawler, play softball, and collect shells."[1]

Two years later, Piper pulled out the article and read this opening paragraph in his most unforgettable sermon—a sermon on retirement—oddly enough preached to a field of college students. At Passion's OneDay conference in Memphis, Tennessee, on May 20, 2000, Piper spoke to an outdoor crowd of about forty thousand students (his largest audience to that point). A whole generation of men and women would look back on that moment in a field as personally defining. Still a decade shy of sixty-five, Piper wasn't thinking about his legacy at the time. He was just trying to endure the elements. Strong wind gusts blew his notes off the podium, and eventually the *Reader's Digest* pages too—blown away and never seen again. He gave up half the fight, relinquishing to the wind his *used* notes in order to hold down the *unused* notes he hadn't gotten to, in effect preaching as a "one-armed paperhanger." The sermon would become legendary. But the preaching experience was "very distracting."[2]

---

1 Deborah Rankin, "Start Now—Retire Early," *Reader's Digest*, February 1998, 98.
2 APJ 1200: "Reflections on the Seashells Sermon, 18 Years Later" (May 21, 2018). Of note, the *Reader's Digest* article appeared nineteen months earlier in Piper's sermon at the Finishers Conference in Chicago, "Finishing What?," desiringGod.org (October 1, 1998).

From the stage, Pastor John contrasted Bob and Penny's story with the story of two older women—Ruby Eliason and Laura Edwards—one a widow, one never married, both in their eighties, partnered to serve the poor and sick of Cameroon, Africa. Their service ended when a car's brakes failed, and they careened out of control and plunged over a cliff. Both were killed instantly. "Is this a tragedy?" he asked. "Two women in their eighties, a whole life devoted to one idea—Jesus Christ magnified among the poor and the sick in the hardest places—and twenty years after most of their American counterparts had begun to throw their lives away on trivialities in Florida and New Mexico, fly into eternity with a death in a moment—is this a tragedy? It is not a tragedy. I will read to you what a tragedy is." And then he read the opening paragraph from *Reader's Digest*. "That is a tragedy. And there are people in this country that are spending billions of dollars to get you to buy it. And I get forty minutes to plead with you: *Don't buy it!* With all my heart I plead with you, don't buy that dream. The American dream—a nice house, a nice car, a nice job, a nice family, a nice retirement, collecting shells as the last chapter before you stand before the Creator of the universe to give an account with what you did. 'Here it is, Lord, my shell collection. And I've got a good [golf] swing. And look at my boat, God.' Well, not for Ruby and not for Laura. Don't waste your life. Don't waste it." The famous punchline in the "seashell message" would later become the title for his best-selling book *Don't Waste Your Life* (2003).[3]

Years later I asked Piper about the sermon, the book, and their effect on college students and retirees. It reminded him of a story that was earlier and more foundational in his life than the *Reader's Digest* article. He recalls a story his father told from an evangelistic crusade. After pleading with a group to give their lives to Christ, Bill Piper noticed an old man sitting on the front pew with his face in his hands, saying over and over: "I've wasted it. I've wasted it." "I can remember my dad telling that story over and over, and everything in me as a kid said, 'I don't want that to happen to me.'"

Spurned by all these life examples, the "seashell sermon" was actually a rigorous exposition of Galatians 6:14. But "hardly anybody knows that, I think." It was a sermon on Paul's claim that he boasted in nothing but the cross. And yet Paul boasted in many other things, like in his converts and in his sufferings. "He uses the word *boast* or *exalt* all over the place for other things besides the cross, it seems. So I worked and worked and worked to try to figure out what he means." His conclusion was that as "hell-bound, God-belittling sinners, none of us deserves one good thing from God—not one.

3   APJ 535: "How to Make a Difference in the World" (February 18, 2015).

We don't deserve one millisecond of good health or anything else. Because of the cross—covering our sin and securing God's everlasting favor for us as sinners—every single *good thing* that comes into our life as part of the blessings we will enjoy forever in God's favor was purchased by the cross. Every *painful thing* that comes into our life that God turns for good was purchased by the cross. Therefore, the cross is the foundation and the central glory of grace and every moment of our lives."

The message on retirement became a book intended as a graduation gift, although "I think I can say, with pretty serious confidence, that more people in their fifties and sixties have thanked me for that book." The graduation gift speaks loudly to retirees, and it makes sense. Even in the famous illustration, the four prominent figures are in their fifties and eighties. "I suppose it's not so ironic that the book not only confronts young people with the plea, 'Don't get sucked into the so-called American dream!' But it also shakes fifty-somethings who were just about to step into it. They were just about to spend the last twenty or thirty years of their lives dinking around. That message shakes them free from their comfort trance and catapults them into something way more significant than collecting shells." In this way, the book is not unique, because "virtually everything I write aims to help people not waste their lives. But this one, this book, more than any other, cuts to the chase, puts the finger on the chest, and says, 'Don't do that. Don't waste your life!'"[4]

No surprise, retirement was featured in episode 1 of APJ, on John Piper's sixty-seventh birthday. As he wrapped up his pastorate and entered a new ministry era, he was most certainly not entertaining thoughts of retirement and seashells and golf. "I want to go hard after God in this new season. What strikes me about retirement and the way the world conceives of it is that generally the world recommends pretty poor ways of getting ready to meet King Jesus."[5]

Retirement is not the end

In 2009 Piper spent a day inside Angola, a notorious maximum-security prison in Louisiana, home to 6,300 inmates, mostly habitual felons, armed robbers, rapists, and murderers. Nine of ten inmates will die there.

While inside the prison, Piper met individually with Gerald Bordelon, a "sexual sadist," rapist, and murderer sentenced to execution. "Never have I felt a greater urgency to say the good news plainly and plead from my heart," he reminisced of the meeting. A little later, with the meeting fresh on his mind,

---

4   APJ 1200: "Reflections on the Seashells Sermon, 18 Years Later" (May 21, 2018).
5   APJ 1: "Reflections from John Piper on His Birthday" (January 11, 2013).

Piper preached in the prison chapel with the same urgency. "I preached with all my heart to all those who could fit in the chapel," working through John 6 to convince the inmates that "Jesus did not come into the world mainly *to give bread*, but *to be bread*" (John 6:35, 48, 51). Christ came, Piper pleaded, not to be *useful* "but to be *precious*. Oh, how many Christians receive him as *useful*. Or another way to put it is this: Jesus Christ did not come into the world to assist you in meeting *desires you already had*, before you were born again. He came into the world to *change your desires*, so that he's the main one. That's the reason he came."[6]

Piper pleaded with Bordelon (via CCTV) and eight hundred other inmates (in the chapel) to embrace Christ as their greatest treasure. "Paul says, 'I count everything as loss because of the surpassing worth of knowing Christ Jesus my Lord. . . . That I may know him and the power of his resurrection, and may share his sufferings, becoming like him in his death, that by any means possible I may attain the resurrection from the dead' (Phil. 3:8, 10–11). Next stop after Angola: heaven—if he's precious beyond anything in this world that you've already had to lose. When you eat of the bread of life, you get eternal life—that is, a new chapter is added to your life. Angola is not the last chapter."

At this point in his prison sermon, the topic of retirement surfaced (yet another seemingly odd place for a riff on the senior years). "So many Americans work their fingers to the bone to have twenty years of so-called retirement, thinking that retirement is the last chapter. It isn't. It's the next-to-last chapter. Too many of us have this little, puny, fragile hope that as an old, wrinkled, aching, aged person you're going to go golf somewhere for twenty years or go fish somewhere for twenty years. But, instead, you can have absolute certainty—all of us—of an everlasting cabin by the lake with Jesus, an everlasting ocean cruise with Jesus, an everlasting evening by the fire with a good book and Jesus. Now, you men don't dream that way, like most Americans, or even the people in my church. And that's very good."

The last chapter of life is not retirement, but what follows death: eternity. This finale is true for Bob and Penny collecting shells but also for the prisoners who will die inside Angola. Set your eyes on the next chapter, the endless chapter to come. "This life is very short, brothers," he pleaded. "It may seem long. It's short. And eternity—it's really long. It's really long, and it's really good—ten thousand times will you be rewarded for every kind deed you ever do, every act of faith that ever comes forth from you." And such an eternity is free in Christ.[7]

---

6   APJ 1445: "John Piper's Death-Row Plea" (March 11, 2020).

7   APJ 1454: "Plan for Something Greater Than Retirement" (April 1, 2020).

Seven weeks after the prison visit, Bordelon was executed in Angola's lethal injection chamber.[8]

Should we save for retirement?

Financial planning is prudent for all Christians. But an aspiring financial counselor asked if he could help others "plan for retirement—even a very typical American retirement—with a clear conscience."

Five points should lead retirees.

1. God owns all our money. "Your money is not yours—period. Which puts you in a very, very precarious position. It's God's, and you got it in your bank and your pocket. Watch out. You might become a thief or a mismanager." We must exercise stewardship, not ownership, of the money God gives us.

2. Money is a currency we use to obtain what we love. How we spend money reveals who we are. "Therefore, money becomes a means of worship and witness and love—or selfishness. We can put out of our minds any thoughts that money is *intrinsically evil*." But it is "*intrinsically dangerous*, because Jesus said that it's hard for the rich to get into the kingdom of heaven (Matt. 19:23). Money exerts a tremendous power to try to enslave us to this world. But if we are born again with new values, new preferences, new things that we cherish and treasure, then money can become an instrument to show that we value God more than money."

3. With sufficient boldness, a wise investment counselor can bring perspective. "People need help. Rich people need help. They look powerful, but they need help. They need to be shaken loose from the assumptions of our culture. You can be a great help in that regard if you have the courage to speak to very wealthy people about what they should do with their money."

4. "There is no such thing as retirement from ministry in the Bible. Everybody who is a Christian is a minister serving people's needs by whatever gifts they have. In retirement, you may stop doing a paid vocation. Our culture calls that 'retirement.' That is not a good word. But you never retire from active service. In a world like ours, which is so broken, so needy, you never retire."

5. So can a Christian vocationally help others plan for a very typical American retirement and do so with a clear conscience? "No, no, no, no. Your aim is not to counsel a typical American retirement. You want people to break free from that." You can offer rare and precious counsel. "Many could use a specialist in helping people know ways to use their money wisely to maximize that kind of active, ministry-oriented, end-of-life season."[9]

---

8   APJ 1445: "John Piper's Death-Row Plea" (March 11, 2020).
9   APJ 1206: "Should Christians Save for Retirement?" (June 4, 2018).

Do godly parents leave an inheritance?

The Bible says, "A good man leaves an inheritance to his children's children" (Prov. 13:22a). So godly couples leave their children a financial inheritance, right?

Not exactly. This text doesn't mean a man has a "duty" to save up an inheritance but that he "has the resources and the ability" to do so. Such an inheritance is a divine blessing, not a command. Nothing guarantees that parents' wealth, set aside for their kids, will reach their children, as the second half of the proverb makes clear (13:22b). Proverbial generalizations should be balanced with the rest of Scripture. Heirlooms are not inherently virtuous. The ungodly leave "huge inheritances to their children, often to their ruin" (Ps. 17:13–14). And it's better for a father to have no inheritance to offer and live with integrity than to be rich and corrupt (Prov. 28:6). So there are greater legacies than money, as Proverbs 13:22 demonstrates. This man's "children and grandchildren will experience blessing because they had a good man for a father and a grandfather."

In a related New Testament text, Paul seems to say that parents are obligated to pass along an inheritance (2 Cor. 12:14). But this text is less about inheritance and more but about the money parents earn to support their children "while they're growing up."

With those clarifications in place, as you think of your legacy, consider five points. (1) Be generous with your money while you're alive. Meet the financial needs of your adult children now and "bear witness to the sufficiency of Jesus by being generous to them according to their real needs rather than waiting for the blessing to come only when you're gone." (2) Leave a greater legacy than money. Wealth is dangerous (Matt. 19:23). "There are many legacies to leave children that are vastly more important than money." (3) See the dangers of wealth, especially quickly and easily gotten wealth (Prov. 13:11; 20:21). The prodigal son demanded his entire inheritance, ran off, squandered it, and ruined his life with the money (Luke 15:11–32). Wealth is dangerous, but especially when "gotten quickly and easily." (4) Fix dollar amounts to the inheritance. Consider leaving "a fixed amount to each son or daughter" with the estate balance going to ministries. This was the Pipers' decision. Each child gets a "significant" and "generous" (but limited) number, with the estate balance managed by the National Christian Foundation that will distribute the money as the Pipers pre-determined (to the church, Desiring God, Bethlehem College and Seminary, etc.). (5) Make special considerations to support disabled adult children for lifelong needs that will prove disproportionate to those of the other children.

So, yes, leave a legacy for your children and their children. And know that "vastly more important than any financial legacy is the legacy of biblical truth, and the glorious gospel of Christ, and a life showing the love of Christ."[10]

On snowbirding

A concerned pastor needs wisdom to address the church-life disruption caused by "snowbirding"—the habit of retirees who seasonally migrate between warm climates (during cold months) and cooler climates (during hot months).

Piper took up the question as a seventy-year-old man who lives in Minneapolis year-round and still endures the harsh winters. "So I feel an increasingly privileged position from which to make pronouncements about the evils of the American dream of so-called retirement." It's a larger question about how "those of us who have stepped away from our lifelong means of livelihood should be spending the last twenty years of our lives." These last two decades, "the period between sixty-five and eighty-five, is called *life*. It is not something else. In fact, it is a crucial part of life because it is the last period of preparation before we stand before the Lord face-to-face and give an account for every idle word and moment" (Matt. 12:36).

Snowbirding itself is a particular issue for the wealthy in the West, not for most people in the world. But it's also a question that encompasses a much larger discussion: the size of your home, your neighborhood choices, owning multiple homes, the expense and frequency of vacations, and weekends spent skipping out on church to be at the lake. What does that say to the grandkids? Instead of setting out prohibitions, "it seems to me that the Bible goes about it in a much broader, more general way." And that broader way is a call for "a radical, Christian, wartime lifestyle based on clear biblical passages of love and sacrifice and suffering in ministry and the brevity of life and the lostness of the world and the suffering of those around us." The Bible does not call us to maximize our comforts and luxuries in life; it calls all Christians to "move toward need rather than toward comfort and security" and "toward generosity and simplicity."

A pastor concerned with snowbirding shouldn't scold his people in sermons. He should labor toward a culture that embraces the fact that "self-sacrifice and generosity and ministry in love are where true joy is found. And I would try to show over and over from the Bible, from modern life, that following the mindset of the world to maximize comfort and escape hardship is the path of boredom and guilt and emptiness in the end." From here you build a vision for retirement as a "golden opportunity, not for coasting and resting and playing

10   APJ 1729: "Should I Leave an Inheritance for My Children?" (January 10, 2022).

and self-indulgence, but for ministry and service and meeting needs and making disciples and showing love—maximizing usefulness, not maximizing physical pleasures through leisure and luxury. God has not given us seventy-somethings a lifetime of experience with God and with the world to be shelved while we putz around endlessly with our hobbies and games and leisures." Use that experience for good.

Pastor, get everyone over the age of sixty reading J. I. Packer's book *Finishing Our Course with Joy: Guidance from God for Engaging with Aging.* And stress the issue of personal ministry impact. "Florida, Mexico, New Mexico, Phoenix—wherever you move—do you move as a means of maximizing spiritual growth and impact? Is there a greater impact for ministry in Florida than in northern Minnesota? Will you have a more integral influence for Christ in a big megachurch that you visit in Florida than you would have if you stayed in your rural church in Wisconsin or Kentucky or wherever? Are you thinking mainly of comfort, or are you thinking mainly of meeting needs?"

Once such a culture is established, a pastor can pull aside his older members for more pointed and personal questions in private conversations.[11]

We're retired and want to go to the nations—what's first?

A retired couple wants to bring the gospel to unreached peoples around the globe. "This is amazing. This is glorious. I just want to come out of my seat when I hear that." The potential is huge among America's seventy-four million baby boomers, a fourth of whom are self-professed, Bible-believing Christians. And most are financially stable. "And by global standards, rich—*really* rich. I don't care if they're on fixed income. By global standards, they are really rich."

Four tips for maximizing the global impact of your "retirement" years. (1) Be involved in the local church to discern your call for the future. There are no "Lone-Ranger Christians or Lone-Ranger missionaries or Lone-Ranger, post-retirement, radical servants of Christ." Lean on your church to help determine gifting, confirm calling, discern the needs you can meet, and help formulate a plan for the next chapter of your life. (2) Reach out to a missions agency serving those with a similar burden. You're not alone; other retirees share your passion. (3) Know that "God is so full of joy over your resolve not to waste this last chapter of your life." He won't fail you here. "When you call out to him for help and for guidance in this matter, you are not going to be left to yourselves." His heart is with you. (4) "Be on guard against being lulled to

---

11 APJ 819: "A Plea for a Radical Christian Wartime Lifestyle in the Retirement Years" (March 21, 2016).

sleep by a dozen conversations that you're going to have with retired believers who have no dream of making their lives count for the glory of Christ and the suffering of the world. They will be talking about their different toys and their different houses and their different travels and their different vacations and on and on and on." That will be normalized. Don't buy it. "You're going to get sucked in and formulate your dreams that way—where the new condo is going to be, how free from yard work you're going to be, how many fun things you can do, and on and on. Only a mighty work of grace—a glorious work of sovereign grace—can keep you from fitting into the American way of acting as if heaven and all its rest and pleasure begins at retirement instead of death. Heaven begins at death, not sooner. Let me say it again. Trouble-free heaven begins at death."[12]

What's next for the retired pastor?

Handing off the baton to a younger senior pastor is commendable, but retirement from ministry is unthinkable. "It is not biblical to lay down ministry and play games till you are dead at sixty-five or ninety-five. That is the typical American view of retirement, and it strikes me as unbiblical."[13]

So then what's next for the retired pastor? This may be an easy answer for John Piper, but what about the pastor who isn't anticipating book deals and speaking invitations? What's he to do?

First, don't fall for the world's definition of retirement: "fishing, golfing, cruises, resorts, shopping. There's not anything like that in the Bible: minister for forty or fifty years, and then indulge yourself with worldly leisure and play for the last chapter of your life as you prepare to give an account to the judge of the universe, while putting all the accumulated knowledge that God has given you over the years on the shelf, unused. That's insane!" Instead, be poured out, fight the faith, and finish the race well (2 Tim. 4:6–8). The *race of life* is the *race of ministry*, thus, the race of ministry "did not end for Paul until he hit the finish line—and the finish line was death." So "don't think in terms of retirement. Think of pulling back from one kind of ministry when the time seems right but pursuing other ministry when that happens."

Retired pastors serve the church in ongoing roles by meeting the needs of the seniors, the sick, the addicted, the homeless, the orphaned, the lost, the inner city, or a younger generation of men. Doors are open in your own hometown and among the nations. At stake is the question, "Are you committed to what

---

12   APJ 1139: "I'm Retired and Want to Do Missions—What's My First Step?" (December 29, 2017).
13   APJ 427: "Explain Your Title 'Pastor Emeritus'" (September 11, 2014).

Paul calls 'abounding in the work of the Lord'" (1 Cor. 15:58)? It's a call to every Christian, in light of the resurrection, to be abounding in the work of the Lord, meaning "doing lots and lots of it" and "filling our days with work that has the Lord as its conscious source and the Lord as its conscious goal. That's the work of the Lord."

Don't rest on previous work. Forget the past. Press forward to new opportunities (Phil. 3:13–14). Think less in terms of titles and more in terms of deeds for others. "Get up in the morning and say, 'I want to do something good for somebody today. I'm not content to sit around and watch TV or play games. There is in me this Holy Spirit–given energy. I want to do some good in the world." To that end, ponder a life of good works (Eph. 2:10; Titus 2:14; 3:8, 14; Heb. 10:24). "God will not leave you without a significant work to do. He does not waste his children."[14]

Should aging parents live in retirement homes or with their family?
The Bible does not dictate protocols for caring for aging parents, but we see three pointers.

1. Scripture is clear that we should serve others, modeled in the humility of Christ (Phil. 2:3–8). "That is one of the most convicting, one of the most beautiful, one of the most transforming texts in the Bible. The great mark of Christians, Paul says to the adult Christian child, is that they look not just to their interests in midlife as their careers reach their capstone. They look toward the interests of others, including aging parents. They count others, like their parents, as more significant than themselves. They don't sit atop some pinnacle of privilege, but, like Jesus, they come down to where the need is and serve even unto death. There's a basic principle and a call in it."

2. Love your parents as you wish to be cared for in old age (Matt. 19:19). Jesus parallels our parent honoring and neighbor love. We are to love our parents to the end, just as Christ modeled his own love and care for his mother (John 19:26).

3. Families are called to care for older parents in 1 Timothy 5:4, "the most to-the-point text in the Bible" on the topic. The church steps in to care for widows who have no family, "implying that the first and foremost responsibility is for the families to care for widows." This love of family for aging parents is God-honoring, and it rightly repays a "return" (ἀμοιβή) on the investment of the parents to their children earlier in life. God delights in this care role reversal.

"The main issue is if the heart of the children is a selfish heart or a servant heart. Are we ready to make sacrifices for our parents? Or are we resentful that

---

14 APJ 1452: "What's Next for an Aging Pastor?" (March 27, 2020).

they are becoming a burden? That's the real test. All of this may or may not mean that the parents come to live with us or near us. There are innumerable variables that make one situation right for one family and another situation right for another." But these circumstances are secondary. Primarily, "are we servants or are we selfish? Are we ready to sacrifice and trust God with the joy to meet every need?"[15]

The dignity of the elderly

Even with dementia and prolonged suffering, the dying bear God's image. They may require increasing care and extra patience, but they always command our dignity. "That applies to an eighty-pound, arthritic, diapered, drooling, glazed-eyed human being that we love, lying in bed and praying for death in the nursing home or in the jungle hut." Consider this: in Christ, those standing on the brink of death are standing on the brink of glorification (1 Cor. 15:43). "Paul is telling us that the weak, inglorious, demented shadow of a once-strong Christian in front of us is on the brink of glory and power. You need to go to nursing homes and think that way. These people are on the brink of glory and power." Because of the resurrecting power of Christ, these old and bent and withered men and women are moments away from becoming "gloriously superhuman." And even as the body shrivels, the soul is alive in ways God sustains.[16]

15 APJ 1078: "Retirement Homes and Caring for Aging Parents" (August 9, 2017).
16 APJ 1115: "The Dignity of Those with Dementia" (November 3, 2017).

On Suicide, Euthanasia, and the Will to Live

I will die young—how do I fight for hope?

A man wrote us who will likely die in his late twenties or early thirties. How does he live out his final years with courage? How can he fight the temptation to become jaded and bitter toward God?

Such a question brings "quiet reverence." To be in the presence of a believer whose life will be cut short, "I feel as though I'm on sacred ground." For such a believer, Piper shared four thoughts. (1) Don't feel bad for asking *why—why* God made your life the way he did. This is a legitimate question within a submissive and faith-filled spirit. Paul doesn't forbid asking it (contrary to a popular misinterpretation of Romans 9:20–21). In fact, "my guess is," in your remaining months and years, "God is going to give you some very precious answers to the *why*. It's not wrong to humbly ask God for those answers and accompany that request with a willingness to say *yes* to his answers." (2) Desire to honor Christ in your final days and in your death. This was Paul's prayer. Christ is honored at the end of life when we begin to truly "see and savor Christ as more precious than life." So "it's no accident that some of the greatest Christians, as they approached the end of their lives, shifted all their focus onto seeing and savoring the glories of Christ in his Scriptures" (Phil. 1:20–23). (3) Avoid becoming jaded against the Lord. The opposite of becoming *jaded* toward the Lord is to *bless* the Lord (Job 1:20–21; 2:9–10). In the words of Paul, "Do not lose heart" (2 Cor. 4:16–18). (4) Anticipate eternity. Eternity is forever, and there we find our true calling, a true calling "which always seemed just out of reach here on earth." So *the life to come* "is not a postscript to *this true life*; rather, *this life* is a prelude to *real life*." Or as Paul calls eternity: "that which is truly life" (1 Tim. 6:19). So begin, even now, to "feel the amazing, immeasurableness of the kindness that is about to be poured out on you forever."[1]

Is the desire to hasten death a sinful longing?

A teenage Christian boy named Austin, sick with cancer, emailed to say he was ready to die and go home to be with his Savior. He was praying to this end, that his life would end sooner than later. The teen was not bitter or angry, and he seemed to demonstrate an extraordinary amount of faith and courage. Suicide was not mentioned but inferred from the question.

"Frankly," Piper said, "I think that a person who has been a follower of Jesus for some time and has never prayed to go home to heaven with him either hasn't seen Jesus very clearly or has not been involved in much misery over our own (and others') sins. Paul had zero shame in saying that he wanted to die and be with Christ" (Phil. 1:23). We should all long for the same. "But you, Austin, clearly are right in believing this is God's decision, not yours." Suicide isn't an option. "Suicide—assisted, merciful, or otherwise—is not just self-murder; it is role-reversing with God, and you are right to leave it with him. So your great struggle is how to make it to God's appointed end—short or long—with joy, when your life is painful." The key in this final season of life is to focus on eternity, meditate on God's electing love, and rehearse his love to us in Christ.[2]

Terminal cancer does not warrant euthanasia either. Even then, "life is a glorious thing." Cherish your days, use them, and don't waste them. "Whether for one year or four years, whether I'm feeling good or feeling miserable, whether death is tomorrow or years away, I would seek to treasure Jesus Christ above all things and to bring as many people with me as I can into the everlasting enjoyment of his presence."[3]

Likewise, "hastening death" through the "selfish pleasures" of smoking and drinking "is not submission to providence, but the failure to value a precious gift."[4]

My life is ruined—is it wrong to want to die?

The life of a thirty-one-year-old woman has been "ruined" by her sin. She has alienated her friends, family, and (soon to be) ex-husband. She repented, but her life seems irreparably ruined. Her future seems bleak. Is it sinful for her to desire death?

No, "it is not a sin to long for heaven, and for the presence of Christ, with a sense of aching dismay over the sin and sorrows of this world and of our own

1   APJ 1286: "I Will Die Young—How Do I Fight for Hope?" (December 7, 2018).
2   APJ 692: "When Should We Pray for God to Take Us Home?" (September 24, 2015).
3   APJ 1723: "End-of-Life Medical Intervention—or Not?" (December 27, 2021).
4   APJ 1702: "On Cigarettes, Vaping, and Nicotine" (November 8, 2021).

lives. In fact, I would say that the more one knows of the real condition of this world, and the more one grieves over the remaining corruption of our own hearts, the more natural it is to long for heaven and Christ." We long for "that day when, freed from sinning," we will see Christ's "lovely face" (as Robert Robinson's hymn put it). "That's what we long for; we long for the day when we'll be free from sinning. The thing we want most to be free of in this life is dishonoring the Lord by our own sin," because while "there are troubles in the world, and there's pain in the world, the most grievous thing is sin in our own soul in the world."

Two texts illustrate the longing. Paul said he wanted to depart this life (Phil. 1:23–25), a holy longing for any Christian. We all would prefer to be at home with Christ (2 Cor. 5:6–9). Such a desire—for our earthly life to be shortened so that we can be with Christ—is not only *not a sin*; it is "biblical and healthy." But note that in both texts, Paul is clear that God's will says not yet. We continue living out this life on earth because God has use of us, and because we don't walk by the sight of life's seeming potential but by faith that God is governing this life for his glory (Phil. 1:24–25). Paul knew that his future on earth would be full of sorrow and pain (Acts 20:23).

So, *yes*, "long for heaven, long for Christ, long for the day when we will sin no more. But trust his promises now, like Paul as he faced a painful future and walked by faith, not by sight. God's promise for you is fruit in the midst of this sorrow." Cling to God's promises to the afflicted (Isa. 56:5; 58:10–11). And then walk by faith, not by sight (2 Cor. 5:6–7).[5]

Can a doctor help a suffering patient die if it's legal?

In 2016, Canada passed bill C-14, called "medical assistance in dying" (MAID). It prompted an email from a Canadian physician. Now legalized, would it ever be permissible for a Christian doctor to participate in "assisted dying"?

Note the change in language from "assisted suicide" to "assisted dying." Such subtle changes muddy the water and make it hard to see what's at stake. This is a *suicide* question.

Four convictions guide us. (1) A Christian doctor's first obligation is to God's commands, not to legal options. In obedience we are not given all the rationale for God's commands. "Sometimes God commands us to do something, and only much later do we or the world discover how many good effects come from obeying God, and/or would have come if we had obeyed God." We cannot see all the future good, so we obey in the present. Murder—the

5   APJ 1342: "Is It Sinful to Want to Die?" (May 13, 2019).

"shedding of innocent blood"—is prohibited all over the Bible. (2) Human life is created in God's image and "designed to exist forever." Animals are not. Only God can take human life when he pleases, without wronging anyone, all by "his unique prerogative" (Deut. 32:39; 1 Sam. 2:6; 1 Tim. 6:13; James 4:15). "Human life in its fullest sense is a miracle that only he can create and only he has the right to take, unless he has given the state the right to use the sword in various settings to take life." (3) The Hippocratic Oath calls physicians to be "life givers and life sustainers, not life takers." This role applies to the unborn, the elderly, and the terminally ill. Yet in the most horrific suffering, "it is right and loving for physicians to use whatever medicines they have at their disposal, if the patient wants it, to minimize the pain." (4) Preemptive death undermines God's purposes. Human suffering can be redeemed by God for good. Therefore, "suffering never becomes such an evil so great that it justifies disobedience to one of the commands of God, like the command not to take innocent life."

So Christian doctors will not take lives or hasten death. But "here is what remains ambiguous: the line between *taking life* and *not unduly sustaining life* is not always clear." There are clearly times "when death should be allowed to run its course or to arrive naturally without any extraordinary efforts to keep a person alive. Clearly death comes to all of us." But discerning this line "is not easy in these modern, remarkably wonderful medical days in which we live, which have created new possibilities for sustaining life beyond all ordinary means of life." The patient's will to live is key. "Yes, strive to sustain life for a patient who desires life. But the will of the patient to die is not a decisive word for the simple reason that many patients in the crisis of depression have attempted suicide, been rescued, and gone on to be thankful for the rest of their lives that someone contradicted their dark desires at that moment." In the end, "we do not have the right to help a patient take his own life or the right to take it ourselves. The laws that put such things into our hands are bad laws and should not constrain Christian physicians to act against their convictions even if they must lose their job in the process." Yet "the ambiguities of end-of-life decisions regarding what is fitting life support and what blocks a timely, natural death—those decisions remain very, very difficult."[6]

Given all the medical options to choose from and the ambiguities that surround decisions about end-of-life medical intervention, and how far to go (or *not* go), we can be governed by seven biblical hopes, prayers, and convictions.[7]

6   APJ 812: "May Christian Doctors Help Patients Die If the Law Permits?" (March 10, 2016).
7   APJ 1723: "End-of-Life Medical Intervention—or Not?" (December 27, 2021).

How do we serve the dying?

Dying believers are still running the race of faith. And their race "is not a race against wind or hills or heat or burning muscles; it's a race against temptations that would make them doubt God's goodness, God's love. It's a fight to stay restful and content in God through broken hips and cancer and lost sight and failed memory. It's not an easy race. They may not be moving their legs or even their arms, but, oh, the difficulty of this race! It's harder than the Olympics, and it may have to be run flat on your back. For most of us at the end, it will be run that way"—in bed. The goal is to keep the faith to the end (2 Tim. 4:7). To finish without shifting away from the gospel (Col. 1:22–23). To know these present pains are culminating in a future glory (2 Cor. 4:16–17).

So "weakening saints need the constant reminder that the finishing line is crossed not by a burst of human energy but by collapsing into the arms of Jesus." This is our opportunity to serve the dying, who "are often not mentally or physically able to feed themselves with the promise-sustaining word of God. I hope my family remembers that when I'm in my final weakness. The last caregivers should be speaking, maybe even singing, gospel-sweet promises into the life of the dying person, whom they may think no longer can hear us. You don't know that. I sat beside my dying father, counting his breaths, wondering when the gaps would stop. I was there at midnight when they stopped, and I never stopped speaking God's word into his ear."

So how do we serve dying believers? "Spare the dying as much pain as you can" and "use the prayer-soaked word of God to keep Christ before the dying, to help them fight the fight of faith, to keep believing that even this final, painful push will be rewarded by God's grace."[8]

How do we serve dying unbelievers? An oncology nurse asked about how to bring the good news of the gospel to the dying patients she serves. It is "a beautiful gift to quietly and calmly and lovingly speak words of hope into the ear of a person who is unable to respond." But this is also a gift that requires a great deal of professional wisdom and gospel sensitivity.[9]

Can a Christian commit suicide and be saved?

It is maybe the hardest and most sensitive question a pastor will ever get. Did my loved one who just ended his own life go to heaven?

For a pastor of thirty-five years, this is no abstract question. "I have been involved closely in several suicides. I cleaned up the basement after the police

8   APJ 1605: "How Can I Serve the Dying?" (March 26, 2021).
9   APJ 1636: "How Do I Serve Dying Unbelievers?" (June 7, 2021).

removed the body of a man who shot himself in the head, and I used a broom to sweep the blood, and other stuff, into a dust pan and poured it down the laundry sink so his wife would not have to see what we found. And then I did his funeral five days later. He was a professing believer. I have done a funeral for a young woman who died by leaping from the window of the locked ward at the hospital down the street from my house, where she was being safely kept in her psychological distress."

First, the biblical principles. "Let's be clear now. Self-murder is serious. We are playing with fire here. It is spiritually and eternally serious to murder yourself. It is not a light thing. And anyone listening to me now who is contemplating suicide should hear me say don't do it. There is a better way. I promise you, in the name of Jesus Christ, there is a better way. You don't feel that perhaps right now, but your feelings are not true. They are deceiving you." Self-murder is murder, and "no murderer has eternal life abiding in him" (1 John 3:15). "Now that should scare the wits out of people who are contemplating ending their life with murder." So is the apostle John suggesting that everyone whose last act in life is murder is finally a murderer? That's an open question.

Second (and where the pastoral discretion kicks in), the Bible is very clear that we must persevere to the end to be saved (Mark 13:13; Heb. 3:14). "But it does not mean that our experience of confidence in God to the end is perfect, or that we don't have lapses of sin which betray that we are not fully trusting Christ. All sin, all my sin—the sin that I do this afternoon, tomorrow, yesterday—is all rooted in some level of distrust in the superior goodness of God. And I don't go in and out of being a Christian when I sin. And that measure of distrust becomes manifest in sinning. I don't cease to be a Christian. So saying that we must persevere to the end in confidence doesn't mean that you must persevere to the end in sinlessness or perfect trust in Christ. There is imperfection in our trust." So the answer will require clarity on final acts. "If people have been trusting in Christ as their Savior, their Lord, their treasure, does the last act of their life prove the decisive one in showing their true standing as a child of God?" Is their entire life defined by one final act of self-murder?

He drove home the point with a vivid analogy. Imagine John Piper storming out of the house after an argument with his wife. He drives off in such sinful anger and reckless rage that he eventually loses control of his speeding car, hits a telephone pole, and dies. "Now, my last act was sin. I killed myself by my sin. I didn't intend to kill myself, but I did. And it was sin that made it happen. So the last thing I did was sin. Is that last sin decisive in determining whether John Piper was born again?" No. "God will look at my whole life, and the evidences of whether I belong to him will be assessed not because of that failure alone any more than any other failure alone. Why would the last one be decisive when the others are just as serious?"

So we should be "terrified to try to meet Jesus by means of murder," and yet "I am waving a flag of hope that true faith can have a season that dark."[10]

Does suicide atone for a murderer's sins?

In an act of unspeakable evil, Adam Lanza, twenty, shot and killed twenty-six people, including twenty children, at Sandy Hook Elementary School (2012). Then he shot himself. In suicide, was justice served? "Can you hatefully, wantonly slaughter people created in the image of God and then get away with it through suicide, a millisecond of pain?" The emphatic answer is *no*. "This world is not one long injustice ending in nothingness." No, justice must be met. Lady Justice stands with scales in hand, blindfolded for impartiality. But even blindfolded, no one escapes justice's final decree. "That last *pop* of the gun to your own head is heard on the other side of hope like a slamming door, and the guilty who have spurned the grace of God all their lives suddenly realize, 'I am not dead.' There she stands with perfect recompense in her hand."[11]

This point should not be taken to mean that a killer who lives to be arrested and convicted cannot be forgiven of his wickedness. David was pardoned for his scandalous lust and what it led to in rape and murder (2 Sam. 12:1–15).[12]

On spiritual suicides

Physical suicides are stark, troubling, and decisive. Spiritual suicides are normally subtle, slow, and potentially more catastrophic. In reality, all sinning is self-killing.[13] In particular, self-trust is suicidal.[14] And the idolatry of money, power, success, or romance—treasured above Christ—amounts to "eternal suicide."[15]

In particular, the "love of money" is how hordes of sinners wander away from the faith and self-puncture themselves "with many pangs" (1 Tim. 6:10). Lust for wealth amounts to self-inflicted soul stabbing. Thus, "the very thing that leads people to suicidal piercings of pangs—namely the desire to be rich— is nurtured and cultivated by prosperity preachers. They are encouraging that this suicidal behavior happen. That is abominable."[16]

---

10 APJ 352: "Suicide and Salvation" (May 29, 2014).
11 APJ SE02: "Explain Your New Poem 'Grace Forfeited'" (May 17, 2013).
12 APJ 1322: "He Killed His Wife and Children—Can He Really Be Forgiven?" (March 27, 2019).
13 APJ 588: "Why Is Radical Islam Alluring to Westerners?" (May 4, 2015).
14 APJ 1465: "Is the Christian's Heart Deceitfully Wicked?" (April 27, 2020).
15 APJ 1460: "More Precious Than Praise and Possessions" (April 15, 2020).
16 APJ 231: "Why I Abominate the Prosperity Gospel" (December 6, 2013).

The love of money is spiritual suicide. In the case of Judas, the sin manifested in physical suicide (Matt. 27:5; John 12:1–8). "If you want to be rich, you are on a suicidal track"—at least one suicidal track, maybe two. You can't serve God and money (Matt. 6:24; Luke 16:13). In effect, Jesus said: "'You are devoted to *money*, Judas. You get up in the morning, you think *money*. You go to bed at night, you think *money*. You open the newspaper and go to the stock page, you think *money, money, money, money, money*. It's the hope and the god that you have. It's your security. It's your pathway to pleasure. If that is true, you are dead. You are going to die, Judas, and never see me again.'"[17]

Likewise, the homosexual lifestyle is also spiritual suicide, and any pastor who officiates a "so-called same-sex wedding" is "blessing" an "eternal suicide," and "solemnizing and making official their choice *not to enter* the kingdom of heaven." Such a pastor "has given a signal that he is disqualified from his role of leading the sheep into the kingdom of heaven." When asked to officiate such a "union," the pastor should confront the lifestyle, share the good news of Christ, and invite them to attend church.[18]

So if unrepentant homosexual sin amounts to spiritual suicide, the public celebration of it amounts to murder-suicide (Rom. 1:32; Phil. 3:18–19). Of Romans 1 and the culture, "Not only do they know that it's wrong, and not only do they know that it deserves death, and not only do they practice it, but they recruit others to do the same and die with them. So, the sin is not just self-destructive but others-destructive" (Rom. 1:32).[19]

How do I know if I'm ready for heaven?

Well, "nobody is ready for heaven" because "nobody deserves heaven." Not naturally. How we get into heaven requires the supernatural answer from a "short book you can read in an hour" called Romans. It's in the Bible. There we find that we have all sinned by failing to honor and glorify God, who made us (Rom. 3:23). We're selfish. Born selfish. We cannot work our way out of this scenario. And keeping a list of our good deeds will never placate a holy and just and perfect God (Rom. 3:20). All our acts of obedience are dead-ends for trying to get right with God. He must act.

The "breathtaking news" is that even though we don't deserve heaven—and none of us can get to heaven by our goodness—"God made a way for us sinful human beings to be accepted as righteous, good, just, and law-abiding, and to be accepted as righteous in his presence." How on earth is this possible? God did

17 APJ 706: "Loving Money Is Suicide" (October 14, 2015).
18 APJ 586: "What to Say to a Pastor Who Wants to Officiate a Gay Wedding" (April 30, 2015).
19 APJ 1380: "What Does the Bible Say about 'National Coming Out Day'?" (October 11, 2019).

it. He managed to find a way to remain unwaveringly holy and yet graciously merciful to justify us, the ungodly (Rom. 3:26). And that way is the only way. In his son, Jesus Christ. He came to pay with his holy life and his perfect blood to bear the judgment we deserve for our sin (Isa. 53:5–6).

But it gets better! Not only are *our* sins put on Jesus, but *his* perfect righteousness is now ours (2 Cor. 5:21)! In him—united to him by faith—we get God's righteousness. "That is what the Bible calls 'justification': being declared just or declared righteous in God's presence on the basis of the justice and the righteousness of Jesus, not ourselves." It's the "great exchange" and "glorious mystery of how a sinner can be accepted in the presence of God."

So how do I get Christ? We don't earn him. We receive him. "We receive Jesus as a precious Savior. We receive him as a perfect Lord. We receive him as an infinite treasure. *Believing* is *receiving* him for who he is—for the treasure that he is" (Phil. 3:8). In him we are justified and changed. "When you put your trust in Christ, your life takes on a new direction, not a new perfection. The river turns, but it doesn't yet run with perfectly pure water. The perfection is Jesus. And then, when we die or when Jesus comes back, we will share in that complete perfection."[20]

20 APJ 1008: "Am I Really Ready for Heaven?" (February 27, 2017).

APPENDIX

Favorite Episodes

AS FOR YOUR FAVORITE EPISODES, go to the *Ask Pastor John* website (AskPastorJohn.com) and click the "popular" tab for a real-time list, organized in descending order, with the most played episodes at the top.

Occasionally, listeners ask me about my favorites. I have six.

My favorite episode of all time: APJ 729. This miniature theology of glory is a theme that must become a full book from Piper at some point (and, yes, I've been asking). No one better explains the universe along the lines of glory, here applied particularly to sin, redemption, and atonement.

My second favorite episode: APJ 670. An exceptional episode on smartphone overuse, made more remarkable by a paradigm that applies to all of sanctification. We fight sin and temptation as one war in two theaters—the theater of the *internal desires* (the fight to be most satisfied by Christ). But we also fight in the theater of *outward means* (safeguards and limits and restrictions). Pastor John masterfully balances this dual strategy.

My third favorite episode: APJ SE10. No context better suits John Piper's ministry ethos than a funeral, particularly on stage with a casket in the foreground leading the congregation in prayer. The few funeral prayers of his that I have witnessed in person have been profound, and none more than his funeral prayer for a family of five, a missionary couple in training with three young children, all killed in one fatal interstate car accident. As you can hear in a later episode, we had to work through "misgivings" about whether this prayer recording should be broadcasted online because "the thought that we would exploit that moment and that pain to put ourselves forward would be absolutely loathsome in the eyes of God."[1] The potential benefits would have to warrant the sharing.

1 APJ 931: "How Do You Pray in Public, without Performing?" (August 31, 2016).

It did. The prayer episode garnered 320,000 plays in twenty-four hours, seven hundred thousand in four days, and over two million to date.

The episode I seem to suggest most: APJ 352. A stellar example of Pastor John's pastoral sensitivity coming alongside his biblical clarity on the very delicate topic of suicide and salvation. The episode is a masterpiece of pastoral carefulness, theological boldness, and moral imagination.

The episode I most return to as a dad: APJ 255. A dad's role in the home is key. Among other things, a father carries the primary responsibility for "cultivating joy as the indomitable atmosphere" of the home, rooted in "the gospel and the sovereignty of God." A dad not only leads his family *to* this joy in Christ, but he serves his family *from* his joy in Christ "so that the kids realize that to be happy in God is really what life is about." Dad sets the tone of the home and tunes it to joy in Christ.

The episode with the timeliest personal impact: APJ 1173. The episode tackles the midlife years and was recorded just as I entered my forties and first felt the pinch of caring for teens and their pressing challenges. The episode landed in my life at the exact right moment—echoing the testimony of so many of you listeners. You know what it feels like to be met in a moment of personal need by a sovereignly timed episode.

Full Index of Episodes Featuring John Piper (2013–2022)

THE FOLLOWING INDEX is an exhaustive chronology of every episode featuring John Piper in the first ten years of the *Ask Pastor John* podcast. Only guest episodes are excluded. I frequently return to this index to browse titles, listen, and jot down personal notes. For a season I used the list to relisten to a few years' worth of episodes, ticking off the titles as I progressed through the archive. Simply browsing this list will lead you to a lot of hidden gems. The full audio and transcript for every episode—tallying over 2.3 million words, *ten times the length of this book*—can all be accessed online at AskPastorJohn.com. Happy browsing, listening, and discovering!

2013

1   Reflections from John Piper on His Birthday (January 11, 2013).

2   Who Was George Herbert? (January 12, 2013).

3   How Important Is a Christian Writer's Influence? (January 13, 2013).

4   Was Adam for Real, and Does It Matter? (January 14, 2013).

5   Why Adam Matters for Global Missions (January 15, 2013).

6   What Is It Like Preaching to 60,000 People? (January 17, 2013).

7   What Are Your Takeaways from Passion 2013? (January 18, 2013).

8   Leadership Lessons from Martin Luther King (January 21, 2013).

9   Arrests and Imprisonments in Opposing Abortion (January 22, 2013).

10   Safety Is a Myth (January 23, 2013).

11   What Is the Difference between Right Risk and Wrong Risk? (January 24, 2013).

12   Exercising the Body (for the Sake of the Soul) (January 25, 2013).

*   Episode numbers preceded by SE denote special episodes.

2015

2016

2017

2018

2021

Also Available from Tony Reinke

For more information, visit **crossway.org**.